The Founding of Modern States

The Founding of Modern States is a bold comparative work that examines the rise of the modern state through six case studies of state formation. The book opens with an analysis of three foundings that gave rise to democratic states in Britain, the United States, and France and concludes with an evaluation of three formations that birthed non-democratic states in the Soviet Union, Nazi Germany, and the Islamic Republic of Iran. Through a comparative analysis of these governments, the book argues that new state formations are defined by a metaphysical conception of a "will of the people" through which the new state is ritually granted sovereignty. The book stresses the paradoxical nature of modern foundings, characterized by "mythological imaginations," and the symbolic acts and rituals upon which a state is enabled to secure political and social order. An extensive study of some of the most important events in modern history, this book offers readers novel interpretations that will disrupt common narratives about modern states and the state of our modern world.

RICHARD FRANKLIN BENSEL is the Gary S. Davis Professor of Government at Cornell University. He is the author of *Yankee Leviathan: The Origins of Central State Authority in America, 1859–1877* (1991), *The American Ballot Box in the Mid-Nineteenth Century* (2004), *The Political Economy of American Industrialization, 1877–1900* (2000; J. David Greenstone Prize, 2002), *Passion and Preferences: William Jennings Bryan and the 1896 Democratic Convention* (2008), and *Sectionalism and American Political Development, 1880–1980* (1984).

The Founding of Modern States

RICHARD FRANKLIN BENSEL

Cornell University

CAMBRIDGE
UNIVERSITY PRESS

Shaftesbury Road, Cambridge CB2 8EA, United Kingdom

One Liberty Plaza, 20th Floor, New York, NY 10006, USA

477 Williamstown Road, Port Melbourne, VIC 3207, Australia

314–321, 3rd Floor, Plot 3, Splendor Forum, Jasola District Centre, New Delhi – 110025, India

103 Penang Road, #05–06/07, Visioncrest Commercial, Singapore 238467

Cambridge University Press is part of Cambridge University Press & Assessment, a department of the University of Cambridge.

We share the University's mission to contribute to society through the pursuit of education, learning and research at the highest international levels of excellence.

www.cambridge.org
Information on this title: www.cambridge.org/9781009247207

DOI: 10.1017/9781009247245

First published 2022

A catalogue record for this publication is available from the British Library

Library of Congress Cataloging-in-Publication Data
NAMES: Bensel, Richard Franklin, 1949– author.
TITLE: The founding of modern states / Richard Franklin Bensel.
DESCRIPTION: Cambridge ; New York, NY : Cambridge University Press, 2022. | Includes bibliographical references and index.
IDENTIFIERS: LCCN 2022031225 (print) | LCCN 2022031226 (ebook) |
ISBN 9781009247207 (hardback) | ISBN 9781009247214 (paperback) |
ISBN 9781009247245 (epub)
SUBJECTS: LCSH: State, The–Case studies. | Constitutional history. | Dictatorship. | World politics. |
BISAC: POLITICAL SCIENCE / General
CLASSIFICATION: LCC JC11 .B46 2022 (print) | LCC JC11 (ebook) | DDC 320.1–dc23/eng/
20220816
LC record available at https://lccn.loc.gov/2022031225
LC ebook record available at https://lccn.loc.gov/2022031226

ISBN 978-1-009-24720-7 Hardback
ISBN 978-1-009-24721-4 Paperback

To Eliza and Seth

Contents

Tables

Boxes

Preface

Cornell requires all first-year undergraduates to enroll in a writing seminar that combines intensive writing and discussion of a particular theme. When I taught these small seminars, the theme that I offered my students (they can choose their seminar from over a hundred different options) was titled "Utopia" and involved the semester-long construction of a blueprint for an imaginary society that they individually considered viable and virtuous. Every week they added features to their blueprint such as "religion" and "economic organization" and then explained to their peers how those new elements could be reconciled with whatever they had hitherto laid out in their plan. But the most important step, as I emphasized, and as they readily accepted, was the "launch": the way in which that society, structured by the blueprint they had created, came to life. The vast majority of my students designed this launch as a consensual separation from the rest of human society. In many cases, they imagined an extraterrestrial settlement on the moon, a planet, or an artificial satellite. And then they imagined a process through which individual people would "volunteer" to join the new society after studying what passed for a prospectus. Although they acknowledged that their society (which almost always was imagined as "democratic") would evolve once it was set in motion, they always contended that their design would ensure that the society would nonetheless enjoy a deep, abiding consensus over a wide array of issues. This consensus would, among other things, guarantee a fit between the organization of the polity and the will of the people.

What they almost always did not recognize was that the way in which they imagined the launch also evaded the dilemma that otherwise attends the founding of all democracies. Their design (1) designated the members of the proposed polity before they organized their government (e.g., through the admission of individuals onto the spaceship that would take them to their new world); (2) implicitly anointed a temporary political leadership that arranged their transportation to the new world after attending to its physical construction; and (3) settled, through the winnowing process of individual selection, most of the broad issues of political rules and governmental form (e.g., the prospectus described, in very broad terms, the kind of society that was on offer and individuals self-selected because that was the kind of society in which those individuals wanted to live).

Voilà! Their society maximized the fit between a democratic will and governmental form because the most basic questions of governance were solved before people even began to govern themselves. But, in theory and, all too often, in practice, the democratic dilemma "does not go gentle into that good night." When founding a new polity, people cannot simultaneously decide (1) who will belong; (2) what the political rules will be; and (3) who will preside over them while they decide who will belong and what the political rules will be. At least, they cannot decide these things "democratically." And this book is about how, in practice, that dilemma is evaded, encountered, or simply ignored in real societies in which real people live.

All modern foundings justify the state's right to rule in accordance with a social purpose arising from the very existence of the people. This social purpose transforms the merely instrumental survival of the state as the guarantor of a stable social order into an agency in which the people are obliged to obey because the state fulfills their normative destiny. By way of the founding, the state becomes the facilitating agent for the realization of the collective destiny of a people, whether it be their racial superiority within the community of nations, their glorification of a deity through religious discipline, their responsibility for the construction of a proletarian utopia, or the creation and preservation of democratic rights and principles. For both democratic and non-democratic states, this social purpose arises out of the state's subordination to the collective will of the people at the moment of its founding. The flip side of this subordination is the imagined consent of the people to the formation of a new sovereignty. In one way or another, all modern states, including those that cannot be classed as democracies, meld together sovereignty, the will of the people, and a transcendent social purpose as a carapace for securing social and political order. That social and political order is conceived and dedicated to the transcendent social purpose recognized and instantiated at the state's founding.

The will of the people is not an objective fact that can be ascertained empirically. It is, instead, inextricably and normatively bound up in the notion of the "people" as a collective; the very reason that a people take on an identity as a collective body contains or, better stated, confers upon them a goal or purpose that they *necessarily* "will." There is no way to independently ascertain whether or not the people actually "will" that goal or purpose because the two are inextricably embedded, one within the other. However, the connection between the elite who found a new state and the erection of the state itself must still, within their own logic and ideological understandings, be legitimated with respect to the will of that people. Put another way, both the elite and the state they erect must somehow demonstrate that the people consider them to be the agents who embody, in their actions and decisions, the collective will. In turn, the relation of the agents and the state they found are only legitimate to the extent that they authentically correspond to what the people consider to be their collective goal and purpose. The method in which the people reveal that correspondence is implied by that transcendent social purpose, while the method for determining that correspondence is democratic only within the ideology and logic of that collective purpose.

One of the tasks of this book is to demonstrate why a people cannot collectively participate in the founding of a new state without prejudging and predetermining the outcome of their participation. For that purpose, I focus on the "opening dilemma" confronted by any legislative assembly at the moment of its organization. At that moment, three fundamental elements of any legislature must be created: a formally defined membership, a presiding officer, and rules of procedure. The dilemma necessarily attending the convocation of a constitutional assembly is that none of these elements can be created if the other two do not exist already. For example, a presiding officer cannot be elected unless the members have been formally recognized as voting delegates and procedural rules have been adopted that allow motions to be proposed and decided. For the same reason, the members cannot be formally recognized (usually in the formal acceptance of their credentials, whatever form they might take) unless a presiding officer has been elected and procedural rules have been adopted. And procedural rules cannot be adopted unless members have been formally recognized and a presiding officer has been elected. The dilemma facing any constitutional assembly, at the moment of its convocation, arises out of both the necessity to create these elements and the fact that they must be created by fiat.[1] The justification for the otherwise arbitrary decisions that allow the assembly to organize arises out of and thus reveals the influence of preexisting social formations on how the will of the people is imagined and what the transcendent social purpose of the state should be.

Put another way, the political process of a founding must be mediated by a priori decisions that: (1) designate the people who are to offer their consent; (2) conceptualize how that consent is to be manifested; (3) create a process through which that consent can be transformed into a constitution; and (4) identify the political agents who will make these three decisions. Those are the practical problems that must be solved. The normative challenge is that the solution must also both create and draw upon a mythology that veils these a priori decisions in a shroud of historical inevitability which maintains that: (1) the people have always existed as a social unity; (2) the way in which consent is and should be manifested is intimately bound up with the historical destiny of that people;

---

[1] For a formal explication of this dilemma, see Richard Bensel, "The Opening Dilemma: Why Democracies Cannot Found Themselves," *Studies in American Political Development* (forthcoming 2022).

(3) the procedure through which the will of the people is translated into a constitution will result in a document consistent with that historical destiny; and (4) the political elite who actually decide how the process unfolds have the ability to correctly anticipate that result. In all these ways, myth always precedes the founding (e.g., in the imagined distinctive identity and unity of the people), attends the founding during the performance of its rituals (e.g., in the imbrication of the historical destiny of the people into the transcendent social purpose of the new state), and persists after the founding (e.g., that the people had consented to the founding because the latter properly embodies the historical destiny and will of the people). These challenges and the mythological elements that meet them are present in all foundings, both democratic and non-democratic alike.

Like most books, this one began as a dream. That dream has changed substantially over the last decade – so substantially that some of the people who once entertained its possibility may no longer remember that they did so. But I warmly thank them nonetheless: John Brooke, Dan Carpenter, Douglas Dion, Jason Frank, Ira Katznelson, Keith Krehbiel, Aziz Rana, Silvana Toska, Greg Wawro, and Pablo Yanguas. As the years passed and I began to write, I periodically revised the prospectus describing that dream. Advising me on those revisions (which were much like course corrections) were Uriel Abulof, Ivan Ermakoff, Jill Frank, Isabel Perera, and Nic van de Walle. Nic was tasked with reading both very early and very late versions of the plan for the book. Several people deserve even more thanks for indulging the details: David Bateman (who carefully read several long chapters and gave me pages and pages of comments), Jordan Ecker (who painstakingly worked through the section on the American founding, both editing the text and pointing out the errors), and Yuqing Weng (who has, often unwittingly I suspect, shaped my thinking over the years as we discussed many issues both central and peripheral to this book). Elizabeth Sanders, my colleague and partner for almost half a century now, once again wielded her legendary sharp pencil. Many of my most cherished footnotes have been banished from this book as a result. However painful it is to admit it, on this she was correct. In some respects, however, she was following in the footsteps of the reviewers for Cambridge University Press who (more gently) recommended much the same thing. I thank them as well, along with Rachel Blaifeder, my editor at Cambridge University Press. Rachel intervened at just the right time and her suggestions have, among many other things, radically rearranged the structure of the book. I very much appreciate everyone's help. One of the things that I hope to have learned over the years is how to listen, not just to what people say but to what they mean to say, sometimes inadvertently. The latter is often more important.

I

Introduction

Six modern foundings are examined in this book. Three of them involved the creation of non-democratic states: the dictatorship of the proletariat that arose out of the Russian Revolution; the fascist regime brought to life in 1933 Germany; and the Islamic republic that emerged during the Iranian Revolution. While fascinating in their own right, these will serve as a useful foil for the founding of three states whose sovereignty rests, in whole or in part, on their dedication to those principles we have come to associate with traditional democracies: the unwritten English Constitution as the embodiment of the rights of Englishmen; the American Constitution that was created after those rights of Englishmen were denied to the colonists; and the French Revolution that asserted the rights of man as a justification for its demolition of monarchy and the decadent remains of feudalism. However, as will become clear in the examination of these cases, the distinction between non-democratic and democratic foundings largely depends on the normative commitments of the beholder.[1]

That is the case for two reasons. First, all modern foundings have been committed to the existence of a mythological conception of the will of the people, including a belief that that will can be revealed only through a properly conceived and performed political practice. In democratic foundings, the will of the people is more freely conceived and openly solicited than in non-democratic

---

[1] Studies of the relation between democracy and the state generally conceive of democracy in two different ways: (1) as an end unto itself that is grounded in a belief that there really is a "will of the people" and that the study of politics should be focused on how to *perfect* the relation between that will and the rule of the state; and (2) as a means to other ends such as political stability and freedom of thought in which the notion of democracy is a necessary fiction. In the second, the will of the people is not immanent in social reality but it is nonetheless necessary that the masses *believe* that it both exists and is faithfully translated into the way in which the state rules society. This book falls into the latter category.

foundings, but all modern foundings constrain its expression to some extent. Second, all modern foundings have been grounded in a priori normative decisions concerning the identity of a people, the transcendent social purpose associated with their historical destiny, and the practice through which the popular will is and should be manifested. In the founding of the Soviet state, for example, the Bolshevik revolutionary elite identified the proletariat as "the people," declared the global communist revolution to be their destiny, and asserted that their party was the vehicle through which, with minor caveats, the will of the proletariat would be manifested.

Although modern foundings have dramatically varied in their details, they have nonetheless shared a common form. For example, they have all created a sovereign state through a ritual performance in which a revolutionary elite presumes to enact the will of the people.[2] In this founding ritual, the people are imagined to demand the creation of a state that will carry out a purpose that is immanent in the very existence of the people and thus transcends the personal interests, opinions, and desires of individuals. Because the transcendent social purpose of the new state is immanent in the very existence of the people, the way in which this melding proceeds is largely determined by a conception of the historical destiny of the people: That destiny is what gives the people a collective purpose and, in fact, their very identity as a people.

All modern states claim that they rule by popular consent and that this consent arises out of the state's commitment to what we will call a "transcendent social purpose" demanded by the citizens. This "transcendent social purpose" is "transcendent" in the sense that it transcends the interests of individuals and generations; is "social" in the sense that it both identifies and bonds a people within a collective existence; and has a "purpose" in the sense that it articulates a destiny for that people. While enabling and fulfilling the

---

[2] All modern states have had a founding, a real or imagined moment in which sovereignty was originally claimed by a new government. See, for example, Martin Loughlin and Neil Walker, "Introduction" in Martin Loughlin and Neil Walker (eds.), *The Paradox of Constitutionalism: Constituent Power and Constitutional Form* (New York: Oxford University Press, 2007), p. 3. On the ubiquity of the framing of constitutions by duly authorized assemblies after a revolution, what became a universal practice after American independence, see Hannah Arendt, *On Revolution* (New York: Penguin Books, 2006), p. 116. Charles Taylor, for example, describes the American Revolution as:

[a] watershed. It was undertaken in a backward-looking spirit, in the sense that the colonists were fighting for their established rights as Englishmen. Moreover, they were fighting under [the auspices of] colonial legislatures [originally established by Britain that had then] associated in a Congress. But out of the whole process emerges the crucial fiction of "We, the people," into whose mouth the declaration of the new constitution is placed ... the idea is invoked that a people, or, as it was also called at the time, a "nation" can exist prior to and independently of its political constitution.

Charles Taylor, *Modern Social Imaginaries* (Durham, NC: Duke University Press, 2004), pp. 156–7.

transcendent social purpose is the reason why the people grant sovereignty to their state, the state cannot simply declare what that purpose might be. It must, instead, appear to arise from the people themselves as a spontaneous and natural affirmation of their very existence.

The founding thus requires an ideological framework within which the identity of the people, their transcendent social purpose, and the granting of sovereignty can be melded into the creation of the state. In each instance, that melding has been largely determined by the role of history in the conception of the founding, in particular the conception of the historical destiny of the people. The central question animating this study is thus as follows: How have (1) the metaphysical conception of a will of the people, (2) the ritual granting of sovereignty to a new state, and (3) a transcendent social purpose been combined in the creation of modern states? For example, in the founding of the Third Reich in 1933, Nazi ideology melded the identity of the German people (as the Aryan race), their transcendent social purpose (as the realization of their historical destiny), and sovereign authority (formally recognizing Hitler as the Leader who embodied the will of the German people in realizing that destiny).

All modern foundings embed the state's right to rule in a social purpose arising from the very existence of the people. This social purpose transforms the merely instrumental survival of the state as the guarantor of a stable social order into an agency that the people are obliged to obey because the state fulfills their normative destiny. By way of the founding, the state thus becomes the facilitating agent for the realization of the collective destiny of a people, whether it be their racial superiority within the community of nations, their glorification of a deity through religious discipline, their responsibility for the construction of a proletarian utopia, or the creation and preservation of democratic rights and principles.

Alternative conceptions of the transcendent social purpose of the new state compete with one another in the period leading up to the founding moment. As we will see, this competition inevitably takes the form of alternative practices through which the will of the people can be revealed. This antecedent period sets the stage on which the revolutionary elite performs what we might well call "the enchantment" through which the transcendent social purpose, the will of the people, and the newly created state are melded. That enchantment requires sincere belief on the part of the sorcerers, and thus this book is about what those beliefs have been and how they have prescribed the forms through which founders have enacted the melding.[3]

---

[3] In all the cases we will study in this book, the founders of modern states have combined sincere belief with instrumental tactics that, at times, cannot be easily reconciled with their belief. These tactics have often been pragmatically justified as either exceptions or necessary amendments to the doctrinal dictates of revolutionary ideology. Either way, the founders have usually, as Carlo Ginzburg (quoting Tacitus) put it, come to "believe what they just made up." Carlo Ginzburg, *Fear, Reverence, Terror: Five Essays in Political Iconography* (Calcutta: Seagull Books, 2017), p. xii.

The authentic manifestation of the will of the people at the founding requires that no authority other than the people themselves can influence the expression of the will. ("Authentic" here means "truthfully revealed within a specific logic and ideological understanding." There is nothing in social reality, including the will of the people, that is "universally authentic.") In classical political theory, the only situation in which this precondition can be met is the state of nature – the pristine social and political condition in which no government has ever before existed. In this original state of nature, a people who have never experienced a state come together voluntarily to write and promise to abide by a social contract that simultaneously creates the state and confers upon it a sovereign right to rule. In the modern world, however, almost all societies have been ruled by a state at one time or another, some of them for several millennia. For them, it is the emphatic rejection of the sovereignty of the ruling state that returns the people to something like a state of nature.

A modern founding is thus the event following a revolution in which a constitutional assembly enacts that will in the form of a new social contract, a social contract that we commonly call a constitution. This description, however, overstates the distinction between the state and the people because the political elite simultaneously defines who the people are, what people demand as a transcendent social purpose, and how the sovereignty of the new state will be created. What we might otherwise interpret as a social contract between the state and the people is, in fact, thoroughly imbricated in the very identity of both of them.

The founders of all modern states have presumed to call upon, be guided by, and thus enact the will of the people as they deliberate on the institutional form and social commitments of the new government.[4] In that process, they have all contended that the people who are to be governed by the new state have consented to its creation.[5] However, that consent has always been

---

[4] This is an empirical claim. However, the ways in which founders have interpreted the will of the people have been so varied and complex that we should probably recognize that it is also a frame for conducting research. It is possible to imagine the creation of a personal dictatorship in which hired sycophants cynically assert that they both represent the people and grant sovereign authority to their leader. The key distinction between such a case and a modern founding is that these sycophants do not sincerely believe in the interpretation of the will of the people that they ostensibly enact. In modern foundings, such as that of the Soviet Union, the founders sincerely believed in the logic through which they interpreted that will. Unlike a personal dictatorship, there is a complex logic and ideological world view in modern foundings that legitimates the creation of a new sovereignty as the expression of the will of the people. It is the analysis of that logic and ideology that forms the central focus of this book and the six cases that are studied.

[5] In their otherwise exhaustive study of constitution-making and survival, Zachary Elkins, Tom Ginsburg, and James Melton inadvertently illustrate some of the complexities of the relationship between foundings and constitutions. For example, because they are interested in empirically cataloging the provisions contained in constitutions, they exclude the English Constitution

imagined and that imagination has taken radically different forms. In the case of the English Constitution, for example, consent was imagined to have occurred deep in the "mists of history" and was more or less simultaneous with the emergence of the English as a people. The precise identity of the first king of England and the exact moment when parliament was created were (and are) relatively unimportant when compared with the massive fact of a long, unbroken constitutional tradition that frames, defines, and documents the consent of the people. The English case exemplifies just one instance of imagination, an imagination that always rests on some combination of historical fact, cultural and ethnic identity, and myth-making. Writing in 1988, Edmund Morgan maintained that the "popular governments of Britain and the United States rest on fictions as much as the governments of Russia and China."[6] He drafted this passage just before the socialist regimes of the latter began their radical transformation, but his observation would have been equally valid and more theoretically powerful had he simply said: "The sovereignty of all modern governments rests on fictions."[7]

---

from their data set because it was never codified and thus contains no "provisions." They also regard the Third Reich to be nothing more than a continuation of the Weimar Constitution, which thus, as they see it, "endured" for thirty years (from 1919 to 1949). While they (correctly) count fifteen constitutions for France, they consider each of them to be the equal of the 1791 Constitution that enshrined the Declaration of the Rights of Man and the Citizen, a declaration that became the ideological litmus test for all the others as well as the most influential totem in French public life. The explanation for these discrepancies between their catalog and the cases studied in this book is that they needed a large data set for their analysis and that led them to include hundreds of prosaic constitutions that we should not consider foundings because they had little or no resonance with the popular culture within which they were written. At the same time, they exclude or belittle some of the major foundings that have shaped the world in which we live. Zachary Elkins, Tom Ginsburg, and James Melton, *The Endurance of National Constitutions* (New York: Cambridge University Press, 2009), pp. 49, 217. I should note, however, that the authors certainly understand that some constitutions "engender norms of attachment" in the citizenry while others do not, and that is also something that they want to explain (pp. 78–81).

[6] Edmund Morgan, *Inventing the People: The Rise of Popular Sovereignty in England and America* (New York: W. W. Norton, 1988), p. 13, also see p. 153 and, more generally, pp. 13–15. Morgan is overly cynical with respect to the ways in which "the opinions needed to make the many submit to the few are often at variance with observable fact." While he is certainly correct when asserting that founding elites often use symbols and concepts that are incompatible with their ideological beliefs (e.g., referenda attending the creation of the Islamic Republic of Iran), he merely views these instrumental enhancements of their popular credibility as pragmatic tools enabling the creation of the new state, a state in which the people will later come to recognize their authentic will and the tools, like the proverbial ladder, can be discarded. For a more positive view, see Arendt, *On Revolution*, p. 136, where she notes "the enormous difference in power and authority between (1) a constitution imposed by a government upon a people and (2) the constitution by which a people constitutes its own government."

[7] Perry Anderson has provided a very thoughtful Marxist interpretation of the "fiction" underlying representative government that nonetheless recognizes its popular appeal within Western political culture:

Because the transcendent social purpose of a people is an immanent part of their very nature, the people must give their consent when that purpose is embedded in the new state. In that sense, all modern foundings are "democratic" because they give the purpose of a people an actuating state form. All modern foundings thus claim to embody the will of the people.[8] However, the will of the people is emphatically *not* an objective fact that can be empirically demonstrated because, in all cases, it is defined by the mythological ground through which the people come to be.[9] Instead, the will of the people is inextricably and normatively bound up in the notion of "the people" as a collective; the very reason why a people take on an identity as a collective body contains – or, better stated, confers upon them – something (a goal or purpose) that they *necessarily* "will." There is no way to ascertain whether or not the people actually "will" that goal or purpose because the identity of the

Parliament, elected every four or five years as the sovereign expression of popular will, reflects the fictive unity of the nation back to the masses as if it were their own self-government. The economic divisions within the "citizenry" are masked by the juridical parity between exploiters and exploited, and with them the complete separation and non-participation of the masses in the work of parliament. This separation is then constantly presented and represented to the masses as the ultimate incarnation of liberty: "democracy" as the terminal point of history.

And the attending note:

In other words, it is quite wrong simply to designate parliament an "ideological apparatus" of bourgeois power without further ado. The ideological function of parliamentary sovereignty is inscribed in the formal framework of every bourgeois constitution, and is always central to the cultural dominion of capital. However, parliament is also, of course, a "political apparatus," vested with real attributes of debate and decision, which are in no sense a mere subjective trick to lull the masses. They are objective structures of once-great – still potent – historical achievement, the triumph of the ideals of the bourgeois revolution.

Perry Anderson, *The Antinomies of Antonio Gramsci* (New York: Verso, 2016), pp. 64–5.

[8] The concept of a will of the people requires an "imagined community" that is both the "collective that wills" and creates, as a direct implication of its emergence, an agency (the state) that can embody and act upon that will. In many ways, the circumstances that led to the emergence of these "imagined communities" were the same events and developments that engendered the will of the people in political imagination. See, most generally, Benedict Anderson, *Imagined Communities: Reflections on the Origin and Spread of Nationalism* (London: Verso, 2006).

[9] There is no such thing as the "will of the people." This is not because such a will must be constantly in flux and thus cannot, like Heisenberg's electrons, be precisely identified without artificially assigning a location to an object that essentially has no location. And it is not because the empirical identification of the will of the people must necessarily alter the will itself. And it is not because the people who will cannot articulate with specificity what it is that they will. And it is not even because the will of the people is a Platonic construction ushered in by the Enlightenment. All of these things are true in their own way but none of them has prevented the will of the people from becoming a fundamental principle of modern politics. The universality of that principle instead rests upon the plasticity of the concept in conjunction with the tribal passions that it enlists. While the will of the people does not exist, its imagination is nonetheless necessary for the sovereignty and stability of the modern state.

people and what they are said to "will" are inextricably embedded, one within the other.[10]

The elite who found a new state must create a conception of the will of the people before they can erect the state, and that conception must be consistent with the logic and ideological understandings that underpin how they imagine the transcendent social purpose of the people. Their conception of the will of the people is not a testable proposition. For example, the Bolsheviks believed that the proletariat could not help but support the communist revolution even though many workers were clearly not aware that they should do so. In turn, the way in which the revolutionary elite conceives of the will of the people underpins and legitimates the claim that the political elite represent and embody the will of that people as they perform the rituals that found the new state. Put another way, the elite must somehow demonstrate that the people actually consider them to be the agents who embody, in their actions and decisions, the collective will. In turn, the relation of the agents to the state they found is only legitimate to the extent that the relation authenticates what the people consider to be their collective goal and purpose. The processes through which the people reveal that correspondence is implied by the transcendent social purpose that they are said to embrace. As a result, those processes can be considered to be "democratic" only within the ideology and logic of that purpose.[11]

Sovereign states, for that reason, have always justified their right to rule in the name of something other than themselves, whether it is the remaking of society in conformance with God's design, enabling the historical destiny of a class or a people, or the realization of individual freedom and liberty. No state has ever justified its right to rule solely in its own name, putting its own survival and interests before and above the people it rules.[12] States founded on principles other than the Western notion of a "democratic will" have conceived of consent in dramatically different ways. A theocracy, for example, commits its

[10] While foundings are often interpreted as the creation of a social contract between a people and a state, in reality they embed a people *in* the new state.

[11] Western democracies have created metrics for evaluating the validity of other states based on, among other things, freedom of the press, the breadth of suffrage, and the frequency of elections. In the twenty-first century, these metrics are often characterized as universal truths. However, they ultimately rest on myths and fictions just as much as does any theocracy or authoritarian state. For example, the Islamic Republic of Iran has as much warrant for judging the validity of the USA as does the USA in judging the Islamic Republic. Both states draw their legitimacy from their own, particular, conceptions of the will of the people; and, in both instances, there exists no metric for evaluating their claims to rule outside the ambit of those conceptions.

[12] Richard Bensel, "Valor and Valkyries: Why the State Needs Valhalla," *Polity* 40: 3 (2008), pp. 386–93. In his study of the French Revolution, Georges Lefebvre stated that one of the two most important political principles is that "the state does not find its end in itself." Georges Lefebvre, trans. Elizabeth Moss Evanson, *The French Revolution from Its Origins to 1793*, vol. I (New York: Columbia University Press, 1969), pp. 146–7.

energies and purpose to the greater glory of God and the realization of God's will in human affairs. As a collateral byproduct, its subjects usually gain an enhanced opportunity to achieve salvation. Since the hallmark of a theocracy's legitimacy is its conformity to God's will, and since all of a theocracy's subjects can be assumed to desire salvation, there is simply little or no need to ask whether or not those subjects consent to the founding and rule of the state. Similarly, a state founded by a political party that mobilizes and directs the proletariat as the vanguard of history presumes that the passage of time will ultimately validate its sovereign claims. The revelation of popular consent is thus pushed forward to a moment when it is no longer meaningful; it is no longer meaningful because no one contemplates an alternative to the communist utopia once it has been established and no one retrospectively denies sovereignty to the state that has made that utopia possible. In fact, once the class destiny of the proletariat has been realized, the very reason for the state's existence vanishes.

THE ASSUMPTIONS UNDERPINNING A CONSTITUTIONAL ASSEMBLY

Before proceeding any further, we must distinguish between two different but ultimately intertwined arguments. On the one hand, all modern foundings – regardless of how exquisitely they are choreographed – are grounded in mythological, utopian pretensions even though these pretensions are not always obvious even to the disinterested observer, and often much less so to the passionate participant. Modern foundings are emphatically not a charade in which political elites foist a mythological fiction upon an unwary people. For example, the 1787 Constitutional Convention in Philadelphia was a legislated founding that was both acutely self-conscious of the formal requisites of a democratic social contract *and* unaware of how much of that social contract was already predisposed by the cultural and personal understandings with which the delegates entered into the proceedings.

On the other hand, modern foundings are not logically coherent, even on their own terms. Like all legislative assemblies, the Constitutional Convention in Philadelphia had to create three organizational elements before it could even begin to deliberate: a presiding officer, a formally defined membership, and a set of parliamentary rules. Because a founding assembly must emerge from a state of nature (in which the people can freely recognize and act upon the principles that legitimate the creation of a new state), these elements cannot be dictated to the assembly by an authority greater than itself. On the one hand, the founding assembly must self-consciously "convene itself" because it draws its sovereign authority directly from the will of the people. On the other hand, the founding assembly cannot formally recognize any organizational antecedents or prior institutional relations that might designate who might preside over its deliberations, constitute its membership, or decide what its rules of procedure might be.[13]

As a result, there is an irresolvable "opening dilemma" that attends all modern foundings. That dilemma arises from the combination of the premise that there is a pristine will of the people and the pragmatic reality that an institutional form is a prerequisite for constructing a constitution. More precisely, the opening dilemma originates in the fact that the assembly writing the constitution must (1) specify the people who will be encompassed by the social contract, (2) devise a process through which these people will designate agents (delegates) to represent their will, (3) create a procedure through which those delegates can communicate the people's will, and (4) select a leader who will preside over the deliberations of the assembly. In parliamentary terms, these prerequisites are satisfied when the members are formally identified, procedural rules are formally adopted, and a presiding officer is formally elected.

The opening dilemma thus arises from the fact that none of these prerequisites can be met if the other two have not already been fulfilled. Simply put, there is no way to begin. A presiding officer, for example, cannot be elected without (1) a membership that is qualified to vote and (2) formal rules that specify how the election is to be conducted. Rules for deliberation cannot be adopted in the absence of (1) a presiding officer who can recognize a motion for that purpose, (2) rules that specify how that motion might be adopted, and (3) a membership that is qualified both to offer and to ratify that motion.[14] And members cannot be officially recognized as such without (1) a presiding officer who can recognize a motion for that purpose and (2) formal rules that specify how that motion might be approved.[15]

---

[13] This is so even though the decisions that create these elements constitute the preconditions for the assembly's deliberations. For a narrower discussion of the initial adoption of these arrangements, see Douglas W. Rae, "Decision-Rules and Individual Values in Constitutional Choice," *American Political Science Review* 63: 1 (1969), pp. 40–56.

[14] Rules are particularly interesting because the adoption of a set of rules of procedure requires a set of rules of procedure and thus results in an infinite circularity.

[15] From a rational choice perspective, this dilemma is similar to Arrow's paradox in that it both lies at the very core of democratic theory and yet presents an irresolvable puzzle. Arrow's paradox arises when a legislative body cannot definitively choose between distinct alternatives because the members form rotating majorities whenever the alternatives (there must be at least three alternatives) are sequentially paired with one another. Kenneth J. Arrow, *Social Choice and Individual Values*, third edition (New Haven, CT: Yale University Press, 2012). Both Arrow's paradox and the opening dilemma have rarely been observed empirically. With respect to Arrow's paradox, this rarity is because the distribution and ordering of individual preferences rarely align in such a way as to induce cycling in a public choice context. For the founding of modern states, this is because revolutionary elites have already made the decisions that would have otherwise attended the opening dilemma. However, unlike Arrow's paradox, the opening dilemma has much more serious and general consequences for democratic theory because it *must* always be resolved, regardless of the distribution of preferences.

The opening dilemma thus arises from the fact that the utopian pretensions of democratic foundings preclude their very possibility in reality.[16] All founding assemblies have therefore had to "cut the Gordian knot" in practice by making an arbitrary "first move." This first move is always inconsistent with utopian principles because whatever arbitrary act is chosen cannot be traced back to a pristine will of the people.[17] The only solution to the opening dilemma is for some agent (i.e., the revolutionary elite) to make these decisions by fiat before the constitutional assembly actually meets. While those decisions allow an assembly to create a constitution that commits the state to the transcendent social purpose of the people, they also predetermine the outcome of the legislative process. In short, the opening dilemma precludes an answer to the question of "where to begin" and thus precludes any possibility that "the people" have freely decided the form and purpose of the state their agents have created.

How the will of the people can be manifested, and thus known before the constitutional assembly is organized, raises all sorts of problems that can only be resolved in a particular historical and cultural context. However, the fact that the will of the people can be known to at least some individuals prior to the organization of a constitutional assembly dramatically improves the standing of that assembly as an interpreter and agent of that will. This is the case because prior knowledge of the will places constraints upon what the assembly can do. For example, if the will of the people is already known before the assembly convenes, then the identity of "the people" must also be known (otherwise, their will could not be known). If the identity of "the people" is already known before the constitutional assembly convenes, then the assembly cannot do anything other than recognize that identity. Other constraints, such as the method for selecting delegates, are more subtle in their implications. Even so, the dilemma can still erupt in everyday political life.

Reason and logic can only tell us that an arbitrary act must precede and accompany every democratic founding; reason and logic cannot tell us which of the many arbitrary acts that might resolve the opening dilemma should be chosen. In fact, because any one of those arbitrary choices unavoidably prejudices the outcome of a modern founding, they are inevitably normative. Because we cannot eliminate the opening dilemma and its normative implications, all foundings that presume, in one form or another, a pristine will of the people are theoretically illegitimate.[18]

---

[16] See, for example, Hans Lindahl, "Constituent Power and Reflexive Identity: Towards an Ontology of Collective Selfhood" in Loughlin and Walker (eds.), *Paradox of Constitutionalism*, p. 18.

[17] The insoluble problem of "where to begin" is somewhat related to the "paradox of constitutionalism" that Martin Loughlin and Neil Walker describe in their "Introduction" in Loughlin and Walker (eds.), *Paradox of Constitutionalism*, p. 1.

[18] "Pristine" means the unmediated expression of the will of the people. Mediation can occur in several ways. For example, a higher power can dictate the convening of a constitutional assembly in terms of where it will take place, when it will begin, who is to participate, what the procedural

In most cases, those who attend founding assemblies do not even recognize that their legislative organization is entirely enabled by arbitrary acts inconsistent with their utopian pretensions. However, these arbitrary acts shape the content of modern foundings by decisively committing the assembly to a particular outcome before it has even begun to deliberate.

Since foundings are the primary philosophical and cultural devices through which the will of the people and state authority are reconciled, we are probably not going to abandon popular celebrations of these events anytime soon. Nor are future constitutional conventions likely to present themselves as anything but the untainted agents of the will of the people. But we should nonetheless acknowledge that the sovereignty of a democratic state is unavoidably dedicated to a social purpose even before the state itself is founded. Not only in theory, but also in practice.[19]

We should emphasize that the opening dilemma does not "cause" the founding of modern states to be shrouded in metaphysical assumptions about the nature and content of the will of the people. Those assumptions necessarily exist independently of the opening dilemma. However, the opening dilemma nonetheless reveals their metaphysical status because they cannot, within their own logic and understandings, enable the creation of a modern state. By clearly identifying the decisions that must be made by revolutionary fiat, the opening dilemma becomes a diagnostic tool for examining modern foundings.

Modern foundings are fragile because they rest on symbolic acts and rituals that are ultimately grounded in mythological imagination.[20] We believe in

---

rules might be, and even who will call the assembly to order. Any of these dictations would infringe upon the pristine expression of the will of the people at the founding. However, mediation also occurs whenever an assembly attempts to resolve the dilemma on its own. Simply put, mediation is as unavoidable as it is contaminating.

[19] The most common resolution of the opening dilemma has been a reliance on political tradition, cultural understandings, and social folkways. Whatever an assembly does first is thus almost always thickly embedded in the political culture and power relations that gave rise to the assembly itself and is thus socially (but not logically) legitimated as an acceptable (if not the best) resolution of the dilemma.

Legislative assemblies that are not "continuing" bodies must also confront the dilemma attending "where to begin." In Britain, for example, custom and tradition greatly determine how the dilemma at the opening of a new House of Commons is resolved: "[T]he Clerk of the House rises in his place and points with his finger to the member who is to propose the name of the Speaker." Once the Clerk's finger has pointed: "The duty of proposing and seconding the name of the Speaker is usually entrusted to the two old and influential members of the House who are not at the time Ministers of the Crown." And everything else proceeds from there. For this and other arrangements that resolve the opening dilemma for parliament, see Earl of Halsbury, *The Laws of England, Being a Complete Statement of the Whole Law of England*, vol. XXI (London: Butterworth, 1912), pp. 691, 693–5. The selection of the Speaker is not, of course, arbitrary but determined in advance by decisions that these rituals veil in ceremony. But these rituals also veil the opening dilemma itself.

[20] Political elites do, in fact, attempt to design such symbols and orchestrate appropriate performances but they are always and everywhere compelled to implement only those that effectively

foundings because they are necessary for establishing and maintaining a stable social order. But, in the end, there is nothing supporting that belief but belief itself.

REFLECTIONS, REFINEMENTS, AND QUALIFICATIONS

The founding of a modern state must rest upon the freely given consent of the people. That much is clear. But there is also a second, often overlooked, reason that the founding of a modern state must be justified as the will of the people: The purpose to which the state is dedicated at the founding is always something considered to be immanent in the social reality of the people. However, the immanence of that purpose in social reality can be identified and thus acted upon only if the will of the people is directly revealed without mediation. Because the will of the people (an abstract concept) melds with the founding purpose of the state only at the moment of the latter's creation, only the expression of the pristine will of the people can securely anchor the foundational purpose for which the state is granted sovereignty. That is the reason why the utopian pretensions of legislated foundings are absolutely essential to the transcendent justification for the state's right to rule. Only through such pretensions can the collective destiny of a people be freely revealed and thus validate the purposes to which the sovereignty of the new state will be dedicated.

In reality, however, the decisions made before the assembly begins to deliberate have already implemented assumptions with respect to the ways in which the will of the people will be expressed, the ritual forms that will create the new state, and the identification of the transcendent social purpose to which the new state will be dedicated. The assumptions that enable those decisions are profoundly metaphysical and rest on doctrinal commitments that are unique to each founding. Every founding thus entails a unique metaphysical understanding of the relation of the state to its host society.

---

make a connection with what the people intuitively and emotionally feel. During the French Revolution, for example, the people were serially presented with various depictions of "who they were and what role they played" in the matrix that connected the exercise of political power to the cosmological order that ordained, to put it quaintly, "justice, equality, and fraternity." The problem was to find the right depiction, the one that resonated with the national culture. That depiction could not be "designed," only (somewhat experimentally) "offered" as possibility.

Such a depiction locates what Clifford Geertz has called the "sacred center" of all political regimes, where political rule is connected to and is partially conflated with a sort of cosmological (often divine) purpose. From that perspective, the founding of a modern state must recognize and align with the cosmological order to which the people have already subscribed. Clifford Geertz, "Centers, Kings, and Charisma: Reflections on the Symbolics of Power" in Clifford Geertz, *Local Knowledge* (New York: Basic Books, 2000), pp. 121–46. For an application of Geertz's theory to the founding of the French Republic, see Lynn Hunt, *Politics, Culture, and Class in the French Revolution* (Berkeley: University of California Press, 2004), p. 87.

The mythical status of founding conventions as the pristine revelation of the will of the people confers an unlimited sovereignty upon these assemblies. For example, the 1787 Constitutional Convention in Philadelphia was called together to revise the Articles of Confederation but immediately discarded that document as a framework for its deliberations. Similarly, after Louis XVI convoked the Estates-General in order to raise revenue for the French state, that body turned itself into the French National Assembly and ultimately beheaded the king. As it turned out, the French and American foundings were much more disorderly and openly fraught with contradictions than the other cases we will examine in this book. However, their messiness was a direct result of their (failing) attempts to resolve the opening dilemma.[21] In England, the Soviet Union, Nazi Germany, and the Islamic Republic of Iran, things were simpler precisely because their foundings made very strong assumptions as to the nature and substance of the will of their respective peoples, assumptions that the Americans and French were unwilling to make.[22]

A people revolts because the state is not committed to the social purpose for which it is willing to cede sovereignty. The content of that rejection (i.e., the ways in which the people explain their resistance to the state) thus implies the social purpose upon which the new, succeeding state should be founded. A *revolution* decisively rejects the legitimacy of the ruling regime in the name of an alternative transcendent social purpose; a *founding* melds that purpose with a new state's right to rule. Revolutions are celebrated as national holidays because they both liberate the will of the people and reveal the transcendent social purpose that should underlie collective political life. The most persuasive rhetorical statements of that purpose, such as the right to "life, liberty, and the pursuit of happiness," emerge during the revolution and become the doorway through which the people pass into a new political order. Foundings are usually not celebrated in the same way because they are, in theory, merely the formal ratification of what was revealed in the revolution.[23] However, foundings must still be democratic in the sense that the will of the people is the only proper authority for the construction of the new state. Because the constitution is regarded as an authentic expression of the will of the people, consent becomes a mere formality (although the people are often asked to consent to what, in

---

[21] For a discussion of the influence of the opening dilemma on the politics of the French Revolution, including the role of the abstract conception of the "will of the nation" as a remedy that caused as many problems as it solved, see Arendt, *On Revolution*, pp. 154–5.

[22] As Charles Taylor puts it, the "common will is even the grounding of fascist regimes, it being understood that the real will of the people is expressed through the Leader." Taylor, *Modern Social Imaginaries*, p. 188. In such cases, the theoretical problem of how the will of the people is to be revealed is ultimately reduced to the empirical identification of the Leader.

[23] "A successful revolution directly establishes a new status and *eo ipso* a new constitution." Carl Schmitt, *Constitutional Theory* (Durham, NC: Duke University Press, 2008), p. 61. However, Schmitt would not otherwise distinguish a revolution from a founding.

theory, they have already mandated). In all these things, I am most interested in the concrete forms in which these fictions are materialized in practice.

There are at least three perspectives on constitutions: (1) a normative perspective that dictates "how they should be constructed" and provides reasons for why they should be constructed in just that way; (2) a sociological or anthropological perspective that describes how constitutions are, in fact, constructed and why they have particular political and cultural effects on their host societies; and (3) a positivist perspective that locates and analyzes the logical contradictions and empirical fantasies that constitutions must embody in order to have those political and cultural effects on their host societies (the primary effect of interest is the maintenance of social order). This book is not interested in (1), will theorize and analyze some aspects of (2), but is primarily interested in (3), where political practice (in terms of behavior and the construction and operation of social organizations) comes into direct contact with theory (the symbolic assumptions and constructions that give those social organizations the authority to do what they do).

PART I

THE FOUNDING OF DEMOCRATIC STATES

Almost all democratic theorists in the West either assert, assume, or imagine that all peoples desire a democracy as the political system in which they live.[1] This belief is, in fact, the most important a priori assumption that the founders of a democracy make, and in many ways it resembles the a priori assumption that non-democratic founders must make as well. For example, the Bolsheviks imagined that the Russian proletariat – and, indeed, workers everywhere – desired the communist revolution even if they did not yet recognize that they did.[2]

Both democratic and non-democratic founders comprehend these varying desires in one of two ways. If the beliefs and will of the people are imagined to be well defined and stable at the beginning of a national existence, then the state should be designed in such a way as to facilitate the revelation of the popular will and its imbrication in policy decisions. Although this is the universal ideal, neither democratic nor non-democratic founders have fully imagined their respective peoples in this way at the moment of the founding of a new state. If, on the other hand, the beliefs and will of the people are conceived as

[1] I do not know of a democratic theorist in the West who would concede that a people might actually prefer a non-democratic state, although there are certainly theorists who might accept the founding of a non-democratic state if the alternative were massive and extended communal violence. Perhaps the last important Western theorist to maintain that a formally democratic process was not necessary for the embedment of the will of the people in the constitution of a new state was Carl Schmitt. See, for example, Carl Schmitt, *Constitutional Theory* (Durham, NC: Duke University Press, 2008), pp. 131, 136.

[2] Orlando Figes, for example, contends that most of the Russian peasantry simply could not comprehend the notion of a will of the people that went beyond the bounds of the small community in which they lived, let alone the vanguard role of a proletariat that they had never seen and could scarcely imagine. Orlando Figes, *A People's Tragedy* (London: Penguin, 1997), pp. 98–101, 518–19.

malleable and unstable, then the political system should be designed to reshape the citizenry to enable the state to *recreate* the people so that their beliefs and their will are properly and fully articulated. The metric with which the beliefs and will of the people are compared is the transcendent social purpose of the state. The alignment of the will of the people with this transcendent social purpose is thus manufactured, at least in part, by the state after the founding.

In Western democracies, the manufacturing of this alignment is more or less invisible because most observers, participants, and theorists share the basic assumption that a people *must* desire a democracy as a natural impulse of the human condition. That assumption veils the fact that democracy is nonetheless a fantastic realm in which imaginary spirits such as electoral mandates, public opinion, the rights of citizens, freedom, and liberty mutually validate and authorize each other's (otherwise ethereal) existence.[3] The founding that ostensibly creates a democracy is just as fantastic as the rest of this realm.

There is an irresolvable paradox in all foundings that arises from the fact that a people cannot be conceived without first articulating the transcendent social purpose immanent in their collective social life. This is easy to see in the case of non-democratic foundings (e.g., the proletariat for the Soviet Union, the German race for Nazi Germany, and the Shi'ite devout for Iran). But Western democracies also make such fundamental assumptions because they identify and declare the transcendent social purpose of the new state to be the will of the people even before they define whom the people might be. The English, for instance, made "the rights of Englishmen" the transcendent social purpose of the English state, thus implicitly declaring that other peoples were not to be consulted or included in its (quite extended) founding. The American founding emerged out of complaints that the colonists were not granted "the rights of

---

[3] Recognition of the ways in which these things are related and manifested in the political process can provide tools for "assaying the ground of sovereignty" upon which a new state is founded. For example, there is a moment at the very beginning of a constitutional assembly when the practical problems of constituting that body and the presumptions of its legitimating ethos must be simultaneously reconciled. This moment involves questions that must be answered (1) in terms of procedural acts within a very material social reality and (2) in terms of the legitimating ethos that confers authority upon the constitutional assembly. Because the ethos that legitimates the constitutional convention was created and defined well before such an assembly organizes, it resolves many of the pragmatic problems attending the opening before the delegates even recognize them. In effect, the ethos veils the opening dilemma but does not eliminate it. The Bolsheviks, for example, assumed a "consensus" on proletarian preferences (which, in their view, could only be expressed collectively, even within the party) and then declared that they were acting as the vanguard of the people (and their will, even if the workers were not able, at that moment, to fully express it). That is the hard form in which a consensus can efface the dilemma. Much of the time, the USA has practiced a softer form that sometimes allows that consensus to be questioned; and, when it is, the dilemma erupts in full view. See, for example, the opening sessions in *Debates and Proceedings of the Constitutional Convention of the State of Illinois: Convened at the City of Springfield, Tuesday, December 13, 1869* (Springfield, IL: E. L. Merritt & Brother, 1870).

Englishmen" and only later and incompletely attempted to conceive of a transcendent social purpose that was not, in fact, profoundly English in content. Because the American founders did not try very hard, they failed. Heroically insisting on the universal rights of man, the French Revolution began as a utopian embrace of those universal rights as the common entitlement of all humanity; then, through progressive steps, it limited them to the French nation and thus aligned the people with the state. Along the way, the political elite excluded the vast majority of the nobility and Catholic clergy from the French nation because they did not subscribe to the transcendent social purpose as set out by the National Assembly. Behind all foundings there lurks an irresolvable paradox: the people cannot reveal, through an exemplification of their will, the transcendent social purpose of their collective existence without at the same time being fundamentally defined by that very purpose. If this material reality were not veiled, it would puncture the bubble in which democracy has been otherwise suspended in defiance of reason and logic.

Given the almost totemic position of legislative assemblies as the political manifestation of the will of the people, they have occupied a central role in democratic foundings.[4] In the democratic imagination, delegates representing the people come together to craft a constitution to which the people subsequently consent, sometimes through a separate ritual (e.g., a referendum) and sometimes not. That constitution melds the transcendent social purpose of the people, the sovereignty of the new state, and the consent of the people, and thus establishes the new state's right to rule.

These legislative assemblies all share at least three characteristics. They have presiding officers who orchestrate the proceedings; they have precisely defined memberships; and they operate under formal rules of procedure.[5] From a purely instrumental perspective, these features are shared by all legislative assemblies because they are essential to their primary functions: (1) the proposing of alternatives; (2) the disposing of those alternatives; and (3) the collective recognition of these motions in making decisions. From a theoretical perspective, these functions underpin the fiction that the delegates, as agents of the

---

[4] Legislatures, for example, have been described as the "principal embodiment of popular sovereignty," a role firmly instantiated as an "axiom of Western political thought." Charles R. Wise and Trevor L. Brown, "Laying the Foundation for Institutionalisation of Democratic Parliaments in the Newly Independent States: The Case of Ukraine," *Journal of Legislative Studies* 2: 3 (1996), p. 216.

[5] For example, in the British House of Commons, "it is absolutely necessary that the Speaker should be invested with authority to repress disorder and to give effect, promptly and decisively, to the rules and orders of the House. The ultimate authority upon all points is the House itself; but the Speaker is the executive officer by whom its rules are enforced." E. May, *Treatise on the Law, Privileges, Proceedings and Usage of Parliament*, nineteenth edition (London: Butterworths, 1976), p. 436; quoted approvingly in Stanley Bach, "The Office of Speaker in Comparative Perspective," *Journal of Legislative Studies* 5: 3–4 (1999), pp. 211–12.

people, are freely and collectively crafting a new sovereign authority.[6] Put another way, organizing a deliberative assembly in this way supports, from the perspective of normative theory, the claim that the delegates accurately and truthfully represent the will of the people as they deliberate.[7]

In democratic foundings, the collective will of the people is usually imagined as something that is revealed by this deliberative process because the popular will is assumed to exist in a more or less fully fledged form prior to the convening of a constitutional assembly. The delegates attending a constitutional assembly merely register the content of the collective will as they create a constitution. Non-democratic foundings are more complex because the collective will is imagined as partially unformed, although the general impulse toward imbricating the transcendent social purpose in the new state is imagined to be immanent in social reality. The political elite in such cases registers, refines, and corrects this impulse because it has special expertise or knowledge of what it is the people should (and imperfectly do) desire. After the state has been created, one of the most pressing tasks is to perfect the will of the people so that it aligns with the understanding of the political elite.[8] In sum, we could say that democratic foundings imagine that the deliberations of a constitutional assembly "reveal" the collective will of the people, while those in non-democratic foundings "create" that will. While overdrawn, this generalization does identify a major difference between the two kinds of foundings.

---

[6] There are at least two obvious exceptions to the need for a formal organization of a legislative assembly: very small bodies in which the costs of coordination are greatly reduced and assemblies of any size in which the wills of the members are so closely aligned that they unanimously agree on almost all issues. The First Continental Congress, for example, was an exception in both respects: the membership was very small and the members almost unanimously knew how they wanted to address the major issues. As a result, it could dispense with all but the most rudimentary parliamentary formalities. However, this assembly did not found a state because it only coordinated protest for the individual American colonies and compiled grievances to present to the British crown.

[7] All parliamentary procedures are rituals but not all legislative rituals are parliamentary procedures. For example, the election of a presiding officer is both a parliamentary procedure (in that the context and criteria for making a decision are well defined under the rules) and a ritual (in that the election is a necessary step in the recognition of a leader by the collective body). However, almost all such elections (at least in the USA) are followed by the appointment of a small committee that then ceremonially "escorts" the newly elected leader to the chair at the head of the assembly. This ceremony is clearly a ritual in which respect and deference are shown to the new leader but it is not a parliamentary procedure (because it is rarely written into the rules and could be dispensed with without affecting the substance of the election). However, there is little reason to attempt to draw a firm distinction between rituals and procedures because they often shade into one another in practice.

[8] If a people wanted only to create God's estate on earth and they believed that only holy men knew how to do this, then only holy men should be involved in the drafting of the constitution and a constitutional assembly would be, at best, irrelevant to the project. What is important here is the strength of the a priori assumptions regarding a people's desires and beliefs. It is one thing if a prospective people freely selects delegates to a founding assembly in which the delegates then decide that only holy men should be involved in the drafting of the constitution and quite another if a prospective people is simply assumed to consent to a process involving only holy men. The founding of the Islamic Republic in Iran was much closer to the latter than the former.

However, we should always keep in mind that political elites in all foundings have a clear conception of what form the state should take and that conception is conceded to be more or less different from that expressed, in whatever way, by the people themselves.[9] As we shall see, the American founders imagined that the collective will of the people desired limits on its expression in the new state in the form of: (1) the creation of some institutions that were only remotely influenced, if at all, by elections; (2) the erection of filters through which the individual wills of only some people could be formally expressed in politics; and (3) the generation of rights, both as individual rights beyond the reach of the collective will of the people and as institutional limits beyond which neither the national nor the individual states could legislate. The American elite thus imagined a collective will that, recognizing its own inherent and irremediable imperfections, placed limits on what it could do.

The French National Assembly, on the other hand, imagined very few limits to the perfectibility of the common man. While there were procedural requirements to which the exercise of state authority must conform, there were no substantive limits to what it could do. Standing at the heart of the French state, as conceived in the Declaration of the Rights of Man and of the Citizen and the Constitution of 1791, was the National Assembly in which the delegates infallibly registered the collective will of the French people. At least at the beginning of the revolution, what the people willed was what the National Assembly willed and vice versa. At the same time, however, the Assembly pragmatically conceded a role for the king in its constitutional design, temporarily creating a constitutional monarchy that was at odds with the theoretical presumptions of the new state. Once the king was gone, many of the delegates came to believe – like Rousseau, who was in many ways their leading light – that the people needed to be correctly educated in order to realize their perfectibility. From that point forward, the French Revolution took a much more authoritarian direction, a direction that inspired much of Bolshevik thinking a little over a century later.

The ancient English Constitution had none of these problems because the state (king and parliament) emerged in tandem with the identity (and thus the will) of the English people. The customs and traditions of the state, particularly those setting out relations between the king and parliament, were simultaneously the product of and shaped the identity of the English people. There could be no contradiction or discrepancy between them because state and people had mutually constituted each other.[10] The English polity could and did change

---

[9] In the American founding, for example, James Madison had a very clear, detailed plan for what became the constitution before the Philadelphia Convention even met. While he understood that parts of his plan would have to be pragmatically modified and even jettisoned altogether, he nonetheless anticipated that the opinions of the convention delegates and a process through which the constitution would be retrospectively "ratified" would be conceived and represented as a revelation of the will of the people.

[10] "[I]t was no accident that the word *democrat* did not enter the English language until 1790, under the influence of events in France: even within the theoretical framework of the most radical

over time, but any alteration was imagined as an incremental improvement on a governing framework that had existed "time out of mind."

As a result, England had no written constitution; instead, it possessed a pastiche of customary practices, proclamations, rulings, principles, and traditions that had accumulated over hundreds and hundreds of years. In its contemporary form, however, Britain does have a constitutional assembly because parliament, over the last two centuries or so, has taken on unilateral authority to "revise" that unwritten constitution and, somewhat ironically, it now resembles in some ways the French National Assembly that Edmund Burke so roundly denounced in the late eighteenth century. In theory and in practice, the British constitutional assembly now reconvenes every time a new House of Commons is organized.

In the next three chapters, we will review each of these democratic foundings in detail, examining how it is that the founders of the English, American, and French states imagined the will of the people, how they believed that will was manifested, and how they justified their authority to interpret that manifestation. When juxtaposed against the backdrop of the non-democratic foundings that we will study later in this book, there are striking similarities between these three foundings. However, if viewed only in relation to each other, the dissimilarities may be equally striking to the reader. The ancient English Constitution, for example, was so completely shrouded in thick layers of cultural tradition and custom that a distinct conception of the popular will, independent of its embedment in these layers, was almost entirely precluded as a possibility. The English people could not judge the state in terms of the realization of its transcendent social purpose because, to all intents and purposes, they *were* the state.

At the beginning of what became the American Revolution, the colonists conceived of their relation to the mother country in the same way; that conception became the basis for their claims for political inclusion. When those claims were rejected, the American founding necessitated a break with ancient English customs and traditions as the mother country interpreted them and, by way of a quite haphazard and opportunistic refashioning, their reinstantiation as the ground for the new American state. In effect, the American founders invented new customs and traditions that were, for the most part, only revisions of those that they had originally understood as the "rights of Englishmen." The French both were much more original than the Americans and mimicked some of their forms.[11] By explicitly rejecting custom and tradition in the name of "reason,"

English-speaking republicans, it simply did not make much sense to talk of a personal or party allegiance to a democracy." James Miller, *Rousseau: Dreamer of Democracy* (New Haven, CT: Yale University Press, 1984), p. 159.

[11] See, for example, William Doyle, *The Oxford History of the French Revolution*, second edition (New York: Oxford University Press, 2002), p. 118; Lynn Hunt, *Politics, Culture, and Class in the French Revolution* (Berkeley: University of California Press, 2004), pp. 13–15; Annie Jourdan, "Tumultuous Contexts and Radical Ideas (1783–89): The 'Pre-Revolution' in a Transnational

the Declaration of the Rights of Man and of the Citizen was much bolder than either the American Declaration of Independence or the Bill of Rights.[12] The French also embraced a conception of the will of the people that was much more immediate and materially tangible than the Americans had done before them.[13] While both of these innovations have been epoch-making for the history of the world, they were also fatal weaknesses with respect to the political stability of the French state.[14]

Perspective" in David Andress (ed.), *The Oxford Handbook of the French Revolution* (New York: Oxford University Press, 2015), pp. 98, 101; Hannah Arendt, *On Revolution* (New York: Penguin Books, 2006), pp. 139–40; Peter McPhee, *Liberty or Death: The French Revolution* (New Haven, CT: Yale University Press, 2017), p. 80; Jonathan Israel, *Revolutionary Ideas: An Intellectual History of the French Revolution from The Rights of Man to Robespierre* (Princeton, NJ: Princeton University Press, 2014), p. 349. In a speech before a revolutionary court in April 1797, Gracchus Babeuf took one of his doctrinal principles directly from the American Declaration of Independence: "The natural right and destiny of man are life, liberty, and the pursuit of happiness." He was executed about a month later. John Anthony Scott (ed. and trans.), *Defense of Gracchus Babeuf* (Amherst: University of Massachusetts Press, 1967), p. 20.

[12] As Jonathan Israel has so elegantly put it: "Where the American Declaration declares natural rights inherent in British constitutional liberties, the French Declaration invokes rights enshrined in laws yet to be made." Israel, Revolutionary Ideas, p. 84. Charles Taylor has addressed many of these themes, including why the American founding was much less problematic than the French and the importance of Rousseau and the invocation of a secular notion of the "sacred" in the form of the people in the latter. Charles Taylor, *Modern Social Imaginaries* (Durham, NC: Duke University Press, 2004), pp. 29, 111, 113–17, 121–9, 136–8.

[13] Carl Schmitt saw this immediacy as the most important aspect of the French Revolution: "The political greatness of the French Revolution lies in the fact that … the thought of the French people's political unity did not cease to be the deciding directive even for a moment … The constitution was … a political decision affecting the one and indivisible *nation* determining its own destiny. Every constitution presupposes this unity." Schmitt, *Constitutional Theory*, pp. 102–3. We should probably insert "subsequent" before "constitution" in that last sentence. We should also note Schmitt's reference to the "destiny" of the people.

[14] Writing in 1798, after the guillotine had done much of its work, Immanuel Kant still lauded the French Revolution: "[S]uch a phenomenon in the history of the world will never be forgotten, because it has revealed at the base of human nature a possibility of moral progress which no political figure had previously suspected. Even if we must return to the Old Regime, these first hours of freedom, as a philosophical testimony, will lose nothing of their value." McPhee, *Liberty or Death*, p. x. Even though the state founded by the French Revolution proved to be chronically unstable, the experiment with unqualified democracy became an archetype or standard for the analysis of all subsequent revolutions. For example, Carl Schmitt declared that the French Revolution was the first instance "of a people reaching a decision regarding their political existence as a whole" and then used "certain aspects of the French Revolution as a baseline" for analyzing deviations of other revolutions from the French model. Ellen Kennedy, "An Introduction to Carl Schmitt's Constitutional Theory: Issues and Context" in Schmitt, *Constitutional Theory*, p. 32. Hannah Arendt simply concluded that the "sad truth of the matter is that the French Revolution, which ended in disaster, has made world history, while the American Revolution, so triumphantly successful, has remained an event of little more than local importance." Arendt, *On Revolution*, p. 46. Also see Israel, *Revolutionary Ideas*, p. 696; Georges Lefebvre, trans. Elizabeth Moss Evanson, *The French Revolution from Its Origins to 1793*, vol. I (New York: Columbia University Press, 1969), p. 91.

2

"The Rights of Englishmen" and the English Constitution

Although commonly considered to be the birthplace of constitutional liberty and democratic rights, England did not have a distinct founding moment in which the people consented to the creation of a state. Such moments, I have argued, presume a people (as those who can and must consent to the creation of a state), a transcendent social purpose (that animates the state at and after the founding), and a leader (as the person and/or party that both articulates that social purpose and calls the people forth into mutual consultation). Perhaps paradoxically, these elements are often more apparent in the founding of otherwise non-democratic states than they are in democratic states. And nowhere are they more ambiguous than in the founding of what became English democracy.[1] In fact, the emergence of the English people, recognition of their immanent social purpose, and the creation of the English Constitution have been more or less intentionally shrouded in the mists of history.[2]

The vast majority of national states have an imagined history that both creates an identity for the people and defines their collective social destiny.

---

[1] As I will show, the emergence of a democratic state was, in both theory and fact, confined to England. While we now commonly speak of "Great Britain" and the "British" parliament, Scotland and Northern Ireland (and to a lesser degree Wales) are appendages to the primary historical trajectory of the English people and their democracy. I will address the political implications of this relationship between England and the other regions later in this chapter.

[2] For example, Frederick Pollock and Frederic William Maitland stated: "On the whole the state of English law before the [Norman] Conquest presents a great deal of obscurity to a modern inquirer." They nonetheless spent almost seventy pages attempting to discern what this law might have been. There are many things we do not know about the past but we try to reconstruct only those things that serve a purpose in the present. In their case, their purpose was to provide an anchor for a linear narrative of the development of English law. Frederick Pollock and Frederic William Maitland, *The History of English Law before the Time of Edward I*, vol. 1 (Indianapolis: Liberty Fund, 2010), pp. 33, 45.

At the founding, both that history and that destiny became enshrined in the state. Because that history assumes a more or less fixed meaning at the founding, historical research is subsequently confined to confirming that meaning (particularly in non-democratic states) or becomes an academic exercise in parting the veils of antiquity. In the latter case, the investigation usually reinforces the legitimacy of the state whatever the findings might be. For the English, however, the mists of history both shroud and constitute the very essence of national identity and the social purpose of the state precisely because there has been no founding moment in which the meaning of these things was clearly asserted. As a result, English historians have assiduously tilled the fields of prehistory as they search for the time in which the English became a people, a ruler became their monarch, and the common law first enshrined their (English) liberties.[3] When English historians put down in words what they have uncovered, the political stakes are thus higher than in those states with clearly defined founding moments.

At the very end of the nineteenth century, Pollock and Maitland wrote: "Such is the unity of all history that any one who endeavours to tell a piece of it must feel that his first sentence tears a seamless web."[4] With many English historians, that observation could be turned on its head: The very first sentence begins the construction of a seamless web that imposes a unity upon all history. With respect to the English nation, this seamless web has a name: "Whig history." First articulated as a political defense of parliamentary prerogatives, the Whigs constructed an interpretation of the past that viewed "the progress of English society" as a more or less inexorable expansion of liberty, germination of national identity, and emergence of parliament as the embodiment of the popular will.

Whiggish history insists, on the one hand, that the present has descended gradually and inevitably from the past; and, on the other, that this descent has, notwithstanding a few detours and side steps, incrementally perfected the English state and nation.[5] William Blackstone, for example, declared that

---

[3] For Edmund Burke, the very fact that institutions such as the common law had existed from time immemorial demonstrated both their venerability and their virtuous relevance in the present. The "rights of Englishmen" resided in the customs of the people and, when incorporated into political practice, became, in Burke's own words, "the disposition of a stupendous wisdom, moulding together the great mysterious incorporation of the human race," which, in turn, "is placed in a just correspondence and symmetry with the order of the world." As Pocock put it, the "body of rules" expressed in the common law and "English political thought ... contained all that was necessary" for understanding and realizing the relationship between politics and the nature of English society. However, the mists of history obscure the precise way in which this relationship had arisen and, as a result, "the law ... cannot be reduced to general principles, or scientific laws." J. G. A. Pocock, "Burke and the Ancient Constitution: A Problem in the History of Ideas," *Historical Journal* 3: 2 (1960), pp. 128, 130–1, 133; also see pp. 125, 136, 140.

[4] Pollock and Maitland, *History of English Law*, vol. 1, p. 3.

[5] See, for example, David Bateman, *Disenfranchising Democracy: Constructing the Electorate in the United States, the United Kingdom, and France* (New York: Cambridge University Press, 2018), pp. 202–3. For a brief account of the origin of what became the English state from a

"the history of our laws and liberties" has involved a "gradual progress, among our British and Saxon ancestors, till their total eclipse at the Norman conquest; from which they have gradually emerged, and risen to the perfection they now enjoy." He went on to say that "the fundamental maxims and rules of the law ... have been and are every day improving, and are now fraught with the accumulated wisdom of ages." As a result, England enjoys "a constitution so wisely contrived, so strongly raised, and so highly finished, [that] it is hard to speak with that praise, which is justly and severely its due." Blackstone concluded that the English Constitution was the "noblest inheritance of mankind."[6] This Whiggish perspective both explains how England (now Britain) came to be and anchors the legitimacy of the state in the dim recesses of the past.[7]

THE MISTS OF HISTORY

Given the absence of a definitive founding moment, many English historians have pressed their research deep into the mists of prehistory. In these forays, the ways in which evidence survived the passage of time have often shaped the arguments that they make. For example, Pollock and Maitland recognized "a temptation of some practical danger, that of overrating both the trustworthiness of written documents and the importance of the matters they deal with as compared with other things for which the direct authority of documents is wanting."[8] We know much more, for instance, about the wardrobes of monarchs and courtiers, the weaponry and battle armor of knights, and the castles and manor houses of the nobility than we do about their attitudes toward and understandings of political identity and the proper role of government.[9]

slightly different perspective, see Thomas Ertman, *Birth of the Leviathan: Building States and Regimes in Medieval and Early Modern Europe* (Cambridge: Cambridge University Press, 1997), pp. 156–69.

[6] William Blackstone, *Commentaries on the Laws of England*, Book IV, eds. Edward Christian, Joseph Chitty, Thomas Lee, John Eyken Hovenden, and Archer Ryland (Philadelphia: J.B. Lippincott, 1855), p. 342 [442–3 in the original manuscript].

[7] J. C. Holt, *Magna Carta* (Cambridge: Cambridge University Press, 1969), p. 8.

[8] Pollock and Maitland, *History of English Law*, vol. 1, p. 29. In order to survive, documents must first be written. In the centuries preceding the Norman Conquest, however, much of the business of government was conducted orally. Those serving a monarch depended on their memories when attempting to recall what orders had been given, and those memories, fragile as they were in their own time, are forever lost to us in ours. Even when written, these records have, as Pauline Stafford notes, their own biases. For example, clerics did most of the writing in the tenth and eleventh centuries and historical interpretation of the documents created then "is inseparable from that of the intellectual milieu of the church." Pauline Stafford, *Unification and Conquest: A Political and Social History of England in the Tenth and Eleventh Centuries* (London: Edward Arnold, 1989), pp. 3–4.

[9] Modern interpretation of written documents assumes knowledge of an indefinite mass of "custom and practice" for which we have little or no information. For example, there is a complex relation

Much of early English history, not only the lived experience of the masses but even the most pertinent facts of state formation, is forever lost.[10] Even where evidence has survived, the form and content sometimes frustrate those who would project an "English" existence into the remotest regions of the past. Although he was one of the most daring and persistent of these historians, David Hume did not attempt to reconstruct the ancient lineage of Saxon kings and the peoples they ruled before their invasion of Britain in the mid-fifth century:

We shall not attempt to trace any higher the origin of those princes and nations. It is evident what fruitless labour it must be to search, in those barbarous and illiterate ages, for the annals of a people, when their first leaders, known in any true history, were believed by them to be the fourth in descent from a fabulous deity, or from a man, exalted by ignorance into that character. The dark industry of antiquaries, led by imaginary analogies of names, or by uncertain traditions, would in vain attempt to pierce into that deep obscurity, which covers the remote history of those nations.[11]

English scholars have attempted to "pierce into that deep obscurity" with varying degrees of courage. William Stubbs, for instance, believed that he could clearly see the pattern that the English had woven into the development of their civilization even though he recognized that many of the details had been lost.[12]

---

between historical custom that defines, on the one hand, the respective duties and responsibilities of lord and serf, and, on the other, the legal principle that articulates and enforces an obligation or privilege. The former rests on unwritten communal understandings, the latter on formal institutions and their officers. If we have access only to the latter, we cannot reconstruct political and social reality. Pollock and Maitland, *History of English Law*, vol. 1, pp. 30, 454.

[10] For example, there exists "very little information" on the constitutional history of the Normans before the Conquest. William Stubbs, *The Constitutional History of England in Its Origin and Development*, vol. 1, fourth edition (Oxford: Clarendon Press, 1883), p. 270. Pollock and Maitland similarly confessed that "the principles which regulated the existence and the competence of seigniorial courts are very dark to us." They also observed that "the law of property [was] almost entirely left in the region of unwritten custom and local usage" during the Middle Ages because people did "nearly all their business in person and by word of mouth with neighbours whom they know" and thus left behind almost no written records of their transactions. Pollock and Maitland, *History of English Law*, vol. 1, pp. 79, 49, 63–4.

[11] David Hume, *The History of England from the Invasion of Julius Caesar to the Revolution in 1688*, vol. 1 (Indianapolis: Liberty Fund, 1983), p. 17. Also see Henry Loyn, *The Making of the English Nation: From the Anglo-Saxons to Edward I* (London: Thames and Hudson, 1991), p. 10.

[12] Stubbs admitted that he was only able "for the first time ... to grasp an idea of [England's] condition" around the beginning of the seventh century. Stubbs, *Constitutional History of England*, vol. 1, p. 187. Chadwick similarly stated that "our knowledge of English history begins" at the very end of the sixth century. H. Munro Chadwick, *The Origin of the English Nation* (Cambridge: Cambridge University Press, 1907), p. 1. Stenton is a little more adventurous in that he concludes that "an outline of continuous English history begins to appear" around the year 550. F. M. Stenton *Anglo-Saxon England*, third edition (Oxford: Oxford University Press, 1971), p. viii.

Whatever the quality of the evidence, the reason for persevering has always been clear. B. Wilkinson, for instance, was "acutely aware of the continuity of history" as both a principle and motivation for research.

Today, we are perhaps more acutely aware of the continuity of history. We value the Middle Ages as providing not so much the foundation as the pattern of our civilization. We appreciate more the underlying identity of our twentieth-century way of life with that of our medieval predecessors. We have to study the Middle Ages not merely as a foundation but for their own sake. They were a period when our own constitutional ideals and traditions, which still continue and without which our civilization cannot live, were simply and vigorously expressed.[13]

One of the reasons for insisting upon historical continuity is that it bestows legitimacy upon the present.

THE ORIGIN OF THE ENGLISH PEOPLE

Histories of the English people often announce the identity of the protagonist in their very title and thus immediately announce what facts and information will be pertinent to the narrative.[14] From the very outset, one necessary element in such narratives is the construction of the protagonist itself: Whom should we regard as the English people and from whence did they come? This question is distinct from but clearly related to a second: When did the English people become a nation? Both of these are almost always associated, at least remotely, with a third: When did the English Constitution begin to enshrine English liberties?[15]

David Rannie begins his book on the English Constitution by stating that the Angles, Jutes, and Saxons were the three German tribes that occupied Britain after the Romans left the island. Although the Saxons were the most numerous and powerful of the three, the name of "the new German colony ... came to be called the land of the Angles – Angleland, England." He then enjoins the reader

---

[13] B. Wilkinson, *Constitutional History of Medieval England, 1216–1399*, vol. I (London: Longmans, Green, 1948), p. xv.

[14] Green, for example, titled his two-volume study *A Short History of the English People* and announced in the very first paragraph: "For the fatherland of the English race we must look far away from England itself [to] what we now call Sleswick, a district in the heart of the peninsula which parts the Baltic from the Northern seas." Although Green was referring to the fifth century and a people then residing in what we now call Denmark, he identified this people as the "English." The English people thus emerged from the mists of history after their migration to the island of Britain and their destiny has subsequently unfolded as a teleological march into the present. John Richard Green, *A Short History of the English People* (London: J. M. Dent & Sons, 1960 [1915]), p. 1.

[15] For dissent from "the obsessive teleology that is the Original Sin of English historians," see Patrick Wormald, *The Making of English Law. Volume 1: Legislation and Its Limits* (Oxford: Blackwell, 1999), p. 11; G. O. Sayles, *The King's Parliament of England* (New York: W. W. Norton, 1974), p. 136.

that "you must learn to call them [the three tribes] by one name, a name you know very well. You must learn to call them the English." By 600 AD, "a great number of Germans, called the English, were firmly settled in every part of the present England."[16]

There was thus, in at least some versions of the standard historical narrative, an "English people" even before they arrived in Britain. As the "English" made their new homes on the island, their language began to drift away from the original Germanic tongues and became distinct as, first, Old English and then the modern vernacular. The evolution of the language paralleled in many ways the development of the English nation. In fact, that nation, if we think of it as a consciousness of a single people, emerged more or less in lockstep with the increasing distinctiveness of the language. If we conceive of the nation as comprising a people who desire a state that would unify their community under one government, then the English nation emerged somewhat later than both the people and the language. All of this presumes that the peoples who inhabited Britain before the invasion did not play a significant role in the emergence of the English people and nation.

THE LEGACY OF THE ROMAN EMPIRE

Britain was inhabited by Celts when Julius Caesar invaded the island in 55 BC. Hume reports that the Britons, as they were called, were "a military people" divided into many tribes. Their "sole property was their arms and their cattle" and, in their simplicity, "they had acquired a relish for liberty" that made it impossible "for their princes or chieftains to establish any despotic authority over them." Although Caesar clearly demonstrated Rome's ability to conquer these people, he did not then occupy the island. However, the Romans came for good in 43 AD. After the Romans had pacified Britain, the Britons, now "disarmed, dispirited, and submissive," lost "all desire and even idea of their former liberty and independence."[17] They were then incorporated into the Roman Empire for the next 400 years. When Roman rule came to an end in the first part of the fifth century, the history of the Britons came to an end with it.[18]

---

[16] David Watson Rannie, *Historical Outline of the English Constitution for Beginners* (New York: Charles Scribner's Sons, 1887), p. 4.

[17] Hume, *History of England*, vol. 1, pp. 4–5, 10.

[18] When the Romans left Britain, Burke wrote, "the fabulous and heroic age of our nation" began and "the stage is again crowded with enchanters, giants, and all the extravagant images of the wildest and most remote antiquity." Onto "this darkened theatre ... some old writers have introduced those characters and actions which have afforded such ample matter to poets and so much perplexity to historians." Edmund Burke, "Abridgment of the English History" in *The Works of the Right Honorable Edmund Burke*, vol. VII, third edition (Boston, MA: Little, Brown, 1869), pp. 233–4. Also see Loyn, *Making of the English Nation*, p. 19; Hume, *History of England*, vol. 1, p. 162.

The only thing known for certain (and even that is known very imperfectly) is that the Britons were unable or unwilling to maintain the institutions and the material infrastructure (e.g., the roads and towns) that the Romans had erected.[19] Some historians contend that Roman influence was in gradual decline even before the end of the fourth century and that the Celts became dominant once more. Others argue that Roman and Celtic institutions, beliefs, and practices merged into something like a "hybrid" culture. A third possibility is that the eastern portion of the island remained more or less Roman in its institutions and culture while these reverted to something much more Celtic in the western regions. But most such interpretations simply attempt to explain in what way Roman influence declined and how long it persisted before it disappeared. Almost all historians concede that the Romans ultimately left little behind aside from mounds of stone and ruined roads.[20]

Pollock and Maitland, for example, flatly stated that "there is no real evidence" that "Roman institutions persisted after Britain was abandoned by the Roman power." Both "the language and the religion of Rome were effaced" and "there is no trace of the laws and jurisprudence of imperial Rome." In their view, the complete disappearance of Roman influence made way for the later emergence "of our Germanic polity" following the Anglo-Saxon invasions.[21]

In the absence of solid evidence, English historians have been tempted, in good faith, to fill in the gap with interpretations that support their own grand developmental narratives. One of the most widely accepted narratives describes an invitation to Saxon "adventurers" by the Britons in the middle of the fifth century, not long after the Romans had finally abandoned the island for good. By this time, as Stenton noted, Britain had entered a period "outside the range of recorded history" and accounts of the invitation depend on untrustworthy "British traditions." However, we are more interested in the way in which the narrative is structured than in its accuracy as historical fact. In that vein,

---

[19] Loyn, *Making of the English Nation*, p. 13. After 420, no coins were apparently minted in Britain until the seventh century because the "need for coined money [had] disappeared" (pp. 18–19).

[20] Burke wrote:

> When the Romans deserted this island, they left a country, with regard to the arts of war or government, in a manner barbarous, but destitute of that spirit or those advantages with which sometimes barbarism is attended ... After a peaceable possession of more than three hundred years, the Britons derived but very few benefits from their subjection to the conquerors and civilizers of mankind. (Burke, "Abridgment of the English History," pp. 224–5)

> For a review of the historical literature on the decline of Roman rule in Britain, see Don Henson, *The Origins of the Anglo-Saxons* (Ely: Anglo-Saxon Books, 2006), pp. 49–51.

[21] Pollock and Maitland, *History of English Law*, vol. 1, pp. xlii–xliii. When the principles of Roman law do reappear in Britain, they are imported from the Continent as antique political practice or in the form of canon law by way of the Catholic Church after the Norman Conquest (pp. xliv, 57, 124, 130–1, 373). Also see Loyn, *Making of the English Nation*, p. 19.

Stenton reported that a Saxon chief named Hengest brought his men across the North Sea and entered "the service of a British king." Hengest subsequently revolted and fought several battles that prepared the ground for the occupation of what became Kent by the Saxons.

Because Hengest had served a British king, however disloyally, instead of ruling in his own right, Stenton concluded that he "belongs to the history of Britain rather than to that of England" because the history of "England" begins with the replacement of the Britons by the Saxons. However, the Saxons became "the English" so soon after their original arrival that the two events were almost simultaneous. When discussing the Saxon origin of place names in Sussex, for example, Stenton reported that many of them denoted "groups of persons" and would have been "familiar to the English peoples before their migration to Britain" at the beginning of the sixth century.[22] Burke similarly refers to the Saxons as "the English" from the very moment of their invasion of Britain.[23] Ann Williams, writing some 200 years after Burke, also describes the period from 400 to 600 AD as the "period of English settlement in Britain."[24] The Saxons, it seems, were "English" either before or shortly after they arrived in "England."

THE ANGLO-SAXON CENTURIES

Hume describes the Saxon invaders as "fierce conquerors" who "threw every thing" that the Britons had inherited from the Romans "back into ancient barbarity" as they proceeded with "the total extermination" of the original inhabitants. He concludes that there have been "few conquests more ruinous than that of the Saxons."[25] Loyn similarly describes the Saxon invasions as

---

[22] Stenton, *Anglo-Saxon England*, pp. 1–2, 17–19, 29, 81. Also see Hume, *History of England*, vol. 1, p. 15.

[23] Burke, "Abridgment of English History," p. 233.

[24] Ann Williams, *Kingship and Government in Pre-Conquest England, c. 500–1066* (New York: St. Martin's Press, 1999), p. xiv. Hume, however, first referred to the "English" when he recounted the "vigour" with which they "vanquished an invasion by the Danes" in 851. Hume, *History of England*, vol. 1, p. 59. Burke, for his part, wrote that the "southern part" of Britain was "for the first time authentically known by the name of England" in 827. Burke, "Abridgment of English History," p. 258. Dating the emergence of the nation somewhat later, Pollock and Maitland said that an "English nation is gradually forming itself" during the reign of Henry II (1154–89). By that time, there could be heard "a cry of 'England for the English.'" Pollock and Maitland, *History of English Law*, vol. 1, p. 488.

[25] Hume, *History of England*, vol. 1, pp. 16, 23–4, 227. Although Stenton rejected the notion that Britons were "deliberately exterminated" by their "English conquerors," he did maintain that the original inhabitants had no influence over the post-invasion "fabric of the social order, the fundamental technicalities of law," or organization of government. Stenton, *Anglo-Saxon England*, pp. 314–15. Also see Loyn, *Making of the English Nation*, p. 25–6. While Burke said that "the British race ... was not wholly extirpated," he also noted that they left almost no evidence of influence on their Saxon conquerors. Burke, "Abridgment of English History,"

"one of the truly regressive periods in British history."[26] At first, the Saxon invaders are said to have kept "links with their homelands and the wider north-western Germanic world." Over time, however, "an insular Germanic culture" emerged as "self-consciously Anglo-Saxon" kingdoms provided a cultural sub-strate that facilitated both the subsequent conversion of the population to Christianity and the propagation of a "national myth" in which the Saxon migration became interpreted as the arrival of a "chosen people."[27]

The "chosen people" were emphatically German. Pollock and Maitland, for example, insisted that the legal culture that organized Anglo-Saxon society rested upon "pure Germanic law" right up to the Norman Conquest. They found no evidence that "ancient British custom" or any "Celtic element" had shaped what was becoming an English legal tradition.[28] Stubbs wrote that the Saxons brought with them the "common civilization" that they had shared with "their German kinsfolk." Their social structure, for instance, imposed a three-tiered system of ranks: nobles, freemen, and "the laet" (the latter occupying a position somewhere between a freeman and a slave). Following German tradition, they divided their territories into communal townships, used "the mark system of land-ownership," relied on kindred as a source for legal rights and responsibilities, and elected their governing officials.[29] This emphasis on a German inheritance as the wellspring of English law and culture creates, in the traditional narrative, a sound foundation for English identity, but, as I shall discuss later, it also asserts that no other element (e.g., the Welsh, the Scots, or the Irish) significantly influenced the origins and evolution of English society. England was the core of what became the United Kingdom and that core was German.

Soon after the invasion, the Saxons began to call themselves "Angelcyn" and "Englisc."[30] Later, in the early seventh century, Pope Gregory the Great "coined" the term "gens Anglorum ... to describe the Germanic inhabitants of south-eastern Britain" and used the term "Anguli (or Angli), to describe the

---

pp. 232–3. Kirby, however, notes that at least some historians maintain that the Britons, although a conquered people, were still able to influence their Saxon overlords. Nevertheless, the evidence for influence remains weak and the debate itself only testifies to the intense pressure to impose very large conclusions on the nature of social change even in the absence of evidence. D. P. Kirby, *The Making of Early England* (New York: Schocken Books, 1968), pp. 29–32.

[26] Loyn, *Making of the English Nation*, p. 25. In Kirby's words, "the darkness of the Anglo-Saxon Conquest descends" almost immediately after the Romans abandoned Britain. Kirby, *Making of Early England*, pp. 14, 36.

[27] Henson, *Origins of the Anglo-Saxons*, p. 163.

[28] Pollock and Maitland, *History of English Law*, vol. 1, pp. xxxix–xli. They concluded that "in its general features, Anglo-Saxon law is not only archaic but offers an especially pure type of Germanic archaism" (p. 49).

[29] Stubbs, *Constitutional History of England*, vol. 1, pp. 68–9, 71.

[30] Chadwick, *Origin of the English Nation*, pp. 88–9. Henson, however, contends that the term "English" did not come into common usage until the tenth century. Henson, *Origins of the Anglo-Saxons*, pp. 35, 108.

Germanic inhabitants of Britain." Bede, perhaps the most noted contemporary chronicler, believed that "the Anglo-Saxon peoples ... were united" by both their common language, which distinguished them "from their British, Irish and Pictish neighbors," and "their shared Christian faith into one gens Anglorum in the sight of God. Bede wanted the Church to not only create but [also] name this new communal identity and thus to make the *gens Anglorum* a people with a covenant, like Israel." In the centuries following the creation of an archiepiscopal see at Canterbury, the Roman Catholic Church consistently favored political unification as a means of furthering "the ideal of a single English (indeed a single British) church." The ambitions of the Church and the Saxon kings were thus aligned and, in the ninth century, King Alfred "adopted the vernacular label of the *Angelcynn* to denote a people with a shared, Christian, past, united under West Saxon rule," confirming "that English self-consciousness" must acknowledge "a common Christianity centered on Canterbury."[31]

The *Encyclopaedia Britannica* may be the premier authority on such matters. In the ninth edition, the *Encyclopaedia* reported that the "Teutonic settlers themselves would not give their country a common name till they had reached some degree of political unity; but when they gave it a name, that name was naturally *England*. England, in short, as a political unity, began to be formed in the ninth century; it received its name in the tenth."[32] By the early seventeenth century, the realm and the people had become fully united under English law. Any child born in a place where the king of England exercised sovereignty was considered a "natural-born subject," while, with few exceptions, every child born in any other place was "an alien," regardless of the nationality of his or her parents.[33] This principle rested on the direct relationship between the king and the subject: To be born in a place where the king exercised sovereignty automatically both granted the protection of the king and compelled allegiance to the crown. Except in rare cases, the standing of the parents did not determine the status of the child.[34] To be an Englishman one had to be a subject of the king, not a citizen of the state.

---

[31] See the entry "English People" in Michael Lapidge (ed.), *The Blackwell Encyclopaedia of Anglo-Saxon England* (Oxford: Blackwell, 1998), p. 170. Williams, *Kingship and Government*, p. 12. "Angelcynn" can be roughly translated as "Englishkind" and "directly translates the Latin gens Anglorum."

[32] *The Encyclopaedia Britannica ... with American Revisions and Additions*, vol. VIII, ninth edition (Chicago: Werner, 1896), p. 283.

[33] As in other things, the emergence of this legal principle enshrining English nationality was delayed by the Norman Conquest because the crown's possessions on the Continent contained many people who could not, in any sense, be considered "English." Pollock and Maitland, *History of English Law*, vol. 1, pp. 483, 486.

[34] Herbert Broom, *Constitutional Law*, second edition (London: W. Maxwell & Son, 1885), pp. 26–7, 32–3. To be the king's subject was to be involved in a reciprocal relationship in which the subject owed allegiance to the king and, in return, the king extended the crown's protection

Although people, language, and nation are usually distinguished from one another, the standard historical narrative nevertheless conceives them as different aspects of the same process through which the people become a nation. This notion of a nation then anchors a conception of the collective that progressively consents to the formation of the English state. The origin of the people is "natural" in that no one designed or dictated its emergence. However, the transformation of the people into a nation was intentionally willed by the people themselves. One of the most significant events, for example, was King Alfred's occupation of London in 886; this sparked spontaneous recognition of his political leadership and thus, in Stenton's words, "marked the achievement of a new stage in the advance of the English peoples towards political unity." Within Stenton's teleological rendering of the rise of the English nation, this "acceptance of Alfred's overlordship expressed a feeling that he stood for interests common to the whole English race."[35] But was Alfred the first "English king"? Put another way, was he the first monarch who could lead the people as they came to recognize and realize their natural rights and liberties?

THE FIRST KING OF ENGLAND

Most of the history of the period between the fifth and eleventh centuries is framed as an inevitable progress toward the unification of the English under one king. From that perspective, most historians consider the first king of England to be the ruler who first politically unified the nation. Political unification, in turn, has been variously defined as either universal recognition of personal primacy within a system of kingdoms (with little or no formal institutional integration between them), durable ties of family alliance once that system begins to consolidate (again with little or no formal institutional integration), or formal political integration (including ritual acknowledgment in coronation ceremonies and exchanges of documents). However defined, political unification identifies the onset of an unbroken line of monarchs who have

to the subject. The development of this notion of "allegiance" coincided with the increasing centralization of sovereign authority and the resulting conflation of crown, state, and nation (pp. 26–8). Also see Pollock and Maitland, *History of English Law*, vol. 1, p. 316.

[35] Stenton, *Anglo-Saxon England*, p. 259. Stenton in much the same way interpreted King Edwin's military victory over the Northumbrians in 616 as enabling the formation of a "confederation" that "foreshadowed a kingdom of all England," but he described this as a precocious, imperfect "confederation of a barbarian type" grounded in "the mere allegiance of individuals" (pp. 79–80). For a more contingent interpretation of the political consolidation of England, see Stafford, *Unification and Conquest*, pp. v, 103, 128. She, for example, states that "the boundaries of England" were the product of "kingly aspiration, external development and accident" during the tenth and eleventh centuries and that there was "little of English nationalism" in the years following the Norman Conquest.

ruled England up to the present.[36] One exception to that unbroken sequence occurred in the middle of the seventeenth century, when Oliver Cromwell ruled over most of the nation. But that exception has usually been viewed as confirming the rather teleological unfolding of the intertwined destinies of crown and state.

Another possible exception occurred in 1689 when William of Orange was invited by parliament to assume the throne after James II had fled to France. At the time, the convention (a name parliament took upon itself because only a king could call the latter into session) had an "opportunity we are like never to have again in the World" to remake the form of the state and its relation to the people it governed (the quote comes from a tract published in that period). However, Edmund Morgan notes that most writers at the time "agreed that the best form was the ancient constitution, distinguished by the sharing of authority among a hereditary monarchy, a hereditary nobility, and a popularly elected body of representatives." Morgan also says that, by "the 1760s," the conventional view of the Glorious Revolution was that it "had restored the original constitution established by the people during a time to which the memory of man ran not."[37]

Because it restored England to what it had more or less been before 1688, the Glorious Revolution might have been "Glorious" but it was not a "Revolution." Even so, the deposition of James II and the crowning of William and Mary still appeared to be, at least technically, somewhat akin to a coup d'état. Despite appearances, the standard historical narrative has had little difficulty squaring the exchange of rulers with the "natural" evolution of the English nation. As Charles Dickens put it:

[A]ll those who had served in any of the parliaments of King Charles the Second ... resolved ... that the throne was vacant by the conduct of King James the Second; that it was inconsistent with the safety and welfare of the Protestant kingdom to be governed by a popish prince; that the Prince and Princess of Orange should be king and queen during their lives and the life of the survivor of them; and that their children should succeed them, if they had any. That if they had none, the Princess Anne and her children should succeed; that if she had none, the heirs of the Prince of Orange should succeed.

And thus the "Protestant religion was established in England" while, at the same time, the succession was spliced together in such a way that Anne, the daughter of James, ultimately came to the throne in 1702.[38]

---

[36] For example, the half-century between 1016, when Cnut ascended the throne, and 1066, when William the Conqueror was crowned, witnessed four changes in dynasty. However, there was always a "king of England." Loyn, Making of the English Nation, pp. 73–4.

[37] Edmund Morgan, *Inventing the People: The Rise of Popular Sovereignty in England and America* (New York: W. W. Norton, 1988), pp. 108, 230–1; also see p. 120.

[38] Charles Dickens, *A Child's History of England* (New York: Frank F. Lovell and Co., n.d.), p. 363.

While religion played a central role, Richard Kay stresses that "it was a revolution ostensibly undertaken to save the law [the principles of the ancient English Constitution]." However, "[e]very step of the process by which William and Mary became King and Queen was unauthorized under any plausible conception of English law." In order to reconcile this contradiction,

the revolutionaries of 1688–89 ... crammed irregular decisions into the regular forms; they described illegal actions with legal terminology. In short, they faked it. But, in their circumstances, it is hard to imagine any other course was possible. Such evasion was ubiquitous during and after the events of the Revolution. In a society with the reverence for law and the fear of disorder that stamped late seventeenth century England, only obfuscation could justify the change of regime.

Kay quotes Edmund Burke, who wrote in his *Reflections on the Revolution in France* a century after the fact that, "unquestionably," there was "a small and a temporary deviation from the strict order of a regular hereditary succession." However, Burke went on to say: "At no time, perhaps, did the sovereign legislature manifest a more tender regard to that fundamental principle of British constitutional policy [than] when it deviated from the direct line of hereditary succession ... When the legislature altered the direction, but kept the principle, they showed that they held it inviolable."[39]

Because historians have differed on when England was unified politically, they have also differed on who first unified the nation.[40] David Hume favored a relatively early date and, implicitly at least, proposed criteria through which we might evaluate political unification.

Thus were united all the kingdoms of the Heptarchy in one great state, near four hundred years after the first arrival of the Saxons in Britain; and the fortunate arms and prudent policy of Egbert at last effected what had been so often attempted in vain by so many princes. Kent, Northumberland, and Mercia, which had successively aspired to general dominion, were now incorporated in his empire; and the other subordinate kingdoms seemed willingly to share the same fate. His territories were nearly of the same extent with what is now properly called England; and a favourable prospect was afforded to the Anglo-Saxons, of establishing a civilized monarchy, possessed of tranquility within itself, and secure against foreign invasion. This great event happened in the year 827.

Hume then went on to describe the celebratory sentiment with which the English people greeted their political unification.

---

[39] Richard S. Kay, *The Glorious Revolution and the Continuity of Law* (Washington, DC: Catholic University of America Press, 2014), pp. 14, 16–17, 280. Kay discusses the immense and irresolvable constitutional quandaries confronting the revolutionaries at length. See, for example, pp. 53, 75, 125, 168–80.

[40] This question did not trouble Sir Matthew Hale, who openly admitted that "we cannot know the Original of the planting of this Kingdom" and thus "cannot certainly know the Original of the Laws thereof." Nonetheless, he concluded that those laws "may be well presum'd to be very near as ancient as the Kingdom itself." Matthew Hale, *The History of the Common Law of England* (Chicago: University of Chicago Press, 1971 [1739]), pp. 40–1.

The kingdoms of the Heptarchy ... seemed to be firmly cemented into one state under Egbert; and the inhabitants of the several provinces had lost all desire of revolting from that monarch, or of restoring their former independent governments. Their language was every where nearly the same, their customs, laws, institutions civil and religious; and as the race of the ancient kings was totally extinct in all the subjected states, the people readily transferred their allegiance to a prince, who seemed to merit it, by the splendor of his victories, the vigour of his administration, and the superior nobility of his birth. A union also in government opened to them the agreeable prospect of future tranquility.[41]

Although there is some discrepancy concerning dates, Hume considered the crucial events attending unification to be Egbert's military victory over the rival kingdom of Mercia, which brought that realm under his rule, and the ritual submission of Northumberland during the same year (827).[42] As a result, Egbert was no longer just the King of Wessex but had become the king of England.[43] Despite Hume's description of Egbert's kingdom as "one great state," it was, in fact, mostly a patchwork of personal alliances. Egbert's unified kingdom lasted but a year, after which Mercia once again became independent.

Perhaps recognizing that Egbert's claim was weak, Hume later backtracked a bit and stated that King Alfred (871–99) "was, more properly than his grandfather Egbert, the sole monarch of the English" because he had "established his sovereignty over all the southern parts of the island, from the English channel to the frontiers of Scotland." Bolstering Alfred's claim, Hume also wrote that this monarch had "framed a body of laws" that gave birth to the common law of England.[44] Blackstone similarly argued that "we owe" to King Alfred the consolidation of government authority "under the influence and administration of one supreme magistrate, the king ... which wise institution has been preserved for near a thousand years unchanged."[45]

---

[41] Hume, *History of England*, vol. 1, pp. 50–1, 55. The "Heptarchy" was a somewhat idealized conception of an England divided, after the Saxon invasions, into seven kingdoms: East Anglia, Essex, Kent, Mercia, Northumbria, Sussex, and Wessex. Lapidge (ed.), *Blackwell Encyclopaedia*, p. 233. In the standard historical narrative, one of these seven kingdoms was always destined to unify England and the only outstanding questions concerned which of them it would be and how it would be achieved.

[42] Stenton mentioned an even earlier claim when he cited a practice in which King Offa (757–96) called himself *rex Anglorum*. However, the tenth-century charters in which this title appears have turned out to be forgeries. Stenton, *Anglo-Saxon England*, pp. 211–12; Lapidge (ed.), *Blackwell Encyclopaedia*, p. 341. While forgeries are clearly not historical evidence in the traditional sense, in this case their production and the significance that was later attached to them demonstrate just how important it has been to project "the conception of a kingdom of all England" as far back in history as possible.

[43] Blackstone also considered Egbert to be "the founder" of "the monarchy of England." Blackstone, *Commentaries on the Laws of England*, Book IV, p. 323 [410].

[44] Hume, *History of England*, vol. 1, pp. 70, 75.

[45] Blackstone, *Commentaries on the Laws of England*, Book IV, p. 323 [411].

In many ways, then, King Alfred is the most important protagonist in this unification narrative. For one thing, Alfred repulsed the advances of the Danes who had occupied northeastern England in the late ninth century. Although Alfred was not strong enough to expel the Danish invaders, that struggle both stabilized the boundary between the Danes and the English and, more importantly, strengthened English identity and the desire, more or less choate by that time, for a unified kingdom. Alfred was also the first English king who was recognized as "overlord" by all the Welsh kings. Although Alfred was not able to politically integrate Wales into his West Saxon kingdom, the close affinity of the two regions in the rest of English history dates from his overlordship.

Lastly, in addition to his quite considerable martial abilities, Alfred was a student and patron of the arts and made his court into a prodigious intellectual center that strengthened and deepened the moral culture of his realm.[46] Burke stated that Alfred brought "into England men of learning in all branches from every part of Europe" and, among many other cultural achievements, founded Oxford University.[47] Much of that cultural ripening can be traced the Catholic Church, which provided most of the literate and scholarly talent that served the crown. Catholic clerks, for example, reduced the customary laws of the Saxons to writing and infused them with principles of canon law in the process. The clergy also participated in the drafting of legislation and the rendering of justice in Saxon courts.

Nonetheless, Loyn considers Alfred's "little Christian kingdom" to be nothing more than a "springboard towards the creation of a kingdom of England."[48] That springboard launched the reign of Alfred's son, King Edward the Elder, who then consolidated and extended his father's realm. As a result, Edward came to rule over everything south of the Humber while Wales and most of the lands below Scotland to the north recognized his dominance. According to Kirby, Edward had thus "attained a position of pre-eminence unequalled by any previous king in England."[49] *The Blackwell Encyclopaedia*

---

[46] David M. Dumville, *Wessex and England from Alfred to Edgar* (Woodbridge: Boydell Press, 1992), pp. 143–4. Also see Stenton, *Anglo-Saxon England*, p. 257; Kirby, *Making of Early England*, pp. 76–82. Kirby states that historians have "generally" concluded that Alfred "guaranteed the survival of a Christian Anglo-Saxon culture" by defeating the Danes at Edington in 878. After that battle, the Danish leader agreed to be baptized with Alfred acting as his godfather. This did not end the Danish threat, because, as Loyn relates, "English political history was dominated by the need to defeat and contain the Danes" for another three-quarters of a century, which thus occupied the attentions of both Alfred's son and grandson. However, this long campaign "ensured that Wessex emerged as the dominant Christian kingdom of England, the basis for the unitary kingdom over all England." Loyn, *Making of the English Nation*, pp. 46–7.

[47] Burke, "Abridgment of English History," pp. 266–8.

[48] Loyn, *Making of the English Nation*, p. 65. Loyn strongly suggests that the English kings "made" the people that they then came to "rule," rather than the reverse (that the people first constituted a nation that called forth a king to unify them).

[49] Kirby, *Making of Early England*, pp. 86–7.

of Anglo-Saxon England, in fact, considers "Edward the Elder and his sons" to be the first "kings of England."[50] But preeminence as a king *in* England did not make Edward a king *of* England. Most historians have given that honor to Æthelstan, Edward's son, because he was able to negotiate "real control" over Northumbria where his father had merely received ritual submission. This completion of the English realm in 927 made Æthelstan "king of the English."[51] Dynasties rose and fell after Æthelstan's reign but there was always an English throne.[52]

The development of an English state followed political unification. The most important development was the expansion and increasing uniformity of the shire, which gradually came to align with exercise of royal authority. As a result, England became a more or less uniform network of local governments that were, in theory at least, directly responsible to the king. The shires also became the most important institution through which the "king's justice" ultimately supplanted the seigniorial courts of the manor.[53]

As "late as the fourteenth century," jurists sometimes considered the origin of English laws to have arisen from "the utterance of some divine or heroic person." Legal institutions were thus the creation of "a deified or canonized legislator" such as King Alfred, whose acts and decisions were thought "to be especially national and excellent." The very concept of an English Constitution thus required a separation between the king and the body of laws that rule the realm.

There are several aspects to this separation. One, as seen here, concerns the origin of that body of laws; for example, the king as "lawgiver" denies the existence of a constitution as long as the king continues to pronounce laws.

---

[50] Lapidge (ed.), *Blackwell Encyclopaedia*, p. 271. I should note that the various entries for kings and kingship sometimes disagree on the identity of the first king of England because they were authored by different historians.

[51] Lapidge (ed.), *Blackwell Encyclopaedia*, pp. 16, 514. For alternative dates for the emergence of "an English state" or kingdom, see Henson, *Origins of the Anglo-Saxons*, p. 15; Rannie, *Historical Outline of the English Constitution*, p. 15; Stafford, *Unification and Conquest*, pp. 32, 37; Dumville, *Wessex and England*, pp. xii, 142, 148–9, 168, 173.

[52] In what became a precedent for later monarchs, King Edgar celebrated his ascension to the throne in an elaborate coronation ceremony at Bath in 973. Dumville, *Wessex and* England, pp. 144–5.

[53] Thomas N. Bisson, *The Crisis of the Twelfth Century: Power, Lordship, and the Origins of European Government* (Princeton, NJ: Princeton University Press, 2009), pp. 88–9; Williams, *Kingship and Government*, pp. 90, 107–9; Loyn, *Making of the English Nation*, pp. 77–8, 177, 180. On the gradual development of the "king's peace," see Stubbs, *Constitutional History of England*, vol. 1, pp. 201–2. Stubbs interpreted the "king's peace" as both material evidence of royal sovereignty and a symbol of the mutual obligations of king and subject. Even after the distinction between the "two capacities" of the king had fully emerged, his or her subjects owed primary allegiance to the mortal body of the king (as opposed to the immortal crown). Broom, *Constitutional Law*, pp. 13–14.

King Alfred was a "lawgiver" in that sense. However, those kings who followed him became increasingly subject to a constitution not of their own making. A second aspect concerns the notion of the king as "above the law." As long as English law is the "king's law," a constitution cannot be said to exist. However, the emergence of an English state required the separation of the king from the crown and, even by the thirteenth century, there was little in English law that suggested "that the king is other than a natural person." As Pollock and Maitland put it: "No medieval king is tempted to say 'I am the state,' for '*Ego sum status*' would be nonsense."[54]

THE RIGHTS OF ENGLISHMEN AND THE ENGLISH CONSTITUTION

Blackstone described England as "perhaps, the only [land] in the universe, in which political or civil liberty is the very end and scope of the constitution."[55] Although most contemporary historians would now qualify that claim, the transcendent social purpose of the English state has traditionally been viewed as the protection of the "rights of Englishmen" and the preservation of "English liberty." These transcendent social purposes have been evidenced by their historical descent into the present, a descent in which an evolving English Constitution provided the framework for the simultaneous emergence and maturation of the English people, the English crown, and the English common law as distinct bodies and institutions. While these processes are usually described as intertwined and mutually constructing, English "liberty" was always immanent.[56] Put another way, these political institutions and identities merely realized an ideal that had always existed in the English consciousness. There is, accordingly, an English Constitution that has existed as long as the English people have walked the earth, but that constitution has neither a written text nor a single founding moment in which it was formally adopted.[57]

---

[54] Pollock and Maitland *History of English Law*, vol. 1, pp. xxxviii, 193–4, 545, 547. On the increasing independence of royal judges from the king during the twelfth and thirteenth centuries, see pp. 147, 162–4, 217–18. On the development of parliament's authority to enact laws that the king cannot alter or amend, see Broom, *Constitutional Law*, pp. 385–7.

[55] Blackstone, *Commentaries on the Laws of England*, Book I, p. 3 [6].

[56] Stubbs, for example, viewed Henry I's campaign to put down a rebellion by Norman barons as a "battle of English liberty." Stubbs, *Constitutional History of England*, vol. 1, p. 334.

[57] Historians and political theorists sometimes refer to documents as the equivalent of a "constitution" in some sense. See, for example, G. O. Sayles, *The Functions of the Medieval Parliament of England* (London: Hambledon Press, 1988), p. viii; Carl Schmitt, *Constitutional Theory* (Durham, NC: Duke University Press, 2008), p. 92. The fact that the English Constitution was unwritten has encouraged, even compelled, legal historians to continuously enlarge the boundaries of their discipline; this is because what might appear to be legal principles primarily rested, on further inspection, on social practices that, in turn, were often embedded in cultural norms.

The English Constitution has its origins in Anglo-Saxon law, which historians have often viewed as "forming the bedrock ... of English Liberty. It was ancient; and antiquity belonged to the people." From that perspective, "Anglo-Saxon law was ... the province not of royal power but of popular liberties," and, as such, it remained almost unaltered for 500 years, from the seventh to the eleventh century.[58] Saxon laws thus laid the basis for the future development of the English legal system, including: the "constitution of parliaments"; the "election of their magistrats by the people"; "the descent of the crown" according to "hereditary principles"; the relative infrequency of "capital punishments"; and trial by jury.[59] The "peculiarly English" idea of the king's peace also came from Germanic traditions associated with "the homestead of a freeman" as they first became applied to "the special sanctity of the king's house" and then were extended to the king's retinue and anyone else the monarch wished to protect.[60]

Although he was an American, Henry Adams enthusiastically traced the customs and traditions that gave rise to Saxon law back to "the entire Germanic family," which, "in its earliest known stage of development, placed the administration of law, as it placed the political administration, in the hands of popular assemblies composed of the free, able-bodied members of the commonwealth." When Saxons of "the purest Germanic stock" settled in what became England, they brought with them an even "sturdier independence" and "tenacious conservatism to their ancient customs and liberties" than the other "German races" possessed at the time. Admitting that almost "nothing is known with certainty" regarding the century following the Saxon invasion, Adams concluded that the law was then "administered in the popular courts, theoretically as the act of the freemen." In his interpretation, the "philosophic continuity" of English institutions was securely suspended

---

To study the development of the English Constitution has thus been to venture forth onto an uncertain historical terrain in which both the "mists of history" and the problematic conception of the constitution often made evidence and facts the offspring of interpretive predilection. For these and other reasons, Pollock and Maitland "kept clear of the territory over which [these historians of the constitution] exercise an effective dominion." Pollock and Maitland, *History of English Law*, vol. 1, p. xlvii. They believed that "the history of English law could not be profitably traced for practical purposes" before 1189. After that date, the "historian of law and constitution has no longer to complain of a dearth of authentic materials; soon he is overwhelmed by them" (p. 179).

[58] Wormald, *Making of English Law*, vol. 1, pp. 13–14, 26–7.

[59] Blackstone, *Commentaries on the Laws of England*, Book IV, pp. 324–5 [412–13]. Blackstone was conforming to "established usage" when he collected custom, tradition, and formal legislation "under the common heading of 'Anglo-Saxon laws.'" This heading unifies a body of historical evidence in such a way as to promote a larger narrative (e.g., that English liberties descended from Anglo-Saxon legal practice). Pollock and Maitland, *History of English Law*, vol. 1, p. 32.

[60] Pollock and Maitland, *History of English Law*, vol. 1, p. 50. After the Norman Conquest, the king's peace became "the normal and general safeguard of public order."

by "a slender thread of political thought" that traversed the centuries through "the confusion of feudalism" – and, even further back, out onto "the wide plains of northern Germany."[61]

Hume also traced the ethos that informed this subculture back to the Continent, where the "government of the Germans ... was always extremely free; and those fierce people, accustomed to independence and enured to arms were more guided by persuasion than authority." He went on to say that Europe owed its values "of liberty, honour, equity, and valour ... to the seeds implanted by those generous barbarians."[62] Even as the nobility came to dominate Anglo-Saxon political authority, the "still considerable remains of the ancient democracy" offered an often effective defense of "general liberty."[63]

However, Adams' "slender thread of political thought" has been entangled in social institutions that raise difficulties for this interpretation of historical continuity. For example, it is difficult to identify the "freeborn Englishman" in an early tenth-century ordinance issued by King Æthelstan that declares a "lordless man" to be a "suspicious if not dangerous person; if he has not a lord who will answer for him, his kindred must find him one." If they cannot find him a lord, the man "may be dealt with ... as a rogue and vagabond." The fundamental organizing device of this feudal society was the solemn ceremony of homage in which, in England as on the Continent, the serf or subordinate noble placed "his hands between the hands of the lord" in a symbolic admission "that the man has come helpless to the lord and has been received into the lord's protection." This ritual imposed communal and hierarchal bonds that were obviously incompatible with both individual freedom and social equality.[64]

---

[61] Henry Adams, "The Anglo-Saxon Courts of Law" in Henry Adams, J. Laurence Laughlin, H. Cabot Lodge, and Ernest Young, *Essays in Anglo-Saxon Law* (Boston, MA: Little, Brown, 1876), pp. 1, 6, 26. All four essays in this volume grew out of a seminar on the origins of English constitutional law that Adams taught during his early years at Harvard.

[62] Hume, *History of England*, vol. 1, pp. 15, 160–1. Stubbs similarly praised "the primitive German constitution [in which] the free man of pure blood is the fully qualified political unit; the king is the king of the race; the host is the people in arms; the peace is the national peace; the courts are the people in council; the land is the property of the race, and the free man has a right to his share." Stubbs, *Constitutional History of England*, vol. 1, pp. 184–5.

[63] Hume, *History of England*, vol. 1, p. 172.

[64] Pollock and Maitland, *History of English Law*, vol. 1, pp. 34, 314–15. They also described at least fourteen additional legal and social categories into which the English people could be placed in the thirteenth century. For example, Jews were considered to be "the king's serfs" and thus occupied a special relationship to the crown not shared by the much more numerous Christians (pp. 430, 493–501). Although distributed unevenly through England, "unfree" serfs and villeins probably composed more than half of the rural population in the latter half of the thirteenth century (pp. 454, 456). However, the villein was protected by a "positive morality" that rested in local custom and community sentiment (pp. 381, 393–5).

As a problem for the ostensible continuity of the "freeborn Englishman," this feudal relation pales before the English experience with slavery. In the sixth and seventh centuries, English slaves were sold to buyers throughout Europe and the Middle East; this export trade was so profitable that D. P. Kirby concluded that it "must have been one of the economic foundations of emerging Anglo-Saxon kingdoms."[65] When William the Conqueror landed in England in 1066, he was entering a society in which slaves were bought and sold.[66]

Both slavery and serfdom played an important role in English history, because, as Pollock and Maitland noted, to "turn a thing into a person is a feat that cannot be performed without the aid of the state." The English crown was thus a necessary enabling agent as slaves turned into serfs. And serfs, for their part, could participate in their own emancipation because a person "who is already free as against all" people other than his or her lord can leverage other relations against those with the lord.[67] Serfdom thus contained the impetus of its own abolition. However, the justices of the king's court facilitated this process by "openly ... leaning in favour of liberty."[68] The legal principle that "all freemen are in the main equal before the law" regardless of whether or not they are noble facilitated this process. While only a minority of

---

[65] Kirby, *Making of Early England*, p. 277.

[66] Pollock and Maitland, *History of English Law*, vol. 1, pp. 39, 83. In 1086, the entries in the Domesday Book indicate that one in every ten persons was a slave. Lapidge (ed.), *Blackwell Encyclopaedia*, p. 423. David Pelteret, the author of this entry on "Slavery," goes on to say:

> However, the status of slaves was converging upon that of serfs by that time. The two were so close that the Normans preferred serfdom as a means of organizing exploitation of the rural laborers and slavery, as a distinct status, disappeared early in the twelfth century. It should be noted that English slavery did not entail the horrific brutality or inhumane subordination as we commonly associate with, for example, the American version of the nineteenth century.

> Pollock and Maitland also noted that the sale of Christian slaves outside of England had been forbidden by Æthelred and that the prohibition had been confirmed by Cnut, his successor, around 1000 CE. While such laws recognized Christian slaves as having a special, higher status compared with non-Christian slaves, they did not confer any direct benefit upon or reduce the subordination of slaves to a lord. The distinction rested, rather, upon communities, one Christian and the other not. Pollock and Maitland also noted that some "freemen enslaved themselves in times of distress" and their masters later manumitted them as a virtuous act, in effect making enslavement a charitable act. Pollock and Maitland, *History of English Law*, vol. 1, pp. 40–1. However, they also reported that a thief might be enslaved if he could not compensate the owner for the latter's loss. In that event, the thief's "whole family" was in danger of losing "their freedom" as well (p. 62).

[67] Pollock and Maitland, *History of English Law*, vol. 1, pp. 438, 441.

[68] For example, the justices enforced a principle under which "a serf who fled [his lord] had to be captured within four days; otherwise he could not be captured." The authors call this "one of the great constructive exploits of medieval law." Pollock and Maitland, *History of English Law*, vol. 1, p. 452. See p. 453 for ways in which a serf might leverage other social relations against the claims of the lord.

the population was both "free" and "men," the principle was still there to be had as "free" became an ever more encompassing category.[69]

Under the Saxons, when someone was charged with treason against the king, guilt or innocence was sometimes determined by "ordeal." In one variant, the defendant must hold a "hot iron" of varying weight. In another, his "arm had to be plunged elbow-deep ... into ... boiling water." Lesser crimes were tried in much the same way. As irrational attempts "to elicit the judgment of God," trial by ordeal demonstrated that English society was still looking "to the supernatural for proof of doubtful facts." Ordeals gradually disappeared as the crown extended its sovereignty and insisted on material evidence.[70]

In tandem, the conception of an "outlaw" also evolved. The notion that someone had placed himself "outside the law" was originally intended to compel a person to give himself up to the courts. If they did not do so, their property could be taken by the king and they could be killed with impunity. On the one hand, this concept had a modern quality in that the community at large (not just kinship ties) possessed a common orientation toward the law. On the other hand, the concept conceded that the effective authority of the state did not yet encompass all parts of society and, thus, the local community had to be enlisted on its behalf.[71]

Within this traditional narrative of progress, however, England was also developing legal and institutional arrangements that are usually interpreted as at least a detour on the road to a modern state. The most important of these were the seigniorial courts in which the administration of justice was inevitably dominated by the great and lessor lords.[72] In addition, the tightening of feudal relations converted "a peasantry ... composed essentially of free men" into serfs whose very place and survival in the social order depended on reciprocal rights and obligations with their lords. In the centuries preceding the Norman Conquest, "the general drift of English peasant life" was thus from "freedom

---

[69] Pollock and Maitland, *History of English Law*, vol. 1, pp. 431, 435. They noted that

> the king was the only person who was always lord and never tenant; that his greatest feudatories had one interest as lords, another as tenants; that the baron, who did not like to see his vassals creating new sub-tenancies, could not forget that he himself had a lord. The conflict of interests takes place within the mind of every magnate of the realm. (Pollock and Maitland, *History of English Law*, vol. 1, p. 350)

> The competing interests of feudalism as they applied to one and the same person meant that the formulation of any royal command or law was almost always not in the undivided interest of anyone, excepting the king and the simplest villein. In some ways, this may have made allies of the king and villein in the creation of a universal legal system, but the latter had very little to offer the former in terms of influence.

[70] Pollock and Maitland, *History of English Law*, vol. 1, pp. 57–8, 80.
[71] Pollock and Maitland, *History of English Law*, vol. 1, pp. 52, 54–5.
[72] Stubbs, *Constitutional History of England*, vol. 1, pp. 204–5.

towards servitude."[73] In fact, the emergence of feudal relations is often viewed as the ground upon which the Normans consolidated their rule.

THE NORMAN CONQUEST

The Norman invasion in 1066 raises a number of difficult issues for the traditional narrative. Perhaps the most general of these is whether or not the Norman Conquest interrupted the continuity of English history.[74] That question is usually modified by asking: To what extent and in what ways did the Conquest alter the trajectory of what had been Saxon development? The answer to this question, in turn, is often divided into two parts. At the elite level involving the construction and powers of the king, particularly in relation to the nobility, the Norman Conquest is commonly viewed as invigorating the English crown by centralizing and rationalizing authority.[75] While viewing the Conquest as an interruption in the developmental narrative with respect to national politics and government, English historians often interpret it as necessary for the emergence of a crown strong enough to pursue modernizing projects such as the creation of a national revenue system and an effective system of national defense. However, at the level of peasants and common people, the vitality of popular culture created a subterranean society in which English values not only survived but were enhanced by an awareness of how distinct they were from those of the invaders.[76] In terms of individual rights and national identity, the continuity of the English narrative thus lies with the popular classes who resisted the imposition of a foreign culture and values until the Normans themselves became "English."

The invigoration of the monarchy by the Norman Conquest was not the product of a sweeping reform of Saxon governance.[77] There was, for example,

---

[73] Stenton, *Anglo-Saxon England*, p. 470.

[74] Hume, for example, viewed the Norman invasion as a violent interruption of the otherwise fairly continuous transmission and development of Saxon customs and traditions. For example, he reports that "many Englishmen fled into foreign countries, with an intention of passing their lives abroad free from oppression, or of returning on a favourable opportunity to assist their friends in the recovery of their native liberties." Hume, *History of England*, vol. 1, p. 199.

[75] On the centralization of English courts and law after the Conquest, see R. C. Van Caenegem, *Birth of the English Common Law*, second edition (Cambridge: Cambridge University Press, 1988), pp. 17–28.

[76] Wormald summarizes Stubbs' argument this way: "[T]he resources for Englishmen's long struggle with would-be tyrants were being stored during [the Middle Ages] in the barns of local institutions" where "the energies of the political nation lurked at a barely visible level, to be brought to the fore by the demands of Norman and later regimes." The historical responsibility for the origin and persistence of English liberty thus lay with the English people regardless of who ruled them (in this instance, the Normans). Wormald, *Making of English Law*, vol. 1, pp. 13–14, 26–7.

[77] Liebermann stated that William the Conqueror was "so little a revolutionist" that "the essence of the old English constitution" had been confirmed by his successors by 1135 and the already

no "abrupt break in English administrative contrivances" because William the Conqueror and his successors basically absorbed most of the institutions that existed before the invasion. In fact, Sayles contends that the Normans found English institutions to be "much more sophisticated" at all levels of government than those that had governed Normandy.[78] The inhabitation of these English institutions by the Normans permitted a centralization of authority that, in turn, "made possible the emergence of the idea of the 'community of the realm'" as a conjunction of nation and kingdom.[79] Both Edward Coke and Matthew Hale, two of the most respected English historians, characterized the Conquest as "the greatest apparent trauma in English history" but nonetheless concluded that it had produced "hardly a tremor in the history of English law."[80]

ancient witenagemot had once again "appeared ... as the national protector of popular liberties." F. Liebermann, *The National Assembly in the Anglo-Saxon Period* (New York: Burt Franklin: 1961 [1913]), p. 88. "Our English law shows itself strong enough to assimilate foreign ideas and convert them to its own use. Of any wholesale 'reception' of Roman law [after the Norman Conquest] there is no danger." Pollock and Maitland, *History of English Law*, vol. 1, p. 144. They consistently identify their conceptualization of "English law" with what we might call the "spirit of the English people" and that equivalence provides much of the theoretical and normative backbone of their study.

[78] Sayles, *Functions of the Medieval Parliament*, pp. 2–3; Loyn, *Making of the English Nation*, p. 75. Burke said that William "fortified his throne yet more strongly by the policy of good government. To London he confirmed by charter the liberties it had enjoyed under the Saxon kings, and endeavored to fix the affections of the English in general by governing them with equity according to their ancient laws." Burke, "Abridgment of English History," pp. 335–6. By this time, London "was rapidly developing the dignity and the political self-consciousness appropriate to a national capital." Stenton, *Anglo-Saxon England*, p. 539. For a description of those very substantial portions of "Old English law" that were adopted more or less unchanged by William the Conqueror, see Pollock and Maitland, *History of English Law*, vol. 1, pp. 95–6; Stenton, *Anglo-Saxon England*, pp. 545, 683. Pollock and Maitland nonetheless regard the Norman Conquest as "a catastrophe" that may very well have diverted "the whole future history of English law" from a trajectory that otherwise might "have closely resembled the history of law in Germany" (p. 86). For summaries of the varying interpretations of the impact of the Norman Conquest on English society and politics, see Henry Loyn, *Society and Peoples: Studies in the History of England and Wales, c.600–1200* (London: University of London, 1992), pp. 106, 322–38; Bisson, *Crisis of the Twelfth Century*, pp. 168–81.

[79] Martin Loughlin, "Constituent Power Subverted: From English Constitutional Argument to British Constitutional Practice" in Martin Loughlin and Neil Walker (eds.), *The Paradox of Constitutionalism: Constituent Power and Constitutional Form* (New York: Oxford University Press, 2007), p. 29. Stubbs contended that the consolidation of Norman rule superimposed a "superstructure" of strong relations between the king and nobility upon a "substructure" composed of the well-developed communal associations in the lower reaches of government. In his view, the amalgamation combined the "strongest elements of both" aspects. Stubbs, *Constitutional History of England*, vol. 1, pp. 302, 365–6. Also see Van Caenegem, *Birth of the English Common Law*, pp. 11–12.

[80] Charles M. Gray, "Editor's Introduction" in Hale, *History of the Common Law*, p. xxviii. Even so, Hale still devoted much of his text to an analysis of why and how the Norman occupation of England was consistent with the historical continuity of the common law before, during, and after the Conquest. See, for example, pp. 5, 47–106.

In 1069, a "national revolt" erupted in which the "English every where, repenting their former easy submission [to the Normans], seemed determined to make by concert one great effort for the recovery of their liberties, and for the expulsion of their oppressors."[81] After this revolt was put down, William replaced the few remaining English lords with loyal Normans and further strengthened crown authority.[82] By 1086, when the Domesday Book was written, 96 percent of the land in England was controlled by the highest-ranking Norman lords.[83] The "exceedingly strong kingship" arising from the Conquest, along with the English legal system inherited by the Normans and the isolation of England from the Continent, subsequently allowed and encouraged the emergence of a powerful central state that was later able to impose a uniform system of laws upon the nation.[84] In addition, Norman imposition of continental theory and practice made the king the supreme lord and, thus, ultimate "owner" of all the land in the kingdom. As time passed, this principle indirectly enabled the "king's justice" to become the basis for national law.

Although Norman feudalism strengthened the crown, the blurring of the boundary between private and public authority limited how far that strengthening might progress. As a result, the centralizing impact was almost entirely restricted to high politics with respect to the relation of lords to the king and matters such as taxation. Feudalism strongly influenced the crown as well because it more or less fused king and state: The king was little more than the "supreme lord" in a country composed entirely of lords. England had already developed some feudal arrangements and traditions, but, many historians argue, the invasion vastly strengthened them.[85]

One way of minimizing the disruption to the standard narrative is to view William as one of the claimants to the throne in the succession crisis brought on by the death of King Edward the Confessor. In this interpretation, the Battle of

---

[81] John Richard Green, *History of the English People*, vol. 1 (Chicago: Belford, Clarke, 1886), p. 111; Hume, *History of England*, vol. 1, p. 201. As Stubbs put it, "the embers of English independence burst into flame." Stubbs, *Constitutional History of England*, vol. 1, p. 316. Green titled the section of his book dealing with the Normans "England under Foreign Kings."

[82] Stenton, *Anglo-Saxon England*, pp. 624–5. As Stenton noted, there were other forces working toward the elimination of the old English nobility: intermarriage of English daughters with Norman lords and the incompatibility of English military traditions with those of the Normans (pp. 680–1). For a discussion of why the consolidation of Norman rule depended so heavily on a feudal organization of society and how the military aspect of feudal organization evolved in the subsequent two centuries, see Pollock and Maitland, *History of English Law*, vol. 1, pp. 266–7.

[83] Loyn, *Making of the English Nation*, p. 102.

[84] Pollock and Maitland, *History of English Law*, vol. 1, p. 102.

[85] Sayles, *Functions of the Medieval Parliament*, p. 3. Stubbs stated that "feudalism in both tenure and government was, so far as it existed in England, brought full-grown from France." Stubbs, *Constitutional History of England*, vol. 1, pp. 173n, 681–3. Also see Van Caenegem, *Birth of the English Common Law*, pp. 6–7, 109.

Hastings in 1066 becomes the event in which William successfully pressed his claims against Harold, Edward's brother-in-law. In terms of feudal tradition and practice, William the Conqueror had legitimate, although not conclusive, rights to the throne and was, in that sense, a thoroughly "English king."[86] Many of the English lords accepted him as such, if only because they pragmatically acquiesced to the realities of military power. From this vantage point, the consolidation of Norman rule introduced only minimal discontinuities with feudal traditions even as challenges to the crown later led to a wholesale replacement of English lords by Normans.[87]

However, Norman feudalism was incompatible with the precursors of English nationalism that historians contend was developing in the pre-Conquest centuries.[88] From that angle, the Normans, including William the Conqueror, were simply aliens who were "Frenchmen, French in their language, French in their law, proud indeed of their past history ... who regarded Normandy as a member of the state or congeries of states that owed service ... to the King at Paris."[89] In the very last passage of his book, Stenton wrote:

---

[86] William, in fact, strove to present himself as the legitimate successor to King Edward by observing all the formalities of coronation and ritual. Stenton, *Anglo-Saxon England*, p. 622. Stubbs, however, maintained that William's claim to the crown was a "fallacy ... which the English did not admit." Stubbs, *Constitutional History of England*, vol. 1, p. 280.

[87] Stafford, *Unification and Conquest*, p. 102. Under the principle that William was the legitimate English king, all those lords who had sided with Harold were traitors and, under English law, their lands were forfeit. While this facilitated the consolidation of Norman rule, it also brought the new Norman lords who replaced them under English land law. At the same time, these new lords were also subject to feudal obligations that had been carried over from Normandy. In this way, Pollock and Maitland conclude, William and his successors combined "all that was favourable ... in the Norman, with all that was favourable ... in the English system." Pollock and Maitland, *History of English Law*, vol. 1, pp. 99–100.

[88] Pollock and Maitland described England as "the most perfectly feudalized" of all countries if "mere property law" is the central aspect in its definition. This thorough embrace was the result of the Conquest, which, among other things, imposed feudalism from above. As a result, the feudal principle with respect to the merging of property and social relations penetrated all strata of English society as an organizing device. However, the very universality of its insinuation in otherwise very different social contexts also meant that it was weaker in some ways in England than in other countries because it had to be malleable in its application. Pollock and Maitland, *History of English Law*, vol. 1, p. 250. They, however, regarded "feudalism" as "an unfortunate word" because the varieties of social relations that the term attempted to encompass were just too great for a single heading (pp. 72–3). Stubbs himself embraced the term. Stubbs, *Constitutional History of England*, vol. 1, pp. 273–4.

[89] Pollock and Maitland, *History of English Law*, vol. 1, p. 72. Although Van Caenegem believed that "the documents tell a different story," he also noted that those "historians, who admire the legal achievements of the Anglo-Saxon and the genius of the Angevin kings, cannot say a good word for the Normans, who constitute a sort of *medium aevum* between two glorious epochs. In their view the barbaric Normans brought utter darkness, which was relieved only by the light of Henry II's reign." Van Caenegem, *Birth of the English Common Law*, p. 45.

The Normans who entered into the English inheritance were a harsh and violent race. They were the closest of all western peoples to the barbarian strain in the continental order. They had produced little in art or learning, and nothing in literature, that could be set beside the work of Englishmen. But politically, they were the masters of their world.[90]

Hume condemned the Normans as "so licentious a people, that they may be pronounced incapable of any true or regular liberty; which requires such improvement in knowledge and morals, as can only be the result of reflection and experience, and must grow to perfection during several ages of settled and established government."[91] In Hume's view, the "reflection and experience" of the ages were retained in the local governments, where, as Stenton put it, the "framework of the Old English state survived the Conquest" and "the accustomed course" of government continued more or less as it always had.[92] In this interpretation, the enduring substructure of society was composed of the English people and the popular traditions and practices of local government.[93]

Even as the Normans occupied the higher reaches of the state, the persistence of this subterranean culture meant that the English people still lived, for the most part, within local communities and institutions that they themselves controlled.[94] Constructed by the English people during the six centuries since the Saxon invasion, these institutions were thoroughly tailored to (indeed, synonymous with) the values and norms of popular society. Within their communities and institutions, the common people thus tended the hearth of English liberty even as they were subjected to Norman authority by force of arms.

For example, the persistence of English as the language of the people is often cited as evidence that Norman influence never penetrated the cultural core of the nation, despite the fact that William ordered all schools in the kingdom to use French as the medium of instruction. French also became the language of the royal court and was accordingly taken up by those English who feigned in polite society "to excel in that foreign dialect." While French became much of the idiom through which the common people were subordinated by the

---

[90] Stenton, *Anglo-Saxon England*, p. 687.   [91] Hume, *History of England*, vol. 1, pp. 254, 486.

[92] Stenton, *Anglo-Saxon England*, pp. 683–4, 686.

[93] On the persistence and autonomy of local government under the Normans, see Loyn, *Making of the English Nation*, p. 79. Loyn, in fact, cites the persistence of the forms of local government "well into the modern world" as "the most enduring testimonial, short of the monarchy itself, to positive Anglo-Saxon success in the art of government."

[94] In Kirby's words:

[T]he English peasantry ... constituted a solid belt of social and agricultural continuity across the divide of 1066. In the Anglo-Saxon period were laid the foundations of the English language, of English literature, art, government and administration, of English ecclesiastical organization and of English medieval piety. Against such deeper currents of continuity, the Norman Conquest and its immediate consequences were but ripples on a troubled surface. (Kirby, *Making of Early England*, pp. 137–8)

Norman elite, English was commonly used by the people of the town and countryside and was also preferred by most of those who could read and write. The persistence of English among the common people both ensured and evidenced the strong identity and culture of the nation in the century or so after the Norman Conquest.[95]

Although French was the language of the law courts and legal documents, the Normans brought little in the way of written law with them because, according to Hume, the invasion "occurred in the very midnight of the legal history of France; indeed they brought the midnight with them." In rather sharp contrast, English law was already available in law codes and treatises and, in this form, influenced Norman judges as they otherwise centralized and adapted judicial practice to meet their needs. Thus, the central precepts and construction of the national law remained English even as legal proceedings were conducted in French. English provided both the grammar and the general framework of the law while French contributed only technical terms.

In 1362, a statute finally acknowledged that "the French tongue was but little understood" by the English people and thus stipulated that legal documents and proceedings should henceforth be "pleaded, shown, defended, answered, debated and judged" in English.[96] This statute merely recognized that, as the Norman successors to William became increasingly intertwined with and encompassed by English culture, the English language became insinuated into the sinews of formal state practice and the vernacular of royal rule.

Even after all power in the upper reaches of the English state had "passed from native into alien hands," the Normans themselves became increasingly domesticated by English society.[97] The most important event in their domestication may have come when, soon after assuming the throne in 1100, Henry I wed Matilda. Because she was a distant "heir of the Saxon line," the union dramatically increased Henry's popularity among his English subjects, who, reflecting "with extreme regret on their former liberty," hoped for better times now that "the blood of their native princes should be mingled with that of their new sovereigns."[98] But the process of integrating Norman lords with the native English was otherwise slow.

In the standard historical narrative, the Norman Conquest shaped "the character and constitution of the English" in several ways. Perhaps most importantly, "Norman rule invigorated the whole national system" by

---

[95] Stubbs, *Constitutional History of England*, vol. 1, p. 587; Hume, *History of England*, vol. 1, pp. 208–9; Pollock and Maitland, *History of English Law*, vol. 1, pp. 71, 86–9, 91, 93–5.

[96] Pollock and Maitland, *History of English Law*, vol. 1, p. 92. This statute, somewhat paradoxically, was written in French. Latin, for its part, remained the language in which state and judicial records were compiled until 1731 (p. 90). Van Caenegem described both the 1362 statute and "Cromwell's attempt in 1650 to impose English as the language of the law" as failures. Van Caenegem, *Birth of the English Common Law*, p. 141n.

[97] Stenton, *Anglo-Saxon England*, p. 680; Kirby, *Making of Early England*, p. 137.

[98] Hume, *History of England*, vol. 1, p. 256.

imposing strong leadership on a people who had hitherto been languishing in isolation from the rest of Europe. To the extent that the Normans "became English," they "added nerve and force" to the national system. On the other hand, to the extent that the Normans remained aliens, their often oppressive rule brought out "the latent energies of the English" and thus "stimulated the growth of freedom and the sense of [national] unity." Although the Norman Conquest thus strengthened the monarchy and the unity of the English nation, it had little or no impact on English identity. In many respects, then, the Norman Conquest was but a transient catalyst for the development of England.[99]

By the end of the twelfth century, a little more than a century after the Conquest, Hume described both "nations" – the Norman/French and the English – as acting "in the government, as if they were the same people." At the higher reaches of the realm, the "more homely, but more sensible manners and principles of the Saxons" had been "exchanged for the affectations of chivalry" and "Romish sentiments in religion ... had taken entire possession of the people" as the Catholic Church consolidated its hold. But the Norman lords and their families "had now struck deep root" and had become "entirely incorporated with the [English] people." As a result, the lords now shared their "memory ... of a more equal government under the Saxon principles" and their "spirit of liberty." The barons both were "willing to indulge" this spirit among their people and desired "more independence" for themselves.[100] The Norman Conquest thus paved the way for the Magna Carta.

THE MAGNA CARTA

If we were compelled to assign a date to the founding of the English state, that date would probably be 1215, when the Magna Carta was signed. Blackstone, for example, venerated the Magna Carta because it "protected every individual of the nation in the free enjoyment of his life, his liberty, and his property, unless declared to be forfeited by the judgment of his peers, or the law of the land."[101] Hume provided more context when he viewed the signing of the Magna Carta as the renewal and elaboration of "the liberties, however imperfect, enjoyed by the Anglo-Saxons in their ancient government." The Magna Carta thus released the English people from the "state of vassalage" that had

---

[99] Stubbs, *Constitutional History of England*, vol. 1, p. 269.

[100] Hume, *History of England*, vol. 1, pp. 371–2. On Hume's dim view of the influence of the Roman Catholic Church, see, for example, pp. 50–1. Like Hume, Blackstone was very hostile to the Catholic Church and contended that the Normans were responsible for the enslavement of the "consciences of men" to the papacy, "a foreign power ... unconnected with the civil state under which they lived." The "whole *farrago* of superstitious novelties" was "now imported from Rome." Blackstone, *Commentaries on the Laws of England*, Book IV, p. 328 [419].

[101] Blackstone, *Commentaries on the Laws of England*, Book IV, p. 331 [424].

been imposed by the Norman Conquest and demonstrated that the "nation, by a great confederacy, might still vindicate its liberties."[102]

Burke also thought the barons "had always kept up the memory of the ancient Saxon liberty" and that the Magna Carta was not "renewal ... of the ancient Saxon laws" but instead a "correction of the feudal policy" of the Norman kings. However, he still called the host raised by the barons that brought King John to his knees "the army of liberty."[103] Pollock and Maitland more carefully interrogated the meaning of clauses in the Magna Carta, including "all its faults," but nonetheless they contended that the barons had produced what "rightly becomes a sacred text, the nearest approach to an irrepealable 'fundamental statute' that England has ever had ... For in brief it means this, that the king is and shall be below the law."[104]

Calling the Magna Carta "a treaty between the king and his subjects," Stubbs effusively labeled it the "first great public act of the nation, after it has realized its own identity: the consummation of the work for which unconsciously kings, prelates, and lawyers have been laboring for a century." On the one hand, it was "the summing up of a period of national life." On the other, it was "the starting-point of a new period." Only sixty years earlier, according to Stubbs, the English "nation" was "scarcely conscious of its unity," but at Runnymede it was able "to state its claims to civil liberty and self-government as a coherent organized society." By setting those claims down in words, the Magna Carta thus recognized "the rights and duties that have been growing into recognition whilst the nation was growing into consciousness." Stubbs then concluded that "the whole of the constitutional history of England is little more than a commentary on Magna Carta."[105]

---

[102] Hume, *History of England*, vol. 1, p. 437. Because he viewed the Magna Carta as a recovery of "ancient liberties," Hume minimized the document's novel quality by stating that it apparently did not change "the distribution of political power." However, it nonetheless "became a kind of epoch in the constitution" and thus entered into the grand narrative of national existence (pp. 487–8).

[103] Burke, "Abridgment of English History," pp. 456, 459, 463. All leading English historians are critical of King John and his reign. Rannie, for example, described John as "thoroughly treacherous." Rannie, *Historical Outline of the English Constitution*, p. 44.

[104] Pollock and Maitland, *History of English Law*, vol. 1, pp. 182–4. Also see Rannie, *Historical Outline of the English Constitution*, p. 46. Loyn, however, called the Magna Carta a part of "the national myth" that nonetheless "caught the imagination of later generations." Loyn, *Making of the English Nation*, pp. 140–1. While referring to the document as "a sacred text," Holt says that the meaning given the Magna Carta was a "myth." He also notes the ways in which the fourteenth- and seventeenth-century parliaments reworked the language of Magna Carta in order to make claims that the original text could not have supported. Holt, *Magna Carta*, pp. 8–13, 18.

[105] Stubbs nicely combined the Norman Conquest, which provided the monarchy with sufficient strength to unify the nation, with the Magna Carta, which then redressed the balance of power between the monarchy and the people without impairing the strength of the English state. Although he was careful to qualify the claims he made, he nonetheless crafted a quite teleological narrative. This teleology is also evident in the phrase "unconsciously ... laboring"

Hume recognized that the great lords who compelled King John to sign the Magna Carta were themselves Normans and that they had their own personal interests in mind when they reined in a rapacious monarch. However, he nonetheless praised those great lords as "gallant and high-spirited barons" who intended to "vindicate the honour, liberty, and independence of the nation, with the same ardour which they now exerted in defence of their own." These barons, Hume contended, had been "seized with the national passion for laws and liberty; blessings, of which they themselves expected to partake."[106] When King John "threatened to destroy both church and state, the barons were ready to become patriots and to lead the constitutional progress of the nation."[107] According to Stubbs, it was "the collective people" who authored the Magna Carta because

the demands of the barons were no selfish exaction of privilege for themselves ... [T]he people for whom they acted were [also] on their side. The nation in general, the people of the towns and villages, the commons of later days, the Englishmen who had fought the battles of the Norman kings against the feudatories, had now thrown themselves on the side of the barons.[108]

As a founding for the English state, the signing of the Magna Carta has several flaws. That it was Norman lords who compelled King John to recognize English liberties has already been noted. The response is that the great barons had become acculturated in the century and a half following the Norman invasion and now appreciated the "ancient liberties" that they had initially suppressed when they occupied England. When Henry II ascended the throne in 1154, the "Normans and the English had ... lived so long together that they were really blended into one nation. The union was hastened by the fact ... that they belonged to the same race. And the nation which resulted from the union was not a new Norman, but the old English nation, influenced, modified, and strengthened by the Norman blood, laws, and character."[109]

Another problem was the text of the Magna Carta itself. Hume, for example, stated that the document contains "all the chief outlines of a legal government," including "the equal distribution of justice, and free enjoyment of property; the great objects for which political society was at first founded by men, which the people have a perpetual and unalienable right to recal [sic], and which no[t]

---

quoted in the text. Stubbs, *Constitutional History of England*, vol. 1, pp. 482–3, 569, 570, 572, 579. For an interpretation of the articles, see pp. 572–9.

[106] Hume, *History of England*, vol. 1, p. 440. As Stubbs put it, "the division of interest between the two races" had disappeared and the "Norman and Englishman are now one." Stubbs, *Constitutional History of England*, vol. 1, p. 482.

[107] Rannie, *Historical Outline of the English Constitution*, p. 45. Rannie also contended that "the barons ... were still the leaders of progress" almost a century later when they attempted to correct the mistakes and abuses of Edward II.

[108] Stubbs, *Constitutional History of England*, vol. 1, pp. 570–1.

[109] Rannie, *Historical Outline of the English Constitution*, pp. 34–5.

time, nor precedent, nor statutes, nor positive institution, ought to deter them from keeping ever uppermost in their thoughts and attention." But he then conceded that the actual provisions might be "too concise" and narrowly drawn for achieving those great purposes. He explained this discrepancy between the text and its importance as a fundamental document in the ancient English Constitution as something to be attributed "to the genius of the age" in which it was formed. Even though they acted within the context and beliefs of their own time, the great lords had nonetheless "demanded the revival of the Saxon laws" in a way that they thought "sufficiently satisfied the people" and thus put English history back on its original trajectory. Their efforts, in Hume's view, bore fruit because "time gradually ascertained the sense of all the ambiguous expressions" in a way that conformed with the expectations and desires of the nation.[110]

Even if the Magna Carta comes too late and is too imperfect to constitute a founding for the English state, its role in uniting the Norman overlords with the subterranean popular culture of English liberty is still extremely important in the standard historical narrative. Created by Norman barons as they contested the despotic authority of a Norman king, the Magna Carta is considered thoroughly and indubitably English – and an invaluable legacy given to the world.

HENRY VIII AND THE ROMAN CATHOLIC CHURCH

In its broadest outline, the standard narrative has three central protagonists: the crown, the Roman Catholic Church, and parliament. They each have moments in which they represent and act in accord with the aspirations of the English people. The influence of the Roman Catholic Church, for example, was felt very early in English history when St. Augustine arrived in Kent in 597 and subsequently converted Æthelberht, one of the many Saxon kings at that time, to Christianity. Over the next century or so, the other Saxon kingdoms also joined the Church.[111] Their conversion, according to Stubbs, "not only revealed to Europe and Christendom the existence of a new nation, but may be said to have rendered the new nation conscious of its unity in a way in which, under the influence of heathenism, community of language and custom had failed to do." In fact, Stubbs maintained that Pope Gregory, when he sent St. Augustine on his mission to Kent, had already conceived of "the whole cluster of tribes" as

[110] Hume, *History of England*, vol. 1, pp. 445–6. For Hume's narrative of how the Magna Carta came to be, see pp. 438–42, 446–7. For his interpretive summary of the articles and clauses, see pp. 442–5.

[111] Henson, *Origins of the Anglo-Saxons*, pp. 132–3; Stenton, *Anglo-Saxon England*, pp. 105–6; Loyn, *Making of the English Nation*, pp. 30–1. Before their conversion, Loyn states that the Saxons "were pagan and polytheistic, worshipping the gods of the German pantheon – Woden, Thor, Tiw, Freya – and tracing the ancestry of their rulers back to Woden himself" (p. 12).

comprising one "English" people and accordingly partitioned the nation into ecclesiastical provinces, one centered in York and the other in London. Very early on, then, the Roman Catholic Church both recognized the existence of the English people and facilitated their self-recognition as that people.[112] The Church also brought civilization to England, both in terms of moral sensibility and in the material form of literacy.

After the conversion, Catholic clerks and prelates played a very important role in the affairs of state and the administration of justice, so important that "[s]ecular rulers had to learn the very notion of a national state from the clergy."[113] As a matter of high ecclesiastical policy, the Roman Catholic Church consistently and strongly desired the unification of the English nation so that the spiritual and the secular realms might reinforce one another.[114] For very different reasons, the rival Saxon kings also desired unification, as long as it was their kingdom that brought together the nation.[115] As a result, the interests and policies of the Church and the most powerful Saxon kings were usually aligned and mutually cooperative up until the eleventh century or so.[116]

After the Norman Conquest, the "churches," according to Stubbs, "were schools and nurseries of patriots; depositories of old traditional glories and the refuge of the persecuted ... They trained the English people for the time when the kings should court their support and purchase their adherence by the restoration of liberties that would otherwise have been forgotten." Even more importantly, the Roman Catholic Church educated "the growing nation for its distant destiny as the teacher and herald of freedom to all the world."[117]

However, cooperation between the Church and the state became increasingly difficult because the monarchy came to regard papal influence as at least irritating and sometimes dangerous. The complex saga of the Magna Carta, for example, demonstrated both the independent interests of the papacy in English affairs and the increasing national character of the English branch of the

---

[112] Stubbs, *Constitutional History of England*, vol. 1, p. 237. Also see Williams, *Kingship and Government*, p. 13; Stenton, *Anglo-Saxon England*, pp. 103–4.

[113] Pollock and Maitland, for example, state that "popish clergymen" converted "our English common law ... from a rude mass of customs into an articulate system." Pollock and Maitland, *History of English Law*, vol. 1, p. 142. As a result, the "boundary between lay and spiritual authority was never defined in pre-Conquest England." Stenton, *Anglo-Saxon England*, p. 546; Liebermann, *National Assembly*, p. 4. The cooperation between crown and Church was so close that Alfred did not distinguish between the synod, as the ecclesiastical council, and witenagemot, as the "secular national assembly" (p. 13).

[114] Stubbs, *Constitutional History of England*, vol. 1, pp. 266–7.

[115] On the role of monarchical ambitions in the unification of England, see, for example, Stafford, *Unification and Conquest*, p. 35; Stubbs, *Constitutional History of England*, vol. 1, p. 159.

[116] For examples of the reciprocal synergy between the Roman Catholic Church and the emerging unification of the secular realm, see Dumville, *Wessex and England*, p. 147; Stubbs, *Constitutional History of England*, vol. 1, p. 136. On the growth of collaboration between state and Church, also see Stenton, *Anglo-Saxon England*, pp. 154–5, 368.

[117] Stubbs, *Constitutional History of England*, vol. 1, pp. 267–8.

Roman Catholic hierarchy. Briefly recounted, King John's excommunication by Pope Innocent opened the way for an invasion of the island by the French king. John's submission to the pope returned the crown to the Church and the French invasion was canceled. However, the English barons then rose up against King John when his abuses of power became intolerable. Compelled to choose sides between the king and the barons, Pope Innocent supported the "base and degenerate" King John because, Hume argued, he feared that the "gallant and high-spirited barons," if they prevailed, "would vindicate the honour, liberty, and independence of the nation, with the same ardour which they now exerted in defence of their own" freedoms. And such a vindication was not in the interests of the papacy.[118]

However, the Archbishop of Canterbury, Stephen Langton, took the part of the barons, first convening a meeting in which he urged them to demand their rights from the king, subsequently serving as an intermediary between the barons and the king as they negotiated terms, and finally translating those terms into what became the text of the Magna Carta. The differing geopolitical interests of the papacy and the national sentiment of the archbishop were thus starkly displayed.

Edmund Burke described Archbishop Langton as "distinguished for his learning, or irreproachable morals, and free from every canonical impediment." When the archbishop administered the oath to King John that removed his excommunication, Langton manifested these virtues by going beyond the ecclesiastical elements of the oath and compelling the king to "swear to amend his civil government, to raise no tax without the consent of the Great Council, and to punish no man but by the judgment of his court. In these terms we may see the Great Charter traced in miniature." After he had thus anticipated the Magna Carta, Langton then "put himself at the head of the patrons of civil liberty" in the ensuing struggle with both the pope and the king.[119] After Pope Innocent excommunicated the barons, Langton refused to publish the sentence, thereby nullifying its effect. Hume described the barons as so "seized with the national passion for laws and liberty" that "even the power of superstition" could no longer control them. More pragmatically, the barons also anticipated that "the thunders of Rome, when not seconded by the efforts of the English ecclesiastics," would come to nothing.[120] Even after the pope excommunicated the barons by name, the English "nobility and people, and even [the] clergy, adhered to the defence of their liberties."[121]

In the years following the Magna Carta, the Roman Catholic Church became more hierarchically disciplined and the English clergy were, as a consequence, increasingly "prevented from being patriots by their allegiance to the

[118] Hume, *History of England*, vol. 1, pp. 439–40.
[119] Burke, "Abridgment of English History," pp. 447, 455, 457.
[120] Hume, *History of England*, vol. 1, p. 440.
[121] Hume, *History of England*, vol. 1, pp. 448–9.

Pope." During the fourteenth century, King Edward III partially restored the national autonomy of the English clergy by insisting on the crown's right to propose the appointment of bishops. According to Rannie, this was important because popes had "almost always appointed foreigners," and, as a result, "the Church of England more and more lost its national character." Even worse, these foreign bishops, by "sitting in the House of Lords and governing the country, were apt to serve the cause of the country's enemies." A similar retrenchment of papal authority occurred when Edward's successor, Richard II, restricted ecclesiastical jurisdiction over clergy whenever the rights of the crown were implicated.[122]

When subsequent popes sought to evade these statutes, the English "nation" became "more discontented with the Pope and the clergy who obeyed him than it had ever been." After Martin Luther defied the authority of the Catholic Church in 1517, English discontent began to merge with what became the Reformation as much of northern Europe redefined relations with the papacy. All of this set the stage for Henry VIII, who was able to combine his quest for a divorce from his first wife, Catherine of Aragon, with the disestablishment in 1534 of the Roman Catholic Church. Erecting the Church of England in its place, with the king as its head, the nation was now independent of Rome. In all this, the "king and the nation were ... working together; what the king did was for the good of the nation."[123]

According to the standard historical narrative, some of these events have been characterized as the products of intention and, in that way, rulers and subjects alike have been regarded as visionaries who anticipated the consequences of what they wrought. Others have been depicted as the inadvertent results of random events or petty self-interest. The break with Rome during the reign of Henry VIII, for example, contained a little of both. On the one hand, the need for a male heir was a matter of grave importance to the crown and the coming of the Reformation was a powerful catalyst for freeing England from papal influence. However, by breaking with the Roman Catholic Church, Henry also "ensured the emergence of an English protestant church, from which he himself would have recoiled in horror." Henry also found parliament very pliable when he asked for support in his struggles with the pope. As a result, parliament became "first and foremost a legislative assembly."[124]

---

[122] Rannie, *Historical Outline of the English Constitution*, pp. 83, 85–6. Note that Rannie referred to the English branch of the Roman Catholic Church as the "Church of England" more than a century before Henry VIII actually broke with Rome.

[123] Rannie, *Historical Outline of the English Constitution*, pp. 109–10. By the late eighteenth century, Burke could plausibly maintain that "the majority of the people of England" considered the Church of England to be "the foundation of their whole constitution" and that "Church and State are ideas inseparable in their minds, and scarcely is the one ever mentioned without mentioning the other." Quoted in Bateman, *Disenfranchising Democracy*, p. 224.

[124] Sayles, *Functions of the Medieval Parliament*, p. 57.

Chance and accidents, however, are not materials out of which a state can legitimate its sovereignty.[125] There must be a point at which a people consents to its government and, as a consequence, commits the state to a transcendent social purpose. That transcendent purpose, as characterized in the standard historical narrative, is the creation and protection of the traditional "rights of Englishmen" and the preservation of "English liberties."

THE ORIGIN OF THE "RIGHTS OF ENGLISHMEN"

In many ways, the king's evolving relationship with the law has paralleled the development of the English Constitution. At first, the emergence of a king of England politically consolidated the English people and thus provided the possibility of a constitution that they might share. Later, the expanding sovereignty of the king coincided with the consolidation and centralization of a national law and the king was the agent of – or, better put, the primary force behind – that consolidation and centralization.[126] During this period, the struggle for primacy between the king and feudal lords facilitated that consolidation as the "king's justice" slowly displaced seigniorial courts and thus, in theory at least, extended royal (national) law throughout the land. At the same time, parliament gradually came into its own as a national assembly in which the crown competed with feudal lords for political dominance.

The relationship between crown and parliament remained primarily symbiotic up until the mid-seventeenth century. At that point, parliament became the primary bearer of constitutional development, as, on the one hand, the personal power of the king became increasingly distinct from the crown (with the latter becoming the primary repository of national authority), and, on the other, the roles of statutory law and judicial decisions expanded with the institutional development of what became the central state.

More than anything else, the English Constitution is an orientation toward history in which the past is considered a repository of those customs that created and bound together the English people and their state. In 1784, for example, Lords Mansfield and Loughborough, Chief Justices of the King's Bench and Common Pleas, respectively, rendered an opinion in which they decided that a naval commander could not be sued for (allegedly) maliciously prosecuting a subordinate on the high seas. They stated that the "wisdom of ages hath formed a sea military code, which in the last reign was collected and

---

[125] On the problematic place of chance and contingency in the standard historical narrative, see Van Caenegem, *Birth of the English Common Law*, pp. 106–8. While Van Caenegem describes the origin of the English common law as "a freak event in western history," he also says that "historical fact ... detracts in no way from the admiration one feels for this deviation from the common European pattern and the global importance it acquired in modern times" (pp. 104–5, 145n).

[126] Pollock and Maitland, *History of English Law*, vol. 1, pp. 49–51, 221–2.

digested into an Act of Parliament." Although they thought the statute still did not cover the case at hand, the relevant part of their decision for us is the passage in which the "wisdom of ages" was said to have "formed a sea military code." This fiction was then reconciled with the statute passed by parliament by simply assuming that the latter was merely codifying what was already known to be the law. The ostensible perfect correspondence between the "sea military code" wrought by the "wisdom of ages" and the parliamentary statute precisely anchored the latter in a history that, although largely unrecoverable, could still legitimate sovereignty in the present.[127]

No one has articulated this orientation toward history better than Edmund Burke, who ascribed those customs to decisions made by people whose identities and opinions were now lost in the mists of history. In his view, the English Constitution had slowly emerged over the course of history as the people and their leaders confronted challenges and problems that were now often incomprehensible in the present. But the way in which they had met those challenges and resolved those problems nonetheless embedded reason and experience in the matrix of the ancient English Constitution. From this repository of reason and experience had emerged principles of politics and practices of judgment that reflected a collective wisdom far beyond the ken of any individual or the comprehension of abstract ideology. In Burke's words:

Our constitution is a prescriptive constitution; it is a constitution whose sole authority is that it has existed time out of mind ... It is a presumption in favour of any settled scheme of government against any untried project, that a nation has long existed and flourished under it ... [A] nation ... is a deliberate election of ages and generations; it is a constitution made by what is ten thousand times better than choice, it is made by the peculiar circumstances, occasions, tempers, dispositions, and moral, civil and social habitudes of the people, which disclose themselves only in a long space of time ... The individual is foolish; the multitude, for the moment, is foolish, when they act without deliberation; but the species is wise, and, when time is given to it, as a species it always acts right.[128]

As early as 1600, if not before, the expression "ancient constitution" already referred to a "habit of mind" in which political debate in England often turned "upon the assumption that there existed an ancient constitution which was the justification of all rights and was itself justified primarily by its antiquity." In 1608, for example, Sir Edward Coke rendered a decision in which he said that

our days upon the earth are but as a shadow in respect of the old ancient days and times past, wherein the laws have been by the wisdom of the most excellent men, in many successions of ages, by long and continued experience, (the trial of light and truth) fixed and refined, which no one man, (being of short a time) albeit he had in his

---

[127] *Sutton v Jonstone* [1784] 1 Tr. 493 (24 Geo. 3). The House of Lords had asked the judges for their opinion and then affirmed it. Broom, *Constitutional Law*, pp. 709, 656–711.
[128] Pocock, "Burke and the Ancient Constitution," p. 140.

head the wisdom of all the men in the world, in any one age could ever have effected or attained unto.[129]

Matthew Hale similarly insisted that some of "the Laws of this Kingdom have obtain'd their Force by immemorial Usage or Custom," even though they originated *"before Time of Memory."* This ancient common law is

[n]ot only a very just and excellent Law in it self, but it is singularly accommodated to the Frame of the English Government, and to the Disposition of the English Nation, and such as by a long Experience and Use is as it were incorporated into their very Temperament and, in a Manner, become the Complection and Constitution of the English Commonwealth.

However, Hale may have recognized that he had not adequately incorporated the Irish, Welsh, and Scots into this narrative because he added separate chapters "Concerning the Settling of the Common Law of England in Ireland and Wales" and "Concerning the Communication of the Laws of England into the Kingdom of Scotland."[130]

The intimate and mutually constitutive relationship between the English Constitution and the English people solved several otherwise intractable problems for the traditional narrative. On the one hand, the origins of the constitution, like the origins of the English people, were "lost in the mists of time." The search for a definite beginning was both fruitless (because the past had left little or no record) and pointless (because the coevolution of the constitution and people was otherwise apparent). This interpretive posture both explained the absence of a distinct founding moment and evaded interrogation of the conditions under which the English state was created.

Such an interrogation was otherwise strongly implied in English political theory because the latter emphasized an original "social contract" as the legitimating act grounding the creation of a state. A social contract in that sense was unnecessary because the constitution and the people had been inextricably intertwined and had emerged in parallel. This orientation toward the past thus turned the absence of a distinct founding moment into a virtue. For one thing, "the origins of society are," like the constitution, "lost in the mists of time immemorial." We cannot recover popular consent to the creation of the

---

[129] Given this orientation, Pocock concluded, the purposes of the constitution "can only be inferred from its structure, and if the structure is immemorial nothing can be inferred about its functioning at any particular time." For Coke, "there was little to be known about the history of the law except that it was immemorial." Pocock, "Burke and the Ancient Constitution," pp. 128–30, 132–3, 140–1. Charles Taylor notes that, "when eighteenth-century Whigs defended their oligarchic power in the name of the people ... they were drawing on an older understanding of 'people,' one stemming from a premodern notion of order ... where a people is constituted as such by a Law that always already exists, since time out of mind." Charles Taylor, *Modern Social Imaginaries* (Durham, NC: Duke University Press, 2004), p. 16; also see p. 9.

[130] Hale, *History of the Common Law*, pp. 2, 44, chapters IX and X.

English state except through the historical record of coevolution in which the mutually constitutive relationship between people and state emerged hand in hand. At every point in time that relationship demonstrates, in theory at least, an evolving consent that is thus not given at one definitive moment but granted naturally and almost unconsciously throughout history. In fact, as Ernest Young puts it,

Burke's conception of the social contract deemphasizes consent altogether, using the contract instead as a metaphor for the obligations that bind individual to individual and generation to generation. For Burke, individuals are bound to members of the national community, as well as to generations that are dead or yet to be born, by moral obligations arising out of a common history; the community is a permanent body composed of transitory parts ... there can never be a single isolated point in time to which we can appeal to find the complete meaning of our mutual commitments.[131]

When Edward II ascended the throne in 1307, he presided over an English constitution that was already "the best the world had or has ever seen."[132]

The "rights of Englishmen" were embedded in this constitution and none of these rights is more sacred than trial by jury. Burke called the article in the Magna Carta that provided that "no freeman shall be taken, or imprisoned, or disseized, or outlawed, or banished, or in any wise destroyed, but [by the] judgment of his peers" the capstone of that great document and stated that it "cemented all the parts of the fabric of liberty."[133] Blackstone similarly termed trial by jury the "most important guardian both of public and private liberty." That institution, he contended, "hath been used time out of mind in this nation, and seems to have been coeval with the first civil government." Although Blackstone was reluctant to credit the Britons with originating trials by jury, he said that they "were in use among the earliest Saxon colonies." As in many other respects, he viewed the Norman Conquest as an interruption in the otherwise majestic development and historical descent of English liberty. In this instance, the Normans brought with them and imposed upon the English "the impious" trial by battle.[134]

Hume called trial by jury an institution "best calculated for the preservation of liberty and the administration of justice, that ever was devised by the wit of man" and claimed that its origin could be traced as far back as the reign of King Alfred (871–99).[135] On this, Burke dissented: "Historians, copying after one another, and examining little, have attributed to [King Alfred] the institution of

---

[131] Ernest Young, "Rediscovering Conservatism: Burkean Political Theory and Constitutional Interpretation," *North Carolina Law Review* 72 (1994), pp. 650, 668, 673.

[132] Rannie, *Historical Outline of the English Constitution*, p. 71.

[133] Burke, "Abridgment of English History," p. 466.

[134] Blackstone, *Commentaries on the Laws of England*, Book IV, pp. 271, 325, 328 [349, 414, 419].

[135] Hume, *History of England*, vol. 1, p. 77.

juries, an institution which certainly did never prevail amongst the Saxons."[136] Pollock and Maitland, in fact, maintained that jury trials originated in "the prerogative rights of the Frankish kings" and, sharply contradicting Blackstone's interpretation, stated that the institution "would have perished and long ago have become a matter for the antiquary" if William the Conqueror had not carried it to England. While conceding that there is a "natural disinclination of Englishmen to admit that this 'palladium of our liberties'" originated in Normandy rather than England and in royal prerogative rather than popular custom, they nonetheless firmly ruled out Anglo-Saxon law as the birthplace of the trial by jury.[137]

Whatever its origin, English judges have long held the view that the autonomy of jurors from the authority of the court is a bedrock principle of English liberty. In 1670, for example, this autonomy was confirmed in a court decision that contended that "the time-honoured institution of trial by jury merit[s] protection," especially

when questions evolved by political agitation are raised between the subject and the Crown – questions the solution of which most nearly touches the privileges of the one or the prerogatives of the other – it is conceived that, by the wit of man, no system could be devised more fitted to insure the rights of individuals, and give confidence and stability to the public mind, than that of trial by the country, which has descended to us from our ancestors, and which we in turn, if we rightly appreciate our liberties, ought to transmit to our posterity.[138]

The writ of habeas corpus has had a similar history.[139] Rannie, for example, stated that "the commitment of any person to prison, without due cause assigned, was contrary to the aboriginal English legislative traditions, or common law," from "the very earliest times." This longstanding "immunity from arbitrary imprisonment" was merely confirmed by the Magna Carta and

---

[136] Burke, "Abridgment of English History," p. 264n.

[137] Pollock and Maitland, *History of English Law*, vol. 1, pp. 101, 149–53. On the development of trial by jury more generally, see pp. 158–9, 161–2, 213–14. For other views on the origin of jury trials, see Loyn, *Making of the English Nation*, p. 139; Stubbs, *Constitutional History of England*, vol. 1, pp. 658–9; Stenton, *Anglo-Saxon England*, pp. 510–11, 651–2; Wormald, *Making of English Law*, vol. 1, pp. 4–9, 17–18; Van Caenegem, *Birth of the English Common Law*, pp. 71–80, 133n, 134n; Rannie, *Historical Outline of the English Constitution*, p. 38. The latter was published in Boston, written by a Canadian, and closely edited by an English lord and thus amply illustrates the importance of English history to all three nations. For a discussion of the jury under the common law, see Theodore F. T. Plucknett, *A Concise History of the Common Law* (Indianapolis: Liberty Fund, 2010 [1956]), pp. 106–38.

[138] *Bushell's Case* [1670] Vaughan, r.135; 6 St. Tr. 999 (22 Car. 2). Broom, *Constitutional Law*, pp. 156–7. The case involved the refusal of jurors to convict Quakers who had been prosecuted for practicing their faith. The royal authorities had claimed that the jurors should be compelled to render a verdict of guilty in conformance with the evidence and should be punished for their refusal to do so.

[139] Broom, *Constitutional Law*, pp. 158, 163–4, 175.

thus entered into statutory law. In 1679, imperfections in this law were corrected in the Habeas Corpus Act, which stipulated: "(1) that any of the judges of any of the Courts ... might issue the writ ...; (2) that the law should apply to imprisonment in the colonies or other countries; [and] (3) that the gaoler should return the prisoner within twenty days."[140]

While trial by jury and the writ of habeas corpus have been the most cited English contributions to Western democracy, historians have long viewed the "rights of Englishmen" the product of a much more extensive political culture. From that perspective, English towns have long been considered one of the incubators of the "rights of Englishmen" because they largely lay outside feudal law; and, where feudal law did apply, they transformed much of it into communal arrangements. The emergence of the "peculiarly corporate character" of these early towns has, for example, been called "one of the greatest moral and legal achievements of the middle ages." As lord of the court and lord of the market in these towns and villages, the king could grant a wide variety of privileges and exemptions from feudal law that became, over time, customary "liberties" jealously guarded by town elites. In the assertion of these liberties, particularly those that produced revenue, the towns developed their "ideal will" in the form of "a permanent purpose" that both conferred unity on their collective existence and distinguished that collective from the rest of the kingdom.[141] Even more important was the emergence and development of the English common law.

THE COMMON LAW

Writing in 1974, Sayles concluded that "we remember Athens and Rome not so much for their transient empires as for their permanent contributions to art, philosophy, and jurisprudence"; in just that way, "England, now bereft of empire, will remain honoured for its development of the common law, which spread over half the world."[142] The common law, like the English Constitution, has no clearly defined origin and, in many ways, has been viewed as emerging more or less in tandem with the consciousness of the English people, the unification of the English nation, and the transfer of sovereignty from the crown to parliament.[143] But that is essentially where scholarly agreement ends.

Broadly speaking, there are two contending schools of thought with respect to the origin of the English common law. The first views the common law as almost synonymous with the "spirit" of the English people and places its origin

---

[140] Rannie, *Historical Outline of the English Constitution*, pp. 142–3.
[141] Pollock and Maitland, *History of English Law*, vol. 1, pp. 669–71, 706, 722; see pp. 676–702 for a detailed description of these privileges and exemptions.
[142] Sayles, *King's Parliament*, p. 3.
[143] See, for example, Pollock and Maitland, *History of English Law*, vol. 1, pp. 196–7, 423.

in the misty shrouds of history.[144] This school sees the common law as emerging in the Anglo-Saxon centuries. Hume, for example, contended that "the judicial power" was "always of greater importance than the legislative" among the Anglo-Saxons.[145] As a result, the dominance of the common law over statutory law naturally arose out of English history.[146] The second interprets the common law as a formal legal system in which compilations of cases and precedents are called upon when rendering legal decisions and routinized procedures organize the legal purview of the courts.

These schools have been speaking past one another to a large extent because they each conceive of the common law in a different way.[147] Those advocating an expansive conception often conflate the common law with the political traditions and history of the English Constitution.[148] By the beginning of the seventeenth century, for example, the common law was already bound up with "the doctrine of the ancient constitution" on the basis of three assumptions that lawyers and judges unquestionably accepted: "[F]irst, that all the law in England might properly be termed common law; second, that common law was common custom, originating in the usages of the people and declared,

---

[144] As Maitland once wrote: "National character, the genius of a people, is a wonder-working spirit which stands at the beck and call of every historian." Quoted in Van Caenegem, *Birth of the English Common Law*, p. 87.

[145] Hume, *History of England*, p. 173.

[146] The tension between the common law and parliamentary statutes appeared as early as 1674 when Baron Francis North, Lord Chief Justice of Common Pleas, noted that "the common laws of England ... are not written, but depend upon usage" and, thus, "the laws are fitted to the genius of the nation." However, only parliament should be "entrusted to judge" if and "when that genius changes," and, if it so decides, it should change the law so that it again fits "the genius of the nation." Broom, *Constitutional Law*, p. 804. However, this tension only became important long after the thirteenth century. Before then, only four legal documents are usually regarded as "statutes": the Magna Carta (1215), the Charter of the Forest (1217), the Provisions of Merton (1236), and the Provisions of Marlborough (1267). Pollock and Maitland, *History of English Law*, vol. 1, pp. 190–1.

[147] In fact, the distinction between these schools was often unclear because many scholars both affirmed that the customs and practices of the common law, although unwritten for the most part, formed a political culture that carried the English up to and through the Norman period and clearly recognized that it was the Norman kings, particularly Henry II, who gave the common law a modern form and procedure. Plucknett, for example, cited thirty Anglo-Saxon laws in what was otherwise a treatise overwhelmingly dedicated to the period after the Norman invasion. Plucknett, *Concise History of the Common Law*, p. xix. Also see John Hudson, *The Formation of the English Common Law: Law and Society in England from the Norman Conquest to Magna Carta* (London: Longman, 1996), pp. 20–1, 23.

[148] Broom attempted to distinguish between constitutional law and the common law by defining the former as "the aggregate of doctrines and sanctions directly tending to the maintenance of our social union" and the latter as "the aggregate of rules and maxims written or customary, directly tending to maintenance of private rights." He particularly maintained that constitutional law concerned matters "regulating and assuring the stability of the Empire." However, in practice, he also conceded that the two bodies of law were intertwined. Broom, *Constitutional Law*, pp. viii–ix.

interpreted and applied in the courts; third, that all custom was by definition immemorial, that which had been usage and law since time out of mind, so that any declaration of law, whether judgement or (with not quite the same certainty) statute, was a declaration that its content had been usage since time immemorial." Taken together, these assumptions crafted an interpretation of history that presumed that the common law "had existed from the obscure beginnings of English history ... from a time earlier than the earliest historical evidences." In turn, this orientation toward English history generated "an elaborate body of myths, maintained with great tenacity by Englishmen of the seventeenth century and after, which taken together form the cult of the 'ancient constitution.'"[149]

This cult has been nurtured by English jurists for centuries.[150] In fact, no one was more devoted to nurturing this cult than Blackstone, who wrote:

That ancient collection of unwritten maxims and customs which is called the common law, however compounded or from whatever fountains derived, has subsisted immemorially in this kingdom; and, though somewhat altered and impaired by the violence of the times, had in great measure weathered the rude shock of the Norman conquest. This had endeared it to the people in general, as well because its decisions were universally known, as because it was found to be excellently adapted to the genius of the English nation.[151]

Stubbs similarly maintained that the common law was based "to a far greater extent than is commonly recognized ... on strictly primitive custom" and "usages" that arose long before the onset of feudalism; even those elements of the common law that are feudal in nature were fully compatible with Anglo-Saxon traditions that can be traced back to "common Germanic sources."[152] In sum, the first school views the common law as developing much earlier than the

[149] Pocock, "Burke and the Ancient Constitution," pp. 129–30. On the linkages between the concept of "immemorial" custom, the common law, and "the ancient constitution," see pp. 131–2.

[150] In 1637, for example, Sir John Finch, Chief Justice of the Common Pleas, rendered an opinion in which he maintained that the "first precedents" under the common law were set "before the Conquest ... [in] the times of Edgar, Alfred, Ethelred, &c." Cited in Broom, *Constitutional Law*, pp. 357–8. Also see Hume, *History of England*, vol. 1, p. 78; Burke, "Abridgment of English History," p. 264; Blackstone, *Commentaries on the Laws of England*, Book IV, p. 324 [412].

[151] Blackstone, *Commentaries on the Laws of England*, Book I, p. 9 [17]. In Blackstone's view, Norman "scholastic reformers" undermined "the more homely, but more intelligible maxims of distributive justice [that had previously existed] among the Saxons ... Statute after statute has in later times been made to pare off these troublesome excrescences, and restore the common law to its pristine simplicity and vigour; and the endeavor has greatly succeeded" because English judges have sought "to recover that equitable and substantial justice, which for a long time was totally buried under the narrow rules and fanciful niceties of metaphysical and Norman jurisprudence" (p. 327 [418]).

[152] Stubbs, *Constitutional History of England*, vol. 1, pp. 10–11.

Norman Conquest, although the precise origin is considered to have been lost in the mists of time.[153]

Those in the second school contest this interpretation on several grounds. For one thing, where Blackstone views the Norman Conquest as a "rude shock" that interrupted the continuity and development of the common law, those in the second school often view the Normans as the major influence on its creation.[154] However, they also contend that the Norman Conquest encouraged the writing of law books in England for two reasons: (1) The compilation of laws had become an entrenched practice in England before the invasion occurred; and (2) the "very collision between two races" had made older law books increasingly obsolete. As a result, new law books had to be compiled in which feudal principles were written down in England to a greater extent than on the Continent.[155]

The organization of power and authority under Norman feudalism encouraged the development of the common law for several more reasons. First, the centralization of crown administration fostered the emergence of "a specialist judiciary, a vital step towards an ever more specialized law, distanced from ordinary social life, and understood and practiced primarily by professional lawyers." As the administration of the law became a profession, its practitioners cobbled together principles from "existing materials" and then transformed them into a system "by routine application."[156] As the royal courts became known for the greater predictability of their new brand of justice, popular demand for access to their rulings and decisions enhanced their prestige, and, as a result, the royal tribunals rapidly displaced the classically feudal forms available in seigniorial courts.[157]

Second, in imposing a full-blown feudal regime upon England, the Normans made rights and obligations attached to land the primary focus of the law.[158]

---

[153] For other historical interpretations that date the origin of the common law before the Conquest, see Hudson, *Formation of the English Common Law*, p. 20; Hume, *History of England*, p. 493. On Saxon legal codes see Kirby, *Making of Early England*, p. 125.

[154] Pollock and Maitland, *History of English Law*, vol. 1, pp. 23–4.

[155] Pollock and Maitland, *History of English Law*, vol. 1, pp. 113–14. On the inhospitably of feudalism to written law more generally, see Van Caenegem, *Birth of the English Common Law*, p. xi. On the gradual mixing of Norman feudal law and English custom, see p. 12.

[156] Hudson, *Formation of the English Common Law*, p. 22. On the centralizing predilections and orientation of the legal profession in which a preference for the "utmost generality and simplicity" went hand in hand with the unification of a national legal system under crown sovereignty, see Pollock and Maitland, *History of English Law*, vol. 1, p. 455; also see pp. xxxvii–xxxviii, 226–7, 230. As they noted, the king himself was outside the common law (p. 329).

[157] Much of this increased predictability arose from the expansion of trial by jury within the royal courts. Van Caenegem, *Birth of the English Common Law*, pp. 61, 72, 80.

[158] As a result, "feudal land law has been the core of the Common Law for centuries." Van Caenegem, *Birth of the English Common Law*, p. 23. Also see Pollock and Maitland, *History of English Law*, vol. 1, pp. 238–9. Edmund Burke, in Pocock's words, believed that it was

As already noted, there is a potential inconsistency here. On the one hand, feudal institutions are often viewed as hostile to legal development and England was thoroughly feudalized after the Norman Conquest. On the other hand, the rapid emergence and development of the common law after the Normans invaded produced a precociously modern legal system in England.[159] One way out of the inconsistency is to propose that "the better feudalism works the more rapidly it generates a political structure which is no longer completely feudal."[160]

In the English case, the Conquest imposed a very coherent feudal order both because the Normans possessed the power to do so and because that order effectively enabled their occupation of what was in many respects an alien society. However, within this feudal order, authority was centralized around the crown because the king, in theory and often in practice, owned all of the land in the kingdom.[161] Much of that land, in turn, was allocated to those who owed him homage; they, in turn, provided military support to the crown. These barons and earls subsequently distributed rights to their land to minor lords who did the same thing. And so on down the line. The rights and obligations attached to these relations and to the land, along with the fact that land was by far the major source of wealth in the kingdom, naturally, in this view, became the focus of English administration and law. The inordinate power and authority of the crown permitted and encouraged the movement of litigation over the rights and obligations attached to the land into royal courts.[162] The common law thus primarily originated as the administrative superstructure for a profoundly feudal order, precociously modern in its system of principles and centralization and fundamentally premodern in its substance and purpose.[163]

In what is probably the most authoritative presentation of the Norman case, Van Caenegem contends that "the English common law started in fact as Anglo-Norman law, which was shared by one and the same feudal society on both sides of the Channel" and became "English" only after the Norman kings were evicted from their original home on the Continent.[164] Much of the

fortunate "when a people lay claim to their liberties on exactly the same principles as those on which they inherit their estates" and that English land law was a "simple device [and] the most superb of all legal fictions" that identified "the principles of political liberty with the principles of our law of landed property." Burke saw this identification "as an act of conformity with the order of nature" and "the greatest accomplishment of our thought." Pocock, "Burke and the Ancient Constitution," pp. 130–1.

[159] Van Caenegem, *Birth of the English Common Law*, pp. 90, 92.
[160] J. R. Strayer and R. Coulborn, "The Idea of Feudalism" in R. Coulborn (ed.), *Feudalism in History* (Princeton, NJ: Princeton University Press, 1956), p. 9. Quoted in Van Caenegem, *Birth of the English Common Law*, p. 93; also see pp. 6–7.
[161] Plucknett, *Concise History of the Common Law*, p. 13.
[162] Van Caenegem, *Birth of the English Common Law*, pp. 40–1.
[163] Van Caenegem, *Birth of the English Common Law*, pp. 96, 104–5.
[164] Van Caenegem, *Birth of the English Common Law*, p. viii. After the loss of Normandy in the thirteenth century, the Anglo-Norman monarchy turned "into an English state" and the

argument for an "Anglo-Norman" interpretation of the origin of the common law depends on some combination of the following: (1) a definition of the common law that is weighted heavily toward official acts by the king and royal courts as opposed to unwritten custom and tradition; (2) hence the use of French and Latin as the language of the law instead of English; (3) the imposition of feudalism upon England by the Normans; and (4) the identification of Henry II as a "Norman" as opposed to an "English" king.

Historians from both schools have praised Henry II as the English monarch who contributed most to the development of the common law. Those who date the origin of the common law in the far distant past view Henry II as more English than Norman and view his reign as one in which English customs and traditions were once more attached to the crown. Those who insist on a more formal conception of the common law as a repository of precedents, rulings, and statutes view Henry II as the originator of the common law.[165] For them, whether or not Henry was more English than Norman is largely immaterial because what mattered was that he was able, through his "genius," to reconcile the strong Norman monarchy with forms of law that protected and enhanced English liberties.[166]

Even if the Normans are conceded to have originated the common law, the role it played in creating a distinctive English identity and binding that identity to the English state is still immensely important. As Van Caenegem puts it, the common law "became a real hallmark of English life" even though it "was originally not English at all." Although the common law was, instead, "a species of continental feudal law developed into an English system by kings and justices of continental extraction ... this exotic innovation [soon] took on the protective colouring of a thoroughly native species."[167]

While Burke believed that the distinctive nature of the English people and nation had been produced and revealed by their mutually constitutive history, he also maintained that the historical repository of political principles and practices in the common law safeguarded the English as they made their way

---

Normans and English melded into one nation. It was only then that the "Common Law, which bound together freemen of every descent became truly English, distinct from continental law and part of the country's identity" (p. 97). Van Caenegem then adds that "countless generations of English lawyers later turned it into a very English monument indeed."

[165] As Wormald put it, the common law suddenly appeared "with all the qualities of Athena, from the head of King Henry II." Wormald, *Making of English Law*, vol. 1, p. x.

[166] Van Caenegem, *Birth of the English Common Law*, pp. 2-4, 29, 83, 87, 89, 106. Henry II could well afford these judicial reforms because the efficiency of his financial administration might have made him the wealthiest monarch in Europe. In at least some years the crown's revenue in England probably equaled that of all the barons put together (pp. 102-3). Also see Hudson, *Formation of the English Common Law*, p. 19.

[167] Van Caenegem, *Birth of the English Common Law*, pp. 87, 98, 110.

into the future.[168] As a repository in which the otherwise incomprehensible wisdom of the ages was stored and organized, the English people drew upon the common law as they adjusted the realm to the material particularities of the present.[169] As Hale put it, the common law was like "the Argonauts Ship" which, as it traversed the centuries, might be replaced one plank at a time until none of "its former Materials" still existed. It was nonetheless still a more than serviceable vessel for the maintenance of English liberty.[170]

THE TRANSFER OF SOVEREIGNTY FROM CROWN TO PARLIAMENT

The standard narrative usually maintains that democratic traditions and customs emerged before parliament came into existence. One of the most important of those traditions was the "hundred," the existence of which cannot be firmly documented before the tenth century but, according to Stenton, must

---

[168] A "nation," Burke wrote, "is not an idea only of local extent, and individual momentary aggregation, but it is an idea of continuity, which extends in time as well as in numbers and in space. And this is a choice not of one day, or one set of people ... It is a vestment, which accommodates itself to the body." Quoted in Young, "Rediscovering Conservatism," p. 649.

[169] The common law embodied the wisdom of the past but this was a wisdom unique to the English people. Pollock and Maitland, for example, attributed the emergence of the distinctive characteristics of English law to the nation's exceptional history:

(1) In the first place, we should have to remember the small size, the plain surface, the definite boundary of our country ... England is small: it can be governed by uniform law: it seems to invite general legislation ... (2) the kingship of England, when once it exists, preserves its unity: it is not partitioned among brothers and cousins ... (3) the Northmen were so victorious in their assaults on our island that they did less harm here than elsewhere. In the end it was better that they should conquer a tract, settle in villages and call the lands by their own names, than that the state should go to pieces in the act of repelling their inroads ... (4) a close and confused union between church and state prevented the development of a body of distinctively ecclesiastical law which would stand in contrast with, if not in opposition to, the law of the land. Such power had the bishops in all public affairs, that they had little to gain from decretals forged or genuine. (Pollock and Maitland, *History of English Law*, vol. 1, p. 24)

Sayles similarly contended that the emergence of parliament required "centuries during which the English people have been sheltered from invasion and, very largely as a result, have been protected from tyranny ... When the environment differed, as it does so clearly, for example, in the states of Africa, English parliamentary institutions transplanted abroad are not likely to function." Sayles, *Functions of the Medieval Parliament*, p. 58.

[170] Hale, *History of the Common Law*, pp. 59–60. Hale also noted that "Titius is the same Man he was 40 Years since, tho' Physicians tells us, That in a Tract of seven Years, the Body has scarce any of the same Material Substance it had before." On the intimate connection between the common law and the "ancient constitution," see, for example, Glenn Burgess, *The Politics of the Ancient Constitution: An Introduction to English Political Thought, 1603–1642* (University Park: Pennsylvania State University Press, 1993), p. 4.

have played a role in governing the social order in "every part of England for many generations" before that time. The hundred had "all the features of an ancient popular assembly. It met in the open air" and rendered decisions arising from "the deliberations of peasants learned in the law."[171] Such assemblies and practices created a cultural substructure of popular custom and attitudes that traversed the centuries somewhat independently of the formal institutions surrounding the crown and the emerging national state.[172]

In the standard historical narrative, parliament emerged in a symbiotic relationship with the crown with respect to the production of political legitimacy. However, this symbiosis did not preclude a competition for power, a competition that became entwined with the ever expanding influence of the popular will within what became the national state. At first, the crown represented that popular will because the king was the leading agent in the formation of the English people and nation. Once England was politically unified, the gradual transfer of sovereignty from the crown to parliament has been viewed as the melding of the state and the people around the transcendent social purpose of perfecting political liberty. In this process, the people came to have a collective identity increasingly capable of articulating a "common will" through democratic institutions.

There is something very Burkean about the relationship between the "will of the people" and the "mists of history" in this characterization of the now forgotten reaches of the past. While acknowledging, for example, that "the growth of the medieval constitution" was primarily the product of competition "between the monarch and the magnates," Wilkinson contended that this was only the superficial appearance of more important "deep forces."

In a strong and progressive polity like that of medieval England clashing interests do not determine the pattern of the state. This is determined, not by what divides a nation but by what unites it. The true pattern was created in the thirteenth and fourteenth centuries, not by the great political struggles ... but by the common effort of Englishmen, within and outside the periods of crisis, to translate their common heritage into the institutions and practices of the state ...

The great struggles were not simply for power. They were the outcome of a clash of principles and ideals. They were based on conflicting interpretations of the common good. Nothing less would have gained sufficient support for the great movements of baronial opposition which repeatedly brought England into, or to the verge of, civil war.

---

[171] Stenton, *Anglo-Saxon England*, pp. 298–9. Stenton also states that "it is not the [noble] manor, but the community of free peasants, which forms the starting-point of English social history" (p. 314).

[172] In almost all accounts of English history, custom and tradition are the allies of "rights and liberties." However, the codification of custom and tradition tends to strip them of much of their meaning by rationalizing them into a unified, logically coherent system. In some ways, then, the development of central state capacity was hostile to the preservation of ancient rights and liberties. Pollock and Maitland, *History of English Law*, vol. 1, p. 143.

This is what makes these conflicts supremely important for the historian of the medieval English constitution.[173]

This translation of a "common heritage into the institutions and practices of the state" was nothing less than a process in which Englishmen were making themselves into Englishmen.

The origin of parliament can be traced as far back as the eighth century, when the witan, "the great council of the realm," advised the king on whatever matters he chose to refer to them. Composed of the king's immediate company, churchmen, and earls, the witan's advice at times crossed over into consent and the early kings often stated that the witenagemot, as a meeting of the council was called, shared responsibility for whatever public act was adopted. Whenever the throne became vacant and the successor was not obvious, the witan also decided who should be king.[174]

Up until the end of the tenth century, however, the witan was never considered a "corporate body." When it was obliged to consent, for example, it was the individual "crosses" of its members that stood by "the truth of the record," not the signature of a presiding officer. The witan, up to that point, was thus little more than a group of individuals and was not yet an institution that could exercise authority in its own name.[175] Even so, Stubbs argued that "the national assembly must have comprised a much wider class than the witan" even before Alfred ascended the throne and that "such gatherings ... might, by an easy and welcome fiction, be considered as representing the nation, although they were really the mere retainers of the nobles or the inhabitants of the neighbouring villages." As a "great council," this assembly of barons and servants of the king "represented the collective wisdom ... of the land in legislation, taxation and judicial matters."[176]

The word "parliament" first appears in the legal record in 1236; two decades later, in 1258, the Provisions of Oxford marked the point at which "the conception of organized parliaments" was solemnized as "an established part

---

[173] Wilkinson, *Constitutional History of Medieval England*, pp. ix–x. Within the standard historical narrative, the opposition of the great feudal lords to King John gave rise to "a continuous tradition reaching back to Runnymede." However, "the barons built better than they knew, for there was no conscious pursuit of political or constitutional ideals." Sayles, *Functions of the Medieval Parliament*, p. viii. Also see Stubbs, *Constitutional History of England*, vol. 1, p. 604.

[174] Stenton, *Anglo-Saxon England*, pp. 550–2; Liebermann, *National Assembly*, pp. 1–6, 7, 10–11, 14–15, 19, 21–2, 52; Kirby, *Making of Early England*, p. 168; Stubbs, *Constitutional History of England*, vol. 1, p. 138. Burke called the witenagemot the "Saxon Parliament." Burke, "Abridgment of English History," p. 308.

[175] Liebermann, *National Assembly*, p. 6.

[176] Stubbs, *Constitutional History of England*, vol. 1, pp. 135, 606. For criticism and reservations concerning the accuracy of the teleological implications of this orientation toward the past, see Sayles *Functions of the Medieval Parliament*, pp. vii–viii; Stenton, *Anglo-Saxon England*, pp. 553–4; Liebermann, *National Assembly*, pp. 23–4, 40–1; Stafford, *Unification and Conquest*, p. vi.

of the machinery of administration."[177] When parliament subsequently became the "testing ground where the king and the barons could try out their respective strengths," an unintended consequence of this competition was that the "knights of the shire and the burgesses of cities and boroughs" became an "indispensable element in the functioning of parliament," thus transforming it into a representative assembly.[178] As the nobility increasingly assumed a judicial role in what became an internal division of labor, the knights, burgesses, and proctors of the clergy began to meet separately as "a representative house of commons." While the emergence of a bicameral parliament was extremely important for the future evolution of the English state, "it was one of those events that are unremarked at the time as though nothing out of the way had occurred" because "previous developments had quietly prepared for the change." In that sense, the emergence of parliament "had no architect."[179]

Characterizing the subsequent growth of the English Constitution as an incremental transfer of authority from the crown to the House of Commons, Rannie described the fourteenth century as "a period of steady progress" in which parliament "showed its sovereignty by twice setting aside a King," took control of taxation and spending, and "claimed and exercised the right of impeaching ministers when they deemed it necessary." In 1322, for example, parliament asserted that all legislation, "whether affecting king or people, should henceforth be invalid without the consent of the Commons ... this statute marks a great advance in the direction of theoretic self-government, the goal of all British constitutional progress."[180]

The decisive transformation of the relationship between king and parliament occurred during the seventeenth century. With reference to that period, Loughlin describes three stages in the transfer of sovereignty: In the first, the "sovereign right was ... bestowed from above (by God)" upon the king; in the second, under Cromwell, this sovereign right "was conferred from below (by the people)," resting "on a belief that the ultimate power to make or alter the

---

[177] Sayles, *Functions of the Medieval Parliament*, pp. 12, 14–18; Sayles, *King's Parliament*, p. 48.

[178] Sayles, *King's Parliament*, p. 60. Also see Paul Brand, *Kings, Barons and Justices: The Making and Enforcement of Legislation in Thirteenth-Century England* (Cambridge: Cambridge University Press, 2003), pp. 15–105; Sayles, *Functions of the Medieval Parliament*, p. 42. Sayles interprets the entry of knights and burgesses into parliament as a melding of the latter with the practices and substance of popular representation that had long typified local government.

[179] Sayles, *Functions of the Medieval Parliament*, pp. 21, 44. Also see Hume, *History of England*, pp. 466–7.

[180] Rannie, *Historical Outline of the English Constitution*, pp. 73, 83, 88. According to Rannie, England in 1702 solved "the last and not least important problem of government, namely, how to make the Privy Council, and especially that active section of it known as the 'Ministry,' responsible to the House of Commons. The solution, like most other solutions in English politics, was worked out gradually and by means of circumstances." It was through this reform that political parties ultimately came to control the executive departments through the ministries (p. 155).

framework of government vests in the people"; and in the third, a "a conscious effort of British statecraft" subsequently created "the doctrine" in which "absolute authority" was given "to the Crown-in-Parliament to speak for the British nation ... This was achieved by eulogizing the status of parliament in the modern constitution" as "an omnicompetent representative forum of the 'community of the realm.'" After the 1688 Glorious Revolution, political parties emerged in parliament that both loyally supported the English state and yet, when in opposition, provided "an alternative government constantly standing at the ready." These developments, in turn, brought about

the triumph of the representative role of the MP, championed by Edmund Burke in his speech to the electors of Bristol in 1774, in which he explained that, while he might owe his constituents the courtesy of listening to their opinions, they had no authority to impose instructions and mandates; although the member for Bristol, his duty was to act for the best interests of the whole country.[181]

Observing that "most gentlemen of considerable property, at some period or other in their lives, are ambitious of representing their country in parliament," Blackstone enjoined them to recognize and act in accordance with the grave responsibilities that came with the office.

They are the guardians of the English constitution; the makers, repealers, and interpreters of the English laws; delegated to watch, to check, and to avert every dangerous innovation, to propose, to adopt, and to cherish any solid and well-weighed improvement; bound by every tie of nature, of honour, and of religion, to transmit that constitution and those laws to posterity, amended if possible, at least without any derogation.[182]

By then, as it is now, parliament's interpretation of the good of the community had become synonymous with the "will of the people."[183]

Carl Schmitt offered an even more Whiggish account of how parliament became the embodiment of the will of people. Although his narrative was not quite framed in stages, he recognized no historical backtracking in the transfer of sovereignty from the crown to parliament and then from parliament to the people. For him, "genuine parliamentary cabinet government" rested on "the basic principle of a political agreement between cabinet and parliament." This principle began to operate in 1689 after the Glorious Revolution when William

---

[181] Loughlin, "Constituent Power Subverted," pp. 27, 46.

[182] Blackstone, *Commentaries on the Laws of England*, Book I, p. 4 [9].

[183] Loughlin, "Constituent Power Subverted," pp. 27–9, 31–5, 38–42, 46–7. Loughlin goes on to say that, since the seventeenth century, there has "been an almost deliberate fudging of the issue of who holds the supreme legislative power. It is not held strictly by the people's representatives in the commons" but, instead, "rests in the king, lords, and commons representing the three estates and acting as the crown-in-parliament." This "obfuscation" has lodged "popular sovereignty" in parliament by characterizing the transfer as a restoration of "the ancient constitution." However, "the modern British system has thrived" on this obfuscation (pp. 42–3).

of Orange appointed a cabinet composed of members of the party that had offered him the crown.[184] In 1695, according to Schmitt, this principle was strengthened when "the cabinet was in complete harmony with the parliamentary majority for the first time." He called this the "birth of the first cabinet." In 1700-1, partisan rotation of the cabinet began as the Tories replaced the Whigs as the majority in parliament and, as a consequence, were appointed to the cabinet by the king. The minority party now constituted the potential "alternative government" in waiting. While Schmitt called this "the beginning of parliamentary government," partisan rotation was viewed at that time only as accepted practice; it was not yet obligatory custom. In addition, it was not entirely clear whether the "majority party" was determined by counting the membership of the House of Commons or enumerating the House of Lords. Furthermore, the king still possessed full authority over the composition of the cabinet and could appoint or dismiss its members at will during the eighteenth century. He also personally presided over the cabinet and decided all major policy questions.

The king's role changed dramatically with the reign of George I, who, either because he could not speak English or due to lack of interest (or perhaps both), chose not to participate in the deliberations of the cabinet. In 1803, parliamentary dominance was further strengthened when William Pitt the Younger, as leader of the majority party, himself appointed a cabinet. Over the following century, Schmitt noted two intertwined developments that progressively increased parliament's subordination to the people and to public opinion. The first was the expansion of the electorate and redefinition of parliamentary constituencies in the electoral reforms enacted in 1832, 1867, 1884-5, and 1918. Mass participation in the selection of members of the House of

---

[184] The Glorious Revolution of 1688 provided decisive confirmation by the crown of what eventually became parliamentary supremacy. As the *Encyclopaedia Britannica* puts it, William of Orange was invited by parliament "to come to the rescue of the religion and laws of England" and, accepting that invitation, "transferred the ultimate decision in the state from the king to parliament." *Encyclopaedia Britannica*, eleventh edition (New York: Encyclopaedia Britannica Co., 1910), vol. IX, p. 542. The Glorious Revolution was both a necessary but not sufficient event in the march of the English toward their historical destiny as "freemen" and, at the same time, provided much of the narrative ground for what became known as the Protestant Constitution, an ideological justification for the political dominance of the landed aristocracy and the Anglican Church that persisted for the better part of two centuries. Bateman, *Disenfranchising Democracy*, pp. 209–27; also see Broom, *Constitutional Law*, pp. 32–3. For a very strong argument that the Glorious Revolution should not be interpreted "as a great moment in which the English *defended* their unique way of life" but was, instead, an event in which "English revolutionaries *created* a new kind of modern state," see Steve Pincus, *1688: The First Modern Revolution* (New Haven, CT: Yale University Press, 2009), p. 3, emphasis in the original, and, more generally, the Introduction. Pincus would distinguish between the impact of the Glorious Revolution and the way in which it was justified. Without engaging the impact (which was, perhaps, not fully anticipated by the participants in any case), I would stress that the justification was not "modern."

Commons made the latter much more sensitive to public opinion. In addition, the House of Commons developed the right to compel the resignation of the cabinet through the operation of a vote of no confidence. When the cabinet fell, either a new cabinet had to be constituted that enjoyed the support of a majority of the chamber or new elections were held. A somewhat softer tradition also emerged in which the government was required to hold new elections if the majority party proposed a radical change in their policy program.

As "the culmination" of this historical process, parliament became "a mere expression of public opinion" and "the authority to topple the cabinet passed from the king to the lower house and then from the lower house to the people." However, the seamless manner in which these transitions evolved historically has left the nation with a monarch who retains, in practice, almost none of the discretionary sovereignty of the past while, in theory, he or she still holds "all the government's grants of authority and is only compelled to exercise them through his [or her] ministers." In the seventeenth century, "the King governed through his ministers"; now, "the ministers govern through the king."[185]

While there has never been a founding moment in which the adoption of a constitution clearly coincided with the creation of a state, parliament now sits as a constitutional convention whenever it convenes as a legislative body.[186] When considered within the historical context of English political development, this unusual combination of roles is fully compatible with the mutual evolution of the people, their transcendent social purpose, and the state that enfolds them both. However, there is a potentially serious tension between "the ordinary rights of Englishmen, the right to personal liberty and the right to private property" and the role of parliament, which, as the "great and powerful Assembly in the land," can alter the English Constitution at will.[187] Parliament formally acquired authority to alter the constitution in the Reform Act of 1832, but this act merely confirmed in principle what had already evolved historically in practice.[188] As a kind of permanent "constitutional

---

[185] Schmitt, *Constitutional Theory*, pp. 343–5.

[186] Earl of Halsbury, *The Laws of England, Being a Complete Statement of the Whole Law of England*, vol. XXI, article 1065 and note G (London: Butterworth, 1912), p. 616. On the nature of the English Constitution as an "open" process in which "numerous individual constitutional laws [have been] issued in the form of statutes," see Schmitt, *Constitutional Theory*, pp. 69–71.

[187] Broom, *Constitutional Law*, pp. 225, 231–2, 237, 799. Noting that parliament is often "assumed to be in some sense above the law," Broom asked "how and to what extent the ordinary rights of Englishmen ... may be affected or jeopardized by the existence of this great and powerful Assembly in the land." Broom, *Constitutional Law*, p. 799. Although Broom was writing over 130 years ago, this remains an open question.

[188] The Reform Act was passed after the House of Lords finally yielded to the entreaties of the king and violence in the streets. "Thus was England spared the crisis of a bloody revolution, and proof given to the world that her ancient constitution was sufficiently elastic to expand with the needs of the times." *Encyclopaedia Britannica*, vol. IX, p. 538. Among other things, the Reform Act transferred "a large share of political power from the landed aristocracy to the middle

convention" unconstrained by any other political institution, parliament has come to embody the unalloyed "will of the people" in a way that Rousseau would have warmly applauded in some ways.[189] However, this authority also means that parliament can create and destroy individual rights by passing a simple statute. This possibility has made political tradition and custom, as interpreted and apprehended by society, the keeper of "the rights of Englishmen" and thus has elevated history to the position of guarantor.[190]

THE ENGLISH NATION AND THE WELSH, SCOTS, AND IRISH

In the concluding passage of *The History of English Law before the Time of Edward I*, Pollock and Maitland describe the organic unity of the nation at the end of the thirteenth century in terms that leave no doubt that Wales, Scotland, and Ireland played little or no role in the English founding: "The England that saw the birth of English law, the England of Magna Carta and the first parliaments, was a much governed and a little England."[191] The king, the people, and the law evolved over the course of the following centuries, but the distinctive qualities of the nation indisputably originated and subsequently devolved from the English inhabiting that "little England."

The Welsh fare best in the standard historical narrative because they joined the English nation fairly early; the Scots are viewed as worthy partners who come in after most of the work is completed; and the Irish have been viewed as alien by almost all historians. In 1991, Loyn, for example, concluded "that the idea of an English nation was fully formed by 1307." At that time, England dominated Wales "and a high proportion of the Welsh people, if turbulently, was successfully slotted into English methods, English law and English enterprise." However, while the potential incorporation of Wales and Scotland into the English nation "was much more than a pipe-dream," those events still lay in the future.[192] Prior to that incorporation, Welsh laws were "barbarous, barely Christian," and Welshmen had to "be made into Englishmen."[193]

---

classes" by redistributing seats in the House of Commons from rural constituencies and "rotten boroughs" to the industrial regions of the nation.

[189] Loughlin, "Constituent Power Subverted," p. 46.

[190] Loughlin views this guarantee as grossly inadequate. Loughlin, "Constituent Power Subverted," p. 47.

[191] Pollock and Maitland, *History of English Law*, vol. 1, pp. 724–5. In their magisterial history, Pollock and Maitland identified a heartland or core region within what became England (and then Great Britain) as the central object of study because what became English law descended through time within the community that resided within this territory. Ireland, Scotland, and even Wales and the northern counties of Northumberland and York were treated as outliers that contributed little or nothing to the emergence and development of English law.

[192] Loyn, *Making of the English Nation*, pp. 177–81.

[193] Pollock and Maitland, *History of English Law*, vol. 1, p. 98. They cite, in particular, the persistence of the wergild "as a trait of Welsh barbarism" (pp. 234, 237). For a slightly different

In the centuries prior to their incorporation, the "Celts ... had been driven westward by the waves of German conquest" and "were gradually compressed into ever smaller space. It was absurd for such a people to hope for independence of their great and ambitious English neighbours, even though different blood flowed in their veins." Still, the subjection of Wales "took much fighting," because, "[l]ike other Celtic races the Welsh had much poetry and sentiment; and the great object of their poets was to stir the people to resistance to the English." After their defeat, Wales became "a part of England" and thus "shared the benefits of the constitutional system which Edward I was perfecting."[194]

Developments between Scotland and England followed roughly parallel trajectories because their respective royal houses intermarried on several occasions and their shared "Norman and English blood ... made the early governing arrangements in Scotland very similar to those in England." However, "the absence of the English popular assemblies from the greater part of Scotland prevented the early growth of self-government" and, for that reason, "the Anglo-Norman Constitution was much more despotic and oligarchic in Scotland than it ever was in England." Scottish feudal lords harshly exercised their relatively great power and, as a result, parliamentary democracy was slower to develop than in England.[195] Scotland thus never influenced English development and only imperfectly realized the potential of English institutions.

Hume noted that Ireland had "never been conquered or even invaded by the Romans" and had therefore been denied the benefits of Roman "civility." As a consequence, the Irish persisted "in the most rude state of society, and were distinguished by those vices alone, to which human nature, not tamed by education or restrained by laws, is for ever subject." They thus, "from the beginning of time, had been buried in the most profound barbarism and ignorance" and, while "never fully subdued, still retained their animosity against" their English conquerors. Their hatred of the English, in fact, was one reason the Irish "remained still savage and untractable." It was only in the beginning of the seventeenth century, after 400 years of English subjugation, that Ireland could become "a useful conquest to the English nation."[196]

Although his account might appear to be more charitable in some respects, Rannie still described the Irish as "sunk in barbarism" in the decades following the Norman Conquest. The invasion of the Danes in prior centuries

interpretation of Welsh incorporation into the English state, see Stubbs, *Constitutional History of England*, vol. 1, pp. 68, 595, 597.

[194] Rannie, *Historical Outline of the English Constitution*, p. 71.
[195] Rannie, *Historical Outline of the English Constitution*, pp. 67–8.
[196] Hume, *History of England*, vol. 1, p. 339.

had never progressed much further than the eastern seaboard. Furthermore, the Danes "neither mixed with Irish nor subdued them; they merely ... drove them to sullen isolation among their morasses, with the seeds of deadly enmity to the German races sown in their hearts." Later, Henry II attempted to conquer Ireland but succeeded only in installing a few barons. In fact, English control was almost entirely restricted to the eastern and southeastern coastal regions, where "the mass of the English immigrants" intermarried with the Danes. Beyond the pale, the Irish lived much as they always had, and, over time, even the descendants of the English lords "sunk to [the] depressed level of Celtic civilization." By 1300, the Irish were ruled by "an aristocracy of English origin ... who were now barbarians," an English "Constitution whose workings were confined to the district near Dublin," and "two races, alien in blood, who could neither believe in, govern, nor exterminate one another." While the Irish were nominally Christian, that religion's "influence was gone."[197]

Writing in 2006, Henson describes "a Britain that is divided, with a core that is England and what is sometimes referred to, rather dismissively, as the Celtic fringe." He attributes the existence of separate Scottish, Welsh, and English identities to "a feeling" among the English "that the Anglo-Saxons had a divine right to be in Britain and had a superior right ... to rule the whole of the island."[198] Although Henson was referring specifically to the centuries leading up to the Norman Conquest, the attitude he describes persisted well into the modern era.

Support and opposition in the referendum on British membership in the European Union in 2016 had many different causes. However, if we knew only one thing and that thing were the standard historical narrative of the emergence and rise of the English nation, we would have been able to anticipate much of the geographical distribution of the vote. Where the native-born, ethnically identified English resided, the vote was overwhelmingly in favor of exiting the Union. In the Celtic fringe and among those communities (such as London) where immigrants have settled in large numbers, the vote was just as overwhelmingly in favor of remaining in the European Union. The referendum was thus, simultaneously, a demonstration of the power of the standard historical narrative as a ground for national identity and its utter impotence among those peoples denied participation in and responsibility for the founding of the English nation.

---

[197] Rannie, *Historical Outline of the English Constitution*, pp. 69–71. Even when Henry VIII formally added Ireland to his title in the sixteenth century, the king's claim to sovereignty was largely symbolic because the native Irish had been "driven into semi-barbarism" and those who were nominally English "were scarcely subject even in name to the English crown." Stubbs, *Constitutional History of England*, vol. 1, p. 599.

[198] Henson, *Origins of the Anglo-Saxons*, p. 187.

THE RITUAL OPENING OF PARLIAMENT AND THE WILL OF
THE PEOPLE

In 1912, the Earl of Halsbury published one of the great compilations of
English law, in which, among a great many other things, he described the
powers and authority of parliament. In the first of three successive articles, he
stated: "The Parliament of the United Kingdom consists of the Sovereign and
the three Estates of the Realm, namely, the Lords Spiritual and the Lords
Temporal, who sit together in the House of Lords, and the elected representatives of the people, who sit in the House of Commons." While entirely
consistent with the historical order of their importance, he thus inverted their
prominence and role in the early twentieth century. The next article declared:
"The two Houses of Parliament are summoned, prorogued and dissolved by
the Sovereign by the exercise of his Royal Prerogative, and his assent must be
given to any Bill passed by the Lords and Commons before it can have the
force of law." With respect to ritual formalities, this statement was correct,
but, again in practice, the sovereign merely rubber-stamped legislation that
was passed by the House of Commons. While the House of Lords might
quibble a bit before approving legislation sent from the lower house, in
practice its role was also more or less perfunctory. Halsbury then proceeded
to the crucial statement of the powers exercised by parliament: "Parliament is
the supreme legislative authority, not only in the United Kingdom, but also
throughout the whole British Empire, and there is no legal limit to its power of
making and unmaking laws." The only limitation on that power was that one
parliament "cannot bind a succeeding Parliament." Just like the kings of
England from whom this authority historically devolved, each parliament
reigns supreme. However, it is not, in practice, the parliament of "the
Sovereign and the three Estates of the Realm" that reigns but, instead, the
House of Commons alone.[199]

In these articles, Halsbury had reconciled the historical traditions and
customs of "the ancient constitution" with the practice of politics in the modern
era. Everyone who read these articles realized that the monarch would never
withhold his or her approval from legislation passed by the House of Commons
but everyone also understood that the legitimacy of the state and the identity of
the nation rested on the Whiggish narrative of a gradual historical devolution
of authority from the crown to the lower house of parliament.[200] What the

---

[199] Halsbury, *Laws of England*, vol. XXI, p. 616.

[200] As one of those most hallowed traditions, the speaker of the House of Commons was,
"immediately after the confirmation of his election," to demand "from the Crown the rights
and privileges of the Commons, and, throughout the duration of the Parliament, he is responsible for the preservation of the dignity, the maintenance of the privileges, and the due
enforcement of the rights of the House of Commons." Halsbury, *Laws of England*, vol. XXI,
p. 664. These ritual forms originated in contests for supremacy between the crown and
parliament that the latter had won long ago. For other examples of the complex rituals and

latter now exercised was, in fact, authority once exercised by monarchs more than a millennium in the past. That ancient authority had made the English people, the English nation, and the English state; the task of the modern House of Commons was now to carry and preserve those identities and institutions into the modern era.

In his compilation, Halsbury hastened to recognize this modern reality, stating: "Parliament is not an executive authority, but either directly or indirectly it exercises a dominating control over the action of the Crown and of the Executive Government and the administration of the laws which it has enacted." One of the attending notes to this article elaborated on what Halsbury meant by "dominating control" in the field of foreign policy:

It is a recognised convention of the Constitution that, although the declaration of peace or war or the making of treaties with foreign Powers rests with the Sovereign acting upon the advice of his Ministers, all such acts must conform with the wishes of Parliament, and in certain cases the direct action of Parliament may be required to carry out the obligations incurred by a treaty.[201]

The phrase "a recognised convention of the Constitution" refers to a tradition never expressly set down in law because, of course, "the Constitution" was and is unwritten. Parliamentary authority in this area rests on a custom within a large bundle of associated political traditions.[202]

Halsbury also stated that "[t]he House of Commons consists of 670 members, 495 of whom are elected as representatives of England and Wales, 72 of Scotland, and 103 of Ireland."[203] This apportionment recognized the relative standing of the regions under the English Constitution in two ways. First, the regions appear in the order of their historical incorporation into the English state: England, Wales, Scotland, and, lastly, Ireland. Second, England

---

symbolic emblems setting out relations between the crown and parliament, including relations between the House of Commons and the House of Lords, see pp. 692–6.

[201] Halsbury, *Laws of England*, vol. XXI, p. 617.

[202] Similar conventions require that only members of the House of Commons or the House of Lords may serve in the cabinet and that "a Government" must resign if it loses a vote of confidence in the House of Commons. Halsbury, *Laws of England*, vol. XXI, p. 618. With respect to voting for candidates who stand for election to the House of Commons, most suffrage qualifications were explicitly set down in statutes. Statutes also determined eligibility for membership in the House of Commons (p. 656). However, Halsbury also reported an exception for membership that, at the time, seems to have rested on the denial of suffrage eligibility: "It is clear at common law that a woman cannot be elected to serve in Parliament" (p. 655). This, of course, has changed. Halsbury also stated that "[m]inisters of Protestant nonconformist religious bodies are capable of being elected to membership of the House of Commons" but, under either tradition, law, or sometimes both, clergy of the Church of England, the Church of Scotland, and "the Church of Rome" were barred from membership (p. 657).

[203] Halsbury, *Laws of England*, vol. XXI, p. 655.

and Wales are, apart from the order of their names, considered as one, consolidated region, while Scotland and Ireland have remained distinct.[204]

Every new session of parliament begins with a concatenation of rituals called the state opening of parliament. Much of the pageantry associated with these rituals dates back to the fourteenth century and reflects events and historical relations from the distant past. For example, the ceremonies begin with a formal search of the cellars in Westminster in commemoration of the attempt by Guy Fawkes to blow up parliament in November 1605. That search is followed by a procession from Buckingham Palace to Westminster in which the queen rides in the same Irish state coach that carried Queen Victoria in 1852. The Household Cavalry provides her escort and the Imperial State Crown rides in a separate coach just ahead of the queen. Arriving at the Sovereign's Entrance, the Union Flag is replaced by the Royal Standard. After entering Westminster, the crown is placed on the queen's head in the Robing Room and she then leads the Royal Procession through the Royal Gallery to the House of Lords. The Sword of State and the Cap of Maintenance are carried just ahead of her. These symbols, along with the Imperial State Crown and the Robe of State that she wears, represent the majesty and dignity of the sovereign.

Once the queen arrives at the House of Lords, the members of the House of Commons are summoned in a ceremony arising from the English Civil War in the seventeenth century. An officer of the House of Lords entitled the Black Rod approaches the House of Commons where the door is slammed in his face. That act symbolizes the independence of the lower house from the sovereign. After the Black Rod gives three strikes to the door, it is opened and the members then follow the officer, the speaker, the prime minister, and the leader of the opposition party back to the House of Lords. Further demonstrating their independence from the sovereign, they move slowly and the members in the body of the procession behave boisterously. When they reach the House of Lords, the members stand at the "bar" that blocks the entrance.

Inside the chamber, members of the House of Lords are dressed in red robes and, along with other high-ranking members of the Royal Procession, surround the throne. At that point, the queen reads a speech outlining the legislative program of the majority party in the House of Commons. Although the queen has no role in its preparation, it is delivered as a policy pronouncement of Her Majesty's Government. The queen then retires and the members of the House of Commons return to their own chamber. As a result of history, the pageantry

---

[204] There are many such discriminations between the different regions of the United Kingdom. See, for example, the distinction between Scottish and Irish peers with respect to eligibility for service in the House of Commons in Halsbury, *Laws of England*, vol. XXI, p. 625. Also see the various ways in which judges of contested elections are designated when the results are disputed (p. 787, note O).

and symbolism associated with the participants in the ceremony are inversely related to their actual political influence: The queen who is, in actuality, almost bereft of practical authority over the government, is the center of all attention; the House of Lords provides the primary site and the members are in close attendance in the chamber although they have little to say on how the government will be run; and the members of the House of Commons are summoned by the sovereign to attend the proceedings but not allowed inside the chamber even though it is they who will actually rule the nation.[205]

CONCLUSION

All foundings are mythological because they invariably entail an imagined "will of the people" that is melded into and thus becomes the transcendent social purpose of the state. Although these things are tangible in some ways (e.g., the conduct of elections), they are also constructed out of historical and cultural materials that have little grounding in material reality. The founding of the English state clearly entails these qualities. In the standard historical narrative, the origin of the people lies beyond the ken of history in the lowlands between what is now Denmark and Germany. English historians accept that beginning without asking who these people might have been before they migrated to the island Britain. However, the political traditions and customs within what becomes England are at least as old as the people who migrated to Britain. When they came to the island, the Angles and the Saxons brought with them a kingship as the form of governance. While this kingship is often portrayed as a kind of proto-democracy, it is not yet a state. Emerging out of competition between Anglo-Saxon kingships, the English state gradually took form as English people became united under one sovereign. Over time, the practices and routines of the crown gave rise to the common law, which is, in some ways, as much an imagination of historical tradition and custom as it is a formal statement of legal principles and devices.

In the standard historical narrative, the precise origins of the people, the sovereign, and the common law are now lost in the mists of history. In that way, the standard historical narrative relies upon the mists of history to solve the great dilemma attending all foundings by positing a people, a leader, and a common law. For example, there is no controversy over whether or not there was a first king, even though English historians continue to debate when the first "king of England" appeared in history.

---

[205] Members of the House of Commons must also take an oath: "I, [name], do swear that I will be faithful and bear true allegiance to His Majesty King George, his heirs and successors, according to law. So help me God." Halsbury, *Laws of England*, vol. XXI, p. 687, note U. Those who have a religious objection to taking this oath may swear a slightly different version.

These imagined artifacts have invented an historical narrative describing the creation of the ancient English Constitution, a social contract that guarantees that the English state will always conform to the will of the people even as it continues to evolve. The unquestioned consensus that the ancient English Constitution enjoys also creates expectations with respect to the exercise of legislative and executive authority that ostensibly constrain the modern parliament. Most importantly, members of the House of Commons themselves share those consensual beliefs and voluntarily, even unconsciously, act in accordance with the English Constitution. And, if they did not, the people would clearly recognize the violation of their rights and take appropriate remedial action.[206]

The rituals attending the opening of parliament basically conform to and recapitulate the standard historical narrative: (1) by symbolically demonstrating the continuity of popular consent from the beginning of time; (2) by characterizing that consent as an exercise that is ostensibly voluntary in that it is hallowed and dictated by tradition; and (3) by thus underpinning the organic unity between the English people and the English state. This ritual is so perfected to these purposes that the transfer of sovereignty from the crown to the House of Commons has not significantly changed its performance. The ceremonial opening of parliament salutes the fundamental concepts of sovereignty, people, and rights while leaving them ambiguously wrapped in the enigmatic "ancient constitution." On the one hand, the English state is refounded every time a new parliament is opened because the House of Commons now sits as a constitutional convention in full control over the rights and duties of the English people. On the other hand, the ritual attending that opening shrouds that fact in the mists of history, a history in which the English are said to have consented long ago to the founding of the state.

And it is emphatically an English, not a British, state. The people of England do not negotiate the terms of its association with this state because, ostensibly, the people and the state are the same thing. The position of the Welsh is somewhat more distant, but, despite their somewhat tardy incorporation, they are considered participants in the founding. The Scots, on the other hand, belong to the United Kingdom only through negotiation with what is otherwise an alien nation. There is little in the standard historical narrative that obligates loyalty to the English state. And the rump of Ireland that still adheres to this United Kingdom does so out of pure and simple self-interest. The unique founding that the English have crafted works, as they invariably report, superbly for England but very poorly for the rest of the United Kingdom.

And there is little, if anything, the English can do to solve the problem. If they try to rewrite the standard historical narrative so as to include Scotland

---

[206] Broom seems to believe that a harsh judgment in "public opinion" would be enough to bring parliament back to its senses, but he doubtless would have recognized that revolution in the defense of English liberty has always been a possibility. Broom, *Constitutional Law*, p. 982.

and Ireland as participants in the founding, the exercise would be transparently vacuous and would probably invite destructive inspection of just how purposeful traditional academic interpretations have been in creating a usable past for the English state.[207] If they hold a constitutional convention that does not require that the Scots must commit themselves in advance to membership in a united state, then the subsequent bargaining might very well result in the separation of Scotland. The very bonds that created the English people, the English state, and English common law repel the Scots, who, in the standard historical narrative, are *not* English.

---

[207] Traditional academic interpretations of English history more or less served this purpose up until 1950 or so. Since then, revisionist treatments, some of which have been cited in the text, have often undermined those accounts by demythologizing both events and actors, including revelation of the mixed motivations and beliefs of the latter. The late nineteenth century was the heyday in which the standard historical narrative was constructed. Although scholars quibbled over the details, almost all of them agreed on the purpose of their historical research.

3

The Will of the People and the American Founding

SECTION I: FROM THE RIGHTS OF ENGLISHMEN TO THE DECLARATION OF INDEPENDENCE

English political customs, traditions, and institutions profoundly shaped the American founding, so much so that the major difference between them was that, following the break with Britain, the Americans "wrote down" those customs, traditions, and institutions into their constitutions and statutory laws.[1] In 1760, both the British people and the American colonists held that the unwritten English Constitution had created and guaranteed the "rights of Englishmen."[2] This ensemble of abstract principles, maxims, and institutional relations gradually came to supersede the comparatively specific claims based on the individual charters of the separate colonies. For example, when the royal governor of Georgia rejected the man elected by the Georgia Assembly as speaker, John Zubly, in 1772, Zubly first cited the history of parliament as support for the assembly's right to choose whomever it wanted as a presiding officer and then added: "[A]n Englishman I should think [is] entitled to English laws, which I suppose implies Legislation any where and every where in the British dominions, that this right is prior to any charter or instruction,

---

[1] "[T]he Americans could easily conceive of themselves as simply preserving what Englishmen had valued from time immemorial. They sincerely believed that they were not creating new rights or new principles prescribed only by what ought to be, but saw themselves claiming 'only to keep their old privileges,' the traditional rights and principles of all Englishmen, sanctioned by what they thought had always been." Gordon Wood, *The Creation of the American Republic, 1776–1787* (Chapel Hill, NC: Omohundro Institute of Early American History and Culture, 1998), p. 13.

[2] For a succinct description of colonial understanding of the English Constitution, see William E. Nelson, *The Common Law in Colonial America: Law and the Constitution on the Eve of independence, 1735–1776* (New York: Oxford University Press, 2018), pp. 4–6.

and is held not by instructions to a Governor but is his [in this instance, the colonist's] natural right."[3]

This embrace of the ancient English Constitution and rights of Englishmen both facilitated the development of a common political ideology across the individual colonies and encouraged a comprehensive assimilation of the procedures and substantive doctrine of the English common law in colonial courts in the years prior to the revolution.[4] That assimilation was so thorough that American lawyers found it difficult (and often impossible) to think of the law in any other way.

The rights of Englishmen were emphatically not democratic in the sense that people could, by majority vote or by any other demonstration of the popular will, either give them up or expand upon them. They were part of the "given" of British political life. In fact, they were the very stuff of English ethnic and national identity, both collectively and individually. This, as we shall see, had several consequences for colonial–metropole political relations during the revolutionary crisis. First, the colonists' insistence that they had inherited the rights of Englishmen meant that American political identity was profoundly English in the early eighteenth century. Second, this political identity meant that those rights could not be compromised or violated by the metropole without undermining colonial allegiance to the home country.

The colonists and the metropole fundamentally disagreed about how those rights might be extended and applied to the colonies; the dispute ultimately boiled down to an assertion by parliament that the rights of Englishmen, whatever their relevance to the colonies, could be ignored, transgressed, or redefined by legislative fiat. For the colonists, this was absolutely intolerable. In some respects, then, the colonists entered into the revolutionary crisis by staking out a position that could be characterized as "more English than the English."[5]

---

[3] Zubly's pamphlet was entitled "CALM AND RESPECTFUL THOUGHTS on the NEGATIVE of the CROWN on a SPEAKER chosen and presented by the REPRESENTATIVES of the PEOPLE." Jack P. Greene and Craig B. Yirush (eds.), *Exploring the Bounds of Liberty: Political Writings of Colonial British America from the Glorious Revolution to the American Revolution*, 3 vols. (Carmel, IN: Liberty Fund, 2018), p. 2146.

[4] Lord Beloff, "American Independence in Its Constitutional Aspects" in A. Goodwin (ed.), *The New Cambridge Modern History. Volume 8: The American and French Revolutions, 1763–1793* (Cambridge: Cambridge University Press, 1965), p. 451.

[5] On the very "Englishness" of the colonists, including their self-conception as "free-born Englishmen," see Gordon S. Wood, *The Radicalism of the American Revolution* (New York: Vintage, 1991), pp. 12–18, 25–6, 33, 40–2, 52, 57–60, 64–5, 77–92, 105, 109–10, 123, 146. On the complicated social and cultural comparisons the colonists made between themselves and the metropole, see Gordon S. Wood, "Search for Identity: An Interpretation of the Meaning of Selected Patterns of Social Response in Eighteenth-Century America," *Journal of Social History* 3: 3 (1969–70), pp. 213–18. Also see Bernard Bailyn, *The Ideological Origins of the American Revolution* (Cambridge, MA: Harvard University Press, 1967), p. 82n.

But a new state cannot be founded through revolution if it is merely a carbon copy of what an old state had once been or should have been. The American Revolution thus transformed the rights of Englishmen (which the colonists fervently claimed at the onset of the revolutionary crisis) to the will of the people (which became, once the colonists became committed to an independent national existence, at least a coequal principle for founding the American state). In pursuing independence, colonial leaders faced several challenges. First, they had to construct a mass, popular coalition that would oppose imperial rule. Specification of the imperial violation of the colonial rights of Englishmen provided only a justification for protest against the actions of British authorities. When those protests came to naught, colonial leaders resorted to armed insurrection, but, at first, they combined organized violence with an insistence on the possibility of a reconciliation of differences with Britain. When the possibility of reconciliation became utterly unrealistic, colonial leaders had to persuade their people that independence was preferable to political submission. It was at that point that insistence on the rights of Englishmen became theoretically and practically problematic. As a result, the British could no longer be the authoritative source for the meaning of these rights; that meant that the colonists themselves were compelled to set down exactly what these rights entailed.

This is precisely what the colonists did when many of the colonies adopted new constitutions that included bills of rights while eliminating all references to British officials.[6] In effect, each bill of rights specified what the rights of

---

[6] Maier calls these "the world's first written constitutions," distinguishing them, of course, from the unwritten ancient English Constitution. Pauline Maier, *Ratification: The People Debate the Constitution, 1787–1788* (New York: Simon & Schuster, 2010), p. 17. This is a little exaggerated in that the Ancient Greeks had drafted constitutions some two millennia earlier, collected and classified by Aristotle in his *Politics*. Mogens Herman Hansen, *Polis and City State: An Ancient Concept and its Modern Equivalent* (Copenhagen: Royal Danish Academy of Sciences and Letters, 1998), pp. 73–4, 103–5. On the ancient Athenian constitution, see Josiah Ober, *The Rise and Fall of Classical Greece* (Princeton, NJ: Princeton University Press, 2015), pp. 232–6. However, the word itself took on a new meaning during the revolution, shifting "from a description of the entire political system of government toward a specific written document establishing the frame of government." Mary Sarah Bilder, *Madison's Hand: Revising the Constitutional Convention* (Cambridge, MA: Harvard University Press, 2017), p. 37. Bailyn agrees but gives the change in meaning a slightly different formulation. Bailyn, *Ideological Origins*, pp. 67–8. On the novelty of a written constitution as well as an interpretive account of the framing of the revolutionary constitutions in the colonies, see Wood, *Creation of the American Republic*, pp. 132–73, 259–60, 430–63. Also see Esmond Wright, "American Independence in Its American Context: Social and Political Aspects: Western Expansion" in Goodwin (ed.), *New Cambridge Modern History. Volume 8*, p. 528. The first of these, adopted by New Hampshire on January 6, 1776, was intended to be temporary, providing for a government outside imperial rule only until a reconciliation with England was effected (which many had come to doubt would ever occur). Even if reconciliation was regarded as imaginable, the moment was pregnant with immense possibility. Just as the Continental Congress was about to suggest to the colonies that they might now construct new constitutions, John Adams sent a letter to a colleague in Virginia celebrating

Englishmen actually entailed in that colony. The rights set down in these new constitutions were not intended to be new or invented; they were, instead, interpretations of the unwritten, historical inheritance they shared with the British metropole. However, in setting them down in words, there was an inevitable expansion and transformation of meaning. The problem was to legitimate this otherwise authoritative statement of rights.[7]

There were several ways to legitimate these statements. On the one hand, they could be viewed as authorized by English common law and, thus, by the historical inheritance the colonies shared with the metropole.[8] But, as already noted, this raised its own problems. On the other hand, they could be understood as an explication of the will of the people. The will of the people, however, was not viewed as whimsical, open-ended, or volatile. It was instead constructed as the natural recognition of eternal political principles by the people. These principles were, of course, almost identical to the rights of Englishmen because the latter rested on the same political principles. And the people could naturally recognize these principles because they inhabited a culture in which these rights constituted the very foundation of social and political community. And, for these reasons, the will of the people was both enabled and strongly constrained: enabled in the sense that the people were called upon to legitimate the founding of the new states (and, later, the founding of the national state) and strongly constrained because political elites sought to ensure that the will of the people would not itself violate the very rights that were to be legitimated. As in all other modern foundings, the role of the will of the people was only intended to legitimate a particular form that the new state could assume. In the American state, that form was profoundly English, and a new bill of rights thus stood at the apex of the US Constitution as both a reinstantiation of the rights of Englishmen and a

---

the fact that: "You and I, my dear friend, have been sent into life at a time when the greatest lawgivers of antiquity would have wished to live. How few of the human race have ever enjoyed an opportunity of making a election of government, more than of air, soil, or climate, for themselves or their children!" Willi Paul Adams, *The First American Constitutions: Republican Ideology and the Making of the State Constitutions in the Revolutionary Era* (Chapel Hill: University of North Carolina Press, 1980), pp. 3, 21, 56–7.

[7] On the content of these bills, see Leonard W. Levy, *Origins of the Bill of Rights* (New Haven, CT: Yale University Press, 1999), pp. 22–4, 265–8, 272–4.

[8] Bailyn, for example, elegantly summarized the American attitude this way:

To the colonists [the common law] was a repository of experience in human dealings embodying the principles of justice, equity, and rights; above all, it was a form of history – ancient, indeed immemorial, history; constitutional and national history; and, as history, it helped explain the movement of events and the meaning of the present ... English law – as authority, as legitimizing precedent, as embodied principle, and as the framework of historical understanding – stood side by side with Enlightenment rationalism in the minds of the Revolutionary generation. (Bailyn, *Ideological Origins*, p. 31)

justification for revolution against the home country that had originally discovered and articulated those very rights.

The political culture in both Britain and the colonies thus imagined an ancient English Constitution that was the ground from which the rights of Englishmen had sprung. This political culture made law in the form of custom and tradition the determinant of what, in fact, the rights of Englishmen were and how, in theory, their exercise and vitality constituted preconditions for individual membership in the polity.[9] The reasoning behind these connections was complex and political contestation between the colonies and the metropole often involved abstruse legal arguments grounded in historical cases and precedents that were beyond the ken of the vast majority of colonists.[10] These arguments were, for that reason, largely constructed by the elites, including newspaper editors, journalists, merchants, wealthy landholders, and legislators. Even so, the larger political community also viewed the metropole as a threat to their identities and were consequently willing to act in defense of their rights as Englishmen.[11] As a consequence, abstract contestation over constitutional principles between the colonial elite and the British authorities became thickly

---

[9] These rights became embodied and enshrined in the political practice of the colonial assemblies, that practice evolving into a foundational basis for colonial claims to legislative governance even as it became quite distinct from the way things were done in the metropole. See, for example, Bernard Bailyn, *The Origins of American Politics* (New York: Vintage, 1967), pp. 7–10, 59–63, 66–70, 107–24.

[10] For a succinct summary of Greene's interpretation of the constitutional controversies leading up to the revolution, see Jack Greene, *The Constitutional Origins of the American Revolution* (New York: Cambridge University Press, 2011), p. 184. As a legal interpretation, Greene's analysis coherently describes a trajectory that made collision between the colonies and the metropole inevitable. However, the connection to popular mobilization is left largely unexplained in that this very sophisticated line of argument was probably much too complex for popular consumption and thus itself needed to be explicated before it could encourage popular mobilization. The process through which it was popularized thus shaped both its expression (as, for example, in slogans such as "no taxation without representation") and content.

[11] On the breadth of the social base supporting the revolution, see R. R. Palmer, "Social and Psychological Foundations of the Revolutionary Era" in Goodwin (ed.), *New Cambridge Modern History. Volume 8*, p. 424. One of the questions seldom addressed in the historiography of the American Revolution is how the thirteen colonies came together so rapidly in opposition to imperial rule after 1765. Some of them were separated from one another by well over a thousand miles, had very different political economies, and had much stronger interactions, both social and political, with the metropole than with each other. Reid's explanation for the alacrity with which they unified was that these otherwise different communities nonetheless "used similar language to enunciate similar principles and responded uniformly to perceived political dangers. They did so because eighteenth-century Americans everywhere had internalized the same constitutional program." John Phillip Reid, *Constitutional History of the American Revolution: Abridged Edition* (Madison: University of Wisconsin Press, 1995), p. xv. This interpretation of an "internalized" political identity is strengthened if we also note that colonial corresponding societies transmitted constitutional arguments and language and thus facilitated local convergence on a continental understanding of political identity. We need not assume that a thick uniformity of meaning had emerged before the colonies began to communicate with one another,

intertwined with popular action in the streets, with the latter often dramatically strengthening the position of the former.[12]

Colonial elites and their communities thus met on the common ground of an interpretation of the English Constitution: elites emphasizing abstract legal claims that underpinned identity in the form of "the rights of Englishmen" and their communities acting in defense of that identity. This common ground in the law had two major effects on the American Revolution. First, it provided the link between popular action and elite ideology, including the coordination of protest with formal politics and the assignment of meaning to popular insurgency.[13] Second, the common ground of the law profoundly shaped the ways in which popular political identities entered into conceptions of the will of the people, in the first instance under the ancient English Constitution and later in the new republic.[14]

On both sides of the Atlantic, the most important constitutional issue concerned the exercise of arbitrary power, but that issue assumed very different

only that they shared the basic principles of a political culture that they all had inherited from the metropole.

[12] For examples of popular protests in opposition to the Stamp Act, see Barbara Clark Smith, *The Freedoms We Lost: Consent and Resistance in Revolutionary America* (New York: New Press, 2010), pp. 91–5. Much historiography on the American Revolution has been loosely categorized as the "ideological school" in which "republicanism" has been cited as a major motive force in explaining popular mobilization. The "constitutional school," to which Reid belongs, has offered a more persuasive explanation for the translation of "republicanism" (to the extent that they would concede its existence) into actual political claims that then became the spark driving mobilization. This distinction between the two "schools" can easily be overstated because they are complementary rather than competing explanations in many respects. Law (as an element of institutional design shaping the behavior of citizens) and virtue (as the political practice that should be engendered by that design) can, for example, be conceived as different sides of the same coin. In the same way, legal argument and popular mobilization were merely different aspects of the revolutionary movement in the middle of the eighteenth century. See, for example, Reid, *Constitutional History*, p. xiv.

[13] In Reid's words, "the discourse that shaped the 'reality' of American whigs was framed in constitutional terms, and ... the assumptions, traditions, conventions, and values were all to a large extent constitutionally based. A culture of constitutionalism pervaded that epoch more than in any previous times and certainly more than during the two centuries since." Reid, *Constitutional History*, p. xii. Greene proposes a very similar interpretation of the origins and unfolding of the revolutionary crisis in his *Constitutional Origins*. For a succinct summary, see pp. ix–xviii. Bailyn, on the other hand, contends that the lack of rigor in colonial legal thinking created an opening for the primacy of popular ideology in the revolution. See, for example, Bailyn, *Ideological Origins*, pp. 212–13.

[14] In the metropole, English identity was composed of a commitment to Protestant religion, the prestige and power of the nation, and, most importantly "the systems of law and liberty that ... distinguished English people from all other peoples on the face of the globe." Greene, *Constitutional Origins*, pp. 5–6. The new American nation was, practically speaking, Protestant but did not enshrine that commitment in law. It was also an emphatically weak player in the international arena. But that most salient component of English identity, the belief in the rule of law as the fount of individual liberty, became the very heart of the transcendent social purpose of the new state.

forms in the colonies and the metropole. In the colonies, the apprehension of arbitrary power by the metropole drove an insistence on what Americans interpreted to be their rights under the English Constitution.[15] The colonial position was that the customary rights of their communities arose under a contractarian tradition that originated in their founding as colonies, a founding that was structured by the grant of royal charters that were, forever afterward, beyond the authority of parliament to alter.[16] Attempts to alter what colonists interpreted as their rights under these charters violated the rule of law and were, for that reason, an arbitrary exercise of despotic authority. During the colonial crisis, this led colonists to oppose acts of parliament as illegitimate, while simultaneously insisting that their opposition arose out of rights guaranteed them as Englishmen.[17] They contended, often passionately, that parliament was bound by the English Constitution and that its acts had to conform to the rule of law.[18]

The colonists could not recognize the metropole's changing interpretation of the rule of law without abandoning their own claims. After they fully realized that the king would unequivocally side with parliament, the colonist interpretation of the rule of law was no longer even remotely tenable under the metropole's version of the English Constitution. Viewed in another way, the

[15] In the formulation of their claims and arguments, colonial elites heavily relied on English constitutional history. With respect to the concept of arbitrary power, for example, they relied on the same arguments that parliament had made little more than a century earlier in overthrowing Charles I and even used "similar modes of expression." From the colonial perspective, England in 1640 and the colonies in 1765 were in similar situations. However, these two situations differed with respect to the institution (the crown earlier and parliament later) that exercised arbitrary power. Reid, *Constitutional History*, pp. xii–xiii.

[16] For a succinct summary of this contention, see Greene, *Constitutional Origins*, p. 118.

[17] The colonists contended that "all the settled inhabitants of this vast [British] empire" were, rightly, "called Englishmen," but that did not mean that they all belonged to "a single state." As Samuel Adams put it, each colony had "a right equal to that of the people of Great Britain to make laws for themselves" because each of them constituted "a separate body politick." The various parts of the empire were, in Franklin's words, "all united in allegiance to one Prince, and to the common law," but shared no other institutional connection. Greene, *Constitutional Origins*, p. 122.

[18] With respect to the rule of law, the colonies persisted in viewing customary rights embedded in legal tradition as formal constraints on the exercise of arbitrary power. By the 1760s, the colonists were, as a consequence, citing and constructing "anachronistic fundamental-law arguments" in order to protest "new imperial regulations." Daniel J. Hulsebosch, *Constituting Empire: New York and the Transformation of Constitutionalism in the Atlantic World, 1664–1830* (Chapel Hill: University of North Carolina Press, 2005), p. 6, and, more generally, 7, 19–20, 73–4, 90–2. On the importance of customary practices and community consensus in colonial understanding of the rule of law, see Greene, *Constitutional Origins*, p. 141. In the metropole, the rule of law had come to mean only that parliament must have passed a statute enabling the exercise of power; law was no longer above and beyond the reach of the ruler. Put another way, the rule of law in the metropole required only that the exercise of authority be procedurally correct, while, in the colonies, the principle retained the substantive prescriptions as they descended from history and tradition. Reid, *Constitutional History*, pp. 22–3.

colonists perceived an institutional shift (by the king) rather than a constitutional shift (the increasing empowerment of the House of Commons within an evolving legal tradition). The former was a more persuasive way of presenting the cause of independence to the American people because it preserved English constitutional tradition and forms as the template for erecting a new state and a new political order.[19] In this and other ways, the transition to independence was a culmination of miscommunication in which neither side properly understood the argument the other was making. However, even if they had, given the intransigency of parliament, the differences were probably irreconcilable. Over the long term, measured in centuries, the revolutionary emphasis on the rule of law and a written constitution produced an American identity in which an adherence to abstract principles embedded in highly adjudicated political institutions stood in the place of the ethnic, religious, and class foundations on which other modern states rested.[20]

Until late in the colonial crisis, Americans relied on the royal prerogative (e.g., the rights granted under crown charters) as a bulwark against the exercise of authority by parliament.[21] For the metropole, on the other hand, acts of parliament *were* the law; as a consequence, the rule of law and acts of parliament were essentially the same thing. On the eastern side of the Atlantic, parliament was a bulwark against the possibility of despotic authority by the crown and law was what bound the monarch. The reconciliation of these two positions was, from a theoretical perspective, probably impossible. From a realist perspective involving the practice of governance, reconciliation could only be had if parliament voluntarily refused to exercise the authority that it otherwise claimed.[22]

---

[19] Reid, *Constitutional History*, p. 24.

[20] On the importance of the rule of law in the American founding, see, for example, Reid, *Constitutional History*, pp. 104–5. In some respects, the American Revolution transformed the English tradition into something related and yet substantively novel. For example, where the Magna Carta had, in the traditional interpretation, subjected the otherwise discretionary authority of the king to the "law of the land," the American emphasis on the "due process of law" subjected the enforcement of that law to a determination as to its applicability in a particular case. In a sense, the former "creates" a "law of the land" while the latter, presuming its creation, constrains its application. Both English phrases played a role in the New York ratification convention where Hamilton successfully promoted "due process of law" as an affirmation of judicial authority. Maier, *Ratification*, p. 379.

[21] For a concise description of the historical primacy of the crown in colonial governance, see Benjamin Franklin's summary (written in 1766) in Greene, *Constitutional Origins*, pp. 52–3. For increasing colonial insistence that parliament had no constitutional authority to legislate on internal affairs in the colonies, see pp. 58–9. On the king's prerogative, see Eric Nelson, *The Royalist Revolution: Monarchy and the American Founding* (Cambridge, MA: Belknap Press, 2014), p. 35.

[22] Reid, *Constitutional History*, pp. ix–x. Reid describes the clash between the colonies and parliament as a "constitutional dilemma" in which "American liberty – the right to be free of arbitrary power – could not be secured under parliamentary supremacy [and] British liberty – the representative legislature over the crown – could not be secured without parliamentary sovereignty"

We can distinguish four periods in the evolution of American political identity between the original creation of the colonies and the ratification of the United States Constitution. In the first, from the granting of colonial charters up to 1730 or so, the colonies were part of a trans-Atlantic community with Britain as the mother country. Although there were exceptions, political relations were complacent, largely because the colonies were left alone to govern themselves. In the second period, from 1730 to 1775, Britain asserted authority in the colonies in ways that increasingly transgressed against what the colonists understood to be the customs and traditions that defined their relationship to the metropole within the imperial system. Parliament became both the provocateur in these transgressions and the audience before which the rights of Englishmen were asserted by colonial leaders (with the increasingly active support of the colonists generally). In these two periods, the will of the people was thoroughly wrapped up in the rights of Englishmen because the latter were inseparably entwined with the identity of the colonists and were thus not "willed" but instead rightfully claimed as a natural birthright.

When war broke out in 1775, the rights of Englishmen became an increasingly inadequate basis for mobilizing the colonists because (1) the colonists were fighting the nation the originally gave rise to those rights; (2) that nation did not recognize those rights as applying to the colonies; and (3) there was almost no possibility that recognition of those rights would ever be granted by the metropole. Put another way, the colonists found it increasingly difficult to be "more English than the English" and, at the same time, mount a war against the mother country. As the war became increasingly violent, the political elite in the colonies transformed, with uneven success, the rights of Englishmen into the natural rights of all men.[23] The revival of natural rights

(p. 99). I rely heavily on Reid and Greene in this discussion. Their arguments are not quite the same in that Reid displaces royal prerogative onto the customary practice of colonial governments (the "rule of law," from a colonial perspective). That displacement can be seen as immaterial in that royal prerogative was, ultimately, the source of that customary practice.

[23] In some quarters, however, this transformation was well underway even before hostilities commenced. For example, on June 15, 1762, the Massachusetts General Assembly proclaimed, as part of its instructions to its agent in London:

The natural Rights of the Colonists, we humbly conceive to be the same with those of all other British Subjects, and indeed of all Mankind ... This Liberty is not only the Right of Britons, and British Subjects, but the Right of all Men in Society, and is so inherent, that they Can't give it up without becoming Slaves, by which they forfeit even life itself. ("Instructions to Jasper Mauduit" in Greene and Yirush, *Exploring the Bounds of Liberty*, pp. 1725–6)

Bushman states that the Massachusetts Assembly "thought of itself as claiming English rights, natural rights, and charter rights imperceptibly blended," even combining them "in the same sentence." He then cites an example from 1728. Richard Bushman, *King and People in Provincial Massachusetts* (Chapel Hill, NC: Institute of Early American History and Culture, 1985), p. 93n, and, more generally, pp. 88–132.

theory had several effects: (1) It detached colonial constitutions from the English tradition (i.e., they no longer rested on the rights of Englishmen but became universal principles that applied to all humanity); (2) it meant that Americans no longer had to persuade metropolitan opinion because the rights of Englishmen no longer constrained how Americans presented their case (e.g., those rights were "English," and thus the English had some say in what they were); and (3) it promoted, for both reasons, the construction of an autonomous American identity that, in addition to all these things, conferred a much larger framework within which political action and institutions could emerge. But, unlike the rights of Englishmen, these natural rights did not have a firm grounding in custom and tradition, and the elite, for that reason, had to carefully lodge them within a new conception of the will of the people.[24] The last period, following the treaty of peace in 1783 until the ratification of the Constitution, completed this transformation while, somewhat instrumentally, creating reservoirs of rights where the will of the people could not go and crafting institutional filters that the elites believed would induce political and economic stability. In the end, a government grounded in the will of the people had become a natural right of all peoples and nations, but most of the supporting infrastructure of rights and institutions through which it operates in the United States is thoroughly English.

THE INTERTWINED AMERICAN AND BRITISH TRAJECTORIES

Colonial elites never mapped out a general strategy during the crisis leading up to the revolution because it was the British who almost always held the political initiative. With a centralized political apparatus that the colonists could not match, the British were more able to develop and implement a unified program that, in turn, drove events forward. The American colonial elite was certainly opportunistic at times but it more often simply reacted to events that had been provoked by the British. Even so, the British made serious mistakes in the decades leading up to the American Revolution. Most fundamentally, they repeatedly underestimated American resolve, including the extent to which their own ancient English Constitution facilitated unity between colonial elites and the rest of the people. This miscalculation, in turn, led the British to insist upon policies that clearly transgressed against American conceptions of the English Constitution; these transgressions lent crucial legitimacy to American popular and elite resistance during the decades preceding the Declaration of Independence. The colonists, as it turned out, were anything but an adventurous people, at least when it came to politics. However, British policy, with its

---

[24] On varying interpretations of natural rights within traditional English thought, see George Van Cleve, *A Slaveholders' Union: Slavery, Politics, and the Constitution in the Early Republic* (Chicago: University of Chicago Press, 2010), pp. 43–4.

arrogant and blunt assertion of the metropole's right to rule by fiat, ultimately made revolution seem conservative.[25]

In addition, the British did not develop a plan for integrating the American colonies within the imperial system on terms other than absolute dominance by the metropole. In the short term, the British articulated a coherent legal argument that gave the metropole control of the colonies (that argument was tenable but also eminently debatable). However, over the long run, political relations between the American colonies and the metropole were simply unsustainable within the political framework the British sought to impose. Demographically and economically, the colonies were expanding so rapidly that some form of political integration was almost certainly inevitable if the colonies and the metropole were to remain within the same political system. Parliament, however, failed to recognize that the colonies must be either incorporated into the political system of the home country or permitted such extensive political autonomy that they might as well be regarded as independent.[26] In sum, the British simply could not imagine a viable political future within which they and the colonies could coexist. As a result, it was British mistakes, both in theoretical understanding of the situation and in concrete policy decisions, that created the material with which the colonists crafted their own identities and their own conception of the will of the people.[27]

---

[25] While providing an exhaustive and balanced account of British imperial policy toward the colonies, Justin du Rivage stresses the internal divisions in parliament between what he terms the "authoritarian reformers," "radical Whigs," and "establishment Whigs." The "authoritarian reformers" made most of the crucial decisions involving the American colonies while both groups of Whigs repeatedly warned that these decisions would have dire consequences. Justin du Rivage, *Revolution Against Empire: Taxes, Politics, and the Origins of American Independence* (New Haven, CT: Yale University Press, 2017), pp. 24–111, 131–77, 225–42.

[26] For instance, the British interpreted military protection of the colonies as a contractual relation, as opposed to a sovereign responsibility for the protection of a part of the realm. In that contractual relation, the colonies had to pay for that protection in order to uphold their part of the bargain. That argument only reminded the colonists that the metropole did not regard them as "Englishmen" because "Englishmen" did not have to "contract" for their own protection. That refusal was reinforced when the 1765 Stamp Act denied the colonists the right to be tried by a jury (which, of course, would often exonerate those who refused to pay the stamp tax) and instead required appearance before a judge appointed by the crown. Reid, *Constitutional History*, pp. 35–7, 41.

[27] For example, the British seriously underestimated the strength of colonial opinion with respect to opposition to taxation. Greene, *Constitutional Origins*, pp. 93–4. When this misapprehension led to the Boston Tea Party in 1773, the British compounded the error by assuming that imperial punishment of the city would politically isolate Massachusetts from the other colonies. Rallying to the commonwealth's defense, the colonies instead created the First Continental Congress. M. A. Jones, "American Independence in Its Imperial, Strategic and Diplomatic Aspects" in Goodwin (ed.), *New Cambridge Modern History. Volume 8*, pp. 484–5.

THE "MISTS" OF EARLY COLONIAL HISTORY

Even in 1750, most records of governance in the decades following the original settlement of the American colonies had been lost. The death rate among early settlers was very high and mere survival was a much higher priority than the keeping of records. In addition, the very small size of these communities made formal government by edict and statute unnecessary. As a result, the practices and traditions that colonial elites cited in the run-up to independence were often the products of informed imagination as opposed to retrievable historical facts. What can be retrieved is an uneven record of governing arrangements that relied on some form of consultation with the local population.[28]

In 1619, the first representative assembly in the colonies was created upon instructions issued by the London headquarters of the Virginia Company. The company subsequently encouraged settlement by granting settlers the right to make the laws under which they would live – in the words of a 1621 ordinance: "to imitate and follow the policy of the form of government, laws, customs, and manner of trial; and other administration of justice, used in the realm of England." Under this warrant, the new Virginia assembly naturally claimed the right to approve taxes in the new colony just as parliament did on the other side of the Atlantic.[29]

Other colonial charters, patents, and proclamations similarly promised that there would be no distinction drawn between the political rights of settlers and those of people who resided in the home country.[30] Colonists were considered

---

[28] Edmund S. Morgan, *Inventing the People: The Rise of Popular Sovereignty in England and America* (New York: W. W. Norton, 1988), pp. 210–13. For a description and interpretation of what is available in the New England records, particularly with reference to conceptions of democratic practice, see J. S. Maloy, *The Colonial American Origins of Modern Democratic Thought* (New York: Cambridge University Press, 2008).

[29] When he compared political institutions in Massachusetts, Pennsylvania, and Virginia, Pole concluded that Virginia bore "the most significant resemblance to England" and, for that reason, provided the most apt illustration of "the application of Whig principles [and] the most illuminating test of their meaning in practice." J. R. Pole, *Political Representation in England the Origins of the American Republic* (New York: St. Martin's Press, 1966), p. 125 and, more generally, pp. 125–65. Also see Paul Musselwhite, Peter C. Mancall, and James Horn (eds.), *Virginia 1619: Slavery and Freedom in the Making of English America* (Williamsburg, VA: Omohundro Institute of Early American History and Culture, 2019), pp. 138–40, 142–5.

[30] On the one hand, the variation in charters became an advantage during the struggle with the metropole because it implied a unique arrangement between each colony and the metropole, one that could not be reduced to a generic formulation within a general constitutional framework. In addition, this diversity in colonial governance implicitly conferred respect for their particular customs and traditions in that the crown accepted, in each one, whatever were the original terms of settlement as the basis for governance. However, that same diversity complicated efforts to bring the colonies into alignment with one another since disputes with the crown in one place may very well have been moot in another. At several points in the late seventeenth and early eighteenth centuries, the crown contemplated unification of colonial governance but always backed away. It is an interesting question whether unification would have strengthened the impulse toward independence (because the colonies would have been able to work out their

the "natural born subjects of England" and none of the laws governing them were to be repugnant to "Laws, Statutes, Customs, and Rights of our Kingdom of England." As the Maryland charter proclaimed in 1632, colonists were to enjoy "all Privileges, Franchises and Liberties of this our Kingdom England, freely, quietly, and peacefully ... in the same manner as our Liege-Men born, or to be born within our said Kingdom of England."[31]

After William Penn, along with other Quakers, purchased the colony of West Jersey, he offered would-be settlers "Concessions and Agreements" that granted "the inhabitants more political and legal rights than most people enjoyed anywhere in the world then and now," including a representative assembly elected annually by the universal suffrage of free men. In 1681, when Penn was given the colony that later became Pennsylvania, he allowed the members of the lower house "to write their own constitution." When they did, they abolished the upper house and thus gave themselves a monopoly on legislative authority, qualified only by the governor's veto.[32]

The colony of Massachusetts was originally a creature of the Massachusetts Bay Company and rule there did not require the consent of those the company governed. However, the company transferred its meetings of stockholders to the colony in 1629 and sometime after that permitted "all orthodox male Puritan church members" to participate in their proceedings. From that point onward, Massachusetts rapidly evolved governing arrangements involving an elected governor and "assistants," the latter acting as a legislative assembly in the customary English tradition. When the community of Watertown, for example, protested against the imposition of a tax in 1632 because the colonial government could not "make laws or raise taxations without the people," the governor contended that the assistants were very much like parliament and thus played the same role in soliciting and

---

shared needs and reconcile their differences in a common forum) or frustrated separatist sentiment (because the colonies would have fought with one another as they considered legislation that affected each of them differently). Their diversity later became a liability once the colonies attempted to found a new state because the prior existence of thirteen constitutional regimes, each of them unique, frustrated consolidation into one polity. In practice, however, the variation in political arrangements and institutions in the several colonies tended to converge on a common form composed of an elected assembly, a governor appointed by the crown, and an appointed council. Beloff, "American Independence," pp. 448–53.

[31] Greene, *Constitutional Origins*, pp. 9–10. In 1728, Daniel Dulany published an emphatic declaration, "The RIGHT of the Inhabitants of MARYLAND, to the Benefit of the ENGLISH LAWS," including colonist rights arising from both this charter and the subsequent history of governance under its terms. Greene and Yirush (eds.), *Exploring the Bounds of Liberty*, pp. 651–75. And in 1768 the Virginia House of Burgesses asserted that "their ancestors brought over with them intire, and transmitted to their descendants, the natural and constitutional rights they had enjoyed in their native country." Reid, *Constitutional History*, p. 15.

[32] For an overview of politics in colonial Pennsylvania, see Pole, *Political Representation*, pp. 76–124.

recording popular consent to taxation.[33] That satisfied the community and was one of the many precedents the colonists were to cite when, over a century later, they fervently protested against parliament's right to tax them without their consent. Consent could be manufactured only in the colonies because tradition and custom had always held that was so.[34]

While the circumstances and details differed from colony to colony, there was thus a pastiche of legal instruments and pronouncements upon which the colonists very plausibly rested their claims to an English identity with all the institutions and rights that that identity implied. This pastiche provided the legal scaffold upon which the colonists rested their claims for self-governance, but it was political practice that conferred plausibility on this scaffold.[35] That political practice, in turn, was the product of an indifferent mother country that had not paid much attention to the colonies until they became a potentially significant source of wealth and revenue. Until then, the colonies were so small and insignificant that British officials probably considered them, when they thought of them at all, as "so many petty Corporations at a distance" with almost no independent identity. But the colonies had nevertheless independently evolved into distinct political communities and "it was natural," in the words of Edmund Burke, "that they should attribute to [their] assemblies, so respectable in their formal constitution, some part of the dignity of the great nations which they represented."[36]

---

[33] Morgan, *Inventing the People*, pp. 39–40, 43–6, 124–30. In 1669, John Locke tried his hand at creating constitutions for the Carolina colonies but these were rejected by the settlers because he assigned too little authority to representative assemblies (p. 129). For the origins of traditional English practice and custom, particularly with respect to the possibility and responsibility of representation by members of the House of Commons, see pp. 47–121.

[34] On the connection between "a customary constitution" and the notion of political consent, see, for example, Greene, *Constitutional Origins*, pp. 181–2. Mary Sarah Bilder provides a superb overview of the relation between the colonial and metropole legal systems in her *The Transatlantic Constitution: Colonial Legal Culture and the Empire* (Cambridge, MA: Harvard University Press, 2004), pp. 1–7; also see pp. 38–9 on the extent to which English law applied to the colonies; pp. 136–42 on the importance of precedent, particularly with respect to Privy Council rulings; and pp. 192–6 on the ways in which Privy Council supremacy over colonial legislation was later drawn upon as a rough model for judicial review of state law by the US Supreme Court. On the construction of politics and institutions in colonial Massachusetts, see Pole, *Political Representation*, pp. 33–75. Pole notes that the Massachusetts House of Representatives built "a public gallery" just after the Stamp Act crisis in 1765 in order to "publicise its proceedings and by so doing to strengthen the bonds holding the colonists together" while bolstering the reputations of "the representatives who were engaged in the exalting business of defying the Crown to their electors in scattered home towns" (p. 69).

[35] Pole, *Political Representation*, p. 31. More generally, see Sheldon D. Pollack, *War, Revenue, and State Building: Financing the Development of the American State* (Ithaca, NY: Cornell University Press, 2009), pp. 118–24.

[36] Greene, *Constitutional Origins*, p. 26. Burke also thought that the colonies "formed within themselves, either by royal instruction or royal charter, assemblies so exceedingly resembling a parliament, in all their forms, functions, and powers, that it was impossible they should not imbibe some opinion of a similar authority" (p. 48).

By the time the metropole began to pay attention, imperial ability to overawe the colonies through the threat of military force had declined because the British Empire had vastly expanded and had thus multiplied the material commitments of British military and naval forces. In addition, the population of the American colonies had grown and, along with that growth, it had become increasingly conscious of its own existence as a distinct political community.

The conception of consent that arose in the colonies was grounded in this parallel between the provincial assemblies and parliament.[37] For that reason, the authority of colonial assemblies was constructed as one of the rights of Englishmen as opposed to an abstract notion of the will of the people.[38] The people were "represented" by those who lived among them and these representatives were assigned responsibility for ensuring that the colonial governor (and, later, the king himself) did not overstep his authority. While the colonists conceded that royal governors (and the king) could veto legislation passed by the assembly, use of the veto was strongly constrained by the fact that assemblies controlled the purse strings of governors, including the salaries of these governors and the expenses of the administrations they oversaw.[39] This responsibility, in turn, was grounded in traditional and customary relationships that those who served in colonial assemblies were expected to respect and enforce. Policymaking, in the sense of translating the will of the people into law, was distinctly secondary if recognized at all. The colonial assemblies were thus the protectors of the rights of Englishmen and, in that sense, in direct, unmediated correspondence with the crown.[40]

---

[37] See, for example, Greene, *Constitutional Origins*, p. 32. As James Otis proclaimed in his pamphlet "A vindication of the Conduct of the House of Representatives of the Province of the Massachusetts-Bay," written in 1762, "the general assembly ... however contemptably some may affect to speak of it, is the great council of this province, as the British parliament is of the kingdom." Greene and Yirush, *Exploring the Bounds of Liberty*, p. 1721.

[38] Several groups flirted with a more full-bodied notion of the will of the people during the seventeenth century, most notably the Levellers and parliament after Charles I was beheaded. Morgan, *Inventing the People*, pp. 64–5, 72–3. However, advocates of popular sovereignty were generally suppressed. Algernon Sidney, for example, was executed in 1683 as a traitor and John Locke, noting the fact, fled to Holland in the same year (pp. 104–5). Later, of course, Locke became the major theorist justifying the legitimacy of the Glorious Revolution, but his view of popular sovereignty was basically restricted to the right of parliament to depose and recognize a monarch (pp. 104–6).

[39] The British unsuccessfully attempted to compel the colonial assemblies to permanently appropriate money for governors and other imperial officials. Greene, *Constitutional Origins*, p. 29. The British could have achieved the same result if the metropolitan government had simply paid for imperial administration out of its own pocket. The general shortage of revenue was, perhaps, the primary reason why they did not do so. This failure had the paradoxical result of increasing colonial demands for autonomy, which, ultimately, gave rise to quite an expense in itself.

[40] Because the assemblies had traditionally advocated the rights of colonists, this role would come back to haunt the Federalists as they crafted a new constitution. When that time came, these same assemblies were reluctant to cede that responsibility and their reluctance was immensely strengthened by popular appreciation of their historical role.

The colonists' political relationship with the metropole provided strong support for their interpretation of colonial standing under the ancient English Constitution in several ways.[41] For one thing, none of the colonies had been created or authorized by parliament; they were all creatures of crown prerogative. In the first decades of settlement, the significance of this fact was generally unrecognized because the colonies were then of little importance to the empire. Parliament was preoccupied with much more important business, including a civil war, and even the crown, distracted by many of the same concerns, delegated its authority over the colonies to court favorites in the form of royal charters. Almost as an afterthought, and perhaps as an inducement to immigrants in some cases, the crown either required the creation of popular assemblies when a charter was granted or confirmed their legitimacy if they emerged naturally.

Another factor was the location of the colonies across an ocean that made communication difficult and direct rule from London inefficient. Messages sent either way took many weeks to arrive at their destination and during that elapse of time were often rendered obsolete or inappropriate by changing conditions on either side of the Atlantic.[42] In addition, the colonies, despite the naming of many towns as the "new" versions of "old" cities in Britain, were not much like the mother country. Commerce and agriculture, for example, often involved novel crops, in some cases produced by very different labor regimes. And settlers were constantly moving to a frontier that was almost always beyond the reach and support of government institutions. In addition, there were, just at the edge of that frontier, an indigenous people who must be dealt with one way or another. Effective imperial rule of the American colonies required both knowledge and cooperation; that knowledge could come only from regular consultation with the colonists themselves, and that consultation required their cooperation. Cooperation, in turn, required that the colonists be treated as if they, like their counterparts in the metropole, enjoyed the rights of Englishmen. And so it was that representative assemblies emerged almost naturally in the colonies because they served as panels for

---

[41] On the acceptance of the notion of the ancient English Constitution in the colonies, see Morgan, *Inventing the People*, p. 109.

[42] Here are two examples in which very important information moved, although slowly, across the ocean. On January 27, 1775, Lord Dartmouth, secretary of state for the colonies, sent an order to General Gage in Boston, commanding him to prevent the Massachusetts militia from further perfecting their military preparations. Gage did not receive the order until April 14, 1775, two and a half months later. Five days after receipt, on April 19, 1775, Gage moved on Concord, initiating hostilities there and at Lexington. Similarly, George III had announced that the colonies were now considered to be in rebellion on August 23, 1775, but news of his proclamation arrived at the Continental Congress only on November 9, again some two and a half months later.

regular consultation and, both symbolically and in practice, as the protectors of the rights of Englishmen.[43]

The one prominent exception to this relative colonial autonomy involved the Navigation Acts passed by parliament in 1660 and 1663. This legislation was intended to benefit English merchants and thus transfer at least some wealth from the colonies to the metropole. However, Massachusetts claimed exemption from acts of parliament because its royal charter gave its own assembly exclusive jurisdiction over statutes applying to its people. The king negated that interpretation but Massachusetts ignored his ruling until 1684, when an English court revoked the colonial charter. When James II abdicated the throne in 1688, the colonists sent the royal governor he had appointed back to England. Under King William, Massachusetts again received a royal charter in 1691 and the customary practice in which colonial assemblies played an almost autonomous role in governance was resumed.[44]

The extent of crown authority varied enormously from colony to colony. Because Connecticut and Rhode Island were not governed by royal officials, the crown exercised almost no direct authority. In Maryland and Pennsylvania, crown influence was circumscribed by the fact that the proprietors of these colonies appointed the governor and council. The 1691 royal charter made the governor a crown appointee in Massachusetts but gave the colonial assembly predominant control of the council. In all the other colonies, the king appointed both the governor and the council, the latter serving as an upper house much like the House of Lords in the mother country. Whatever the roles and powers of the governor, council, and assembly, they all strove for primacy, appealing to the authorities in the metropole or to voters in the colonies.[45]

These seventeenth-century contests for primacy were intense in the colonies but only of secondary interest in the metropole. In fact, the British government was often indifferent as to how the colonies were governed as long as they did not cause problems for the imperial system as a whole. Sporadic confrontations with the mother country tended only to accentuate and sharpen the English identity of the colonies – an identity that, in turn, reinforced and strengthened their claims to autonomy. Most colonists were first- or second-generation immigrants from the mother country who either believed or could be easily persuaded to believe that the rights of Englishmen had been

---

[43] Reid has this to say with respect to the sincerity of the colonists as they asserted their rights as Englishmen: "We read their words – there are certainly enough of them, for they were always boasting of their rights – yet it is hard to believe how completely they basked in its security and gloried in the fact that it made them the freest people in the world." Reid, *Constitutional History*, p. 27. The colonists simply inhabited an understanding of the world that was very different from those in the metropole, even as they claimed the protection of metropole customs and traditions.

[44] Morgan, *Inventing the People*, pp. 131–4. More generally, see Greene, *Constitutional Origins*, p. 13; Beloff, "American Independence," p. 450.

[45] Morgan, *Inventing the People*, pp. 135–7.

convoyed across the Atlantic in the same ships that had brought them or their forebears to the New World.

From the colonial perspective, the ancient English Constitution determined the theory and practice of governing relations between the colonies and the crown in several ways. First, and what became foremost, parliament had no right to control the internal affairs of the colonies because the constitutional relationship between local assemblies and the crown excluded its jurisdiction. Within each of the colonies, the local assembly essentially claimed to enjoy the same standing vis-à-vis the king as parliament occupied in the metropole. And just as it would have been absurd for, say, the assembly in New York to legislate with respect to domestic affairs in London, it was wrong (if otherwise more easily imaginable) for parliament to dictate internal affairs in the colonies. Second, the colonial position depended almost entirely on the acquiescence of the king. In theory, the crown never explicitly conceded that the colonial assemblies were like "little parliaments" or that parliament had no jurisdiction in the colonies. However, in practice, both the crown and parliament appeared to concede these things from the onset of colonial settlement and they had thus become more or less fixed expectations that shaped both how politics would be carried on and how the political identity of the colonists was understood.[46]

Third, the colonial perspective placed the royal governors on the western side of the Atlantic in an almost untenable position. On the one hand, they were responsible for carrying out crown policies, policies that were ambiguously grounded in a notion of apparently qualified imperial sovereignty. That ambiguity encouraged royal governors to cajole, coax, persuade, and otherwise entice colonial assemblies to support these policies in order to effectively implement them. On the other hand, by controlling the power to tax their constituents, colonial assemblies often held the upper hand because the metropole refused to fund colonial administrations. In order to carry out their duties, royal governors were thus compelled to treat with the assemblies.[47]

---

[46] Morgan, *Inventing the People*, pp. 140–1.

[47] In practice, metropolitan policies intended to promote the growth of the colonial economy also tended to encourage the development of customs and traditions that enhanced colonial political autonomy. The colonists were better able, for one thing, to mold government policy to local conditions (which were very different from those in the home country) and political autonomy was also an inducement attracting migrants. The effect of these policies was reinforced by a reduction in the political resources available to royal governors, which led them to drift toward an accommodation with colonist demands. "As a consequence, royal and proprietary governors in many colonies were fully integrated into the local political community and came to identify and to be identified as much with the interests of the colonies as with those of the metropolis." Greene, *Constitutional Origins*, pp. 10–18, 21, 22–5, 130. For exceptions in which governors opposed what colonists believed to be their rights, see pp. 135, 137. In addition to the relative lack of coercive capacity (in the form of a royal constabulary or soldiers), governors and judges appointed by the crown were often rendered almost powerless by the autonomy of colonial juries, who constantly insisted that legal enforcement conform to local custom and opinion (pp. 142–3, 180).

Fourth, and finally, the traditional and customary rights of Englishmen upon which the colonial position rested were not grounded in a notion of a sovereign will of the people. As deployed by the colonists, these rights were almost exclusively defensive in the sense that they were arrayed against perceived infringements by the metropole. They were thus very much like immovable theoretical fortifications that could not be altered without impairing the security of those they protected. Furthermore, those fortifications largely rested on the passive consent – or at least tolerance – of authorities in the metropole because, after all, they were the rights of *Englishmen*.[48] The sovereign will of the people, on the other hand, was ever changing and aggressively reconstructive. In fact, in what ultimately became one of the problems of constitution-making for Americans, some of the sovereign claims of the will of the people threatened to transgress some of the rights of Englishmen. The most distinctive and salient aspect of the American Revolution was thus the transition from the rights of Englishmen to the will of the people as the animating ground of the state.[49]

[48] Even after the initial eruption of revolutionary crises in 1763, the colonists were very reluctant to abandon the rights of Englishmen for the sovereign authority of the will of the people. Morgan gives several reasons for this reluctance: (1) The imperial system, however jerry-rigged in theoretical terms, had worked in practice up to then; (2) the colonists realized that the abandonment of one set of "first principles" for another would create great political uncertainty and risk; and (3) the colonial assemblies already rested on a more democratic foundation, in terms of representation and the assignment of suffrage rights, than did the House of Commons in the metropole. This last reason may be the most important for Morgan because it rendered more or less invisible the tension between the rights of Englishmen and the will of the people. That invisibility arose because the colonial assemblies could, with much justification, claim to be both asserting those rights and simultaneously representing the will of the people when they opposed parliament's claims to jurisdiction over the colonies. Morgan, *Inventing the People*, pp. 144–7. On suffrage and electoral campaigns in Britain and the colonies during the eighteenth century, see pp. 174–208. Also see Wright, "American Independence," p. 511. While Wright notes that suffrage eligibility in the colonies was limited, he contends that political practice (e.g., participation in the county courts and town meetings) gave rise to "a vitality in public controversy and in the election of representatives and selectmen ... that belied, and was in the end to challenge, the authority of Whitehall." However, if we measure suffrage eligibility by the rather exacting metrics of the twenty-first century, democracy, as Bateman points out, "did not exist in colonial America," largely due to gender, racial, and property restrictions. David Bateman, *Disenfranchising Democracy: Constructing the Electorate in the United States, the United Kingdom, and France* (New York: Cambridge University Press, 2018), p. 49 but also see, more generally, pp. 44–69. While the need to mobilize the people behind protest and the subsequent war for independence led colonial elites to expand suffrage eligibility, the will of the people was still strongly filtered through conceptions of political and social propriety that were inherited from the ancient English Constitution. Bateman emphasizes that this is one instance in which "relatively low levels of economic inequality" in the colonies rendered suffrage expansion much less "threatening [to] elite privileges or property" than it would have been in Britain (p. 44).

[49] Charles Taylor describes a similar "transition" (his term as well) in his *Modern Social Imaginaries* (Durham, NC: Duke University Press, 2004), p. 110. Morgan also provides a very similar description in *Inventing the People*, p. 290. J. R. Pole, describing the transition in Virginia, stated that the "immediate constitutional result of discarding all shadow of royal authority was to base the whole of the government on the authority of the people." Pole,

This transition was never completed.[50] We could even say that the transition never even made it to the halfway mark.[51]

THE EMERGENCE AND DEVELOPMENT OF THE
REVOLUTIONARY CRISIS

As Greene notes, European states during the seventeenth and eighteenth centuries simply lacked the material capacity to directly rule far-flung peripheral territory; instead, they indirectly exercised authority by negotiating with local elites.[52] In the seventeenth century, the American colonies were peripheral to Britain in both senses of the term: They were far away and relatively unimportant. The pragmatic decentralization of administration unintentionally gave rise to legal traditions and customs that, in turn, came back to haunt the metropole once it did attempt to impose authority on the colonies.[53] By that time,

---

Political Representation, p. 281. Also see Bailyn, *Ideological Origins*, p. 300. For a very different interpretation that involves a questioning of the legitimacy of the "legal order" once the authority of the crown was denied, see Michael Warner, *The Letters of the Republic: Publication and the Public Sphere in Eighteenth-Century America* (Cambridge, MA: Harvard University Press, 1990), p. 98.

[50] Up until the Declaration of Independence, the colonists understood their participation in the political crisis as a "British" revolution entirely oriented toward a correction of their relations with the mother country. As "an episode in British imperial history" in which Englishmen (albeit as colonists) claimed their rights, it was emphatically not "the first step in the creation of the American nation." The formation of that nation involved, instead, a wrenching transformation in political belief and political principles that has never been completed. Greene, *Constitutional Origins*, p. xxi.

[51] Morgan, however, states that "in every state the government [that had previously been] authorized by the king [during the colonial era] had given way to government authorized by the people [during the drive to independence] with a minimum of disorder." Morgan, *Inventing the People*, p. 257. As a broad description of the transformation in the political authorization of sovereignty, this is clearly correct. However, this authorization by the people was never unqualified and, as we shall see, the qualifications almost always descended from the (monarchical) rights of Englishmen, both in form and, often, in the language of the relevant texts. It is in that sense that the transition was never and is not now complete; any interpretation of the will of the people in the American constitutional regime was and is thoroughly hedged about and conceptually informed by inheritance from British customs, traditions, and theoretical presumptions.

[52] Greene quotes Edmund Burke: "[The] immutable condition, the eternal law, of extensive and detached empire" was that "the circulation of power must be less vigorous at the extremes." Even the Turkish sultan recognized that "the force and vigor of his authority in his centre ... derived from a prudent relaxation in all his borders" and thus governed his far-flung provinces "with a loose rein" in order to "govern [them] at all." Greene, *Constitutional Origins*, p. 164.

[53] Greene contends that, after 1720, "the unstated strategy of the [colonial] assemblies seems to have been to secure local rights against metropolitan power in much the same way that those rights had been achieved within the metropolis itself: Through practice and usage that with the implicit acquiescence of the metropolis would gradually acquire the sanction of custom." Greene, *Constitutional Origins*, p. 25. However, this process could also have been the natural inclination of a people thoroughly accustomed to the practices and ethos of the English Constitution.

however, the colonies had recreated "little Englands" in which, inevitably, they had drifted apart from the mother country.[54]

By 1730, the colonists believed their assemblies to be, in the words of Governor Francis Bernard of the Massachusetts Bay Colony, "perfect states" whose only link to the metropole was their subservient relation to the British crown. The colonial interpretation of the ancient English Constitution regarded principles such as the rule of law and "no taxation without representation" as the inviolable rights of Englishmen that their assemblies, like parliament before the Glorious Revolution, were sworn to uphold and respect.[55] But Britain had had that revolution in 1688, and parliament now reigned supreme in the metropole.[56] From that vantage point, parliament regarded the colonial assemblies and the royal charters that had created them as little more than statutory creatures. Parliament could thus alter the powers of these assemblies and, if need be, even utterly destroy them.[57] By 1775, the colonies and Great Britain were thus irreparably divided by a common political culture.

From a broader perspective, there are several ways to explain the growing discrepancy in constitutional thinking. On the one hand, the development of custom and tradition on the American side of the Atlantic was not affected by

---

[54] "Belief in a fundamental correspondence between the English Constitution and the separate colonial constitutions [had become] almost an axiom of political thought in eighteenth-century America." Bailyn, *Origins of American Politics*, p. 60.

[55] Wright, "American Independence," p. 517. As a result of the 1688 Glorious Revolution, "the English Parliament [had seized] supremacy over the monarchy [and the] constitutional issue ... was whether Parliament's *supremacy* over the throne also meant *sovereignty* over the law and constitution." Parliament, in effect, maintained that it had inherited what the king's prerogatives had originally granted to the colonies (in the form of a constitutional contract) and, for that reason, could not violate colonial rights if it altered those governance arrangements. Parliament could not violate those rights because it now enjoyed the same prerogatives as the king had possessed before 1688. Reid, *Constitutional History*, p. 17; Greene, *Constitutional Origins*, p. 38; also see Jennifer Carter, "The Revolution and the Constitution" in Geoffrey Holmes (ed.), *Britain after the Glorious Revolution, 1689–1715* (New York: St. Martin's Press, 1969), pp. 39–40. The distinctions here between king and parliament and between before and after the Glorious Revolution did not much matter to the colonists because they interpreted the original colonial charters as conferring upon them "the rights of Englishmen" and those rights could be defended from all directions. For more on the relationship between parliament's claims to legislative supremacy and the American Revolution, see Nelson, *Common Law in Colonial America*, pp. 1–3, 46, 97, 113–18, 127–9, 150–5.

[56] As Nelson puts it: "Patriots of the late 1760s and 1770s were effectively proposing to turn back the clock on the English Constitution by over a hundred years – to separate the king from his Parliament and his British ministers and to restore ancient prerogatives of the Crown that had been extinguished by the whig ascendancy" following the Glorious Revolution. Nelson, *Royalist Revolution*, pp. 2–3; also see Hulsebosch, *Constituting Empire*, pp. 138–9.

[57] Greene, *Constitutional Origins*, pp. 96–7. Blackstone, for example, provided a detailed, if somewhat nuanced, justification for the supremacy of parliament over the colonies in William Blackstone, *Commentaries on the Laws of England*, Book I, eds. Edward Christian, Joseph Chitty, Thomas Lee, John Eyken Hovenden, and Archer Ryland (Philadelphia: J.B. Lippincott, 1855), pp. 77–8.

events in the metropole and thus continued to adhere to older principles and practices under the English Constitution. On the other hand, the colonists might have been instrumentally choosing those older constitutional under-standings and practices because they were more advantageous for achieving their goals, most importantly local political autonomy. Both might have been (and probably were) true at the same time: The lack of metropolitan involve-ment in the colonies after the Glorious Revolution allowed custom and trad-ition to develop in an "unreformed" manner, and, later, when parliament did intervene, the colonists rather stubbornly refused to update their constitutional understandings so that they would conform to those of the metropole.[58]

The colonies and parliament first came into serious conflict after the end of the French and Indian War, when military expenditures in that conflict had created a large debt that now had to be serviced.[59] In response, Britain attempted to impose new taxes on the colonies. Passed in the form of the Sugar Act of 1764 and the Stamp Act of 1765, these levies raised revenue for the British government by imposing duties on the importation of sugar and compelling the purchase of stamps that were to be attached to all newspapers and legal documents before they could be sold or entered into the public record.[60] The ostensible justification for these taxes was that the colonists had an obligation to help support British troops stationed in America.[61] The more pressing reason was that the British government desperately needed more revenue in order to relieve the tax burden in the metropole. Colonial opposition to these taxes arose out of their interpretation of the relation of the colonies to the metropole, on the one hand, and their interpretation of the rights of Englishmen, on the other.[62]

---

[58] See, for example, Greene, *Constitutional Origins*, pp. 63–5; Beloff, "American Independence," p. 453.

[59] Goodwin cites several ways in which the increasing revenue demands that the British made on the colonies affected imperial policy: a desire to suppress smuggling and other forms of evasion of the Navigation laws (which by most accounts was quite common); the affirmation of parliament's right to impose taxes on the colonial economy; and attempts to free imperial administration from financial dependence on colonial assemblies so that British officials could enforce revenue policy. "Introductory Survey" in Goodwin (ed.), *New Cambridge Modern History. Volume 8*, p. 8.

[60] Jones, "American Independence," p. 482.

[61] Reid, *Constitutional History*, p. 26. There is an interesting parallel here between (1) this scenario in which the expenses of a previous war precipitated a budgetary crisis in the metropole that ultimately led to a revolt in the colonies and (2) the French Revolution, in which the expenses of the involvement in that revolt led to the same thing in France. But the British case seems more avoidable in that the budgetary crisis was not as severe, both because the national debt was not as large and because the fiscal machinery was much more efficient in collecting revenue. On the impact of the Seven Years' War on British ability to coerce the colonies and on the metropole's finances, see Greene, *Constitutional Origins*, p. 55–6.

[62] Reid consistently maintains that the colonists distinguished between a statute's "illegality" and "unconstitutionality." For example, the stamp tax was not "illegal" in late eighteenth-century legal thought but it was "unconstitutional" because it laid a tax without the consent of the

In what became an intricate and sometimes abstruse debate over the meaning and application of the unwritten English Constitution, three themes took center stage. First, the colonists claimed the rights of Englishmen by contending that they had not consented, through their assemblies, to the imposition of these taxes.[63] In Reid's words:

[The] doctrine of consent to taxation was the bone and marrow of the revolutionary controversy [and] was not only one of the best known legal premises in English history, but was also believed to be one of the oldest-traceable, some experts thought, to time immemorial, even to the gothic constitution in the Saxon forests on the continent ... It was the quintessential constitutional custom.[64]

The colonial contention, of course, rested on two additional axioms: that the only link tying the colonies to the metropole ran through the king and that the colonial assemblies bore the same relation to the king as parliament occupied in the metropole. In effect, the colonists were claiming a political relation to the king that would exclude parliament's legislative authority. The colonists had very strong evidence of a direct relationship to the king in the form of royal charters that originally established and enabled settlement. Although they varied quite a bit in their details, most colonies had them and they could, without too much difficulty, be viewed as organic constitutions on the order of, say, the Magna Carta.

In 1764, the year before the Stamp Act was enacted, the Connecticut Assembly announced that the royal charter granted to the colony by Charles I gave it "full power of legislation" and that it had assiduously conformed to and exercised that authority ever since.

---

colonial assemblies. Reid, *Constitutional History*, pp. 81–2. He insists on the distinction because modern notions in the United States that conflate the two are, he contends, anachronistic in the colonial context. Although it is a little unclear what implications we should draw from the distinction, we might conclude that (1) if a law is "illegal," you do not have to obey it, while (2) if the law is "unconstitutional," you have a right to rebel. But this seems a little odd in that it would require simultaneously obeying a law that, at the same time, justifies rebellion.

[63] Burke also opposed these taxes, contending that "governing the whole body of the people contrary to their inclinations" was impossible; it was particularly impossible, if that were not an oxymoron, when those "inclinations" and the notion of "governing" were profoundly English. Many others in the metropole shared the same opinion. Greene, *Constitutional Origins*, pp. 133, 175. In a speech in the House of Commons, Burke attempted to show his colleagues that it was they themselves that they saw reflected in the colonial mirror when Americans asserted their rights as Englishmen: "To prove that the American ought not to be free, we are obliged to depreciate the value of freedom itself; and we never seem to gain a paltry advantage over them in debate, without attacking some of those principles, or deriding some of those feelings, for which our ancestors have shed their blood." David C. Hendrickson, *Peace Pact: The Lost World of the American Founding* (Lawrence: University Press of Kansas, 2003), p. 86. It is thus no surprise that Burke would be sympathetic to the American cause and that the United States, once formed, would warmly embrace Burkean principles as a fundamental part of its national philosophy toward politics and government.

[64] Reid, *Constitutional History*, pp. 41–2.

[T]hese powers, rights, and privileges the colony has been in possession of for more than a century past. This power of legislation necessarily includes in it an authority to impose taxes ... These privileges and immunities, these powers and authority, the colony claims not only in virtue of their right to the general principles of the British constitution and by force of the royal declaration and grant in their favor ... but also as having been in possession, enjoyment, and exercise of them for so long a time, and constantly owned, acknowledged, allowed to be just in the claim and use thereof by the crown, the ministry, and the Parliament, as may evidently be shown by royal instructions, many letters and acts of Parliament, all supposing and being predicated upon the colony's having and justly exercising these privileges, powers, and authorities, and what better foundation for or greater evidence of, such rights can be demanded or produced is certainly difficult to be imagined.[65]

In this interpretation, parliament had no role whatsoever.

However, the colonists could not persuasively impose this interpretation without the public consent of the king himself.[66] There was, for one thing, no constitutional court of last resort to which the colonies might appeal through the logic of legal argument.[67] The ancient English Constitution did not work

---

[65] Reid, *Constitutional History*, p. 40.

[66] Colonial recognition that George III utterly rejected the colonial interpretation of crown prerogatives was very slow in coming. Reid explains this reluctance as a product of an English constitutional tradition in which the wrongful acts of a monarch were to be attributed to crown ministers who had led him or her astray. Constitutional tradition, for that reason, provided a reason for hope that the king might change his attitude (under the cover of a change of ministers), when, objectively, they more realistically recognized that the basis for that hope was slim. Reid, *Constitutional History*, pp. xiii–xiv. As late as December 6, 1775, the Continental Congress continued to recognize this constitutional tradition: "[T]o support our laws, and our liberties established by our laws, we have prepared, ordered and levied war: But is this traitorously, or against the King? We view him as the Constitution represents him. That tells us he can do no wrong. The cruel and illegal attacks [prosecuted by parliament], which we oppose, have no foundation in the royal authority." Worthington C. Ford (ed.), *Journal of the Continental Congress* (Washington, DC: US Government Printing Office, 1904), vol. 3, p. 411. On February 13, 1776, Congress again took up that "Part of our Constitution" that placed the colonists "under Allegiance to the Crown," acknowledging "*that a King can do no wrong*" (emphasis in the original) while attributing "your [the colonists'] Calamities to the House of Commons." But the endorsement of kingly virtue and prerogatives was much more limited and contingent. Ford (ed.), *Journal of the Continental Congress*, vol. 4, p. 145. When the king clearly aligned with parliament, this presumption that wrongful acts by the king should be attributed to crown ministers (and not to the throne) disappeared; its disappearance (e.g., that the king could now be unambiguously recognized as a perpetrator of wrong) was one element in the transition from the rights of Englishmen to the will of the people. For a concise overview of the increasing disaffection of the American colonists toward the king, see Brendan McConville, *The King's Three Faces: The Rise and Fall of Royal America, 1688–1776* (Williamsburg, VA: Omohundro Institute of Early American History and Culture, 2006), pp. 268–86.

[67] As Greene notes, the colonies recognized no court of last resort for the adjudication of constitutional disputes with the metropole and instead increasingly turned to the judgment of "the people" as a vindication of their defense of colonist rights as Englishmen. This tactic ultimately had the paradoxical effect of loosening popular identity "as English" while calibrating popular

that way. As long as the king did not conclusively affirm or deny that these royal charters excluded parliament from assuming jurisdiction over the colonies, the colonists could make formal constitutional arguments and place them in the public arena but they could not bring the constitutional dispute to a close. But once the king explicitly denied that these arguments were legitimate interpretations of the acts involving the crown, the colonists would be (and ultimately were) placing their contentions before an audience that rejected their premises out of hand.[68]

The second theme developed out of parliament's rejection of the claim that the colonies had not consented to the sugar and stamp taxes. This rejection also rested on two axioms: (1) that the colonies were represented "virtually" in the House of Commons in the same way that British women, children, and men who did not possess the right to vote were nonetheless represented by members of parliament; and (2) that parliament, including the king and the House of Lords, constituted the sovereign authority over the imperial system, including the American colonies.[69] The British government rejected, more or less in passing, the interpretation that royal charters constituted a direct link between the colonies and the crown that excluded parliamentary authority. Parliament was emphatically clear on all these points.

In their response, the colonists had to address two facts of political practice under the ancient English Constitution. On the one hand, the existence of "virtual" representation was both empirically undeniable in the sense that a large proportion of the British citizenry did not participate in the selection of members of the House of Commons and yet these members did take their interests (if not their desires) into account when legislating for the common interests of the realm. In fact, although British authorities did not make much use of the parallel, members of the colonial assemblies also "virtually"

---

insurgency with the assertion of their rights as Englishmen. Greene, *Constitutional Origins*, pp. 60, 127.

[68] In the 1740s, before the colonial crisis had become acute, the colonists even entertained the notion that they might be able to play off parliament against the crown because the former had been the traditional protector of the rights of Englishmen in the metropole and, it was thought, would be correspondingly sympathetic to colonial claims to those same rights. The colonists, however, were soon disabused of that notion. Greene, *Constitutional Origins*, pp. 61–2.

[69] Nelson, *Royalist Revolution*, pp. 80–98. Although Burke was very sympathetic to American complaints about the lack of representation in parliament, he also strongly advocated the principle of virtual representation. To him, parliament was not

a *congress* of ambassadors from different and hostile interests, which interests each must maintain, as an agent and advocate, against other agents and advocates; but parliament is a *deliberative* assembly of *one* nation, with *one* interest, that of the whole, where, not local purposes, not local prejudices ought to guide, but the general good, resulting from the general reason of the whole. (Bailyn, *Ideological Origins*, p. 163)

On the notion of virtual representation of the colonies in parliament and colonial rejections of that notion, see Wood, *Creation of the American Republic*, pp. 173–81.

represented many (and, in some instances, most) of their own constituents. On the other hand, most members of the House of Commons either resided in or at least had some first-hand acquaintance with the constituencies that sent them to London. Given that fact, the colonists could contend that those members who ostensibly represented them should reside in America, or at least visit the colonies from time to time. And there was some support "in the British tradition" in that, as Greene puts it, "true liberty always required a community of interest between legislators and constituents." Greene then paraphrases David Hume: "[F]or a legislature to have a right [to rule], it had to have a common interest and direct connection with the people for whom it presumed to legislate."[70]

The American colonists nevertheless had difficulty rebutting metropole arguments for several reasons. For one thing, parliament contended that the ostensible imperfections in the theory of representation cited by the colonists were, in fact, deeply embedded in the rights of Englishmen because they had arisen out of more than a thousand years of tradition, custom, and practice.[71]

---

[70] Greene, *Constitutional Origins*, pp. 70-1. On November 11, 1765, Samuel Adams and several other members of the Massachusetts Assembly wrote a letter in which they "clearly admitted" the "general superintending Power of the Parliament over the whole British Empire" and acknowledged that, properly exercised, that power was "consistent with the Enjoyment of our essential rights, as Freemen, and British Subjects." However, they also asserted "an exclusive Right to make Laws for our own internal Government" because the colonists "are not represented in the British Parliam[en]t & their great Distance renders it impracticable." Greene, *Constitutional Origins*, pp. 82-3. These passages neatly combine (1) the fact of non-representation in parliament with (2) the (alleged) impossibility of effective representation (if it were offered) with (3) the necessity of representation as a fundamental right of Englishmen in order to conclude that (4) the colonies must be internally self-governing. As is the case with all such citations, we should keep in mind the distinction between quoting the words of leading figures and describing the course of mass colonial opinion. We now see these men as leaders, in part, because of the consequent course of the revolution. If the British had turned the current of opinion in an alternative direction (which was certainly within their power), these same men would have been, from our perspective, much less prominent.

[71] By the tenets of custom in the eighteenth century, whatever had been done in the nation or community from time immemorial was constitutional and legal. Whatever consciously had been abstained from in the nation or community from time immemorial was unconstitutional or illegal. Immemorial time was a relevant segment of time during which the memory of the law did not show a contrary custom. From the perspective of custom the constitution was a collection of legal principles established through the discovery of precedential usages. It was, in other words, a combination of: (1) inductive revelation drawn from appropriate principles by examining past experiences; and (2) deductive application of these principles to current constitutional issues. The eighteenth-century legal mind assumed a universally known constitutional law existing independent of will or command for which custom was the best evidence. (Reid, *Constitutional History*, p. 5; also see pp. 19-20)

This is a splendid description of legal and constitutional "custom." It is particularly important in that the last sentence explains why the colonists could present their claims on the metropole without risking their rejection (in the colonies) as "self-interested." They were, instead, the mere statement of historical "fact," a fact embedded in a constitution of "rights."

Furthermore, those same traditions, customs, and practice, including the notion of "virtual representation," had shaped the relation of members of the colonial assemblies to their constituencies. The colonists could and did claim that their own relations to their assemblies were more intimate because a larger proportion of the people could participate in the selection of members and because the members themselves resided near, if not within, the constituencies they represented.[72] But those facts (and they were facts) did not vitiate parliament's contention that "virtual" representation could extend across the Atlantic Ocean and thus authorize the House of Commons to represent colonists in America.[73] On the contrary, the colonial position meant only that the colonies preferred their own assemblies to parliament.

The problem, however, had another aspect that ultimately proved intractable. The most apparent solution to the problem of representation would have been to create colonial constituencies in the House of Commons so that the colonists were directly (and not "virtually") represented when taxes were imposed on them. However, both parliament and the colonists rejected this solution. The colonists rejected formal representation in the House of Commons because they believed that the sheer distance between the colonies and the metropole would mean that whomever they sent to London would become, over time, increasingly unfamiliar with conditions in and the interests of their constituencies. Supporting those members at such a distance would also be expensive.[74] These contentions might seem weak if not for two other, probably more important, considerations. On the one hand, parliament was unlikely to allocate more than a small number of members to the colonies and those members would thus be swamped by those residing in the British Isles. In addition, if the colonists were to seek formal representation in parliament, they would be conceding that parliament had a right to legislate in the colonies, thus abandoning what was their most fundamental principle in the struggle with the metropole. If they conceded that parliament could legislate in the colonies, the autonomy of colonial assemblies would be fatally undermined, thus eliminating

---

[72] On the quality and characteristics of the relation between representatives and their constituencies in the colonies, see Morgan, *Inventing the People*, pp. 243–8.

[73] On the notion of "virtual" representation, see Reid, *Constitutional History*, pp. 45–8.

[74] On the reasons colonists opposed representation in parliament, see Morgan, *Inventing the People*, p. 242. As Beloff notes, most colonists considered formal representation in parliament "technically impossible" because of the distance imposed by the Atlantic Ocean. Beloff, "American Independence," p. 455. However, once the colonies became independent, the continental expanse of the new nation ultimately imposed distances almost as great on the quality and practice of representation. The size of the new nation, in fact, was one of the sources of opposition to ratification of the new constitution. Arising out of what Beloff describes as an "antique republicanism," opponents believed that representation of the democratic will would be frustrated by the remoteness of the center of government, the large size of constituencies, and the smothering of local concerns in what would become an arena in which only national interests could participate. Beloff, "American Independence," pp. 475–6.

the major institutional bulwark of colonial rights. Taken as a package, the strength of these objections meant that no important colonial leader ever sought representation in parliament for the colonies.[75]

By comparison, parliament's objections to colonial representation seem obscure at best. As with most official British policy, arrogance appears to have motivated some of that rejection in that parliament had already asserted its responsibility to "virtually" represent the colonies and, as part of that responsibility, to legislate for them.[76] And that was that. However, there were two rather long-term considerations lurking on the distant horizon that may also have motivated parliament's rejection of formal representation. For one thing, the colonies were rapidly growing and, if the principle of "local" representation were granted to them, the number of members coming from across the Atlantic would probably increase in the years to come. There would come a time, albeit in the distant future, when the colonial population and economy would likely surpass those of the home country. From that perspective, holding the line in the present might have been seen as fundamentally important for future political dominance of the metropole in the imperial system. Over the same political horizon, parliament may also have been reluctant to set a precedent for colonial representation in general. By the late eighteenth century, Britain had many colonial possessions, and, while many of them were more directly ruled from the metropole through a wide variety of arrangements, at least some of the settlers in those possessions were likely to want representation in the House of Commons if that privilege were granted to the American colonies. But neither of these considerations appear to have been discussed during the revolutionary crisis and, for that reason, arrogance (or, perhaps, stubbornness) would be a better explanation. And, of course, parliament might have been unwilling to grant representation to the colonists if they were likely to refuse the offer.

The colonial interpretation of the English Constitution drew a line between the internal and external affairs of the colonies. The internal affairs of the colonies were those pertaining to their domestic relations and commercial transactions between the thirteen colonies. These were conceived as internal in the sense that they had no implications for or effects on other parts of the imperial system, including the metropole. For that and other reasons, the internal affairs of the colonies, the jurisdictional ambit of their assemblies, and the colonial rights of Englishmen coincided precisely. The colonists thus maintained that parliament could not impose taxes on the internal affairs of the colonies because there could be no taxation without representation and the colonies were not represented in parliament.[77] However, the colonists also

---

[75] Pauline Maier, *American Scripture: Making the Declaration of Independence* (New York: Vintage, 1997), pp. 21–3; Nelson, *Royalist Revolution*, pp. 93–4.

[76] Morgan, *Inventing the People*, pp. 240–3.

[77] Reid, *Constitutional History*, p. 27. As Morgan points out, this colonial reduction of the presumed rights of Englishmen (i.e., "no taxation without representation") must have seemed

conceded that parliament could legislate with respect to the external affairs of the colonies because it was responsible for managing the imperial system as a whole.[78] On October 13, 1774, the Continental Congress clearly and precisely stated the distinction between internal and external trade in a resolution that, on the next day, became Proposition Four of the Declaration of Rights.

[F]rom the necessity of the case, and a regard to the mutual interests of both countries, we cheerfully consent to the operation of such acts of the British parliament, as are bona fide, restrained to the regulation of our external commerce, for the purpose of securing the commercial advantages of the whole empire to the mother country, and the commercial benefits of its respective members, excluding every idea of taxation, internal or external, for raising a revenue on the subjects in America without their consent.

The words "cheerfully consent" were intended both to indicate the delegates' eagerness to remain within the empire if their rights were respected and also to reserve for the colonies the right to interpret those rights under the English Constitution. As Proposition Four states, colonial interpretation of the external affairs of the colonies encompassed customs duties intended to regulate commercial relations between the various parts of the empire. For example, parliament could legitimately require that all trade between the metropole and the colonies be carried in British or American vessels. Parliament could also impose duties that favored imperial interests over trade with foreign nations.[79]

And therein arose a potential problem. If parliament were to impose duties in colonial ports that were intended to raise revenue for the metropole, those levies would be illegitimate because colonial assemblies had not consented to their imposition. However, if parliament imposed the same duties for the purpose of regulating relations within the empire (including commerce with other nations), the colonists would consider them legitimate. In the former case, parliament would be violating the constitutional jurisdiction of the colonial assemblies because revenue-raising fell within the internal affairs of the colonies. In the latter, parliament's acts would be permissible as an exercise of regulatory

---

quaint to actual Englishmen who resided in the metropole because parliament's dominance over the British government made control of taxation an ordinary fact of political life. Morgan, *Inventing the People*, p. 239.

[78] Greene, *Constitutional Origins*, p. 38; also see Carter, "Revolution and the Constitution," pp. 39–40.

[79] As Reid repeatedly emphasizes, the distinction between internal and external regulation of trade was not grounded in "commercial practice" but was, instead, intended to demarcate the constitutional spheres within which the colonial assemblies and parliament could, respectively, legislate. See, for example, Reid, *Constitutional History*, pp. 75–8. As the crisis intensified, it became apparent that the colonies were not molded out of the same clay and forming a consensus often meant balancing between the more radical and more conventional responses to British policies. In this case, this meant a partial retreat from the most expansive assertion of legislative rights. On the variation between the colonies in the interpretation of these rights, see Greene, *Constitutional Origins*, pp. 78–80, 116.

authority over the management of the empire as a whole. In theory, depending on the intention of parliament, the same act could be interpreted either way.[80]

In sum, the colonists contended that: (1) Parliament could tax and provide for the common defense of the empire but those taxes must be on trade between the colonies and the rest of the world; (2) the colonists were not represented in parliament because MPs were not "of them" (e.g., they were foreign to America because all of their constituencies were in Great Britain); (3) it was impossible for the colonists to be represented in parliament because it was too far away; and, in any case, (4) the customs and traditions that had grown up under royal charters gave them all the rights of Englishmen, including a right to self-government under their own representative assemblies.

If parliament had been primarily interested in raising revenue, it could have argued that duties imposed on colonial trade were merely intended to regulate relations between parts of the imperial system. However, while raising revenue was certainly one goal in the passage of duties, it rapidly became secondary to parliament's desire to thwart colonial interpretations of the English Constitution. That desire compelled parliament to emphasize that the imposition of taxes on the colonies was for the purpose of raising revenue, even when, as in the actual event, the return to the metropole was minuscule (or even negative). Parliament thus went out of its way to join the struggle over the colonist assertion of the rights of Englishmen on the constitutional ground that the latter had creatively constructed.[81]

---

[80] For example, the motive for imposing the stamp tax was decisive for the colonists because it implied a relation between the colonies and the metropole. If the purpose of the tax was to regulate trade within the empire, it was constitutional because the colonies and the metropole had "external relations" with one another that must be governed in some way. (Such an interpretation would have been difficult to sustain because the tax was levied on "internal" civil and economic relations within the colonies.) However, if the purpose of the tax was to raise revenue, it was unconstitutional because the tax would transfer wealth from the "interior" of the colonies to the "interior" of the metropole. There is a distinction here but in practice it primarily rests on the determination of motive as opposed to substantive design.

Parliament, however, solved what might have been a difficult interpretive problem by openly declaring that the motivation behind the tax was to raise revenue. The colonists then rejoined that the tax was unconstitutional and thus invalid. From a formal perspective, the constitutional question was ultimately rendered moot because parliament simply refused to engage in that debate (if parliament had agreed to such a debate, it would have begun by asserting that it held all the cards with respect to interpreting the English Constitution). For the colonists, the question was not whether parliament agreed or did not agree with their constitutional position but whether their position facilitated the mobilization of popular sentiment in the colonies. In the near term, that mobilization was intended to compel parliament to relent on the general question of colonial autonomy. When that failed, the long-term purpose became the establishment of a new state and political order. On the application of the "internal/external" distinction to the Stamp Act, see, for example, Nelson, *Royalist Revolution*, pp. 32–3.

[81] Although Burke could not have known that war had, in fact, broken out at Lexington and Concord on the very day on which he spoke, he warned his government that the motive for imposing "the 3d duty" in the Tea Act had been primarily to produce "litigation and quarrel.

Legal precedents, when uncontested, give rise to custom over time. For example, a statute sheds the specificity of its enactment as memories fade and it merges into a larger realm of abstraction and principle. If parliament were to successfully impose the Stamp Tax, it would, over time, bolster general authority to impose direct taxes on the colonies and the tax would thus become an element in the construction of an ideological principle (e.g., unlimited parliamentary sovereignty). At the time of its creation, the Stamp Tax was intentional and specific as to its object, purpose, and implementation. However, it was not yet custom.[82] But, as a statutory precedent, it could plainly transgress on custom. The possibility of such transgressions made timely inspection of the acts of parliament a necessary corollary in the protection of the customary rights of the colonies.[83]

The colonial reaction to the 1765 Stamp Act demonstrates that the colonists clearly understood the importance of precedent.[84] Immediately after it was

The 3d is not the object; it's the principle that the Americans could not submit to; they would be slaves if they did." Reid, *Constitutional History*, p. 86; also see Greene, *Constitutional Origins*, pp. 149–50. For a graphic analysis of the varying grounds for contention over taxes imposed by parliament, see the chart and description in John Murrin, *Rethinking America: From Empire to Republic* (New York: Oxford University Press, 2018), p. 171.

[82] In a letter to his son, written on March 13, 1768, Benjamin Franklin suggested: "Something might be made of either of the extremes; that Parliament has a power to make *all laws* for us, or that it has a power to make *no laws* for us." Because parliament held that sovereignty was defined by unlimited government authority and, in Greene's words, "was either complete or nonexistent," "no middle doctrine" was possible. Greene, *Constitutional Origins*, pp. 98–9, 116, 176. Parliament's conception of sovereignty was, however, also widely shared in the colonies both during and after the revolution and played an important role in Antifederalist arguments against adoption of the Constitution (p. 118).

[83] Custom was not an instrumental strategy, opportunistically chosen simply because it supported the colonial cause. It was, instead, a reflexive orientation toward the legitimate exercise of government authority. As such, the "chief function of custom ... was to restrain power. It was not helpful to arbitrary command ... [Custom was] the guarantor of political neutrality. Immanent, unmade, and rooted in the past, custom was thought to be independent of human judgment and human choice, not only relatively neutral but politically benign, the legal opposite of the feared bane of constitutionalism, sovereign command." Reid, *Constitutional History*, p. 7.

[84] As Van Cleve notes, "colonial Americans were among the most lightly taxed people in the world." It was thus the constitutional principle, not the substance of the Stamp Act, that was important. That was true for the British as well because the tax would not have yielded much revenue if it had been implemented. George William Van Cleve, *We Have Not a Government: The Articles of Confederation and the Road to the Constitution* (Chicago: University of Chicago Press, 2017), p. 76; Goodwin, "Introductory Survey," p. 11; Palmer, "Social and Psychological Foundations," p. 438. On the significance of the Stamp Act as a rupture in traditional imperial governance of the colonies, see Greene, *Constitutional Origins*, pp. 68–70. For a description of the distribution of opinion in Britain during the Stamp Act crisis, see pp. 93–4. The political crisis sparked by the Stamp Act was eminently avoidable because it was initiated by British authorities who could have chosen to raise revenue in another way (e.g., through indirect levies on commerce between the colonies and the metropole), and, in any case, the amount of revenue expected from the tax was very small. After repealing the act, parliament still persisted in an assertion of authority that was clearly, at least to Burke and other observers, counterproductive.

promulgated, crowds of colonists began to harass those imperial officials who were to sell the stamps. By preventing their sale, the colonists solved the collective action problem that might otherwise have attended a voluntary boycott. Popular mobilization ultimately led to the resignation of the imperial officials involved and, because there was now no one to distribute stamps, the tax failed to create the precedent that the British so ardently desired.[85] When the Stamp Act proved unenforceable (an attempt would have cost far more money and political capital than parliament was willing to expend), the statute was repealed on March 18, 1766.

On the same day, however, the British government promulgated another statute, the Declaratory Act, proclaiming that parliament "had, hath, and of right ought to have, full power and authority to make laws and statutes of sufficient force and validity to bind the colonies and people of *America* ... in all cases whatsoever." For the metropole, this statute settled the issue because parliament was pronouncing, as was its right to do, a constitutional principle. For the colonies, the Declaratory Act was empty verbiage because it conflicted with the custom and tradition of the English Constitution. But the colonists could also ignore the Declaratory Act because there was no accompanying practice in the colonies that might set a dangerous precedent.[86] Unlike the Stamp Act, there was no material activity by the imperial authorities against which they would be obliged to protest. That is the legal explanation for colonial indifference. The political reason was that the colonial elite needed an on-the-ground practice in order to connect the constitutional principle of "no taxation without representation" to the mobilization of the masses. From the latter perspective, the Declaratory Act simply did not create a material opportunity for protest.[87]

The revolution was not inevitable because the British willfully dictated the pace at which relations with the colonies deteriorated and they could have reversed, halted, or deflected that trajectory at any point up to and, perhaps, including the Declaration of Independence.

[85] Reid, *Constitutional History*, pp. 30–1, 84. On the nature of precedents during the colonial crisis, see pp. 12, 59–66. Even while both the colonies and the metropole subscribed to the importance of precedent, there were those who were skeptical that custom and tradition could be a satisfactory guide to political practice. For example, Sir George Saville, a member of parliament, wrote in 1768: "I believe [that] principles have less to do than we suppose. The Critics['] rules were made after the poems. The Rules of architecture after ye houses, Grammar after language and governments go *per hokum & crookum &* then we demonstrate it *per bookum*. There is not that argument or practice so bad that you may have precedents for it." Greene, *Constitutional Origins*, p. 50.

[86] While repeal of the Stamp Act was material evidence that the British had concluded that they could not enforce their edicts in the colonies, the Declaratory Act, by its lack of substance, seemed only to confirm that inability. Greene, *Constitutional Origins*, p. 101.

[87] Reid, *Constitutional History*, pp. 49–50. On May 9, 1770, Burke argued that "Parliament had no need to tax the colonies because the Declaratory Act already 'sufficiently establish[ed] the sovereignty of this country over its plantations and colonies.'" Greene, *Constitutional Origins*, p. 106. If parliament had resisted the temptation to again impose taxes, this would have been a pragmatic solution to the constitutional problem in that the act would have asserted sovereignty but would have otherwise left undisturbed the local autonomy of the colonies.

In the following years, however, parliament did pass several statutes that did provide such opportunities.[88]

The most important of these statutes was the 1767 Townshend Acts, which imposed duties on the importation of paper, lead, glass, paints, and tea into the colonies. Duties, from the colonial perspective, were not objectionable as long as they were intended to regulate trade within the empire. The problem, however, was that the announced intention of these tariffs was to support British troops and imperial officials serving in the administration of civil government in North America and would have thus shifted the tax burden for their support from the metropole to the colonies. That intention moved the levies into the contentious category in which the "no taxation without representation" principle was to apply. By the end of 1769, all the colonies (with the exception of New Hampshire) had joined in a boycott of British goods that reduced imports into the colonies by almost 40 percent. The boycott was particularly effective in New York City and Philadelphia. Since the duties were not producing revenue, the British repealed all but one of them in April 1770. Parliament regarded repeal of the Townshend duties as an act of conciliation with which, at this point, the colonists were quite willing to reciprocate. Repeal thus broke the back of the boycott.[89]

The Townshend episode was important for several reasons. First, parliament took the initiative but clearly failed to anticipate the end game. It escalated the already heated disputes over colonial governance but seriously underestimated the commitment of the colonists to their (interpretation of) constitutional rights.[90] The episode also demonstrated how tactical maneuvering in disputes over taxation became inextricably bound up in the traditional and customary dynamics of the ancient English Constitution. These dynamics were clearly very different from those of a written constitution since they did not turn upon the interpretation of a text but upon the historical and evolving record of political relations. They were, in a word, dependent upon the contesting "wills" of

---

[88] One of these statutes suspended the New York General Assembly. Another authorized the government to move trials for treason from the colonies to the metropole. The latter was based on a 200-year-old statute from the reign of Henry VIII that was reinterpreted so as to place the colonies "out of this realm of *England.*" In effect, the colonists were "English" to the extent that they could commit treason against the British government but they were not "English" in terms of constitutional rights. We should note, however, that the Henry VIII statute was never enforced in the colonies. Reid, *Constitutional History,* pp. 66–70, 83.

[89] Greene, *Constitutional Origins,* pp. 113–14.

[90] As was the case with the Stamp Act, parliament intentionally asserted an unqualified authority of "sovereign command," knowing full well that the assertion would instigate intense resistance in the colonies. Given the fact that the tax revenue this legislation would produce, even if it were enforceable, was relatively small, it is difficult not to reach the conclusion that it was obedience, not money, that parliament really sought. Reid, *Constitutional History,* pp. 84–6. In 1764, for example, custom duties collected in the American colonies covered only a little over a quarter of the cost of their collection. Richard B. Morris (ed.), *Encyclopedia of American History: Revised and Enlarged Edition* (New York: Harper & Brothers, 1961), p. 73.

parliament and the colonists, because there was neither a text that might adjudicate between them nor an authority that might interpret that text if one had existed. Finally, this was also clearly a much more subtle "game" than the public at large could comprehend.[91] Colonial leaders had to translate its more arcane elements into slogans, such as "no taxation without representation," that could motivate popular action.[92]

After the Townshend Acts were repealed, the one tariff that was retained was on the importation of tea. In May 1773, the British government revised the terms of that levy by passing the Tea Act. The new tax was primarily designed to rescue the East India Company from bankruptcy by giving it a practical monopoly on the sale of tea in the colonies. However, the colonists interpreted the statute as an infringement of their rights and the major American ports instituted boycotts against importation of the tea. These were successful everywhere except Boston, where one ship, the *Dartmouth*, threatened to set, for complex legal reasons, a constitutional precedent if it remained in the harbor on December 17, 1773. Thus ensued one of the many instances in which popular protest was motivated and inspired by legal arguments over the rights of the colonies: the Boston Tea Party.[93]

The colonists waited as long as they could and then, dressed up in the costume of Indians, they boarded the *Dartmouth* the night before the precedent would be set and cast the offending tea into the harbor. Thomas Hutchinson,

---

[91] Greene, for example, emphasizes "the strength of the conciliatory thrust on both sides of the Atlantic during the quarrel over the Townshend Acts," even while, at the same time, stressing the resolve of the colonies in their resistance to "metropolitan conceptions of sovereignty." Greene, *Constitutional Origins*, p. xvi. The arguments that he and Reid have made often assume a consensus on constitutional questions between elite and popular views in the colonies. That assumption prevents them from attributing "the conciliatory thrust" during the Townshend episode to a reluctance of erstwhile revolutionary "radicals" to get too far ahead of the people they wished to lead. They instead explain the wish to conciliate to a simultaneously felt desire, on the part of the political elite and the people, to remain within the British Empire (and, as they often called it, "nation") if compromise were possible. The colonial elite and the people they led shared a common political culture that led them naturally to think in the same way. During the transition to independence, this popular culture would come under great stress when loyalists chose an alternative path.

[92] On the constitutional issues that motivated colonial and metropole maneuvering during the Townshend Act's brief existence, see Reid, *Constitutional History*, pp. 70–1. As a part of that maneuvering, smuggling became an act of legitimate political resistance when British duties were viewed as constitutionally unjustified. Greene, *Constitutional Origins*, p. 46. For a list of the most prominent incidents in which popular demonstrations were closely coordinated with the substance of ongoing constitutional disputes between the colonies and the metropole, see pp. 140–1, 143–8. One of the results of these protests was intervention by the British military in support of imperial officials and a suspension of legal institutions in the colonies. These, in turn, only increased popular resistance.

[93] For an account of the Boston Tea Party and the more general boycott of tea in the colonies, see T. H. Breen, *The Marketplace of Revolution: How Consumer Politics Shaped American Independence* (New York: Oxford University Press, 2004), pp. 294–329.

the royal governor, conceded that the colonists "had tried every method they could think of to force the tea back to England, and all in vain ... and in two or three hours destroyed three hundred and forty chests."[94] The Boston Tea Party marked another step in the transition from the rights of Englishmen to a comprehension of another foundation for the relation between the subject (who was fast becoming a citizen) and the state. The colonists had not quite abandoned an English identity but the symbolism of Indian costumes under-lined the emerging construction of an American alternative. In this instance, colonial leaders needed the public to deny the creation of a precedent (i.e., unloading and selling the tea); the timing is conclusive proof of the connection between constitutional claim-making and popular protest. There were thus two modes during the early stages of colonial resistance: the popular and the legal. For both of them, the momentum of events became self-propelling, but for different reasons.[95]

In response to the Tea Party, the British government passed what became known as the Boston Port Act, which closed the port to all non-military trade.[96] Nothing could move through Boston until the city had made restitution to the East India Company for the tea that had been destroyed. This act was followed by a second that suspended trial by jury in some instances by removing cases to venues outside of the colony; by a third that suspended most aspects of popular

---

[94] Reid, *Constitutional History*, pp. 87–8.

[95] For a succinct description of how the contradictory constitutional stances assumed by the colonies and the imperial authorities almost insensibly drove escalation of the crisis, see Reid, *Constitutional History*, p. 91. Popular mobilization is often irrepressible when aroused to action. See, for example, the description of "the Boston mobs" in Pole, *Political Representation*, p. 67. Also see, more generally, McConville, *King's Three Faces*, pp. 311–21. Frank views this irrepressibility as a popular corrective to more rigid and arbitrary legal constructions of "the people." Jason Frank, *Constituent Moments: Enacting the People in Postrevolutionary America* (Durham, NC: Duke University Press, 2010), particularly chapter 1. With respect to the transition, he writes: "The people petitioning Parliament in defense of the [English] constitution slowly gave way to the people surpassing the Parliament's constitutional power altogether and proclaiming separate sovereignty" (p. 16). However, Pole described the colonial elite as more circumspect. To them, "[n]o instrument had been more terrifyingly powerful in the not infrequent moments of crisis under late British rule than the Boston mob. On certain well-remembered occasions it had perhaps done its job to satisfaction. But the performance was not to be repeated." Pole, *Political Representation*, p. 211. John Adams, for his part, enthusiastically embraced the event: "This is the most magnificent Moment of all ... This Destruction of the Tea is so bold, so daring, so firm, intrepid and inflexible, and it must have so important Consequences, and so lasting, that I can't but consider it an Epocha in History." Mark Peterson, *The City-State of Boston: The Rise and Fall of an Atlantic Power, 1630–1865* (Princeton, NJ: Princeton University Press, 2019), p. 341. During the French Revolution, the Parisian people were similarly indispensable on at least three occasions: the storming of the Bastille, the taking of the king from Versailles to Paris, and the deposition of the king. However, many revolutionaries viewed most of the many other instances of street demonstrations, some of which invaded the French Assembly itself, with apprehension.

[96] Beloff, "American Independence," p. 458.

government in Massachusetts by consolidating power in the royal governor; and by a fourth providing for the quartering of British troops in privately owned buildings. In enacting these measures, parliament either underestimated the depth of colonial sentiment or was simply indifferent to the political risk it was assuming.[97] Either way, the primary purpose was not to collect damages for the lost tea but to punish the city, and, in that way, to clearly demonstrate parliamentary supremacy over the colonies. Parliament also enacted legislation that, among other things, unilaterally altered the royal charter of the colony. Parliament assumed that Massachusetts would stand alone because the other colonies would either not care what happened to Boston or would be too intimidated to come to its aid. In what should not have surprised the British government, the colonies instead convoked the First Continental Congress on September 5, 1774.[98]

On September 6, the day after the delegates first assembled, they passed a rule prohibiting public attendance at their sessions and enjoining secrecy as to what transpired as they deliberated: "That the door be kept shut during the time of business, and that the members consider themselves under the strongest obligations of honour, to keep the proceedings secret, until the majority shall direct them to be made public."[99] Given that the British would otherwise be closely monitoring their discussions, this was probably a very reasonable

[97] In the House of Lords, a few voices were raised against this act on the grounds that "[t]he legal Condition of the Subject [e.g., the city of Boston] ought never to depend upon the arbitrary Will of any Person whatsoever [in this instance a government minister]." Reid, *Constitutional History*, p. xvii. While Reid uses this example to illustrate the parallel legal arguments made by whigs in the metropole and the colonies, the argument made by these dissenting lords appears to presume that it would be possible to punish Boston if the legislation did not permit excessive discretion; the colonists would have opposed punishment in any form. Note that Reid uses the label "whigs" to denote colonial advocates of rights under the English Constitution and that usage implies a shared ideological heritage between them and Whigs in Britain. However, colonial advocates themselves seldom described themselves as whigs.

[98] Reid, *Constitutional History*, pp. 88–90. Georgia was the only colony that did not send delegates. During this period, Massachusetts was rapidly moving toward the construction of new political institutions that would be independent of all royal authority. However, even though "[r]oyal administration collapsed," Massachusetts downplayed the revolutionary character of its actions for fear that the other colonies might not support its confrontation with the British. Richard D. Brown, *Revolutionary Politics in Massachusetts: The Boston Committee of Correspondence and the Towns, 1772–1774* (Cambridge, MA: Harvard University Press, 1970), pp. 210–36.

[99] Ford (ed.), *Journal of the Continental Congress*, vol. 1, p. 26. The opening dilemma for the First Continental Congress was largely solved by unanimously accepting Peyton Randolph, the oldest member of the Virginia delegation, as the presiding officer because Virginia had issued the call to which the other colonies had responded. The credentials of the delegates were easily determined by the assumption that each colony had absolute control over the election or appointment of its delegates. These questions were settled on the first day. On the second, the delegates adopted an extremely spare set of rules in the form of four resolutions and then immediately began their substantive deliberations. Ford (ed.), *Journal of the Continental Congress*, vol. 1, pp. 13–14, 25–6. On these and other matters attending the initial organization, also see Calvin Jillson and Rick Wilson, *Congressional Dynamics:*

precaution. But it also liberated the delegates from close control by the state assemblies that had sent them to Philadelphia. Seven weeks later, on October 26, the Continental Congress sent a petition to the king:

We ask but for peace, liberty, and safety ... We wish not for a diminuation of the prerogative, nor do we solicit the grant for any new right in our favour. Your royal authority over us and our connexion with Great-Britain, we shall always carefully and zealously endeavour to support and maintain ... We therefore most earnestly beseech your majesty ... that your royal authority and interposition may be used for our relief and that a gracious answer may be given to our petition.

The colonies were simultaneously pledging complete and enduring loyalty to the king and asking him to intercede on their behalf in their dispute with parliament.[100]

In 1775, protest turned into treason. At that point, colonial identity was no longer primarily focused on the rights of Englishmen in their relations with the metropole; instead, they became increasingly grounded in their membership of a new and independent polity. The change was irreversible. But the transition from a constitutional debate over how the rights of Englishmen were to be applied in the colonies to a new identity in which American rights were to be wrested from the British did not occur overnight.[101] In 1776, the freeholders of Concord, Massachusetts, declared: "[A] Constitution in its Proper Idea intends a System of Principles Established to Secure the Subject[s] in the Possession and enjoyment of their Rights and Priviliges [sic], against any Encroachments of the Governing part." Since this declaration was made a year after the opening clash between American militia and British troops, it would have been obvious to the freeholders that the English Constitution was not "proper" because "the Governing part" (parliament) now controlled its meaning. Americans now saw themselves as the legitimate heirs of a constitutional tradition that the English themselves had abandoned. As a consequence, the rights of Englishmen to which the colonists subscribed were becoming detached from

---

Structure, Coordination, and Choice in the First American Congress, 1774–1789 (Stanford, CA: Stanford University Press, 1994), pp. 48–53.

[100] Reid, *Constitutional History*, pp. 92–3.

[101] While much of this transition spontaneously evolved as the public digested the meaning of political events, catalysts, in the form of agents and theorists clothed with community authority (e.g., delegates serving in the Continental Congress and members of colonial assemblies) also shaped the change in public opinion. These agents not only articulated why and how the intellectual, political, and cultural orientation of the people should change but also how that change would alter the practice of politics within legitimate (and legitimated) institutions. The transition thus moved "through" the agency of colonial governments which were considered legitimate precisely because they had been, for over a century, synonymous with the enjoyment of the rights of Englishmen. Greene, *Constitutional Origins*, pp. 159, 172. The transition was neither monolithic with everyone turning the page at the same time (some forged ahead while others were left behind) nor a linear process, because trial and error, as opposed to "discovery," dictated where "the logic of the situation" would take the colonists.

the mother country and were on the way to becoming the rights of men. As the opening paragraphs of the Declaration of Independence amply demonstrate, the next step was both natural and easy.[102]

Intermixed with a continuing debate over interpretation of the ancient English Constitution was the sporadic eruption of a new national identity. In 1765, for example, Christopher Gadsden declared during the Stamp Act Congress that "[t]here ought to be no New England man; no New Yorker, known on the continent, but all of us Americans." In 1774, Patrick Henry eliminated the "ought" from Gadsden's injunction and simply stated that the "distinctions between Virginians, Pennsylvanians, New Yorkers and New Englanders are no more. I am not a Virginian, but an American ... All distinctions are thrown down. All America is thrown into one mass."[103]

Despite Patrick Henry's nationalist oratory, there were deep and abiding divisions over whether or not the colonies should break ties with the British empire.[104] On the one hand, these divisions could be traced back to differences in the social conditions and economic interests of individual communities; for example, many on the southern frontier remained loyal to the crown while those to the north were ever more emphatically committed to rebellion.

On the other hand, the emerging distinction between American patriots and British loyalists compelled a wrenching reorientation of politics itself. As long as the colonists demanded their rights as Englishmen, unity was so likely that it could be implicitly assumed because all colonists shared a common status in relation to the metropole. That common status in the pursuit of those rights also conferred a legitimacy on colonial assemblies as the unquestioned repository of those rights. Grounding themselves in the customs and practices of traditional colonial governance, these assemblies embodied the English notion of representation in their very institutional existence. Demands for republican democracy, for example, were suppressed by the need for these assemblies to present themselves to both the colonial and metropolitan audience as the ancient vessels of historical experience and tradition. If they had experimented in new and radical political forms, they would have undercut their claims in the debate over constitutional interpretation because those claims had to be wrapped in the shroud of English constitutional history.

The transition to independence, however, dramatically changed the orientation of colonial politics.[105] On the most fundamental level, the colonial

---

[102] Reid, *Constitutional History*, p. 3.   [103] Wright, "American Independence," p. 524.
[104] Wright, "American Independence," pp. 526–7.
[105] The transition also radically altered American culture from an already weak attachment to "the traditional ethnic, religious, and tribal loyalties of the Old World" to "new democratic adhesives" arising from "the actual behavior of plain ordinary people." Wood, *Radicalism*, p. ix; also see p. 105. As Wood emphasizes throughout his text, the political and legal order laid down and perpetuated in the British monarchy and constitution was a social order as well. Although he does not say so, the colonial political and legal order probably changed less than the social habits, presumptions, and attitudes of the people. Put another way, there was more

assemblies and their leaders could no longer wrap their claims in tradition and custom because those things were grounded in fealty to the crown. There was also a more subtle difficulty: If the colonists still insisted on the preservation of the rights of Englishmen even as they also sought to break their ties with Britain, they would be in the rather odd position of asserting rights, along with an associated political identity, that were native to what would now become a foreign country. Although much of what transpired during the American Revolution – and, even more emphatically, during the crafting of the United States Constitution – reflected an enduring respect for English political tradition and institutions, the revolutionary elite was compelled to reconceive the ground of sovereignty in new and distinctively American terms.[106]

THE CONTINENTAL CONGRESS

The First Continental Congress met for only two months and its deliberations focused on the articulation of American rights, British wrongs, and the coordination of colonial protest that was intended to protect the former and rectify the latter. For example, the resolution empowering the delegation from New Hampshire to act as that colony's representatives merely authorized the delegates

[t]o attend and assist in the General Congress of delegates from the other Colonies ... to devise, consult, and adopt measures, as may have the most likely tendency to extricate the Colonies from their present difficulties; to secure and perpetuate their rights, liberties, and privileges, and to restore that peace, harmony, & mutual confidence which once happily subsisted between the parent country and her Colonies.

Virginia similarly instructed its delegation

[t]o consider of the most proper and effectual manner of so operating on the commercial connexion of the colonies with the Mother Country, as to procure redress for the much

---

continuity between colonial and post-independence political forms and practices than in the social and economic relations of the daily life of the people (see, for example, pp. 4–6).

[106] The social implications of this reconception were dramatically revealed in the division between, on the one hand, "patriots" who "were free of dependent connections and influence" and whose social "position or rank came naturally from their talent and from ... recognition by the people" and, on the other, "loyalists" who often were "well-to-do gentry operating at the pinnacles of power and patronage – royal or proprietary officeholders, big overseas dry-goods merchants [with thick, ongoing relationships with their British counterparts], and rich landowners." Wood estimates that the latter comprised approximately one in five whites residing in the colonies when the revolution began. Almost one in six of these loyalists left the new American states during and after the revolution. Wood, *Radicalism*, p. 176. The revolution also ended entail and primogeniture, which had previously anchored what passed for an American landed aristocracy, eliminated tax support for the Anglican Church, and hastened the abolition of slavery in the northern states. Otherwise, the American Revolution did not significantly change the relative social position or political status of the major economic classes in the colonies. Wright, "American Independence," pp. 529–30.

injured province of Massachusetts-Bay, to secure British America from the ravage and ruin of arbitrary taxes, and speedily as possible to procure the return of that harmony and Union, so beneficial to the whole Empire, and so ardently desired by all British America.[107]

While the credentials authorizing the Massachusetts delegates adopted a stronger tone, they also anticipated the reconciliation of differences with the home country. Revolution and independence were not yet in the air the delegates breathed. As a result, when the Congress first convened, it represented only a loose confederation of colonial sentiment, a debating society in which the delegates sent by the colonies were authorized to do little more than discuss matters of mutual concern, primarily British imposition of taxes upon the colonies and the dismantling of colonial government in Massachusetts.[108]

Both of these discussions took a slightly radical turn when Paul Revere brought to Philadelphia the "Suffolk Resolves," nineteen declarations adopted by the county that we now know as the city of Boston. The preamble urged the Congress to "nobly defeat that fatal edict [issued by parliament] which proclaims a power to frame laws for us in all cases whatsoever, thereby entailing the endless and numberless curses of slavery upon us, our heirs and their heirs forever." However, the resolves themselves alternated between expressions of loyalty to the crown and radical measures for correcting relations with the mother country. The first "resolve," for example, announced that "we, the heirs and successors of the first planters of this colony, do cheerfully acknowledge the said George the Third to be our rightful sovereign," while the third condemned "the British parliament" for violations of "the laws of nature, the British constitution, and the charter of the province." The fourth resolve characterized these violations as "the attempts of a wicked administration to enslave America" while implicitly absolving the king of any responsibility for their enactment.

The eighth went on to declare that any "persons" who accepted an official role in the implementation of these oppressive acts were to "be considered by this county as obstinate and incorrigible enemies to this country." The twelfth reaffirmed loyalty to the crown and declared that it was because of "our affection to his majesty, which we have at all times evidenced, [that] we are determined to act merely upon the defensive, so long as such conduct may be vindicated by reason and the principles of self-preservation, but no longer." The fourteenth recommended a boycott of British goods and, in fact, "all

---

[107] Ford (ed.), *Journal of the Continental Congress*, vol. 1, pp. 15, 23.
[108] "As a practical matter, Massachusetts became a republic in September 1774," when, upon the assembling of the Provincial Congress, royal government was at an end. However, "Massachusetts was not [yet] independent" because the people were still pledging their "allegiance to the monarch." The colony had entered a nether world in which the "province was bound to the monarch not by affection, but by a principle: the belief that a true legislature was a meeting of king and people." Bushman, *King and People*, pp. 212–13.

commercial intercourse with Great-Britain, Ireland, and the West-Indies," in order to compel the British to change their colonial policies. The penultimate resolve, like the instructions and credentials that have already been cited, urged "the continental Congress, now sitting at Philadelphia" to pursue "the restoration and establishment of our just rights, civil and religious, and for renewing that harmony and union between Great-Britain and the colonies, so earnestly wished for by all good men." However, as the nineteenth and last resolve announced, "should our enemies, by any sudden manoeuvres," commence hostilities, the county of Suffolk stood ready to meet the challenge by mobilizing its citizens.

The Massachusetts delegation feared that the Suffolk Resolves might be too radical for their colleagues when they were formally presented on September 16, 1774, the eleventh day of deliberations. However, the Continental Congress warmly and unanimously endorsed the resolves and declared "[t]hat contributions from all the colonies for supplying the necessities, and alleviating the distresses of our brethren at Boston, ought to be continued, in such manner, and so long as their occasions may require." In his diary, John Adams declared: "This was one of the happiest days of my life ... because this day convinced me that America will support ... Massachusetts or perish with her."[109]

When the delegates subsequently decided to create an "association" in order to boycott British goods and to establish local committees for its enforcement, they took the first step toward something more than a loose confederation of sentiment, but that step, like many that were to follow, still presumed that the individual colonies could refuse to cooperate and thus held effective veto power over everything the Congress would propose. By the end of its deliberations on October 26, 1774, the First Continental Congress was neither a sovereign state nor a debating society. However, its ambiguous status was not a serious issue because many, if not most, of the delegates did not anticipate that the Congress would ever meet again.

When the First Continental Congress adjourned in October 1774, the delegates provided that a second congress would meet in May 1775, but only if the British had not yet acted upon American grievances. The possibility that their disputes might be amicably settled without further agitation then seemed very real. In pursuit of such a reconciliation, the Continental Congress had repeatedly affirmed American loyalty to the mother country while also couching its demands as the expression of the "most sacred" rights of Englishmen. While praising the people of Massachusetts for their firm resistance to British oppression, for example, Congress also urged them to remain "peaceably and firmly ... on the defensive" in order to avoid involving the colonies in "the horrors of a civil war" before the king could make amends.[110]

---

[109] Ford (ed.), *Journal of the Continental Congress*, vol. 1, pp. 32–40.
[110] Maier, *American Scripture*, p. 3.

When the Second Continental Congress convened on May 10, 1775, after the bloody skirmishes at Lexington and Concord, it became the central institution of an emerging nation.[111] However, the delegates were still uncertain as to whether or not reconciliation with the mother country was possible. The colonies were not, in fact, on the same page until the Declaration of Independence was proclaimed on July 4, 1776. Some, like Massachusetts, moved toward a radical rejection of British rule much earlier and more rapidly than others.[112] But even Massachusetts wavered. Even as the Massachusetts Provincial Congress was raising troops and requesting military assistance from neighboring colonies, it also issued an address to the British people in which it pledged to remain the king's "loyal and dutiful Subjects" who would willingly "defend his person, Family, Crown and Dignity" with their own "Lives and Fortunes." This address was penned one week after blood had been shed at Lexington and Concord.

On June 15, Congress appointed George Washington as commander-in-chief of a new continental army, and, on June 17, 1775, colonial troops (neither led by Washington nor properly enrolled in the continental army) fought one of the bloodiest battles of the Revolutionary War at Bunker Hill and Breed's Hill just outside of Boston.[113] At about the same time, many of the other colonies were ordering their delegates to find ways to assert "American rights and liberties" while simultaneously restoring "harmony between Great-Britain and the Colonies." Even the more passively inclined delegates did not find any inconsistency in supporting military action and, at the same time, compromise solutions that would keep American colonists within the British nation.[114]

---

[111] The Continental Congress received and printed personal accounts from several of the militia who fought at Lexington and Concord. Ford (ed.), *Journal of the Continental Congress*, vol. 2, pp. 27–44.

[112] When they entered the First Continental Congress in September 1774, the Massachusetts delegates deported themselves "with great Delicacy and caution" because many of the other delegates thought the colony they represented to be "intemperate and rash." Some even believed that Massachusetts had already decided that independence from Britain should be the goal of colonial policy. When the Massachusetts delegation arrived for the convening of the Second Continental Congress some seven months later, their entrance into Philadelphia was, in sharp contrast, "verry grand" and they were celebrated as they moved through the streets. In the intercession between the two congresses, the Minutemen had fought the British at Lexington and Concord and radicalism was on the upswing. Maier, *American Scripture*, p. 6.

[113] Maier, *American Scripture*, pp. 10–11.

[114] On May 9, 1775, the day before the convening of the Second Continental Congress, colonial troops surprised the British garrison at Fort Ticonderoga and seized cannon and other war materiel. While the occupation of the fort was bloodless, the British considered it an act of war. Congress, on the other hand, promised to compile an inventory of all the property that had been seized. That property would, the delegates pledged, be "safely returned when the restoration of the former harmony between great Britain and these colonies so ardently wished for by the latter shall render it prudent and consistent with the overruling law of self preservation." Maier, *American Scripture*, pp. 7–10. The delegates pinned their hopes for a reconciliation on the king,

In the mass of apparent contradictions that accompanied the transition from assertion of the rights of Englishmen to the struggle for independence, we might include the shifting policy of the Continental Congress toward Quebec. On May 29, 1775, Congress invited Quebec to join the thirteen colonies in their resistance to British oppression by claiming that "the fate of the protestant and catholic colonies" was "strongly linked." Three days later, the delegates declared that, because "this Congress has nothing more in view than the defence of these colonies . . . no expedition or incursion ought to be undertaken or made, by any colony, or body of colonists, against or into Canada." This declaration was fully consistent with the invitation extended to Quebec and with the (already fraught) position that armed hostilities against the British would be undertaken only in defense of colonial rights as Englishmen. However, Quebec did not accept the invitation to join the thirteen colonies to her south, probably because, as Maier notes, the other colonies were hostile to Catholicism. So, less than a month later, on June 27, the Continental Congress ordered the invasion of Quebec, a decision that could not be described as either defensive or consistent with the latter's ostensible status as a sibling colony.[115]

On May 16, 1775, the Massachusetts Provincial Congress asked the Continental Congress for advice on how it might reconstitute its government now that they had cast off royal authority. In response, the Continental

---

unanimously resolving on May 26 "[t]hat his Majesty's most faithful subjects, in these colonies, are reduced to a dangerous and critical situation, by the attempts of the british Ministry to carry into execution, by force of arms, several unconstitutional and oppressive acts of the british Parliament." Ford (ed.), *Journal of the Continental Congress*, vol. 2, pp. 64–5.

[115] Maier, *American Scripture*, p. 12. For the texts of the invitation, the promise not to invade, and the order to Major General Schuyler to mount an invasion, see Ford (ed.), *Journal of the Continental Congress*, vol. 2, pp. 68–70, 75, 109–10. At the beginning of hostilities, the revolutionary elite believed that all British colonies in North America, including Newfoundland and the Floridas, might follow their lead in rebelling against British rule. On the one hand, the more widespread the rebellion, the more difficulty the British would have in suppressing it. On the other hand, the elite believed that they were advocating rights that all those who lived under the British flag would recognize and honor as their own. Goodwin, "Introductory Survey," pp. 11–12. Perhaps paradoxically, once the elite had turned away from the rights of Englishmen and more fully embraced natural rights as the justification for independence, they became much less interested in the export of their political principles. On the reluctance of the colonies in the British West Indies to join the mainland colonies in resisting metropole policies, see Andrew Jackson O'Shaughnessy, *An Empire Divided: The American Revolution and the British Caribbean* (Philadelphia: University of Pennsylvania Press, 2000), pp. 65–8, 137–8, 146–7, 151–9. One of the problems was the competing economic interests of the Caribbean sugar planters and their mainland consumers (the latter also providing food and other supplies to the former). The Caribbean islands also contained much larger slave populations who became, somewhat like the Haitians during the French Revolution some fifteen years later, increasingly restless during the revolutionary period. O'Shaughnessy concludes that the "British West Indies stood to gain nothing from the American Revolutionary War." In fact, the Continental Congress never invited the British West Indies to join the Articles of Confederation even as they pursued Quebec.

Congress recommended that the colony elect an assembly and council in accordance with its 1691 charter and then regard the positions of royal governor and lieutenant governor as vacant until officials who pledged "to govern the colony according to its charter" presented themselves. This minimalist proposal both enabled effective provincial government and, at the same time, would allow a return to the royal fold without much institutional adjustment if the British were to make appropriate concessions to colonial claims.[116] In subsequent months, several other colonies asked for and received the same advice.

These actions were significant for several reasons. For one thing, the colonies that made these requests tacitly acknowledged the role of the Continental Congress as a legitimizing authority. This acknowledgment, however, was qualified by the fact that the colonies requested "advice," as opposed to asking "permission." In addition, the reliance on royal charters, albeit sans royal officials, maximized continuity with pre-revolutionary traditions, customs, and practices. Both the Continental Congress and the colonies were thereby acting upon the premise that it was the current king and parliament that had departed from the rightful principles of the rights of Englishmen, not the colonists; the latter, in resisting imperial rule, were merely affirming custom and tradition.[117] Finally, the advice given by the Continental Congress once again evidenced the persisting ambiguity of the transition to political autonomy in that the delegates appeared to be awaiting, even anticipating, the return of crown authority once differences with the mother country had been resolved.[118]

---

[116] Wood, *Creation of the American Republic*, p. 130.

[117] Edmund Burke's insistence on the primacy of custom resonated more deeply in the colonies than in the metropole because colonial claims of customary rights were rejected by most of the British political elite. However, it was precisely this mode of constitutional theorization that made him so favorable to the colonist position. There was a difference, however, in that Burke also held that custom and tradition had now grown up around the 1688 revolution and its reaffirmation of the principle that the monarchy could not be trusted. As a consequence, he supported "unlimited" parliamentary sovereignty within the metropole. Because custom and tradition had also grown up around the colonial institutions, this left him in a potentially uncomfortable position. If parliament was not willing to respect colonial autonomy in local governance, the only alternatives were either colonial representation in parliament (which both the British and Americans rejected) or American independence. Reid, *Constitutional History*, p. 96.

   Burke and the colonists thus interpreted the customary history of the English Constitution in slightly different ways. From Burke's perspective, custom and tradition reflected the wisdom of the past, but, because they descended from "time out of mind," they could not articulate the specific nature of the origins or content of that wisdom (which has been lost forever and is hence unknowable). Burke, nevertheless, and everything else being equal, held that we should give our consent to custom because it is usually (but not infallibly) wiser than our passions and opinions in the moment. However, from the colonial perspective, parliament and the colonies "had irrevocably" consented to custom and it was therefore absolutely binding on our passions and opinions (e.g., "custom" had turned into "inalienable rights").

[118] Maier, *American Scripture*, p. 13.

Up until the end of 1775, on every occasion that Congress issued a statement, published a declaration, or passed a resolution describing what it considered instances of "American Oppressions" by the British, it would simultaneously append an insistence that the colonies sought only a resolution of their difficulties with imperial rule. Independence was not on the table.[119] Even those who might otherwise be considered radical opponents of imperial rule did not advocate separation. On August 25, 1775, for example, Thomas Jefferson privately stated a fervent desire for a resolution of differences because he "would rather be in dependence on Great Britain, properly limited, than on any nation on earth, or than on no nation" (meaning, by the latter, independence).[120] However, even as Congress was giving conservative advice to the provincial governments on how to reform their institutions, it was itself taking on many of the trappings of an independent state by, among other things, establishing an inter-colonial postal system, carrying on negotiations with Indian tribes on the frontier, regulating American trade, directing the treatment of loyalists (who were being progressively transformed into "traitors"),[121] and, of course, creating an army.[122] At the same time, several provincial assemblies formally instructed their delegates in the Continental Congress to oppose all attempts to separate from Britain.[123] The Continental Congress was still on the cusp of the transition between colony and nation, between loyalty to the crown

---

[119] Maier, *American Scripture*, p. 18. Even after Bunker Hill, a battle in which colonial and imperial troops met as fully fledged armies, the Continental Congress on July 8, 1775, adopted an appeal "to the Inhabitants of Great-Britain" in which the colonists were described as the rightful "Descendants of *Britons*" who were only defending their "glorious Privileges" for which their common "gallant and virtuous Ancestors" had previously "fought, bled, and conquered" (p. 20). Given that some of these protestations were voiced after many months of bloodshed, Maier describes these continuing "expressions of allegiance to the King absurd" (p. 79). However, when we consider that the colonists were, somewhat paradoxically, affirming both their rights as Englishmen and the violation of those rights by the government that had originally created them, this "absurdity" becomes more understandable. Also see Beloff, "American Independence," pp. 461–2.

[120] Maier, *American Scripture*, p. 21.

[121] For instances of this transformation, see the way in which traitorous conduct was defined and punished on January 2, 3, 11 and February 8, 1776. Ford (ed.), *Journal of the Continental Congress*, vol. 4, pp. 18–20, 25–8, 49, 121, 205. These can be contrasted with the protest to a British general on the treatment of American prisoners "who while fighting bravely in their country's cause, are sent to Britain in *irons*, to be *punished* for pretended treasons" (p. 22). All of these examples occurred well before Congress had declared American independence.

[122] Maier, *American Scripture*, pp. 13–14. On the same day that Massachusetts asked for advice on how to reconstitute its government, the Continental Congress discussed "the state of America." While the delegates debated whether and how to raise an army, John Rutledge of South Carolina suggested that more fundamental issues must be settled first: "[D]o We aim at independency? Or do We only ask for a Restoration of Rights & putting of Us on Our old footing?" At that time, none of the delegates appeared to favor independence (pp. 17–18).

[123] Maier, *American Scripture*, p. 30.

within the ambit of the rights of Englishmen and the founding of a new nation in which those same rights were transformed into American principles.[124]

The intertwined destinies of the colonies and the metropole were shaped by mutual misrecognition of the other's intentions and resolve. American policy pronouncements were hedged with qualifications of loyalty to the crown in ways that may have misled British policymakers. Although colonists were willing to shed blood in defense of their rights, those rights were always presented as the rights of Englishmen, not the universal rights of all men.[125] British authorities thus thought that they were dealing with rebels, not potential revolutionaries, and the way to deal with rebels was to brutally repress them. In a very real sense, American political leaders were responsible for this misunderstanding, although it is difficult, given the political problems associated with mobilizing popular support for their policies, how they could have proceeded very differently.

The British, on the other hand, made it crystal clear that the colonial interpretation of the English Constitution (which, among other things, held that the governance arrangements in the colonies created by royal charters could not be altered by parliament) was never going to be accepted. Up until 1774, the colonists had relied on an ever weakening belief that King George would reaffirm his, in their eyes, royal prerogative with respect to colonial governance and thus overturn parliament's insistence that its authority was absolute. On November 18, 1774, the king unambiguously affirmed the crown's alignment with parliament's position. Writing to Lord Frederick North, the prime minister of his majesty's government, the king declared that "[t]he New England Governments are in a state of rebellion" and "blows must decide whether they are to be subject to this country or independent." Twelve days later, King George publicly declared that Massachusetts was displaying a "most daring spirit of resistance and disobedience to law" and announced his "firm and steadfast resolution to withstand every attempt to weaken or impair the supreme authority of this Legislature over all the Dominions of my Crown."

---

[124] The transition from the rights of Englishmen to the will of the people was not only effected through the conversion of individuals from one to the other but also by the replacement of an older generation with the new. This can be seen in Maier's distinction between the generation who led the independence movement (men who "had learned their politics as colonists under a distant monarchy") and those who came to maturity during the subsequent revolution (men who "had learned their politics during the resistance to Britain, which was founded on popular support"). Maier, *Ratification*, p. 268.

[125] The rights of Englishmen were not and could not be the universal rights of all men for two related reasons. First, the former had arisen and taken shape within a particular political history that clearly was not shared by other nations (or even by some parts of the United Kingdom, such as Scotland and Ireland). Second, the rights of Englishmen were the product of a custom and tradition in which logic and reason played a subordinate role in constitutional interpretation. The universal rights of all men, in rather sharp contrast, rested on nothing but rational deduction from abstract principles.

King George, in fact, may have been a little ahead of his government, because three months elapsed before parliament formally declared Massachusetts to be in a state of rebellion in February 1775. As punishment, it then passed the New England Restraining Act, which both blocked American access to the fishing banks of the North Atlantic and restricted foreign trade. Originally applied only to Massachusetts, these policies were subsequently extended to the sympathetic colonies of Maryland, New Jersey, Pennsylvania, South Carolina, and Virginia.[126]

Some months later, on August 23, 1775, the king formally declared that the colonies had "proceeded to open and avowed rebellion"; two months after that, in a speech before parliament, he told the members that this rebellion was "manifestly carried on for the purpose of establishing an independent Empire." In response (as if they needed any prodding), parliament then passed a "Prohibitory Act" that blocked all commerce with the American colonies "during the continuance of the present Rebellion." In addition, all Americans were to be denied the king's protection and all their vessels and cargoes were to be treated as if they "were the ships and effects of open enemies." American seamen were also subject to impressment in the Royal Navy, where, colonists could not help but note, they might be compelled to fight against their own people.[127]

On October 16, a British naval captain told the people of Portland (then Falmouth), Maine, that they were rebels and gave them two hours to vacate their homes. He bombarded the town on the following day. On November 7, the royal governor of Virginia offered emancipation to those slaves who enlisted in the British effort to suppress their masters.[128] According to Merrill

---

[126] Maier, *American Scripture*, pp. 23–4. Up until the Boston Tea Party, George III's attitude toward the colonies was more indulgent than sentiment in parliament and the colonies rightly considered him to be more sympathetic. However, by 1775, even those most hopeful of royal intervention against parliament's claims were forced to concede that "the fiction of opposing Parliament and not the king could not last." Lord North, who served as prime minister from 1770 through the end of the war, traversed the opposite path, moving from a staunch and unalloyed assertion of parliament's prerogatives with respect to colonial policy to a much more lenient and compromising attitude after the Tea Party. North, in fact, spent much of his tenure after 1773 attempting to resign from office because he doubted that the king's uncompromising policies would succeed. Andrew Jackson O'Shaughnessy, *The Men Who Lost America: British Leadership, the American Revolution, and the Fate of the Empire* (New Haven, CT: Yale University Press, 2014), pp. 21–5, 47–71.

[127] Maier, *American Scripture*, pp. 25–6. When the king accused the colonists of "forgetting the allegiance" to the "power that has protected and sustained" the colonies, Congress unhesitatingly replied, on December 6, 1775, with its own proclamation: "What allegiance is it that we forget? Allegiance to Parliament? We never owed – we never owned it. Allegiance to our King? Our words have ever avowed it, – our conduct has ever been consistent with it." Ford (ed.), *Journal of the Continental Congress*, vol. 3, p. 410.

[128] In return for their freedom, thousands of slaves enlisted in both the American and British armies during the war. Those who served in British armies were evacuated after the peace. Bateman, *Disenfranchising Democracy*, p. 60.

Jensen, this appeal persuaded more Virginians to break with the mother country "than all the acts of Parliament since the founding of the colonies." At the end of November, Jefferson privately lamented that he considered it "an immense misfortune to the whole empire to have a king of such a disposition at such a time. We are told and everything proves it true that he is the bitterest enemy we have."[129] In all these declarations, policies, and actions, the British were steadily transforming "rebels" who insisted on their rights as Englishmen into "revolutionaries" who had no recourse but independence if those rights were to be realized. It is thus remarkable that the British were willing to charge the colonists with desiring independence when the colonists themselves, in both their communications with one another and their public proclamations, were openly denying that they entertained that goal.

The Americans misread the British in at least three ways. First, as just noted, the British repeatedly and absolutely rejected the colonial contention that parliament did not have a constitutional right to govern American affairs. While parliament did, from time to time, retreat from policies that did not "work" (in varying senses of that term), it never indicated any hesitancy with respect to asserting its authority. Second, the king was even more enthusiastic about the exercise of that authority than parliament was. There was thus never any realistic possibility that the crown might intercede on behalf of the colonies.[130] Finally, Americans consistently misinterpreted the state of the English Constitution as it applied to domestic affairs in the metropole. As a

---

[129] Quoted in Maier, *American Scripture*, p. 26.
[130] The persistence with which the Continental Congress pursued the crown was truly remarkable. On July 8, 1775, for example, Congress adopted what became known as the "Olive Branch Petition," which, once it arrived in London, the king refused to receive. And, because he never received it, he also refused to reply to its contents. In fairness to the delegates, adoption of the petition may have been primarily motivated by a wish to mollify the moderates among them and thus might not have been a misapprehension of political possibility on the part of the majority. Maier, *American Scripture*, p. 24. Much of the tone of the petition was obsequious. For example, the delegates

> solemnly assure your Majesty, that we not only most ardently desire the former harmony between her and these colonies may be restored, but that a concord may be established between them upon so firm a basis as to perpetuate its blessings ... the apprehensions that now oppress our hearts with unspeakable grief, being once removed, Your Majesty will find your faithful subjects on this continent ready and willing at all times, as they ever have been, with their lives and fortunes, to assert and maintain the rights and interests of your Majesty, and of our Mother country.

For the full text of the petition, see Ford (ed.), *Journal of the Continental Congress*, vol. 2, pp. 158–61. The king's unqualified endorsement of parliamentary supremacy fatally undermined the colonial constitutional argument, while, at the same time, demolishing the ground upon which Americans could identify as Englishmen. Both of these make the manner in which the colonists referred to the king the most important barometer of colonial change in political identity, moving from allegiance (to the king) to charges of tyranny (by the king) to irrelevance (of the king). Jones, "American Independence," pp. 488–9.

result of the Glorious Revolution of 1688, parliament had embarked on a constitutional program in which its authority was to become paramount – and had already done so to a large extent – within the British political system.[131] American appeals to the intercession of the crown in colonial affairs raised profound apprehensions that this new and evolving state of affairs in the home country might be upset by, among other things, qualifying the authority of parliament in the colonies and thus, as a byproduct, awarding the crown a substantial and unrestricted source of revenue.

In Pauline Maier's words, to British political leaders, Americans seemed to want to "leap not toward the future but backwards, toward royal absolutism."[132] Put another way, the autonomy of governance sought by the colonies through an assertion of the royal prerogative would, in British eyes, have seriously compromised the same, hard-won autonomy sought by the House of Commons.[133] On one side of the Atlantic, the Americans presented themselves as more English in their politics and ideological principles than the English themselves.[134] On the other side, the British considered the colonists to be, at best, little more than bone-headed commoners and, at worst, uncouth miscreants. In such a context, American insistence on their English rights,

[131] Greene contends that the colonists turned the Glorious Revolution on its head: To the extent that the Glorious Revolution strengthened parliament, as the defender of liberty and the English Constitution in its relations with the crown, the colonial assemblies were also strengthened in their own relations with the king because they thought of themselves as having their own "little parliaments." Greene, *Constitutional Origins*, p. 53. Put another way, the Glorious Revolution did not change the relation between the colonies and parliament but instead strengthened the colonies in their relations with the crown (pp. 120–1). Somewhat aside from the question of parliamentary sovereignty, Murrin contends that the political development of the United States after adoption of the Constitution "mimicked or even repeated English developments" after 1688 to "an almost incredible degree." Murrin, *Rethinking America*, pp. 62–5.

[132] Maier, *American Scripture*, p. 22; also see Reid, *Constitutional History*, pp. 24, 94–5; Morgan, *Inventing the People*, p. 244.

[133] "Same" in the sense that both the colonial assemblies and the House of Commons sought to dominate their respective polities.

[134] Before the adoption of the Declaration of Independence, colonists sometimes grounded the rights they claimed in what now appears to be a theoretical muddle; natural rights, the common law, statutes, historical practice and precedent, the logic of reason, and the will of God were all bundled together as if they were entirely consistent, each one with the others. So, for example, Dulany's 1728 tract on the "The RIGHT of the Inhabitants of MARYLAND to the Benefit of the ENGLISH Laws" described "the Law of *England*" as consisting

of the Common and Statute Law. That the Common Law, takes in the Law of Nature, the Law of Reason, and the revealed Law of God; which are equally binding, at All Times, in All Places, and to All Persons, And such Usages, and Customs, as have been experimentally found, to suit the Order, and Engagements of Society; and to contain Nothing inconsistent with Honesty, Decency, and Good Manners; and which by Consent, and long Use, have obtained the Force of Laws. (Greene and Yirush (eds.), *Exploring the Bounds of Liberty*, p. 653)

paradoxically, was inexorably pushing them out of the very nation in which those rights had been created.

The British, for their part, misread the Americans in several ways. On the one hand, they overestimated the size of the loyalist community in the colonies. There were, in fact, many in the colonies who warmly supported imperial policy and closely identified with the metropole. While their ranks included those who held government offices or who had personal ties to people living in Britain, other colonists so strongly identified with the status of Englishmen under the unwritten constitution that they could not imagine forsaking allegiance to the most perfect government man had ever created.[135] Such identities had been strongly reinforced during the French and Indian War, a conflict that resulted in a victory mutually celebrated by the British and the Americans when the Treaty of Paris was signed in 1763. Only twelve years had elapsed between that peace and the eruption of revolutionary violence in Massachusetts, and some Americans simply could not shift their identities, allegiances, and future destinies in so short a time.[136]

But the size of the loyalist community was neither as large nor as influential as British officials assumed.[137] Much of their information on the state of colonial politics came from loyalists who served the government and those loyalists were caught between a rock (the need to explain to their supervisors in London why they were failing to keep the public order) and a hard place (the equally pressing need to cajole Americans into accepting policies that, to the colonists, were unjust and oppressive). The easiest way to negotiate between these two imperatives was, on the one hand, to describe unruly colonists as a mob without principles and, on the other, to weakly enforce,

---

[135] Before 1763, for example, even John Adams regarded the unwritten British Constitution as "the most perfect combination of human powers in society which finite wisdom has yet contrived and reduced to practice for the preservation of liberty and the production of happiness." Bailyn, *Ideological Origins*, p. 67. Some fifteen years later, Adams published his *Defence of the Constitutions* in which he declared that "the English Constitution is, in theory, the most stupendous fabric of human invention, both for the adjustment of the balance, and the prevention of its vibrations; and that the American ought to be applauded instead of censured, for imitating it, as far as they have." Nelson, *Royalist Revolution*, p. 206. As Pole put it, Adams "wanted to reproduce in America, in perfect and uncorrupted form, those virtues of balance which were the ideal (not the actual or contemporary) merit of the British Constitution. For these ideal virtues Adams shared all the enthusiasm that Burke poured out on the British Constitution in its capacity as a venerable pile." Pole, *Political Representation*, p. 221.

[136] Maier, *American Scripture*, p. 36.

[137] Jones, for example, estimates that around half of all colonists had come to support independence by mid-1776 with the remainder divided between neutrals and loyalists (with the latter marginally more numerous). Loyalists may have been in the majority in New York and New Jersey and composed sizable proportions in Pennsylvania and Georgia. But in the oldest colonies (Virginia, Maryland, and New England) they were insignificant. Some 80,000 loyalists emigrated to Canada and other British possessions by the end of what he describes as a "civil war." Jones, "American Independence," pp. 489–90.

if at all, imperial edicts.[138] But such a path could, in the long run, only produce an ever more untenable combination of more stringent policies emanating from London and increasing colonial contempt for the substance and principles of imperial policy.

The Continental Congress is often described as a failure, an institution that was fatally cursed, internally, with rules and procedures that hamstrung the possibility of decisive action and, externally, with almost no authority to enforce the legislation that it enacted.[139] Much of this criticism, however, presumes that the delegates and the states that appointed or elected them desired the construction of a central state with the capacity to identify national policies that would respond to collective needs and with the power to compel compliance throughout the country.[140] This presumption became increasingly valid in the years following the surrender of the British army at Yorktown in 1781 and ratification of the peace treaty in 1783. However, it is untenable during the early years of the Continental Congress when the delegates and the states were debating how to respond to British policies that violated the rights of the colonists and, after those responses failed, how to encourage their compatriots to support and participate in the war for independence.

The major task in this earlier period was the development and maintenance of consensus and cohesion within the colonies. Consensus with respect to the coercive exercise of government authority was only available at the state level for several reasons. First, the colonists were accustomed to the exercise of government authority by colonial governments and thus did not fear or resent the imposition of policies by their respective assemblies. Second, because the colonies had long existed as political communities, colonists drew much of their social and political identity from membership within them. Finally, each of the colonies had a distinct relationship with imperial Britain that had both shaped their institutions in different ways and colored the construction of what the colonists had come to view as their rights as Englishmen. When Massachusetts broke with the crown in 1775, for example, it could easily and naturally claim a sovereign relationship with its people without relying on the approval or even passive acceptance of the other colonies. Such a claim was not available to the Continental Congress when it first met in 1774. Furthermore, it was probably beyond the ability of the new states to transfer to the Continental Congress the elements upon which their own sovereignty rested. In any event, the question was moot because none of the political elite in the new states were willing to subordinate their own government to the Continental Congress.

---

[138] On the lack of enforcement of imperial policy in Maryland, see Maier, *American Scripture*, p. 36.

[139] Much of this section is indebted to Calvin Jillson and Rick Wilson, whose *Congressional Dynamics* provided much of the evidentiary detail for its preparation.

[140] For ease in exposition, I often refer to "states" in this section even though they were, of course, colonies before the Declaration of Independence transformed them.

All of this determined the shape of the Continental Congress, both before and after adoption of the Articles of Confederation. The primary factors were: (1) that the people could consent to continental policies only through the delegates elected or appointed by their states because the latter were the only governments to which they felt personal allegiance; and (2) that the war effort required the unity of all the states and that unity was possible only if each and every one of them consented to those policies. Many scholars have referred to the delegates sent to the Continental Congress as "ambassadors" from the respective states.[141] The analogy makes a lot of sense in that it emphasizes that the locus of sovereignty remained with the states, which could, in theory and often in practice, always opt out of whatever policies the Congress proposed. But the analogy also distorts the priorities and orientations of the delegates and the institution that they inhabited. Those delegates shared a project – winning the war with imperial Britain – that was a matter of life and death to them individually and to those that they represented. As the last sentence in the Declaration of Independence stated, they had "mutually pledge[d] to each other our lives, our Fortunes, and our sacred Honor." No ambassador has ever pledged such things to other ambassadors.

The Declaration of Independence, in fact, recognized the twin imperatives under which the Continental Congress was compelled to operate. On the one hand, the Declaration had to be the consensual agreement of each and every one of the states in order to achieve the unity necessary to wage war upon the British Empire. In the process of crafting the text, Congress waited upon the several states as they individually came to support the decision. The states thus agreed, in advance, to become severally independent within a yet-to-be-determined political structure that presumed that they would be both autonomous and yet cooperating closely. On the other hand, the delegates signed as individuals with no sign or marker identifying the states that they represented. Their signatures are scattered randomly at the foot of the document, profoundly attesting to their individual commitments to one another. The delegates were, at one and the same time, agents of the states that they represented and individuals who, in the absence of the sovereign authority of the Congress in which they served, pledged themselves, to one another, to faithfully pursue their common cause.

THE DECLARATION OF INDEPENDENCE

By the winter of 1775–6, the colonists were on the verge of a transition from a defense of the rights of Englishmen within the imperial order to a realization of

---

[141] Jillson and Wilson, for example, do so repeatedly in *Congressional Dynamics*, pp. 43, 71, 91, 136. On "the longstanding and deeply ingrained sense of loyalty and attachment that citizens felt for their local state governments," see Pollack, *War, Revenue, and State Building*, p. 103.

those rights in a new and independent nation.[142] Just at that time, almost as if he had been waiting in the wings to be called upon the stage of history, Thomas Paine brought out a pamphlet, *Common Sense*, which was intended to resolve the contradictions in current political contention. Copies of this tract first hit the streets in Philadelphia, a city where revolutionary angst and conservative anxiety had more or less paralyzed the political community. Published in early January 1776, *Common Sense* addressed the mass public in its own vernacular, launching a direct and unmediated assault on the very foundation of monarchy and the ground of kingship. Since the very idea of legitimate authority was, for Paine, incompatible with the divine pretensions and arbitrary origins of monarchs, there could be no social contract between the colonies and the government of King George III. And, since the English Constitution was inextricably infused with monarchical principles and rituals, a hypothetical restoration of the rights of Englishmen to the colonists was as absurd as it was delusional. This sweeping condemnation of colonial attempts to reconcile with the imperial order was, perhaps, the most successful of Paine's several purposes. The very vigor with which he asserted what the British considered to be treasonous arguments created a new public space in the colonies where the status of the king and the justification of kings in general could be discussed without fear or apprehension.

Paine was less successful, however, in weaning colonists from their attachment to the rights of Englishmen, which, as we will soon see, ultimately became the warp and woof of the new American constitutional order. Paine would have preferred the construction of a new government arising out of a philosophically consistent application of his republican principles. Deriving his plan from what he contended were the immanent meanings and imperatives of the natural order of existence, Paine proposed a unicameral legislature in which the public will would flow seamlessly into government practice and policy. There was to be, no separation of powers and no institutional variation with respect to how the people rule themselves.[143] On these two points – rejection of the ancient English

---

[142] When the colonists abandoned all hope that the king might intercede between them and parliament, they also had to abandon their identity as Englishmen, an identity in which competitive relations between parliament and the crown had given rise to a very particular composition of liberty as resistance to the royal prerogative (the colonial assembly assuming the historical role of parliament). Freed from this particular composition, liberty became defined as a specific relation between the citizen and the government in which the rule of law became the guarantor of American rights. But the colonial assemblies (and the Continental Congress) could no longer be the guarantor of liberty because the crown, and with it the kingly prerogative, had vanished. As a consequence, Americans floundered about as they tried to reconcile their historical inheritance from the British with the absence of those institutional relations that had given that inheritance substantive meaning.

[143] Paine's proposals later found an echo in the thinking and writing of many of those who opposed ratification of the Constitution. See, for example, Saul Cornell, *The Other Founders: Anti-Federalism and the Dissenting Tradition in America, 1788–1828* (Chapel Hill, NC: Omohundro Institute of Early American History and Culture, 1999), p. 120.

Constitution and the institutional realization of the will of the people – *Common Sense* failed to achieve its purpose. But Paine still played an important role in shifting public opinion toward independence and thus transforming debate from how the British ruled the colonies to the ways in which the colonies would have to rule themselves.[144]

This transformation was not simple. For example, On February 13, 1776, a draft proclamation, "To the Inhabitants of the Colonies," was considered by the Continental Congress. On the one hand, it asserted that "all Power was originally in the People – that all the Powers of Government are derived from them – that all Power, which they have not disposed of, still continues theirs." However, it then immediately claimed that these were "Maxims of the *English* Constitution." Much later in that same document, the committee rather timidly recommended that Congress also affirm that "[w]e are too much attached to the English Laws and Constitution, and know too well their happy Tendency to diffuse Freedom, Prosperity and Peace wherever they prevail, to desire an independent Empire."[145] Congress had not yet detached the will of the people from the rights of Englishmen. But the rhetorical deployment of the will of the people as a mobilizing frame for the revolution subsequently took on a life of its own and resulted in a series of unanticipated, from the perspective of the elites, changes in American society and politics as "many soldiers and urban workers came to believe that they had a right to participate in both the economy and politics on equal level with their former gentry superiors."[146]

Four months after *Common Sense* first appeared, the Continental Congress considered a resolution recommending that those colonies that had not yet reconstructed their institutions now proceed to "adopt such government as shall, in the opinion of the representatives of the people, best conduce to the happiness and safety of their constituents in particular and America in general." Believing that this resolution required a preface explaining its purpose, Congress appointed a committee of three members (John Adams of Massachusetts, Richard Henry Lee of Virginia, and Edward Rutledge of South Carolina) to compose a text. When the committee reported three days later, on May 13, 1776, the preface they presented could have been written by Paine himself (it was, in fact, written by Adams):

[I]t is necessary that the exercise of every kind of authority under the said crown should be totally suppressed, and all the powers of government exerted, under the authority of the people of the colonies, for the preservation of internal peace, virtue, and good order, as well as for the defence of their lives, liberties, and properties, against the hostile invasions and cruel depredations of their enemies; therefore, resolved, &c.

---

[144] Maier, *American Scripture*, pp. 31–4, 90–2, 95.
[145] Ford (ed.), *Journal of the Continental Congress*, vol. 4, pp. 134–46, emphasis in the original. The delegates tabled this draft.
[146] Van Cleve, *We Have Not a Government*, pp. 19, 26–8.

Adams considered this preface, along with the resolution, to be the practical equivalent of "a total, absolute Independence," but he conceded that a formal declaration was still necessary. One reason why it fell short was that the delegates were still not of one mind. Although they approved the preface after two days of debate, they were bitterly divided: Six or seven colonies voted for it, four opposed, and the rest either abstained or did not vote. However compromised by dissent, the sweeping renunciation of crown authority and the detailed list of charges brought against the king were a major step toward a complete break with the mother country. While the break with parliament was old news, the slender thread binding the colonies to the crown was now rending.[147]

Things were now moving rapidly. On June 7, Adams and Richard Henry Lee moved the adoption of resolutions that would completely sever relations with Britain:

That these United Colonies are, and of right ought to be, free and independent States, that they are absolved from all allegiance to the British Crown, and that all political connection between them and the State of Great Britain is, and ought to be, totally dissolved.

That it is expedient forthwith to take the most effectual measures for forming foreign Alliances.

That a plan of confederation be prepared and transmitted to the respective Colonies for their consideration and approbation.

While these resolutions were not taken up immediately, four days later, on June 11, Congress appointed a committee of five (Adams, Thomas Jefferson, Benjamin Franklin, Robert Livingston of New York, and Roger Sherman of Connecticut) to prepare a draft of a declaration of independence.[148] While that draft was in preparation, Congress received, on June 25, a "[d]eclaration of the deputies of Pennsylvania ... expressing their willingness to concur in a vote of Congress, declaring the United Colonies Free and Independent States." A similar declaration was received from New Jersey three days later.[149] When the committee reported back on June 28, that draft was tabled because several provincial delegations were still bound by instructions that prohibited them from voting for independence. On July 1, Congress took up the draft declaration but delayed its deliberations until the next day for the same reason. By July 2, New York was the only delegation that could not vote for independence.[150]

---

[147] Maier, *American Scripture*, pp. 37–8, 82, 252 n. 72.

[148] Jefferson's appointment to this committee would not have been unusual even if he was not recognized as a wordsmith. During one period of six months spanning 1775 and 1776, he served on thirty-four committees in the Continental Congress, more than one every week. Maier, *American Scripture*, p. 103. It is simply amazing how such a small group of founders, including Franklin, Jefferson, John Adams, James Madison, and John Jay, carried on so much of the work during the revolutionary crisis. Adams and Franklin, for example, also served with Jefferson on this committee.

[149] Ford (ed.), *Journal of the Continental Congress*, vol. 5, pp. 478, 490.

[150] Maier, *American Scripture*, pp. 41–5.

Congress now began to revise the committee's draft declaration in earnest. As the lead author, Jefferson had drawn on the preamble he had previously written for the new Virginia constitution, cribbing from the English Declaration of Rights of 1689. When revised by the Virginia Convention and subsequently ratified on June 29, the preamble declared that all ties between the province and Great Britain were now "totally dissolved" because of the crown's "several Acts of Misrule." Between April and July 1776, there were many such pronouncements that could be considered "declarations" of independence, more than ninety of them by Pauline Maier's count. Like previous addresses, letters, and resolutions addressed to the people of England and other parts of the empire, members of the Continental Congress, the provinces, and local governments, these intentionally mimicked English antecedents.

Some of that mimicry was the product of their common political, cultural, and legal heritage in which concepts and phrases came to mind simply because they had become customary forms of thought for the colonists. Someone like Jefferson could distinguish between those forms and the meaning that they conveyed when deployed in a text, but, for most colonists, these forms of thought were in and of themselves a legitimation of argument and action.[151]

This conformity to English constitutional custom and tradition constrained the revolutionary elites as they coaxed their people into the transition to independent nationhood. For one thing, these elites had to demonstrate that all remedial alternatives under the English Constitution had been tried and failed before they could contend that the colonies had no choice but to break with the mother country. This intentional continuity with English constitutional tradition up to and during the drive to independence profoundly shaped much of the Declaration of Independence and the United States Constitution but did so in quite different ways.

The Declaration of Independence both fully embraced English constitutional tradition and formally severed all connection between the colonies and Great Britain. Thanks to Pauline Maier and many other historians, we know a great deal about how these two seemingly contradictory purposes were reconciled in the writing of the Declaration. After Jefferson had completed his draft, the other four committee members revised the text and presented their product to the entire Congress.[152] The delegates then labored over the text, significantly changing some of the parts but leaving much of it more or less the same as the committee had proposed. As finally ratified on July 4, 1776, the Declaration of

---

[151] Maier, *American Scripture*, pp. 48–58, 75, 89–90, 126.

[152] On the relative contributions of the other committee members in revising Jefferson's draft, see Maier, *American Scripture*, pp. 98, 101, 150. In general, Maier carefully balances her praise of Jefferson's creativity and inspiration with an insistence on the collaborative contributions of other delegates, both in the committee and in Congress as a whole. However, she also notes that in 1826 Jefferson proposed an epitaph for his tomb that, in part, read: "Author of the Declaration of American Independence" (p. 186).

Independence contained two distinct sections that addressed very different purposes and audiences. The opening paragraphs read, in part:

When in the Course of human Events, it becomes necessary for one People to dissolve the Political Bands which have connected them with another, and to assume among the Powers of the Earth, the separate and equal Station to which the Laws of Nature and of Nature's God entitle them, a decent Respect to the Opinions of Mankind requires that they should declare the causes which impel them to the Separation.

We hold these Truths to be self-evident, that all Men are created equal, that they are endowed by their Creator with certain unalienable Rights, that among these are Life, Liberty, and the Pursuit of Happiness – That to secure these Rights, Governments are instituted among Men, deriving their just Powers from the Consent of the Governed, that whenever any Form of Government becomes destructive of these Ends, it is the Right of the People to alter or to abolish it, and to institute new Government, laying its Foundation on such Principles, and organizing its Powers in such Form as to them shall seem most likely to effect their Safety and Happiness.[153]

On the one hand, this ringing affirmation of the eternal and universal rights of mankind clearly justified the sacrifice of life and limb that war would require.[154] And, as an affirmation of the goals worth fighting for, these passages also implied that British troops were fighting for the suppression of those rights. On the other hand, the "sentiments Jefferson so eloquently expressed were ... absolutely conventional among Americans of his time." As principles of politics, they were well ensconced in eighteenth-century Whig tradition. In a letter to Madison written in 1823, almost half a century after the fact, Jefferson recalled that he "did not consider it part of my charge to invent new ideas" and that he

---

[153] Some of these passages had clear antecedents in earlier proclamations. For example, the "Declaration and Resolves of the First Continental Congress," October 14, 1774, had declared

[t]hat the inhabitants of the English Colonies in North America, by the immutable laws of nature ... have the following Rights:

1. That they are entitled to life, liberty, and property, and they have never ceded to any sovereign power whatever, a right to dispose of either without their consent.

The "Virginia Bill of Rights" issued on June 12, less than a month before the Declaration of Independence, had similarly affirmed

[t]hat all men are by nature equally free and independent, and have certain inherent rights, of which when they enter into a state of society, they cannot by compact deprive or divest their posterity; namely, the enjoyment of life and liberty, with the means of acquiring and possessing property, and pursuing and obtaining happiness and safety. (Adams, *First American Constitutions*, pp. 170–1)

[154] As Morgan notes, "self-evident propositions are not debatable" because challenges "would rend the fabric of our society." Morgan, *Inventing the People*, p. 14. But challenges to these passages would later emerge as Americans came to recognize the ever more complicated and often unanticipated implications of Jefferson's rhetorical flourishes. At the time of its adoption, however, the Declaration of Independence was a formality whose language was little more than a placemark for the act itself.

did not know whether he had drawn the ideas he had put to paper from reading or reflection. He knew "only that I turned to neither book nor pamphlet while writing it."[155]

At the end of the second paragraph appear two sentences that were intended to provide a transition to the other, and much longer, section of the Declaration:

The History of the present King of Great-Britain is a History of repeated Injuries and Usurpations, all having in direct Object the Establishment of an absolute Tyranny over these States. To prove this, let Facts be submitted to a candid World.

What follows is a very long list of grievances the colonists had lodged against the king.[156] Most of these grievances would not have made much sense to the "candid World" because they were, in fact, violations of the traditional rights of Englishmen. As such, they were, in the first instance, thoroughly ensconced in a political culture that only those who breathed the air of that culture would have understood; and, in the second and more narrow instance, they were an interpretation of those rights from the colonial perspective. Thus, the Declaration asserted that the king

has forbidden his Governors to pass Laws of immediate and pressing Importance, unless suspended in their Operation till his Assent should be obtained; and when so suspended, he has utterly neglected to attend to them.

Outside of the English-speaking community, this grievance would not have made much sense because it described what seemed to be a royal prerogative that almost all monarchs naturally possessed.[157] To those who lived in Britain,

---

[155] Maier, *American Scripture*, pp. 95–6, 124, 135.

[156] Reid persuasively contends that any "reasonable" reader of the entire text will readily recognize that the Declaration "accused the king of Great Britain of violating only the legal and constitutional rights of American colonists. It did not, in a single instance, accuse George III of violating a natural right ... Natural law simply was not a significant part of the American whig constitutional case." Reid, *Constitutional History*, p. 14. From that perspective, the Declaration of Independence should be interpreted as a transitional document, evidencing the incomplete abandonment of English political identity.

[157] The conventional position was much closer to that set down by Lord Granville, president of the Privy Council. The following is from a letter written by Benjamin Franklin to the proprietors of Pennsylvania on August 20, 1757, in which he relayed Lord Granville's position:

You Americans have wrong Ideas of the Nature of your Constitution ... you contend that the King's Instructions to his Governors are not Laws, and think yourselves at Liberty to disregard them at your own Discretion. But, those Instructions [cannot be treated by the colonists] as not binding, and no Law ... they are first drawn up by grave and wise Men learned in the Laws and Constitutions of the Nation; they are then brought to the Council Board, where they are solemnly weigh'd and maturely consider'd, and after receiving such Amendments as are found proper and necessary, they are agreed upon and establish'd. The Council is over all the Colonies ... The King and Council is THE LEGISLATOR of the Colonies; and when his Majesty's Instructions come there, they are the LAW OF THE LAND; they are, said his L[ordshi]p, repeating it, the Law of the Land, as such ought to be OBEYED. (Greene, *Constitutional Origins*, p. 32)

this passage would have made sense but would have been rejected because the colonists were implicitly asserting that their assemblies bore the same relation to the king that parliament bore to the crown in Britain. If that were so, then the king, in refusing to act upon duly passed legislation in a timely manner, would have been violating the rights of the popular assembly, which, in turn, was the protector of the rights of Englishmen. But the British asserted that parliament, not the several colonial assemblies, was the protector and interpreter of colonial rights.[158] The colonial assemblies were merely a political and administrative convenience that facilitated imperial governance. That position, staunchly defended by the British authorities, left the colonists standing alone in presenting to "a candid World" a grievance that was probably inconsequential to most of the globe and utterly denied by the one audience that mattered most. However, to the colonial audience this particular grievance and the other grievances were utterly and transparently important.[159] In fact, many of the grievances in the Declaration of Independence had already appeared, in one form or another, in state and local pronouncements and resolutions.[160]

The Declaration of Independence was many things. Most importantly, the document justified the revolution in terms that the colonial audience would both understand and accept by providing a summary statement of grievances against the crown. From that angle, most of the document simply restated British violations of colonial rights and framed those violations in the language of the rights of Englishmen. Independence was thus portrayed as an eminently conservative response that had been forced upon the colonies. Even so, this was a rather peculiar format in which to justify the founding of a new state. These violations of the rights of Englishmen could easily justify rebellion as a means of redressing wrongs but there was still a qualitative leap between rebellion and independence. When the colonists asserted that crown violations of their rights justified the severance of ties with the mother country, they then had to explain how the rights of Englishmen would be conceived and ensured once they were no longer tied to that country. While the founders attempted, more or less

---

[158] British radicals, however, accepted the spirit motivating the Declaration of Independence. John Wilkes, for example, praised the document. Maier, *American Scripture*, p. 162.

[159] Maier stresses that the long list of grievances was "essential to the Declarations' central purpose, not subordinate to an assumed premise" precisely because only irrefutable "charges against the King" would "warrant the dissolution of his authority over the American people." She later adds that most modern scholarship devotes "little serious attention to the charges against the king" because they seem to "lay in the obscure quarrels of provincial politics." Maier, *American Scripture*, pp. 105, 123. When we focus attention on the opening paragraphs with their resounding assertion of "unalienable Rights," we risk overlooking, first, the importance of the transition from the rights of Englishmen to the rights of man and, second, that the latter actually meant, in context, the rights of Americans, which were very much the legitimate descendants of the rights of Englishmen. We might also add that those now famous opening passages became notorious precisely because the founding that they helped to enable subsequently became very powerful in the modern world.

[160] For a summary of these documents, see Maier, *American Scripture*, pp. 89–90.

successfully, to portray independence as a recovery of hallowed tradition and custom, not as a radical step into the unknown, that unknown still lurked in everything they did.

As a partial response, the Declaration went beyond a mere statement of irresolvable differences with the mother country in the opening paragraphs and stated how Americans conceived of the traditional and customary formulation of the rights of Englishmen now that they were on their own. This reconception was ostensibly set upon a new foundation for those rights in the form of "self-evident ... Truths." But these truths were, in fact, self-evident precisely because the colonists were so thoroughly accustomed to English political principles that they could not conceive of a political system founded on anything else. This conservative reformulation profoundly limited an otherwise new and quite visionary proclamation of the transcendent social purpose to which the American independence was dedicated: "life, liberty, and the pursuit of happiness" (a phrase deeply rooted in the English political tradition). Despite their thorough embedment in English political tradition, these were now proclaimed to be the legitimating purposes of any state (including those that were neither American nor English).

Although most of the text was dedicated to a recitation of violations of the rights of Englishmen, what we remember most today is the more abstract opening paragraphs that progressively supplanted the backward-looking elements in pre-revolutionary thinking with a more distinctively republican conception of political and social life. In the process, these opening paragraphs helped create the new national identity that was simultaneously arising out of the ever deepening material commitments in blood and treasure that the long war demanded.[161]

The Declaration of Independence is thus a composite document containing internal contradictions arising from its position on the cusp of the transition in colonial identity. Far from attempting to create a new theory of politics, the delegates who labored over Jefferson's draft considered the Declaration to be an instrumental text, one of many that they and the colonies crafted at the time. Like those other documents, the text had to be legible to the audience that was addressed but it was not intended to be a creative work of political philosophy that broke new theoretical ground or presented new justifications for the break with Britain.[162] However, the open-ended language and resounding rhetoric of

---

[161] We should also note that, while the British refusal to recognize their rights as Englishmen was the primary cause of the disaffection of colonists of English descent, those who were not of English stock had other, sometimes very different, reasons for breaking with Britain. For many of them, support for American independence arose out of an ethnically rooted antipathy to British culture and international ambitions. As Wright put it, "Germans and Scots-Irish, Dutch and French ... had no natural reason to venerate the British connection." Eighteen of the fifty-six men who signed the Declaration of Independence were, in fact, "not of English descent." Wright, "American Independence," p. 516.

[162] Maier, *American Scripture*, pp. xvii–xviii.

these opening paragraphs were also intended to create the patriotic emotions that would justify the sacrifices that the struggle would require and were thus crafted in a way that would facilitate their oral recitation to public audiences, including the troops in the field. In this respect, they could appeal to a sympathetic global audience as well. That global audience, however, was not their primary target.

One of the instrumental purposes of the Declaration was served by the simple announcement that the thirteen colonies had broken all political ties with imperial Britain. That public statement coordinated resistance to imperial rule by confirming that each of the colonies individually and all of them collectively were now committed to independence. Each and every colony had "signed on" to the same project and had done so in a way that all the world, including people residing in the several colonies, could see. In some respects, this announcement was merely a formality because the colonies had already been at war with the mother country for over a year.[163] But the bare fact that each of the delegations to the Continental Congress had given their consent to a common text strengthened and facilitated their cooperation by mutually committing themselves to a new frame for their existence.

The Declaration also announced to other nations that the colonies had now irretrievably broken with the British; it thus increased the likelihood of foreign, particularly French, assistance by formally creating a new nation with which those nations might negotiate.[164] The possibility of those

---

[163] Reid, among many others, dates the beginning of the war for independence with the outbreak of military action at Lexington and Concord on April 19, 1775. But that, of course, was over a year before the colonies actually declared independence. Reid, *Constitutional History*, p. 86. Reconciliation with the mother country, however, was still considered possible even as war became an acknowledged political fact. For example, on August 26, 1775, Rhode Island issued instructions to its delegates "[t]hat this Colony most ardently wishes to see the former friendship, harmony and intercourse between Britain and these Colonies restored," but went on to say that "this colony will most heartily exert the whole power of government in conjunction with the other colonies for carrying on this just and necessary war ... in the most vigorous manner, until peace, liberty and safety are restored." Ford (ed.), *Journal of the Continental Congress*, vol. 3, p. 274. While waiting for reconciliation, the Congress proceeded to create the necessary institutions for conducting war. See, for example, the November 28, 1775, congressional consideration of "The Rules for the Regulation of the Navy of the United Colonies" (pp. 378–84). When "Articles of War" were adopted on September 20, 1776, they were "modeled upon those of Great Britain." Ford, "Prefatory Note" in *Journal of the Continental Congress*, vol. 4, pp. 9, 788–807. In effect, the Continental Army was conducting much of its operations under regulations copied from the very army that it was fighting.

[164] As Maier points out, "the Declaration was nothing less than a public confession of treason" and it was understood that the "outcome of the war ... would decide whether they would be remembered as the founders of a nation or be hanged by the British as traitors." While the British certainly could collect sufficient evidence to pursue such convictions without a public signature, the founders were making it flagrantly obvious that they were crossing a bridge of no return and thus strengthening, from the French perspective, the credibility of their personal and collective commitments to independence. These public commitments would have been similarly

negotiations was further enhanced because the Declaration also raised the (already high) personal stakes for the American leaders. While much of what they had done up to then could be and often was regarded as treason against the crown, there was no question that they crossed a Rubicon in signing the Declaration of Independence.[165] Foreign nations would no longer worry that their aid (and its attendant costs in terms of British hostility) would be squandered if the Americans somehow changed their mind and sought rapprochement with the mother country. Changing their mind was now impossible.[166] What the text actually said was not very important for the purposes of coordinating colonial cooperation or attracting foreign aid.[167] In fact, we might even surmise that Louis XVI might have been offended if he had actually studied the document.

monitored by other colonists. On all these purposes, see Maier, *American Scripture*, pp. 44, 130–1, 152–3. The Continental Congress had already initiated contact with the French in December 1775, and the French had proven receptive. Four months before the Declaration, Congress sent an emissary to Europe in order to purchase war materiel from the French and, on April 6, 1776, had opened all the colonial ports to trade with all nations except Britain. At the time, there were no British troops stationed in the colonies who could prevent that declaration from taking effect. Jones, "American Independence," p. 487; Ford (ed.), *Journal of the Continental Congress*, vol. 4, pp. 257–9. This same act ordered "[t]hat no slaves be imported into any of the thirteen United Colonies." By that time, Congress had also authorized the capture of British vessels (November 25, 1775), sanctioned privateering (March 19, 1776), and begun to issue letters of marque and reprisal (March 23, 1776).

[165] On June 12, 1775, just five days before the battle on Breed's Hill and Bunker Hill, General Gage declared that all colonists who had taken up arms, along with all those who aided them, were traitors, but he offered a pardon to those who returned to allegiance to the crown. However, Gage excluded Samuel Adams and John Hancock from that offer. This was over a year before the Declaration of Independence.

[166] The French offered remarkably generous terms to the Americans when an alliance was formally ratified in 1778. Spain, on the other hand, refused to recognize or support American independence even as it joined the French in declaring war on the British. For their part, the Russians did not consider the colonies important enough to warrant diplomatic recognition but did indirectly aid the American war effort by defying the British blockade of France and Spain. In the end, it was the intervention of the French navy, along with financial aid, that "proved decisive" in the war. Goodwin, "Introductory Survey," p. 13.

[167] When the Declaration of Independence was written, each of these purposes was transitory or time-bound in the sense that they applied to very specific political and social contexts that would change very rapidly. The Declaration was thus a mere "fact" that, although noted as marking a transition in politics, was otherwise not particularly important. It was only some fifty years later that "the document assumed a function altogether different from that of 1776: It became not a justification of revolution, but a moral standard by which the day-to-day politics and practices of a nation could be judged." When that transformation occurred, the long list of grievances lodged against the king became almost invisible because Jefferson's opening paragraphs were far more and spectacularly relevant. Maier, *American Scripture*, pp. xvii–xviii, pp. 154, 160. Even so, it is truly remarkable that the text of the Declaration of Independence with its sweeping assertion that "all Men are created equal" has never had formal standing in an American court of law (p. 192).

SECTION II: FROM THE DECLARATION OF INDEPENDENCE TO THE CONSTITUTION

After the Continental Congress had proclaimed that the colonies were now independent, colonists tore down all "portable signs of royalty" in many major towns and cities. Representations of the crown and displays of the king's name on commercial establishments and government buildings were destroyed in public demonstrations that cleansed the colonies of the trappings and symbols of imperial authority and power.[168] While the colonists thus made it very clear what they were rejecting, it was not at all clear what they wanted to erect in its place. The war delayed that decision.

THE ARTICLES OF CONFEDERATION

On November 15, 1777, the Continental Congress proposed the Articles of Confederation to the states. By then, the war with the British was in full swing.[169] The Articles were thus primarily intended to formally grant Congress the authority to mobilize men and materiel.[170] However, ratification required the unanimous consent of all thirteen states and three (Delaware,

---

[168] Maier, *American Scripture*, p. 157. Almost exactly fifteen years later, the French were to do the same thing after the king tried to escape from Paris. In both instances, these mass demonstrations emphatically confirmed the end of monarchy.

[169] Jones, in fact, describes General John Burgoyne's surrender of some 5,700 British troops at Saratoga on October 17, 1777, as "the war's turning point" because it convinced the French that active support of American independence might actually succeed. Jones, "American Independence," p. 495. The notion of a "turning point," however, can be conceived from either the perspective of the participants at the time (when it must have seemed almost imperceptible and highly contingent on subsequent events) or from the hindsight of later observers (such as historians), for whom it serves to organize a narrative that otherwise might appear messy. In any event, after Burgoyne's surrender, Lord North attempted to head off an American–French alliance by offering the constitutional settlement that the colonies had previously been seeking. However, once the decision had been made to seek independence, the revolutionary elite could not step back and make it a negotiating position because men had died and, if they were to continue to be willing to die (a necessary condition for enforcing a constitutional settlement with the British), they had to be motivated by something more than "terms of agreement" (pp. 497–8).

[170] About a third of all free males of military age served in either the Continental Army or one of the state militias. Of these 200,000 men, somewhere between 10 and 20 percent died in battle, from disease, or in British prisons. In addition, the British burned the cities and towns of Norfolk (Virginia), New London, Groton, and Fairfield (Connecticut), and Portland (then Falmouth) in Maine. The British also seized some 1,100 American vessels. The South generally suffered more than the North. Rhode Island and South Carolina were particularly hard hit while Pennsylvania and the inland reaches of Virginia were mostly spared. Van Cleve, *We Have Not a Government*, pp. 19–22.

Maryland, and New Jersey) withheld their approval for several years.[171] In fact, it was not until March 1, 1781, that Congress could announce that the Articles of Confederation had been accepted by all the states.[172] This was, as it turned out, less than eight months before Cornwallis surrendered at Yorktown. Congress thus conducted almost all of the war effort through ad hoc administrative arrangements and exhortations.

Although Article I stipulated that "[t]he style of this Confederacy shall be, 'The United States of America,'" Article II immediately provided that "[e]ach state retains its sovereignty, freedom and independence, and every power, jurisdiction and right which is not by this Confederation expressly delegated to the United States in Congress assembled." This and other provisions meant that the Articles more or less assumed the form of a treaty between independent states, and continued membership in the Confederation was always conditioned on the self-interested calculations of the several states. These self-interested calculations were strongly reinforced by the method through which the states selected their delegates. With the exception of Connecticut and Rhode Island (which chose their members by popular vote), delegates were selected by their state legislatures, which in turn jealously monitored their actions and at times instructed them on the positions they were to take. In addition, the delegates could be recalled at any time by the states and no delegate could serve for more than three years in any six-year period. The term limit on the president of the chamber was even more strict: at most only "one year in any term of three years." Each state had to send a delegation of no fewer than two members and no more than seven. These delegations would caucus separately and determine among themselves how to cast the one vote awarded to each state. All important matters required the consent of at least nine states; this meant, among other things, that abstentions could prevent enactment even if eight states unanimously favored passage. A state's failure to send a delegation to Congress had the same effect as abstention.

Although the Continental Congress and the revolutionary army gave both symbolic and substantive form to a collective unity that transcended the

---

[171] Michael J. Klarman, *Framers' Coup: The Making of the United States Constitution* (New York: Oxford University Press, 2016), p. 14.

[172] Beloff, "American Independence," pp. 466–7. The major reason that ratification took so long was that those states that did not have claims (arising out of royal charters) to land extending across the American continent wanted that land ceded to the Continental Congress, where it would become part of a jointly administered public domain. It is worth noting that those states that held land claims arising out of their royal charters were contending that those charters were legally valid even after they had revolted against royal rule. In the end, the ceding of western land claims gave a material heft to the Continental Congress that it would not have otherwise had, because leaving the Confederation meant abandoning any participation in the disposal of these lands. Wright, "American Independence," pp. 530–1. When Virginia gave up its claim to westerns lands on January 2, 1781, ceding them to Congress, Maryland (the last holdout) signed the Articles on February 27.

individual states, it was the individual states to which Americans were primarily loyal and from which they drew their identities.[173] Prior to 1775, for example, colonial assemblies had claimed the authority both to raise and to spend revenue. Under the Articles of Confederation, some of the authority to spend money was granted to Congress but the states retained exclusive power to raise revenue. The bifurcation arose because it was British violation of colonial rights over taxation that had originally motivated the people to resist. For that reason, the locus of sovereignty had to remain with colonial assemblies and nothing was more important to that locus than the power to tax.[174] The fact that the locus of sovereignty was lodged with the colonial assemblies meant that it was there that the will of the people operated as well.

In general, these concessions to the sovereignty of the colonial assemblies were the most important flaw in the design of the Confederation.[175] However, sheer necessity meant that mobilization of an effective military effort required a central authority (the Continental Congress) to combine and coordinate the material capacities of the individual colonies. Therein lay the reason that Congress had to have the authority to spend. But the disjunction between the

---

[173] Klarman, *Framers' Coup*, pp. 14, 725–6n. The clearest exception to this orientation toward the individual states was the Continental Army that Congress consistently treated as a national institution. This solicitude, which continued even after the war had been won, was probably a precondition for the subsequent creation of a national political identity because it was the most important concrete symbol that could be associated with the existence of an American nation. But military policy also illustrated that Congress was much more nationalistic than the states that its delegates represented. Van Cleve, *We Have Not a Government*, pp. 57–61. Also see Stephen Conway, *The War of American Independence, 1775–1783* (London: Edward Arnold, 1995), p. 175.

[174] It was in that vein that David Howell, a delegate from Rhode Island, wrote on February 5, 1784: "The pretensions of the particular States to Sovereignty after they have parted with the control of their purses will be no less ridiculous than the claim of the man in the Fable to enjoy the Shadow after he had sold his Ass, alleging that although he had parted with his Ass, he had not parted with his Shadow." Van Cleve, *We Have Not a Government*, pp. 85–6. However, Van Cleve, in another place, states that "[s]lave states' political influence also led to a permanent Confederation stalemate on issues of taxation and representation." Van Cleve, *Slaveholders' Union*, p. 57. Also see, Robin L. Einhorn, *American Taxation, American Slavery* (Chicago: University of Chicago Press, 2006).

[175] On the institutional flaws that frustrated elite efforts to make a nation out of the Articles of Confederation, see Van Cleve, *We Have Not a Government*, pp. 51–4, 74–101, 324 n. 27. See pp. 61–9 for a summary review and interpretation of Confederation difficulties in collecting requisitions from the individual states, including: (1) the reluctance of states that depended on ports in other states for imports to pay as much as the those other states because they were already contributing revenue to the latter through duties; (2) the sectional imbalance in the holding of Confederation debt, with southern states generally holding much less than northern states and with the result that the former were much more reluctant to redeem the debt; and (3) the inability of western land sales to make a substantial contribution to the redemption of Confederation debt. For Madison's description of the "Vices of the Political System of the United States" under the Articles, see Hendrickson, *Peace Pact*, pp. 212–19.

motivation to resist the British and the material requirements of the war effort opened a huge chasm between revolutionary theory and pragmatic possibility.

By appealing to the broader sensitivities of the people, Congress played the leading role in attempting to transit from the several independent states to a new national ("consolidated," in the vernacular of the time) government. The constant appeals to a moral responsibility to pay the debts incurred during the war and the invocation of a shared fate that transcended individual states kept the possibility of a national government before the people even when the prospects for constructing such a government were widely acknowledged to be slim.[176] The failure of these efforts emphatically demonstrated that a flawed institutional structure could frustrate even the most otherwise capable elites from constructing a national political culture.[177] In a letter to Washington written on April 9, 1783, Robert Livingston, then the secretary of foreign affairs for the Confederation, expressed doubts that Americans would comply with the terms they had agreed to in the treaty of peace with the British because "national faith, and national honor are considered things of little moment" by "the mass of the people" and their state legislatures. "Faith" and "honor" were characteristics assigned to individual political identity and the absence of personal identification with the Confederation, revealed in this failure to abide by the treaty, demonstrated that the locus of political sovereignty resided with the states, not with their ostensible union.[178]

During the American Revolution, the colonies were united by their opposition to the British and their shared vulnerability if they were to lose the war. But, once the war was won, the new states that emerged with the Treaty of Paris rediscovered their diversity, a diversity that made political cohesion extremely problematic.[179] On July 8, 1783, almost two years after Cornwallis had surrendered at Yorktown and a little less than two months before a formal treaty of peace was signed with the British, George Washington privately denounced the lack of respect given to the Continental Congress: "For Heavens sake who are Congress? Are they not the Creatures of the People, amenable to them for their conduct, and dependent from day to day on their breath? Where then can be the danger of giving them such Powers as are adequate to the great ends of government?"[180] Two years later, Washington was still pounding on this theme:

---

[176] For examples of such appeals, see Van Cleve, *We Have Not a Government*, pp. 50–1.

[177] Van Cleve, for example, concludes that the institutional form of the Confederation was simply not viable under any circumstances, including administration by very talented leaders, and that fact underpinned his view that it was not and could never be a sovereign state. Van Cleve, *We Have Not a Government*, pp. 284–5.

[178] Van Cleve, *We Have Not a Government*, p. 53.

[179] On the economic, social, ethnic, and religious heterogeneity of the colonies, see Wright, "American Independence," pp. 513–16; Van Cleve, *We Have Not a Government*, p. 319, n. 66.

[180] Morgan, *Inventing the People*, p. 265n.

[I]t is one of the most extraordinary things in nature that we should confederate for national purposes, and yet be afraid to give the rulers [in Congress] who are the creatures of our own making, appointed for a limited and short duration, who are amenable for every action, recallable at any moment, and subject to all the evils they may be instrumental in producing – sufficient powers to order and direct the affairs of [the] nation.

In 1786, Washington was still thumping on that drum when he wrote to John Jay: "To be fearful of vesting Congress, constituted as that body is, with ample authorities for national purposes, appears to me the very climax of popular absurdity and madness."[181]

But the problem primarily lay with the Articles of Confederation as a governing framework, not with the Congress. Congress was very weak because the Articles had made it so, and, although Congress proposed amendments that would have given it some of the necessary trappings of a national government, one or more of the individual states always withheld their approval.[182] The most contentious of those amendments involved the raising of revenue, which, under the Articles, was to be provided by the states when Congress requested money. Because Congress could neither compel the states to honor the requisitions their delegates had agreed to pay nor possessed its own sources of revenue, Congress was always short of money, and, near the end of its life, it chronically teetered on the edge of bankruptcy. In January 1783, for example, Robert Morris, the superintendent of finance for the Confederation, was compelled to write checks drawing on funds that he knew the government did not have. Worried that the troops might revolt if he did not pay them, he secretly requested permission from a congressional committee. Writing checks with no funds to cover them presumed a public sovereignty (in the form of creditworthiness) that the Confederation simply did not possess. Hence the secrecy. On the other hand, that Morris was willing to risk his reputation in this operation does demonstrate that, for him, keeping up the appearance of the Confederation as a sovereign entity was worth that risk.[183] Even so, the longer that the Articles of Confederation remained the only bond between the individual states, the stronger the loyalties and identities of most Americans to the latter became.[184]

Most of the political elite thought that the Articles of Confederation were deeply flawed in ways that threatened the independence of the several states. Perhaps the most serious flaw was the unanimity requirement for changes in its

---

[181] Klarman, *Framers' Coup*, p. 43; also see Van Cleve, *We Have Not a Government*, p. 121.

[182] On attempts to amend the Articles of Confederation, see Klarman, *Framers' Coup*, pp. 24–41.

[183] Van Cleve describes the "Confederation's last years [as] a marvelous peacetime experiment in republicanism ... marked by deep divisions about whether and how two fluid, potentially conflicting ideas – empire and republicanism – should be embodied in any new central government." Van Cleve, *We Have Not a Government*, pp. 2, 18–19. This was, in practice, a contest between an elite interpretation of what a viable state required and the will of the people as the transcendent social purpose of a government.

[184] On the financial insolvency of the Confederation, see Van Cleve, *We Have Not a Government*, pp. 18–19, 54.

provisions; this made addressing the other flaws through amendment of the Articles more or less impossible. Even within the ambit of its very weak constitutional authority, Congress could not enact legislation unless a supermajority of nine of the thirteen states approved the measure. The sheer impotence of Congress aggravated this problem because the individual states often found it difficult to encourage its delegates to attend the proceedings. In addition, many of the delegates were not paid enough to maintain adequate living arrangements in a distant city (usually New York or Philadelphia), cities that were also hard to get to.[185] Advancement in a political career was thus more promising in one of the individual states than it was in a largely powerless debating forum that also necessitated personal sacrifice and inconvenience. One of the net results was that Congress was often left without a quorum to conduct business. And that fact further strengthened the harm inflicted by the supermajority requirement for approving legislation.

The delegates themselves, even when they chose to attend congressional sessions, were strongly controlled by the individual state legislatures, most of which appointed them, imposed very short terms in office, could recall delegates at will, and set their salaries. In fact, after the war was won, delegates were even more like ambassadors representing independent nations than they were representatives of the people. Turnover in Congress would have been high in any case, but the Articles made rotation mandatory and even those delegates who would have otherwise dedicated themselves to strengthening the institution could serve only half of the time under the best of conditions.

There were other serious problems arising out of the inability of Congress to impose legislation and authority on recalcitrant states. While Congress, for example, had the power to negotiate treaties, it lacked authority to compel the individual states to abide by their terms.[186] Even the terms of the Treaty of Paris, which formally ended hostilities with Great Britain in 1783, could not be enforced by Congress. Willfully defying those provisions that required Americans to repay debts to British citizens and make restitution for property confiscated from loyalists during the war, the individual states practically vitiated much of the treaty. Congress was thus placed in the almost impossible position of attempting to coax the British into honoring provisions that benefited the Confederation while trying to explain why its own obligations under the treaty could not be fulfilled.[187] In retaliation for the American failure to

---

[185] The parochialism of the early American elite was, in fact, quite remarkable. George Mason, a Virginia delegate to the Constitutional Convention, played a prominent part in the proceedings. However, when he traveled to Philadelphia, his journey "took him farther from home than he had ever gone before." Maier, *Ratification*, p. 41.

[186] For example, New York negotiated a treaty with the Iroquois, flagrantly violating the Articles of Confederation that made the Confederation Congress the sole authority over treaty-making. Maier, *Ratification*, p. 13.

[187] Klarman, *Framers' Coup*, pp. 43–6, 129–30; Van Cleve, *We Have Not a Government*, pp. 4–5, 69–72, 281–2. For a somewhat different perspective, see Wright, "American Independence,"

honor their obligations, the British refused to abandon the forts they occupied in the western territories, a refusal that became a standing affront to the international respectability and status of the Confederation.[188]

The Confederation had no administrative structure for carrying out the terms of the treaty with respect to the property claims of British subjects and loyalist Americans because the states controlled the courts in which these claims would be adjudicated. As a result, the claims could not be enforced if the states and their juries would not comply. And even if the claims could have been enforced, we still might ask whether the central government would have adhered to the terms of the treaty. Although such a prediction is hazardous, the answer would probably be "yes." And the explanation would be that the advantageous parts of the treaty (e.g., territory and navigation rights) would have been in the same hands as the disadvantageous parts. The consequences for non-compliance would have been clear. On the other hand, once one small state refused to comply with the treaty, the other states had no incentive to conform with its provisions, particularly when public opinion was hostile to compliance in any case. While this was a collective action problem, it was certainly aggravated by the fact that the Confederation could "receive" the benefits of compliance as a unitary actor but could not "deliver" on its obligations in the same way.[189]

One of the most serious flaws in the Articles of Confederation arose out of its impact on the legislative process in Congress. During the war, the Continental Congress had given up navigation rights on the Mississippi in return for Spain's recognition of American independence. In 1781, Spain had opened up the river to American traffic but again closed the Mississippi in July 1784. Under intense

---

pp. 531–2. Wright, for example, considers the Northwest Ordinance, the legislation passed by the Continental Congress that organized governance in the western territories north of the Ohio River, as "fully as important as the [ratification of the United States] Constitution." Also see Peter S. Onuf, *Statehood and Union: A History of the Northwest Ordinance* (Notre Dame, IN: University of Notre Dame Press, 2019), pp. xiii–xx. The Northwest Ordinance was adopted by the Continental Congress on July 13, 1787, after several delegates who were members of both the Congress and the Constitutional Convention traveled north from Philadelphia to New York in order to establish a quorum for its passage. This and other evidence has led some scholars to suggest that passage of the ordinance was part of a "grand bargain" in which northerners consented to the three-fifths clause for representation in the Constitution in return for a prohibition of slavery in the Northwest Territories. See, for example, Van Cleve, *Slaveholders' Union*, pp. 154–65; Klarman, *Framers' Coup*, p. 296. Even if that were not the case, passage of the Northwest Ordinance by Congress in New York while the Constitutional Convention was meeting in Philadelphia may have anticipated the new constitution by removing one of the likely impediments to adoption because the often nasty dispute over the western territories had bitterly divided the states for some time. Beeman believes that there was no agreement. Richard Beeman, *Plain, Honest Men: The Making of the American Constitution* (New York: Random House, 2009), pp. 216–18.

[188] Van Cleve, *We Have Not a Government*, p. 249.

[189] For a synopsis of the peace treaty and the failure of the Confederation to enforce American obligations, see Van Cleve, *We Have Not a Government*, p. 34.

pressure from the southern states to reopen navigation, Congress attempted to negotiate with Spain. In these negotiations, Spain offered a lucrative trade agreement conferring access to Spanish markets for American fish and flour, which were prominent New England exports, but refused to reopen the Mississippi. This package deeply divided the Congress. On the one hand, the South wanted navigation rights on the Mississippi because commerce via the river was vital to the western settlement of Kentucky and Tennessee, which were western extensions of Virginia and North Carolina, respectively. On the other, the northeastern states were mired in a deep recession and the trade agreement was very tempting. Sectional conflict over both the negotiation and the adoption of the proposed treaty was so intense that both the North and the South threatened to quit the Confederation over the treaty.

Unlike most domestic policies, authority to negotiate this treaty was solidly lodged with the Continental Congress, but, because of its weakness in other areas, Congress was unable to effectively broker the conflicting interests of the southern and northern states. There is also some evidence that Spain was well aware of the problem and may have been negotiating in bad faith in order to stir up trouble within the American Confederation.[190] While the conflict over navigation rights was never resolved under the Articles, the process highlighted several defects in the legislative process.

The most important of these was the fact that little or nothing bound the several states to the Confederation. Whenever conflict became intense, one or more states could threaten to secede. As in this instance, such threats were more credible when they arose out of sectional interests because a geographically contiguous alternative federation would be more viable in the international arena than one that was composed of isolated states. In addition, legislative conflict was aggravated by the fact that serious issues were taken up serially with little connection to one another. Problems in which Congress might effectively act came up in isolation from one another and the delegates could not thus compromise between them by creating "bargains" entailing side payments. In addition, the supermajority rules, combined with high turnover and absenteeism, made serious policy conflicts extremely difficult to resolve. Threats, not bargaining, became the primary way in which delegates legislated their differences.[191]

The rejection of attempts to amend the Articles of Confederation encouraged the more ardent nationalists to begin to consider extralegal proposals for altering the terms of union between the individual states.[192] The most active of these nationalists was James Madison, who persuaded the Virginia

---

[190] For legislative conflict over the proposed treaty with Spain, see Van Cleve, *We Have Not a Government*, pp. 6, 161–85.

[191] Klarman, *Framers' Coup*, pp. 48–69.

[192] For unsuccessful attempts to rectify these and other problems, see Klarman, *Framers' Coup*, pp. 46–7, 102.

legislature in January 1786 to call for a joint meeting of the states "to consider how far a uniform system in their commercial regulations may be necessary to their common interest and their permanent harmony." When it met, this convention would craft an amendment to the Articles that would then be considered under the regular process (first by Congress and then by the states). When only nine states appointed commissioners to the convention, the prospects for effective action appeared dim. They grew even dimmer when commissioners from only five of the nine (two of these sent only "unofficial observers") actually arrived in Annapolis. On September 11, the commissioners began to deliberate but, recognizing that the small attendance would fatally impair their efforts, they instead called, on September 14, for another convention "to devise such further provisions as shall appear to them [the delegates to this second convention] necessary to render the constitution of the federal government adequate to the exigencies of the union." This convention was to meet on the second Monday of May the next year. This call was formally directed only to the states represented in Annapolis (Delaware, New Jersey, New York, Pennsylvania, and Virginia) but, ostensibly out of courtesy, letters were also sent to the eight states that had not attended and also to Congress.[193]

Almost half of the members of Congress in 1786 were new to the chamber and attendance was poor; Rufus King of Massachusetts grumbled that nine states were present on only three days from October 1785 until April the following year. From November 1786, after the Annapolis Convention met, until August 1787, just before the Philadelphia Convention finished its deliberations, four or more state delegations were absent on all but three days. These absences made the institution almost entirely moribund.[194]

On February 21, 1787, the Continental Congress, operating under the Articles of Confederation, adopted a resolution stating:

> [I]n the opinion of Congress it is expedient that on the second Monday in May next a convention of delegates who shall have been appointed by the several states be held at Philadelphia for the sole and express purpose of revising the Articles of Confederation and reporting to Congress and the several legislatures such alterations and provisions therein as shall when agreed to in Congress and confirmed by the States render the federal Constitution adequate to the exigencies of Government ["Confederacy" in the original] and the preservation of the Union.[195]

Between September 1786 and February 1787, Shays' Rebellion had changed the minds of many in Congress and in the individual states so that they came, however reluctantly, to support the proposed convention.[196] Even so, the

---

[193] Klarman, *Framers' Coup*, pp. 103–10; Van Cleve, *We Have Not a Government*, pp. 124–9.

[194] Maier, *Ratification*, p. 13; Van Cleve, *We Have Not a Government*, p. 251; Bilder, *Madison's Hand*, p. 32.

[195] Roscoe R. Hill (ed.), *Journal of the Continental Congress*, vol. 32, p. 74.

[196] For a short biography of Daniel Shays, see Dumas Malone (ed.), *Dictionary of American Biography* (New York: Charles Scribner's Sons, 1943), vol. 17, pp. 49–50. Shays had served

committee appointed to consider the advisability of the convention only narrowly (by one vote) recommended that Congress transmit the call to the states. After Congress limited the proposed convention to a revision of the Articles and an amendment process that would follow the regular order, eight of the nine states then in attendance approved the call.

Before Congress acted, only seven states had indicated that they would send delegates to Philadelphia. With congressional endorsement, five more appointed delegations. Only Rhode Island, by rather large majorities in its legislature, refused to participate. On March 28, after much cajoling and many entreaties by friends and advisers, George Washington agreed to go to Philadelphia as the head of the Virginia delegation. His consent came after ten states had already responded to the call (Connecticut and Maryland were very close to responding as well).[197]

Van Cleve describes Congress' endorsement of the Philadelphia Convention as a "definitive 'no confidence' vote" on the Articles of Confederation. The Continental Congress was deciding to go out of the business of governance solely because it considered itself unfit to enact public policies that would ensure effective governance.[198] The Annapolis Convention had also sidestepped Congress, which was, under the Articles, the only institution that could propose reform. The curiosity is how the founders could, at the same time, both appeal to political legitimacy in the sense of personally carrying out the (however filtered) will of the people and also, at least by clear implication, recognize that that same will had created a political impossibility (i.e., the inability of the Congress to reform itself).

THE 1787 CONSTITUTIONAL CONVENTION

Unlike the promulgation of the Declaration of Independence, the writing and making of the United States Constitution were almost entirely bereft of inspiring emotion. It was fear that most drove the delegates who gathered in Philadelphia

---

with distinction in the revolutionary army and his loyalty to revolutionary principles was unquestionably sincere. However, his leadership of the rebellion in 1786–7 led the state of Massachusetts to condemn him to death. Later, recognizing his devotion to revolutionary principles, the state pardoned him and the federal government even gave him a pension for his military service during the revolution. The ambivalence on both sides of this rebellion amply demonstrates the ambiguity of principles and sovereignty during the transition from colony to state to federal government.

[197] Klarman, *Framers' Coup*, pp. 111–24. Washington was reluctant to serve as a delegate because, for one thing, his health was not good and, for another, his personal reputation might be damaged if the convention failed. However, he apparently had no other plan for strengthening the Confederation, something that he thought vitally necessary for preserving American independence. It was James Madison who ultimately convinced Washington to attend. Van Cleve, *We Have Not a Government*, pp. 240–2, 246, 266–70; Maier, *Ratification*, pp. 1–24; Beeman, *Plain, Honest Men*, pp. 30–3.

[198] Van Cleve, *We Have Not a Government*, p. 3.

to devote their energies and reputations to the making of a new constitution – fear and a calculated judgment that this was their last chance to make the new republic a viable political project. Internally, the delegates feared that popular challenges to the sanctity of private property would both seriously damage their own estates and livelihood and fatally undermine the general prosperity of the communities they represented. Externally, the predatory designs of foreign nations threatened the very survival of the individual states, particularly the smaller ones, if they were to continue to insist on their separate existence.[199] While they often referred to abstract notions of political representation, the location and quality of sovereignty, and the advantages of a separation of powers between institutions, much of "their ostensibly principled arguments simply served as rationalizations for the interests being advanced."[200] There was

---

[199] On the inability of the Confederation to negotiate trade treaties and credibly support an effective military capability, one that would persuade European powers that it could retaliate against aggression and also might make a useful ally, see Van Cleve, *We Have Not a Government*, pp. 102–24. On the strengthening of the international standing and viability of the United States following ratification of the Constitution, see Max M. Edling, *The Creation of the Constitution* (Washington, DC: American Historical Association, 2018), pp. 6–7, 23–9, 59–61; Max M. Edling, *A Revolution in Favor of Government: Origins of the US Constitution and the Making of the American State* (New York: Oxford University Press, 2003), pp. 47–59, 73–88. In the latter, Edling notes that the delegates recognized that the new central government required a military establishment supported by an effective revenue system, a recognition that arose from both their own experience and the general history of European states. In his most recent work, he concludes that the "Constitution mattered much more to the international than to the domestic history of the United States." Max M. Edling, *Perfecting the Union: National and State Authority in the US Constitution* (New York: Oxford University Press, 2021), p. 134.

[200] "To an astonishing degree, the drafting and ratification of the Constitution were shaped by conflicts of interest that derived from fairly transient episodes and disputes ... such conflicts would quickly recede in significance." Klarman, *Framers' Coup*, p. 604. Klarman concludes that "the Constitution was a conservative counterrevolution against what leading American statesmen regarded as the irresponsible economic measures enacted by a majority of state legislatures in the mid-1780s, which they diagnosed as a symptom of excessive democracy" (p. x; also see pp. 6, 600–6). Van Cleve similarly considers the Constitution to be "an intersectional elite power-sharing agreement, a 'grand bargain' that had profound long-term economic and political consequences." Rejecting both the view that the Constitution was a reaction to the profound political and economic crisis of the 1780s and the often related interpretation that the Constitution was a counter-revolutionary document, Van Cleve contends that

Confederation reform was riven most heavily by the perceived need to create a sovereign national government that could [a] preserve American independence, [b] protect western expansion, [c] combat foreign trade aggression, [d] provide unified continental government and law enforcement, and [e] maintain internal order. The Confederation lacked every one of those capabilities. Reform efforts were also motivated by [f] a desire to protect wealthy conservatives' property against popular economic redistribution demands, but such concerns played a subsidiary role. (Van Cleve, *We Have Not a Government*, pp. 7–11)

Van Cleve is, in fact, much closer to the "crisis" position than the "counter-revolutionary" perspective. But, more importantly, these are not necessarily competing interpretations, because the latter might have been a necessary condition for a response to the crisis. The crisis itself had

little romanticism in the proceedings and even less in the ratification conventions that followed.[201]

Experience with popular democracy at the individual state level after the war ended convinced many of the elite that an unfettered democracy could be – and, in many instances, would be – a threat to the viability of republican government.[202] The primary threat was to property and came in two forms: the printing of paper money, which produced rampant inflation, and, in connection with legal tender provisions, the impoverishment of creditors who had to accept that money in satisfaction of debts; and simple refusal to pay those debts at all, regardless of the form that money assumed.[203] The most serious and notorious episode in which popular democracy seemingly raised its unlovely head in this way was Shays' Rebellion, which began in August 1786 and was not finally put down until February the following year, less than four months before the Constitutional Convention convened.[204] For the delegates meeting in

to be interpreted from some perspective; although economic distress was certainly an objective fact, its consequences, such as radical claims on wealth, could be viewed only from a normative perspective. Put another way, there were many plausible responses to the crisis, each of which involved a commitment to a particular complex of normative principles. While Van Cleve wants to maintain that the motivation for a new constitution was a response to a political crisis and not to poor economic performance, the distinction between economics and politics does not seem tenable. However, he is correct when he maintains that the Constitution did not directly address the political causes of economic distress and, instead, grappled with the impact of that distress upon political stability. Also see Simon Gilhooley, "The Framers Themselves: Constitutional Authorship during the Ratification," *American Political Thought* 2 (2013), pp. 62–88.

[201] While the Fourth of July is the most important secular holiday celebrated in the United States, most Americans probably do not realize that there is a day set aside for the Constitution, in part because they must still go to work. But we should also note that the Fourth was celebrated for two decades before the Constitution was ratified and thus had a substantial head start. On celebrations of the Fourth of July between 1776 and 1787, see Len Travers, *Celebrating the Fourth: Independence Day and the Rites of Nationalism in the Early Republic* (Amherst: University of Massachusetts Press, 1999), pp. 15–69.

[202] Skepticism regarding the viability of republican government was, in fact, generally deep-seated among the political elite. In his "Notes of Debates in the Continental Congress," John Adams recorded a delegate from Georgia, John Zubly, as saying on October 12, 1775, that "[a] republican government is little better than government of devils." Ford (ed.), *Journal of the Continental Congress*, vol. 3, p. 491.

[203] On the different types of paper money issued by the states and the Confederation and their depreciation, see, for example, Van Cleve, *We Have Not a Government*, pp. 22–3, 189–213, 345–6 n. 3, 347 n. 20; on the root causes of the popular demand for paper money, see pp. 37, 46.

[204] Klarman, for example, states that "Shays's Rebellion … had a profound impact on the Philadelphia convention and its handiwork" and "played a critical role in the creation of the Constitution." Klarman, *Framers' Coup*, pp. 5, 92, 163–4, 604–5. For a detailed description and account of the insurgency, see Leonard L. Richards, *Shays's Rebellion: The American Revolution's Final Battle* (Philadelphia: University of Pennsylvania Press, 2002). Also see Van Cleve, *We Have Not a Government*, pp. 214–29. When Abigail Adams roundly condemned the rebellion, Thomas Jefferson replied that periodic rebellions were nothing more than a "storm in

Philadelphia, the most pressing priorities were to somehow prevent the individual states from threatening the private rights of property while, at the same time, filtering the will of the people so that popular democracy would not threaten those rights in the new national government.[205] On the one hand, the individual states could otherwise be as democratically inclined as they wished, but the national government would not permit them to threaten private property. On the other hand, the design of the national government, while also, like the states, ostensibly resting on the will of the people, would constrain their will in such a way that threats to those rights would never rise to that level.[206]

Despite its instrumental purposes, the making of the Constitution nonetheless melded a transcendent social purpose, the will of the people, and the founding of a new state.[207] As the delegates deliberated over the several Articles and their attendant provisions, they anticipated a ratification process in which the people would approve their work, thus placing the imprimatur on the document that would confer sovereignty on the new republic.[208] On the one hand, they recognized that there already existed a political culture in

the Atmosphere" and were usually a good thing (p. 236). In a letter written to Samuel Kercheval in 1816, Jefferson later railed against those who "look at constitutions with sanctimonious reverence, and deem them like the ark of the covenant, too sacred to be touched." Hannah Arendt, *On Revolution* (New York: Penguin Books, 2006), p. 225.

[205] For a summary of the reasons that delegates overwhelmingly rejected direct, popular election of a president, see Klarman, *Framers' Coup*, p. 228. On the hostility of the delegates toward popular democracy (which Klarman summarizes as: "Behind the closed doors of the Philadelphia convention, the delegates outdid one another in the contempt they expressed for democracy"), see pp. 243–50. In the midst of the ratification process that followed, Benjamin Rush wrote in a private letter that only a "vigorous and efficient government can prevent" the people from "degenerating into savages or devouring each other like beasts of prey" (p. 347). But, of course, the founders could not tell the people that they were "savages" or "beasts." They had, instead, to be distracted by the promise of a democracy that then unobtrusively redirected their attention and energy.

[206] Klarman, *Framers' Coup*, p. 101.

[207] By "instrumental purposes" I am referring to the complex composed of the self-interest of the delegates, their understanding of the interests of the states they represented, motivations arising out of a general wish to ward off predation by foreign powers, and a desire for political and social stability. For a strong interpretation of "economic interest" as the primary motivation in the crafting of the Constitution, see Robert Maguire, *To Form a More Perfect Union: A New Economic Interpretation of the United States Constitution* (New York: Oxford University Press, 2003), pp. 5, 211.

[208] Although placing the Constitution before popularly elected conventions instead of the state legislatures was not particularly contentious, Madison still gave the matter careful thought. In a letter to Jefferson written before he went to Philadelphia, Madison stated that popular conventions would be "expedient" because they would "lay the foundation of the new system ... by the people themselves." At the Constitutional Convention, Madison also contended that such a process would compel recognition that legislation enacted by the new Congress would be "legally paramount to the acts of the states" and would distinguish the new Constitution from "a league or treaty." If the people themselves ratified the Constitution, they would constitute "a union of people." Klarman *Framers' Coup*, pp. 415–16.

which conceptions of the popular will, among other things, would set a standard against which their work would be judged and accepted (or rejected). These conceptions of the popular will thus acted through their anticipations and interpretation of that culture. However, they also expected that the Constitution, if ratified, would itself reshape that political culture in ways that would, they hoped, make the new republic self-sustaining by engendering patriotic emotions that were almost non-existent when the new state was created.[209]

From that perspective, the delegates wagered that their efforts to reshape popular culture would not fatally undermine ratification. The Constitution thus had to work on several levels at once, as responses to: a popular culture that, while impulsive and intense, had a very abbreviated time horizon in which long-term consequences (particularly on changes in their own political attitudes) were largely unimportant; the erection of a political framework that would work both in practice (i.e., create institutions and institutional relationships that would enable effective governance) and in reshaping popular culture (i.e., engendering properly affective attitudes); intense disagreements over particular issues (such as the allocation of representation in Congress among the several states and the regulation of commerce and trade); and, not least of all, the threats of foreign intervention from abroad and popular insurgency at home.[210] These various considerations gave rise to deliberations in which changes in one part of the working draft often affected their attitudes toward other parts, including sections that they had already considered settled. The result was a frequently circular process in which some sections were taken up and approved, then taken up again and changed.

Because the delegates belonged to the political elite, many of them had previous experience in making a constitution for the states they now represented in the convention.[211] They thus fully realized that constitution-making was both a practical and theoretical project and that their disagreements reflected not only the conflicting interests to which they responded but also the unavoidable uncertainty that any of the provisions, let alone the framework as a whole, would ever work in the way they had planned. Realism, fear, and pragmatic imagination strongly discouraged sentimentality in their deliberations. In fact, had it not been for "some important strategic blunders by their

---

[209] As Klarman notes, a "self-conscious sense of nationalism among Americans" had arisen earlier but "only as a result of organizing their shared opposition to British policies." Klarman, *Framers' Coup*, p. 13. On the emergence of nationalism, see Benjamin E. Park, *American Nationalisms: Imagining Union in the Age of Revolutions, 1783–1833* (New York: Cambridge University Press, 2018), pp. 1–112.

[210] All of these dimensions were also involved in ratification debates. Bailyn, *Ideological Origins*, p. 351.

[211] The states elected or appointed seventy-four delegates but only fifty-five actually went to Philadelphia. The average attendance at the sessions was about thirty. Beloff, "American Independence," pp. 470–1.

adversaries" during the process of ratification, the Constitution they had made would have been stillborn.[212]

This exercise in constitution-making did have precedents. The most apt was set in 1779 when Massachusetts elected delegates to a constitutional convention, perhaps the first such convention that had been held anywhere in the world.[213] Massachusetts established an important principle by placing the people in direct communication with the creation of the new state and convening, for that purpose, an assembly that was superior to a mere legislature (which was, of course, operating under the aegis of the existing constitution).[214] Popularly elected constitutional conventions possessed an authority unconstrained by any other institution precisely because (1) the will of the people was supreme and (2) any constraint on its expression would distort what the people willed. The only exception, not always followed in subsequent practice, was that the people should ratify the work of the convention before the new state began to operate. The delegates to a constitutional convention, even if popularly elected and faithful to their task, were still imperfect interpreters and transmitters of the will of the people. So the people themselves had to judge the fruit of their labors. By spring 1787, however, only Massachusetts and New Hampshire had made and ratified a new constitution in this way. All the other colonies made the transition from colony to state in a theoretically compromised fashion with respect to the primacy of the popular will.

These state constitutions occupy an odd position in the American founding in that, on the one hand, their creation was encouraged by the Continental Congress, which was not itself a sovereign institution, and, on the other hand, they were ultimately superseded by the 1787 Constitution, a document that could have required their subordination to the new national government but, by intention and design, did not demand much revision. It should also be noted that these individual constitutions were, for a time, the carriers of the "transcendent social purpose of the state" in that, while the Declaration of Independence outlined that purpose, the Continental Congress had no way of

---

[212] Klarman, *Framers' Coup*, p. 8.

[213] Morgan, *Inventing the People*, p. 258. Also see Mary Handlin and Oscar Handlin (eds.), *The Popular Sources of Political Authority: Documents on the Massachusetts Constitution of 1780* (Cambridge, MA: Belknap Press of Harvard University Press, 1966); Beloff, "American Independence," p. 464. Beloff describes these early efforts at constitution-making as the emergence of a "typically American method" involving a convention, popular ratification (usually through a referendum), and, once implemented, judicial review and enforcement. In all of these respects, the focus of attention was on a written document that could be displayed and presented to the people. The contrast with the unwritten English Constitution, which could not be summarily described, let alone reduced to a formal text, could not have been more stark. Also see Wood, *Creation of the American Republic*, pp. 306–19.

[214] The notion of a "constitutional convention" was itself a product of this ideal form, a conclave in which the state was created out of whole cloth without preconceived notions of custom, tradition, or cultural prejudices. In practice, of course, it was the very opposite but the mythical status of constitutional conventions still served and continues to serve that purpose.

pursuing it because "life, liberty, and the pursuit of happiness" were almost entirely within the jurisdiction of the individual states.[215]

As a vehicle for expressing the will of the people, the 1787 Constitutional Convention in Philadelphia was also compromised in at least six ways: (1) The convention was in fact organized under false pretenses, so that the people, however they might be conceived, did not realize that they were authorizing the construction of a new constitution; (2) the delegates to the convention were designated by the individual state legislatures, as opposed to the people themselves in direct elections; (3) the proceedings in Philadelphia were secret, so the people did not know what was afoot and thus could not monitor the delegates even if they had known that a new constitution was in the making; (4) the goal of the convention was to rectify flaws in the union but many of those flaws arose from the desires and wishes of the people themselves; (5) while the United States Constitution was intended to encompass the entire American community, the delegates required that the consent of the people be given in thirteen conventions, one in each of the states, thereby fragmenting what was, theoretically, supposed to be an unmediated consultation with the people as a national community; and (6) the ratification procedure contemplated (and ultimately resulted in) a take-it-or-leave-it process in which the people, when finally consulted, could not amend the document in ways that might have reflected their collective will.[216]

These six compromises can be boiled down to a tension between, on the one hand, the founders' beliefs and instincts with respect to attributes that a stable, republican government must possess and, on the other, what they anticipated the people of the several states would accept as legitimate.[217] For some of the delegates – among them James Madison, who had more influence over the framing of the Constitution than anyone else in Philadelphia – this tension was between the creation of a theoretically coherent design that would last through the ages and pandering to the momentary interests and passions of public

---

[215] For an overview of the contents of these constitutions, see Beloff, "American Independence," pp. 464–5.

[216] See, for example, Morgan, *Inventing the People*, p. 267.

[217] A few delegates strenuously objected to the crafting of an entirely new constitution because the Continental Congress had authorized the convention only "for the sole and express purpose of revising the Articles." In fact, two of the twelve state delegations in attendance (Rhode Island never attended) were explicitly bound to abide by this limitation. When the delegates finally voted to proceed with the crafting of a new compact, they clearly understood that they were not formally authorized to do so and that, had they formally requested authorization, that authorization would not have been granted. Klarman, *Framers' Coup*, pp. 141–4. The result, as Jameson persuasively contends, was the implicit creation of a precedent under which constitutional conventions could not be bound by the legislatures that created them. John Alexander Jameson, *The Constitutional Convention: Its History, Powers, and Modes of Proceeding* (New York and Chicago: S. C. Griggs, 1867), pp. 293, 355–6, 358.

opinion.[218] Pierce Butler of South Carolina, for example, tended toward the latter when he contended that his colleagues should "follow the example of Solon, who gave the Athenians not the best government he could devise, but the best they would receive" (by which he meant accept).[219]

The delegates repeatedly sought to resolve this tension through deflection, subterfuge, appeals to self-interest, fear of foreign intervention, and obfuscation.[220] But, despite their best efforts, that tension nevertheless profoundly structured the ratification process in which the people had their turn at constitution-making. To be sure, the Constitution was not imposed on the people, because those participating in the ratification conventions were fully aware that they could approve the text with qualifications in the form of amendments and those amendments could have radically transformed the document. Those amendments even, conceivably, could have taken the form of an entirely new text. But the process strongly discouraged such creativity because, for one thing, each of the states held their conventions at different times and coordination between them was difficult. Even more problematically, the states often differed on the kinds of changes they would have liked to see made in the Philadelphia draft.

Many of the delegates who met in Philadelphia had served in the Continental Congress and the legislatures of the several states and were thus familiar with legislatures and legislative procedure.[221] They were aware that, in the event that the Philadelphia Convention failed to produce revisions in the Articles, the Confederation, however inadequate its performance, would have still existed. Both practically and theoretically, they thus recognized that the Philadelphia Convention was deeply enmeshed in a political environment composed of quasi-independent states and an ostensibly national congress. When the

---

[218] While Robertson regards Madison the pivotal actor in the Constitutional Convention, he also notes that Madison often, sometimes at critical junctures, failed to sway the other delegates. Nonetheless, his major goals, bound up in what Robertson terms a "Broad Nationalism," still managed to form the backbone of the Constitution and thus determined the course of subsequent American political development. David Robertson, *The Original Compromise: What the Constitution's Framers Were Really Thinking* (New York: Oxford University Press, 2013).

[219] Klarman, *Framers' Coup*, pp. 131, 166. For points in the convention deliberations in which delegates cited the impact of a decision upon the prospects for ratification, see pp. 171, 173, 177–9, 188, 207, 238, 243.

[220] On the compromises through which the delegates attempted to both respond to public opinion and create what they believed to be a durable governing framework, see Alfred F. Young, "Conservatives, the Constitution, and the 'Spirit of Accommodation'" in Robert A. Godwin and William A. Schambra (eds.), *How Democratic Is the Constitution?* (Washington, DC: American Enterprise Institute, 1980), pp. 117–18, 130–8.

[221] Forty-two of the fifty-five delegates had previously served in the Continental Congress. In addition, some of them had even served as speakers in their state legislatures. All had held public office of some sort and more than half of them were lawyers. Christopher Collier and James Lincoln Collier, *Decision in Philadelphia: The Constitutional Convention of 1787* (New York: Random House, 1986), p. 76.

Continental Congress stipulated that the Philadelphia "delegates ... shall have been appointed by the several States," this meant that the states would determine who would serve as members of the convention and that that determination would be made before the convention met. There would be no uncertainty as to who would be authorized as members of the convention. The delegates still had to settle on a presiding officer and the rules of procedure under which they would deliberate, but their easy familiarity with each other and the depth of experience they brought to bear in their proceedings made these decisions almost perfunctory. The Philadelphia Convention thus dealt with the opening dilemma with an aplomb that seemed to preclude its very possibility.

On May 14, 1787, the day designated for the opening of the Philadelphia Convention, only a few of the delegates from the several states appeared at the State House. Five days later, at least two delegates had arrived from each of four states: New York, Pennsylvania, South Carolina, and Virginia. Those who were in attendance continued to adjourn from day to day until, finally, on May 25, delegates from a majority of the thirteen states assembled at the State House and established a quorum. The convention then opened.

Mr. Robert Morris informed the members assembled that by the Instruction & in behalf, of the deputation of Pena. he proposed George Washington Esqr. late Commander in chief for president of the Convention. Mr. Jno. Rutledge seconded the motion; expressing his confidence that the choice would be unanimous, and observing that the presence of Genl Washington forbade any observations on the occasion which might otherwise be proper.

General [Washington] was accordingly unanimously elected by ballot, and conducted to the chair by Mr. R. Morris and Mr. Rutledge; from which in a very emphatic manner he thanked the Convention for the honor they had conferred on him.[222]

The opening move of the convention was thus the election of a leader and clearly displayed both the opening dilemma that the convention had to face and the way in which the delegates immediately dealt with it. With respect to the dilemma, Morris had no formal right to claim the attention of the other delegates when he first proposed that the convention proceed to the election of a presiding officer and then nominated Washington for the post.[223] In the absence of a presiding officer and procedural rules, there was no one who could recognize him for the purpose of offering these motions. However, there were equally clear sociological and political reasons why the other delegates accepted his initiative.[224]

---

[222] Max Farrand (ed.), *The Records of the Federal Convention of 1787*, revised edition (New Haven, CT: Yale University Press, 1966), vol. 1, p. 3. The account is taken from James Madison's notes on the proceedings. For an exhaustive analysis of Madison's notes, see Bilder, *Madison's Hand*.

[223] The official records state that Morris made two separate motions. Farrand (ed.), *Records of the Federal Convention*, vol. 1, p. 2.

[224] The orchestration of Washington's election was, of course, facilitated by the small number of delegates, each of whom could have been (and probably were) consulted before the event.

For one thing, Pennsylvania was the ostensible host of this convention and Morris was acting upon the authority of the Pennsylvania delegation. For another, Benjamin Franklin was the only other widely recognized possibility as a candidate for presiding officer.[225] Even if Franklin had been considered a competitive alternative (he was almost certainly not), he was from Pennsylvania and, therefore, somewhat of a favorite son of that delegation. By proposing Washington for the post, Morris was implicitly announcing that his election would be acceptable to Pennsylvania, the state most likely to object if any state objected.[226]

When Jonathan Rutledge of South Carolina seconded Washington's nomination, he was conforming to parliamentary practice that was probably universally familiar to the other delegates. That familiarity with a common parliamentary practice underlay an acceptance of motions and seconds that had, as of yet, no formal standing because rules embodying that practice had not yet been adopted by the convention. Put another way, the delegates had not yet formally agreed to conduct their deliberations in the way in which they usually had in their individual careers, but they found the concept of motions and seconds so agreeable that most of them probably did not notice that they were irregular.

More problematic, at least potentially, was the balloting during the election itself. The delegates apparently voted by states, a majority of the delegates from each state determining how that state's vote would be cast. Since that voting method was also used in the Continental Congress under whose auspices the Philadelphia Convention was called, that probably seemed to the delegates the normal course to follow.[227] However, this method weighted each of the states equally, giving small states such as Delaware a vote equal to large states such as Pennsylvania. And, in preparations for the convention, the Pennsylvania delegation had suggested to their Virginia counterparts that, from the very

---

[225] Washington himself facilitated his election in several ways. When he arrived in Philadelphia for the convention, his first move was to make a social call on Franklin. Washington also lodged as a guest at the Morris home during the summer of 1787 while the convention deliberated. One of the reasons was that their spouses were very good friends, but another factor in Washington's decision "was that Washington's longtime mulatto manservant, Billy Lee, could be at his beck and call" because Morris could provide lodging for the latter in his servants' quarters. Beeman, *Plain, Honest Men*, p. 35.

[226] In fact, Franklin himself had intended to nominate Washington but rain and an attack of gout kept him at home that day. Charles L. Mee, Jr., *The Genius of the People* (New York: Harper & Row, 1987), p. 79; Max Farrand, *The Framing of the Constitution of the United States* (New Haven, CT: Yale University Press, 1913), p. 55. Also see Madison's notes in Farrand (ed.), *Records of the Federal Convention*, vol. 1, p. 4. Bilder describes Washington's selection as presiding officer as "obviously choreographed" but also suggests that Franklin's absence may have reflected disappointment that his home state favored Washington. Bilder, *Madison's Hand*, p. 54. For an interpretation of Franklin's complex participation in colonial Pennsylvania politics, see Pole, *Political Representation*, pp. 251, 254–8, 262, 267, 277.

[227] Mee, *Genius of the People*, p. 78.

beginning of the convention, the votes should be allocated to the several states in proportion to their size.[228] If this were not done, the Pennsylvania delegates contended, the small states would be in a position to block a change in the voting rules later on.[229] So an objection to the voting method was at least conceivable and, if it had been lodged, formally irresolvable. However, in the event, no one challenged the allocation of one vote to each state.[230]

Immediately following Washington's election, the convention selected a secretary. After that was done, the delegates presented their credentials evidencing their appointment by their several states. In effect, the delegates reciprocally approved each other's membership in the convention by offering no objection to these presentations. If someone had so objected, there would have been, of course, no formal method for resolving the dispute because there were no rules governing the determination of eligibility. However, most if not all delegates considered the membership of the convention to have been set before they even gathered in Philadelphia. For one thing, the resolution passed by the Continental Congress calling for the convention had indicated that the states were to appoint the delegates. Even though the resolution was practically non-enforceable, it did create an expectation as to the process through which delegates were to be selected.[231] In the absence of any countervailing impulse,

[228] In writing to Washington before the convention met, Madison contended that northern states would support proportional representation in the new Congress because they now contained more people than the South, while southern states would also support proportional representation because they expected to grow faster than the North. Neither these calculations (which were based on the allocation of regional power) nor the wish to reduce the prominence of the states in the new republic was grounded in a theoretical justification arising out of what should be the proper weighting of the will of the people. Van Cleve, *We Have Not a Government*, pp. 271–2.

[229] Virginia opposed the Pennsylvania suggestion for fear that the small states would simply walk out of the convention before it had begun to deliberate. Mee, *Genius of the People*, pp. 82–3; Farrand, *Framing of the Constitution*, p. 57.

[230] Because Washington was elected unanimously, either voting method (one vote per state or weighted votes) would have produced the same result. That fact, plus the prestige that Washington enjoyed at the convention, may have even further discouraged an objection. The unanimity of the delegates, in turn, rested on the fact that the entire nation venerated Washington and, in addition, that the delegates thought that he would facilitate their deliberations by sublimating his own opinions and desires for the sake of managing conflict. On the nation's veneration of Washington as a factor that facilitated ratification of the Constitution in the state conventions, see Klarman, *Framers' Coup*, p. 3. Jefferson wanted a term limit on the service of a president placed in the Constitution but thought that the founders had not included one because they had succumbed "to the unlimited confidence we all repost in the person to whom we all look as our president [i.e., Washington]. After him inferior characters may perhaps succeed and awaken us to the danger which his merit has led us into" (p. 368).

[231] The resolution passed by the Continental Congress was practically non-binding because the Constitutional Convention was the sole judge of the credentials of its members. For example, if two delegations had claimed to represent the same state, the Constitutional Convention would have had to decide which delegation was to serve and the Continental Congress would have had no way of overturning that decision. This was true, in fact, for all other matters that came

that expectation and the objective fact of individual state sovereignty over the matter served to make the reading of credentials uneventful.[232] This process recognized the very real sovereignty of the several states as an objective fact. To question the credentials of the delegates from one of the states would have been to compromise that state's sovereignty and, in all likelihood, would have led that state to withdraw from the convention.

The convention completed its organization by appointing a committee "to draw up rules to be observed as the standing Orders of the Convention" and then adjourned over the weekend. When the delegates met the following Monday, this committee reported a set of rules that were considered, amended, and then approved or rejected one by one.[233] Here, too, the convention could not have acted without bridging the opening dilemma in some way because they were operating outside any formal parliamentary procedure.[234] However, the question uppermost in the minds of most delegates (concerning the allocation of votes among the individual states) had already been settled with the ballot on Washington's nomination as president of the assembly.

At the onset of its deliberations, the Constitutional Convention more or less conformed to the instructions that it had been given by the Continental Congress. The delegates were duly appointed by the individual states and their credentials were approved by their colleagues. And the parliamentary rules of the Continental Congress more or less structured the proceedings in the

---

before the convention. The Continental Congress retained only the right to approve or disapprove the results of the convention – and even that was, in the actual event, problematic.

[232] Farrand (ed.), *Records of the Federal Convention*, vol. 1, p. 2.

[233] Farrand (ed.), *Records of the Federal Convention*, vol. 1, pp. 2, 4, 7–8, 10, 13, 15. The most important of the rules were those assigning one vote to each state delegation, setting a quorum at seven states, and making a simple majority of the states in attendance necessary for deciding a question (e.g., as few as four states might determine the fate of a motion if only seven were participating). Other important rules prohibited the recording of roll call votes but allowed that any prior decision be reconsidered after one day's notice had been given. Klarman, *Framers' Coup*, pp. 135–6. Like the Continental Congress, the Constitutional Convention barred the public from attending its sessions and ordered that "nothing spoken in the House be printed, or otherwise published, or communicated" to anyone outside its walls without permission. Bilder, *Madison's Hand*, p. 55.

[234] Under the Articles of Confederation, all important measures in the Continental Congress had to be approved by at least nine of the thirteen states in order to pass. This was practically equivalent to a two-thirds vote of the states. Farrand, *Framing of the Constitution*, p. 3. Thus the convention could have confronted, at this stage, a choice between that requirement or a more relaxed simple majority rule. Since the vote on that choice would have necessarily required the very decision that it was ostensibly making (i.e., what the criterion would be for passing a proposal), there would have existed a very real possibility that the convention could not have reached a decision. For example, a simple majority could have favored a simple majority rule while a determined minority might have held that the default rule was the provision laid down from the Articles of Confederation. In the absence of parliamentary rules, there would have been no way to determine which of these two alternatives should determine the outcome and, thus, the convention could not have decided what the voting rule would be.

convention, at least until the formal rules had been adopted.[235] But a very serious deviation from congressional instructions soon appeared. The Constitutional Convention had been instructed to confine its attentions to "the sole purpose of revising the Articles of Confederation and reporting to Congress and the several legislatures such alterations and provisions therein."[236] Almost immediately after they began deliberations, however, the delegates discarded the Articles of Confederation as so much waste paper and began to draw up plans for an entirely new government. And, as subsequently became the nature of founding legislative assemblies once they begin to deliberate, the delegates recognized no authority to whom they might have to answer as they did so. In this, too, they were both apparently radical and, from our modern perspective, more or less ordinary.

As the delegates began their deliberations, they believed that failure to design a foundation for their union would result in either foreign entanglements in which some of the states would lose their independence or the emergence of new federations as the union broke up.[237] If the latter were to occur, these new federations might very well transform what were now internal, domestic disputes into international military conflict. If the union still held together despite the failure of reform, many delegates believed that it would ultimately evolve into a monarchy with an American king. While some delegates regarded monarchy, at least a watered-down version of monarchy, an attractive model for designing a unitary executive, others, such as James Madison, felt that this

---

[235] The procedural rules under which the convention operated were, in fact, almost a carbon copy of those that governed the Continental Congress. In this and other ways, the Constitutional Convention resolved the opening dilemma in an emphatically ordinary fashion. Most constitutional conventions in the United States authorized by the individual states have proceeded in the same fashion in that they have begun with the election of a leader (presiding officer), then approved the credentials of the delegates, and, finally, adopted parliamentary rules.

[236] Several states had written in this purpose as a part of the credentials they provided their delegates, ostensibly constraining what they could do in the state's name once the convention began. Catherine Drinker Bowen, *Miracle at Philadelphia: The Story of the Constitutional Convention, May to September 1787* (New York: Bantam, 1968), pp. 23–4. And the point was not entirely lost on the delegates themselves. As James Madison reported in his minutes of the convention, "Genl Pinkney expressed a doubt whether the act of Congs recommending the Convention, or the Commissions of the Deputies to it, could authorise a discussion of a System founded on different principles from the federal Constitution ... Mr. Gerry seemed to entertain the same doubt." James Madison, *Notes of Debates in the Federal Convention of 1787 Reported by James Madison* (Athens, OH: Ohio University Press, 1966), p. 35. In fact, many delegates planned to replace the Articles with a more or less entirely new governing framework even before the convention formally convened. See, for example, Beeman, *Plain, Honest Men*, pp. 42–4, 54–6.

[237] At the end of deliberations in the Constitutional Convention, Benjamin Franklin declared that the new union that it was to create would "astonish our enemies, who are waiting with confidence to hear, that our councils are confounded like those of the builders of Babel, and that our States are on the point of separation, only to meet hereafter for the purpose of cutting one another's throats." Hendrickson, *Peace Pact*, p. 4.

would be "a much more objectionable form" of government than the republic they would like to strengthen.[238]

While the delegates started with a blank slate as they began to deliberate, the English Constitution, with its distinct institutions and working relationships, dominated much of their thinking on how their own institutions should be constructed and how they might operate once they were up and running. From that perspective, the president occupied the place of the British monarchy, the House of Representatives stood in the role of the House of Commons, and the Senate paralleled the House of Lords. Each of the now proposed American branches was, of course, a more "republican" version of its British counterpart. That was in keeping with the American founding as the instantiation of rule by the will of the people. But much of the debate in the Constitutional Convention centered on how to make those several branches as much like their British antecedents as possible without openly negating the transcendent social purpose of the revolution.[239] The presidency, for example, was modeled on a watered-down version of kingly prerogatives while the construction of the Senate was intended by many delegates to encourage an aristocratic detachment from popular passions and narrowly conceived interests. The House of Representatives, like the House of Commons, was always destined to be the most popular branch of the new government. That destiny was preordained by the expectation that direct, popular election of at least one national institution was necessary to establish a claim on the affection and loyalty of the American people.[240] Direct, popular election of the House of Representatives also allowed the delegates to strengthen the far more indirect arrangements for the selection of senators and the president. Because most states had also modeled their governance arrangements on those of the English Constitution, almost all the delegates had long practical experience of what the separation of powers among these institutions promised to produce in terms of political practice.

The attitudes of the delegates toward the British "model" ranged from admiration (and a corresponding willingness to copy some aspects) to wariness (and a suspicion that advocates of the British system were crypto-monarchists) and hostility (an open rejection of what would otherwise have been a British inheritance). Regardless, however, of the stance they assumed, all the delegates drew upon the British model as a source of evidence for their reflections upon

---

[238] Klarman, *Framers' Coup*, p. 127.

[239] Madison, for example, viewed the Senate "as a check on the democracy. It cannot therefore be made too strong" as a counterbalance to more popular institutions in the national and state governments." Klarman, *Framers' Coup*, p. 209. Rejecting the possibility that a president might be directly elected by the people, George Mason of Virginia contended that that would be like allowing "a blind man" to render a decision in "a trial of colors" (p. 607).

[240] Klarman, *Framers' Coup*, pp. 170–9. In an explicit emulation of the House of Commons, the House of Representatives was also given exclusive authority to originate appropriations (p. 681n).

what should be the American form of government.[241] For example, when Antifederalists later criticized the new Constitution because the separate branches shared many powers and were not, for that reason, competing centers of political authority, the Federalists responded that the British system was even more intertwined and that they had thus improved on what was already a good model.[242] Montesquieu greatly admired British institutions for their explicit commitments to different social bases (crown, aristocracy, and commoners), commitments that depended, in part, on an independence of authority and responsibility in governing relations.[243] The American Constitution recognized and realized the latter more clearly than had the British while wrestling with the problem of distinguishing and empowering competitive social bases in a much more homogeneous society.

One of the two major deviations from the English Constitution involved the partial sovereignty of the individual states; that only realistically acknowledged an irreducible political fact in that it would be the states, through the Continental Congress and ratifying conventions, that must ratify the new constitution. Federalism was a massive inheritance from colonial and revolutionary history and the delegates spent much of their time and energy in reconciling that inheritance with what they regarded as the minimal requirements of central state authority. Federalism, however, also presented serious problems for any theory of the will of the people. Under the Confederation, state delegations had jealously monitored national policies in order to somehow determine their "fair" share of the burden of governance; in practice, this preoccupation with the determination of a "fair" share tended to lodge the will of the people solidly within the states, reinforcing the weakness of the Confederation's claims to represent the people as a whole.

The Philadelphia Convention was well aware of this problem and this was one of the reasons why it swore the delegates to secrecy: The states could struggle over their "fair" shares of influence, rights, and responsibilities in the construction of the document while preserving the rather fig leaf presumption that their representatives were somehow in communication with the will of what would become the American people. If the delegates had deliberated in a truly democratic body, directly elected by and fully responsible to the people, they would have been unable to distance themselves from political self-interest

---

[241] Bilder, *Madison's Hand*, p. 102.

[242] The unicameral Congress empowered by the Articles of Confederation lacked both an executive and a judicial branch, let alone a legislative chamber whose members were directly elected by the people. In these and other respects, the institutions created by the Constitution reproduced the British model much more faithfully. For convenience, I use the term "Antifederalists" to designate those who strongly opposed ratification of the Constitution but recognize the limitations of the label noted by, among others, Maier, *Ratification*, pp. xiv–xv, pp. 93–4; Jackson Turner Main, *The Antifederalists: Critics of the Constitution, 1781–1788* (Chapel Hill: University of North Carolina Press, 1961), pp. xi–xiii.

[243] Klarman, *Framers' Coup*, p. 372.

as they calculated the long-term consequences of the institutional arrangements that entered into the constitutional framework. Even with the combination of stealth in the setting of the convention agenda, indirect election of the delegates, and secrecy in the proceedings, the political elite still found it difficult to overcome their conflicting commitments to their states, to their class, and to the future of the nation they were attempting to create. Matters would probably have been much worse if the convention had been more democratically organized and responsible.

The delegates spent much less time and energy on the design of the Supreme Court, the other major deviation from the English Constitution. Much of colonial claim-making during the pre-revolutionary crisis had taken the form of legal arguments as to what the unwritten English Constitution mandated and did not mandate in terms, for example, of parliamentary authority and kingly prerogatives. That claim-making had come to naught, in part because there was no adjudicating authority to which the colonies might refer their disputes with parliament and the crown. Both long experience with the law as a vindication of rights and authority and the realization that adjudication between the competing claims of institutions required an umpire of sorts led the delegates to create the Supreme Court, but what that body could and would do was largely left up in the air.[244]

Madison drew upon the British Declaratory Act of 1766 when designing his proposal that Congress be given veto authority over all laws passed by the individual states. That Declaratory Act had assigned to parliament "full

---

[244] During the ratification convention in Virginia, however, John Marshall, a delegate who would later become chief justice of the United States Supreme Court, clearly anticipated the emergence of judicial determination of constitutional validity – what we now call "judicial review." Maier, *Ratification*, p. 290. On convention deliberations over the scope and content of judicial authority, see Klarman, *Framers' Coup*, pp. 158–61, 164–9. The delegates left much of the detail about how the federal courts should be structured and what their jurisdiction might encompass up to the new, proposed Congress to decide. This delegation of design responsibility can theoretically be interpreted as appointing Congress, on the one hand, to manage of the detail of the Constitution (e.g., in light of what actual experience might dictate) or to determine more accurately what the will of the people might reveal (once the new Congress had been elected and for which the Philadelphia Convention was, at least as far as this issue was concerned, an inadequate substitute). Although these are not mutually exclusive possibilities, the delegates probably leaned toward the former because they were, at least in most respects, firmly committed to specifying in the Constitution exactly what they had in mind if they knew what that might be and if it were politically palatable. They were not shrinking violets when it came to claiming an ability either to recognize the requirements of political reality or to correctly interpret the will of the people. Madison offered an alternative but related perspective when he said, in reply to Elbridge Gerry of Massachusetts, that "if the opinions of the people were to be our guide, it would be difficult to say what course we ought to take" because no delegate "could say what the opinions of his constituents were at this time; much less could he say what they would think if possessed of the information and light possessed by the members here; and still less what would be their way of thinking 6 or 12 months hence" (p. 175). That position could justify the exercise of almost unlimited discretion.

power" to make laws "to bind the colonies and people of America ... in all cases whatsoever" and had been, of course, one of the most serious provocations during the colonial crisis leading up to the Declaration of Independence. Madison now drew upon the act as inspiration for empowering the new national government in its relation to the individual states in a form that, ironically, mimicked the prior relationship between the British parliament and the individual American colonies. He also "analogized" the national veto over laws passed by the individual states "to the British Privy Council's authority to block colonial legislation," a parallel more consistent with colonial interpretations of the states' constitutional relationship with Britain before independence.[245] Either way, however, the parallel with British governance arrangements must have struck his colleagues in the Constitutional Convention as, at best, politically awkward.

John Dickinson also called on British precedent when contending that those who composed the American Senate should be "distinguished for their rank in life and their weight of property, and bearing as strong a likeness to the British House of Lords as possible." Hamilton went even further down that road when he declared the House of Lords to be "a most noble institution" and insisted that senators should be given life tenure because "[n]othing but a permanent body can check the imprudence of democracy" and "induce the sacrifices of private affairs which an acceptance of public trust would require."[246] In fact, Hamilton thought that the judges, senators, and the chief executive of the new nation should all hold office for life – or for as long as they exhibited "good behavior" – because that was the practice in Britain.[247]

When the delegates considered whether or not a president should be given exclusive power to make executive appointments, they were haunted by the thought that that authority had, in Klarman's words, "enabled the Crown to corrupt Members of Parliament with the enticement of appointments to lucrative offices." This possibility so worried Pierce Butler of South Carolina that, citing instances in which members of the House of Commons had sought

---

[245] This congressional veto was part of the so-called "Virginia plan" that was offered at the beginning of deliberations. Klarman, *Framers' Coup*, pp. 139, 155, 666n. For a general survey of the Virginia plan and its influence on the framing of the Constitution, see Robertson, *Original Compromise*, pp. 57–72. One of the committees in the convention even proposed the creation of a "Privy Council" in the new government, composed of the chief officers of the two branches of Congress and the Supreme Court, along with the leaders of important executive departments. Bilder, *Madison's Hand*, pp. 144–5, also 77, 113; also see Van Cleve, *We Have Not a Government*, p. 274. On the king's authority to veto colonial legislation, see Greene, *Constitutional Origins*, pp. 28–9.

[246] Klarman, *Framers' Coup*, p. 210, also 607. Other delegates resisted these proposals to create "an elective version of the British House of Lords." Bilder, *Madison's Hand*, pp. 101, 103.

[247] Maier, *Ratification*, p. 37; Bilder, *Madison's Hand*, p. 93. Robertson contends that "[m]any of the delegates cited the English constitutional monarchy as the best government in the world," even though "they considered the British model unsuitable for American circumstances." Robertson, *Original Compromise*, p. 41.

election solely for the purpose of accepting lucrative appointments from the crown, he contended that members of the new Congress should be prohibited from taking up an executive appointment for at least one year after leaving the House or Senate. James Wilson, however, argued that the continental expanse of the new nation probably required "the vigor of monarchy," even though public opinion (Wilson referred to "manners" here) was "purely republican" and thus opposed to "a king." Dickinson also thought that a constitutional monarchy was "one of the best governments in the world" but also that the "spirit of the times – the state of our affairs – forbade the experiment."

Hamilton even contended, in Klarman's paraphrase, that "the British king was the only sound model for the American executive and that an executive vested with lifetime tenure or at least tenure during good behavior" would add "stability and permanency" to the new government.[248] At one point, Hamilton openly admitted that "in his private opinion he had no scruple in declaring, supported as he was by the opinions of so many of the wise & good, that the British Govt. was the best in the world: and that he doubted much whether any thing short of it would do in America." However, he also admitted that the time was not right for the convention to "join in the praise" of the English Constitution. In opposing these arguments, Edmund Randolph denied that the delegates should take "the British government as our prototype" when he supported the idea that the presidency should be occupied by more than one person to avoid that branch from becoming "the fetus of monarchy."

In defending an executive veto on legislation passed by the new Congress, Gouverneur Morris offered his own comparison with the British monarchy, contending that, as matters then stood in their deliberations, the delegates had constructed an office in which "[t]he interest of our executive is so inconsiderable and so transitory, and his means of defending it so feeble, that there is the justest ground to fear his want of firmness in resisting encroachments" by legislators.[249] In that debate, James Wilson warned his colleagues against their apparent "prejudices against the executive," prejudices arising out of their past experience with the British monarchy.[250] The problem in all these instances

---

[248] Klarman, *Framers' Coup*, pp. 214–16, 244.

[249] Later, as the convention was winding up its work, a committee was appointed "to revise the stile of and arrange the articles which had been agreed to by the House." The five members of this committee included both Hamilton and Morris, with the latter responsible for much of the revision. Among other things, the committee decided that "the executive power shall be vested in a President of the United States." The language in this passage has been interpreted quite expansively over the years. Since Morris (and Hamilton) were strong advocates of a powerful presidency, it has been suggested that this provision was intentionally crafted with that very end in mind. Charles C. Thach, Jr., *The Creation of the Presidency, 1775–1789: A Study in Constitutional History* (Baltimore: Johns Hopkins Press, 1969), pp. 138–9.

[250] Klarman, *Framers' Coup*, pp. 214n, 215–16, 219–21, 224, 228–9, 688–9n; Nelson, *Royalist Revolution*, p. 191. Wood contends that Hamilton and other Federalists who favored a strong executive "were not monarchists" even though the British monarchy was often the model that

could be boiled down to two dilemmas: on the one hand, most of the delegates wanted the chief executive to have enough authority to become a decisive leader in the new nation but feared that such an office would evolve into a monarchy. On the other hand, they believed that popular resentment of King George as an oppressor of colonial rights hampered the construction of an office in which effective leadership would be possible. Part of that problem was resolved by permitting Congress to impeach and remove a president for "high crimes and misdemeanors." As Madison pointed out, vulnerability to impeachment would make the American president much more accountable for his actions than was the British king, who, theoretically at least, was not subject to removal by parliament.[251] Whatever positions they assumed on the construction of executive authority, almost all the delegates drew upon what they believed were the lessons of colonial and British history.

The Constitutional Convention often confronted the irreducibility of "interests" arising out of the varying occupations of the citizenry, the political economies of the several states, the different labor regimes of the separate regions (most importantly, their relative dependence on slavery), the investment of elites in the securities and moneys of the Continental Congress, and the cultural inheritance of the people (particularly their familiarity with the forms of English governance).[252] The delegates, for example, "overwhelmingly

they wanted to emulate. This distinction between theory and reality was, however, sometimes difficult to detect. John Adams, for example, was "accused of being a crypto-monarchist: his conception of an independent disinterested executive standing above and balancing all the interests of the society was as close to a monarchy as a republic could get." Wood, *Radicalism*, pp. 261, 267; also see Bilder, *Madison's Hand*, p. 65. In chapter 10 of her book, Bilder discusses at length Jefferson's very strong apprehension, after 1792 or so, that Hamilton was plotting to turn the early republic into a monarchy. For a very nice description of Alexander Hamilton and his participation in the convention, see Beeman, *Plain, Honest Men*, pp. 164–70.

[251] Klarman, *Framers' Coup*, pp. 373–4. "Theoretically" in the sentence in the text recognizes the rather checkered history of parliament's relations with the monarchy during the seventeenth century. However, Americans rarely mentioned that history in their discussions of the advantages and disadvantages of the British system.

[252] There is very little romance in either the deliberations of the convention or in the process of ratification. Where abstract notions of liberty surfaced – rare in Philadelphia but more common in the ratifying conventions – they often cloaked narrowly conceived interests. On the opportunistic mobilization of theoretical arguments in support of specific governing arrangements during the ratification process, see Klarman, *Framers' Coup*, pp. 376–96, 609–16, particularly 376, 393–5. On the whole, Klarman regards the Federalists as being far more "disingenuous" than were their opponents. With respect to the creation of a strong national government, Main agreed. Main, *Antifederalists*, pp. 120–1, 127. George Van Cleve similarly notes "the Federalists' lack of candor on slave representation" during debates on ratification. Van Cleve, *Slaveholders' Union*, p. 137. Madison explained the absence of romance in public debate over the Constitution in a letter to Jefferson written in February 1790, after the Constitution had been ratified and Washington had been inaugurated. In that letter, Madison rejected the notion that French revolutionary ideals could serve as a ground for American politics: "[O]ur hemisphere must be still more enlightened before many of the sublime truths which are seen thro' the

agreed" that "state laws issuing paper money and providing relief to debtors" should be prohibited by the new constitution.[253] But there were many other issues upon which they had very different conceptions of what the new compact should and should not permit. As a result, exchanges between delegates during the first weeks of the convention often took the form of uncompromising stances that seemed to deny altogether the possibility of common ground. After a little over a month of rather fruitless debate, George Washington confessed to Alexander Hamilton that "I almost despair of seeing a favorable issue to the proceedings of the convention, and do therefore repent having had any agency in the business."[254]

While the interests of the states and of the delegates (individually and as a collective, propertied elite) shaped much of the deliberations, the issues that they had to decide often indirectly indicated where they thought sovereignty and legitimacy should reside. Sovereignty and legitimacy were not empty categories because they entailed an interpretive translation of where and how, in practice and thus in theory, the will of the people was to be enshrined. For example, the ways in which elections, suffrage eligibility, and representation were determined would define how the will of the people would be conceived and how it would operate upon political institutions. That conception and operation, along with the political practice that they engendered, would determine where legitimacy would be created; that legitimacy, in turn, would be the ground of sovereignty. During the debate over whether representation in the Senate should be based on relative population or, alternatively, on an equal allocation to each state, James Wilson of Pennsylvania posed a question: "Can we forget for whom we are forming a government? Is it for *men*, or for the imaginary beings called states? ... We talk of states, till we forget what they are composed of." Hamilton made the same point, contending that "the rights of the people" composed the states, which were, as a result, little more than "artificial beings resulting from the composition."

Madison firmly rejected the notion that the states "possessed the essential rights of sovereignty" and contended that they "ought to be placed under the control of the general government – at least as much as they formerly were under the King and British Parliament." (Given the history of the relationship between the colonies and the mother country, this may have been seen as a less than apt parallel.) While advocating equal state representation in the Senate,

---

medium of Philosophy, become visible to the naked eye of the ordinary Politician." Bilder, *Madison's Hand*, p. 203.

[253] Klarman, *Framers' Coup*, p. 161. Even as staunch an advocate of popular sovereignty as Thomas Paine believed that the protection of property rights, in the form of corporate charters and a prohibition on the issuance of paper money, was a contractual arrangement that should not be violated by the people. Van Cleve, *We Have Not a Government*, pp. 201–2.

[254] Klarman, *Framers' Coup*, p. 127.

Luther Martin of Maryland offered a very different understanding of the sovereign status of the states, contending that the revolution had put them "in a state of nature towards each other" and that, as a consequence, they "like individuals, were equally sovereign and free." That was, he maintained, how the states had entered into the Confederation and that was how they must go about amending their mutual compact with one another.[255]

With respect to that compact, the frontier made the notion of a state of nature an apparently tangible reality to settlers. When, for example, the Confederation army attempted to remove settlers who had crossed the Ohio River despite a prohibition upon infringement on Indian lands, one of the settlers publicly proclaimed that "all mankind, agreeable to every constitution formed in America, have an undoubted right to pass into every vacant country, and to form their constitution" and then denied that the Confederation had any right to prevent the exercise of this right. This stance combined a notion of the "state of nature" with the rejection of Confederation sovereignty (even though the latter ostensibly "owned" the land). And it also implicitly refused to recognize the complicating reality that Indian tribes were both in de facto possession of that land (contradicting the Confederation claim of ownership) and constituted a preexisting political organization (contradicting the "state of nature" position of the settlers). In this respect, the conception of the state of nature on the frontier simplified and strengthened the claims of original (white) settlement. In a somewhat different way, the same conception also worked to cleanse, simplify, and broaden the canvass upon which the individual state and national constitutions were written.

There are at least nine different ways in which "popular sovereignty" (the degree to which the people could directly control government with minimal mediation by intervening officials or institutions) was discussed during the revolutionary period: (1) the election of government officials (the larger the proportion, the better); (2) periodic election of officials (the more frequent, the better); (3) the power to recall elected representatives (the more unconstrained, the better); (4) term limits for elected officials (the lower the number of terms or years, the better); (5) the size of the constituency (the smaller, the better); (6) suffrage eligibility (the broader, the better); (7) the instructing of a representative on how to vote (the more detailed and coercive, the better); (8) unicameralism (so that the popular will is not bargained away in inter-chamber interactions – many radical democrats, such as Tom Paine, similarly opposed an independent executive branch); and (9) a residency requirement for elected

---

[255] Klarman, *Framers' Coup*, pp. 185–6, 188, 241, 678n and, more generally, 182–205. In his conclusion, Klarman writes: "Equal state representation in the Senate fitted awkwardly in a national government ostensibly grounded in popular sovereignty" (p. 600). Also see Carroll Smith-Rosenberg, *This Violent Empire: The Birth of an American Identity* (Chapel Hill, NC: Omohundro Institute of Early American History and Culture, 2010), pp. 119–20.

officials (the longer, the better).[256] At least eight of these nine dimensions are variable (even the residency requirement, which can, for example, stipulate "must have lived in the district for five years" as opposed to, say, one year).

Although each is distinct, they were often viewed as interdependent in the sense that manipulation of the requirements for one affected how another was considered. For example, longer terms often encouraged colonists to view a broader power of recall more favorably. That interdependency is one of the reasons why we would have difficulty trying to scale the proclivity of the different colonies to adopt measures strengthening popular democracy. In general, these dimensions closely align with Burke's distinction between "trustee" and "delegate" representation (with Burke, of course, at the least responsive end in each instance). But, in the opposite direction, they also align even more closely with Rousseau's notion of the "General Will" (e.g., the idea that only a city-state can provide an adequate institutional framework for government). However, Rousseau was generally quite hostile to "representation," which, however constrained, these dimensions presume would be an operative part of governance.

In the convention deliberations, it was clear that equal state representation in the Senate was ultimately grounded in the belief that it was the states that would act as the agents of representation in the national government (an attitude reinforced by the selection of senators by the legislatures of the individual states), while proportional representation presupposed that individuals, not states, were the legitimate bearers of political will.[257] This was one of the most important conflicts that arose in the convention but it was primarily a contest between the large states (which would benefit from proportional representation) and the small states (which would gain from an equal allocation). Although the debate sometimes addressed more fundamental considerations of political theory, the issue was settled by the relative material interests of the several states. The smallest states, for one thing, made a credible threat that they would leave the convention if they did not have their way.

The references to the states as "imaginary" or "artificial beings" are noteworthy because Wilson and Hamilton, both of them nationalists, were of course embarked on the project of creating their own (national) "imaginary

---

[256] Max Weber compiled a similar list of "the principal technical means of attaining" direct democracy "in large groups." Guenther Roth and Claus Wittich (eds.), *Economy and Society* (Berkeley: University of California Press, 1978), vol. I, p. 289.

[257] This point was explicitly made by Roger Sherman of Connecticut: While "the people ought to have the election of one of the branches of the legislature" (i.e., the House of Representatives), "the legislature of each state ought to have the election of the second branch, in order to preserve the state sovereignty." Klarman, *Framers' Coup*, p. 206. However, as Klarman hastens to note, "considerations of political expediency rather than genuine policy preferences probably motivated" the other delegates because "[s]tate legislatures would inevitably play a major role in determining whether the constitution … was ratified, and they would be unlikely to approve a system that denied them any direct influence upon the national government" (p. 207).

being." Convention debates were thus not just about the material allocation of power and authority; they also concerned the very foundation of governance. As the delegates, for example, deliberated on the potential authority of the national government over interstate commerce, they were not only deciding how that authority would operate from a practical, material perspective but whether or not the national government would, in that respect, be assigned a power that implied a sovereign status vis-à-vis the states, a sovereign status that would both require and, in the best of all possible worlds, also engender legitimacy. But most of their decisions concerning the location of sovereignty and legitimacy were determined by the narrow material interests of the delegates and the states from which they hailed.

Slavery provoked similar conflict over the location and expression of the will of the people. The most important problem again involved the allocation of representation among the several states: Should slaves be counted in the formula determining the apportionment of members in the House of Representatives (and, thus, in the Electoral College as well)? Slaves were definitely people but they were a people who were denied an autonomous (free) political will. Since the apportionment formula directly implicated the allocation of political power, this was not a theoretically subtle issue for the South. The material and political interests of the southern delegations in Philadelphia thus dictated that slaves be counted as though they were equivalent to free whites. But the issue was more complex for the North. On the one hand, southerners held that slaves were property, a peculiar form of property that both needed political protection and supplanted, by its existence as a labor force, what otherwise would have been greater numbers of free whites. The South thus had a greater capital to population ratio than the North (although how that would have been calculated exactly was unclear). Many of the northern delegates could entertain such a logic up to a point. In fact, the Constitutional Convention at times considered property and population as possible alternative methods for allocating representation among the several states.

On the other hand, once population was chosen as the basis for determining representation, the logical rationale was that it was people who voted and thus, through voting, revealed their collective will. Although they were people, slaves could not freely exercise their will. Southerners might have argued that slaves were "virtually" represented by the political elite (composed primarily of their masters), but this parallel was not an attractive defense, given the use parliament had made of that notion during the colonial crisis. In addition, more than a few of the northern delegates (and some of the southerners as well) rejected the very notion that slavery was compatible with the ideals of a republic.[258] The

---

[258] However, David Brion Davis "doubts that the inconsistency of revolutionary ideals with slavery was a 'pressing concern to the majority of Americans, even in New England.'" Paraphrase and quote taken from Van Cleve, *Slaveholders' Union*, p. 43. There is a vigorous debate over the extent to which slavery influenced the construction of the Constitution. After nicely

solution – as crudely crafted a material compromise as ever was devised in a constitutional convention – was to count each slave as three-fifths of a free person.[259] The delegates also euphemistically referred to slaves as "all other

summarizing that debate, Waldstreicher states "that slavery was as important to the making of the Constitution as the Constitution was to the survival of slavery." He concludes his book with these lines: "[S]lavery did not itself cause the Civil War. Slavery's Constitution did." David Waldstreicher, *Slavery's Constitution: From Revolution to Ratification* (New York: Hill and Wang, 2009), pp. 17, 157. However, as Wilentz notes, "[s]omehow, a nation with a Constitution that was strongly entwined with slavery also generated political and legal forces that eventually destroyed slavery." Sean Wilentz, *No Property in Man: Slavery and Antislavery at the Nation's Founding* (Cambridge, MA: Harvard University Press, 2018), p. x. Tomlins is skeptical: "Those who celebrate the American Revolution and its aftermath as the beginning of American slavery's end do history no favors." He also notes that "in 1800, 89 percent of blacks were enslaved [in the United States]," even though many northern states had abolished the institution. Christopher Tomlins, *Freedom Bound: Law, Labor, and Civic Identity in Colonizing English America, 1580–1865* (New York: Cambridge University Press, 2010), pp. 504, 506. Van Cleve similarly concludes that "[s]lavery emerged from the Revolution stronger than it had been within the framework of the Empire." Van Cleve, *Slaveholders' Union*, p. 41; for a detailed history of the development of slave law before the revolution, see pp. 418–504. For African American reactions to white political rhetoric before and during the revolution, see Douglas R. Egerton, *Death or Liberty: African Americans and Revolutionary America* (New York: Oxford University Press, 2009). Although this debate is tangential (but not irrelevant) to this book, we might note that it has three dimensions. First, everyone seems to agree that slavery presented material political and economic facts that the delegates in Philadelphia had to confront and that most of them went about that task in a "realpolitik" fashion. Second, the result was a document that incorporated provisions in which the interests of slaveholders and the political economy of their states were protected. The final dimension concerns the extent to which the language of the Constitution, including the institutions and processes that it created, spawned a "democratic ethos" that ultimately brought down slavery. A good case might be made that the rise of national political parties, along with the expansion of suffrage eligibility and a relatively unregulated national economy, made the formation of a major party hostile to slavery quite likely. However, the rise of the party system and the expansion of suffrage rights were largely unintended consequences of the Constitution (although a national economy of some kind was envisioned). In any event, unequivocal announcement in the Declaration of Independence that "all Men are created equal" probably influenced the development of a democratic ethos more than did the Constitution. All this aside, a more interesting line of speculation might start with a (plausible) counterfactual in which the American colonies remained within the British Empire after the metropole government compromised on the issues of taxation and representation. As the colonies developed during the nineteenth century, would increasing anti-slavery sentiment in the metropole and the American North have more or less peacefully dismantled southern slavery? Or, alternatively, would the prosperity of the American South have weakened metropole anti-slavery sentiment in such a way that the institution would have survived longer than it did? There is no way to conclusively answer these questions but they seem at least as important as those involving the imbrication of slavery into the Constitution. For further discussion of the salience of slavery in the construction of the Constitution, see Beeman, *Plain, Honest Men*, pp. 308–36.

[259] At least some of the delegates in Philadelphia were familiar with this formula because it had been proposed previously in the Confederation Congress as a method for apportioning requisitions among the several states. Klarman, *Framers' Coup*, p. 641n; Van Cleve, *We Have Not a Government*, pp. 93, 101; also see Bilder, *Madison's Hand*, pp. 30–1, 68–9, 81–3. In February

persons" who were not "free Persons, including those bound to Service for a Term of Years." That outcome is not logically compatible with any known political theory but made (barely) the crafting of the Constitution possible.[260]

The last Article (number seven) of the Constitution set out how the people would express their will with respect to its adoption: stated in its entirety, "The Ratification of the Conventions of nine States shall be sufficient for the Establishment of this Constitution between the States so ratifying the Same." This process was grounded in two principles, one of them originating in democratic theory and the other in practical political reality. With respect to democratic theory, the delegates wanted the American people as a whole to ratify the Constitution they had made. Their consent, as an American people, would create a direct link between the citizenry and the new national state, a link that was emphatically necessary for the success of the new government. The convention, for that reason, stipulated that the will of the people would be revealed in conventions in the several states (with a constitution-making authority much like their own) and not in the state legislatures.[261]

With respect to practical political reality, the delegates also realized that the thirteen states enjoyed much more affection and prestige than did the Continental Congress.[262] During the ratification process, those opposed to the Constitution often cited the states as the true repositories of the popular will, both because they were closer to the people and because the expression

---

1783, Congress had used this formula to determine the tax liability of the individual states but, in the Constitutional Convention, it was primarily used to allocate representation among the individual states in the new House of Representatives. This flexibility in application underscored the importance of property in defining the legitimacy of the will of the people. In the end, the justification for the formula was neither that slaveholders would represent their slaves in Congress as a form of property that both displaced free people in the South (who otherwise would have been counted in the "whole") nor that slaves constituted a property interest that was far less prominent (although it existed in most of the states) in the North (and thus had to be accounted separately) but that pragmatic compromise was the only way to found the new state. For interpretive accounts of deliberations on the clause, see Van Cleve, *Slaveholders' Union*, pp. 120–34; Wilentz, *No Property in Man*, pp. 60–70.

[260] Almost half of the delegates owned slaves. Klarman, *Framers' Coup*, p. 263. For background on the social and economic importance of slavery, as well as debate during the Constitutional Convention on the allocation formula and prohibition of the future importation of slaves, see pp. 258–97. This broad distinction between the expression of clearly material interests by southerners and the more philosophical, often anguished, reflections of northerners also characterized many of the discussions in the state conventions during the ratification process (pp. 297–304). Also see Robertson, *Original Compromise*, pp. 178–91.

[261] This stipulation, however, was not written into the text of the Constitution but instead was set down in the order transmitting the document from the Constitutional Convention to Congress. Klarman, *Framers' Coup*, p. 421.

[262] The founders also recognized political reality by requiring that only nine states approve the Constitution in order for the new government to be created (thus avoiding the unanimity requirement that the Articles of Confederation would have otherwise imposed). Klarman, *Framers' Coup*, pp. 412–14.

of the popular will was more directly translated into government action. In some respects, this became a debate between opponents who advocated more fulsome popular democracy and proponents who stressed individual liberty and freedom.[263] The latter had a particularly difficult task because, unlike the pre-revolutionary crisis in which the British were the primary threat to liberty and freedom, they were compelled (implicitly at least) to characterize the American people as the source of danger. However, when proponents stressed the fragility of the Confederation when threatened by either insurrection at home or invasion from abroad, they were on much stronger, albeit extremely pragmatic, ground.[264]

The ratification process was intended to frame popular consent through the social and political aura of the individual states, attaching the latter and, thus, the people to the new national government.[265] This strategy, of course, consciously recognized that the people were not in anything like a state of nature when they consented to this national contract.[266] They were, instead, bringing their own, preexisting political relationships (encompassed by the states in which they resided) into the new national government. From that perspective, the ratification process was inconsistent with the founding of a national state because it recognized the existence and sovereignty of the individual states.[267]

---

[263] In August 1787, just a few weeks before the Philadelphia Convention adopted the text of the Constitution, the French government sent its *chargé d'affaires* in the United States a secret message:

> It appears, sir, that in all the American provinces there is more or less tendency toward democracy; that in many this extreme form of government will finally prevail. The result will be that the confederation will have little stability, and that by degrees the different states will subsist in a perfect independence of each other. This revolution will not be regretted by us. We have never pretended to make of America a useful ally; we have had no other object than to deprive Britain of that vast continent. Therefore, we can regard with indifference both the movements which agitate certain provinces and the fermentation which prevails in congress. (Van Cleve, *We Have Not a Government*, p. 1)

[264] See, for example, Van Cleve, *We Have Not a Government*, pp. 29–32, 281.

[265] Robertson, *Original Compromise*, p. 221.

[266] William Findley, who later became one of the delegates to the Pennsylvania ratification convention, strongly denied that Americans were in a "state of nature" as they deliberated on the new constitution. In his view, the Articles of Confederation were "federal ground" that made the new constitution, with its alteration in the process of amendment, illegitimate. One of his colleagues in the Pennsylvania Assembly rejected that argument, contending that Americans, in fact, were "on the wild and extended field of nature, unrestrained by any compact." Maier, *Ratification*, pp. 61–2; also see Pollack, *War, Revenue, and State Building*, p. 173. At the convention, Edmund Randolph regarded the constitutional project as one in which "we are not working on the natural rights of men not yet gathered into society" because those rights have been "modified by society and interwoven with what we call ... the rights of states." Levy, *Origins*, p. 15.

[267] Van Cleve, *We Have Not a Government*, p. 144.

Those who opposed ratification of the Constitution usually rested their case on three things: (1) that the delegates had met in Philadelphia under what became false auspices when it transformed a meeting to consider changes in the Articles into a full-blown constitutional convention; (2) that the Continental Congress had transmitted an illegitimate document to the states under a decision rule (i.e., only nine of the thirteen states need approve before the new state would go into operation) that violated the Articles of Confederation; and (3) that there were no provisions for the protection of individual rights.[268] In response, the founders contended (perhaps immodestly) that the document was simply a proposal placed before the people to accept or reject. The process through which it came before the people was far less important than the fact that it was the product of the informed judgment and thought of those men whom the people otherwise honored and respected. However, by merely asking the Continental Congress to transmit the Constitution to the states, the Federalists practically conceded most of the first and second points.

The Antifederalists noted that the procedure created by the Federalists turned the Constitution into a more or less take-it-or-leave-it proposition because the people had not had a chance to participate in its construction before it appeared before them. They thus contended that the people, through their ratifying conventions, had a sovereign right and duty to consider and, if they thought it best, make changes in the text. These changes would then become conditions under which they would approve the document and enter into the new union. As an appeal to the sovereignty of the people, this contention was irrefutable. The (somewhat lame) response of the founders was that changes in the document would be impossible to reconcile because the states would inevitably have varying concerns and objections. The construction of a new document in which those concerns and objections were compromised would thus necessitate another, new constitutional convention, after which, it could be plausibly imagined, more objections would be lodged. Full

---

[268] Under the Articles of Confederation, any amendment to that document must be approved by the legislatures of each of the thirteen states. For that reason alone, the transmission of the new Constitution to the states under a process that required the consent of only nine states before going into effect was a clear violation of the Articles. As a result, the Continental Congress either had no authority to transmit the Constitution because it was altogether outside the confines of the Articles or, the more likely interpretation, had knowingly violated the very document upon which its authority was grounded. Also see Klarman, *Framers' Coup*, pp. 310–12. In addition to setting an achievable threshold for ratification, the nine-state requirement somewhat unexpectedly created a very interdependent process in which members of the state conventions became very aware of the actions of the others as the number of ratifications crept up toward the threshold. The difference between the failure of ratification by nine states and being left out of the union if nine states created a new government was immense, particularly for the smaller states whose relations with the new government might determine their very survival. In addition to those described in the text, there were, of course, other arguments that opponents made. One of those was that the continental United States was simply too large for a democracy. See, for example, Cornell, *Other Founders*, pp. 72–3.

participation by the people, it seemed, was thus beyond practical possibility. To this, of course, the Antifederalists could and did respond that full participation by the people had not yet been tried.

Basically, the Antifederalists contended that the founders had not, in fact, provided any warrant for the first fifteen words of the document: "We, the People of the United States, in Order to form a more perfect Union."[269] When the phrase "the People of the United States" is appropriately excised, the "We" refers only to the delegates who signed the document. In terms of abstract political theory, the Antifederalists were on perfectly solid ground. And the pretension of the founders to present their handiwork as the product of the will of the people even as they denied that the people could revise its provisions was flagrantly hypocritical. But that hypocrisy did not originate with them but with the necessity for any founding to presume the existence of a political authority before that political authority can, in fact, be created. That contradiction arose from the fact that a people could not spontaneously (i.e., in the absence of formal political institutions) authorize anyone to act in their name (e.g., call a constitutional convention). The founders were pragmatically attempting to bridge that unavoidable contradiction by imagining, in the first instance, that they were "the people" in that opening sentence. No doubt about it, that pretension was hypocritical, but, from a practical standpoint, they could make a very good case that it was inevitable and thus necessary. And, "once the new national government had commenced operations, most Antifederalists quickly abandoned their legitimacy challenges."[270]

But the ratification process itself was quite contentious and the outcome was very uncertain. Contending that only a strong central government could prevent the individual states from sliding back into colonial dependency, Federalists accused the Antifederalists of secretly desiring reunification with Great Britain. Given that many of the most prominent Antifederalists had devoted their lives and fortunes to the American cause during the revolution, the evidence supporting this charge was very weak. In fact, many Antifederalists believed that their opponents were conspiring to foist an oppressive government on the American people in much the same way as the British crown and parliament had attempted to do during the colonial crisis. But that did not prevent the Antifederalists from citing British governance principles when they seemed to aid their cause. Noting that the House of Lords could not amend bills making appropriations that originated in the House of Commons, they asked the Federalists why the proposed American Senate was not similarly restricted. That criticism was primarily motivated by hostility to the indirectly

---

[269] This opening language was more or less copied from the preamble of the 1780 Constitution of Massachusetts. Maier, *Ratification*, p. 140.

[270] Klarman, *Framers' Coup*, pp. 9, 619–21. Morgan also concludes that Americans were clearly "ready" for this new national contract because it was almost immediately accepted "as a legitimate expression of popular authority." Morgan, *Inventing the People*, p. 285.

selected Senate, against which the direct election of the House of Representatives was favorably compared.[271]

As an opponent of ratification, Patrick Henry expressed contempt for a Senate, a body formally assigned responsibility to advise the president, by noting that senators could not be impeached if they were bribed or otherwise improperly influenced in the course of their duties. If they did "anything derogatory to the honor or interest of their country ... they are to try themselves," a totally unacceptable arrangement that parliament had avoided by making ministers subject to impeachment.[272] Henry also contended that the Constitution contained "an awful squinting ... toward monarchy" and would thus easily evolve into a kingship with "the President's enslaving America." On the other hand, he also thought that the British system was much better with respect to actual checks and balances between the several branches.[273] Sorting through the varying implications of all these parallels with British experience is enough to make one's head spin.[274]

In Philadelphia, many Federalists had favorably drawn on the prerogatives of the British king when attempting to strengthen the authority of the presidency.[275] Subsequently faced with criticism from Antifederalists that the executive branch might be too powerful, they now emphasized that a president would in fact be much weaker than a king with respect to declaring war, the crafting of international treaties, appointments to government office, and raising an army or navy. They also noted that a king served for life while a presidential term was only four years. Finally, they turned the popular election of the House of Representatives, which they had only grudgingly conceded in Philadelphia as a political necessity, into a virtue by contending that the British House of Commons, less democratic than the proposed House of Representatives, had still proved to be more than a match for a rogue king.

---

[271] Klarman, *Framers' Coup*, pp. 307, 348, 366.   [272] Klarman, *Framers' Coup*, p. 363.

[273] Maier, *Ratification*, p. 266. In New York, however, Albany Antifederalists declared that the Constitution would erect a government "more arbitrary and despotic" than the British system (p. 333).

[274] In the convention in which Pennsylvania considered ratification, James Wilson distinguished the Constitution from the Magna Carta and the British Declaration of Rights, contending that the latter had been wrested from the overweening authority of kings while the former was the voluntary compact of a sovereign people. In the Massachusetts Convention, a delegate noted that "[w]e contended with Great-Britain" during the revolution "because they claimed a right to tax and bind us in all cases whatever." The proposed constitution threatened to do the same thing. Maier, *Ratification*, pp. 107, 185; for other references to the British government during the ratification debates, see p. 189.

[275] See, for example, Bilder, *Madison's Hand*, p. 148. When the Constitutional Convention discussed how to define treason, Madison reported that Gouverneur Morris and Edmund Randolph attempted to use "the words of the British Statute" under which, presumably, they themselves might have been tried had the revolution failed (pp. 135, 191). For the many and various ways in which the founders used the British monarchy as a model and a foil for the construction of the American presidency, see Nelson, *Royalist Revolution*, pp. 185–226.

In effect, the delegates transformed pragmatic necessity into a theoretical asset by emphasizing that the direct election of members of the new House of Representatives promised to check and balance whatever powers might accrue to the president through practice.[276]

Many of these arguments, of course, opportunistically cloaked the real motives, fears, and apprehensions of both Federalists and Antifederalists alike. But they were nonetheless revealing because they relied on American experience with the only national government they had ever known. That experience was, on the one hand, a storehouse of examples, precedents, and anecdotal evidence upon which both sides in the ratification debate could draw; it thus became the shared frame through which they perceived political possibility. Neither side could do without either that storehouse or that frame because they simply could not think in any other way. But – and this is fundamentally important – they appropriated more than the storehouse and the frame because they also, neither inadvertently nor intentionally, instantiated the rights of Englishmen along with the forms of their political practice. Those rights were so familiar that they trotted, on silent cat's paws, right into the Constitution and American political practice when no one was paying particular attention to them. And those that did not trot so silently were almost immediately added to the Constitution by the Bill of Rights.

Congress sent the Constitution to the states on September 28, 1787.[277] As the ratification process got underway, only six states (Connecticut, Delaware, Georgia, Maryland, New Jersey, and Pennsylvania) were expected to easily approve the new constitution. And, in fact, these six were among the first seven states to do so (Massachusetts was the seventh).[278] The last state to ratify the Constitution was Rhode Island, which was also the only state that never sent delegates to the Philadelphia Convention. The Federalists heaped scorn on Rhode Island for that and for many other reasons. Charles Pinckney of South Carolina, for example, denounced its government for oppressing "the people by laws the most infamous that have ever disgraced a civilized nation." By that he meant that popular rule had endangered the rights of property through, among other things, the printing of paper money and laws favoring debtors.[279] During the convention in which Pennsylvania considered its own ratification of the Constitution, James Wilson asked one of his Antifederalist opponents

---

[276] Klarman, *Framers' Coup*, p. 369. For Antifederalist fear that the Constitution would create an executive "vested with power dangerous to a free people," see Main, *Antifederalists*, pp. 140–2.

[277] For an account of the sometimes acrimonious discussions that preceded referral to the states, see Maier, *Ratification*, pp. 52–9.

[278] For an account of the ratifying conventions in the several states, see Klarman, *Framers' Coup*, pp. 417–539, also 616–19. Maier provides even more exhaustive accounts in *Ratification*, pp. 59–472.

[279] In both Rhode Island and North Carolina (the second to last state to ratify) the strongest opposition to the Constitution probably came from the advocates of state paper money. Van Cleve, *We Have Not a Government*, pp. 364 n. 19.

whether he wanted to risk "a great part of his fortune" in a Rhode Island court where the outcome would be popularly decided by a jury.

Federalists were not the only critics. Melancton Smith, a leading Antifederalist delegate in the New York ratifying convention, also damned Rhode Island: "[S]he deserves to be condemned. If there were in the world but one example of political depravity, it would be hers. And no nation ever merited or suffered a more genuine infamy than a wicked administration has attached to her character." When Rhode Island rejected the congressional call for a ratifying convention in the fall of 1787, a merchant in Philadelphia wrote that the "unhappy deluded state still adds infamy to infamy." Another Pennsylvania Federalist contended that Rhode Island's rejection of the Constitution would provide "a greater proof of [the document's] excellence" than "the best reasons yet given by the wisest politicians" who favored ratification; that state's rejection would convince "[m]any worthy men" to "now attach themselves to" the Constitution in order to avoid being associated "with men who for years have been a disgrace to human nature." When the state legislature met again in February 1788, the *Newport Herald* (a local newspaper) urged it to take the opportunity to call a ratifying convention rather than "persist in our obstinacy and be the butt of ridicule." But the legislature again refused; it refused a third time in the fall of 1788. During 1789, the legislature rejected calls for a ratifying convention on four more separate occasions. By that time, Federalists in Newport and Providence were openly discussing secession from the rest of the state.[280] Referring to Rhode Island's refusal to ratify the Constitution long after the federal government was up and running, George Washington wrote that he would have no doubt that the state would ultimately join the union "had not the majority of that people bid adieu, long since, to every principle of honor, common sense, and honesty."

By September 1789, the new Congress had had enough and gave Rhode Island an ultimatum: Ratify the Constitution and join the union or discriminatory tariffs would be placed on its commerce with the rest of the states. That threat, along with the completion of the funding of the state debt with worthless currency, finally convinced the legislature (with the governor breaking a tie in the upper chamber) to call a ratifying convention for March 1790. Congress, in return, extended the deadline in its ultimatum. Even so, Antifederalists comprised a majority of the delegates elected to that convention and sought to delay ratification as long as possible. The United States Senate responded by escalating the severity of the punitive actions contemplated in the ultimatum and set a new deadline of July 1, 1790. Rhode Island surrendered on May 29, 1790, but

---

[280] In 1774, Newport, with 9,208 people, was far and away the largest town in Rhode Island. Providence was second with 4,321. Together, though, they comprised only 22.7 percent of the colony's population. John R. Bartlett, Secretary of State, *Census of the Inhabitants of the Colony of Rhode Island and Providence Plantations ... 1774*, reprint (Providence, RI: Knowles, Anthony & Co., 1858), p. 239.

the margin was close (delegates approved the Constitution by a vote of thirty-four to thirty-two).[281]

THE BILL OF RIGHTS

During the state ratifying conventions, many Antifederalists criticized the Constitution because it failed to explicitly protect traditional English individual and collective rights.[282] Some of that criticism was probably opportunistic in the sense that adding such rights to the document during the ratification process would have defeated adoption because the people in the several states did not agree on what those rights might be or how they should be set down in words. At best, opening up the Constitution to amendment would have necessitated a second constitutional convention so that a common text could be agreed upon; at worst, it would have doomed ratification altogether and compelled the states to go their separate ways. Most Federalists were taken aback by the passionate insistence that the Constitution endangered American liberty by failing to stipulate and protect individual rights. In fact, their stupefaction demonstrates that this was one of the few instances in which the delegates had failed to anticipate public opinion. There were other instances in which they knew that they would encounter resistance from the public but they calculated that those provisions were worth the risk.[283] Their failure to include what ultimately became the Bill of Rights was simply a mistake.[284]

In Philadelphia, Madison contended that a bill of rights would be superfluous, both because the Constitution explicitly limited national authority in ways that prevented transgressions on American liberty and because, in a somewhat contrary vein, mere words on paper would not prevent impassioned majorities

---

[281] Klarman, *Framers' Coup*, pp. 320, 354, 516–17, 520–1, 527, 529, 605. In very sharp contrast to the founders' condemnation of Rhode Island as a benighted cesspool, Gordon Wood praises it as "the most liberal, the most entrepreneurial, and the most 'modern' of the eighteenth-century colonies," in part because it was a society "where nearly everyone seemed to be participating in trade." Wood, *Radicalism*, p. 140. Wood even appears to applaud Rhode Island's enthusiastic reliance on paper money in the satisfaction of debts, something almost all founders found morally reprehensible because the consequent inflation of market prices undermined the property rights of creditors.

[282] Main, *Antifederalists*, pp. 158–61.

[283] The "greatest political risk" knowingly taken by the delegates may have been the expansive taxing authority granted to the federal government. Van Cleve, *We Have Not a Government*, p. 288.

[284] Morgan, for example, partially explains the absence of a statement of rights as "simply an oversight on the part of the Philadelphia convention." When the question finally emerged toward the end of their deliberations, "everyone was impatient to go home" and they simply tabled the issue. Morgan, *Inventing the People*, p. 282; also see Klarman, *Framers' Coup*, pp. 548–9. Maier agrees. Maier, *Ratification*, pp. 44–5. While Levy considers the omission of bill of rights "a deliberate act of the Constitutional Convention," he also states that it was "a colossal error of judgment," a "mistake," and a "blunder." Levy, *Origins*, pp. 12, 25, 31, 103.

from violating those rights.[285] But he later became persuaded that a bill of rights, added separately to the Constitution, would nonetheless cultivate a more enlightened public opinion concerning the rights of the people and responsibilities of the government and, at the same time, set down abstract criteria upon which the people could evaluate government action.[286]

Although the utility of a bill of rights in developing a popular culture of liberty grounded in natural rights was largely an American discovery, the notion of a bill of rights and its relation to the liberty of citizens was thoroughly English. In 1689, the English Declaration of Rights declared illegal those things that members of the convention (i.e., parliament, although it did not call itself "parliament" at the time because it had not been properly elected) believed to be violations of or otherwise inconsistent with the ancient constitution. Thus, the Declaration of Rights, in Morgan's words, "had to be interpreted not as an innovation but as a restoration of the ancient constitution, first established when wise ancestors emerged from a state of nature." They were, in this sense, natural rights that also formed the very core of the rights of Englishmen and thus English political identity. With William III's consent, the Declaration was read at the beginning of his coronation ritual, but this tacit recognition by the new king was not entirely satisfactory and something more was needed. After the convention had proclaimed itself to (once again) be a "parliament" and thus formally resumed its proper role in the English state, it passed the Declaration of Rights in the form of an ordinary statute that William then signed on December 16, 1689. This process, although taking place a century earlier and in a different country, has notable parallels with the American experience.[287]

But the parallels do not stop there. Most of the state constitutions contained a bill of rights, although they differed on their content.[288] These provisions were, like the English Declaration of Rights, primarily directed at oppressive practices that they associated with the crown. When the new national Congress crafted its own Bill of Rights, this historical inheritance – both directly from England and

---

[285] There was also a larger frame at work in all this. The English Bill of Rights was directed against the crown as protection of the liberty of the people from encroachment by the king. But in post-revolutionary America, where the people now reigned as sovereign, was the purpose of the new bill of rights to protect the people from themselves? In this and other ways, the founders discovered (or, more properly, rediscovered) "natural rights" that were above and beyond popular sovereignty. Wood, *Radicalism*, p. 189. The rights of Englishmen loomed so large during the early stages of the political crisis that Goodwin describes the "struggle" for colonial autonomy as "a second English civil war." The emergence of natural rights rhetoric arose only "after the outbreak of hostilities and the realization of the need for foreign alliances." Goodwin, "Introductory Survey," p. 11.

[286] Klarman, *Framers' Coup*, p. 547, also 549–55.

[287] Morgan, *Inventing the People*, pp. 116–17, 120. For the text of the English Bill of Rights, see Levy, *Origins*, pp. 269–71.

[288] Levy notes that the Northwest Ordinance also contained guarantees to the inhabitants that, taken together, can be considered a bill of rights. Levy, *Origins*, p. 11.

from the colonies that were turning themselves into states – strongly influenced what they saw as requiring protection.[289] This was particularly true of the writ of habeas corpus and the prohibition on bills of attainder, which were, in fact, included in the Constitution and thus not formally part of the Bill of Rights.

But it was also true of the Second Amendment. Radical Whigs in Britain had long opposed a standing army because they believed that a king might use it to suppress political opposition. Under the English Bill of Rights, only the consent of parliament could permit a standing army when the nation was at peace. The arguments of British Whigs and the precedent they had set down in the English Bill of Rights convinced their American counterparts, including many Antifederalists, that a professional army would endanger political liberty. Their experience with crown rule during the colonial crisis only reinforced that belief. Americans were not pacifists. Armies were necessary during times of war or civil insurrection but those armies should be raised directly from the people through the calling out of a militia. And that became the Second Amendment: "A well regulated Militia, being necessary to the security of a free State, the right of the people to keep and bear Arms, shall not be infringed."[290] The Fourth, Fifth, Sixth, Seventh, and Eighth Amendments also had very thick antecedents in English constitutional history.[291] Only the First Amendment's protection of freedom of religion and a free press, the Third Amendment's prohibition on the quartering of troops in houses, the Ninth Amendment's retention of rights by the people, and the Tenth Amendment's reservation of authority by the states were primarily American in origin, although even some of these were reactions to the pernicious (from the perspective of the colonists) exercise of imperial authority during the colonial era.

Of those amendments that protected individual rights (such as freedoms of religion and the press along with the right to a trial by jury in criminal cases), most had previously been inserted by the individual states in their own constitutions. Others (such as freedom of speech, grand jury indictments for felonies, and bans on double jeopardy) appeared in only a few state constitutions. In both instances, the construction of protected individual rights was strongly influenced by both British custom and tradition and, from a very different perspective, American colonial history in which that custom and tradition had been violated.[292]

---

[289] Amar notes many instances in which provisions in the American Bill of Rights can be traced to similar texts in the English Declaration of Rights in Akhil Amar, *The Bill of Rights: Creation and Reconstruction* (New Haven: Yale University Press, 1998), pp. 24–5, 60, 87, 128, 148, 169.

[290] Klarman, *Framers' Coup*, pp. 330–5. On the English origins, see Levy, *Origins*, pp. 133–8. Federalists contended that the Constitution would require congressional consent for a standing army because Congress could not appropriate money for that purpose for any period longer than two years.

[291] On the English origins of these rights, see Levy, *Origins*, pp. 44–56, 68–70, 151–64, 196–204, 210–20, 231–8.

[292] For a detailed account of the crafting of what became the first ten amendments to the Constitution (the Bill of Rights), see Maier, *Ratification*, pp. 440–64.

The American founding was a "blending" of two very different principles – custom and natural law – with the emphasis shifting from the former (e.g., the rights of Englishmen) to the latter (e.g., "all men are created equal") during the course of the revolution. However, these principles are complementary only if we view history as a process of discovery through which natural law is revealed. Custom then becomes a "ratchet-like" sequence in which incremental discoveries in the truth of natural law are recognized and preserved. There are some elements of that view in subsequent American history (e.g., in terms of the constitutional protection of individual rights), but that position would not have been widely shared by Americans in the late eighteenth century.[293]

The colonists turned to natural law only because contention over the interpretation of the English Constitution was at a deadlock once the king had openly and fully aligned with parliament. After that alignment, the colonies could no longer appeal to the English Constitution because there was no longer an audience in the metropole, real or imagined, to whom to address their constitutional claims. Once the sympathy of the king became a transparent fiction, colonial resistance had to move to another basis, "natural law," as the only way to firmly ground their position. When parliament insisted on using force to impose supremacy upon the colonies, the colonies were compelled to resort to force as well and natural law became the way in which they could appeal to the people in the ensuing war for independence. However, the interpretation they placed on natural law was always highly colored by their English inheritance.[294]

The colonists were not being particularly innovative because the English Constitution, with its foundation in the rights of Englishmen, was itself widely

---

[293] Klarman, *Framers' Coup*, pp. 566–90.

[294] On the importance of English legal custom and tradition in the crafting of state constitutions after the Declaration of Independence, see Reid, *Constitutional History*, pp. 101, 140. These state constitutions, in turn, provided many analogous precedents for provisions that later appeared in the United States Constitution. Adams, *First American Constitutions*, pp. 290–300. Fifty years after the Declaration of Independence, the Georgia legislature authorized the publication of a volume primarily authored by William Schley, *A Digest of the English Statutes of Force in the State of Georgia* (Philadelphia: J. Maxwell, 1826). This volume was intended as a convenient reference for lawyers and judges who might otherwise find it difficult to ascertain the legal standing of English laws as they might pertain and influence American practice; it runs to over 400 pages, not including the index or prefatory remarks. Schley begins, naturally enough, with the Magna Carta (acknowledging, in that instance, that "[v]ery few of the provisions of this charter are in force in Georgia, being generally inapplicable, or superseded by our own laws"). That text is followed by the "Statute of Merton" (1235), the "Statute de Anno et die Bissextile" (1236), the "Statute of Marlborough" (1267), and so on, codifying what was already an accomplished fact: the incorporation, in effect, of almost the entirety of English statutory and common law tradition into the Georgia legal system. Nineteen years later, Georgia issued a codification of the state statutes that again incorporated those English laws that continued to be "in force." William A. Hotchkiss, *A Codification of the Statute Law of Georgia Including the English Statutes of Force* (Savannah: John M. Cooper, 1845), especially pp. 5–32.

assumed to be aligned with natural law. For the English, the rights of Englishmen were a unique product of their political and social development as a nation and were thus not "universal" in the sense that any other nation could somehow digest and implement their truth. The colonists merely translated the rights of Englishmen into a new set of abstract principles and thus inaugurated the foundation for a new polity. However, the transition from the rights of Englishmen and those abstract principles was never completed because the Americans absorbed much of English law, thought, and institutional forms as they founded their new nation.[295]

Because something like what became the Bill of Rights was promised by many Federalists in order to secure adoption of the Constitution in the state conventions, and because the necessary amendments were proposed and ratified soon after the new government was up and running, the Bill of Rights is often considered as a part of the original compact that comprised the American founding. Those amendments, however, were the product of much hard work and persistence by James Madison, who had to overcome the indifference of his Federalist colleagues in the First Congress. The latter simply did not believe that those rights needed to be formally recognized because they were already fundamental American principles.

CONCLUSION

The American founding consisted of three separate events, each of which played a role in legitimating the national state. The Declaration of Independence broke the bond with the British crown but did not found a new

---

[295] Reid contends that John Locke's "theory of the social contract" played only a secondary role in the development of colonial constitutional thought and that the primary role was performed by the concept of an "original contract" between the colonies and British crown:

The social contract was a legal fiction explaining the conditions under which individuals left the state of nature and created societies. The constitutional or government contract – called the original contract in the eighteenth century – was an implied agreement between ruler and ruled from which the powers and limitations of government were inferred. The first is a theory of the origin of society, the second a theory of the constitution of government. (Reid, *Constitutional History*, p. 16, also 100–1)

Because "the social contract was a legal fiction," it could not, in the end, be the source of legal rights because there were "no facts to be had" that could enter into the adjudication of contending constitutional claims. However, the "original contract" was, at least in theory, accessible because "the facts upon which it rested" had entered into custom and tradition, which, in turn, had descended into the present. The frames of political practice that had given rise to constitutions in both the metropole and in the colonies had, in Burke's words, been "formed by imperceptible habits, and old custom, the great support of all governments in the world." Greene, *Constitutional Origins*, p. 43. Locke was thus more relevant to the construction of "natural law" once the colonists were compelled to jettison, at least superficially, some of those habits and customs as they abandoned appeals under the English Constitution. Pole, *Political Representation*, p. 17.

national state in its place. It created, instead, a kind of hybrid regime in which the thirteen colonies (now individual states) were independent but nevertheless used the Continental Congress to coordinate their rejection of imperial rule.[296] The Declaration of Independence resoundingly stated the natural rights for which the colonists were fighting in its opening passages but then proceeded to laboriously catalog the many violations of the rights of Englishmen that had been inflicted upon the colonists. These two sections were almost flatly contradictory in that, on the one hand, the opening paragraphs stated what, for many Americans, had become the transcendent social purpose of the new American state, while, on the other hand, the violations charged against the crown seemed to reverently construct an older transcendent social purpose that would have been, from the perspective of the founders, perfectly serviceable if the crown had only honored its principles. What made this contradiction (between the thick embrace of an English political heritage and tradition and a rejection of English rule) tenable, even invisible, was that Americans thought that they were merely realizing the true rights of Englishmen, even as they created a new nation that, ostensibly at least, was grounded on universal principles.

In order to appreciate how fondly the founders recalled their previous existence under imperial rule, we might turn each of these violations into their opposite, transforming them from a condemnatory statement of crown behavior into a laudatory affirmation of the rights that the king had violated. By thus transforming the violations, we can deductively derive the transcendent social purpose of crown rule to which the colonists would have willingly consented had the king only behaved himself. For example, the text of the first violation read: "He [the king] has refused his Assent to Laws, the most wholesome and necessary for the public Good." The reverse would thus be: "[The king should give] his Assent to Laws, the most wholesome and necessary for the public Good." The latter thus describes one of the rights of Englishmen by turning the violation into its opposite. If we were to perform the same operation on each of the other violations and then consider them to be a coherent body of principles, we would arrive at the transcendent social purpose of the ancient English Constitution (or at least a substantial portion of that purpose).

This summary of the rights of Englishmen, taken directly from the text of the Declaration of Independence, is simply incommensurable with, among other things, the opening line of the second paragraph: "We hold these Truths to be self-evident, that all Men are created equal." In short, the Declaration of Independence affirms two very different transcendent social purposes: a new one arising out of very abstract and original principles and an old one that can

---

[296] As Adams points out, the Declaration of Independence "elegantly avoided" any specification concerning the location of sovereignty, whether it was seated in the Continental Congress, each of the thirteen colonies, or some hybridized combination of the two. In effect, the Declaration formally declared the onset of revolution but did not, perhaps could not, initiate a founding at the same time. Adams, *First American Constitutions*, p. 132.

be implicitly reconstructed out of the actual practices of imperial rule. The founders, in crafting the Declaration, knew that they had chosen the former but believed that many of their constituents still subscribed to the latter. The contradiction in meaning arose out of the conflicting purposes of the document, which, in turn, arose out of the historical context within which it was written.

The Declaration of Independence was a "one-time only" event and could not be revised because the change it made in the location of sovereignty was irreversible. It was what it was forever (although we now reverence the opening paragraphs and ignore the rest of the document). The Declaration is sacred in that sense, hallowed in just the form in which it was originally given to the American people, destined to be memorized by generations upon generations of Americans until the government for which it stands falls into ruin.

The Constitution, on the other hand, was the instantiation of the transcendent social purpose in the national state. While that social purpose was compatible with the opening paragraphs of the Declaration, the Constitution added one necessary element. The Declaration enunciated eternal rights that were beyond revision or alteration. The Constitution recognized that, among these rights, the will of the people was not eternal but was and would forever be variable; for that reason, it provided, among other things, that the people themselves could revise its provisions. Thus, unlike the Declaration of Independence, in which the text is eternally the same, the "ideal form" of the Constitution is the revised, printed document that reflects the accumulation of amendments that, through the exercise of the will of the people, have altered the text. We must have an updated, revised copy in order to know what the Constitution says at any given moment; the original is only of antiquarian interest to the citizenry. Put another way, the original text of the Constitution was and is not intended to be a "one-time only" social contract but, instead, a revisable compact that was capable of being further perfected in the future and, perhaps, adapted to changing social and political conditions.

Unlike the Declaration of Independence, the ratification of the United States Constitution established a national state by creating new governmental institutions, by stipulating the relations between these new institutions and between the national government and the individual states, and by embedding the transcendent social purpose (the will of the people) in the maintenance and working of the entire system. But the will of the people was filtered, distorted, shaped, and deflected through institutional forms that should have made Tom Paine (and certainly Jean-Jacques Rousseau) condemn the regime that the founders constructed.[297] The Constitution nonetheless created a democratic regime, particularly with reference to the House of Representatives, and amply provided, throughout its susceptibility to amendment and improvisation

---

[297] With respect to ratification of the Constitution, Paine later took positions much closer to the Federalists than to the Antifederalists, who were in many other respects his ideological allies. For examples, see Van Cleve, *We Have Not a Government*, pp. 201–2, 282–3.

(particularly the emergence of formally organized political parties), for the (albeit filtered) expression of the will of the people.[298]

Radical democrats were suspicious of the new regime and it was at that point that the rights of Englishmen, almost paradoxically, reared their head once again in the form of the Bill of Rights. The first ten amendments to the Constitution, adopted almost immediately after the new national state quickened into existence, resurrected many of the rights of Englishmen and placed them once more at the heart of regime rule. Very much like the rights of Englishmen for which colonists had fought in the revolutionary war, these were constraints on governmental authority. Although they could be theoretically revised when embedded in the new constitution, they were conceived as eternal truths and have never been changed. We might reinterpret their meaning, but a revision of the actual text is almost unthinkable.[299]

The transcendent social purpose of the new American state was the creation and maintenance of a political community in which the will of the people controls the creation and exercise of political power, circumscribed by the protection of individual rights that are essential to the free determination of the will of the people as a collective. That is the ideal construction. The pragmatic construction was the erection of institutions that effectively filtered

---

[298] When the delegates were not preoccupied with other, more instrumental issues, they devoted much of their time to the "process of politics" that the Constitution would create, particularly with the regeneration of the popular will over time as an effective influence on the state. However, they did not subscribe to the ideological conceit that the manipulations of the process that encouraged this regeneration would be "content-free" and thus recognized that there are substantive implications whenever the expression of the will of the people is filtered and deflected. There is a parallel here in that the people can *wish* their will to be fettered by, among other things, the Bill of Rights in precisely the same way that Iranian Shi'ites *wish* to be fettered by the theocratic elements of their own constitutional system.

[299] Because the Bill of Rights placed limitations on the popular will even as it constrained the exercise of state power, Jefferson contended that the justification for these and other constitutional limits on the will of the people expired naturally. In a letter to Madison, he wrote on September 6, 1789:

[I]t may be proved that no society can make a perpetual constitution, or even a perpetual law. The earth belongs always to the living generation. They may manage it then, and what proceeds from it, as they please, during their usufruct. They are masters too of their own persons, and consequently may govern them as they please. But persons and property make the sum of the objects of government. The constitution and the laws of their predecessors extinguished them, in their natural course, with those whose will gave them being. This could preserve that being till it ceased to be itself, and no longer. Every constitution, then, and every law, naturally expires at the end of 19 years. If it be enforced longer, it is an act of force and not of right.

Quoted in Emily Zackin, *Looking for Rights in All the Wrong Places: Why State Constitutions Contain America's Positive Rights* (Princeton, NJ: Princeton University Press, 2013), p. 51n. But Jefferson was in many ways an idealist. For a more pragmatic perspective, see Jed Rubenfeld, "Moment and the Millennium," *George Washington Law Review* 66: 5/6 (1998), p. 1105.

and shaped the ways in which that will could be expressed.[300] In addition, those same institutions and the practices they engendered determined the political (and social) identities of the individuals who could participate in that will.

Those institutions and the identities they engendered would fend off a return to the aristocratic pretensions of monarchy by orienting the people toward a common conception of "proper" politics, a politics in which the personalities of leaders and citizens were distinctly secondary to their identities as virtuous republicans. In describing "Benjamin Franklin's career as a republican states-man," for example, Michael Warner recognized an implicit contradiction between "the statesman's task" as the personal embodiment of "legitimate power," on the one hand, and "the task of republicanism [which] was to remove legitimacy from the hands of persons," on the other.[301] This contradic-tion underlay the transition from English identity (embedded in an emotional attachment to the king's person) to a new republican state (embedded in the abstract rights, liberties, and will of the people).[302]

The founders realized that, in order to survive, this new republican state had to somehow draw upon and cultivate popular emotions, but the transfer from king to nation could not proceed through the personalities of the new leaders. Self-abnegation was thus required and nowhere was this self-abnegation more evident than in George Washington's service as presiding officer of the Constitutional Convention and as the first president of the United States.[303] As Alexander Hamilton noted just after the Philadelphia Convention sent the Constitution to the states, ratification would largely depend on the "very great weight of influence of the persons who framed it, particularly in the universal

---

[300] The revolutionary war had raised some groups, such as war privateers, into the American economic elite while punishing others, such as merchants who previously engaged in foreign trade. Both groups, however, could and did support conservative economic policies. That was the case even though their relative economic positions had been affected in very different ways by the war. Van Cleve, *We Have Not a Government*, p. 25. On the enabling of the will of the people as a secondary aim, at best, in the design of the Constitution, see p. 296.

[301] Warner, *Letters of the Republic*, p. 73.

[302] Popular veneration of new institutions takes time and personal charisma must fill the gap between a founding and the emergence of a self-sustaining political stability. Fischer provides a colorful description of the symbols, songs, and depictions of "liberty" that also played an important role in creating an American identity. David Hackett Fischer, *Liberty and Freedom* (New York: Oxford University Press, 2005), pp. 1–166.

[303] Washington spoke only once at the Constitutional Convention. On that occasion, the final day of deliberations, he contended that a minimum of 40,000 people per member of the House of Representatives was too high. The delegates immediately reduced the minimum to 30,000. Morgan, *Inventing the People*, p. 274; Maier, *Ratification*, p. 38. Wood describes Washington's resignation as commander-in-chief of the American forces on December 23, 1783, as the "greatest act of his life, the one that gave him his greatest fame," precisely because his retirement from public life came at the moment of his greatest public fame and power. Wood, *Radicalism*, pp. 205–6. Washington, of course, came out of this retirement several years later.

popularity of General Washington."[304] Hamilton rather pointedly did not refer to the affection that Americans might hold for their common "country." If Washington had deviated from the role that circumstance had assigned him, he would have endangered the birth of the nation. He enjoyed the almost universal affection of his people precisely because he denied that he was anything but the embodiment of the abstract rights, liberties, and will of the people he ruled. Perhaps more than any other person, Madison understood that deification of the founders, particularly Washington, was necessary in order to impart to "the government ... that veneration which time bestows on every thing."[305] But deification was only possible if the gods themselves denied their divinity.[306]

While many of the founders were mesmerized by short-term economic and political interests, others, such as Madison, Hamilton, Washington, and Jay, envisioned a framework in which the national state would ensure its own success. Like the Bolsheviks, French revolutionaries, and probably all founders of whatever ideological hue, the founders believed that a "properly formed state" would generate "properly formed political beliefs." One of the enduring curiosities of the American founding is, in fact, how the pragmatic and instrumentally dominated process in the Constitutional Convention ultimately created a popular expectation that serious problems would be solved by the new government when, in reality, no one knew how this new political framework would actually work.[307] After wallowing for years in a mire of self-interested and shortsighted contemplations on the problem of governance, the

---

[304] Hamilton also juxtaposed "democratical jealousy" (arising out of the limits of popular influence in the constitutional plan) against the charismatic appeal of Washington and the other founders. Klarman, *Framers' Coup*, pp. 305–6. In a note, Klarman adds: "It is hard to overstate the extent to which most Americans at the time revered Washington."

[305] Klarman, *Framers' Coup*, p. 4; also see Wood, *Radicalism*, pp. 208–9. As Waldstreicher put it: "Washington symbolized the nation and all that was redemptive in it." David Waldstreicher, *In the Midst of Perpetual Fetes: The Making of American Nationalism, 1776–1820* (Chapel Hill, NC: Omohundro Institute of Early American History and Culture, 1997), p. 118.

[306] In this passage from no. 49 of *The Federalist*, Madison was not explicitly referring to the enshrinement of the founders as demigods but was attempting to refute Jefferson's contention that constitutions should be frequently revised because "every appeal to the people would carry an implication of some defect in the government" and thus "deprive the government of that veneration which time bestows on every thing, and without which perhaps the wisest and freest governments would not possess the requisite stability." Alexander Hamilton, John Jay, and James Madison, *The Federalist*, eds. George W. Carey and James McClellan (Indianapolis, IN: Liberty Fund, 2001), p. 262.

[307] Klarman writes:

As Madison explained in *Federalist No. 37*, the need for such compromises [during the Constitutional Convention] compelled the convention "to sacrifice theoretical propriety to the force of extraneous considerations," which ensured that the final product deviated "from that artificial structure and regular symmetry which an abstract view of the subject might lead an ingenious theorist to bestow on a constitution planned in his closet or in his imagination." (Klarman, *Framers' Coup*, pp. 599–600)

American people somehow and in some way found the courage to leap over the chasm of uncertainty and doubt that attended their founding and embrace the new American state as their own.

The Federalist papers are rife with that kind of logic.[308] Put another way, the American founders were guided and driven by a well-disciplined and finely honed hope that things would turn out well.[309] Just after the Constitution had been ratified, George Washington wrote to Henry Lee, Jr.: "In our endeavours to establish a new general government, the contest, nationally considered, seems not to have been so much for glory, as existence. It was for a long time doubtful whether we were to survive as an independent Republic, or decline from our federal dignity into insignificant & wretched fragments of Empire." The problems of designing the mechanics of the new republic so that it might surmount the challenges of nationhood and of somehow charting a path toward successful ratification necessarily meant that the founders hoped that the new nation might attract emotional support and affection without being able to do much to make that likely.[310]

The United States Constitution and, in particular, the Bill of Rights were backward-looking in the sense that they constrained the working of the will of the people in ways that (at least in most modern formulations) compromise democracy.[311] The 1787 Constitution thus marked a transition from an

---

[308] We should, however, not overestimate the influence the essays published in *The Federalist* might have had on ratification debates. For that, see, for example, Maier, *Ratification*, pp. xi, 84–5, 257. And, as Maier also notes, the almost unanimous support for the new constitution among the country's newspapers along with intimidation by the residents of the major cities, ranging "from wealthy merchants to rowdy sailors, dockworkers, and also many tradesmen and mechanics," were more important factors favoring ratification. The *Massachusetts Gazette*, for example, contended: "The proper definition of the word anti-federalism is anarchy, confusion, rebellion, treason, sacrilege, and rapine" (pp. 73–5, 147). On the other hand, Wirls points out that *The Federalist* contains about 200,000 words devoted to explicating the 4,400 words of the Constitution and makes a good case for the volume's importance in creating a distinctive, coherent, and often elegant *American* theory of politics. Its influence endures even if its weight was not fully felt during ratification. Daniel Wirls, *The Federalist Papers and Institutional Power in American Political Development* (New York: Palgrave Macmillan, 2015), p. 6.

[309] Hamilton, for example, believed that the assumption of the debts of the individual states by the federal government would simultaneously create a new class of loyalists for the national government out of those who purchased federal bonds and transpose the primary locus of the will of the people from the states to the federal government. Federal bondholders would, of course, become self-interested agents in this transposition but they would also be caught up within it as they attempted to create a nationalism that would encourage the people to make the new government economically viable. That viability, in turn, depended on whether or not the people themselves were convinced that this new nation warranted their loyalty and affection, above and beyond the mere materiality of its purposes and as something that now and in the future would bulk large in their lives.

[310] Van Cleve, *We Have Not a Government*, p. 279.

[311] The Bill of Rights placed some things, such as freedom of religion and freedom of assembly, beyond the will of the people in the sense that the federal government could not, as the agent of that will, violate them. Individual rights were thus limits on popular sovereignty as well as constraints placed on government. When framed at the founding, these rights were theoretically

emphasis on popular consent with respect to the rights of Englishmen to rights as venerable limitations on government authority. Both were well within the ambit of English constitutional tradition. However, eighteenth-century Britain was in the process of revising that constitutional tradition and was, as a consequence, becoming comparatively "forward-looking" in its warm embrace of parliamentary sovereignty. Although it would take many decades before manhood suffrage became the mode through which the people were represented in the House of Commons, the chamber was already, in theory, the unmediated expression of the will of the people.[312]

The French intellectual and political elite paid close attention to events in America, not only because their own country participated in the war for independence but also because they thought that the Americans were opening up a new age in which enlightened judgment and logic could thoroughly remodel the Old World as well as give birth to the New. But what they learned was not the lesson that the Americans taught.[313] While the will of the people first arises as a modern, democratic principle in the American

created in accordance with the will of the people. That may be so but they were also limits and constraints on the expression of that will as it might change and evolve in the future. As Klarman puts it, James Madison regarded "one of the beauties of popular sovereignty" as a political principle "was that it did not mandate any particular political arrangement, so long as the people endorsed the overall system," and thus it could encompass such limits and constraints. Klarman, *Framers' Coup*, p. 608. From that perspective, the will of the people could (and, in Madison's view, did) bind itself to many of the constraints of English constitutional tradition. In explaining why constitution-making in the United States was so elite-driven, Klarman states that "most Federalists doubted that the people were sufficiently calm, wise, or well informed to play a responsible role in devising their own system of government" (p. 537). But he could also have noted that the people had to have doubted themselves as well.

[312] On this point, see Reid, *Constitutional History*, pp. 4–5.

[313] According to Palmer:

In France, in addition to incredible effusions on the state of nature in which the Americans were supposed to have been living, there was a good deal of serious discussion of the new American governments ... What impressed them the most was that the Americans had created new governments by rational and deliberate planning. In each state delegates had met in an assembly or convention which exercised the sovereignty of the people. This assembly had prepared a written constitution for the state; it created government, calling it into being and issuing authority to it by explicit grant; it set up and defined various offices and functions, which it artfully balanced one against the other to prevent the abuse of power. In short, the Americans seemed to have acted out and thereby proved the idea of the social contract. The American constitutions ... seemed to represent an act of free and rational self-determination. In content, they knew nothing of inherited position, royal, magisterial or lordly; no one possessed any but a delegated authority; there were no governing classes, no legal orders, no estates of society, no one privileged in taxation, and no one with any special or personal right to govern because of birth. All were citizens, all were equal, and all were free.

Although some recognized that the Americans "had carried over a good deal from their English and colonial past," many more "thought of the Americans as having no past, unencumbered by history, free of prejudice, superstition and Gothic night – specimens of man in the abstract." Palmer, "Social and Psychological Foundations," pp. 441–2.

founding and was closely bound up with the emergence of the citizen as the ground for a national political identity, the will of the people was not up for grabs, as it was in the French Revolution. It was, instead, tethered to the rights of Englishmen from the very beginning and, through the influence of those rights, filtered, tamed, and manufactured into a foundation for a politically stable state.

4

The Declaration of the Rights of Man and of the Citizen

The French Revolution

SECTION I: FROM THE ESTATES-GENERAL TO THE EXECUTION OF THE KING

Before 1789, the king was the "sacred center" of French society and his charismatic aura legitimated the political elite who actually governed the nation. The mystique of the monarchy was continuously regenerated by an ensemble of mythological narratives, ritual forms, symbolic regalia, historical tradition, and an attendant nobility; as a result, the king gave the French people a social unity and political coherence that, in turn, conferred order and stability. While political, instrumental calculation shaped much of what went on at Versailles, the charisma of the monarchy psychologically and emotionally connected the common people to the very ground of their collective, cosmological existence. Although, in the words of Clifford Geertz, "majesty is made, not born," the mystique of the monarchy rested on a largely irrational foundation. There are only two origins for such a sacred center: descent from inherited tradition and invention through a revolution.[1]

Because the most striking feature of the French Revolution was the utter destruction of the king as the sacred center of society, the major problem confronting those who made this revolution was how to invent something that could replace the monarchy.[2] There were certainly candidates in the form of

---

[1] Clifford Geertz, "Centers, Kings, and Charisma: Reflections on the Symbolics of Power" in Clifford Geertz, *Local Knowledge* (New York: Basic Books, 2000), pp. 152–3. As Geertz notes, Edward Shils first created the notion of a "sacred center."

[2] Referring to the French Revolution as an illustrative case, Charles Taylor says that the "people" were first "expelled from [the] old forms" that had symbolically stabilized the *ancien régime* and then found it difficult to "find their feet in the new structures." In order to do that, they needed to "connect some transformed practices to the new [revolutionary] principles [in order] to form a viable social imaginary." The period in between these two events was unavoidably chaotic

mystical notions of the "virtuous people," the "General Will," the Nation, and "enlightened reason." We should add to this list a rather vigorous nationalism arising out of a commonly recognized world destiny that emerged, in one way or another, from these things. But there were several apparently insuperable difficulties. First, none of these alternatives clearly dominated the others. Second, they were collectively incompatible in practice. And, lastly, they were each subject to variable interpretation, particularly with respect to the person to whom they should assign power and authority. Power and authority were certainly wielded during the French Revolution but they were wielded, for the most part, in the absence of charismatic legitimation. Much of the history of the French Revolution thus became a serial experimentation with political forms in which alternative constructions of a new sacred center were tried out and found wanting.[3] In the end, the revolution yielded to its lowest common denominator in the form of nationalism and a desire for political stability: Napoleon.

The French Revolution went through several phases, each one contributing something different to the melding of a transcendent social purpose with the state. The first opened with the beginning of the revolution in June 1789, when the third estate successfully transformed the Estates-General into the National Assembly. This phase ended when Louis XVI was sent to the guillotine on January 21, 1793. The primary contribution to the founding during this period was the drafting and passage of the Declaration of the Rights of Man and of the Citizen, which ultimately became the most durable and influential statement of liberal political principles in the history of Western civilization. In addition, much of the governing structure was reformed along Enlightenment conceptions of administrative standardization and efficiency. However, the revolutionary attempt to create a state that embodied the principles pronounced in the Declaration of Rights collapsed when none of the contending political factions would unequivocally embrace a constitutional monarchy. While a constitutional

---

because the new social and political structures for assigning authority and legitimacy did not yet exist. We can here replace "social imaginary" with "sacred center" with little loss of meaning. Charles Taylor, *Modern Social Imaginaries* (Durham, NC: Duke University Press, 2004), p. 18.

[3] For a roughly parallel interpretation, see Lynn Hunt, *Politics, Culture, and Class in the French Revolution* (Berkeley: University of California Press, 2004), p. 26. Hunt concludes that the flip side of a popular desire for a mythic "national regeneration was an enormous, collective anxiety" concerning whether or not a "new consensus" would prove stable (p. 32). More generally, Hunt describes a search for symbols that might constitute a new "sacred center" for the nation. There are two partially contradictory interpretations we might entertain while reading her text. On the one hand, the search appears to be a serial consideration of alternatives in which we might suppose that the people had preexisting, stable cultural preferences or predilections. The perfect (or even adequate) symbolic formulation, in this interpretation, would "feel right" once it was presented. On the other hand, the construction of a new "sacred center" appears to be so novel as to preclude the possibility of preexisting preferences or sympathies. That was what made the process of serial consideration so unstable: Preferences and the orientation toward a collective identity (i.e., the new regime and its relation to the new concept of a citizen) were being created at the same time.

monarchy was the most obvious available compromise, the historical construc-tion of the absolutist kingship in France, unlike the limited powers of the English throne, starkly exposed the contradictions between a monarchy in any form and the logical basis of a republican state.[4] Under stress (and there was plenty of stress), Louis XVI responded to those contradictions by simply refusing to play the part that the revolutionaries had assigned to him.

The second phase opened with the beheading of the king and closed with the execution of the Girondins on October 31, 1793. During this brief period, the deputies drafted a constitution that did, in fact, embody most of the principles in the original Declaration of Rights. However, the democratic republic envi-sioned in this constitution was almost immediately suspended. Even though it never went into effect, the full and almost unqualified endorsement of manhood suffrage in this constitution was a major contribution to the founding of the modern French state. During this phase, the streets of Paris belonged to the people, and the people, in turn, were mobilized by leaders motivated by both personal ambition and populist sympathies.

Although these leaders could and did intimidate the deputies of the National Convention, they ran into a contradiction they could not resolve. On the one hand, their dedication to Rousseau's thought made it impossible to design and erect a stable governance structure. That inability, in turn, compelled a resort to authoritarian terror in order to maintain their authority. On the other hand, the desires of the people of Paris were, as a proxy for the General Will of the nation, an unstable ground upon which to erect even an authoritarian regime. While the period in which the people of Paris constituted the most vital revolutionary force was the most chaotic and violent phase of the revolution, the commitment of the regime to an emotional validation of political legitimacy and to spontan-eous direct democracy nonetheless became durable contributions to the founding of the French state. This phase came to an end with the execution of Robespierre on July 28, 1794.[5] Although Robespierre's fall ushered in a movement back toward Enlightenment principles, little or nothing of import-ance with respect to the founding of the modern French state subsequently occurred until Napoleon took power in 1799.[6]

---

[4] William Doyle, *The Oxford History of the French Revolution*, second edition (New York: Oxford University Press, 2002), p. 135.

[5] These three phases are substantially the same as the "three revolutions" described by Jonathan Israel in his *Revolutionary Ideas: An Intellectual History of the French Revolution from the Rights of Man to Robespierre* (Princeton, NJ: Princeton University Press, 2015), p. 695. For a description of the "three main factions" that corresponded to these revolutions, see p. 66.

[6] As Davidson puts it, "[w]ith the Fall of Robespierre, the French Revolution came to a juddering halt," but he then adds that "it did not come to rest for nothing had been settled." Ian Davidson, *The French Revolution: From Enlightenment to Tyranny* (New York: Pegasus Books, 2016), p. 232. For changes in the policies and politics of the revolution after Robespierre's execution, see Israel, *Revolutionary Ideas*, pp. 583–6, 591, 597, 628. For most purposes, we will consider Robespierre's execution as the end of the revolution. However, as Mason contends, this is as

It is plausible, even likely, that most of those who made the French Revolution would not have embarked on the project had they known what it would entail.[7] For one thing, many of the most active and prominent among them would go to the guillotine at some point. So it is reasonable to ask what caused the revolution. There is broad agreement that social change in terms of economic development and the consequent rise of a commercial class as a political counterpart to the traditional landed nobility was one factor. However, as in England, intermarriage between these classes, along with ennoblement of wealthy merchants, had ameliorated conflict between them.[8] A much more important element was the impending bankruptcy of the French monarchy.[9] This problem was aggravated by antiquated institutions that both balkanized the capital's relations with the provinces and insulated most wealth from taxation. Feudal privileges, for example, exempted most noble and church property from taxation while imposing labor obligations and other dues on agricultural laborers.[10] In the absence of a fiscal crisis, these increasingly antiquated arrangements would only have meant that France, like most of Europe at the time, was still locked into a fading feudal system, stable if stagnant.[11]

much a matter of convenience as it is a settled historical judgment. Laura Mason, "Thermidor and the Myth of Rupture" in David Andress (ed.), *The Oxford Handbook of the French Revolution* (New York: Oxford University Press, 2015), p. 521.

[7] Hunt noted that most interpretations of the French Revolution heavily discount the significance of "intentions" because "what the revolutionaries intended" did not matter if none of their intentions actually came to pass. For her, the explanation for what happened lies in the dynamics of the process within which the revolution unfolded. That process was unpredictably opaque to the participants even as their intentions determined the trajectory. Hunt, *Politics, Culture, and Class*, pp. 9–10.

[8] For debate over how the nobility should be defined, whether or not that class was in decline, and its relationship to the commercial economy, see Jonathan Dewald, "Rethinking the 1 Percent: The Failure of the Nobility in Old Regime France"; Nicolas Tackett, "Violence and the 1 Percent: The Fall of the Medieval Chinese Aristocracy in Comparison to the Fall of the French Nobility" and "Rethinking the 1 Percent: A Response"; Timothy Tackett, "The Nobility and the Long-Term Origins of the French Revolution"; and Gail Bossenga, "The Nobility's Demise: Institutions, Status, and the Role of the State" in *American Historical Review* 124: 3 (2019), pp. 911–54.

[9] This is thoroughly examined and interpreted in Theda Skocpol, *States and Social Revolutions: A Comparative Analysis of France, Russia, and China* (New York: Cambridge University Press, 1979), pp. 47–66.

[10] "Under this accumulation of obligations the peasant felt himself [to be] little more than the beast of burden he was." Georges Lefebvre, trans. Elizabeth Moss Evanson, *The French Revolution from Its Origins to 1793* (New York: Columbia University Press, 1969), vol. 1, p. 48. Also see Peter McPhee, *Liberty or Death: The French Revolution* (New Haven, CT: Yale University Press, 2016), p. 3; Doyle, *French Revolution*, pp. 11–12; D. Dakin, "The Breakdown of the Old Regime in France" in A. Goodwin (ed.), *The New Cambridge Modern History. Volume 8: The American and French Revolutions, 1763–93* (Cambridge: Cambridge University Press, 1965), p. 600. For a general description of the French peasantry, see David Andress, *The French Revolution and the People* (London: Hambledon and London, 2004), chapter 1.

[11] While almost all analysts consider most of the institutions and social relations underpinning the *ancien régime* to be antiquated, some consider those who staffed and advised the highest rungs of

There were, however, several additional factors that undermined the stability of the *ancien régime*. The first was the combination of a growing population and a string of poor harvests that put much of the population on the verge of starvation. Although the monarchy was traditionally responsible for tiding over those at risk, the crown found it increasingly difficult to meet the rising demand for bread. Hunger, as a result, became a major catalyst undercutting the legitimacy of the crown.[12] While the monarchy could do little about either the birth rate or the weather, it simultaneously chose to entertain international ambitions that demanded large military expenditures.[13] In 1789, the French navy was probably the most modern and technologically advanced institution in the country but it was also bankrupting the treasury.[14] One of the ironies of history is that this navy facilitated what might be considered decisive French intervention in the American Revolution while, at the same time, hastening the onset of revolution at home.[15]

The proximate cause of the French Revolution was thus the fiscal crisis brought on by chronic deficits in the royal accounts. This crisis came to a head when domestic and international lenders became increasingly reluctant to fund the shortfall. This reluctance, in turn, originated in the inability of the crown to persuade other institutions, most particularly the Paris *parlement*, to ratify reform proposals that would have both increased the rate of taxation and

state administration to be "a glowing example of advanced liberal culture." Andress, for example, places Simon Schama in that camp. For these analysts, the problem was not the adequacy of reform initiatives proposed by the crown but the array of social interests who had to be persuaded to consent to their enactment and the fact that none of the latter believed that they had much at stake in the success of these proposals. David Andress, *French Society in Revolution, 1789–1799* (Manchester: Manchester University Press, 1999), p. 165. For summary statements of Schama's argument, see Simon Schama, *Citizens: A Chronicle of the French Revolution* (New York: Alfred A. Knopf, 1989), pp. 63, 66.

[12] On the agricultural crisis during the 1780s, see, for example, Lefebvre, *French Revolution*, vol. 1, pp. 116–19.

[13] For an overview of the fiscal crisis engendered by military and naval expenditures, see Thomas Ertman, *Birth of the Leviathan: Building States and Regimes in Medieval and Early Modern Europe* (Cambridge: Cambridge University Press, 1997), pp. 139–51.

[14] Skocpol, *States and Social Revolutions*, pp. 47–67. As Hunt put it, both Tocqueville and Skocpol considered the French Revolution to be the agent of "state modernization." Hunt, *Politics, Culture, and Class*, p. 7. On the impact of participation in the American Revolution on French finances, see Sheri Berman, *Democracy and Dictatorship in Europe: From the Ancien Régime to the Present Day* (New York: Oxford University Press, 2019), p. 54. On the fiscal crisis generally, see Schama, *Citizens*, pp. 62, 70–1, 93, 288, 383. Also see Lefebvre, French Revolution, vol. 1, pp. 97–101; Doyle, *French Revolution*, pp. 131–4; McPhee, *Liberty or Death*, pp. 41–7, 56–7.

[15] Alfred Cobban, *A History of Modern France. Volume 1: Old Regime and Revolution, 1715–1799* (Baltimore, MD: Penguin Books, 1957), p. 122. On the influence of the American Revolution on the French Revolution more generally, see Jeremy D. Popkin, *A New World Begins* (New York: Basic Books, 2019), pp. 71–2.

rationalized those institutions responsible for collecting revenue.[16] The king could still theoretically resort to the absolutist authority of the throne in order to increase revenue, but it was increasingly clear that compliance with such commands would meet intense resistance. The only way out of the fiscal crisis was the construction of a broader popular base for monarchical authority in order to enact financial reform. And that meant that a solution to the fiscal crisis was dependent on political change.

THE MONARCHY, THE NATION, AND THE PEOPLE

There were three alternative sources of political legitimacy at the onset of what became the French Revolution (see Table 4.1). One of them was the monarchy, which, although disparaged by many of the elite, still attracted broad support among the people. As a result, the crown could still display its royal majesty through public rituals and draw upon the spontaneous obedience of its subjects. And these were not mere forms. In 1766, for example, Louis XV appeared before the Paris *parlement* and summarily asserted his divine right to rule France in language that brooked no compromise.

It is in my person alone that sovereign power resides ... It is from me alone that my courts derive their authority; and the plenitude of this authority, which they exercise only in my name, remains always in me ... It is to me alone that legislative power belongs, without any dependence and without any division ... the whole public order emanates from me, and the rights and interests of the nation ... are necessarily joined with mine and rest only in my hands.[17]

While the monarchy drew on the tradition and custom of centuries in creating an aura of rightful authority, crown policy and practices had also insinuated royal prerogatives into almost every aspect of social and economic relations in the country.[18] There were vast interests, in the form of social privileges and the prevailing distribution of wealth, that more or less depended on the crown's political legitimacy. As a consequence, there was thus almost no way of dismantling the monarchy without, at the same time, destabilizing the prevailing social order.

Set against the mythology of divine right and the sacred majesty of the king was the Enlightenment – or, more exactly, the reign of reason – as the arbiter of

---

[16] On the role and structure of the *parlements* before the revolution, see Schama, *Citizens*, pp. 104–5, 260–72; Doyle, *French Revolution*, pp. 2, 37, 39, 76–83, 87–8.

[17] Quoted in Doyle, *French Revolution*, p. 38.

[18] Most accounts of royal authority rightly focus on the crown's alignment with feudal privileges enjoyed by the landed nobility and franchises granted to tax farmers and economic producers of basic commodities. However, the king's representatives also intervened in family relations in ways that both affirmed and extended royal power in some of the most intimate affairs of the common people. Arlette Farge and Michel Foucault, ed. Nancy Luxon, *Disorderly Families: Infamous Letters from the Bastille Archives* (Minneapolis: University of Minnesota Press, 2017).

TABLE 4.1. *The monarchy, the nation, and the people as competing sources of political legitimacy*

Feature	Monarchy	The nation-state	The people
Legitimating ideology	Divine right, sanctioned by tradition and the Catholic Church	The Enlightenment, more particularly, reason and science	Rousseau's conceptualization of the General Will, natural virtue, and direct democracy
Institutional locus	The royal court at Versailles, particularly the king's ministers	Separation of legislative, executive, and judicial functions	Supremacy of the legislature within the government but subordination of the legislature to the people
Role of elections	None, with the exception of the selection of members of Estates-General	Periodic selection of members of the legislature	Periodic selection of members of the legislature
Relation of members of the legislature to the electorate	Members collectively represent the Church, the nobility, and the third estate within the organic unity of the feudal social order	Members represent those who elect them but are expected to use reason, shaped by political debate, in choosing how to act	Members are subordinated to the General Will and must be guided by the wishes of their constituents at all times; they are also subject to recall and dismissal
Conception of justice	The king's will through use of *lettres de cachet*	The rule of law, trial, evidence, and the ability of the accused to mount a defense	Judgment and punishment are often summary and rendered by the people or those who act in their name; personal virtue is independent of evidence and proof of guilt
Federal structure	The relation of the provinces to the royal government varies greatly depending on when and how they were incorporated into the kingdom	Division of authority between the center and local governments depending on which is best suited for carrying out functions	Power and authority are highly concentrated in the central government

Note: This is a highly simplified summary of the varying positions of the monarchists, the Girondins, and the Jacobins, respectively. These are elaborated in detail in the text.

opinion and umpire of evidence. Under its sway, nothing was beyond the capacity of rational possibility and nothing was exempt from logical critique. The political program emerging out of this interpretation of the nature of social and physical reality was hostile to those accidents of history that had morphed into customary and habitual social relations, social relations that had no other justification than unthinking respect for tradition. All institutions and governing arrangements that could not pass the test of reason should be replaced by rational institutions in which all men would be citizens with mutual rights and obligations, both to one another and to the government that they would jointly create.[19]

If the monarchy had any role to play in this transformation, it was to serve as the centralized authority that could prepare the way for reform. The crown, for example, could rationalize state administration by modernizing bureaucratic procedures and simplifying administrative design.[20] Some progress in that direction had already been made but the royal government was still riddled with obligations such as pensions granted to courtiers and practices such as tax farming that were major impediments to modern conceptions of efficiency. Royal prerogatives and authority could also potentially replace the pastiche of feudal arrangements that governed both the center's relations with the provinces and antique social relations between the peasantry and the nobility with a more rational regime in which equality and uniformity would determine the structure of politics and the economy.[21]

The hope that the monarchy could somehow be brought into alignment with this enlightened reform program pragmatically recognized that the call to reason was not nearly as popular with the masses as it was with the commercial and intellectual elite. In the opening stages of what became the revolution, a major and crucial part of the nobility also answered this call; they, together with the commercial and intellectual elite, became the (rational) bridge across which the romantics swarmed as they destroyed the

---

[19] Schama, *Citizens*, p. 475. The Enlightenment, "with its insistent demand for the revaluation of all social institutions ... prepared the great cataclysm of 1789." W. Stark, "Literature and Thought: The Romantic Tendency, Rousseau, Kant" in Goodwin, *New Cambridge Modern History*, vol. 8, p. 55.

[20] Dakin, "The Breakdown of the Old Regime," p. 592.

[21] In a summary of state finance in the late eighteenth century, Bosher concludes that "reforms [begun] during the last years of the *ancien régime* [were] carried further by revolutionary governments." In fact, Bosher so strongly emphasized continuity in administrative development that the revolution seems to have little or no impact. J. F. Bosher, "French Administration and Public Finance in Their European Setting" in Goodwin, *New Cambridge Modern History*, vol. 8, p. 566. Dakin, on the other hand, contended that "the failure to inaugurate revolutionary changes from above" through the exercise of royal authority revealed what turned out to be a fatal contradiction between "the monarchy as a bureaucratic organization and the monarchy as an aristocratic institution" that rested upon the nobility and the Church. Dakin, "The Breakdown of the Old Regime," p. 616.

monarchy. These noble recruits to the Enlightenment program became the first casualties of the revolution.[22]

One of the most important reasons why the monarchy, which was generally sympathetic to much of the Enlightenment program, ultimately resisted alignment with reform was the hostility of many Enlightenment reformers to religion, both as belief (where it was condemned as rank superstition) and as an institution (where the Catholic Church was characterized as a predatory incubus upon the French nation).[23] The Church was, of course, the only institution that could legitimate the divine right of the king to rule the nation and, for that reason, destruction of the Church also meant destruction of the most important pillar of the monarchy. There might have been a remote possibility that the reformers could have convincingly crafted a bargain in which they would have guaranteed a constitutionally circumscribed role for the king in return for his assent to their program. However, Louis XVI was himself a devout Catholic for whom the tending of the spiritual needs of the faithful was a sacrosanct duty and attacks on the Church made such an agreement impossible.

The last potential source of political legitimacy was the French people, whose innate innocence and natural purity had been celebrated by Jean-Jacques Rousseau. Although Rousseau had been dead for over a decade when the French Revolution began, his writings were still the dominant intellectual force in the country. His bestselling novels *La Nouvelle Héloïse* and *Émile* presented readers with a vision "of innocence and virtue preserved and uncorrupted in the face of the snares and iniquities of established society."[24] In sharp

---

[22] Schama notes that there was often little, in terms of social relations, that distinguished this fraction of the nobility from other members of the reform coalition because "they all belonged to a common cultural milieu: the world of the Academies and the Masonic lodges. They all subscribed to the optimistic late-Enlightenment project that saw the sciences as necessarily leading to greater prosperity and more perfect government." Schama, *Citizens*, p. 517; also see pp. 116–17. However, any hope that the monarchy could have been the primary agent of modernizing France was probably dashed by the opposition of the greater part of the nobility that constituted the crown's primary social base. Lefebvre, *French Revolution*, vol. 1, pp. 89–90. On the ultimate incompatibility of the interests of the nobility and the bourgeoisie, see François Furet and Denis Richet, trans. Stephen Hardman, *French Revolution* (New York: Macmillan, 1970), p. 26.

[23] See, for example, Voltaire's discussion of the distinction between the simple belief in a "Supreme Power" and the mythological constructions of organized religion in the entries for "Popery" and "Religion" in M. de Voltaire, *A Philosophical Dictionary* (London: John and Henry L. Hunt, 1824), vol. 5, pp. 271–2, 396–415. However, Voltaire also believed that widespread religious belief was necessary for public morality; he only maintained that this belief should not be cloaked in the power of the state. Schama, *Citizens*, p. 483. On Voltaire's influence upon the revolution, see Doyle, *French Revolution*, pp. 49–50. On the Enlightenment as a critique of ecclesiastical authority, see Israel, *Revolutionary Ideas*, p. 703. On the power and influence of the Catholic Church before the revolution, including the denial of civil rights to Protestants, see Doyle, *French Revolution*, pp. 33, 36, 48, 54.

[24] Doyle, *French Revolution*, p. 52. *Héloïse* was reprinted in seventy-two editions between 1761 and 1800. *Émile* appeared in at least thirty-three editions over the same period. Jim

contrast to the central place of reason and science in Enlightenment thought, Rousseau offered his readers a vision grounded in the primal, innate virtue of man.[25] Depicting modern society as both corrupt and depraved, Rousseau thought that the only way to recover innocence was to empower the General Will of the people, because, when properly elicited, the General Will unfailingly reflected the universal good of society.[26] Under the social contract thus formed: "Each of us puts his goods, his person, his life, and all his power in common under the supreme direction of the general will, and we as a body accept each member as a part indivisible from the whole."[27]

Although those who preferred Enlightenment principles often had little use for Rousseau, his conception of a General Will appeared to transform the people into a single person and thus provided a "theoretical substitute for the sovereign will of an absolute monarch."[28] For monarchists, one of the attractive features of Rousseau's notion of the General Will was that, metaphorically at least, it lined up nicely with the *ancien régime* view that the king's will embodied the nation's interests without the mediation of intervening institutions.[29]

Miller, *Rousseau: Dreamer of Democracy* (New Haven, CT: Yale University Press, 1984), p. 134. However, certain passages on religion and religious belief in both *Émile* and the *Social Contract* were denounced as heretical after the books were published and Rousseau fled the country in order to avoid arrest. Doyle, *French Revolution*, p. 53.

[25] For a discussion of Rousseau's thought as a reaction to the Enlightenment, see Stark, "Literature and Thought," pp. 55–80. Stark, for one thing, contended "that if Voltaire was the spokesman of the *grande bourgeoisie*, still clamouring for reform but already half satisfied with things as they were, Rousseau was the protagonist of the *petite bourgeoisie*, eager for a total revolution and even announcing, to some extent, the proletarian class and the proletarian movement of the future" (p. 68).

[26] Stark summarized one of Rousseau's early essays this way: "We ourselves still bear within us the original of human nature, only that the rubbish of civilization has increasingly overlaid it and must be taken away, or at least thought away, in order to allow the genuine primitive archetype to show itself in its true outline and colours." Stark, "Literature and Thought," p. 62.

[27] The quotation is from *Émile*. McPhee, *Liberty or Death*, p. 31.

[28] Sydenham contended that the "[r]evolutionaries inherited the absolutist belief that the State must be directed towards a single ultimate good by the single will which alone could comprehend that ideal." Michael Sydenham, *The Girondins* (London: Athlone Press, 1961), p. 181. From that perspective, the "attraction of Rousseau's theory for the men of the French Revolution was that he apparently had found a highly ingenious means to put a multitude into the place of a single person; for the general will was nothing more or less than what bound the many into one." Hannah Arendt, *On Revolution* (New York: Penguin Books, 2006), pp. 66–7, 147. This was one instance in which philosophical principles did not create the revolution but, instead, "it was ... the Revolution which created their influence." Joan McDonald, *Rousseau and the French Revolution, 1762–1791* (London: Athlone Press, 1965), p. 10. The quote is from J. J. Mounier.

[29] Some monarchists, for that reason, contended that Rousseau's notion of the General Will could provide the foundation for an enlightened kingship in that the king could express "the constant and general will of the nation, as opposed to the transient will of the deputies who ... were subject to particular interests and personal ambitions." McDonald, *Rousseau and the French*

This commingling of the General Will and a theory of kingship can be seen in one of the grievances (*cahiers*) drawn up as part of the process through which the Estates-General was formed.[30] In the Île-de-France, the electors declared that it was "the general will of the Nation that game [laws that prevented peasants from protecting their fields from rabbits and birds] should be destroyed since it carries off a third of the subsistence of citizens and this is the intention of our good King who watches over the common good of his people and who loves them."[31]

Rousseau held that the people, once they had set aside their own particular interests and private desires, would readily recognize the preeminence of a General Will in which they would all individually participate. Their collective participation in the revelation of that General Will would subordinate the formal structure of government with its agencies, officials, and bureaus to the direct rule of the people. As set down in his *Social Contract*, he proposed that such a politics would both legitimate political authority and, at the same time, preserve natural liberty.[32] For logistical reasons arising out of the need for

---

Revolution, pp. 140, 143. The problem that allowed the monarchists to propose such an apparently perverse reading of Rousseau was that, once the people could not directly legislate, there was no obvious "second-best" mechanism for revealing the General Will. Rousseau himself believed both that either representative democracy or monarchy were necessary for the governance of a large nation *and* that both were to be condemned as "tending always toward despotism" (pp. 148–9).

[30] On the content and role of the *cahiers*, see McPhee, *Liberty or Death*, pp. 60–5; Lefebvre, *French Revolution*, vol. 1, pp. 107–9; Schama, *Citizens*, pp. 309–18. For a very careful, critical survey of the interpretative literature, see Pierre-Yves Beaurepaire, "The View from Below: The 1789 *cahiers de doléances*" in Andress, *Oxford Handbook of the French Revolution*, pp. 149–63. After completing the "immense task" of reading all of the cahiers, Tocqueville concluded "that nothing less is demanded than the simultaneous and systematic repeal of all the laws and the abolition of all the customs prevailing in the country" and that, if he had read them in 1789 when they were written, he would have seen "at once that one of the great revolutions the world ever saw is impending." Quoted in Andress, *French Revolution and the People*, p. 95. As Schama points out, the king's invitation to the people to "register their grievances at the same time they elected their representatives" had no counterpart in the constitutional upheavals in Britain in 1688 or the United States in either 1776 or 1789 (p. 293).

[31] Quoted in Schama, *Citizens*, p. 323.

[32] Rousseau, in his *Les Confessions*, wrote:

I saw that everything depended fundamentally on politics, and that, no matter how one looked at it, no people could ever be anything but what the nature of its government made it; thus this great question of the best possible government seemed to me to reduce itself to this. What is the nature of government suitable for forming a people that is the most virtuous, the most enlightened, the wisest, in short the best, taking the word in its broadest sense. (quoted in Hunt, *Politics, Culture, and Class*, p. 1)

Between 1792 and 1795, thirteen new editions of the *Social Contract* appeared. McPhee, *Liberty or Death*, p. 239. Citing Robert Darnton's work, Burrows notes that much of the popular literature of the period also "put across a simplified Rousseauism to readers unable to comprehend Rousseau's original political texts." Simon Burrows, "Books, Philosophy, Enlightenment" in

constant mutual consultation among the people, such a politics would be practical only in a small city-state.[33]

There were several modes through which Rousseau's thought shaped the politics of the revolution. First, his readership was so vast and the emotional pull of his novels was so strong that the literate French public was thoroughly immersed in his ways of thinking about politics and society.[34] While the frames he offered were not always persuasive to those who read his work, they at least provided a theoretical foil for those who opposed his principles. There was a second mode of influence for those who both fervently accepted those principles and participated in the practical business of politics.[35] In their case, Rousseau's work was both a guide to what should be done and an arsenal of maxims with which they could arm their rhetoric in debate. For them, the urgency of Rousseau's message was communicated in the very first words of the *Social Contract*: "Man is born free, and everywhere he is in chains."[36]

Andress, *Oxford Handbook of the French Revolution*, p. 82. In a speech before the National Assembly on December 29, 1790, one of the deputies described Rousseau as the inspiration behind the new constitution because it was in the *Social Contract* that he and his colleagues "have rediscovered the right usurped from the nation." Miller, *Rousseau*, pp. 133–6. Even so, most of the deputies who served in the National Assembly were apparently not very well versed in either political philosophy in general or Rousseau's writing in particular. Micah Alpaugh, "A Personal Revolution: National Assembly Deputies and the Politics of 1789" and Dan Edelstein, "What Was the Terror?" in Andress, *Oxford Handbook of the French Revolution*, pp. 183, 462. As a result, while both revolutionaries and counter-revolutionaries cited Rousseau, they often incorrectly interpreted his writings. McDonald, *Rousseau and the French Revolution*, pp. 6, 58.

[33] When "Rousseau put forward the theory of inalienable popular sovereignty he visualized his ideal society in the guise of the ancient city state." It is doubtful that Rousseau actually believed that this ideal society could be realized in practice. McDonald, *Rousseau and the French Revolution*, pp. 26, 33–4, 38, 74. "Rousseau himself," as Harkins observes, "was profoundly pessimistic about any realization in France of his ideal state." James Harkins, "The Intellectual Origins of Babouvism" in Morris Slavin and Agnes M. Smith (eds.), *Bourgeois, Sans-Culottes, and Other Frenchmen: Essays on the French Revolution in Honor of John Hall Stewart* (Waterloo, Canada: Wilfrid Laurier University Press, 1981), p. 86. On the role of Sparta, early Rome, and Geneva as examples of "the kind of society which Rousseau envisaged and desired," see Stark, "Literature and Thought," pp. 59–60, 64.

[34] In 1790, for example, the National Constituent Assembly installed a bust of Rousseau, containing copies of *Émile* and the *Social Contract*, in its legislative hall. McDonald, *Rousseau and the French Revolution*, p. 156. The assembly also installed busts of Brutus, Mirabeau, and Helvetius. The latter two were later smashed after a speech by Robespierre in which he condemned the two men. J. M. Thompson, *Robespierre* (Oxford: Basil Blackwell, 1935), vol. 1, p. 294.

[35] On the difficulty of tracing Rousseau's influence on the thinking of individuals who played a prominent role in the revolution, see Harkins, "Intellectual Origins of Babouvism," pp. 75–6. However, Rousseau's influence was both strong and unmistakable with respect to Gracchus Babeuf, Louis Antoine de Saint-Just, Emmanuel Joseph Sieyès, and, most of all, Maximilien Robespierre. Schama, *Citizens*, p. 444; Mona Ozouf, trans. Alan Sheridan, *Festivals and the French Revolution* (Cambridge, MA: Harvard University Press, 1988), pp. 107–8.

[36] In a speech on May 7, 1794, for example, Robespierre paraphrased this passage: "Nature tells us that Man was born for freedom, and the experience of centuries shows him a slave. His rights are

Some passages in the *Social Contract* became almost sacred maxims even though few who read the book fully understood Rousseau's arguments.[37] A report to the National Convention admitted as much in recommending that the great thinker's remains be interred in the Pantheon:

> The *Social Contract* seems to have been made to be read in the presence of the human species assembled in order to learn what it has been and what it has lost ... But the great maxims developed in the *Social Contract*, as evident and simple as they seem to us today, then [when originally written] produced little effect; people did not understand them enough to profit from them, or to fear them, they were too much beyond the common reach of minds, even of those who were or were believed to be superior to the vulgar mind; in a way, it is the Revolution that has explained to us the *Social Contract*.[38]

For those who were not able to comprehend Rousseau's texts, the mode of influence was indirect and selective. The masses often responded enthusiastically: for example, when Rousseau's principles appeared to endorse and even require the direct rule of the people through street demonstrations and other collective actions, even though the demands they made were frequently related to their immediate personal needs, particularly for food, and were thus theoretically suspect. However, the violence associated with these street demonstrations can still be traced to their legitimation within the larger penumbra of Rousseau's thought (as well as the historical practice of the rowdy presentation of mass demands to the monarchy).[39]

Both those who subscribed to the principles of the Enlightenment and those who embraced Rousseau's appeal to innate virtue believed that the social contract between the people and the government could and should be renegotiated and that, in this renegotiation, tradition and custom were at best

---

written in his heart, his humiliation in history." Miller, *Rousseau*, p. 132. On another occasion, Robespierre paraphrased the same passage differently: "Man is born for happiness and liberty and everywhere he is enslaved and unhappy." David P. Jordan, *Revolutionary Career of Maximilien Robespierre* (New York: Free Press, 1985), p. 34.

[37] Patrick concluded that "[n]o one reading the speeches of 1792–93 could doubt that Rousseau had a considerable public, and the quotations (and the disagreements over their implications) suggest that many of the deputies had actually read him." Alison Patrick, *The Men of the First French Republic: Political Alignments in the National Convention of 1792* (Baltimore: Johns Hopkins University Press, 1972), p. 57n. On the other hand, McDonald contended that the *Social Contract* was seldom read and, if read, rarely understood, and, even if understood, even more rarely deployed accurately in public debate. McDonald, *Rousseau and the French Revolution*, pp. 43–50, 63–5. However, McDonald did assign significant influence to both *Émile* and *La Nouvelle Héloïse* and described in great detail the popular "Rousseauist cult" that played an important role in shaping the political culture of the revolution (pp. 51, 155–73). Miller also provides evidence of such a "cult." Miller, *Rousseau*, pp. 136–47, 162–3.

[38] Miller, *Rousseau*, p. 163.

[39] Taylor, *Modern Social Imaginaries*, p. 136. On the popular appeal of Rousseau's thought during the revolution, see Schama, *Citizens*, pp. 293–4; Nigel Aston, *The French Revolution, 1789–1804: Authority, Liberty, and the Search for Stability* (New York: Palgrave Macmillan, 2001), pp. 76–7.

irrelevant.[40] Both camps also believed that the practice of politics within a new regime would produce a new people, but at that point they diverged. Those who enshrined reason as their lodestar believed that education would enlighten the people and thus make them competent to participate in governance. For them, democracy required a knowledge of social relations that would enable proper recognition of political possibility. There would still be debate over what this political possibility might be but informed contestation would entail deliberation in which new knowledge would be created even as political issues were resolved. For those who favored Enlightenment principles, then, discrimination was almost a foregone conclusion because participation in politics required an informed judgment that could be cultivated only through education and leisure. Much of the population was simply not ready to participate because their impoverished circumstances and lack of education rendered them unable to offer an intelligent opinion on the course of government.

For those who favored Rousseau's more "naturalistic" interpretation of the General Will, the issues associated with political participation were more complex. On the one hand, education in the sense of creating a cultivated and learned public was in many ways pointless because the people were naturally virtuous and, when properly consulted, they would spontaneously orient the regime toward the general good. The truth of virtuous social relations and, thus, the proper form of governance was already latent in the "natural" understanding of the people.[41] The task was not the inculcation of reason but the proper orientation of the people so that they would practice politics in such a way as to accord with and thus release this intuitive understanding.[42] From that perspective, a scholarly education impaired the ability of the people to recognize and act upon their natural virtue. In addition, the corruption of French society under the *ancien régime* had contaminated uneducated people in ways that prevented their recognition of that virtue. As a result, even they were not ready for full political participation.

Education was thus the cure for what ailed the body politic for both those who favored Enlightenment principles and those who followed Rousseau. But

---

[40] See, for example, Hunt, *Politics, Culture, and Class*, pp. 12–13, 16.

[41] Robespierre thus believed that the new republic should embark upon "an immense enterprise in moral instruction" so that the people should come to recognize and act upon those "natural" understandings. Schama, *Citizens*, p. 756. Also see Arendt, *On Revolution*, p. 828.

[42] As Lefebvre noted, Rousseau did not reject reason but he did maintain that sentiment and emotion should be given primacy. By loving "his fellows the 'sensitive' man would attain true, altruistic morality; his conscience, the 'immortal and heavenly voice,' would penetrate the phenomenal world to reveal the most important truths, those illuminating his destiny." Lefebvre, *French Revolution*, vol. 1, p. 59. Lefebvre went on to say that "Rousseau's influence spread the preromantic spirit through Europe. Critics reproached both classicism and rationalism for failing to stimulate the imagination, for prohibiting introspection, for scorning the dark and the mysterious, for requiring man to think in terms of utility and ciphers" (p. 68). Also see McDonald, *Rousseau and the French Revolution*, pp. 82–3.

they promoted competing educational programs: the cultivation of scholarship for the former and a rigorous cleansing of social corruption through collective socialization for the latter.[43] Both programs were for the young, who, as far as suffrage rights were concerned, were not considered eligible to vote in any case. In the meantime, the adults had to be separated into two groups: those who were "ready" for the franchise and those who were not. Women, of course, were the largest group excluded from suffrage. For those who favored Rousseau, their exclusion was to be permanent, regardless of how well socialized and virtuous they might be. For those who favored Enlightenment principles, women's suffrage was more problematic but most agreed that women should not vote. In general, suffrage restrictions, along with the dedication to universal education, thus assumed that some part of the people was not yet ready to participate in the expression of the "General Will," but also that the Nation was committed to training them for that role.

Once the king was out of the picture, the basic difficulty facing those who made the French Revolution was that the deputies were evenly and hopelessly divided over what should replace the monarchy as the sacred center of society.[44] On one wing were precocious republican democrats for whom the values associated with democracy, such as freedom of speech and freedom of religion, were at least as important as the more institutional forms of democracy such as elections. They were students and children of the Enlightenment who believed that individual reason would be the fount of political legitimacy if the state were rationally reconstructed.[45] There was a fundamental tension between (1) abstract representations of the General Will in politics (and thus the philosophical ground of political authority and legitimacy) and (2) the Enlightenment reform program, which sought to use "science" as the intellectual findings of reason. The tension arose because the General Will privileged popular sovereignty regardless of the people's reception of the findings of science while the conclusions of reason arose out of the findings of science regardless of popular attitudes and opinions. Unless the General Will and the

---

[43] For summaries of the Enlightenment conception of education, to which Rousseau "turns his back," see A. V. Judges, "Educational Ideas, Practice and Institutions" in Goodwin, *New Cambridge Modern History*, vol. 8, pp. 145–6, 155–60, 163–6, 169–72.

[44] As Taylor writes:

The impossibility remarked by all historians of "bringing the Revolution to an end" came partly from this, that any particular expression of popular sovereignty could be challenged by some other, with substantial support. Part of the terrifying instability of the first years of the Revolution stemmed from this negative fact, that the shift from the legitimacy of dynastic rule to that of the nation had no agreed meaning in a broadly based social imaginary. (Taylor, *Modern Social Imaginaries*, p. 113)

[45] For a discussion of the connection between the Enlightenment and revolutionary thought, see Burrows, "Books, Philosophy, Enlightenment," pp. 75–6. For a description of the Enlightenment as a "self-conscious cultural movement," see McPhee, *Liberty or Death*, pp. 27–30.

findings of science coincided exactly, there would be an irresolvable contradiction between them.

When the National Assembly was created, many deputies wished to erect a political framework grounded in representations of the General Will in order to enact the reasoned findings of science. However, the connection was more or less reversed during the course of the revolution in that science was increasingly used to justify particular representations of the General Will (e.g., in constitutional design). In part, this was due to the increasing realization that the people, however conceived, were not yet "ready" to express the General Will for which they had an innate and unique capacity. "Reason" then indicated the path through which the people would be made competent to express the General Will. The common program uniting those who embraced both the General Will and reason became the simplification of institutional authority (validated by the universal rights of the citizen for the former and by economic efficiency for the latter) and political centralization (justified by political equality for the former and by effective policy direction for the latter). For much of the revolution, the tension between these two groups was manageable even as the balance of power shifted between them.[46]

Their opponents, however, subscribed to Rousseau's notions of the General Will, construction of political virtue, and insistence on direct democracy, and these principles led them to identify collective emotion with virtuous authenticity.[47] This virtuous authenticity, both in practice and in theory, was emphatically hostile to individualism and reason. The French Revolution never resolved the contradiction between these principles and the tenets of the Enlightenment because a large and relatively uncommitted bloc resided between these two camps, shifting between the two but never producing its own political program.

The differences between these two groups, in turn, led to an even more fundamental disagreement over the proper structure of government. Those who accepted Enlightenment principles had complex and detailed blueprints for allocating political power to government officials and institutions. While

[46] In order for a General Will to become manifest, the citizenry had to experience the Nation in more or less similar ways. Given the pre-revolutionary material, ethnic, administrative, and linguistic diversity of France, this meant that the General Will required both a simplification of government authority and political centralization even before the General Will could be revealed, because the latter were preconditions for its manifestation. Thus, the creation of a unified national market, a commonly understood language, a uniform administrative structure in which all local units bore the relation to the center, and, above all else, a universal declaration of rights of the citizen were consensual goals of the revolution. On the diversity of pre-revolutionary France, see Doyle, *French Revolution*, pp. 5–9; James M. Anderson, *Daily Life during the French Revolution* (Westport, CT: Greenwood Press, 2007), pp. 3–4; McPhee, *Liberty or Death*, p. 2.

[47] As Israel notes, other thinkers also contributed to the making of the notion of the General Will. Israel, *Revolutionary Ideas*, p. 23.

these blueprints differed in many ways, the underlying logic that inspired all of them was quite similar. In fact, these blueprints might be characterized as substitutes for one another, depending on which assumptions were adopted concerning the best way in which the people might be incorporated into the governance process. Those who followed Rousseau, on the other hand, were often hostile to anything but improvised governing arrangements that, ostensibly at least, reflected and liberated the General Will of the people.[48] Since the General Will continuously and spontaneously emanated from the people and changed in ways that no person could anticipate, a rigid governing structure would inevitably inhibit and constrain its revelation.[49] However, those who embraced Rousseau had a problem that they more or less recognized but never solved: France was not a city-state in which the people could meet together and thus directly manifest the General Will.[50] The only people who, in practice, could directly manifest their will before the National Assembly were the people of Paris. And thus the street demonstrations and popular assemblies of the city took on a meaning much more profound and politically significant than would otherwise be the case.

Differences concerning the nature of the people who took to the streets of Paris became the most immediate source of conflict between those who embraced the Enlightenment and those who followed Rousseau. Jean-Baptiste-Victor Proudhon spoke for the former when he contended that "the heart of the proletarian is like that of the rich, a cesspool of babbling sensuality, a home of filth and hypocrisy ... The greatest obstacle which [social] equality has to overcome is not the aristocratic pride of the rich, but rather the undisciplined egoism of the poor."[51] In many ways, the French Revolution unfolded inside the National Assembly as a contentious dialogue between the two camps

[48] It did not help that Rousseau was also "vaguest precisely where [the revolutionaries] faced the most momentous decisions." Hunt, *Politics, Culture, and Class*, p. 2.

[49] "Rousseau took his metaphor of a general will seriously and literally enough to conceive of the nation as a body driven by one will, like an individual, which also can change direction at any time without losing its identity ... Rousseau therefore insisted that it would 'be absurd for the will to bind itself for the future.'" Arendt, *On Revolution*, p. 66.

[50] Lefebvre, *French Revolution*, vol. 1, p. 67. For a large nation, the practical implications for governance were, at best, a dominant legislature that recognized and registered the General Will and a subordinate executive mostly, if not entirely, limited to bureaucratic implementation of legislative directives. Harkins, "Intellectual Origins of Babouvism," p. 85. Robespierre himself proposed the erection of "a vast and majestic edifice, open to 12,000 spectators ... Under the eyes of so great a number of witnesses, neither corruption, intrigue nor perfidy dare show itself; the general will alone shall be consulted, the voice of reason and the public interest alone shall be heard." Miller, *Rousseau*, p. 153. For some of Robespierre's thoughts on the impossibility of direct democracy in a large nation, see pp. 157–8.

[51] Quoted in J. F. Bosher, *The French Revolution* (New York: W. W. Norton, 1988), p. 280. Bosher himself believed that the people in the Parisian streets "tended to be fitfully anxious, hungry, envious, violent, and vengeful. They were also gullible and easily led" (p. 154).

on who spoke for the people. Outside the legislative chamber, that dialogue was transformed into a theater in which the people of the street clamored for political dominance.

For those who subscribed to the Enlightenment, the people of Paris were only a small fraction (about 4 or 5 percent) of the nation. What people expressed as their will in the streets of the city was not the same thing as what the people in the provinces might express had they been in Paris. For the latter to be consulted at all they had to be indirectly represented by democratically elected delegates.[52] In September 1791, for example, Isaac René le Chapelier attacked the notion that popular sovereignty was something superior to representative government under a written constitution.

When the revolution is complete, when the constitution is fixed ... Nothing must hinder the actions of the constituted bodies. Deliberation and the power to act must be located where the constitution has placed them and nowhere else ... There is no power except that instituted by the will of the people and expressed through their representatives. There are no authorities except those delegated by the people and there can be no actions except those of its representatives who have been entrusted with public duties. It is to preserve this principle, in all its purity, that the constitution has abolished all corporations, from one end of the state to another, and henceforth recognizes only society as a whole and individuals within it. A necessary consequence of this principle is the prohibition of any petition or placard issued in the name of a group.

In Chapelier's view, nothing should intervene between the citizen and his deputy, because, once elected, the deputy alone could participate in the revelation of the General Will. It was in this vein that the assembly banned the

---

[52] There were thus four major areas in which Enlightenment principles were at odds with Rousseauian prescriptions. The first revolved around the latter's reliance on the natural, intuitive revelation of the General Will within the individual. This revelation required no "learning" in the sense of a formal education but only the elimination of the artificial, corrupting influence of the social forms of modern society. Intimately related to the first was the Rousseauian belief that the "truth" was always "political" in the sense that it arose out of the General Will. This was clearly hostile to the Enlightenment position that "truth" arose out of the gathering and inspection of facts about the world as opposed to personal and collective introspection. For the Rousseauian, individual virtue arose out of the ability to recognize one's contribution to the forming of the General Will and then acting on it (recognition and acting amounted to the same thing, because, once an individual could recognize what was "natural" in man, he would be irresistibly compelled to follow where it led). While those who followed the Enlightenment also esteemed individual virtue, they placed as high or higher value on merit, competence, logical analysis, and rational decision-making. For them, it was possible to be both virtuous and "wrong." Finally, for the Rousseauian, direct democracy was the only way in which citizens could commune with one another in a way that permitted mutual revelation and recognition of the General Will. This presented an insoluble problem because France was a large nation and the citizenry could not possibly commune with one another in the same place. Those who followed the Enlightenment had a much more practical alternative in representative government, but, like other aspects of the Enlightenment position, that never captured the emotional loyalty of the people.

presentation of collective petitions by political clubs or their interference in the legislative or administrative process of government.[53]

In turn, the deputies who served in the assembly should exercise their reason as they deliberated because knowledge and understanding were not evenly distributed among all the people and, in addition, many of the issues that the deputies were to decide could not be anticipated by the people who elected them. Wisdom, education, and personal character should thus be the most important criteria governing the selection of delegates. While those who subscribed to Enlightenment principles wrote most of the four constitutions created during the revolution, they never resolved the contradiction between the representative government that they so elegantly designed and the emotional appeal of direct democracy that Rousseau had so passionately articulated.[54]

A BRIEF DESCRIPTION OF THE REVOLUTIONARY CONSTITUTIONS

Four constitutions were adopted between 1791 and 1799. The first one was drafted rather piecemeal by the National Constituent Assembly and was only ratified as an entire document in September 1791.[55] The most important part of

[53] Malcolm Crook, "The New Regime: Political Institutions and Democratic Practices under the Constitutional Monarchy, 1789–91" in Andress, *Oxford Handbook of the French Revolution*, p. 231. Because all corporate organizations tended to impair the revelation and operation of the General Will, the revolution was also generally hostile to trade guilds and political clubs. On March 2, 1791, for example, the National Assembly ordered the abolition of guilds and corporations. On June 14, 1791, it prohibited all organizations of workers and banned strikes. The latter decree, known as the Le Chapelier law, remained on the books in France for seventy-three years. Lefebvre, *French Revolution*, vol. 1, pp. 150–1, 165; Doyle, *French Revolution*, p. 149; Schama, *Citizens*, pp. 519–20. Just before it was replaced by the newly elected Legislative Assembly, the National Assembly also passed legislation prohibiting almost all political activity by clubs. But this, unlike the abolition of guilds and strikes, was never enforced. Schama, *Citizens*, pp. 576, 580. On the abolition of tax farms, economic monopolies, and other forms of market privileges granted to individuals or corporations, see Doyle, *French Revolution*, p. 131. In many ways, the creation of an unfettered free market in goods and services went hand in hand with the construction of the "citizen" from the Enlightenment perspective.

[54] It was almost as if Rousseau had anticipated the role of the people of Paris in the revolution because he had warned that there was a constant "danger that the administration of the law may fall into the hands of unpatriotic men" and that the only "remedy [was] the unremitting vigilance of the people at large over those entrusted with the execution of the general will." Stark, "Literature and Thought," p. 65. The more general contradiction between the popular will and legislative representation was irresolvable because "the sovereignty of the people could be exercised only through representatives who were at once the agents of particular people in particular communities" and it was the latter who thus became the "wielders of the supreme power that *the* people mysteriously [and mistakenly] conveyed to them." Edmund S. Morgan, *Inventing the People: The Rise of Popular Sovereignty in England and America* (New York: W. W. Norton, 1988), p. 237.

[55] Ambrogio A. Caiani, "Louis XVI and Marie Antoinette" in Andress, *Oxford Handbook of the French Revolution*, p. 313.

that constitution was, of course, the Declaration of the Rights of Man and of the Citizen. This 1791 constitution also provided, both in practice and in theory, for a constitutional monarchy that recognized the political reality of the crown but, for that very reason, was in flagrant contradiction of the abstract, philosophical foundation of the new revolutionary state.

Following the deposition of the king, the new National Convention set about drafting a new constitution that was much more consistent with the foundational principles of the revolution. The convention again provided a preamble in the form of a Declaration of the Rights of Man and of the Citizen but revised the content from the original declaration proclaimed in 1789. The very first article declared that "the goal of society [was] the common happiness." The fourth article conferred citizenship on every man older than twenty-one who was "born and domiciled in France" and on every foreign-born male who met one of four conditions: He had lived and worked in the country for longer than a year, married a Frenchwoman, adopted a French child, or provided support to an elderly person.[56] Entirely new articles set out rights to subsistence and education:

> Article 21. Public aid is a sacred debt. Society owes subsistence to unfortunate citizens, either by obtaining work for them, or by providing means of existence to those who are unable to work.
> Article 22. Instruction is a necessity for all. Society must further the progress of public reason with all its power, and make instruction available to all citizens.

Other provisions elaborated the relation between the General Will and the authority of the state.

> Article 25. Sovereignty resides in the people. It is one and indivisible, imprescriptible, and inalienable.
> Article 26. No portion of the people can exercise the power of the entire people; but every section of the sovereign assembled ought to enjoy, with an entire freedom, the right of expressing its will.
> Article 27. All individuals usurping the sovereign should be immediately put to death by free men.
> Article 28. A people always has the right of revising, of reforming, and changing its constitution. One generation cannot subject future generations to its laws.
> Article 29. Every citizen has an equal right to consent to the formation of the law, and to the nomination of his agents, or of his delegates.
> Article 30. The public functions are essentially temporary: they cannot be considered either distinctions or rewards but only duties . . .

---

[56] Israel, *Revolutionary Ideas*, pp. 372–3.

Article 35. When the government violates the rights of the people, insurrection is for the people, and for each portion of the people, the most sacred of rights and the most indispensable of duties.[57]

As can be readily seen, these provisions both enthusiastically endorse the primacy of the General Will as a constitutional principle and, at the same time, offer nothing that might remedy the contradiction between that principle and the practicalities of national governance. If anything, they might even be interpreted as an open invitation to political instability.

As approved by the National Convention on June 24, 1793, the new constitution also provided for a unicameral national legislature whose members would be elected annually. That legislature would, in turn, appoint an executive council for the day-to-day operation of the government. The convention asked the citizenry to approve the document in a referendum and the final tally was almost two million votes for to 11,600 against. Roughly a third of all of those eligible participated, a remarkably high rate for an election in which the outcome was almost certain.[58] On August 10, 1793, a Festival of the Unity and Indivisibility of the Republic was held in celebration of the adoption of the new constitution.[59] On the very next day, however, the National Convention rejected a proposal to hold new elections that would have put the constitution into effect.[60] Two months after that, on October 10, the convention formally declared that the constitution of 1793 had to be suspended until the crises currently facing the revolution were successfully resolved.[61] Although Israel and others have described the constitution of 1793 as "the first modern democratic constitution," its provisions were never implemented and it has remained a dead letter ever since.[62]

After Robespierre's fall, a third constitution was written. As in the previous two constitutions, this one included a declaration of rights, but it was only a pale shadow of the bold pronouncements that had first appeared in 1789. As Aston put it, the "moderate republicans" who drew up this document downplayed "natural rights" in an attempt to discourage "well-disposed citizens from thinking too strenuously about the theoretical foundations of the Republic."[63] The new constitution of 1795 accordingly eliminated the right to insurrection,

---

[57] Miller, *Rousseau*, p. 154. On the drafting of the constitution of 1793, see Israel, *Revolutionary Ideas*, pp. 346–8, 369, 372–3.

[58] McPhee, *Liberty or Death*, pp. 206–7; Doyle, *French Revolution*, p. 246.

[59] McPhee, *Liberty or Death*, p. 208.

[60] Schama, *Citizens*, p. 756. The constitution was placed in a cedar box which was then hung from the ceiling of the National Convention. Doyle, *French Revolution*, p. 246.

[61] Doyle, *French Revolution*, p. 252.   [62] Israel, *Revolutionary Ideas*, p. 372.

[63] Aston, *French Revolution*, pp. 48–9. Aston nonetheless praises the new constitution as "a bold, pragmatic, and important revolutionary achievement." Israel is even more effusive, calling the document "unparalleled and impressively democratic compared with everything else then available in the world, including the then British or United States constitutions. As an embodiment of modern democratic and egalitarian principles, it assuredly had no rival at all outside France." Israel, *Revolutionary Ideas*, p. 612. Also see McPhee, *Liberty or Death*, pp. 295–6.

emphasized the duties of citizens, and set up a two-stage electoral system in which men who paid direct taxes or had served in the army could participate in the first round (about five million men were thus eligible). However, due to a high property requirement for eligibility, only 30,000 wealthy men would choose deputies in the second round.[64] In addition, a bicameral national legislature was created with a lower chamber called the Council of 500 and a higher Council of Elders. These two chambers were to choose a "directory" of five members who would then exercise administrative authority over the government. After ratifying this new constitution, the National Convention asked voters to approve it in a referendum along with another proposal that two-thirds of the new bicameral legislature be chosen from the 750 deputies who were currently serving in the convention. After that, one-third of the members of the national legislature were to be elected annually. Both were approved but abstention was very high.[65] The Directory created under the new constitution soon vitiated its already limited democratic quality by overturning the results of elections and rapidly putting the revolutionary government on an even more authoritarian trajectory.[66] After the 1799 coup, a new constitution, the fourth in the series, was written; however, since it merely provided cover for Napoleon's assumption of power, its terms need not concern us.[67] In sum, the revolution crafted four constitutions but none of them was ever accepted or put into practice as the foundation of the new French state.

THE FIRST PHASE OF THE REVOLUTION: THE ATTEMPT TO CREATE A CONSTITUTIONAL MONARCHY

The Estates-General first met in Versailles on May 5, 1789. Although no one knew it at the time, this was to be the first of six different legislatures that would

---

[64] In addition, the constitution of 1795 declared that "young people should not be enrolled on civic registers unless they can prove that they can read, write and carry on an occupation." This effectively made literacy a requirement for voting and, as Chappey notes, "excluded the huge mass of the illiterate from political citizenship." Jean-Luc Chappey, "The New Elites: Questions about Political, Social, and Cultural Reconstruction after the Terror" in Andress, *Oxford Handbook of the French Revolution*, p. 558. On April 16, 1796, the Council of 500 (created under the constitution of 1795) decreed that oral or written support for either the 1791 or 1793 constitutions was a capital offence. John Anthony Scott (ed. and trans.), *The Defense of Gracchus Babeuf before the High Court of Vendôme* (Amherst: University of Massachusetts Press, 1967), pp. 10–11; Israel, *Revolutionary Ideas*, p. 632.

[65] Paul R. Hanson, *Contesting the French Revolution* (Chichester: Wiley-Blackwell, 2009), pp. 130–1; Israel, *Revolutionary Ideas*, pp. 607–8, 610–13, 626.

[66] Israel, *Revolutionary Ideas*, pp. 629, 632. For a summary overview of politics during the Directory, see Howard G. Brown, "The Politics of Public Order, 1795–1802" in Andress, *Oxford Handbook of the French Revolution*, pp. 538–54.

[67] For a brief summary of Napoleon's relationship to the French Revolution, see Philip Dwyer, "Napoleon, the Revolution, and the Empire" in Andress, *Oxford Handbook of the French Revolution*, pp. 573–89.

TABLE 4.2. *The names of the various manifestations of the national legislature*

Title	Period in existence	How convoked
Estates-General	May 5–June 17, 1789	Called by the king
National Assembly	June 17–27, 1789	Unilaterally declared by the third estate
National Constituent Assembly	June 27, 1789–September 30, 1791	Clergy and nobility join the National Assembly with the approval of the king
Legislative Assembly	October 1, 1791– September 20, 1792	Formed by elections under the 1791 constitution
National Convention	September 20, 1792– October 26, 1795	Elected by order of the Legislative Assembly following deposition of the king
Bicameral: Council of Elders	October 26, 1795– November 9, 1799	Formed by elections under the 1795 constitution and Council of 500

Source: Adapted with minor changes from Anderson, *Daily Life*, pp. 22–3.

meet during what became the revolution (see Table 4.2). When Louis XVI convoked the Estates-General, he intended the body to conduct its sessions in almost the same way as its last meeting in 1614, some 175 years earlier: The king would play the role of a beneficent ruler and embodiment of the French nation and the Estates-General would consent to the measures necessary to secure the safety of the realm.[68] There were a few changes in form, particularly with respect to the selection of deputies and their respective numbers.[69] The

[68] The *parlement* of Paris supported the king's intention by announcing that the upcoming Estates-General should conform exactly to historical precedent. Schama, *Citizens*, p. 297. The *parlement* of Paris first initiated opposition to the king, making the calling of the Estates-General imperative and then, through its conservatism in interpreting how the Estates-General would be composed and how it would deliberate, lost control of the political process and subsequently became a nonentity. The judges, for example, were almost locked out of the Estates-General when elections were held in the spring of 1789. Lefebvre, *French Revolution*, vol. 1, pp. 101–2; Doyle, *French Revolution*, pp. 88, 91–2, 99–100.

[69] The initial organization of the Estates-General incorporated the "medieval idealization of the society [as] three orders: *oratores, bellatores, laboratories* – those who pray, those who fight, and those who work." Taylor, *Modern Social Imaginaries*, p. 11. This idealization was legitimated by a belief that these social distinctions constituted a natural social order. The French Revolution was the result, in the first instance, that this belief in a natural social order could no longer cloak the inequities of privilege and wealth that it had previously concealed. The deputies from the first estate represented about 130,000 clergy, roughly half of whom were members of religious orders. Many of the clerical deputies were simple priests who closely attended to the spiritual needs of parishioners in their home communities. The second estate represented somewhere between 120,000 and 350,000 nobles. The third estate thus represented the remainder, more than twenty-seven million people. However, no peasants or artisans were elected as deputies and

third estate, for example, was allocated twice as many deputies as either the clergy or the nobility.[70] But the crown expected the three social orders to deliberate separately and, if this had been the case, the larger number of those in the third estate would not have been important.

On May 5, the traditional social hierarchy of clerics, nobles, and commoners was ritually manifested in the costumes and the order in which the three estates marched in the opening procession.[71] From the very beginning, however, those who represented the third estate resisted their subordination. One of the very first steps when a legislative assembly organizes itself is the verification of the credentials of the ostensible members so that the body has an official membership. In this instance, there was not one but three such bodies: the first estate (composed of the clergy's representatives), the second estate (the nobility), and the third estate (commoners). If things had proceeded as they had in the past, each of the estates would have verified the credentials of its own members and then notified the other estates that they were ready to deliberate. The third estate, however, insisted that the three estates meet jointly for this purpose and intended, in that way, to transform the Estates-General into a single legislative body.[72] A stalemate then ensued in which the majority of the first and second estates refused to agree to a joint session for the purposes of verification.[73]

only ninety-nine were drawn from the ranks of trade and industry. Most of these were lawyers or men who had held petty government office. The population of France in the 1780s has been estimated to be twenty-eight million, the largest in Europe after Russia. Lefebvre, *French Revolution*, vol. 1, pp. 36, 41, 43–5; Doyle, *French Revolution*, pp. 2, 22–6, 28–9, 32–3, 99–101; McPhee, *Liberty or Death*, p. 3. On the many issues associated with the opening of the Estates-General, see John Hardman, "The View from Above" in Andress, *Oxford Handbook of the French Revolution*, pp. 136–45.

[70] On the royal decision to double the size of the third estate but, at the same time, to insist on separate deliberations by the three estates, see Doyle, *French Revolution*, pp. 93, 102; Lefebvre, *French Revolution*, vol. 1, pp. 104–5. The crown had earlier, in 1778, created a provincial assembly at Bourges in which "twelve clergy, twelve nobles, and twenty-four commoners ... were to vote by head and not by orders" on taxation and other matters. While this was not in any way a binding precedent, the arrangement now claimed by the third estate did have, at least, a prior example. Dakin, "The Breakdown of the Old Regime," p. 612.

[71] Schama, *Citizens*, p. 338; Doyle, *French Revolution*, pp. 101–2.

[72] The crown's equivocation on crucial aspects of the organization of the Estates-General meant that the Estates-General would determine its own rules of procedure. However, that equivocation also meant that there was no apparent method for adopting those rules, including whether or not to meet together or separately.

[73] Schama, *Citizens*, p. 352; Lefebvre, *French Revolution*, vol. 1, p. 110. Although determination (verification of eligibility to serve) of the membership did not seem to cause any difficulty within the orders, it thus became the process through which the third estate compelled the other orders to merge. Doyle, *French Revolution*, pp. 102–3. Deputies from Brittany and Dauphine warned the third estate that separate verification would lead to separate deliberations. While this was not certain, it was highly likely in practice because determination of the membership would have implied prior decisions on the identity of a leader and rules of procedure, however inchoate those might be. Once those steps had been taken, each legislative body would have been individually

On June 10, a compromise was proposed by the crown that would have created a joint commission for verifying credentials composed of members of each of the three estates. The third estate, however, set this proposal aside and peremptorily demanded that the nobility and clergy join them. If they did not, the third estate threatened to use its own procedure in order to verify the credentials of all three estates.[74] On June 13, some of the parish priests in the first estate came over to the third estate. Other clergy and nobles followed them.[75] Strengthened by these defections, the third estate unilaterally declared itself to be the "National Assembly" on June 17, 1789, preempting whatever legislative prerogatives the other two estates might have insisted upon in their separate chambers.[76] On June 19, a majority of the clergy agreed to merge with the third estate. On June 27, Louis XVI recognized what had become a fait accompli by ordering the other clergy and nobility to join the National Assembly, which was thus transformed into the National Constituent Assembly as it took up the task of drafting a new constitution for the French nation.[77]

During this transformation of the Estates-General into the National Assembly there were several moments during which the deputies were emotionally transfixed by their own unity in the face of political uncertainty and risk. The first of these occurred on June 20, when the third estate found that the crown, without warning, had locked them out of their meeting hall.

formed and merging the three estates would have necessitated a separate process in which those decisions would have been vitiated and thus have had to be made again.

[74] Doyle, *French Revolution*, p. 103. Although there was some semblance of parliamentary order in the third estate's deliberation, there was still no officially recognized leader, membership, or rules. In this instance, Honoré-Gabriel Riquetti, Count of Mirabeau, abruptly interrupted a reading of the compromise proposal so another member, Emmanuel Sieyès, could move the demand described in the text. At that time, the third estate was deliberating more or less by a consensus in which one of the members, Jean Sylvain Bailly, informally presided as "dean" (pp. 106, 111). Mirabeau, who had been elected as a member of the third estate even though he was a noble, described the situation in which the deputies found themselves: "Imagine more than 500 individuals herded into one room not knowing one another, collected from all parts of the country without leaders, without officials, all free, all equal, none of whom had any right to give orders and none any obligation to obey them, whilst everyone – in true French fashion – was more anxious to talk than to listen." Otto J. Scott, *Robespierre: The Voice of Virtue* (New York: Mason and Lipscomb, 1974), p. 42.

[75] McPhee, *Liberty or Death*, p. 69; Doyle, *French Revolution*, pp. 104, 107; Schama, *Citizens*, pp. 355–6, 362–5.

[76] In addition, the National Assembly declared that it had authority to pass tax legislation while recognizing that the king must approve whatever they enacted. Lefebvre, *French Revolution*, vol. 1, p. 112; Schama, *Citizens*, pp. 355–6; Doyle, *French Revolution*, pp. 104–5.

[77] McPhee, *Liberty or Death*, p. 70. Also see Davidson, *French Revolution*, p. 22. After hearing of the king's order, Arthur Young, an English observer of these events, wrote: "The whole business now seems over and the revolution complete." He was then confirming his earlier opinion that "it is impossible for [the Estates-General] to meet without a revolution in the government." Doyle, *French Revolution*, p. 79, 108, 118.

Although the crown's intentions were unclear, the members immediately reassembled in a nearby, enclosed tennis court.[78] That structure was quite barren of amenities but their anxiety and fervor more than compensated for the simplicity of their surroundings.[79] It was there that members of the third estate swore a mutual oath:

The National Assembly, summoned to lay down the Constitution of this realm, to bring about the regeneration of public order and to maintain the true principles of monarchy, considers that nothing must prevent it from continuing its deliberations in whatever place it is compelled to assemble, and that, wherever its members are gathered, there the National Assembly is; this Assembly decrees that all its members will here and now take a solemn oath never to disperse and to continue meeting wherever circumstances allow until the Constitution of this realm has been established on solid foundations; and that, when the aforesaid oath has been sworn, all members will put their individual signatures to this unshakable resolution.[80]

This public, collective commitment irrevocably set the National Assembly down the path toward the creation of a constitutional monarchy whether Louis XVI liked it or not.[81]

The second moment arose on June 23, when the king addressed all three estates in a joint session. In his concluding remarks, Louis XVI commanded the estates to reassemble separately and threatened dissolution of the assembly if they failed to obey. The nobility and most of the clergy then followed the king out of the hall. However, the third estate obstinately remained seated. When the king's command was repeated by a senior royal official, Jean Bailly defiantly replied: "The assembled nation cannot receive orders." While Bailly simply asserted the autonomy of the National Assembly, it was Mirabeau who emotionally stirred the deputies: "Go tell your master that we are here by the will of the people, and that we shall retire only at the point of the bayonet."[82] After noisily seconding Mirabeau's response, the assembly once again swore the "tennis court" oath. While their open defiance put the entire third estate at

---

[78] Lefebvre, *French Revolution*, vol. 1, p. 112; Doyle, *French Revolution*, p. 105.

[79] "Here they were [in the royal tennis court], as Rousseau intended, stripped down to elemental citizenship and brotherhood. There was nothing but their bodies." Schama, *Citizens*, p. 359.

[80] Furet and Richet, *French Revolution*, p. 710. When the oath was taken, Bailly, who had been elected presiding officer on June 3, "stood on the tailor's table, placed one hand on his heart – the gesture *par excellence* of Rousseauean sincerity – and raised the other in command. With right arms outstretched, fingers taut, six hundred deputies" swore fealty to one another. Schama, *Citizens*, pp. 172–4, 359. Only one deputy refused to swear the oath. McPhee, *Liberty or Death*, p. 70.

[81] However, the deputies did believe that the king's consent would be needed in order to ratify the assembly's work. Davidson, *French Revolution*, p. 41.

[82] Mirabeau was one of the most important, if not *the* most important, figures during the opening stages of the Estates-General and National Assembly. For his role in the revolution, see Schama, *Citizens*, pp. 339–45, 347–8, 353, 354–5, 363, 376, 411, 477, 480–2, 532–49.

risk, the crown recognized that repression would have not solved the government's fiscal and political problems.[83]

Over the next five weeks, royal authority rapidly deteriorated in many provinces as peasants took revenge upon the nobles and clerics who had long lived off their labor. While their violence threatened the social and political order, it also created an anxiety verging on panic among the peasants themselves because they often imagined that roving bands of thieves were now on the loose and coming their way. Between July 20 and August 6, something like a national hysteria swept large parts of the French countryside. This later became known as the "Great Fear."[84]

This provided the backdrop for the third moment, when, on August 4 and continuing into the early morning of the following day, the National Constituent Assembly reacted to both the rapidly unraveling social order in the countryside and the contradiction between its insistence on political equality and the social inequality of feudal relations. In what Mirabeau described as an "electric whirlwind" of altruism, noble and clerical deputies, one after another, stood before assembly and renounced their claims to property, privilege, and wealth.[85] As they attempted to outdo each other in their renunciations, the spontaneous emotional relief released by their actions bonded the deputies in a mass rejection of the *ancien régime*. In separate resolutions, they proclaimed, in principle, equality of taxation and the abolition of personal servitude. They also declared that every citizen would be eligible to hold public office and would enjoy freedom of worship. Manorial rights would also be abolished along with venal offices. The only hint of caution was that those holding these rights or offices were to be indemnified for their loss.

All this was done rather haphazardly and had to be written up later in proper legislative language. That process consumed almost all of the next week, during which time the assembly retracted some of what it had earlier so emotionally embraced. Even so, the official decree that translated emotion into legislation began as follows: "The National Assembly destroys the feudal regime in its entirety." This was not quite true because some noble and clerical privileges remained intact and manorial rights would not be vacated until

---

[83] McPhee, *Liberty or Death*, p. 70. There are other versions of Mirabeau's retort. See, for example, Lefebvre, *French Revolution*, vol. 1, pp. 113–14. For a description of the session itself, see Doyle, *French Revolution*, p. 106. Because the hall assigned to the third estate for their deliberations was the same space in which plenary sessions with the king were held, the third estate, in deciding not to disperse at the order of the king, merely remained where it was after the joint session of June 23. Lefebvre, *French Revolution*, vol. 1, p. 110.

[84] Hanson, *Contesting the French Revolution*, pp. 45–7: Lefebvre, *French Revolution*, vol. 1, pp. 127–8; Doyle, *French Revolution*, pp. 114–15; Schama, *Citizens*, pp. 429–36; McPhee, *Liberty or Death*, pp. 75–7.

[85] McPhee, *Liberty or Death*, pp. 77, 98; Doyle, *French Revolution*, pp. 115–17.

compensation could be provided to their holders. In addition, the king had not yet approved the assembly's work.[86]

These moments when passion carried the deputies into what were monumentally important and decisive decisions had several origins. On the one hand, the members of the National Assembly had little or no experience with a legislative process appropriate to a working democracy. They were literally making things up as they went along and many of things that they were improvising imposed upon the historical rights and privileges of the crown. They were also well aware that, even though weakened by the fiscal crisis that had called the Estates-General into being, the crown still controlled the army, the police, and the prisons. There was little or no distinction between making these things up out of thin air (such as the self-declaration that transformed them into the "National Assembly") and flagrantly violating the law. The passion with which they plunged into the unknown registered the anxiety that this fact induced, united them by signaling a mutual commitment to proceed regardless, and merged their individual responsibility into collective action.

The deputies were already imagining that they, in some yet inchoate manner, embodied the General Will of the nation.[87] That General Will had not yet replaced the king as the sacred center of politics but was already the inviolable responsibility of the National Assembly. Many members, in fact, already recognized the contradiction between the divine right pretensions of the monarchy and the legitimating ground upon which the assembly now operated.[88] But the more immediate problem was how they, as deputies dedicated to carrying out the General Will, were to recognize what it demanded of them. In the absence of its material manifestation, the deputies were compelled to recognize the General Will as a largely instinctive and emotionally felt intuition.

This reliance on individual intuition had several consequences. The first was that they were compelled, under Rousseau's theory, to cleanse themselves of parochial identities and self-interest.[89] As a result, complete and uncompromising devotion to the interests of the Nation became the most important defining element in what was considered "virtue."[90] In the opening months of the revolution, this conception of politics was widely shared. (Later, this same conception would send many of them to the guillotine, but that was inconceivable at the time.) This reliance on individual intuition was also the mainspring

---

[86] Lefebvre, *French Revolution*, vol. 1, pp. 130–1, 167; Hanson, *Contesting the French Revolution*, pp. 63–6; Doyle, *French Revolution*, p. 119. Doyle concluded that the clergy lost more privileges than the nobility because tithes, vestry fees, and other revenue sources were abolished without compensation (p. 136).

[87] Israel, *Revolutionary Ideas*, pp. 23–4.   [88] See, for example, Schama, *Citizens*, p. 354.

[89] For example, Guy-Jean Target, who participated in the drafting of the 1791 constitution, wrote: "Each man must forget himself and see himself only as part of the whole of which he is a member, detach himself from his individual existence, renounce all *esprit de corps*, belong only to the great society and be a child of the fatherland." Schama, *Citizens*, p. 291.

[90] Taylor, *Modern Social Imaginaries*, pp. 117–20.

of their episodes of spontaneous collective emotion. To feel what others clearly felt was not to succumb to a kind of collective madness but to verify that their individual intuitions did, indeed, reflect the General Will of the Nation. Lastly, this intuition inseparably aligned the deputies with their conception of "the people." They believed that they felt what the people willed. However, driven by this intuitive emotion, majority opinion within the National Assembly sometimes swayed dramatically on the same day.

THE FALL OF THE BASTILLE

During the early months of the revolution, the most important popular demonstration was the storming of the Bastille on July 14, 1789.[91] The people who attacked this immense fortress were not intending to overthrow the monarchy or to liberate the very few prisoners it held. They were, instead, looking for gunpowder. The thousand demonstrators who demanded the surrender of the fortress had taken over the Invalides military hospital earlier that day, confiscating a few cannon and over 30,000 muskets. The day before they had sacked the Saint Lazare convent, confiscating fifty-three carts of grain and 25,000 liters of wine. They had also, the previous night, wrecked or burned forty of the fifty-five toll gates that ringed the city. Perhaps the most important motivation in all these actions was hunger.[92] The price of grain on July 14 was higher than it had been in over a decade and many of the common people could not afford bread.[93] But they also wanted arms, ammunition, and gunpowder in order to resist the army detachments that the king had deployed in the city. Finally, all these targets, particularly the Bastille, were important symbols of royal authority and power.

If the commander of the Bastille had surrendered the fortress peacefully, the event would have been as historically unremarkable as the attacks on the

---

[91] For descriptions of the Bastille, see Schama, *Citizens*, pp. 389–419.

[92] Many revolutionaries firmly denied that food shortages might be the result of a rising population and poor weather. Turning the shortage of food into a political shibboleth, Robespierre, for example, maintained that it was "a fact generally recognized that the soil of France produces a great deal more than is needed to feed her inhabitants and that the present scarcity is an artificial one" caused by speculators and hoarders. Maximilien Robespierre, *Virtue and Terror* introduction, ed., and trans. Slavoj Žižek, Jean Ducange, and John Howe (New York: Verso, 2017), p. 49.

[93] Doyle, *French Revolution*, pp. 86, 109–10; Schama, *Citizens*, p. 400; Andress, *French Revolution and the People*, pp. 107–9; George Rude, *The Crowd in the French Revolution* (Oxford: Oxford University Press, 1959), pp. 48–51. Even in pre-revolutionary Paris, bread and grain price regulation "was considered a matter of national importance; if the capital went hungry the stability of the state itself might be endangered, and the needs of Paris took priority in all markets within a radius of about 100 miles, and were a powerful influence at up to twice that distance." Doyle, *French Revolution*, p. 21. It was no coincidence, then, that the Bastille was stormed when the price of bread in Paris was approaching its highest level in two decades (p. 109).

hospital and convent. But the Marquis de Launay chose to resist and ordered his men to fire on the demonstrators. Some eighty-three people were killed outright and another fifteen later succumbed to their wounds. Those inside the fortress suffered only four casualties during the fighting, one dead and three wounded. During the fighting, however, several detachments of the militia outside the fortress defected to the demonstrators and brought cannon to bear on the gates of the Bastille. The commander then surrendered the fortress and lowered the drawbridge. The demonstrators pushed inside, took possession of the gunpowder, and liberated the prisoners. There were only seven of the latter: several who were mentally ill, an aristocrat who had been imprisoned with the Marquis de Sade (the latter had been moved elsewhere before the assault), and the rest were forgers. After disarming the defenders, they killed three of the officers and three of the enlisted men. They also took the commander to the Hôtel de Ville, the equivalent of a city hall in Paris, where he was decapitated. Jacques de Flesselles, the mayor, was also killed and decapitated. Both of their heads were put on pikes and paraded through the city.[94]

In Versailles, twelve miles away, the National Constituent Assembly received news of the fall of the Bastille and the associated violence in "a mournful silence."[95] The political consequences were immense. On July 15, the day after the Bastille fell, Louis XVI went to the assembly and announced that he was withdrawing the army from Paris and its environs. While the deputies cheered the announcement, the decision was not entirely voluntary because the minister of war had told the king that he could not rely on the loyalty of his troops in confrontations with the people.[96] That effectively ended royal authority in Paris. In the provinces as well, "the only orders obeyed were those of the National Assembly" after the fall of the Bastille.[97] While the assembly was initially dismayed by the assault, the deputies later embraced July 14 as a national holiday to be celebrated as a patriotic festival. Although all of these consequences were significant, the most important result was the validation of direct popular insurgency as a form of politics. In this instance, the people of

---

[94] Schama, *Citizens*, p. 405; Doyle, *French Revolution*, pp. 112–13; Rude, *The Crowd*, pp. 53–9.

[95] Bosher, *French Revolution*, p. 149. One reason for this silence is that the National Assembly was very afraid that the insurgency in Paris would be crushed and that the crown would then punish them. Alpaugh, "A Personal Revolution," p. 189. One week later, a certain "M. de Robert-Pierre," whose name was mangled in the public prints, was praising the assault on the Bastille: "What happened in this riot in Paris? Public liberty, a little blood spilled, a few heads knocked off no doubt, but guilty heads … So, messieurs, the nation owes its liberty to this riot." D. M. G. Sutherland, "Urban Violence in 1789" in Andress, *Oxford Handbook of the French Revolution*, p. 279.

[96] On June 28, 1789, for example, "mutinying companies of the *gardes françaises*" had publicly announced "that they would under no circumstances fire on the people." Schama, *Citizens*, p. 371.

[97] Lefebvre, *French Revolution*, vol. 1, pp. 124, 126; Doyle, *French Revolution*, pp. 110–11.

Paris came to believe that their insurgencies had saved the revolution; later, they came to believe that the revolution belonged to them.[98]

THE DECLARATION OF THE RIGHTS OF MAN AND OF THE CITIZEN (1789)

As it began to deliberate on what would become momentous changes to the structure of the French state, the assembly did not assume plenary authority over the government; instead, it continued to recognize a monarchical veto over its actions. And even though the deputies from the three estates had been merged into one body, the assembly also continued to recognize their separate identities as nobles, clerics, and commoners. They all had one vote but the constituencies they represented continued to be very strongly skewed in favor of the nobility and the Church. Despite that fact, the assembly did not order new elections. While all of these things of course reflected political reality (e.g., new elections with a semblance of democratic participation would have, at best, delayed political consolidation of the assembly's position or, at worst, allowed the crown to dissolve it altogether), they also reflected the medieval origins of the assembly itself. Thus, while these were compromises with political reality, that political reality was a tapestry woven in feudal thread.[99]

On July 7, 1789, the National Constituent Assembly appointed a committee to draft a new constitution.[100] Four days later, Marie-Joseph Paul Lafayette, who had served as a French general in the American Revolution, placed a draft for a declaration of rights before the assembly.[101] Because the abstract principles in the declaration could sidestep the increasingly serious contradiction between the emerging republican construction of political authority and the continuing role of the monarchy, the Declaration of the Rights of Man and of the Citizen was much easier to draft than the new constitution.[102] In many respects, the task was facilitated by a shared agreement on its tenets by those who subscribed to Enlightenment principles and those who tilted, often heavily, toward Rousseau. The first article, for example, began with what was almost a

---

[98] Taylor, *Modern Social Imaginaries*, pp. 127–8; Albert Soboul, *The Sans-Culottes: The Popular Movement and Revolutionary Government, 1793–1794*, trans. Remy Inlis Hall (Princeton, NJ: Princeton University Press, 1980), p. 254.

[99] Lefebvre, *French Revolution*, vol. 1, p. 114; Doyle, *French Revolution*, p. 118.

[100] Davidson, *French Revolution*, p. 22; Michael P. Fitzsimmons, "Sovereignty and Constitutional Power" in Andress, *Oxford Handbook of the French Revolution*, pp. 207, 209. On the drafting of a constitution and the subsequent history of the National Assembly generally, see Alpaugh, "A Personal Revolution," pp. 180–97.

[101] Lafayette also gave a copy to Thomas Jefferson, who was then serving as the United States representative in the royal court. Lefebvre, *French Revolution*, vol. 1, p. 145. Lafayette's draft was only one of many submitted by the deputies.

[102] For discussions of the declaration, see, for example, McPhee, *Liberty or Death*, pp. 78–80; Lefebvre, *French Revolution*, vol. 1, pp. 145–7; Israel, *Revolutionary Ideas*, pp. 77–84.

direct quote from the *Social Contract*: "Men are born and remain free." The second sentence in that article allowed for "[s]ocial distinctions" but made them dependent on their contribution to "the general good," neatly wrapping in ambiguity any determination of when (and even whether) such distinctions could contribute to "the general good."

The Declaration of the Rights of Man and of the Citizen, adopted by the National Assembly on August 26, 1789

Articles:

1 Men are born and remain free and equal in rights. Social distinctions may be founded only upon the general good.

2 The aim of all political association is the preservation of the natural and imprescriptible rights of man. These rights are liberty, property, security, and resistance to oppression.

3 The principle of all sovereignty resides essentially in the nation. No body nor individual may exercise any authority which does not proceed directly from the nation.

4 Liberty consists in the freedom to do everything which injures no one else; hence, the exercise of the natural rights of each man has no limits except those which assure to the other members of the society the enjoyment of the same rights. These limits can only be determined by law.

5 Law can only prohibit such actions as are hurtful to society. Nothing may be prevented which is not forbidden by law, and no one may be forced to do anything not provided for by law.

6 Law is the expression of the general will. Every citizen has a right to participate personally, or through his representative, in its foundation. It must be the same for all, whether it protects or punishes. All citizens, being equal in the eyes of the law, are equally eligible to all dignities and to all public positions and occupation, according to their abilities, and without distinction except that of their virtues and talents.

7 No person shall be accused, arrested, or imprisoned except in the cases and according to the forms prescribed by law. Anyone soliciting, transmitting, executing, or causing to be executed any arbitrary order, shall be punished. But any citizen summoned or arrested in virtue of the law shall submit without delay, as resistance constitutes an offense.

8 The law shall provide for such punishments only as are strictly and obviously necessary, and no one shall suffer punishment except it

(*cont.*)

be legally inflicted in virtue of a law passed and promulgated before the commission of the offense.

9 As all persons are held innocent until they shall have been declared guilty, if arrest shall be deemed indispensable, all harshness not essential to the securing of the prisoner's person shall be severely repressed by law.

10 No one shall be disquieted on account of his opinions, including his religious views, provided their manifestation does not disturb the public order established by law.

11 The free communication of ideas and opinions is one of the most precious of the rights of man. Every citizen may, accordingly, speak, write, and print with freedom, but shall be responsible for such abuses of this freedom as shall be defined by law.

12 The security of the rights of man and of the citizen requires public military forces. These forces are, therefore, established for the good of all and not for the personal advantage of those to whom they shall be intrusted.

13 A common contribution is essential for the maintenance of the public forces and for the cost of administration. This should be equitably distributed among all the citizens in proportion to their means.

14 All the citizens have a right to decide, either personally or by their representatives, as to the necessity of the public contribution; to grant this freely; to know to what uses it is put; and to fix the proportion, the mode of assessment and of collection, and the duration of the taxes.

15 Society has the right to require of every public agent an account of his administration.

16 A society in which the observance of the law is not assured, nor the separation of powers defined, has no constitution at all.

17 Since property is an inviolable and sacred right, no one shall be deprived thereof except where public necessity, legally determined, shall clearly demand it, and then only on condition that the owner shall have been previously and equitably indemnified.

Anderson, *Daily Life*, pp. 243–5

In the second article, "liberty, property, security, and resistance to oppression" were designated as the "rights of man." While all of these "rights" could be found in both Enlightenment thought and Rousseau's work, they took on vastly different meanings when put into practice. For those who followed the Enlightenment, these were fundamentally individual rights that could not be violated by the state. And, because it was possible for even a properly formed state to violate such rights, these remained outside the social contract. For those who followed Rousseau, these same rights emerged from the exercise of the General Will; they disappeared if and when the General Will revealed their contradiction with the common good. Individual rights that contradicted the common good were thus transformed into "unvirtuous" exceptions and only those who did not recognize the General Will would attempt to insist upon them (or even conceive of them). In effect, those who insisted upon such a construction of rights placed themselves outside the community that granted and protected those rights. And those who were no longer members of the political community could not, by definition, have their rights violated.[103] But the conflict in interpretation between the two camps emerged only later in the revolution. At this point, once again, ambiguity paved the way to consensus.[104]

The third article exclusively lodged political sovereignty in the "Nation." For many of those who subscribed to Enlightenment principles, the "Nation" was something that we now regard as the "nation-state," a state that encompassed and governed a people. From that perspective, the state was an apparatus distinct from but grounded in the people. For those who followed Rousseau, the Nation *was* the people and the state was nothing but an epiphenomenal expression of the General Will. As the revolution developed, the difference between them became increasingly significant as those aligned with the Enlightenment favored more decentralized structural arrangements that appeared, to those who followed Rousseau, to fragment what they regarded as a unitary General Will. The two camps also broke over the concept of "representation," with those who subscribed to the Enlightenment contending that the electorate necessarily and legitimately granted discretion to the deputies it elected while those favoring Rousseau held that deputies should always conform to the General Will, as revealed through direct political participation

[103] In the *Social Contract*, Rousseau had written: "For the state, in relation to its members, is master of all their goods by the social contract, which within the state, is the basis of all right . . . However the acquisition [of property] be made, the right which the individual has to his own estate is always subordinate to the right which the community has over all." In *Émile*, he referred more explicitly to the supremacy of the collective right conferred by the General Will:

The State itself is founded on the right of Property. This right is inviolable and sacred for the State, so long as it remains private and individual. But directly as it is considered a right of all the citizens, it is subordinated to the general will, and the general will can annul it. The Sovereign has no right to touch the possessions of either one individual or several. But it has every right to appropriate the possessions of all. (Harkins, "Intellectual Origins of Babouvism," p. 84)

[104] Articles 4 and 5 can more or less be read through the second article. The definition of "liberty," however, is stretched so as to encompass the other "natural rights" and law may limit all of these rights.

by the people.[105] These two conflicting interpretations were subsequently aggravated by the increasingly direct participation of the people of Paris in the affairs of the National Constituent Assembly.[106] But, for the moment, these differences were but latent possibilities as the two camps confronted the monarchy, the powerful adversary they had in common.[107]

In an apparently clear allusion to Rousseau, Article 6 declared that "[l]aw is the expression of the general will" and that all citizens would enjoy political and legal equality. The article also proclaimed: "Every citizen has a right to participate personally, or through his representative, in its foundation."[108] Although this last sentence ambiguously combined endorsements of what might be interpreted as direct, popular democracy and representative government, it nonetheless implied that, whatever the form, participation would be open to every citizen. However, the article also allowed "distinction" between citizens

---

[105] Those who followed Robespierre, in Israel's words:

> aimed to maximize the people's notional authority over their representatives, and this cornerstone of populist authoritarianism, in turn, relied on the idea that *volonté générale* cannot be represented, so that the legislature's deputies must be rigidly mandated and readily recalled. For this reason, Rousseau's thought was fundamental to the structure of Montagnard Jacobinism in a way that it never was for democratic republicanism. (Israel, *Revolutionary Ideas*, p. 354)

[106] The only way that the people could directly reveal their will to the national legislature was if they were located in the capital. That requirement, in turn, transformed the people of Paris into a proxy for the people in the provinces. To deny that the people of Paris could serve in that role was to assert that the people in the provinces did not necessarily share the same General Will as the people in the capital and, thus, to simultaneously affirm a delegation of discretion to the deputies so that the provinces could be properly represented. But to claim that the people in the provinces did not share the same General Will was to open the door to a decentralization of authority so that government would be more aligned, at least in some cases, with the provincial will.

[107] Even as latent possibilities, the disagreement can be seen in the phrases "a right to participate personally, or through his representative" in Article 6 and "either personally or by their representatives" in Article 14. A citizen could not "participate personally" in the crafting of law in the former or in the determination of taxation in the latter without superseding the discretion of the deputies. In his brief discussion, Lefebvre also underlined the impracticality of these sections by quizzically asking, "In person?" Lefebvre, *French Revolution*, vol. 1, p. 151.

[108] Davidson, *French Revolution*, p. 37. In Arendt's view, this sentence fatefully obliterated the necessary distinction "between the origin of power, which springs from below, the 'grass roots' of the people, and the source of law, whose seat is 'above' in some higher and transcendent region" – what I have referred to as "the transcendent social purpose" that legitimates state authority. In deriving both power and law from the same source (i.e., the General Will), the revolution deified the people and, as a result, "the very process of the Revolution itself . . . became the source of all 'laws,' a source which relentlessly produced new 'laws,' namely, decrees and ordinances, which were obsolete the very moment they were issued, swept away by the Higher Law of the Revolution which had just given birth to them." In many of her comparisons of the American and French Revolutions, Arendt strongly prefers the founding of the United States because the American revolutionaries insisted upon distinguishing between the sources of power and law. This is one of those instances. Arendt, *On Revolution*, pp. 174–5.

in terms of their relative "virtues and talents."[109] With that possible exception, a simple reading of Article 6 appears to endorse full and universal suffrage. In fact, the reference to the "general will" as the legitimating "expression" of the law makes such a conclusion almost unavoidable. However, every election held during the French Revolution discriminated between citizens by imposing suffrage requirements that denied voting rights to a substantial portion of the population.

There were other uncertainties as to what these principles might mean in practice. On the one hand, this article might imply that the law was to be democratically created by the national legislature and then set down, in a relatively stable fashion, as the congealed expression of the General Will. Alternatively, it could also mean that the law was to be the spontaneous expression of the General Will and thus should change whenever the will itself changed. The first interpretation implied a relatively stable and well-defined governing structure. The second implied, among the various possibilities, an authoritarian regime in which the people's will was implemented through otherwise arbitrary decrees.[110] The last clause of Article 6 could also be a source of trouble in that the definitions of "virtues and talents" would distinguish those who enjoyed full equality from those who did not. Although they differed on how these terms should be defined, it was clear from the very beginning that those who subscribed to Enlightenment principles intended to place more emphasis on "talents" as they attempted to create a meritocratic social order while those who followed Rousseau were to place more weight on "virtues" with its attendant subordination of self-interest and parochial identity to the common good. These differences would later emerge as vital, sometimes lethal, political conflicts. For the time being, they were glossed over in ambiguous phrases.[111]

Articles 10 and 11 provide for freedom of personal opinion, including religious belief, and freedom to "speak, write, and print."[112] While there was

[109] This last line is also ambiguous in that it might be read as applying only to eligibility to serve in public office. However, "dignities" is separately referenced and could be interpreted as suffrage rights as well.

[110] Article 16, which sets out a definition of a proper constitution as one in which "the observance of the law is ... assured" and "the separation of powers defined," provides no indication which of the two alternatives described in the text should be preferred.

[111] Articles 7, 8, and 9 lay out procedural protections that articulate some of what is meant by legal equality but do not resolve the fundamental differences in interpretation described in the text. Because it defines taxation as a species of legislation and thus covered by Article 6, Article 14 is more or less superfluous. However, both camps could heartily agree that equality was the negation of feudal privilege and hereditary rank.

[112] Deliberations on the clause referring to religion took about a week because of intense opposition from the clerics. Doyle, *French Revolution*, p. 118. The deputies only gradually enacted legislation with respect to religious freedom. On December 27, 1789, the National Constituent Assembly conferred civil rights on Protestants. One month later, the deputies granted rights to Jews in southern France, followed by those in the eastern part of the nation on September 27,

no disagreement between the two camps on the importance of these freedoms, substantial disagreement later emerged on their limitations. The "manifestation" of opinions and belief, for example, must "not disturb the public order established by law." Those who subscribed to Enlightenment principles tended to view that "public order" through an individualistic lens in which diversity of opinion would be widely tolerated. Those who followed Rousseau, on the other hand, held to a narrower conception in which the "public order" was the creation and embodiment of the General Will. Dissent, for them, often manifested hostility and disaffection from the collective created by that will, and freedom of expression was suspect for that reason. As Timothy Tackett has written, Rousseau's theory regarded any deviation from the General Will "as intrinsically pernicious and counterrevolutionary." He goes on to say that "the violence of 1793 was already inherent in the ideology of 1789."[113]

Articles 12 and 13 set out general principles with respect to the organization and support of the military. Article 14 is remarkable for the way in which a democratic process, involving informed consent, was made the basis for creating taxes. Since the raising of revenue was the original reason for the convocation of the Estates-General, this article, in effect, replaced the Constituent Assembly's feudal authority over taxation, arising out of its relationship with the crown, with a new and democratic process, arising out of its relationship with the people. Although Article 15 appears to simply assert that state officials must publicly report on their administrative conduct, it also designates "[s]ociety," not the national legislature, as the recipient of such reports. Although too much could easily be made of this, the insistence on public transparency was a tilt toward a Rousseauian perspective.

Article 16 sets out conditions that must be met for a valid constitutional order. We might note in passing that the revolution rarely, if ever, met these conditions. The last article, Article 17, declared "property" to be "an inviolable and sacred right."[114] While providing that "public necessity, legally determined" might justify the taking of property, the "owner shall [be] equitably indemnified." As will be described later, this right was most egregiously violated in the expropriation of the Catholic Church very early in the revolution. In fact, most of the other provisions in the Declaration of the Rights of Man and of the Citizen were also violated at one time or another, although a Rousseauian interpretation of the various clauses might render some of those violations acceptable.

1791. Anabaptists were granted citizenship on August 9, 1793. Lefebvre, *French Revolution*, vol. 1, p. 150; McPhee, *Liberty or Death*, pp. 96–7; Israel, *Revolutionary Ideas*, p. 183.

[113] Timothy Tackett, *The Coming of the Terror in the French Revolution* (Cambridge, MA: Harvard University Press, 2015), pp. 2–3.

[114] As Davidson points out, "liberty, property, security and resistance to oppression" were all described as "natural and imprescriptible" rights in Article 2 but property alone was elevated to "sacred" in Article 17. Davidson, *French Revolution*, p. 38.

These interpretations of the individual articles must be qualified in several ways. For one thing, the competing interpretations of their meaning are often retrospective in that they describe ideological differences that only later became evident in practice.[115] They are thus structured by hindsight; we simply do not know to what extent the language in the articles really reflected intentional compromises between conflicting ideological perspectives when they were written.[116] These interpretations also assume the existence of well-defined ideological divisions with the National Constituent Assembly, when, in actuality, most members were much more flexible in both their political beliefs and their factional alignment. While almost all historical accounts of the revolution rely heavily on factional identities in structuring their narrative, these were often merely polar ideological perspectives as opposed to firmly delineated divisions.

What is clear, however, is that this formal statement of the ideology of the French Revolution proposed the liberation and enlightenment of the individual as a citizen of the French nation and that the idealizations of "nature" and "natural" provided the ground upon which rested conceptions of the proper conduct of politics and organization of society. These conceptions assumed the authenticity of spontaneous popular mobilization as an expression of the General Will, the emotional reception of political acts as intuitive recognitions of virtue, and the popular embrace of symbols and social practices as evidence of the virtuous nature of people as they participated in human affairs. Rousseau's followers, for example, expected that a political oration should produce in listeners a spontaneous emotional reaction that, through the natural and undeniable "authenticity" of their collective response, made "citizens ... transparent to each other." The spontaneity and transparency of this emotional arousal constituted intuitive evidence of an authentic articulation of the General Will.[117]

---

[115] Lefebvre, for example, emphasized the consensus among the deputies. For him, the makers of the Declaration of Rights were enchanted with a vision of eternal truths that were in accord "with natural law or the rational will of God." At the same time, these bourgeois deputies who were the bearers of that vision served their own class interests as they imprinted these truths into the fabric of the revolution. Lefebvre, *French Revolution*, vol. 1, p. 148. For an interpretation of the Declaration of Rights from the perspective of the concept of the "citizen" that it created, see Jeremy D. Popkin, "Revolution and Changing Identities in France, 1787–99" in Andress, *Oxford Handbook of the French Revolution*, pp. 242–3.

[116] There were also some who opposed the entire project. During discussion of the advisability of crafting the declaration, for example, Comte de La Blache caustically observed that France was not in some sort of Rousseauian state of nature: "We should not forget ... that the French are not a people who have just emerged from the depths of the woods to form an original association." Quoted in Schama, *Citizens*, p. 443.

[117] Hunt, *Politics, Culture, and Class*, p. 45. Hunt adds: "Politically, transparency meant that there was no need for politicians and no place for the professional manipulation of sentiments or symbols; each citizen was to deliberate in the stillness of his heart, free from the nefarious influences of connections, patronage, or party."

The expansiveness of the language in the articles implied that the Declaration of the Rights of Man set out principles that applied to all of humankind, not only to the French (e.g., the words "France" and "French" appear nowhere in the text). During the early years of the revolution, the universality implied in the declaration was taken seriously because many of the deputies believed that the revolution would inspire the rest of the world to embrace the liberation of mankind. On May 22, 1790, for example, the National Constituent Assembly declared that "the French nation renounces the undertaking of any war with a view to making conquests, and that it will never use its forces against the freedom of any people."[118] Soon after that, on June 19, 1790, Jean-Baptiste Cloots, a wealthy Prussian baron who described himself as "The Orator of the Human Race," persuaded the National Constituent Assembly to receive a diverse group of exiles from surrounding countries, including Geneva, Holland, and Belgium. This delegation asked the assembly if they might have the honor of "representing the universe" at the upcoming Festival of the Federation.[119]

Just over a month after that reception, the Legislative Assembly proposed that the impending elections to the National Convention should produce a "congress of the entire world" in accordance with the Declaration of the Rights of Man and of the Citizen and that the most eminent "apostles of liberty" should be granted honorary citizenship and encouraged to participate in national legislative debates.[120] More than two dozen men, mostly from the United States and Britain, were granted citizenship, including Tom Paine, Joseph Priestley, Jeremy Bentham, Alexander Hamilton, George Washington, and James Madison. Passage of this decree on August 26, 1792, "marked the

[118] McPhee, *Liberty or Death*, p. 152; Lefebvre, *French Revolution*, vol. 1, p. 197.

[119] Lefebvre, *French Revolution*, vol. 1, p. 180; McPhee, *Liberty or Death*, p. 102. Doyle notes that the delegation included a few actors "in fancy-dress" but this did not seem to reduce the enthusiasm with which the group was received. Doyle, *French Revolution*, p. 172. Cloots was made an honorary French citizen on August 16, 1792, and took his seat, as a deputy, in the National Convention in September. McPhee, *Liberty or Death*, p. 165. A year and a half later, after the revolution had turned inward during the Terror, Robespierre accused Cloots of being a foreign agent and he was sent to the guillotine.

[120] At about the same time, the notion of "citizenship" became formalized in what became the constitution of 1791. Title II, Article 6, for example, stated: "The status of French citizen may be lost ... 1) by naturalization in a foreign country, 2) by sentence to punishments implying civic degradation, 3) by sentence *in absentia* until it is annulled, 4) by affiliation with any foreign order of chivalry or any foreign body which requires either proofs of nobility, or distinctions of birth, or religious vows." These conditions clearly identified French identity with at least tacit alignment with the characteristics of an ideal "citizen." Under the monarchy, much of the nobility and almost all of the royal family had intermarried with their foreign counterparts and national identity had thus not been much of an issue (although loyalty to the king, of course, was). Bosher, *French Revolution*, p. 138.

high tide of the Revolution's internationalism."[121] In keeping with this messianic outlook on the revolution's impact on the world, some deputies, including Cloots, believed that neighboring countries, once they had thrown off their feudal chains, should join France in what would be a vast republican federation of the free.[122]

However, even while abetting the creation of other republics founded on the same principles, the revolution focused on the "natural boundaries" of the French republic, both geographical and cultural. The most common conception of those limits proposed the Rhine, the Alps, and the Pyrenees as the boundaries of the French nation and everything within them was to be annexed to France. The revolution, as it expanded abroad, would also create sister republics allied with France but formally independent.[123] France accordingly annexed Avignon (after some hesitation), Alsace, and Savoy.[124] Outside of the national boundaries that those annexations described, the Girondins proposed wars of liberation in which France would wrest other peoples from the yoke of tyranny.[125]

All foundings declare abiding principles that are at least somewhat vague and ambiguous. In this respect, the Declaration of the Rights of Man and of the Citizen is not unusual. What is unusual is that this founding statement never mentions the king. While the National Assembly is implicitly legitimated as the agency through which the General Will reveals and creates law, the monarchy is nowhere to be seen. This omission rather starkly exposed the tenuous status and, soon enough, incompatibility of the monarchy with the revolutionary founding.[126] On the one hand, the continued existence of the monarchy seriously compromised the Declaration of the Rights of Man and of the Citizen as

---

[121] Israel's words. Israel, *Revolutionary Ideas*, pp. 264–6. Also see McPhee, *Liberty or Death*, p. 159. On the reception of French revolutionary ideology abroad, see Mike Rapport, "Jacobinism from Outside" in Andress, *Oxford Handbook of the French Revolution*, p. 514.

[122] Cloots, for example, was quite hostile to the notion that small independent republics were the ideal political form even though they had been designated as such by Rousseau. Writing to republicans in Geneva, he urged them to recognize Paris as the center of a "universal republic" because Rousseau's errors "are just as dangerous as his genius is sublime." Israel, *Revolutionary Ideas*, p. 318.

[123] Israel, *Revolutionary Ideas*, p. 292; Lefebvre, *French Revolution*, vol. 1, pp. 219, 277–8.

[124] Lefebvre, *French Revolution*, vol. 1, p. 196; Doyle, *French Revolution*, p. 139; McPhee, *Liberty or Death*, p. 116.

[125] Lefebvre, *French Revolution*, vol. 1, pp. 273–5; Schama, *Citizens*, pp. 590–2, 597, 642–4. On the night following the first French victory at Valmy, Goethe told his fellow Germans: "From this place and this time forth commences a new era in world history and you can all say that you were present at its birth." Schama, *Citizens*, p. 640. Doyle reports a slightly different version: "Here and today . . . a new epoch in the history of the world has begun, and you can boast you were present at its birth." Doyle, *French Revolution*, p. 193.

[126] Doyle suggests that the third article implied that the king had no authority other than that "expressly emanating from the nation," but that is, at best, a very indirect reference to the monarchy. Doyle, *French Revolution*, p. 118. Also see Schama, *Citizens*, p. 442.

a statement of the transcendent social purpose of the revolutionary state.[127] On the other hand, it was the continuing existence of an obstinate monarchy that bound the deputies together even though their ideological differences were quite serious.

The king was only too willing to play that role. On September 18, Louis XVI indicated that he would approve only those parts of the decree the assembly had crafted after the renunciation of feudal rights on the night of August 4. When pressed by deputies, the king said that he would "publish" the decree but not explicitly endorse it. In early October, he expressed similar reservations concerning the Declaration of the Rights of Man.[128] His reticence, along with a severe shortage of food in Paris and rumors concerning the conduct of the Flanders Regiment posted at the palace, produced a protest march led by women from the city to Versailles on October 5. After arriving at Versailles, the women invaded the National Assembly and "crowded into the benches alongside the startled deputies and, with swords and hunting-knives slung from their skirts," presented their demands for bread and for the punishment of troops who, they believed, had insulted the national cockade.[129]

After they later occupied the palace grounds, the king relented and accepted without qualification both the decree ending feudalism and the Declaration of the Rights of Man and of the Citizen. This, however, did not end the demonstration because the protestors invaded the palace itself the next morning. When several of the king's bodyguards fired on the demonstrators, the guards were killed and their heads skewered on pikes, which the demonstrators then paraded about. When a semblance of order was restored, the king and his family, along with the demonstrators, members of the assembly, and regiments of the army and the National Guard, formed a procession totaling some 60,000 people that escorted the king back to Paris. In the vanguard bobbed the heads of the slain bodyguards. Louis XVI never returned to Versailles.[130]

---

[127] The declaration was intended to serve as the preamble to the constitution, which, of course, had not yet been drafted. For that reason, the deputies only provisionally adopted the Declaration of Rights, reserving the right to revise the articles once the constitution was complete. However, "when that moment came two years later nobody dared [to suggest changes]. The declaration had become the founding document of the Revolution and, as such, sacrosanct." Doyle, *French Revolution*, p. 118. Even so, the Declaration of Rights was revised in both 1793 and 1795 when new constitutions were adopted – and even abandoned altogether when the 1799 constitution was ratified. In some respects, then, the 1789 Declaration of the Rights of Man and of the Citizen has been more important to world history than it was to the French Revolution. See, for example, Doyle, *French Revolution*, p. 119. On the 1793 version of the Declaration of Rights, see Davidson, *French Revolution*, p. 179. For the text of Robespierre's version of the 1793 declaration, see Thompson, *Robespierre*, vol. 2, pp. 40–5. Robespierre's version was not adopted.

[128] Doyle, *French Revolution*, p. 121; Schama, *Citizens*, p. 458.

[129] Rude, *The Crowd*, pp. 75–6.

[130] Schama, *Citizens*, pp. 460–70; Lefebvre, *French Revolution*, vol. 1, pp. 132–5; Rude, *The Crowd*, pp. 72–9; McPhee, *Liberty or Death*, pp. 84–5; Sutherland, "Urban Violence," p. 284.

Although the sweeping rhetoric of the Declaration of the Rights of Man and of the Citizen appeared to encompass all of mankind, two groups were largely excluded from its embrace. For one thing, the revolution was not gender neutral. When the declaration stated the "Rights of Man," it emphatically meant men. In September 1791, the actress Olympe de Gouges published her satirical alternative *Declaration of the Rights of Women*, which, like the original version, contained seventeen articles. Here are the first four:

I   Woman is born free and lives equal to man in her rights. Social distinctions can be based only on the common good.

II The purpose of any political association is the conservation of the natural and imprescriptible rights of woman and man; these rights are liberty, property, security, and especially the right to resist oppression.

III The principle of sovereignty rests essentially in the nation, which is nothing but the union of woman and man. No body or individual can exercise authority that does not derive expressly from the nation.

IV Liberty and justice consist in restoring all that belongs to any, to all. Thus, the only limits on the exercise of the natural rights of woman are perpetual male tyranny. These boundaries are to be reformed by the laws of nature and reason.[131]

Women lost almost every struggle for equal rights during the revolution, even though they played a prominent role in many of the most crucial events, such as the taking of the Bastille and the march to Versailles. Among the few gains for women was the legalization of divorce.[132] The traditional place of women as helpmates to their husbands and nurturing mothers to their children was ideologically reinforced by Rousseau's sentimental understandings of gender

---

[131] Israel, *Revolutionary Ideas*, pp. 125–6. For the full document, including a proposed "Form for a Social Contract between Man and Woman" that would rectify the present inequalities in the institution of marriage, see Lynn Hunt, *The French Revolution and Human Rights* (Boston, MA: Bedford Books, 1996), pp. 124–9. De Gouges dedicated her declaration to Marie Antoinette. She later bravely offered to defend Louis XVI at his trial but the king chose Guillaume-Chrétien de Lamoignon de Malesherbes instead. During the Terror, de Gouges harshly criticized Robespierre and was subsequently convicted of authoring "counterrevolutionary writings." She went to the guillotine on November 3, 1793. Four days before she lost her head, the National Convention banned women's organizations for disrupting the public order. Schama, *Citizens*, pp. 498, 657; McPhee, *Liberty or Death*, pp. 112, 231; Doyle, *French Revolution*, p. 420; Israel, *Revolutionary Ideas*, p. 509.

[132] Andress, *French Society*, p. 112; Lefebvre, *French Revolution*, vol. 1, p. 244; Israel, *Revolutionary Ideas*, p. 279. Georges Couthon, a prominent member of the Committee of Public Safety and a Jacobin, was one of the many exceptions: "Woman is born with as many capacities as man. If she has not demonstrated it until now, it is not the fault of Nature but of our former institutions." However, most deputies would have agreed with Philippe-Antoine Merlin de Douai when he contended that "woman is generally incapable of administration and men, having a natural superiority over her, must protect her." McPhee, *Liberty or Death*, p. 208.

roles. Men had public duties that required their undivided attention; women provided the aid and comfort that allowed them to do that.[133]

The revolution also had difficulty negotiating race and slavery. Although racial discrimination was not common in metropolitan France, the enslavement of blacks was the lifeblood of the colonies.[134] The slave-owning planters in the Caribbean produced goods that, in turn, created vast commercial interests among the shipowners and merchants in the ports of France.[135] These interests were mostly sympathetic to the revolution but only on the condition that their trade relations with the colonies were not threatened. So, while there was a general disposition among the deputies to extend "the rights of man" to men of all races, the National Constituent Assembly supported colonial slavery in practice.

However, what became the Haitian Revolution rapidly turned what might have been a matter of political philosophy into high state politics.[136] At first, the assembly sided with the colonists. However, when the British and Spanish threatened to intervene, free blacks and then slaves became potential allies. In May 1791, the assembly initially conferred citizenship on free blacks who descended from free parents but then attempted to wash their hands of any further involvement in the matter by declaring that "the National Assembly decrees that it will never deliberate on the station of people of colour who are not born of free father and mother, without the prior, free and spontaneous wish of the colonies." Almost a year later, on April 4, 1792, the Legislative Assembly abandoned that position and extended social equality to free blacks. Then, in June 1793, in the midst of fierce fighting on Saint-Domingue, the French commissioners offered freedom to those slaves who would take up arms for France. In October, another edict, issued without the knowledge or consent of the assembly in Paris, abolished slavery on the island. On February 4, 1794, the assembly recognized what had become a reality on the island and formally abolished slavery in all French colonies.[137]

---

[133] Schama, *Citizens*, p. 749; Andress, *French Society*, p. 46. Schama, for example, notes that: "In keeping with Rousseauean doctrine on the sacred nature of the family, 'It is not the legal condition but the act of paternity which constitutes marriage'" (p. 763).

[134] In September 1793, Jean-Baptiste Belley, a former slave from Senegal, joined the National Convention and thus became the first black man to sit in a European parliament. Other black and mixed-race deputies served in the assembly between 1794 and 1799. McPhee, *Liberty or Death*, p. 304; Israel, *Revolutionary Ideas*, p. 411.

[135] McPhee, *Liberty or Death*, pp. 35-7.

[136] For Robespierre, if the assembly had to choose between slavery and the principles of revolution, then he would "perish the colonies" before defiling "liberty." Robespierre, *Virtue and Terror*, p. 21. On the relationship between the Haitian and French Revolutions, see Popkin, *A New World Begins*, pp. 231-5, 354-6, 387-9, 420-1, 537-43.

[137] Lefebvre, *French Revolution*, vol. 1, pp. 172-3; Israel, *Revolutionary Ideas*, pp. 396-8, 403-19; Doyle, *French Revolution*, pp. 13, 151, 181, 212, 411-13; McPhee, *Liberty or Death*, pp. 35-6, 105-6, 145-6, 191-2, 249, 350; Manuel Covo, "Race, Slavery, and Colonies in the French Revolution" in Andress, *Oxford Handbook of the French Revolution*,

SQUARING THE CIRCLE: DESIGNING A CONSTITUTIONAL MONARCHY

On May 3, 1788, about a year before the revolution began, the *parlement* of Paris declared that France had fundamental laws, one of which was that succession to the kingship was hereditary. While that was unproblematic from the king's perspective, the other laws were not because the *parlement* also asserted that only the Estates-General could approve revenue measures, that the king could not arbitrarily order the arrest of his subjects, that judges serving in one of the thirteen *parlements* could not be removed, that *parlements* had the right to register new laws and without registration these laws could not be implemented, and that those customs and privileges tradition-ally enjoyed by the provinces could not be violated.[138] The following day, the Paris *parlement* declared that these fundamental laws were part of an ancient constitution that guaranteed that "[t]he heir to the Crown is desig-nated by the law; the Nation has its rights; the Peerage likewise; the Magistracy is irremovable; each province has its customs, its capitulations; each subject has his natural judges, each citizen has his property; if he is poor, at least he has his liberty."[139]

Although most of the principles annunciated in these declarations were anathema to the crown, the purported existence of an ancient constitution was not. In November 1787, Chrétien François de Lamoignon, the king's keeper of the seals, had previously set out the king's role under the ancient constitution to the *parlement* of Paris.

> These principles, universally accepted by the nation, testify that sovereign power in his kingdom belongs to the king alone;
> That he is accountable only to God for the exercise of supreme power;
> That the link that unites the king and the nation is by nature indissoluble;
> That the reciprocal interests and duties of the king and his subjects ensure the perpetuity of this union;
> That the nation has a vested interest that the rights of its ruler remain unchanged;
> That the king is the sovereign ruler of the nation, and is one with it;
> Finally that the legislative power resides in the person of the sovereign, depending upon and sharing with no-one.

These, sirs, are the invariable principles of the French monarchy.[140]

---

pp. 290–307. Israel estimates that about 15 percent of the deputies owned property in the colonies (p. 398). Napoleon reinstated slavery in the colonies in May 1802. On the Haitian revolt generally, see Lefebvre, *French Revolution*, vol. 1, pp. 171–3; Doyle, *French Revolution*, pp. 181, 210, 212; Hanson, *Contesting the French Revolution*, pp. 101–14; R. A. Humphreys, "The Development of the American Communities outside British Rule" in Goodwin, *New Cambridge Modern History*, vol. 8, pp. 417–20.
[138] Lefebvre, *French Revolution*, vol. 1, p. 100.   [139] Doyle, *French Revolution*, p. 81.
[140] McPhee, *Liberty or Death*, p. 44.

Even before the revolution began, those bent on political reform denied the very existence of an ancient constitution. As Guy-Jean Target put it: "The mere fact ... that antiquarians had to go rummaging around in the history of Charlemagne and the Carolingians was proof enough that France had no constitution and it was now necessary to create one from scratch."[141]

The deputies, however, felt that they could not start from scratch because they felt they needed the king's consent, tacit though that might be. The Declaration of the Rights of Man and of the Citizen had finessed the king's existence by simply ignoring him in its seventeen articles. The new constitution, however, could not do the same thing because this document would construct the institutional framework of governance and, for that reason, was compelled to set out the duties and privileges of the king. Most deputies in the National Constituent Assembly favored some form of constitutional monarchy as a pragmatic solution to this problem and thought that the English model might guide them. But the English model cut both ways: On the one hand, it presented a tangible historical experience that demonstrated the viability of the model, at least in England; on the other hand, it was profoundly English and thus quite repugnant to those who regarded England as a hostile power.

However, the dilemma posed by the king was only part of an even more basic problem: The translation of the Declaration of the Rights of Man into institutional forms threatened to once more divide the people into those who were governed and those who ruled them. Rousseau had solved this problem by identifying the city-state as the appropriate unit of government so that the people could regularly participate in the revelation of the General Will without the aid or intervention of political authorities. This regular participation would have reduced government officials to mere functionaries who executed what the people willed without reinterpreting or exceeding its content. It was this principle of direct, popular participation in government that both legitimated the revolution in its early contests with the king and, later, empowered the crowds in Paris who viewed themselves as the unalloyed expression of the General Will.[142]

As the deputies began to deliberate on the new constitution, they set aside the question of direct popular participation because France was not and clearly could not be a city-state. But the notion that the assembly represented the General Will of the nation was nonetheless very strong. When, on September 10, 1789, those who supported a constitutional monarchy on the English model proposed the creation of something like a House of Lords,

---

[141] Paraphrased in Schama, *Citizens*, p. 299.
[142] After the king had been deposed, Robespierre similarly recognized "the politically active part of Paris as a representative population, expressing the will of all France" and thus interpreted the *sans-culottes* as the empirical manifestation of the otherwise "abstract and even mythical" people of Rousseau's theory. Jordan, *Revolutionary Career of Maximilien Robespierre*, p. 119.

the idea of a second chamber composed of nobles was overwhelmingly rejected (849 to 89).

The next day, the assembly refused to grant the king an absolute veto over legislation and instead opted for what was called a "suspensive veto" (673 to 325). The latter gave the king the right to delay enactment of a decree for three two-year terms. The voting revealed that some 220 deputies did not want the king to have a veto of any kind.[143] The refusal to grant the king an absolute veto made the National Constituent Assembly the sole agent of the General Will of the nation and the dominant institution in the government.[144] While the king could still delay legislation, and even though six years was an eternity during the revolution, the National Constituent Assembly was rapidly developing an understanding of constitution-making that assigned something like absolute power to itself. Many in the assembly now believed that it held full and complete authority to remake the entire French state, including whether or not there should be a monarchy.[145] The crisis of October 5–6, when the people marched on Versailles and brought the king back to Paris, aligned this new theory with political practice. From that point until the new constitution was completed and ratified on September 3, 1791, the assembly constructed a framework for government piece by piece.[146] During this period, most policy decisions were made haphazardly, underlining the contradiction between a more or less democratic assembly (still compromised by the presence of hundreds of noble and clerical deputies) and a monarch who, although now almost devoid of legitimacy, exercised much day-to-day authority over the affairs of government.[147]

The people themselves posed another problem. Although the Declaration of Rights had granted full political equality to all citizens, the deputies created an electoral system that dramatically restricted suffrage rights. Properly stripped of

---

[143] Schama, *Citizens*, p. 458; McPhee, *Liberty or Death*, pp. 81–2; Doyle, *French Revolution*, p. 120; Lefebvre, *French Revolution*, vol. 1, p. 130.

[144] Lefebvre concluded that the "Legislative Assembly was thus made master of the state." In form, "it was a republic" but it had "no real government" because the crown still controlled most administration. Lefebvre, *French Revolution*, vol. 1, p. 153.

[145] Lefebvre, *French Revolution*, vol. 1, pp. 130–1. "The moment at which Louis XVI appeared to have finally turned into a citizen-king was on February 4 [1790], when he appeared before the National Assembly in a simple black suit to swear that he would 'defend and maintain constitutional liberty, whose principles the general will, in accord with my own, has sanctioned.'" Schama, *Citizens*, p. 502.

[146] Doyle, *French Revolution*, p. 157.

[147] Although Robespierre rhetorically contended that "God created tigers; but kings are the masterpieces of human corruption" and subscribed to "that great moral and political truth preached by Jean-Jacques … that only the people is good, just, and generous; and that corruption and tyranny are the monopoly of those who disdain the common crowd," he was willing to tolerate a constitutional monarchy "until," in his words, "the General Will is sufficiently enlightened by ripe experience to proclaim its desire for a happier state." Robespierre, *Virtue and Terror*, p. 93; Thompson, *Robespierre*, vol. 1, pp. 212, 231, 240, 244.

self-interest and parochial sentimentality, any portion of the population could reveal the General Will of the entire nation. However, most deputies believed that the masses were not yet able to properly distinguish the interests of the nation from their own self-interest and, for that reason, could neither act virtuously nor recognize virtue in those who might represent them in the assembly.[148] Only those who were ready for these responsibilities were granted suffrage rights under the new constitution; for them, the practice of politics would perfect their understanding of virtue.

With that understanding, temporary restrictions on suffrage were not entirely inconsistent with Rousseau's theories. Although the restrictions seemed incompatible with the conception of virtue as an inherent quality of the common man that would be invariably expressed through political action, the deputies could attribute the deferral in suffrage rights to the lingering social corruption of the *ancien régime*. Revolutionary socialization and education would later cleanse the people of this corruption and thus permit their innate virtue to be revealed in politics. At least some of those who subscribed to Enlightenment principles expected this cleansing to take a long time. Those who favored Rousseau anticipated a much shorter period and, later, none at all.

Although the Declaration of the Rights of Man and of the Citizen graced the preamble of the 1791 constitution, the governance framework that it created was a compromise that pleased almost no one.[149] On the one hand, those deputies who favored a republic in which no monarch would have a place were nonetheless very reluctant to openly oppose the constitutional monarchy that it constructed.[150] Their numbers were steadily increasing along with their frustration. On the other hand, the constitutional monarchy erected by the constitution, along with the elimination of noble privileges and titles, alienated those deputies who preferred a return to the *ancien régime*. Pragmatism was as unappealing to them as it was to the republicans. After a promising start with the Declaration of Rights, the National Constituent Assembly had ultimately created a state that few people could heartily support.[151] Neither loved nor venerated, "the Constitution of 1791 remained a piece of paper, of more interest to the learned and the experts than to the people."[152] When Louis XVI appeared before the assembly on September 14 in order to give his consent to the new constitution, the deputies refused to stand as royal protocol would have required. When the king noticed that they had all remained seated, he

---

[148] Lefebvre, *French Revolution*, vol. 1, p. 151.
[149] For summaries of the provisions set out in the 1791 constitution, see Doyle, *French Revolution*, pp. 123–8; Lefebvre, *French Revolution*, vol. 1, pp. 152–3.
[150] Israel, *Revolutionary Ideas*, pp. 141–2.   [151] Israel, *Revolutionary Ideas*, p. 141.
[152] Arendt, *On Revolution*, p. 116. Although it was unloved, the constitution crafted by the National Assembly was, in Schama's words, "one of the most astonishing collective personality changes in political history [transforming] a realm based on ceremonially defined orders and corporations [into] that of the uniform entity of the sovereign nation ... In many respects the constitution was the realization of an Enlightenment project." Schama, *Citizens*, p. 574.

interrupted his speech and awkwardly sat down himself.[153] His evident embarrassment confirmed that the social base of the monarchy was incompatible with a Rousseauian insistence on the abolition of self-interest and the elimination of social inequality.

THE ATTEMPT TO FOUND THE FRENCH REVOLUTIONARY STATE

Under different circumstances, the Declaration of the Rights of Man and of the Citizen could have committed the French revolutionary state to a transcendent social purpose. And, however flawed the election of deputies to the Estates-General (now the National Constituent Assembly) might have been as an exercise in democracy, there was no doubt that the people had voluntarily and enthusiastically consented to that declaration. But that was not enough to meld these elements into a new state for two reasons. First, the constitutional monarchy that had been created under the 1791 constitution contradicted the principles proclaimed in the declaration and thus fatally undermined the government's claim to rule.[154] It did not help that the retention of kingly authority was a pragmatic concession to the realities of power. Second, there was no dominant revolutionary party that could convincingly embed the principles of this declaration in the organization and policies of the new state through the imposition of a coherent political program. These problems were clearly related. On the one hand, the survival of the monarchy was, in part, due to the absence of a disciplined revolutionary party. On the other, the absence of a disciplined revolutionary party was, in part, due to the persisting institutional authority of the monarchy.

But these factors cannot, in themselves, account for the failure to meld a transcendent social purpose and the consent of the people in the founding of a new state. There were, in fact, two revolutionary factions in France and these factions had very different ideas about what the broad pronouncements in the Declaration of the Rights of Man and of the Citizen would mean even if the monarchy had not occupied one corner of the political stage. These factions were primarily based in the several incarnations of the National Assembly, although they had affiliates in the provinces (the latter were particularly well developed for the Jacobins). Despite these affiliates, the national legislature was where these factions debated, competed, and evolved. In what follows,

---

[153] Israel, *Revolutionary Ideas*, p. 212. "The transfer of sovereignty away [to the assembly] rendered [the king's role] meaningless, in Old Regime terms, and hard to grasp even within the discourse of the Revolution. He became essentially a scapegoat for the inability of the body politic to function efficiently around him." Andress, *French Society*, p. 119. Also see Lefebvre, *French Revolution*, vol. 1, pp. 134–5.

[154] The arrangement was, as Israel notes, theoretically "illogical" and practically "unworkable." Israel, *Revolutionary Ideas*, p. 261.

I sometimes discuss the Girondins (also often referred to as the Brissotins) and the Jacobins as if they were political parties.[155] However, they were not formally organized and their ostensible members often behaved and voted as undisciplined factions.

The absence of organized, hierarchical parties clearly originated in the assembly's desire to represent and express an unfettered General Will.[156] In fact, Lefebvre attributes the National Assembly's inability even to "agree upon fixed rules to govern their business" to a revolutionary individualism that "rejected party discipline with horror."[157] Thus, the decision to treat the Girondins and the Jacobins as if they possessed formal organizational structures distorts reality. However, those belonging to these factions often went to their deaths while defending the principles in which they respectively believed. One of the paradoxes of the French Revolution is this combination of fluid

---

[155] In his close examination of the extent to which the Girondins could be considered a political party, Sydenham posited four possible grounds upon which they might have presented a united front in revolutionary politics: the advocacy of common policy positions; opposition to the Montagnards; close ties and loyalties arising from personal friendship; and shared interests arising from their respective constituencies. On each count, Sydenham found so much variation in behavior, interpersonal relations, and policy interests that the Girondins were little more than an ill-defined cluster of members. However, he also described the Montagnards, led by Robespierre, as a much better organized and effective political organization: "The Montagnards alone appear as a distinct entity, having a fair measure of unity imposed upon them by the public debates and frequent purges of the Jacobin Club and having their separatism justified in their own eyes by the conviction that they represented, not a party, but the true voice of the sovereign people." He later concluded that they did resemble "a coherent party." The Girondins, on the other hand, "became an entity only in the hour of its downfall." Sydenham, *The Girondins*, pp. 74, 120–1, 143, 165, 176, 179–207. On these points, Patrick concurs. Patrick, *Men of the First French Republic*, pp. 17n, 295–6.

[156] Schama, *Citizens*, p. 354. As Doyle puts it: "[T]he very idea of political parties was abhorrent to a generation whom Rousseau had taught to seek the general will." Doyle, *French Revolution*, p. 235. In Hunt's words, "all organized politics were conflated with conspiratorial plotting." Hunt, *Politics, Culture, and Class*, pp. 3, 43. Also see Bailey Stone, *The Anatomy of Revolution Revisited: A Comparative Analysis of England, France, and Russia* (New York: Cambridge University Press, 2014), p. 189.

[157] Lefebvre, *French Revolution*, vol. 1, pp. 137–8. And, because there was but one General Will, there should be but one chamber in the national legislature and that chamber should continuously supervise the state. Israel, *Revolutionary Ideas*, p. 106. For similar reasons, ministerial service was incompatible with the role of the deputy because members of the legislature must be wholly committed to the General Will. Ministers would have had divided loyalties both because they would have been servants of the king and because they would have been tempted to defend personal reputations associated with the performance of their administrative duties. After the fall of the king, these considerations provided decisive support for a unicameral chamber in which executive authority was exercised by committees that were directly and immediately responsible to the legislature. For Robespierre's role in the construction of these and similar arrangements, see Doyle, *French Revolution*, p. 150. Robespierre even opposed extending to ministers the privilege of addressing the assembly. Thompson, *Robespierre*, vol. 1, pp. 166–7.

factional commitments and uncompromising ideological belief.[158] In this section, I first describe the ideological bases of these two parties and then explain their differing attitudes toward the survival of the monarchy. The fall of the monarchy brought their disagreements over what should have been the transcendent social purpose of the revolutionary state to a head.

In the fall of 1788, the crown lifted a prohibition on political clubs, which rapidly formed in the months that followed. The most important of these was the Society of Thirty, whose members were drawn from the elite salons of Parisian society and who included Lafayette, Mirabeau, Charles Maurice de Talleyrand, and Nicolas de Condorcet. Although almost all of the members were nobles, they were deeply committed to political reform and viewed the convocation of an Estates-General as a means of transforming the French monarchy into a more modern and egalitarian mode of governance.[159] In many ways, the Society of Thirty was the predecessor of the Feuillants, who formed in July 1791 in order to defend the monarchy against the increasing strength of those who preferred a republic.[160] The election of deputies to the new Legislative Assembly that organized after the adoption of the constitution in September 1791 replaced many of these noble reformers with middle-class men, particularly lawyers.[161]

Many of these new members nonetheless shared the political beliefs and intellectual orientation of the noble reformers who had left the assembly.[162] Among them was a prominent cohort from the Gironde, hence the name for what became their faction.[163] Dedicated to reason, logic, and the promise of

---

[158] On the "specious clarity" of the Jacobin and Girondin factions, see Bosher, *French Revolution*, pp. 186–7; Lefebvre, *French Revolution*, vol. 1, pp. 265–6. For a review of the literature on this topic, see Hanson, *Contesting the French Revolution*, pp. 91–4.

[159] Doyle, *French Revolution*, p. 90.

[160] Davidson, *French Revolution*, p. 72; Doyle, *French Revolution*, p. 175.

[161] Doyle, *French Revolution*, p. 174. Although the nobility would have probably been a smaller proportion of the new Legislative Assembly in any case, the fact that the National Constituent Assembly had prohibited all of its members from standing for reelection made a dramatic reduction in their numbers inevitable. An even more important consequence was that many of those commoners who had served in the National Constituent Assembly now transferred their political energy to the political clubs in the capital, thus creating a rival set of political institutions that competed for the attention and loyalty of the people of Paris. Davidson, *French Revolution*, p. 78. On political clubs generally see Crook, "New Regime"; Charles Walton, "Clubs, Parties, Factions" in Andress, *Oxford Handbook of the French Revolution*, pp. 225–8, 362–81.

[162] For a brief overview of these noble reformers and a comparison of their philosophical and political orientation with those who became the Girondins and the Jacobins, see Schama, *Citizens*, pp. 479–80.

[163] On the origin and usage of the name "Girondins," see Sydenham, *The Girondins*, p. 60. Furet and Richet sympathetically described the Girondins this way:

Very much the children of their century, the Girondins had an immense appetite for liberty, a great capacity for optimism and for enjoying life. Above all, they embodied one of the

science, the Girondins were the primary bearers of the Enlightenment in the assembly.[164] They were confirmed democrats but also believed that many French citizens were not yet ready to exercise the franchise. For them, the disparities in wealth, talent, and education that then existed in French society demanded political leadership by an elite – a broadly based elite to be sure, but one consensually recognized as qualified to create a truly democratic society.[165] Their commitment to reason and science also predisposed them to create constitutional forms precisely designed to reconcile the imperfections of the moment with the grand vision they embraced as France's future.[166] They wished for – and, to some extent, pinned their hopes on – the cooperation of a reformed monarchy that already appeared to embrace modern conceptions of expertise as the guiding principle of state administration.[167] On this point, they were closely aligned with the noble reformers who had preceded them. However, they were more interested in the instrumental utility of a cooperative monarchy than in the sanctity of the institution.[168] The Girondins constructed the first constitution around the monarchy for these reasons and, when the king refused to cooperate, he brought the Girondins down with him.

The Girondins attempted to straddle two trajectories that were moving in diametrically opposed directions. On the one hand, the monarchy was increasingly unwilling to play what was fast becoming a figurehead role in a regime that was rapidly destroying the Church and undermining the status of the landed nobility. It was increasingly obvious that the long-term prospects for the monarchy were bleak if these historical supports for the crown disappeared. On the other hand, the promises that the revolution made to the people took on an increasingly millenarian quality. The popular imagination turned the abolition of feudal dues into rent-free occupation of land, the proclamation of social

---

fundamental ideals of the Revolution – the desire to sweep away the old social hierarchies and replace them by a world of opportunity, in which men of talent and eloquence could make their mark. This is why the very name "Girondin" conjures up an image of eternal youth, irresponsible perhaps, but infinitely appealing. (Furet and Richet, *French Revolution*, p. 150)

[164] Sydenham contended that the philosophical differences between Enlightenment thinkers and those who followed Rousseau formed the most significant cleavage between the Girondins and the Montagnards. On the one hand, Brissot thought that "[t]he most durable monument to our Revolution is philosophy. The patriot *par excellence* is a philosopher." On the other hand, Robespierre, in direct reply, condemned "the mathematicians and the members of the Academy that M. Brissot holds up to us as models" as royalist sycophants who had persecuted Jean-Jacques Rousseau, who "is alone among the celebrities of his time in meriting public honour." Sydenham, *The Girondins*, pp. 190–2.

[165] See, for example, Schama, *Citizens*, p. 856.   [166] Lefebvre, *French Revolution*, vol. 1, p. 214.

[167] Schama, *Citizens*, pp. 291, 858–9.

[168] Lefebvre, *French Revolution*, vol. 1, p. 66. On the importance of the Girondin commitment to the king, see Hanson, *Contesting the French Revolution*, p. 94. For a brief review of the varying interpretations of the philosophical and policy inclinations of the Girondins in French historiography, see Sydenham, *The Girondins*, p. 2.

equality into the right of the people to press political demands through direct action in the streets, and the de facto suspension of the judicial system into the application of summary justice through mob execution.[169] In a sense, the Declaration of the Rights of Man and of the Citizen, that splendid product of Enlightenment principles and beliefs, made its own realization impossible in reality as popular demands arising out of a literal reading of its seventeen articles ran up against hard facts such as the prevailing organization of society and the economy. As popular insurgency became routine, many deputies felt compelled to accommodate state policy to popular demands in ways that often violated liberal principles such as the rule of law, an unregulated economy, freedom of speech, and the rights of private property.[170] The Girondins were caught up in the massive contradiction that was the political and social reality of revolutionary France. They would have liked to have slowly but steadily brought that reality into alignment with their utopian vision of national possibility, but they could not buy the time it would take for that process to unfold.

Although the Girondins were partially responsible for creating this problem, their fate was sealed when the Jacobins made the popular demands of the people the basis for their own claims on political power.[171] Taking their name from an old monastery in which they met, the Jacobin Club organized after the removal of the king and the assembly from Versailles to Paris and descended from the Society of the Friends of the Constitution.[172] The Jacobins invited the public into their club where they could participate in discussion and debate on an equal footing with deputies. Their opponents, the Club of 1789 (in some ways one of the predecessors of the Girondins), organized exclusive dinners and breakfasts in which the members, many of them noble reformers, genteelly discussed the great issues of the day. For the Club of 1789, the major threats to the success of the revolution were social anarchy and the impending fiscal

---

[169] Schama, *Citizens*, p. 497.

[170] On Girondin commitment to an unregulated economy, see Hanson, *Contesting the French Revolution*, p. 93; Albert Soboul, *The French Revolution, 1787–1799* (New York: Vintage Books, 1975), pp. 276–7; Doyle, *French Revolution*, p. 236.

[171] Robespierre explicitly linked this claim to a broader interpretation of the Parisian people as proxies for the national citizenry:

We want our enemies to realize that the public does not echo the opinions of the society, but the society those of the public. We want them to realize that the club is nothing but a section of the general public, and that all its energy comes from the fact that the capital is deeply imbued with revolutionary principles – that capital in whose defence it is ready to sacrifice all that it holds dearest in the world. (Thompson, *Robespierre*, vol. 1, p. 202)

Israel describes the differing strategies of the Girondins and Jacobins as arising out of a conflict between "core Revolution democratic republicanism," on the one hand, and "unbending Rousseauist populism," on the other. Israel, *Revolutionary Ideas*, pp. 21–2, 66, 90, 216.

[172] Although the Jacobins did slightly remodel the second-floor library of the monastery for their purposes, they left undisturbed the shelves of books and a fresco of Saint Thomas Aquinas. Jordan, *Revolutionary Career of Maximilien Robespierre*, p. 68.

bankruptcy of the state. The Jacobins, for their part, viewed their rivals as elitist manipulators and suspected them of abetting, consciously or unconsciously, the return of royal absolutism. Since the king appointed many of his ministers from the ranks of the Club of 1789, the Jacobins had more than enough circumstantial evidence to fuel these suspicions. While the Club of 1789 was indeed preoccupied with the pragmatic problems of governing, it was also dedicated to the creation of a modern, dynamic French nation. The Jacobins, on the other hand, sought the subordination of the state to the will of the people and material realization of the abstract principles of the revolution.[173] In theory, these were not incompatible goals; in reality, they pointed toward opposite ends of the earth.

In contrast to the Club of 1789, the Jacobins conducted their affairs in the open, a practice that helped transform their club into a school for training citizens in the ways of political virtue and morality.[174] In August 1790, over 200 deputies belonged to the Jacobin Club, along with another thousand members drawn from Parisian citizenry. At that time, 152 clubs in the provinces had affiliated with the Paris parent. Twelve months later, there were over 900 affiliated clubs.[175] As long as the monarchy was politically relevant, Jacobin membership evolved more or less in tandem with changing attitudes toward the king. Following the unsuccessful attempt of Louis XVI and his family to flee Paris in June 1791, for example, there were several Jacobin factions. The dominant among them still adhered to the construction of a constitutional monarchy despite the king's obvious and intense unhappiness with that arrangement. Another group supported the deposition of Louis XVI but would have retained the monarchy, replacing Louis with the Duke of Orléans, Louis Philippe. At the other end of the spectrum were the radical democrats who proposed to abolish the monarchy and create a republic in its stead. Robespierre's faction was already creating a populist power base within

---

[173] Schama, *Citizens*, pp. 479–80. The Jacobins were, in any case, firmly convinced that anyone who desired to be a minister thereby revealed their disloyalty to the Nation. As Robespierre put it:

> I am in a position to explain myself freely on the subject of ministers: firstly because I do not fear being suspected of speculating on their succession, either for myself or for my friends; secondly because I have no desire to see them replaced by others, being convinced that those who aspire to their jobs would be worth no more than they are. (Robespierre, *Virtue and Terror*, p. 28)

[174] Schama, *Citizens*, p. 528. For most revolutionaries, politics "was not an arena for the presentation of competing interests. It was rather an instrument for reshaping human nature, making citizens out of subjects, free men out of slaves, republicans out of the oppressed." Hunt, *Politics, Culture, and Class*, p. 49.

[175] Schama, *Citizens*, p. 527; Doyle, *French Revolution*, pp. 142, 153; Walton, "Clubs, Parties, Factions," p. 365. McPhee estimates that some "6,000 Jacobin clubs and popular societies" might have been formed nationally during 1793 or the following year. McPhee, *Liberty or Death*, p. 223.

Paris but wanted to preserve the club as a platform for its leader. Condemning the king and demanding his trial by the assembly, they waffled on the monarchy, neither urging that it be retained nor supporting its abolition. All but the first of these groups then joined in passing a resolution demanding that the king be tried before a newly elected National Convention.[176] The constitutional monarchists who supported retention of Louis XVI subsequently seceded from the club.[177]

The seats in the National Assembly were primarily divided into three sections according to the political sympathies of the deputies. On the left, occupying benches high up against the wall of the chamber, were the Jacobins, who were now often referred to as the "Mountain"; the members who sat in that section thus became the "Montagnards." On the far right were the Girondins, who, somewhat reluctantly, had taken up residence in seats vacated by those who had harbored royalist sympathies. Between the Girondins and the Jacobins, both figuratively and physically, were the deputies of the Plain; they were moderates who collectively held the balance of power.[178] The public galleries, almost always filled with the common people of Paris, could thus easily locate their favorite factions even if they did not always understand what it was they were debating.

Where the Girondins favored a constitutional monarchy and, later, a republic in which the protection and enhancement of individual liberty would be a primary commitment of the state, the Jacobins primarily constructed their political principles around Rousseau's conception of the "general will."[179]

---

[176] Davidson states that the name of this proposed assembly was chosen "in homage to the Constitutional Convention" held in 1787 in the United States. Davidson, *French Revolution*, p. 104.

[177] Israel, *Revolutionary Ideas*, pp. 176, 282; Doyle, *French Revolution*, p. 154. On October 12, 1792, Jacques-Pierre Brissot, the Girondin leader, was expelled from the club after publicly attacking Montagnard leaders. This was followed, on March 1, 1793, by the expulsion of all those deputies who voted for a national referendum on whether or not the king should be executed. As a result, Doyle says that the club "now became a Montagnard monopoly" (p. 222).

[178] Schama, *Citizens*, p. 648; Doyle, *French Revolution*, p. 194. At the opening of the Legislative Assembly in October 1791, Davidson estimated the number of Jacobins at 136, Feuillants at 264, and "undeclared" deputies at around 300. Davidson, *French Revolution*, p. 79. For other estimates of factional strength, see Schama, *Citizens*, p. 582; Lefebvre, *French Revolution*, vol. 1, p. 213; Israel, *Revolutionary Ideas*, p. 222. While these estimates vary a bit, the Jacobins were clearly in a minority.

[179] Hanson, *Contesting the French Revolution*, p. 9.

Central to Jacobin ideology was the certainty about the innate goodness of the common people, corrupted by centuries of misery and ignorance and now by the deception, even conspiracy, of those who would prevent them from reaping the revolutionary harvest. The inspiration was Rousseau, now more popular than ever, who in his *Social Contract* had stressed the role of the virtuous legislator in interpreting what was best for the people at a time of lies by those with vested interests. (McPhee, *Liberty or Death*, p. 170)

However, those who later divided into these factions agreed at first on many things. For example, in January 1789, Emmanuel Sieyès, a priest who later renounced his ordination, published a pamphlet entitled *What Is the Third Estate?* in which he asked three questions of those who would elect deputies to the Estates-General. He also provided answers that would later provide a rough and ready catechism during early confrontations with the monarchy:

1 What is the Third Estate? Everything.
2 What has it been until now in the political order? Nothing.
3 What does it want? To become something.

Sieyès then defined the third estate in a way that made its membership identical to the category of "citizen," thus excluding the nobility and clergy until and unless they gave up all of their particular rights and distinctions.

By Third Estate is meant the collectivity of citizens who belong to the common order. Anybody who holds a legal privilege of any kind leaves that common order, stands as an exception to the common law, and in consequence does not belong to the Third Estate ... the moment a citizen acquires privileges contrary to common law, he no longer belongs to the common order. His new interest is opposed to the general interest; he has no right to vote in the name of the people.[180]

He then went on to write:

Who thus would dare to say that the Third Estate does not contain everything that is needed to make up a complete nation? It is a strong and robust man who still has one arm in chains. If the privileged orders were removed, the nation would not be worse off for it, but better. So, what is the Third? Everything, but a fettered and oppressed everything. What would it be without the privileged order? Everything, but a free and flourishing everything ... the fear of seeing abuses reformed inspires more fear in the aristocrats than the desire they feel for liberty.[181]

Sieyès argued that the only appropriate action for the third estate was to have nothing to do with the other two estates and, instead, to immediately transform itself into a national assembly.[182] This, of course, is more or less what actually happened. During the first two years of the revolution, the relative unity of the third estate was enhanced by their common opposition to the monarchy – not as an institution, because most deputies wished to preserve it in some form, but to the royalists who sought to turn back the revolutionary tide. Their unity was also strengthened in this period by the relative moderation of the claims the

---

[180] Hunt, *French Revolution and Human Rights*, pp. 65, 68.
[181] McPhee, *Liberty or Death*, pp. 52–3. For a brief description of Sieyès, see Lefebvre, *French Revolution*, vol. 1, pp. 106–7.
[182] Doyle, *French Revolution*, p. 94. Although he stood apart from most factional politics in the assembly, Sieyès played a major role in most of the committee deliberations over the construction of the several national constitutions. Those roles and his ability as a political theorist thus frequently aligned him with the Girondins and their antecedents.

assembly made on the national political economy. On the one hand, the assembly dismantled many of the feudal impediments to the development of a national market and thus realized some of the most fervent desires of crown reformers. On the other hand, the abolition of feudal privileges and titles invited the nobility to become citizens of a more powerful nation as opposed to petty lords of country manors. As long as the monarchy existed, these moderate policies secured the revolution by bringing together factions that were later to tear one another apart.[183]

The Girondin and the Jacobin deputies came from very similar social, occupational, and political backgrounds. One of their most striking differences was regional: The Girondins were disproportionately drawn from the coastal provinces and port cities and many Jacobin leaders represented Paris. These differences in origin tended to reinforce their attitudes toward revolutionary governance: The Girondins were predisposed to insist upon the constitutional supremacy of the assembly and the responsibilities of parliamentary representation while the Jacobins often favored a more direct form of popular participation in politics in which the Parisian citizenry would often play a decisive role.[184] One of the most important weaknesses in the Girondin position was that the fate of the revolution in fact depended on direct popular action at several points: the storming of the Bastille, the bringing of the king to Paris in October 1789, and the deposition of the king in August 1792. In all those instances, the intransigency of the king threatened to deadlock the revolution and only extralegal intervention by the people resolved the impasse. But these interventions also legitimated direct popular action and thus strengthened the Jacobins. Operating in the opposite direction, the spontaneity and brutality of direct popular action reinforced Girondin resistance to popular insurgency because of its clear violation of the rule of law under the constitution. The Girondin refusal to recognize and accommodate the demands of the Parisian citizenry ultimately placed them in what became an indefensible position because their provincial supporters had no way of counterbalancing Jacobin mobilizations of the people in the city.[185]

---

[183] Schama, *Citizens*, pp. 73, 332, 518; Lefebvre, *French Revolution*, vol. 1, pp. 21, 32–3, 162. While the abolition of noble privileges might be considered a radical repudiation of the feudal social order, the long night of August 4 in which one noble after another warmly embraced their elimination indicated that many noble reformers were more than ready to trade in those privileges for a place in the new regime. All noble "titles, orders, ribbons, and coats of arms" had been abolished on June 19, 1790. Doyle, *French Revolution*, p. 128.

[184] Schama, *Citizens*, pp. 583, 648; Lefebvre, *French Revolution*, vol. 1, pp. 266–7. On tension between Paris and the provinces during the revolution, see Schama, *Citizens*, pp. 536–7, 785–7; McPhee, *Liberty or Death*, pp. 186, 191, 197; Doyle, *French Revolution*, pp. 229–31, 238–43, 248–9, 253–5.

[185] As Doyle writes:

[T]here were certain realities which the Girondins refused to face. (1) Without Paris, the Republic would not have been established and the Convention itself would not have

The Jacobins were thus free to exploit the political opportunity that the Girondins refused to entertain.[186] The Girondins placed individual liberty, human rights, legal reform, and observance of the formal rules of democracy on a par with the reduction of economic inequality and emergency measures to relieve human suffering, particularly the provision of food to the Parisian people. This opened the way for the Jacobins to mobilize the people by promising immediate relief through extraordinary means, including an authoritarian regime legitimated as the clear and unmediated will of the people.[187] Overriding the inconveniences of constitutional rules and legislative prerogatives, their embrace of popular political action became a litmus test for distinguishing patriots from traitors.

In a speech made on July 9, 1794, Robespierre laid out how this test would be applied.

There is a sentiment written in the hearts of all patriots, and it is a touchstone by which they can recognize their friends. A man who is silent when he ought to speak is to be suspected: if he wraps himself in mystery, if he shows a momentary energy which soon passes away, if he limits himself to empty tirades against tyrants, and pays no heed to public morals, or to the general happiness of his fellow-citizens, he is to be suspected. When men are seen denouncing aristocrats merely as a matter of form, their own lives call for severe scrutiny. When they are heard uttering commonplaces against Pitt and the enemies of mankind, whilst at the same time they deliver covert attacks on the

---

existed ... And however abhorrent the forces in control of the capital, (2) it was only sensible for an assembly sitting there (and where else could it credibly sit?) to try to work with them. This was the Montagnard position. [In response to] Girondin intransigence they opposed prudence and practicality. (Doyle, *French Revolution*, p. 236)

[186] See, for example, their endorsement of government regulation of markets, "cheered on by the Convention's public galleries." Doyle, *French Revolution*, p. 229.

[187] The *Social Contract* provides, perhaps unintentionally, ample justification for an authoritarian regime:

The constant will of all the members of the State is the general will; it is by it that they are citizens and free. When one proposes a law in the assembly of the People, what one asks them is not precisely whether they approve or reject the proposal, but whether it conforms or not to the general will that is theirs; each one, by voting, expresses his opinion of this, and by weighing the voices himself obtains the declaration of the general will ... When the opinion contrary to mine then prevails, that proves nothing except that I was deceiving myself, and that what I reckoned to be the general will was not. If my individual opinion had prevailed, I would have done something other than what I wanted [namely, to act in harmony with the wishes of others for the common good], it is then that I would not have been free. (Miller, *Rousseau*, p. 252 n. 72)

As Slavoj Žižek notes, Rousseau describes "the voting procedure not as a performative act of decision, but as a constative one, as the act of expressing the opinion on (of guessing) what the general will is (which is thus substantialized into something that *pre-exists* voting)" and thus "avoids the deadlock of the rights of those who remain in the minority (they should obey the decision of the majority, because in the result of voting, they learn what the general will really is)." "Introduction" in Robespierre, *Virtue and Terror*, pp. xxii–xxiii.

revolutionary government; or when, alternately moderate and extreme in their views, they are forever denouncing and obstructing useful measures; then it is time to be on one's guard against conspiracy.[188]

Robespierre's litmus test can be summed up under three headings: (1) transparency (the citizen must harbor no thoughts that cannot bear scrutiny by his fellows); (2) obedience (the citizen must fully and emphatically embrace the General Will in all his actions); and (3) conformity (the citizen must never dissent if that dissent might give aid and comfort to those who oppose the people). Under Robespierre's leadership, Jacobins embraced this conception of the General Will and identified its popular expression with political virtue and justice.[189]

Even before Robespierre came to power, those nobles who publicly opposed this conception were banished from the political community when, in direct violation of the Declaration of Rights, the National Constituent Assembly instituted controls on "the movement of suspected émigrés," licensing, in Schama's words, "a police state."[190] They were followed by those clergy who chose the pope over the nation as their spiritual leader. In July 1790, the National Constituent Assembly imposed an oath of political loyalty upon Catholic clergy and, adopting a civil constitution, transformed those who swore loyalty into salaried officials of the revolution. Almost all prelates serving in the assembly refused to take the oath. Most priests refused as well and, together with the prelates, left the assembly. In France as a whole, just under half of all clergy refused to swear. Doyle calls the imposition of the oath one of the "turning points" of the revolution and a "serious mistake" because, for the first time, it compelled citizens to declare themselves for or against the new political order.[191] While those who refused the oath "branded themselves unfit

---

[188] Thompson, *Robespierre*, vol. 2, p. 240.

[189] Schama, *Citizens*, pp. 290–2; Arendt, *On Revolution*, pp. 65–6. Once an insistence on class privilege became a clear violation of the General Will, any defense of noble identity became incompatible with recognition as a "citizen." Schama, *Citizens*, p. 293. On the one hand, the revolution was hostile to the nobility precisely because their insignia, privileges, and separate identity embodied a "class." This hostility was, of course, strengthened by their wealth and social pretensions. On the other hand, the revolution was also hostile to working-class strikes because they, too, arose from a particularism of interests. These attitudes also help to explain why the sans-culottes were never referred to as a "class" but, instead, were always termed "the people."

[190] Schama, *Citizens*, pp. 540–1. For punitive measures enacted against émigrés, including some that were never implemented, see Doyle, *French Revolution*, pp. 155, 176; Schama, *Citizens*, p. 815; Aston, *French Revolution*, p. 49; Israel, *Revolutionary Ideas*, p. 681. More generally, see Kirsty Carpenter, "Emigration in Politics and Imaginations" in Andress, *Oxford Handbook of the French Revolution*, pp. 330–45.

[191] Doyle, *French Revolution*, pp. 145–6, 155, 157, 177, 183, 190, 261. Also see McPhee, *Liberty or Death*, p. 123; Fitzsimmons, "Sovereignty and Constitutional Power," p. 210. Israel views anti-Catholic policies adopted during the revolution, up to but not including the later de-Christianization campaigns, as logically implied in Enlightenment principles and thus almost

to exercise public office," they were, somewhat paradoxically, granted a right "to reject the Revolution's work." This "freedom to refuse" was, of course, a violation of Rousseauian principles and this voluntary exclusion from the national community was later made extremely painful. Subsequent legislation, for example, restricted the exercise of religious duties to those who would swear loyalty to the revolution; closed monasteries and "teaching and charity orders"; ordered the deportation of refractory priests; prohibited the public display of crucifixes and crosses; and banned the ringing of church bells, ecclesiastical uniforms, and religious processions.[192]

Although their ultimate fate may well have been sealed from the beginning, the Girondins contributed to their own demise by attempting to combine the making of a liberal regime and at least rhetorical observance of the demands of popular democracy. On the one hand, they sought to preserve a role for the king in the new government and, when Louis XVI proved unwilling to accept that role, to spare his life. These Girondin attempts to preserve some semblance of a central authority outside the legislature were, to at least some extent, incompatible with their support for the export of revolutionary ideals through war because military mobilization required the invocation of popular (republican) sentiment. Even though prosecution of the war, in turn, required political unity, the Girondins felt compelled to attack the Montagnard Jacobins and the Parisian sans-culottes over what were, in fact, fundamental issues of governance. When the war began badly, the contradictions between a liberal regime and the conception of the General Will as the legitimating link to the people were laid bare for all to see. The Montagnards were all too ready to pounce.[193]

THE EXECUTION OF THE KING

On June 20, 1791, Louis XVI and his family attempted to flee France but were apprehended short of the French frontier. As he was brought back to Paris on June 25, the people spontaneously destroyed royal symbols throughout the city.

---

inevitable consequences entailed by the revolution. Israel, *Revolutionary Ideas*, pp. 28, 195–6, 681–2. Also see Lefebvre, *French Revolution*, vol. 1, pp. 169–70, 235, 244; Davidson, *French Revolution*, pp. 63–5.

[192] In May 1791, the pope asked that all clergy refuse to take the oath and condemned the civil constitution of the clergy. Doyle, *French Revolution*, pp. 139, 141, 146. On anti-Catholic policies and agitation during the revolution, see Lefebvre, *French Revolution*, vol. 1, pp. 159–60, 166–8; Israel, *Revolutionary Ideas*, pp. 187, 189–91, 194, 484–5, 604–5; Schama, *Citizens*, pp. 351, 484–90; Doyle, *French Revolution*, pp. 132–3, 137, 140–1; Edward J. Woell, "Religion and Revolution" in Andress, *Oxford Handbook of the French Revolution*, pp. 256–69.

[193] Lefebvre, *French Revolution*, vol. 1, pp. 225, 247, 284.

In order to prevent attacks on the king himself, Parisian officials "posted placards" throughout the city promising that "[t]hose [who] applaud [the king] will be bayoneted; those insulting the king will be hanged." On June 24, the Cordeliers Club led some 30,000 people to the assembly and presented a petition demanding that either the king should be deposed or a national referendum should be held to determine his fate.[194] Although the king had left behind a document condemning the revolution and all of its works, the National Constituent Assembly refused to depose him. On July 14, as the citizenry was celebrating Bastille Day on the Champ de Mars, a committee appointed to investigate his flight announced that Louis had been kidnapped against his will and should be absolved of any responsibility for what most people considered a treasonous act. On the following day, representatives sent by the Cordeliers Club attempted to present a petition asking for a national plebiscite on the deposition of the king but guards prevented them from reaching the National Assembly. Robespierre came out of the hall and told them they were too late because the deputies had already decided to absolve the king from any responsibility for his flight to Varennes. Charles Lameth, the Girondin president of the assembly, sent a written reply that contested the very right of the Parisians to mass in the streets. In Israel's words, Lameth flatly contradicted

their assertion of direct democracy: the crowd represented only the will of a handful of individuals, not that of France. Under the Constitution, the Assembly alone represented the people's will. The Assembly would not defer to theirs but act according to its own will. Petitioning collectively was illegal, their action insurrectionary. Worse, they were permitting a handful of schemers to manipulate them, turning Paris – a city of intrigue – into the foe of all France.[195]

Two days later, on July 17, thousands of protestors gathered on the Champ de Mars in order to sign a petition demanding that the National Assembly remove Louis XVI from the throne. The gathering was peaceful until two men were discovered under the table where the petition was being signed. Believing the men to be police spies, officials attempted to move them to one of the Parisian prisons for their own safety. However, a mob took custody of the men and attempted to hang them. After their purpose was defeated when the rope broke, the two men were killed, their bodies were dismembered, and their organs were placed on pikes and paraded about. Lafayette and a detachment of the National Guard then appeared and attempted to restore order at the petition site.

[194] Micah Alpaugh, *Non-Violence and the French Revolution: Political Demonstrations in Paris, 1787–1795* (New York: Cambridge University Press, 2015), p. 93. Also see Israel, *Revolutionary Ideas*, pp. 176–7; Schama, *Citizens*, pp. 550–61; McPhee, *Liberty or Death*, pp. 132–4.
[195] Israel, *Revolutionary Ideas*, p. 177.

However, the guardsmen opened fire on the protestors after they threw rocks and killed some fifty people.[196]

In absolving the king of responsibility, a majority of the deputies had pragmatically concluded that France had to have a king. With that in mind, if Louis XVI were deposed, they would have to put someone else on the throne. If it were his young son, then a regent would have to be appointed and, whomever that might be, they would not be as useful as a reigning sovereign to ratify the new constitution the assembly was drafting. If it were one of Louis' reactionary brothers, then a confirmed counter-revolutionary would sit on the throne and rejection of the constitution would be almost certain. If it were Louis Philippe, a firm supporter of the revolution, the succession would go to someone the deputies considered dissolute and erratic. Despite his clear antipathy toward the revolution, the deputies thus hoped Louis XVI could be cajoled into cooperation. In any case, he remained the best out of a set of poor alternatives.[197] So the assembly pretended that he had been kidnapped.

About two and a half months later, on September 14, 1791, Louis came to the National Constituent Assembly and accepted the now finished constitution, swearing "to maintain it at home and defend it against attacks from abroad and to use all the means which it places in my power to execute it faithfully."[198] While Louis had, in effect, become a hostage of the revolution, he still exercised some authority under the mixed constitution the assembly had crafted. Over the following year, the crown more or less cooperated with the revolution in most matters but the royal family also secretly communicated with neighboring monarchies, plotting foreign intervention that might enable a return to the *ancien régime*. Although almost everyone suspected that the loyalty of the king and his family to the revolution was seriously compromised, the activist leaders of the Parisian people were in the best position to exploit these suspicions. On August 10, 1792, the people of Paris, along with detachments of the National Guard, invaded the Tuileries and attempted to take physical possession of the royal family.[199]

---

[196] On the background and a description of the July 17 demonstration, see Alpaugh, *Non-Violence*, pp. 94–9. Also see Rude, *The Crowd*, pp. 88–94.

[197] Israel, *Revolutionary Ideas*, pp. 175, 177; Doyle, *French Revolution*, pp. 152–3; Andress, *French Revolution and the People*, p. 86. For a different interpretation of the assembly's motives, see Lefebvre, *French Revolution*, vol. 1, pp. 206–9.

[198] Despite the superficial success of this charade, 150 deputies declared the constitution to be illegitimate because Louis XVI, to all intents and purposes a prisoner of the revolution, consented to its adoption only under duress. Schama, *Citizens*, pp. 568, 573; Doyle, *French Revolution*, p. 157.

[199] Schama, *Citizens*, p. 613. Even before the popular insurrection on August 10, almost three-quarters of the deputies were no longer attending sessions of the Legislative Assembly because they feared for their personal safety (p. 610). For an account of the insurrection, see Davidson, *French Revolution*, pp. 98–102. Davidson concludes: "For more than three years the Revolution had been managed peacefully, and above all legally, by the bourgeois Revolutionaries in the National Assembly. Now the Paris sans-culottes had thrust them

Louis and his family fled to the Legislative Assembly where they were subsequently imprisoned.[200]

Without a king, the constitution was a nullity and the assembly immediately moved to arrange the election of a new legislative body to draft a new document. That new body, the National Convention, assembled on September 20, 1792; it abolished the monarchy the next day. Jacobins now outnumbered Girondins by a relatively narrow margin (approximately 215 to 150) but the balance of power was held by the almost 400 unaligned deputies.[201] One of the most pressing tasks of governance involved the disposition of Louis XVI. After much discussion of the alternatives, the National Convention decided to indict the king and put him on trial. But this decision was much more difficult that it might seem.

On the one hand, the constitution of 1791 explicitly stated that "[t]he person of the king is inviolable and sacred." If the constitution was to be obeyed, the only way in which the king could be tried were if he abdicated the throne. The constitution did, in fact, provide three ways in which abdication might occur: by failing to swear fealty to the constitution; by leading a domestic insurrection against the government; or by emigrating from France and refusing to return. Louis XVI had done none of these things and was thus formally immune from trial and punishment.[202] On the other hand, the king (and his court) had clearly engaged in treasonous conspiracies against the government.[203] In order to prosecute the king, the deputies had to cut a Gordian knot. From that perspective, some (in the end most) deputies sought refuge in the formality of a trial that was, in and of itself, both illegitimate and verged upon farce. Others would

violently aside. From this point on, the central theme of the Revolution was uncompromising power struggle between these two groups." In Alpaugh's words, the people of Paris had announced that "[p]opular sovereignty" now superseded "all other authority" and had itself become both the agent and "the justification for radical change." In general, both "the rise of a Rousseauian ideal of the people as 'good,' together with the political debt owed Parisians for the Bastille insurrection, gave popular activists significant claims to legitimacy." Alpaugh, *Non-Violence*, pp. 17, 123.

[200] The deposition of the king led many European nations to break diplomatic relations with the revolutionary government. The first to do so was Sweden on August 13 followed by Britain four days later. The "Dutch republic, Spain, Denmark, Poland, Russia, the Swiss Confederation and the majority of the Italian states" followed suit over the next two weeks. A. Goodwin, "Reform and Revolution in France: October 1789–February 1793" in Goodwin, *New Cambridge Modern History*, vol. 8, p. 706.

[201] McPhee, *Liberty or Death*, p. 169. The August 10 insurrection had eliminated monarchists as a political force. Schama, *Citizens*, p. 644.

[202] Patrick, *Men of the First French Republic*, p. 43.

[203] From a traditional perspective, "treason" was a label that was difficult to affix to the king since he *was* the French nation in many interpretations, ranging from divine right to the embodiment of the General Will of the people. In effect, in committing "treason," the king would have had to betray himself and such a construction had obvious problems.

have cut the knot cleanly without the ambiguity and political dissimulation attending a trial that was, on the face of it, unconstitutional.[204]

On November 13, for example, Louis de Saint-Just, who was later dubbed the Archangel of the Terror, condemned the king with or without a trial.

[Some would say] that the King should be judged as a simple citizen; and I say that the king must be judged as an enemy . . . I do not see a middle ground: this man must reign or die . . . Louis is a foreigner among us; he was not a citizen before his crime . . . he is even less a citizen since his crime . . . Louis has waged war against the people; he is defeated. He is a barbarian; he is a foreign prisoner of war.[205]

On December 3, 1792, Robespierre also strongly condemned the very notion of a trial in a way that implicitly acknowledged the unsteady foundations of the revolution itself.

Louis cannot be judged, he has already been judged. He has been condemned, or else the Republic is not blameless. To suggest putting Louis XVI on trial, in whatever way, is a step back towards royal and constitutional despotism; it is a counter-revolutionary idea; because it puts the Revolution itself in the dock. After all, if Louis can still be put on trial, Louis can be acquitted; he might be innocent. Or rather, he is presumed to be until he is found guilty. But if Louis is acquitted, if Louis can be presumed innocent, what becomes of the Revolution?[206]

The revolution, of course, had written a constitution in which the king had been given a prominent role. And then, in what could only be interpreted as an action contravening that constitution, the revolution had deposed and imprisoned the king.[207] The constant in these and other actions was not the constitution (as the Girondins passionately wished) but the popular will imagined in the first instance as the entirety of the French people (manifested

---

[204] As Patrick writes:

> It did not matter how many ingenious hairs were split about the people on 10 August as the jury of accusation, the Convention as the trial jury, and the law (laying down the penalty for treason) as the judge, in fact the Convention was acting as prosecutor, judge, and jury in a trial which could produce only one verdict, and the deputies knew it. All of them knew that such a trial . . . could be justified only by the most abstract of general principles; thus Rousseau's name flew backward and forward, being used with equal confidence by both sides. (Patrick, *Men of the First French Republic*, pp. 51, 57)

> For a fine-grained analysis of the theoretical conundrums, emotional investments, and political risks associated with the decision whether or not to try the king, see chapter three.

[205] Davidson, *French Revolution*, p. 138. For the Montagnards, some of the most common labels affixed to political enemies were "alien" and "foreigner" because those who had, in their view, placed themselves outside the General Will should no longer be considered part of the political community. Popkin, "Revolution and Changing Identities," p. 246.

[206] Doyle, *French Revolution*, pp. 194–5.

[207] On the strained logic and convoluted stratagems through which an indictment of the king was justified, see Schama, *Citizens*, pp. 650–1, 659.

in the acts of the assembly) and in the second as the people of Paris (manifested as the popular invasion of the Tuileries).[208] It was the popular will, along with the revolution, that Robespierre contended would be impeached by a presumption of innocence in the trial of the king. As Georges Danton wrote to Charles Lameth, a noble sympathetic to the revolution who had emigrated to Germany after August 10: "Can a king under indictment be saved? He's as good as dead when he appears before his judges."[209]

While the king was already guilty before the trial began, he was not yet "as good as dead." On January 15, 1793, the deputies began to vote on whether the king was innocent or guilty. As they individually gave their votes at the bar, some of the 749 deputies refused to render judgment but the vote was nonetheless 693 to nothing for a verdict of guilty. A proposal to refer the verdict to the people in a national referendum was then rejected by a vote of 424 to 283. On eight o'clock on the evening of January 16, the National Convention began to vote on how the king should be punished. For the next thirteen hours, 721 deputies ascended the podium one by one to announce their vote. Those voting for death were in the majority but the tallies were complicated by the fact that some deputies had qualified their votes in one way or another. While 361 deputies voted for the king's execution without qualification, an additional three dozen who otherwise favored death asked for a delay or suggested the possibility of a reprieve. Those opposing the death penalty numbered 321.[210] Philippe Égalité (formerly Louis Philippe), the Duke of Orléans and the king's cousin, was one of those who voted to send Louis XVI to the guillotine.

On January 21, 1792, National Guard troops lined both sides of the street as Louis XVI was taken to the Place de la Révolution. After his head was taken from the basket and held high so that the people could see it, the executioner then sold bits of the king's clothing, locks of his hair, and other mementos to the crowd. His body was placed in a cheap wooden coffin with his head placed between the legs and was covered in quicklime so that it would rapidly disintegrate.[211]

---

[208] The hostility to the king expressed by the Parisians who thronged the assembly's galleries was so great that, at one point, the president of the assembly described their demonstrations as "the vociferations of cannibals." Thompson, *Robespierre*, vol. 1, p. 302.

[209] Lefebvre, *French Revolution*, vol. 1, p. 270.

[210] The numbers vary slightly from source to source but generally accord with those in the text. The most exhaustive analysis of the voting on the king's trial, verdict, and sentencing is in Patrick's *Men of the First French Republic*, pp. 74–107. For an account of the king's trial, see Schama, *Citizens*, pp. 650–73.

[211] Schama, *Citizens*, pp. 668–70, 673; Lefebvre, *French Revolution*, vol. 1, p. 272; Furet and Richet, *French Revolution*, p. 166; Tackett, *Coming of the Terror*, p. 241.

SECTION II: FROM THE FALL OF THE GIRONDINS TO NAPOLEON

The trial and execution of the king had several important consequences. For one thing, diplomatic relations between the revolutionary regime and foreign powers were seriously compromised. The British government, for example, now considered the revolution to have become "a phenomenon of uncontainable barbarism and irrationality that rendered all further discussions moot." Those monarchies that were nominally at peace with the regime recalled their ambassadors. Even the ambassador from the United States, the most prominent sister republic, gave some thought to returning home.[212] With the king's execution, the nation had also irrevocably become a republic "by indirection, not out of judgment based on theory and formally stated, but because revolutionary France, which for its own safety had dethroned Louis XVI, now had to govern itself."[213] The revolutionary republic would henceforth have to stand entirely on its own legitimating symbols and logics.[214]

Although these consequences were significant, the impact on politics within the revolutionary community was even more important.[215] Although they split their votes, the Girondins had disproportionately both supported a popular referendum on the king's guilt and opposed his execution. In supporting a popular referendum, they had cited Rousseau, contending that only a national vote in which the 44,000 primary assemblies participated would ensure that the convention accurately interpreted the General Will of the French people.[216] The Girondins had thus implied that the revolution itself could, at least theoretically, be overthrown by the General Will of the French nation. The Montagnards, led by Robespierre, emphatically rejected this implication because to them the revolution itself was an irrevocable product of the General Will. But the prior position of the two factions on parliamentary representation was

---

[212] Schama, *Citizens*, p. 687; Doyle, *French Revolution*, p. 197. On French diplomacy generally, see Marc Belissa, "War and Diplomacy (1792–95)" in Andress, *Oxford Handbook of the French Revolution*, pp. 418–35.

[213] Lefebvre, *French Revolution*, vol. 1, pp. 264–5. Also see Doyle, *French Revolution*, p. 194.

[214] Some of the deputies cited the execution of Charles I in 1649 as a warning and, as a result, "the Convention [was] as nervous of a possible Cromwell as the post-1917 Russians were to be of a possible Bonaparte." Patrick, *Men of the First French Republic*, p. 70.

[215] One of the oddities of the revolution is that coins bearing the king's image were struck by the republic for several months after his execution. Thompson, *Robespierre*, vol. 1, p. 311n.

[216] Schama, *Citizens*, pp. 660–1. Although the Girondins were certainly correct when they maintained that Rousseau had insisted that "the people" should directly ratify all legislative acts, they had routinely rejected direct ratification up until this point. McDonald, *Rousseau and the French Revolution*, p. 135. And, as Patrick noted, they downplayed to the point of ignoring the political risks associated with turning over "a highly controversial and vitally important political decision [to] the mainly rural, largely illiterate, and variably informed" primary assemblies. Patrick, *Men of the First French Republic*, p. 59.

reversed on this issue, with the Montagnards implicitly supporting the delegated right of a deputy to interpret and act upon the will of his constituency and the Girondins suggesting that that right should be set aside, at least on an issue as momentous as the execution of the king.[217] Aside from these apparent ideological inconsistencies, those Girondins who supported a national referendum and opposed execution were indelibly marked in revolutionary politics as moderates whose personal commitment to the revolution was suspect.[218] In part this was the product of Montagnard propaganda, which was intended to remove the Girondins as competitors. But Girondin opposition to the expression and integrity of the General Will as manifested by the Parisian masses made this interpretation at least superficially plausible.[219]

THE ELIMINATION OF THE GIRONDINS

With the nobles, the clergy, and now the king out of the way, the Jacobins turned their attention to the Girondins, who, as they saw things, had seriously misconstrued how the General Will should govern the course of the revolution. The pivotal moment came in April 1793, when the Girondins persuaded the National Convention to impeach Jean-Paul Marat, the editor of the *L'Ami du Peuple*, "the most chauvinistic and blood-thirsty of the revolutionary papers." In the months

---

[217] Not that Robespierre did not make a valiant effort to square the Montagnard circle: "In this so-called appeal to the people, I see nothing but an appeal from what the people has willed and done [on August 10] to those secret enemies of equality whose corruption and cowardice were the very cause of that insurrection." Thompson, *Robespierre*, vol. 1, p. 305.

[218] Doyle, *French Revolution*, p. 222. Subsequent support for the indictment of Marat was also important in establishing Girondin identity. Hanson, *Contesting the French Revolution*, pp. 92–3.

[219] Tom Paine proposed that, instead of execution, Louis be sent to the United States for rehabilitation as a citizen. For this and other reasons, the Montagnards considered him to be overly friendly with the Girondins. Writing to Danton on May 6, 1793, Paine said that he now despaired "of seeing the great object of European liberty accomplished" because of "the tumultuous misconduct with which the internal affairs of the present Revolution are conducted." On December 25, 1793, the convention decided that foreigners could no longer serve as deputies and Paine was expelled from the national legislature. He was imprisoned three days later, held for more than ten months, and released only upon the request of James Monroe, who was then representing American interests in Paris. Schama, *Citizens*, pp. 665–7; Israel, *Revolutionary Ideas*, pp. 431, 535, 582, 590. The reluctance of the American government to press strongly for Paine's release can be attributed, in part, to Gouverneur Morris, the United States ambassador to France, who personally disliked Paine. But, perhaps more importantly, this hesitancy underscores the American disinclination to "export" their own revolution by involving the nation in European affairs. American foreign policy considerations, particularly relations with Britain, took precedence over revolutionary principle. In addition, Paine's citizenship status was quite ambiguous. He was claimed by the British (who wanted to hang him), was at least an "honorary" citizen of France (which alternately celebrated him as a fellow citizen of the world and condemned him as a foreigner), and recognized as a leading "patriot" in the United States (which, nonetheless, denied him the right to vote in 1806 because he was not a citizen). A. J. Ayer, *Thomas Paine* (New York: Atheneum, 1988), pp. 127–31, 159–64, 177–8.

prior to his indictment, Marat had played a central role in several popular uprisings in Paris and had repeatedly called for the creation of a dictatorship with Robespierre as the national leader.[220] However, Marat was also a deputy, and in order to get at him the Girondins first had to abolish the immunity of deputies from arrest. That was their first mistake. The second came eleven days later, on April 12, when the Girondins proposed to impeach Marat.[221] The motion carried 222 to 98 with 55 abstentions (311 deputies did not vote because 128 were "on mission" and 183 were absent).[222] Marat's indictment immediately sparked an immense outpouring of opposition among the popular assemblies in Paris, with thirty-three of the city's sections calling for expulsion of leading Girondins from the convention. On April 24, the Revolutionary Tribunal, composed of judges associated with the Girondins, acquitted Marat, who was then carried through the streets in triumph.[223] On April 30, the Girondins began to contend that the National Convention was no longer safe from popular assault and proposed that it be moved back to Versailles.[224]

While they were unable to relocate the National Convention, they did succeed, on May 18, in creating a Commission of Twelve whose mission was to investigate the involvement of the Paris Commune in conspiratorial plots against the revolution. On May 24, the commission ordered the arrest of some of the most radical leaders in Paris as "conspirators." Two days later, Robespierre delivered a speech at the Jacobin Club in which he encouraged the people to rise up and purge the convention of the "corrupt deputies" who had supported creation of the commission: "When all laws have been violated, when despotism is at its height and when good faith and decency are trampled

---

[220] Israel, *Revolutionary Ideas*, p. 724.

[221] On the consequences of these errors in judgment, see Patrick, *Men of the First French Republic*, pp. 134–5.

[222] Deputies "on mission" were appointed by the Committee of Public Safety and served in pairs, with one of them usually from the region to which they were sent. They represented the National Convention in the local implementation of policy and administration and thus constituted in many ways the extension of legislative authority into executive management of the revolution. It was one of several devices through which the legislature could direct the government in the absence of a separate executive branch. Most of those "on mission" were either Montagnards or politically unaffiliated; only a small minority were Girondins, with most of the latter remaining behind in Paris. While this arrangement enabled the Girondins to maintain a majority in the National Convention, it also strengthened Montagnard influence in the provinces. Hanson, *Contesting the French Revolution*, pp. 113–18; Doyle, *French Revolution*, p. 237. While the vote totals are roughly accurate, secondary sources report slightly varying numbers.

[223] For a detailed account of the circumstances of and voting on Marat's impeachment, see Patrick, *Men of the First French Republic*, pp. 108–14. Schama describes Marat's trial as a "dangerous fiasco for the Girondins," adding that to call it "a collective disaster would be to understate the case." Among other things, the precedent set by the removal of Marat's legislative immunity would later be turned against them. Schama, *Citizens*, pp. 718–19. Also see Doyle, *French Revolution*, p. 228; Israel, *Revolutionary Ideas*, pp. 425–6. Israel interprets Marat's acquittal as "a turning point, decisively bolstering authoritarian populism" (p. 432).

[224] Doyle, *French Revolution*, p. 229.

underfoot, then is the time for the people to rise up. This moment has come."[225]
Some of the Parisian sections then began to arrest people who had publicly
criticized Robespierre and Marat. On May 27, the convention abolished the
commission after crowds of people gathered around the hall. Those who had
been arrested were then released. However, the convention reinstated the
commission after the crowds dispersed.[226]

On May 31, the Montagnards mobilized much larger crowds.[227] After
fighting with Girondin supporters in the streets, they purged the Paris
Commune of opponents and cut off all communication between the convention
and the rest of France so that the Girondins could not bring in reinforcements.
They then surrounded the convention and turned the deputies into prisoners.
Demanding that Robespierre and Marat be given dictatorial authority over the
revolution, the people, supported by troops controlled by the commune,
besieged the convention until late in the evening. The deputies, however,
refused to give in to their demands and the people drifted away.[228] They
returned on June 2. Now 80,000 people, according to some estimates, massed
around the convention and demanded the immediate arrest of twenty-two
leading Girondins. After hours of intimidation, including violent threats by
the National Guard, the deputies gave in and ordered their arrest.[229] Some of
the Girondins managed to escape custody; others committed suicide.[230] Five

[225] Furet and Richet, *French Revolution*, p. 180. It is difficult to overemphasize the importance of
speeches as a mode of exercising power for Robespierre. On average, he delivered a major address
to either the National Convention or the Jacobin Club every two days during 1793. McPhee,
Liberty or Death, p. 217. On the frequency with which he spoke to the National Constituent
Assembly, see Jordan, *Revolutionary Career of Maximilien Robespierre*, pp. 47, 272 n. 2.

[226] Israel, *Revolutionary Ideas*, pp. 441–2; Doyle, *French Revolution*, p. 234; Lefebvre, *French
Revolution*, vol. 2, pp. 52–3.

[227] For an account of how the Montagnards used the sans-culottes in order to purge the convention
of the Girondins, see Rude, *The Crowd*, pp. 120–5.

[228] Israel, *Revolutionary Ideas*, pp. 443–5. For the fourteen demands that the Paris Commune placed
before the National Convention on May 31, see Davidson, *French Revolution*, pp. 160–1.

[229] Lefebvre, *French Revolution*, vol. 2, pp. 53–4; Tackett, *Coming of the Terror*, pp. 274–6.
Although the deputies who ordered the arrest of the Girondins were clearly intimidated by the
people, soldiers, and cannons massed outside the convention, they were also, according to
Doyle, pragmatically weighing the alternatives available to them. Girondin refusal to compromise with the demands of the Parisian people was "endangering the very existence of the
Convention." Given that fact, "the practical, experienced men who made up [the convention's]
majority agreed, with anguished reluctance, to sacrifice a handful of their colleagues." Doyle,
French Revolution, pp. 237–8. Although their theoretical commitments to a liberal, parliamentary regime gave them far less justification for authoritarian rule than the ideological beliefs of
the Montagnards, the Girondins, had they been able to gain control of the assembly, might have
been impelled to launch a repression as extensive and complete as the Terror. It is difficult, for
example, to imagine how they would have been able to control Paris if they had not ruthlessly
suppressed the sans-culottes and their leaders.

[230] Israel, *Revolutionary Ideas*, pp. 446–8, 450–1. For a detailed description and interpretation of
Montagnard charges against the Girondins and the latter's response, see Sydenham, *The
Girondins*, pp. 20–38.

months later, most of the Girondins were condemned at trial and guillotined.[231] In the meantime, Robespierre and the Jacobins consolidated power by moving against some of those who had helped them mobilize the Parisian people against the Girondins.[232]

ROBESPIERRE AND ROUSSEAU

In proposing Robespierre as the best person to assume the role of dictator, Marat believed that he had found the ideal leader, "steely, unbending, and uncompromisingly Manichean ... someone who divided all mankind into the good and the evil, oppressed and oppressors, ceaselessly attacking corruption in high places and eulogizing 'the people.'"[233] Robespierre saw himself somewhat differently. As a devoted reader of Rousseau, Robespierre believed himself to be nothing more than the agent of the people's will, and that the primary task of the revolution was to ruthlessly deliver the innocent and pure new order into the world.[234] His interpretation of that mission was simultaneously messianic

[231] Tackett, *Coming of the Terror*, pp. 308–11.

[232] Israel, *Revolutionary Ideas*, p. 449. Also see Doyle, *French Revolution*, p. 228; Alpaugh, *Non-Violence*, pp. 142–7.

[233] Israel, *Revolutionary Ideas*, pp. 164–5. Also see Jordan, *Revolutionary Career of Maximilien Robespierre*, p. 184. Israel describes Marat's ideology as the product of a "polarizing populist chauvinism, a kind of protofascism" in which "a dictatorship of the most uncompromising kind" was considered necessary in order "to rescue 'the people.'" However, he also notes that Marat's position was quite consistent with Rousseau's description in the *Social Contract* of the dire circumstances in which a "dictatorship" should entrust absolute authority in the "worthiest person" (pp. 216–17). However, Marat's public and private evaluations of Robespierre may have differed. After one of the very few private conversations between the two men, Marat wrote: "This interview confirmed me in the opinion I had always had of him, that he joined to the insights of a sage senator the integrity of a truly good man and the zeal of a true patriot. But at the same time he lacks both the vision and the audacity of a statesman." Jordan, *Revolutionary Career of Maximilien Robespierre*, p. 93. Perhaps referring to the same conversation (which he said took place in January 1792), Robespierre reported to the convention that he had told Marat that all "the patriots, even the most ardent," believed "that he [Marat] had himself created an obstacle to the good that might come from the useful truths developed in his writings, by insisting on forever returning to extraordinary and violent propositions (for example the assertion that five or six hundred guilty heads should roll) which revolted the friends of liberty as much as they did the aristocracy." Robespierre, *Virtue and Terror*, p. 39. For a ringing defense of Robespierre as a "statesman" who was compelled to assume "the terrible responsibility for saving the Republic," see Lefebvre, *French Revolution*, vol. 2, pp. 63–4.

[234] Aston, *French Revolution*, p. 77. Robespierre had visited Rousseau not long before the latter's death and wrote more than a decade later: "I saw you during your last days, and the memory remains a source of joy and pride. I contemplated your august features, and saw on them the marks of the dark disappointments to which you were condemned by the injustice of mankind." Thompson, *Robespierre*, vol. 1, p. 9. On Rousseau's powerful influence on Robespierre's own thought and politics, see, for example, Israel's discussion of his speech before the National Convention on May 7, 1794. Israel, *Revolutionary Ideas*, pp. 561–5. On Rousseau's influence on Robespierre more generally, see Miller, *Rousseau*, pp. 147–8; McPhee, *Liberty or Death*,

and apocalyptic, both of these reinforced by a personal discipline that imposed almost unbearable demands upon his own psyche. In effect, Robespierre identified the historical destiny of the French people with the creation of a new political order in which the General Will would be enshrined as the central animating force.[235] In that vein, he stated: "I am not the courtesan, nor the moderator, nor the tribune, nor the defender of the people, I am the people myself!"[236] As the physical embodiment of the people as they would become once the revolution was completed, Robespierre became a living sacrament wholly at one with their future General Will – a will that, at the present, they could only imperfectly reveal on their own.

One of the central problems in the realization of that goal was that many other revolutionaries either interpreted the General Will differently or preferred a more liberal, constitutional vision that would enshrine reason and rational design in the construction of a government. When these revolutionaries stood in the way, Robespierre frequently removed them from politics and, in many instances, sent them to the guillotine. Another, equally serious difficulty was that the people, even in Robespierre's view, were not themselves "ready" to properly manifest the General Will. Although they were the only authentic source of virtue, the people were imperfectly aware of how that should be expressed.[237] Until they were able to properly reveal the General Will, the people must have leaders.

---

pp. 143–4; Jordan, *Revolutionary Career of Maximilien Robespierre*, pp. 31–5; Thompson, *Robespierre*, vol. 1, pp. 54–5, 57, 181; Thompson, *Robespierre*, vol. 2, pp. 47, 51–2, 280.

[235] Robespierre "fully identified" with

> Rousseau's concern with the necessity of "virtue" in the creation of a healthy body politic ... Rousseau's premise, that "the people" are inherently good, however corrupted by poverty and the self-serving behaviour of powerful elites, had become the core principle in Robespierre's understanding of popular sovereignty. He had come to believe that he, too, was "a virtuous man," called to devote his life to creating a state of virtue to serve and enlighten the people. (McPhee, *Liberty or Death*, p. 170)

> After Robespierre's death, a dedication to Rousseau was found among his papers in which his personal fealty to the thinker is clearly stated:

> It is to you that I dedicate this work, manes of the Citizen of Geneva! ... Divine man, you have taught me to know myself ... you made me appreciate the dignity of my nature and reflect on the great principles of the social order ... I want to follow your venerated path ... happy if ... I remain constantly faithful to the inspiration which I have drawn from your writings. (Miller, *Rousseau*, pp. 149–50)

[236] Jordan, *Revolutionary Career of Maximilien Robespierre*, p. 158.

[237] In Taylor's words:

> [If] the general will exists only where there is real virtue, that is, the real fusion of individual and common wills, what can we say of a situation in which many, perhaps even most people are still "corrupt," that is, have not yet achieved this fusion? Its only locus now will be the minority of the virtuous. They will be the vehicles of the genuine common will, which is objectively that of everyone, that is, the common goals everyone would subscribe to if virtuous.

> It is in that situation that the "vanguard politics" theorized and practiced by Robespierre is justified. Taylor, *Modern Social Imaginaries*, p. 124.

In February 1794, Robespierre delivered a speech on "The Moral and Political Principles of Domestic Policy"; on the one hand, this celebrated the virtuous energy of the people and, on the other, it set out the task of their leaders (of whom he, of course, bore the greatest responsibility):

> But when, by prodigious efforts of courage and reason, a people breaks the chains of despotism to make them into trophies of liberty; when by the force of its moral temperament it comes, as it were, out of the arms of death, to recapture all the vigor of youth; when by turns it is sensitive and proud, intrepid and docile, and can be stopped neither by impregnable ramparts nor by the innumerable armies of the tyrants armed against it, but stops of itself upon confronting the law's image; then if it does not climb rapidly to the summit of its destinies, this can only be the fault of those who govern it.[238]

But even if virtuous leaders were found, there were still other problems.

Most importantly perhaps, the people were simply not accessible to the revolution as a collective body because they were distributed throughout France. Only the people of Paris could directly present themselves to the assembly and thus manifest the General Will as a guide to political action. This was, of course, a serious difficulty that Robespierre and the revolution as a whole were never able to solve. In practice, Robespierre and the Montagnards who followed him were compelled to idealize the General Will of Parisians as inseparable from and thus identical with the will of the entirety of the French people. However, the Parisians often manifested narrowly focused demands, most often for food, that clearly indicated that they had not properly subordinated their individual identities and interests to the General Will.[239] Recognizing their imperfections as "citizens of the nation," Robespierre felt compelled to interpret what would have been their will if they had been properly socialized. He thus became an agent for a "future people" whose will could not yet be manifested in the present. But the people in that present, in Robespierre's view (and in the view of many other deputies), nonetheless willed that they become this "future people."

---

[238] Hunt, *Politics, Culture, and Class*, p. 117.

[239] Aside from the ideological dimension, the relationship between the Montagnards and the people of Paris was quite complex. On the one hand, popular mobilization was often spontaneous and focused on demands, such as bread during food shortages, that were not identical or even compatible with Montagnard policy stances. The people thus could and did act independently, often led by men who had their own political ambitions. On the other hand, the people of Paris were an absolutely vital political ally at those moments when the Montagnards moved decisively against their opponents. In late May 1793, for example, Robespierre had come to believe that the revolution could be saved only through the intervention of the sans-culottes for the purpose of removing the Girondins from the convention. But his orchestration of their intervention was limited to a veiled (if clearly implied) invitation in a speech to the Jacobin Club on May 29: "It is not for me to tell the people the means they should take to save themselves." Sydenham, *The Girondins*, p. 177. Sydenham says that this allusion was "so well comprehended that his audience broke into vociferous cheering."

The task then became to lead the people into that future while remaining faithful to what they would will once they arrived.[240] In fulfilling that task, Robespierre devoted himself to the creation of a state that would become "a school of virtue ... capable of bringing about a great moral regeneration in individuals and in its collective life." While all citizens were responsible for the creation of such a state, no individual was more responsible, as he saw things, than Robespierre himself.[241]

One of the most important principles of virtue was personal transparency because it guaranteed that the private self could not cloak corruption or self-interest in the performance of public responsibility.[242] Similarly, "friendship" in the sense of an affectionate and particular relationship between two individuals was suspect because it might harbor private understandings of mutual regard and interest. When Camille Desmoulins was compelled to give evidence of his personal virtue before the Jacobin Club on December 14, 1793, he claimed: "I was always the first to denounce my own friends; from the moment that I realized that they were conducting themselves badly, I resisted the most dazzling offers, and I stifled the voice of friendship that their great talents had inspired in me."[243] Transparency not only required that public performance and the private self be the same thing, but also that public performance be stripped of artifice.[244]

---

[240] This is one way in which the French Revolution was similar to subsequent foundings in Bolshevik Russia, Nazi Germany, and Islamic Iran. In each instance, the people were thought to have willed their "becoming" a new people but, because of their own present imperfections, necessarily subordinated that will to a revolutionary vanguard who could more clearly see what must be done to achieve that goal.

[241] Schama, *Citizens*, pp. 577–80.

[242] "There was nothing Robespierre hated more than crime disguised as patriotism." Arendt, *On Revolution*, p. 814. On the general acceptance of the principle of transparency, see Soboul, *The Sans-Culottes*, p. 136. Within the arc of the General Will, this principle became linked to "an ardent desire for unanimity which animated the sans-culotte: he related himself wholly to the mass movement; he could not conceive of isolating himself from it; conformity of sentiments, of mind and of votes struck him as being not only desirable, but necessary. Unity ... was to be one of the driving powers of their political activity, an almost mystical concept" (pp. 144–5).

[243] Marisa Linton, "Terror and Politics" in Andress, *Oxford Handbook of the French Revolution*, pp. 475–6.

[244] "The revolutionaries had inherited from Rousseau the conviction that the good person should be entirely transparent, with a public identity directly reflective of his or her inner being." Popkin, "Revolution and Changing Identities," p. 238. McPhee describes "emotional honesty and political transparency" as "twin imperatives for deputies [that were] two sides of the same coin, but came from different intellectual threads: the natural virtues of sentiments expressed sincerely, loyalty and sympathy, and the political virtues of transparency, sacrifice and modesty associated with classical republicanism. But the two threads could form a tight web from which protestations of patriotism were not grounds for escape." McPhee, *Liberty or Death*, p. 267. On the relation between transparency and revelation of the General Will, see Taylor, *Modern Social Imaginaries*, pp. 121–2. However, even transparent devotion to the General Will could not guarantee the safety of the individual because changes in revolutionary ideals and the veritable explosion of sometimes contradictory legislative decrees meant "that virtually every

Robespierre thus abhorred the display of symbols, including the red cap of liberty.[245]

As the agent of a General Will that could not yet be perfectly expressed, Robespierre became the unwilling "Law-Giver" as he, on the one hand, liberated the people from the fetters of the past and, on the other, coaxed them into recognizing what they should become.[246] In this role, he denied his own personal ambition, repeatedly offering himself up as martyr to the nation as if to clarify both how he would exit politics once his task was done and why others, in the meantime, should trust and follow his lead.[247] In his speeches to

citizen was now technically guilty of property crimes against the state." Scott, *Robespierre*, p. 221.

[245] Ozouf, *Festivals*, p. 109. For a slightly different interpretation of Robespierre's motives, see Soboul, *The Sans-Culottes*, p. 224. On March 19, 1792, someone attempted to place a red cap on Robespierre's head as he rose to address the Jacobin Club and he threw it to the ground. Thompson, *Robespierre*, vol. 1, pp. 213–14.

[246] "[E]specially where fundamental laws are concerned," Rousseau proposed "the intervention of a law-giver who divines what the general will is and puts it into words. He must say what all would say if only they knew how, and so he is merely their mouthpiece and not their master. For this reason his activity does not infringe upon, but rather implements, the sovereignty of the covenanted people." Stark, "Literature and Thought," p. 65. Recognizing the parallel between Robespierre and Rousseau's Legislator, Thompson titled one of his chapters "The Law-Giver." Thompson, *Robespierre*, vol. 2, p. 32. In many respects, Robespierre's personal identification with martyrdom and the excruciating nurturing, as he saw it, of the General Will were perfectly consistent with Rousseau's "great Legislator." As the leader who is necessary to create the situation and circumstances within which the best institutions for the people could be erected, the Legislator must be above and outside "the people" and his profound personal neutrality must be confirmed by his exit from the political stage once he has performed his role. Martyrdom, once Robespierre felt he had completed the task of the Legislator, was thus a splendid, even glorious, way of exiting the political stage. Miller, *Rousseau*, pp. 64–5. Miller later describes "dictatorial democracy" as a stage at which "the power of government [is concentrated temporarily] in the hands of one man or a cadre of enlightened leaders" so that he or they might transform "the people themselves into dutiful citizens," noting that "few means [for this purpose] are considered unfit" and "human nature [is thus cleansed] of its impurities." Miller then adds that a similar role "can be found in Rousseau's image of the great Legislator" (p. 205). Either Robespierre or the Committee of Public Safety which he led fits this image perfectly.

[247] Following the flight of the king, Robespierre addressed some 800 people at the Jacobin Club, naming himself as "[o]ne man of honesty and courage, prepared to unmask their plots. One man who thinks so lightly of life that he fears neither poison nor the sword, and would be happy if his death contributed to the freedom of the fatherland!" Scott, *Robespierre*, p. 125. On May 8, 1793, Robespierre ended a speech at the Jacobin Club by saying: "I have no more to say to you for unless there is a revival of public spirit, and the genius of liberty makes a last effort, I can but await, in the chair of senatorial office to which the people has raised me, the moment when the assassins come to sacrifice my life." On July 26, 1794, Robespierre similarly ended his last speech to the Jacobin Club: "If you support me, the new traitors will share the fate of the old. If you forsake me, you will see how calmly I shall drink the hemlock." Thompson, *Robespierre*, vol. 2, pp. 20, 252. In a speech to the convention on April 24, 1793, Robespierre said: "If I had been at Valenciennes [a city that fell to the enemy], I would never have been in a position to give you a report on the events of the siege; I would have wanted to share the fate of those brave

the Jacobin Club and before the assembly, he frequently explained how he painfully deduced the proper path of politics in the form of a revelation drawn from excruciating self-examination.[248]

When the revolution began, the path to a properly formed state and nation seemed more or less obvious. Although the royal court at Versailles was the center of French society, it was indifferent to human misery, thoroughly corrupt, and riddled with hypocrisy and false pretense. As Arendt put it,

the wretched life of the poor was confronted by the rotten life of the rich [visibly demonstrating] what Rousseau and Robespierre meant when they asserted that men are good "by nature" and become rotten by means of society, and that the low people, simply by virtue of not belonging to society, must always be "just and good." Seen from this viewpoint, the Revolution looked like the explosion of an uncorrupted and incorruptible inner core [through] an outward shell of decay and odorous decrepitude.[249]

As long as Louis XVI reigned, he and the court over which he presided provided both a foil and a target for the revolution. But once the king went to the scaffold, the deputies were compelled to decide just what political virtue might be and to what extent the people embodied and reflected it.

For Robespierre and the many Montagnards who followed his lead, the virtue of the people was instinctive and natural. They were immune to corruption because "labor, austerity, and poverty ... are the guardians of virtue."[250] The problem, as they saw it, was to eliminate the institutional and social arrangements that distorted the expression of the popular will. Formal education and literary discussion of policy issues, for example, were viewed as, at best, irrelevant and, at worst, positively harmful to the popular revelation of the General Will.[251] Claiming, correctly, that the Girondins

---

defenders who preferred honourable death to shameful capitulation." Robespierre, *Virtue and Terror*, p. 78. For other examples of Robespierre's fatalism, see Jordan, *Revolutionary Career of Maximilien Robespierre*, pp. 42, 210–11, 216. Such rhetoric was not, however, Robespierre's monopoly. Pierre Victurnien Vergniaud once replied to an attack by Robespierre on his Girondin faction in the same vein:

We are being accused and denounced, as we were on 2 September, by a violent mob of assassins! But we know that Tiberius Gracchus perished at the hands of a demented people whose interests he had constantly defended. We are not afraid of sharing his fate: our blood is at the disposal of the people; our only regret is that we cannot offer them more. (Furet and Richet, *French Revolution*, p. 151)

[248] As was almost the universal practice among revolutionary orators, Robespierre invariably posed as the voice of the Nation when he spoke. Hunt, *Politics, Culture, and Class*, p. 44.

[249] Arendt, *On Revolution*, p. 96.

[250] From an address by Robespierre to the convention on May 10, 1793. Miller, *Rousseau*, p. 152, italics omitted.

[251] Rousseau's

educational theories were based on the principle that man should learn those things which were within the range of his sense perceptions at the rate which was natural to the growth of his

sought to place *philosophes* (political and social theorists) in the National Convention, Robespierre asked: "[W]hat need have we of these men who [have] done nothing but write books?"[252] During the summer of 1793, this attitude toward learning evolved into an anti-intellectualism so extreme that the National Convention felt compelled to declare that Rousseau had not claimed that the people have to be "ignorant in order to be happy."[253] On December 25, 1793, however, Robespierre declared that the correct "theory of revolutionary government" was only then becoming clear to true patriots and that it could not possibly be discerned in the writings of political theorists "who had not predicted this Revolution." The "modern" principles of Enlightenment thought were "to the Revolution what impotence is to chastity."[254]

Because Rousseau had claimed that the young were naturally innocent and pure, the revolutionaries believed that the goal of education "should be to liberate the child of nature trapped in the carapace of maturity."[255] For Robespierre and his ally Saint-Just, the goals of the new republic were social equality and popular sovereignty and they were to be reached not through the principles and logic of the Enlightenment but through a struggle in which virtue would triumph over selfishness.[256] That struggle, in turn, required that

needs, and that he should learn only what was directly useful and natural to him ... Man developed as a moral being under the dual guidance of nature and society. Society was good in so far as it afforded him the opportunity for attaining a higher moral and rational existence in harmony with his innate potentialities. (McDonald, *Rousseau and the French Revolution*, pp. 26–7)

[252] Israel, *Revolutionary Ideas*, p. 274. In an address to the Jacobin Club on April 27, 1792, Robespierre claimed that the Girondins had attacked him for adhering to Rousseau's principle that the people are the sole repository of the "good, just, and magnanimous" and that "tyranny is the exclusive attribute of those who disdain them." Pointing to a bust of Rousseau, Robespierre went on to ask: "Who is unaware of the ferocity with which these men [those who trained and taught some of the Girondins] persecuted Jean Jacques" because they despised the "virtue and genius for liberty of he whose sacred image I see here?" (p. 244). These characterizations degenerated as the revolution progressed. In late October 1792, Jean-Baptiste Louvet attacked Robespierre in the National Convention by claiming: "There exist only two parties in France ... The first [the Girondins] is composed of philosophers; the second [the Montagnards] of thieves, robbers, and murderers." Tackett, *Coming of the Terror*, p. 231.

[253] Israel, *Revolutionary Ideas*, p. 477.

[254] Israel, *Revolutionary Ideas*, p. 539. In 1793, the National Convention even abolished military academies under Jacobin prodding (p. 388).

[255] Schama, *Citizens*, pp. 8, 770.

[256] Even before the revolution began, there was a conception among the French intelligentsia that the ideal citizen would be devoted to "Nature, tender-hearted, contemptuous of fashion, scornful of the ostentation of the mighty, passionate in their patriotism and enraged at the abuses of despotism. Above all they were apostles of public virtue who saw a France on the verge of being reborn as a republic of friends." Robespierre was simply articulating this cultural and ideological material. Schama, *Citizens*, pp. 181–2.

human nature be remade through political coercion and a rigorous program of popular education.[257]

In our country we want to substitute ethics for egoism, integrity for honor, principles for habits, duties for protocol, the empire of reason for the tyranny of changing taste, scorn of vice for the scorn of misfortune, pride for insolence, elevation of soul for vanity, the love of glory for the love of money, good men for amusing companions, merit for intrigue, genius for cleverness, truth for wit, the charm of happiness for the boredom of sensualism, the greatness of man for the pettiness of the "great," a magnanimous, strong, happy people for an amiable, frivolous miserable people, that is to say all the virtues and all the miracles of the republic for all the vices and all the absurdities of the monarchy.[258]

In order to create the new people who would be all of these things, Robespierre and the Jacobins proposed a system of elementary education in which children would be taken from their parents at the age of five and ensconced in boarding schools in which society could fully mold their character as citizens. The Jacobin education program emphasized the construction of collective identity through the taking of common meals, the wearing of uniforms, and a Spartan regimen of physical exercise, while deemphasizing the traditional goal of forming enlightened independent thinking and intellectual rigor.[259] Contending that the "nation alone has the right to raise children," Robespierre argued that their socialization and training could not be entrusted "to the pride of families" because that would produce only "aristocracy and domestic feudalism," which, in turn, would destroy "all the foundations of the social order."[260]

On May 10, 1793, Robespierre contended that the "people [are] good but [their] delegates are corruptible"; as a result, the virtue of the people must be "safeguarded against vice and the despotism of the government." The goal of

---

[257] Israel, *Revolutionary Ideas*, p. 368. Israel later states that, under Robespierre's influence, "Jacobin ideology [became] an obsessive Rousseauiste moral puritanism steeped in authoritarianism, anti-intellectualism, and xenophobia" because of "an unrelenting emphasis on the need to purify and equalize the people's *mœurs* (morals and customs)" (p. 521). Also see McPhee, *Liberty or Death*, p. 130; for a broader discussion of education policy during the revolution, see pp. 282–3, 375–7, 392–3.

[258] This passage is taken from Robespierre's report to the National Convention that was submitted in the name of the Committee of Public Safety on February 5, 1794. Jordan, *Revolutionary Career of Maximilien Robespierre*, p. 175.

[259] Israel, *Revolutionary Ideas*, p. 389. In Robespierre's words: "Sparta shines like a flash of lightning amid vast shadows." McPhee, *Liberty or Death*, p. 261. Given this rather martial orientation, it should come as no surprise that the army became an important "Jacobin school" for reeducating adults into the norms and principles of revolutionary citizenship. Hunt, *Politics, Culture, and Class*, p. 69. Along with the Girondins and moderate deputies, the Jacobins also favored repression of regional dialects through the teaching of a common, government-prescribed French language, a universal interpretation of history, and the construction of a public morality independent of religion (p. 383).

[260] Jordan, *Revolutionary Career of Maximilien Robespierre*, p. 147.

the new French republic was not, as the Girondins would have it, individual freedom but the imposition of the popular will throughout all government institutions; political corruption was inevitable if the expression of the General Will were frustrated.[261] In February 1794, Robespierre thus demanded that all laws should be decreed "in the name of the French people" instead of the "French republic."[262]

ROBESPIERRE'S REJECTION OF REPRESENTATIVE DEMOCRACY

Rousseau had imagined a "city-state" in which the General Will might be spontaneously revealed by the people in a common and open assembly. Representative democracy in which deputies acted as constitutionally designated delegates of constituents, each one elected in a different district, was thus in some ways the antithesis of Rousseau's ideal: The people could not mutually consult with one another and the deputies they elected were not beholden to the nation as a whole but to its parts.[263] From the Enlightenment position, the National Assembly generated and responded to the General Will in the clash of opinion and debate. That the deputies "willed" different things did not matter as long as they democratically reconciled their differences in legislation. From the constitutionalist perspective, reason would emerge in formal parliamentary debate as the deputies deliberated over legislation.[264] For Robespierre and those who followed his lead, this theory of politics was anathema because indirect representation within formal constitutional institutions corrupted the General Will beyond all recognition. For them, the General Will was spontaneously manifested when the people directly engaged in politics without the intervention of institutions. As Robespierre put it on June 7, 1791: "The National Assembly being subordinate to the General Will, so soon as it acts contrary to that Will, [it] ceases to exist."[265] And, in practice, the Jacobins – and, above all, Robespierre – would decide when the National Assembly transgressed the General Will.

The problem was that the French people could not possibly assemble in one place and thus spontaneously reveal their will. But the people of Paris could

---

[261] Israel, *Revolutionary Ideas*, p. 367.   [262] Arendt, *On Revolution*, p. 66.

[263] In the *Social Contract*, Rousseau had condemned the British system of representative democracy: "If the British people thinks it is free, it is making a terrible mistake; it is only free while electing a member of Parliament; as soon as these are elected, it is enslaved." Soboul, *The Sans-Culottes*, p. 106. Soboul himself interpreted the resulting tension between direct democracy and representative government in class terms (p. 133). On Rousseau's rejection of representative government, see McDonald, *Rousseau and the French Revolution*, pp. 82–4; Taylor, *Modern Social Imaginaries*, pp. 121–2.

[264] As Sydenham put it: "Paris ... must bow before its master, abandon its pretensions to leadership, and accept complete equality with the other Departments; the Convention alone was the capital of France." Sydenham, *The Girondins*, p. 197.

[265] Thompson, *Robespierre*, vol. 1, p. 243.

engage in direct political action. For their part, Robespierre and the Montagnards were willing to grant the Parisians a role in national politics as a proxy for the French people as a whole.[266] To justify this role, the General Will of the French people was theorized as indivisible when spontaneously manifested. The Parisians were thus idealized as a slice of the morally virtuous French people, who, in their spontaneity, authentically manifested the General Will of the entire nation; direct political action in the capital thereby became a manifestation of the General Will of the French people as a whole.

Most direct political action focused on the national legislature and, by undermining the independence of the deputies, often enabled Robespierre and the Montagnards to consolidate power in the revolutionary state. Popular mobilization in Paris thus became the major political force behind the centralization of political authority in the nation.[267] However, the Parisian sansculottes, like their counterparts in the rest of the nation, did not yet fully understand their obligations and roles as citizens of the republic. In addition, they had much more urgent needs, the most pressing of which was for food. Their spontaneous actions were, for that reason, often erratic and misdirected. Some of the responsibility for their errors as guides to the construction of the ideal republic could be ascribed to their leaders, who, as Robespierre saw them, were motivated by personal ambitions that were incompatible with the spontaneous and natural manifestation the General Will. In addition, direct political action introduced a chronic political instability that the new republic could ill afford as it faced foreign threats to its very existence.[268] These problems thus compelled Robespierre to take on responsibility for determining both when and how the Parisian people should direct the course of the revolutionary regime through what was fast becoming an administrative thicket in which pragmatism and abstract theory were inextricably intertwined.

Because he alone could be depended upon to bring the revolutionary state into being, Robespierre was compelled to resort to authoritarian practices even as he himself felt that he had little, if any, room to maneuver.[269] As Robespierre prophesied in his last speech: "We shall perish because, in the history of mankind, we missed the moment to found freedom." The goal of the revolution was "no longer freedom" but had, instead, become "the happiness" of the people.[270] The "moment" to which Robespierre referred never, in fact, existed,

---

[266] Israel, *Revolutionary Ideas*, p. 358.   [267] Israel, *Revolutionary Ideas*, pp. 89, 360–1.

[268] Schama, *Citizens*, p. 725. George Rude contended that "the most constant motive of popular insurrection [in Paris] ... was the compelling need ... for the provision of cheap and plentiful bread and other essentials." In fact, he concluded that the demonstration in the Champ de Mars in July 1791 "was the only one of the great Parisian *journées* which was not associated in any way with a popular demand for the control of bread or of any other commodity of prime necessity." Rude, *The Crowd*, pp. 199–200, 204, 208. On the "political education" and "indoctrination" of the sans-culottes, see pp. 212–15.

[269] Israel, *Revolutionary Ideas*, p. 303.   [270] Arendt, *On Revolution*, pp. 51, 65.

because the Rousseauian ideal to which he subscribed was simply incompatible with a nation-state.

ROBESPIERRE'S RECONCILIATION OF VIRTUE AND PRAGMATIC NECESSITY

On December 2, 1792, Robespierre outlined a "right of subsistence" that would reconcile the most pressing demands of the Parisian people for food with the Rousseauian notion that self-interested claims were incompatible with a revelation of the General Will. By making the provision of food a fundamental right, the demands of the people were no longer private claims but, instead, the general responsibility of the collective. In practice, revolutionary policy that realized this right would, of course, infringe upon the ostensibly equal right to property. However, Robespierre was less concerned with political economy than with "committing the Republic to a form of social egalitarianism that would be the economic equivalent of the reign of virtue he wished" to create in politics.[271] As in other instances, Robespierre's decision can be interpreted as either a response to political necessity or an evolving theory of politics.[272]

---

[271] Schama, *Citizens*, p. 710. In Robespierre's words: "What I call virtue is love of one's country, that is, love of equality. It is not a moral or a Christian virtue, but a political one; and it is as much the mainspring of republican government as honor is the mainspring of monarchies." Jordan, *Revolutionary Career of Maximilien Robespierre*, p. 160. In one of the few passages in which Robespierre ventured into a discussion of the principles of political economy, he compared the movement of grain within France to the circulation of blood in the body and maintained that shortages in the market were much the same thing as congestion "in the brain or in the chest." Robespierre, *Virtue and Terror*, p. 53. For Robespierre's alternative declaration of property rights in which he generally subordinated individual claims to "the security, or the liberty, or the life, or the property of our fellows," see his speech to the convention on April 24, 1793 (p. 67). On Robespierre's general indifference to economic policy, see Rebecca L. Spang, *Stuff and Money in the Time of the French Revolution* (Cambridge, MA: Harvard University Press, 2015), p. 223.

[272] Perhaps leaning heavily toward the former, Israel contends that Robespierre had, at best, a "threadbare ideology" that was not particularly innovative. Israel, *Revolutionary Ideas*, p. 249. These alternating motives would thus explain Robespierre's vacillation between direct and representative democracy and between censorship and freedom of the press. McPhee, *Liberty or Death*, pp. 242, 254. While censorship had been unevenly enforced before 1789, with much of the emphasis on publications that violated Catholic doctrine or criticized crown policy, the revolution opened amidst an almost unfettered freedom of the press and a consequent flood of political pamphlets. In response, the National Constituent Assembly, following the lead of royalist deputies, decreed on August 23, 1791, that a writer who "deliberately provokes disobedience to the Law [or] disparagement of the constituted powers and resistance to their acts" could be prosecuted or sued for damages by those officials whom they attacked. However, freedom of speech and freedom of the press was not seriously impeded until March 1793, when the National Convention moved aggressively against royalist publications and pornography. This decree was also used against the Girondin papers by the Montagnards. During the Terror, censorship was extended to theaters and performances; scripts were compelled to "promote virtue" by, among other things, depicting popular heroes as they overthrew tyranny. By March

Among the many actions that appear to at least subvert the construction of an ideal republic, Robespierre paid hundreds of sans-culottes to attend meetings at the Jacobin Club, where they were directed to applaud the speeches he delivered while hissing those of his opponents. He also ran a "well-honed intrigue, propaganda, and vote-rigging machine" that effectively dominated electoral politics in the capital.[273] Both paid demonstrations and the manipulative practices of a political machine were clearly intended to distort the spontaneity of Parisian people in a way that strengthened Robespierre's ability to direct the course of the revolutionary regime. They can thus be interpreted in two very different ways: as a means to further a personal ambition or as a pragmatic recognition that the General Will, which he himself embodied, could not be expressed reliably by the people of Paris.

Robespierre's revolutionary career seemingly offers plenty of evidence that he sought power, and his rapid rise to prominence correlates almost perfectly with the increasing authoritarian character of the revolutionary regime.[274] Between the deposition of the king in August 1792 and the adoption of a new constitution in June 1793, France had no formal government apparatus other than the national legislature. Despite the fact that the deputies were making things up as they went along, they were nonetheless able to enact legislation that compelled conscription of men for the nation's armies, established a Revolutionary Tribunal to judge and punish treason, set maximum price controls on the most important commodities (particularly bread), and created what rapidly became a collective ministry of war. Lodged within the Committee of Public Safety, the latter rapidly became the institutional center of Montagnard political strength. By August 1793, all freedom of expression had been stifled and the National Convention, emasculated by the purge of the Girondins, was rubber-stamping committee decisions.[275]

1794, all scripts had to be submitted to censors before a play could open. Schama, *Citizens*, pp. 297, 322, 706; Doyle, *French Revolution*, pp. 46, 56, 89, 155, 227; Israel, *Revolutionary Ideas*, pp. 429, 459–60, 518–19; Andress, *French Society*, p. 141. Even after Robespierre's fall from power, the National Convention was vigorously censoring public speech: On May 1, 1795, the convention passed a decree "demanding exile for life for those publicly defaming Convention deputies in writing or at meetings." Israel, *Revolutionary Ideas*, p. 614.

[273] Israel, *Revolutionary Ideas*, pp. 283–4, 293, 439. On the other hand, Robespierre was also thought to be "one of the few orators to receive applause that was not bought," although he was "often heckled by spectators hired by his enemies." Jordan, *Revolutionary Career of Maximilien Robespierre*, pp. 50, 61.

[274] On Robespierre's rise to public prominence, see Jordan, *Revolutionary Career of Maximilien Robespierre*, pp. 57, 59–60, 70, and, most particularly, the epilogue.

[275] The Committee of Public Safety was created on March 25, 1793, when, in Israel's words, the revolution "stood on the verge of collapse." Robespierre declined to serve at that time because he thought that it would be ineffective; he only joined the committee on July 26. Israel, *Revolutionary Ideas*, p. 420. On the history of the committee, see Doyle, *French Revolution*, pp. 228, 236–7, 244, 246–8, 251, 263–4, 267–8, 277–8, 282; Schama, *Citizens*, pp. 755–6, 808–9, 813, 818, 839; McPhee, *Liberty or Death*, pp. 183, 210, 228, 253, 265, 267, 271,

Dominated by Robespierre, the committee behaved as if most of the members had become his personal "secretaries" as opposed to colleagues. However, Robespierre still depended on the support and loyalty of a small group of allies, so much so that his rule should be characterized as a collective dictatorship in which he was the first among equals.[276] While the more pragmatic attitudes of his friends and allies might offer room for compromise or tolerance for mistakes, Robespierre was often stern and implacable and many deputies feared the moral rectitude underpinning his politics. As he well knew, many deputies called him a dictator, a title he could accept only if they recognized that he was merely realizing the destiny of the people. On January 10, 1794, he declared that those who opposed him were the true "tyrants" and it was they, not he, who threatened the revolution.[277]

Robespierre's policies combined political pragmatism with ideological principle in ways that appeared to explain almost all of his decisions, even if those explanations were often known only to himself.[278] On December 18, 1791, for example, Robespierre gave a speech to the Jacobin Club in which he contended that a declaration of war against Austria would inevitably result in a political dictatorship.

War is always the first wish of a powerful government which wants to become still more powerful ... It is in war that the executive power deploys the most fearful energy and exercises a sort of dictatorship which can only frighten our emerging liberties; it is in war that the people forget those principles which are most directly concerned with civil and political rights and think only of events abroad, that they turn their attention from their political representatives and their magistrates and instead pin all their interest and all their hopes on their generals and their ministers ...

274–5, 293, 338. For short biographies of those who served on the committee between July 10, 1793, and Robespierre's fall, see Davidson, *French Revolution*, pp. 266–8. For the membership of the Committee of Public Safety and the Committee of General Security, see Patrick, *Men of the First French Republic*, pp. 374–6.

[276] Israel, *Revolutionary Ideas*, pp. 503, 506; Lefebvre, *French Revolution*, vol. 2, p. 132. Furet and Richet, in fact, describe Robespierre as "a great parliamentary leader" who "laid the foundations of the modern technique of 'managing' a parliamentary assembly." However, while they regard Robespierre as "realistic and efficient," they also say that he indulged in "Utopian fantasies" and "dreamed," along with Saint-Just, "of creating a world of brotherly love in which people would be bound to one another by solemn declarations of friendship ... but their picture of the future as one long rustic idyll was to be shattered by the realities of the mercantile world of capitalism." Furet and Richet, *French Revolution*, pp. 187, 199. Jordan, however, concludes that Robespierre "was quite unsuccessful as a parliamentary politician or leader" because so few of his proposals were actually passed by his colleagues. Jordan, *Revolutionary Career of Maximilien Robespierre*, p. 48. For a summary of the positions Robespierre took on legislation, see pp. 51–4.

[277] Doyle, *French Revolution*, p. 281; Israel, *Revolutionary Ideas*, p. 541.

[278] McDonald, for example, implied that Robespierre supported representative government up until he left the assembly. After that, he became much more critical of its ability to express the General Will. McDonald, *Rousseau and the French Revolution*, p. 56.

It is during war that a habit of passive obedience, and an all too natural enthusiasm for successful military leaders, transforms the soldiers of the nation into the soldiers of the King or of his generals. [Thus] the leaders of the armies become the arbiters of the fate of their country, and swing the balance of power in favour of the faction that they have decided to support. If they are Caesars or Cromwells, they seize power themselves.[279]

If war must come, the Legislative Assembly must first subordinate the king to its will and purge the army of officers who opposed the revolution. If these things were done, the assembly would then be in a position to direct the war effort. On January 2, 1792, Robespierre also presciently predicted that those countries "liberated" by French troops would come to resent their occupation:

The most extravagant idea that can be born in the head of a politician is to believe that it is enough for a people to enter among a foreign people by force of arms to make them adopt its laws and its Constitution. Nobody loves armed missionaries; and the first advice that nature and prudence give is to reject them as enemies.

He then added that the "declaration of rights is not a ray of sunshine which strikes everyone at the same moment."[280]

While his prediction was probably grounded in a pragmatic analysis of the economic burden that military occupation would impose on foreign populations, Robespierre's position was quite consistent with Rousseau's insistence on a small polity in which direct political participation would be possible. The citizens of occupied countries such as Belgium or the Piedmont were not only physically distant from Paris but were also shaped by different cultures.[281] On January 2, 1792, Robespierre noted that the crown itself wanted war and contended that that fact alone was enough to justify opposition. He then went on to connect Girondin support for war with royalist sympathies, even though

---

[279] Davidson, *French Revolution*, p. 83. Also see Jordan, *Revolutionary Career of Maximilien Robespierre*, pp. 83–95.

[280] Davidson, *French Revolution*, p. 85; Lefebvre, *French Revolution*, vol. 1, pp. 218–19.

[281] This debate over French relations with nations that had been "freed" by the revolutionary army centered on, as Arendt noted, a fundamental contradiction in ideology:

The secret conflict between state and nation came to light at the very birth of the modern nation-state, when the French Revolution combined the Declaration of the Rights of Man with the demand for national sovereignty. The same essential rights were at once claimed (a) as the inalienable heritage of all human beings *and* (b) as the specific heritage of specific nations, the same nation was at once declared (a) to be subject to laws, which supposedly would flow from the Rights of Man, *and* (b) sovereign, that is, bound by no universal law and acknowledging nothing superior to itself.

Hannah Arendt, *The Origins of Totalitarianism* (New York: Harcourt, Brace, 1973), p. 230. The notion of a distinct French people as the very definition of the "Nation" could not be reconciled with the export of the "Rights of Man" as a universal template for new republics in foreign lands. In the end, it was the "Rights of Man" that gave way to French nationalism.

the Girondins had very different motives than the crown.[282] His opposition to the war thus combined opportunism (seizing an opportunity to connect the Girondins to the crown), astute political analysis (the prediction that foreign populations would not welcome occupation by the French), and ideological consistency (the restriction of the scope of the revolution to the French nation, which shared a common culture and political principles).[283]

Robespierre delivered a similar speech to the National Convention on November 5, 1792, in which he opposed punishment of those who led the August 10 insurrection. On the one hand, Robespierre argued that the deposition of the king was now a fact to which the National Convention owed its own legitimacy. Prosecution of the insurrection's leaders would thus undermine the authority of the legislature itself while also strengthening the hand of the royalists who were seeking to return the king to the throne. On the other hand, the deposition of the king by popular direct action, however imperfect as an expression of the General Will, was still to be preferred to legislative fiat. Failure to recognize this act of the Parisian people would only deflect the revolution from its ideological mission.[284]

Perhaps the most striking ideological contradiction in Robespierre's revolutionary career arose some months later during the king's trial. Although, like all the other deputies, the Girondins considered the king guilty of crimes against the revolution, they were reluctant to send Louis XVI to the scaffold. Hoping that the French people might be more forgiving than the deputies in

---

[282] Israel, *Revolutionary Ideas*, pp. 239–40.

[283] Robespierre later adopted a much more favorable attitude toward revolutionary expansionism. Scott, *Robespierre*, p. 216. In fact, on April 24, 1793, as part of a speech in which he presented to the convention his draft of a proposed revision of the Declaration of the Rights of Man and of the Citizen, Robespierre told the deputies that the declaration should not be restricted to "a herd of human creatures parked in some corner of the globe" but should extend to "the immense family to which nature has given the earth as its domain and abode." One of his proposed articles then announced: "The men of all countries are brothers, and different peoples should help each other to the best of their ability, like citizens of the same state." This was followed by: "He who oppresses one nation declares himself the enemy of all"; and "Those who make war on a people to arrest the progress of liberty and annihilate the rights of man should be pursued by all, not as ordinary enemies but as murderers and rebellious brigands." A fourth article grounded all of these on an eternal principle: "Kings, aristocrats, tyrants, whatever they be, are slaves in revolt against the sovereign power of the earth, which is the human race, and against the legislator of the universe, which is nature." Robespierre, *Virtue and Terror*, p. 68. Republics were, it seems, to be fully independent of one another and yet obligated by "the sovereign power of the earth" and universal demand of "nature" to come to each other's aid when threatened by tyrants. Some months later Robespierre addressed his remarks to one of those republics: "And you, brave Americans, whose liberty, established by our blood, was also guaranteed by our alliance: what would be your destiny if we no longer existed? You would fall back under the shameful yoke of your former masters." Robespierre, *Virtue and Terror*, pp. 87–8.

[284] Lefebvre states that this speech greatly enhanced Robespierre's stature. Lefebvre, *French Revolution*, vol. 1, p. 270. For the text, see Robespierre, *Virtue and Terror*, p. 43.

the National Convention, the Girondins proposed that a national referendum be held in order that the people might express their will on whether or not the king should be executed. In Jérôme Pétion's words: "It is not for any individual or minority to diverge from the *volonté générale* or there is no more society." While a referendum was somewhat inconsistent with their general position that the convention was both competent and duly authorized to interpret and carry out the General Will, it presented a much more serious problem for the Montagnards, for whom direct political action (in this case a referendum) was a central principle. Although Fabre d'Églantine repeatedly contended that Rousseau himself believed that the General Will could never be authentically revealed in primary assemblies (where the referendum would have been held), a vote by deputies in the National Convention was clearly an inferior alternative. In response, Robespierre contended that the people had already revealed the General Will in the August 10 assault on the Tuileries that had deposed the king and no further consultation with them was required.[285] In the end, Robespierre and the Montagnards prevailed, but the decision turned on apprehension among moderate deputies, including some Girondins, that a referendum would present an opening that might be exploited by royalists and the recalcitrant clergy.[286]

---

[285] Sydenham, *The Girondins*, p. 138.

[286] Israel, *Revolutionary Ideas*, pp. 306, 308–9. I should note that Israel generally has a more jaundiced view of Robespierre's political motives than I have described here and elsewhere in the text (see, for example, pp. 701–2). One of the reasons for Israel's hostility to Robespierre is that he believes that he corrupted what Israel considers the "core values" of the revolution, values that he identifies as the Enlightenment principles held by those he labels "Left Republicans." With the exception of those Jacobins who followed Georges Danton, these Left Republicans were radical democrats who were almost entirely synonymous with the Girondins (whom Israel prefers to call "Brissotins"). Robespierre built an opposing coalition of Rousseauian populists who desired consensus and brooked no dissent, religious Jacobins who abhorred militant secularism, and those deputies who believed the challenges facing the revolution required a strong, centralized leadership. In Israel's view, Robespierre's coalition was responsible for the destruction of the radical democratic promise of the French Revolution. For example, he writes: "Robespierre's and Saint-Just's rejection of the Revolution's core values [were] the wrecking of the Revolution and a virulent form of Counter-Enlightenment and anti-intellectualism, hostile to freedom of thought, individual liberty, erudition, and the right to criticize. In terms of principles, Robespierre was the Revolution's contradiction, the enlightenment's very antithesis" (p. 697); also see pp. 362, 478, 501–4, 510–11, 530, 545, 616, 691–2, 697, 708. He describes "the Revolution's core values" as "representative democracy, republicanism, freedom of expression, minimal religious authority, legal equality, and human rights against both populism and royalism" (p. 611). McDonald identified the Girondins and their adherence to representative government in much the same way. McDonald, *Rousseau and the French Revolution*, p. 95. Thompson, on the other hand, contended that Robespierre "represented the Revolution: he did not refashion it. He copied its movements as faithfully as a shadow – sometimes going ahead of it, and sometimes following behind, but always impotent to alter its course." Thompson, *Robespierre*, vol. 2, p. 112. It was the Girondins who were out of step.

ROBESPIERRE AND THE TERROR

On February 5, 1794, Robespierre delivered what may have been his most important speech. In an address to the National Convention, entitled "On the Principles of Public Morality," he contended that terror and virtue were inextricably linked:

If the mainspring of popular government in peacetime is virtue, the mainspring of popular government in revolution is virtue and terror both: virtue, without which terror is disastrous; terror, without which virtue is powerless. Terror is nothing but prompt, severe, inflexible justice; it is therefore an emanation of virtue; it is not so much a specific principle as a consequence of the general principle of democracy applied to the homeland's most pressing needs.[287]

Earlier, on August 28, 1792, Robespierre had stated: "The people's justice must bear a character worthy of them; it must be imposing as well as prompt and terrible."[288] But he drew a sharp line between the people, who were naturally virtuous but needed to be properly shepherded, and their enemies, who were beyond the pale:

[T]he first maxim of your policy must be to guide the people with reason and the people's enemies with terror ... Break the enemies of liberty with terror, and you will

---

[287] Hanson, *Contesting the French Revolution*, p. 125. From Robespierre's perspective, "democracy" was nothing more and nothing less than the revelation and implementation of the General Will. However, in this speech Robespierre stepped back from an unequivocal endorsement of direct democracy through popular action:

Democracy is a state where the sovereign people, guided by laws which are its own work, does by itself all that it can do well, and by delegates all that it cannot do for itself. So it is in the principles of democratic government that you must look for the rules of your political conduct ... What then is the fundamental principle of democratic or popular government, that is to say the essential underpinning which sustains it and makes it work? It is virtue ... which is nothing other than the love of the land of your birth and its laws ... this sublime sentiment supposes a preference for the public interests above all particular interests ... The first rule of your political conduct must be to relate all you do to maintaining equality and developing virtue ... In the system of the French Revolution, what is immoral is impolitic, and what corrupts is counter-revolutionary. Weakness, vices and prejudices are the high-road to monarchy. (Doyle, *French Revolution*, pp. 272–3)

During the Russian Revolution, Lenin justified the Bolshevik use of terror in much the same way because he was unable, in Richard Pipes' words:

to perceive politics in hues other than pure white and pure black. It was essentially the same outlook that had driven Robespierre, to whom Trotsky had compared Lenin as early as 1904. Like the French Jacobin, Lenin sought to build a world inhabited exclusively by "good citizens." This objective led him, like Robespierre, to justify the physical elimination of "bad" citizens.

Richard Pipes, *The Russian Revolution* (New York: Vintage Books, 1990), p. 790.

[288] Ronald Schecter, *A Genealogy of Terror in Eighteenth-Century France* (Chicago: University of Chicago Press, 2018), p. 152.

be justified as founders of the Republic. The government of the revolution is the despotism of liberty against tyranny.[289]

The major problem facing the revolution was the continuing presence of those who lacked virtue. In some cases, their flaw was a flagrant refusal to abide by the General Will, but most of those were either royalists or recalcitrant churchmen. By this time, they had either been driven underground or had left France. Others who lacked virtue supported the revolution but were personally corrupt. The revolutionary regime provided many opportunities for fraud because military contracts, the confiscation and distribution of noble and church property, and the marketing of bonds and other financial instruments were rarely audited or otherwise monitored. Personal enrichment thus often went hand in hand with revolutionary loyalty. And there were excesses with respect to the enforcement of revolutionary discipline, particularly in departments somewhat distant from the capital.

On September 17, 1793, the National Convention passed what became known as the Law of Suspects. That law created "surveillance committees in every commune" whose purpose was to arrest those who were not patriots; to that end, the committees were to monitor and investigate both the private and public beliefs of common citizens.[290] Schama calls this law "the charter of the Terror" because it conferred extremely broad powers of arrest and prosecution upon the Committee of Public Safety and its designated agents. Under its authority, individuals were subject to arrest if they "either by their conduct, their contacts, their words or their writings, showed themselves to be supporters of tyranny, of federalism, or to be enemies of liberty." Although noble titles and status had already been abolished, former nobles were still subjected to an even higher behavioral standard than ordinary citizens in that they were subject to prosecution if they "have not constantly manifested their attachment to the revolution."[291]

---

[289] Hunt, *Politics, Culture, and Class*, p. 46. Also see Arendt, *On Revolution*, p. 828. On the Terror generally, see Israel, *Revolutionary Ideas*, pp. 249, 503–73; Edelstein, "What Was the Terror?," pp. 453–69; Furet and Richet, *French Revolution*, pp. 183–4. Some historians believe that the Terror was merely the culmination of what was the almost inevitable development of an authoritarian regime. Schama, for example, considers the creation of the Comité des Recherches in July 1789 to have been "the first organ of a revolutionary police state." Schama, *Citizens*, p. 448. McPhee, however, contends that the application of violence by the state should be viewed as a practical response to "extraordinary circumstances" created by civil and foreign wars. McPhee, *Liberty or Death*, p. 209–10. On the historical literature of the Terror, see Ronen Steinberg, "Reckoning with Terror: Retribution, Redress, and Remembrance in Post-Revolutionary France" in Andress, *Oxford Handbook of the French Revolution*, p. 492. For a rejection of the view that Rousseau's influence on the French Revolution promoted totalitarian visions during the revolution, see McDonald, *Rousseau and the French Revolution*, pp. 27–39, 94.

[290] McPhee, *Liberty or Death*, p. 213.

[291] *Citizens*, p. 766; Doyle, *French Revolution*, pp. 251, 258.

Six days before enactment of the Law of Suspects, the Paris Commune passed a new regulatory regime for the issuance of *"certificats de civisme,"* basically identity cards testifying that the bearer was a good citizen and, for that reason, should be permitted to move about the country and participate in politics. In practice, these certificates operated as "passes" and the holder needed to carry one at all times. Anticipating passage of the Law of Suspects, the Paris Commune revised the criteria for their issuance, denying certificates to individuals who fell into one or more of the following categories:

1 Those who, in assemblies of the people, arrest its energy by crafty discourses, turbulent cries and threats.
2 Those, more prudent, who speak mysteriously of the misfortunes of the Republic, are full of pity for the lot of the people, and are always ready to spread bad news with an affected grief.
3 Those who have changed their conduct and language in line with events ...
4 Those who pity the farmers and greedy merchants against whom the law is obliged to take measures.
5 Those who have the words Liberty, Republic and Fatherland constantly on their lips, but who consort with former nobles, counter-revolutionary priests, aristo-crats [and] moderates, and show concern for their fate.
6 Those who have taken no active part in revolutionary affairs ...
7 Those who received the republican constitution with indifference and have given credence to false fears concerning its establishment and duration.
8 Those who, having done nothing against liberty, have also done nothing for it.
9 Those who do not attend the meetings of their sections and who give as excuses that they do not know how to speak or that their occupation prevents them.[292]

The jails and prisons were already filled to capacity throughout France, so much so that the processions of carts to the guillotine relieved overcrowding even as they discouraged even the slightest behavior that might be interpreted as anti-revolutionary.[293]

---

[292] Andress, *French Revolution and the People*, pp. 204, 206; Israel, *Revolutionary Ideas*, p. 511. Similar certificates were being issued as early as August 1792. Doyle, *French Revolution*, p. 190. The issuance of these regulations by the Paris Commune may have marked the high point in cooperation between Robespierre and the street leaders in the sections. Previously, on March 9, 1793, Jacques-René Hébert led a mob of several hundred as they wrecked Girondin printing presses. Although it is not clear that Robespierre approved of this action, it was directed against his primary opponents in the National Convention. Israel, *Revolutionary Ideas*, p. 312; Sydenham, *The Girondins*, p. 153. By September 1793, Hébert and his allies, the Enragés, had become "the political masters of Paris" through their ability to bring masses of sans-culottes into the streets. McPhee, *Liberty or Death*, p. 224. At that point, those street leaders who had proven so useful to Robespierre in his struggles with the National Convention had themselves become threats to Montagnard dominance. Lefebvre, *French Revolution*, vol. 2, p. 61.

[293] Israel, *Revolutionary Ideas*, p. 569; Schama, *Citizens*, p. 793. There were many earlier instances in which revolutionary authorities enacted or implemented repressive measures. For a sampling, see Doyle, *French Revolution*, p. 190; Lefebvre, *French Revolution*, vol. 1, pp. 241–4; Schama, *Citizens*, p. 624.

Although Robespierre was the revolutionary leader most responsible for the Terror and the thousands of executions between June 3, 1793 and July 28, 1794, his motivations were extremely complex.[294] Robespierre's insistence on the purity of the General Will led him to interpret all political opposition as treason against the people and the Nation. During this period, Robespierre labored under almost unbearable psychological stress as he attempted to balance the pragmatic needs of maintaining power with his compulsion to wrest the ideal regime from the womb of the revolution.[295] Believing that he alone was and could be aligned with a General Will that was still largely inchoate, Robespierre became increasingly paranoid and, as a result, came to identify many of his close friends and allies as potential or actual enemies.[296] Robespierre's insistence on personal transparency as an essential aspect of virtue created a regime in which the unmasking of corruption or personal ambition became a revolutionary duty that almost anyone could carry out.[297] For some of those who stood accused, there were trials whose procedures and verdicts heavily favored the prosecution. For others, due process was set aside as revolutionaries used the state to purge its own ranks. Those who mattered least in revolutionary society were mutilated and slaughtered by the people in the streets and public squares. As Arendt observed: "It was the war upon

---

[294] The dates mark the fall of the Girondins and the execution of Robespierre, respectively, and come from McPhee, *Liberty or Death*, p. 375. One of the great ironies of the revolution was that Robespierre had previously (and unsuccessfully) opposed the legalization of executions by the Legislative Assembly. Doyle, *French Revolution*, p. 183. The Terror "was not conceived as the arbiter of conflicting interests ... but rather as the mechanism for ensuring that individual wills were forged into one, single, general, or national will ... The Terror was the people on the march, the exterminating Hercules. Hercules, the people, was in the eyes of the radicals who had called it into being a potential Frankenstein." Hunt, *Politics, Culture, and Class*, pp. 47, 101. But also see Taylor, *Modern Social Imaginaries*, pp. 134–5.

[295] At two critical moments in 1794, from February 10 to March 13 and from July 1 to July 22, Robespierre suffered nervous breakdowns that prevented him from actively participating in debate and decision-making. Israel, *Revolutionary Ideas*, pp. 546, 574; McPhee, *Liberty or Death*, pp. 252–3.

[296] Doyle, *French Revolution*, pp. 278, 281. Schama contends that "the polemics of paranoia" could be taken directly from Rousseau's writings and that the "unmasking" of fifth columnists by Jacobins was "a good Rousseauean fixation." Schama, *Citizens*, pp. 603, 732. That may be true but Robespierre's insecurities became ever more expansive and concrete. In his last address to the convention, for example, his accusations appeared to encompass almost everyone around him:

So let us say that there exists a conspiracy against public liberty; that it owes its strength to a criminal coalition that intrigues inside the Convention itself; that this coalition has accomplices in the Committee of General Security and in the office of that Committee, where they predominate; that the enemies of the Republic set that committee up against the Committee of Public Safety [of which Robespierre was a member], thus constituting two governments; that some members of the Committee of Public Safety are in this plot; that the coalition thus formed seeks to ruin patriots and the homeland. (Robespierre, *Virtue and Terror*, p. 140)

[297] Schama, *Citizens*, pp. 532, 805.

hypocrisy that transformed Robespierre's dictatorship into the Reign of Terror, and the outstanding characteristic of this period was the self-purging of the rulers."[298]

However, Robespierre was sometimes more magnanimous than other members of his faction. He opposed the execution of Marie Antoinette, for example, because he thought that it would weaken support for the revolution domestically while increasing the hostility of foreign powers.[299] After the purging of the Girondin leaders on June 2, 1793, some seventy-five deputies secretly signed a protest against their expulsion from the National Convention. When the document became public during the trial of the leaders, Robespierre first opposed the arrest of the signers and, when that failed, successfully

---

[298] Arendt, *On Revolution*, pp. 88–9. Arendt also emphasized the strong connection between the notions of transparency and nature:

> [T]he unmasking of the "person," the deprivation of legal personality, would leave behind the "natural" human being, while the unmasking of the hypocrite would leave nothing behind the mask, because the hypocrite is the actor himself in so far as he wears no mask. He pretends to *be* the assumed role, and when he enters the game of society it is without any play-acting whatsoever. In other words, what made the hypocrite so odious was that he claimed not only sincerity but naturalness, and what made him so dangerous outside the social realm whose corruption he represented and, as it were, enacted, was that he instinctively could help himself to every "mask" in the political theatre …
>
> They believed that they had emancipated nature herself, as it were, liberated the natural man in all men, and given him the Rights of Man to which each was entitled, not by virtue of the body politic to which he belonged but by virtue of being born. In other words, by the unending hunt for hypocrites and through the passion for unmasking society, they had, albeit unknowingly, torn away the mask of the *persona* [the legal personality which is given and guaranteed by the body politic] as well, so that the Reign of Terror eventually spelled the exact opposite of true liberation and true equality; it equalized because it left all inhabitants equally without the protecting mask of a legal personality. (Arendt, *On Revolution*, pp. 97–8)

Also see Israel, *Revolutionary Ideas*, p. 507. We can readily recognize the practical implications of the identification of transparency with virtue in Robespierre's demand that the Jacobin Club purge its membership by having individuals stand before their peers and give an account of their political behavior, their ties to those who had been politically discredited, their personal virtue, and the soundness of their political opinions. Scott, *Robespierre*, p. 213.

[299] Doyle, *French Revolution*, p. 267. Earlier, Robespierre had also regretted the necessity of king's execution: "I felt republican virtue wavering in my heart at the sight of the guilty man humiliated before the sovereign power." Furet and Richet, *French Revolution*, p. 165. In a speech before the National Convention on December 3, 1792, he stated: "I myself abhor the death penalty generously prescribed by your laws; and for Louis I feel neither love nor hate." As a result, "I utter this deadly truth with regret, but Louis must die, because the homeland has to live." Robespierre, *Virtue and Terror*, p. 64. Thompson stated that Robespierre, "now that the guillotine had done its work, and Louis is dead," had expressed "the hope [that] the Assembly will abolish capital punishment." Thompson, *Robespierre*, vol. 2, p. 1. By the middle of March, however, Robespierre would claim that execution was appropriate for "every attempt made against the security of the state or the liberty, equality, unity, and indivisibility of the Republic" (p. 8).

opposed their trial.[300] As a result, they owed their lives to their most powerful and otherwise implacable enemy.

THE GUILLOTINE

The guillotine combined three of the strongest impulses of the revolution: technological efficiency and simplicity, social equality, and a brutally Manichaean distinction between the virtuous and the corrupt.[301] In December 1789, what ultimately became the guillotine was first proposed to the Constituent Assembly as a machine that would detach heads "in the twinkling of an eye." At that time the design was dismissed as laughable. However, the proposal was again presented to the assembly several years later. Among its alleged virtues were that it would dispatch its victims with painless efficiency and treat each of the condemned as equals whatever had been their previous station in society. The first head severed was that of a brigand who was executed on April 25, 1792. The first victim accused of a political crime mounted the scaffold on August 21: Louis Collot d'Angremont, an administrative official of the National Guard, who had been accused of participation in a royalist "conspiracy." The people were invited to witness the event.[302]

On June 10, 1794, the National Convention passed the Law of 22 Prairial, which ordered that persons were to be brought before the Revolutionary Tribunal for "slandering patriotism," "seeking to inspire discouragement," "spreading false news," or "depraving morals, corrupting the public conscience and impairing the purity and energy of the revolutionary government." Those who were charged with any of these crimes were not permitted to call witnesses

---

[300] Schama, *Citizens*, p. 813; Israel, *Revolutionary Ideas*, pp. 512–13; Doyle, *French Revolution*, pp. 243, 252–3.

[301] The guillotine was a revolutionary innovation that "purged" the premodern

> popular impulse to punishment ... [of] magicosymbolic elements [in that] punishment ... was carried out in a rational, "clean" form, through a modern, "scientific" instrument ... replacing the gory symbolism of the ancient regime ... [T]he ritual was purged of all that mixture of the festive and the murderous, the carnival promiscuity of laughter and killing, which was integral to traditional popular culture ... one deals death in a direct, almost clinical fashion, by means of a modern, efficient machine. (Taylor, *Modern Social Imaginaries*, pp. 137–8)

> For Pierre-Jean Cabanis, a "physician and anatomist," the guillotine also offered an opportunity for research. Even as some of his friends were being exiled or executed during the Terror, Cabanis was "dispassionately studying the phases in which the extinction of life occurred in the bodies of the victims of the guillotine." Judges, "Educational Ideas," p. 157.

[302] Doyle, *French Revolution*, pp. 183, 190; Taylor, *Modern Social Imaginaries*, pp. 137–8; Schama, *Citizens*, pp. 619, 622–3. Although the device took its name from a deputy, Dr. Joseph-Ignace Guillotin, who had been the first to recommend it to his colleagues, the guillotine was actually designed and constructed by a Dr. Louis who served as secretary of the Academy of Surgery. Bosher, *French Revolution*, p. xli.

and were denied representation by counsel. There were only two possible verdicts: acquittal or death. The efficiency with which revolutionary justice could now be rendered significantly increased the number of executions.[303] From October 10, 1793, when the new constitution was suspended, until Thermidor, when Robespierre himself was executed, over 16,000 men and women were guillotined. Most of them were ordinary people who lived far away from Paris, but the capital itself was also drenched in blood.[304]

The number of those who were imprisoned for crimes against the revolution may have been as high as half a million people, just under 2 percent of all men, women, and children in France. Of these, some 10,000 appear to have died while incarcerated. Excluding the civil war in the Vendée, at least 30,000 people were killed during the Terror.[305] Only one in six of the victims who received officially promulgated death sentences were nobles or members of the clergy. While the middle classes contributed another 25 percent, the vast majority were, in Doyle's words, "ordinary people caught up in tragic circumstances not of their own making." The latter composed an even higher percentage of those who were killed in less formal circumstances.[306]

Between the convocation of the Estates-General in 1789 and Napoleon's overthrow of the Directory ten years later, over 40 percent of all leading revolutionaries died a violent death (see Table 4.3).[307] Over a third were guillotined on the orders of the revolutionary regime (fifty in Paris, two in

---

[303] Schama, *Citizens*, pp. 836–7; McPhee, *Liberty or Death*, p. 264. In Doyle's words, the "enemies of the people were so widely defined that ... almost anybody was vulnerable to the charge." Doyle, *French Revolution*, p. 275. On the establishment of the Revolutionary Tribunal, see pp. 226–7.

[304] Doyle, *French Revolution*, pp. 252–3; Andress, *French Revolution and the People*, pp. 254–5. On executions and other extralegal killings outside of the capital, see Schama, *Citizens*, pp. 781–7; Israel, *Revolutionary Ideas*, p. 527. Many of these did not utilize the guillotine.

[305] Revolutionary violence in the Vendée claimed the lives of between 190,000 and a quarter of a million people or about 4 or 5 percent of the total population in that region. Israel, *Revolutionary Ideas*, p. 545; Doyle, *French Revolution*, pp. 224–6, 232, 243, 255–8; McPhee, *Liberty or Death*, pp. 176–9, 232–3, 271. Schama contends that the violence in the Vendée anticipated "the technological killings of the twentieth century." Schama, *Citizens*, pp. 690–706, 787–92. During the spring of 1795, what is often called the "White Terror" claimed the lives of approximately 30,000 more lives as people took revenge on "terrorists." McPhee, *Liberty or Death*, p. 289. On revolutionary violence in the provinces generally, see Andress, *French Revolution and the People*, pp. 102–3, 110–11, 113–16, 123–8, 135, 141–3, 150, 153, 161–2, 169–70, 173–6, 181–2, 184–8, 192–6, 200–1, 206, 212–13, 215–31, 235–9.

[306] Doyle, *French Revolution*, pp. 258–9. In Paris, the proportions of nobles, clergy, and middle-class victims were considerably higher than in the rest of France (p. 275). One reason that the proportion of upper-class victims was relatively small overall was the fact that many nobles and clergy emigrated before or during the Terror. Israel, *Revolutionary Ideas*, pp. 543–6.

[307] See the note to Table 4.3 for a description of the method used in this compilation. Although Davidson utilized a different method, his results are quite similar to those presented in the table. Davidson, *French Revolution*, pp. 198, 269–77.

TABLE 4.3. *The fates of prominent revolutionaries between May 5, 1789 and November 10, 1799*

Fate	Number	Percentage
Sent to the guillotine	54	34.8
Committed suicide after apprehension	8	5.2
Died while imprisoned in Cayenne	1	0.6
Assassinated by a royalist	1	0.6
Assassinated by another revolutionary	1	0.6
Total of those who died for their politics	**65**	**41.9**
Imprisoned by the revolution	28	18.1
Went into hiding or exile	19	12.3
Total of those who were imprisoned or eluded capture	**47**	**30.3**
Do not fall into any of the above categories	43	27.7

Notes: May 5, 1789, was the day the Estates-General convened. November 10, 1799, was the day when Napoleon overthrew the Directory.

Source: The fates of the revolutionaries were compiled from the brief biographies ("Cast of Main Participants") in Israel, *Revolutionary Ideas*, pp. 709–31. Twelve of the 167 biographies described the careers of men and women who were not revolutionaries or, if sympathetic to the revolution, engaged in politics outside of France: Charles Philippe Comte d'Artois, Charles Alexandre Calonne, Georg Forster, Melchiorre Gioia, Willem van Irhoven van Dam, Friedrich Gottlieb Klopstock, Louis XVII, Jacques Mallet du Pan, Marie Antoinette, Jacques Necker, François-Dominique Toussaint Louverture, and Georg Christian Wedekind. These were excluded from the analysis.

Bordeaux, one in Lyon, and one in Amiens).[308] Eight committed suicide either after apprehension by the authorities or while on the run.[309] One, Louis-Michel Lepeletier, was assassinated by a royalist in a Parisian café. Another, Jean-Paul Marat, was killed by Charlotte Corday while in his bath.[310] In addition to those who died violently, almost a fifth of all revolutionary leaders were also

---

[308] One of those who mounted the scaffold was Antoine-François Momoro, author of the revolutionary slogan "*Liberté, Égalité, Fraternité.*" Antoine Fouquier-Tinville, the chief prosecutor for the revolution, sent many, perhaps most, of these men and women to the scaffold. After the Terror ended, he was arrested on August 1, 1794. After a thirty-nine-day trial conducted with meticulous formality, he himself was sent to the guillotine on May 7, 1795. Just before he met his fate, he wrote a letter in which he asked that his children be told that "their father died unhappy but innocent." Schama, *Citizens*, p. 851; Israel, *Revolutionary Ideas*, pp. 580–1, 606.

[309] For example, the mathematician Nicolas de Condorcet took poison on March 28, 1794, the day after he was caught in a restaurant in a southern suburb. He had been declared an "outlaw," which made him subject to immediate execution. Israel, *Revolutionary Ideas*, p. 554.

[310] Corday, who was politically aligned with the Girondins, was sent to the guillotine. On Corday and the assassination, see Schama, *Citizens*, pp. 729–31, 735–46; McPhee, *Liberty or Death*, p. 205; Israel, *Revolutionary Ideas*, p. 471. Just before her execution, Corday wrote to her father: "Pardon me, my dear Papa, for disposing of my existence without your permission." Bosher, *French Revolution*, p. xxxiii.

imprisoned by the regime at some point during this decade. Since almost all those who died violently were first imprisoned as well, we can conclude that almost 70 percent of all those who were arrested were subsequently executed. In addition to those who died or were imprisoned, one in eight of all leaders either left the country or went into hiding in order to elude capture and imprisonment. Of course, many of those who were imprisoned also attempted (unsuccessfully) to hide from the authorities. Only a quarter of all revolutionary leaders managed to avoid execution, imprisonment, hiding, or exile.[311] Most of them did so either by scrupulously attending to administrative tasks that did not bring them into conflict with one or more of the revolutionary factions or by adroitly shifting allegiance whenever the political winds shifted.[312]

Robespierre was either directly or indirectly responsible for the deaths of most revolutionary leaders. One of his victims was Camille Desmoulins, the editor of *Le Vieux Cordelier*, who had published a condemnation of state-sponsored violence:

You want to remove all your enemies by means of the guillotine! Has there ever been such great folly? Could you make a single man perish on the scaffold, without making ten enemies for yourself from his family or his friends ... I think quite differently from those who tell you that terror must remain the order of the day.[313]

Fifteen days later, on January 4, 1794, Robespierre denounced *Le Vieux Cordelier* as heretical and said that all copies of the paper should be destroyed. Desmoulins retorted: "Well said, Robespierre, but I reply like Rousseau: to burn is not to answer."[314] Because Desmoulins and his ally, Danton, continued to publicly oppose Robespierre's authority as a threat to republican liberty, Robespierre came to see them as political enemies. However, before dealing with them he felt that he must first dispose of those who could lead the Parisian people into the streets.[315] On March 24, Jacques-René Hébert, editor of *Le Père Duchesne*, and nineteen of his street allies went to the guillotine. Although in his paper he had comically described mounting the scaffold as going to "hold

---

[311] Of the 749 deputies serving in the National Convention, 144 died violently during the height of the Terror between March 1793 and July 1794. Most of them were not among the revolution's leaders. McPhee, *Liberty or Death*, pp. 272, 297.

[312] One of those who survived was Jacques-Louis David. David apparently embraced Robespierre after the latter's last address in the Jacobin Club and told him: "[I]f you drink the hemlock, I will drink it too." Although David was imprisoned when Robespierre fell, he escaped the guillotine because he was "esteemed as an artist." Later, after Robespierre had been executed, David decided that he was "repulsive." Israel, *Revolutionary Ideas*, pp. 581, 600.

[313] McPhee, *Liberty or Death*, p. 248.

[314] Israel, *Revolutionary Ideas*, pp. 537, 541, 553–4. For a slightly different rendition of this exchange, see Davidson, *French Revolution*, pp. 211–12.

[315] Doyle states that Robespierre also suspected that the men associated with Hébert – and perhaps Hébert himself – had become British agents. Doyle, *French Revolution*, p. 267.

the hot hand," "look through the republican window," and be "shaved by the national razor," he screamed in fear when he took his own turn at the blade.[316]

Less than two weeks later, on April 5, 1794, Danton and Desmoulins followed Hébert to the guillotine.[317] Although Desmoulins had to be dragged to the scaffold, Danton was impassively defiant, telling the executioner: "Don't forget to show my head to the people. It is well worth the trouble."[318] Five months earlier, on October 31, 1793, the Girondins had sung the "Marseillaise" while they were transported to their execution. At their sentencing, many of them shouted *"Vive la Republique!"* while one of their number, Charles Valazé, committed suicide by stabbing himself in the heart. Although he was already quite dead, the guillotine severed his head from his corpse along with the others.

By this time, executions were so unceremoniously conducted that, on average, each of the twenty-one Girondins were dispatched in less than two minutes.[319] When Philippe Égalité, the Duke of Orléans, was executed six days later, he is reported to have said that he now regretted the part he had played in the fall of the king. However, other reports have him sardonically saying, "Really ... this seems a bit of a joke."[320] Madame Roland mounted the

---

[316] Schama, *Citizens*, p. 816; Pauline Chapman, *The French Revolution: As Seen by Madame Tussaud, Witness Extraordinary* (London: Quiller Press, 1989), p. 162. The "national cleaver," "national ax," and "scythe of equality" were other popular names for the guillotine. Soboul, *The Sans-Culottes*, p. 160. On the arrest and trial of Hébert and his colleagues, see Israel, *Revolutionary Ideas*, pp. 549, 552. Doyle states that the Paris Commune was nothing more than "the docile tool of the Committee of Public Safety" after the execution of Hébert and other sans-culotte leaders. Doyle, *French Revolution*, pp. 270–1.

[317] For accounts of their trial, see Israel, *Revolutionary Ideas*, p. 555; Davidson, *French Revolution*, pp. 216–17.

[318] Israel, *Revolutionary Ideas*, p. 556; Schama, *Citizens*, p. 820; Davidson, *French Revolution*, p. 217. During a discussion of revolutionary virtue with Robespierre, Danton had once said that "[v]irtue is what I practice with my wife every night." Robespierre later commented on the remark in his notebook: "The word virtue made Danton laugh ... How could a man, to whom all idea of morality was foreign, be the defender of liberty?" The incident contributed to the demise of their friendship and political cooperation. Scott, *Robespierre*, p. 219; Doyle, *French Revolution*, pp. 274–5. In one sense Robespierre should not have been surprised by Danton's reply because his rhetoric was often as colorful as it was crude. When Marc-Guillaume Vadier, a member of the Committee of General Security, threatened to "gut that fat turbot Danton," Danton retorted that "he would eat Vadier's brains and shit in his skull." Schama, *Citizens*, p. 814.

[319] Doyle, *French Revolution*, p. 253. The defiant posturing of the Girondins led the Revolutionary Tribunal to forbid the selling of alcohol to the condemned on the last day before their execution so that, in the future, the condemned might be sober as they met their fate. Israel, *Revolutionary Ideas*, p. 513. For Robespierre's campaign against the Girondins and their subsequent trial and execution, see pp. 422–3, 446–8, 512–18. Also see Davidson, *French Revolution*, pp. 156–62.

[320] Schama, *Citizens*, p. 805. Davidson, *French Revolution*, p. 204. Three weeks earlier, Marie Antoinette was executed and her head was lifted high so that the crowd might all view it. The people then cheered *"Vive la nation! Vive le Republique!"* for "many minutes." Israel, *Revolutionary Ideas*, p. 530. Madame Tussaud had been asked to prepare a death mask of the queen and waited for her corpse at the cemetery. When the body arrived, "it was the hour of

scaffold two days after him. As she passed a statue of Liberty in the Place de la Révolution, she loudly cried, "Oh Liberty! How many crimes are committed in thy name!"[321]

On August 1, 1794, the Law of 22 Prairial was repealed and the number of executions dramatically declined. One of the few to be guillotined was Jean-Baptiste Carrier, who had conducted nightly orgies with women he had imprisoned and had presided over the grisly slaughter of thousands of people in the provincial city of Nantes. For these excesses, he was recalled to Paris in disgrace in February 1794. However, he was not referred to the Revolutionary Tribunal until November 23. Protesting that he had only been carrying out orders, he was sent to the scaffold on December 16.[322]

The guillotine was not only one of the most durable images produced by the French Revolution; it was also an integral part of revolutionary political culture. Each execution was a public performance in which the revolution eliminated one of those who did not meet the exacting demands of revolutionary virtue and had therefore forfeited his or her right to exist. The egalitarian characteristics of this performance reinforced the simple, even stark, relation between, on the one hand, the revolutionary people as judge and executioner and, on the other, the condemned as someone who was to be completely and forever exiled from society.

The way in which the condemned acquitted themselves as they went to their fate was publicly noted and remembered as one of the most revealing events in their political career. Most revolutionary leaders accordingly behaved in a manner that affirmed the performance in which they themselves participated. While they certainly believed that they should not die, they also stoically mounted the scaffold while reaffirming their faith in and devotion to the

---

the midday break. The men who unloaded the cart could not see any officials around, no coffins, no grave prepared. They wanted to get off to their own lunch, so they dumped the Queen's body, putting the head between the legs. Marie was able to do her work undisturbed." Chapman, *French Revolution*, p. 150. Tussaud also made death masks of many other victims of the French Revolution, including the king, Robespierre, Marat, Hébert, and the chief executioner of the revolution, Fouquier-Tinville. In some cases, demonstrators spontaneously brought their heads on pikes to her house; in other instances, she was ordered by revolutionary authorities to prepare the masks (pp. 20, 71, 77, 122, 132, 141, 143, 150, 162, 176). On the queen's incarceration and execution, see Schama, *Citizens*, pp. 793–800; Israel, *Revolutionary Ideas*, p. 530. In addition to treason, Marie Antoinette was tried for engaging in lesbian relationships and incest with her son. Andress, *French Society*, p. 137.

[321] Anderson, *Daily Life*, p. 161. Also see Davidson, *French Revolution*, p. 203. In what can only be characterized as a profound mistake in judgment, Roland had long admired Robespierre. Israel, *Revolutionary Ideas*, p. 302. On their increasing alienation, see Thompson, *Robespierre*, vol. 1, pp. 223–4. On Robespierre's own fall from power and execution, see Schama, *Citizens*, pp. 840–5; Israel, *Revolutionary Ideas*, pp. 577–80. For an account of the increasing alienation between the sans-culottes and the Montagnards that made Robespierre's fall possible, see Rude, *The Crowd*, pp. 128–41.

[322] Doyle, *French Revolution*, pp. 282, 285; Israel, *Revolutionary Ideas*, pp. 529, 600.

revolution. Personal rectitude in these last moments of their life was the only way in which they could display their personal virtue, but, somewhat paradoxically, their performance also validated that revolutionary virtue was the appropriate criterion by which they should be judged.

One of the most striking characteristics of the French Revolution is its insistence that betrayal of the people was the gravest crime that a person could commit. To betray the people was to alienate oneself from the Nation through self-centered ambition, avarice, or, as in Carrier's case, a moral impurity that perverted an individual's participation in the revelation (and thus frustrated realization) of the General Will. Offenders had to be eliminated because they were and could only be enemies of the people. While some of these enemies might be only minor hindrances as the revolution was attempting to construct the ideal regime, the process was irreversible in the sense that the revolution must not be permitted to "go back" on itself. Execution of those who betrayed the people guaranteed that the increasing purification of French society would be a one-way street in which those who survived would have the correct character required of the citizen.[323] On March 13, 1793, some months before the Terror began to tally victims, Pierre Vergniaud correctly forecast the result when he addressed the National Convention: "So, citizens, it must be feared that the Revolution, like Saturn, successively devouring its children, will engender, finally, only despotism with the calamities that accompany it."[324] Or, as in

---

[323] It was more difficult to "execute" a rebellious city, but the Committee of Public Safety tried to do that as well. On October 11, 1793, the committee proclaimed that: "The city of Lyons shall be destroyed ... the name of Lyons shall be effaced from the list of cities of the Republic. The collection of houses left standing shall henceforth bear the name of Ville-Affranchie – the Liberated City. On the ruins of Lyons shall be raised a column ... with this inscription: 'Lyons made war on Liberty. Lyons is no more.'" Scott, *Robespierre*, p. 213.

[324] Schama, *Citizens*, p. 714. Rousseau assumed that agreement to an initial social contract would, in McDonald's words, "ensure that society was based on a fundamental community of interests." As a result, minorities on any particular issue could, by definition, not be tyrannized by the majority since they had freely consented to the possibility of being in the minority. Since those who anticipated suppression by the majority would not have consented to the contract, purification of society in that sense was simply a byproduct of the founding of a government. Thus, when Rousseau assumed "that for any society there was only one course of action which could be regarded as just, and that every individual in that society must accept that course as just, owning himself mistaken if he had originally thought otherwise," he did not believe that this would make the state oppressive. McDonald, *Rousseau and the French Revolution*, pp. 33, 39. One of the problems in the French Revolution was the rather poor fit between any of the several constitutions and any notion of a social contract in which consent implied a freedom to leave society. In late eighteenth-century France, that option did not exist for all, but only for a few wealthy people. Thus, purification of society (in the sense of eliminating the particular wills of those who would not conform to the norms required in order to express and participate in the General Will) had to be conducted after the fact of a founding. On the role of this Rousseauian notion of "purification" in the Terror, see Taylor, *Modern Social Imaginaries*, pp. 136–7. On purification as political practice, see Jordan, *Revolutionary Career of Maximilien Robespierre*, pp. 188–90.

the alternative metaphor crafted by Georg Forster, victims of the revolution were consumed by "the majestic lava stream of the revolution which spares nothing and which nobody can arrest."[325]

THE GENERAL WILL AS REVEALED IN SPONTANEOUS DISPLAY AND OFFICIAL RITUAL

The General Will spontaneously generates the people as a collective, gives rise to rules in the form of popular norms, and recognizes the virtuous leader through public performance and direct action. Spontaneous popular action intuitively reveals the correct course of politics because it emerges as the collective will of the people, stripped of individual self-interest and ambition. Much of the revolutionary process in Paris arose from more or less spontaneous expressions of popular sentiment that were filtered through this notion of the General Will as it was interpreted and refined by revolutionary leaders. During the early stages of the revolution, many of these popular acts were genuinely spontaneous in that the political elite had little or no role in their emergence. Later, after popular leaders learned how to mobilize the people in support of particular political goals, spontaneity was largely supplanted by direct appeals and calculated coordination.[326] However, even as the revolutionary elite mastered the tactics of popular mobilization, they remained committed to the revelation of the General Will as the litmus test that proper political decisions must pass.[327]

---

[325] Arendt, *On Revolution*, p. 39. Forster was a German Jacobin who represented the "Republic of Mainz," a city first liberated by French troops but subsequently plundered before being reclaimed by the Prussians.

[326] In Hunt's view, words and symbols, although they have varying meanings, can be used to intentionally reconstitute the very foundation of politics. In the early years of the revolution, the people themselves carried out this reconstitution by spontaneously creating and viscerally responding to new symbols and words. Later, revolutionary authorities attempted, with less success, to divert the revolution using the same tools. Hunt, *Politics, Culture, and Class*, p. 24. "Intention" should be interpreted carefully here because Hunt contends, on the one hand, that both the people and revolutionary leaders were actively searching for a "mythic" grounding for the revolution and, on the other hand, that that grounding, by its very nature, was "continually in flux." In the immediacy of a particular moment, the relative effectiveness of symbols and rhetoric in eliciting an emotional reaction from the people "revealed" what could, possibly, constitute an adequate grounding for the revolution. However, those reactions were unpredictably evolving throughout the period. Intention was, for that reason, not the same thing as effectiveness; in fact, it was more akin to desire (p. 74).

[327] On the decline in the spontaneity of popular demonstrations in Paris, see David Andress, "Politics and Insurrection: The Sans-culottes, the 'Popular Movement,' and the People of Paris" in Andress, *Oxford Handbook of the French Revolution*, p. 407. One of the most ambitious and, perhaps, least successful official attempts to remold popular culture was the adoption of a new calendar with new names for the months and a ten-day week that moved the day of rest (formerly the Sabbath) to the last day of each week. Schama, *Citizens*, pp. 771–4; Hunt, *Politics, Culture, and Class*, pp. 70–1; Ozouf, *Festivals*, pp. 228–31.

Like Robespierre, the revolutionary elite both venerated the people and recognized that they were, as yet, imperfect in the sense that they could not always identify and thus express their innate virtue. As a result, the revolution created festivals, rituals, and symbolic practices through which the General Will might be revealed and could be refined and purified through the increasing perfection of the individual citizen.[328] One of the ways of encouraging this purification of the General Will was the construction of vast public spaces in which, in Israel's words, "the people could appear en masse in national celebrations and festivities as a single body, elevating each other with displays of noble zeal for the public cause."[329] These elaborate constructions became the stages upon which the great festivals of the revolution were performed.

Major festivals held during the French Revolution

Festival of the Federation: Held on July 14, 1790, the first anniversary of the storming of the Bastille. Patriotic celebrations were held throughout France in which the National Guard swore fealty to the nation. In Paris, Louis XVI and the royal family played a central role, along with Lafayette and Talleyrand.

Mirabeau's funeral: Held on April 4, 1791. Some 400,000 people, including almost all of the deputies in the National Assembly, escorted Mirabeau's coffin to the Pantheon where he was entombed after an oration proclaiming him to have been a great revolutionary leader.

Voltaire entombed: On July 10, 1791, Voltaire's ashes were received by the mayor of Paris and placed at the Place de la Bastille where the fortress had once stood. On the following day, Voltaire's remains were escorted to the Pantheon and placed alongside Mirabeau's coffin amid great pomp and ceremony.

Festival of the Unity and Indivisibility of the Republic: Held on August 10, 1793, the first anniversary of the deposition of the king, in order to celebrate the adoption of the new constitution of 1793. A Fountain of Regeneration, modeled on Isis, the Egyptian goddess

---

[328] Hunt emphasizes that the revolutionaries also had to create a new symbolism that could compete with the very powerful image of the king's person as the sacred center of the French nation. That competition coincided with the use of symbolism to "model free men." Hunt, *Politics, Culture, and Class*, p. 55. Taws provides a splendid review of the visual representations and images of the revolution that makes their ephemerality a primary interpretive theme. Richard Taws, *The Politics of the Provisional: Art and Ephemera in Revolutionary France* (University Park: Pennsylvania State University Press, 2013). For particularly evocative discussions of the Festival of the Federation and the Bastille, see pp. 75–95, 97–117.

[329] Israel, *Revolutionary Ideas*, p. 368.

(*cont.*)

of fertility, was constructed on the site where the Bastille once stood. From her breasts spouted water symbolizing virtue. Three thousand doves were released; to each one was attached a banner stating "We are Free! Imitate us!"

Festival of Reason: Held on November 10, 1793. The Cathedral of Notre Dame was chosen as the site in order to make the secular attack on religion more explicit. Inside the cathedral, a mountain, symbolizing the Jacobin left, was constructed with a temple dedicated to "*la philosophie*" at its top. After young girls carrying torches had descended and ascended the mountain, a woman symbolizing "Liberty" came out of the temple and presided over the rest of the proceedings on a throne.

Festival of the Supreme Being: Held on June 8, 1794. A mountain was constructed in the Champ de Mars and a tree of liberty was placed at its summit. Led by Robespierre and the other deputies, an immense procession made its way from the Tuileries to the mountain. Robespierre gave two addresses, one before and one after he had burned a symbolic visage of atheism.

Marat entombed: On September 21, 1794, Marat was entombed in the Pantheon.

Rousseau entombed: On October 11, 1794, Rousseau was entombed in the Pantheon.

Note: Although many of these festivals were held throughout France, the information in this box focuses on the leading celebrations in Paris. Although they were not exactly festivals, I have also included funerals if they entailed mass processions preceding entombment in the Pantheon.

The king, in fact, became one of the most important platforms for displays of the General Will. On July 17, 1789, just three days after the fall of the Bastille, Jean Sylvain Bailly, the newly elected mayor of Paris, presented the king with a tricolor cockade which Louis then put on his hat. That act transformed the cockade from a symbol identifying insurgency into an emblem of the French nation.[330] Three years later, on June 20, 1792, a red bonnet was thrust upon

---

[330] The cockade combined three colors: white, symbolizing the Bourbon monarchy, and red and blue, the traditional colors of Paris. McPhee, *Liberty or Death*, p. 73. The cockade first appeared on June 13, 1789, as a means of identifying the members of the Paris militia who at that time lacked uniforms that might distinguish them from the rest of the citizenry. At first, the cockade had only two colors: red and blue. Lafayette was responsible for the addition of the Bourbon white. Schama, *Citizens*, pp. 387, 454; Lefebvre, *French Revolution*, vol. 1, p. 124.

the king's head.[331] On another occasion, the third anniversary of the fall of the Bastille, the revolutionary government held a celebration on the Champ de Mars where an immense tree, designated "The Tree of Feudalism," had been erected. The tree was decorated with various aristocratic and royal emblems of the *ancien régime* and the king was asked to light what was, in effect, the funeral pyre upon which the tree had been placed. However, he respectfully declined because, in Pauline Chapman's paraphrase, "feudalism no longer existed" and there was thus "no sense in burning it." This was one of the very few occasions in which Louis was not compelled to act upon demand.[332]

The king was also the platform for rhetorical displays. On February 4, 1790, for example, Louis was somewhat reluctantly produced before the National Constituent Assembly, where he swore an oath of fealty to a constitution that had not yet been fully drafted or formally ratified. This occurred after a plot to suppress the assembly and restore the monarchy's full powers had been discovered.[333] On July 14, 1790, the king was again called upon to swear loyalty to the revolution. The occasion was the Festival of the Federation, held in Paris on the first anniversary of the fall of the Bastille.[334] Even the formal title of the king became a symbolic plaything of the revolution in which Louis' consent was imagined as an emphatic marking of irreversible political change.[335] So it was that the National Assembly changed his title from "the King of France and Navarre" to "the King of the French" as he was escorted from Versailles to Paris by "the people" on October 6, 1789.[336]

Revolutionary symbols such as the cockade, the red liberty cap, the figure of Marianne, the tricolor flag, the "Marseillaise," and the slogan "Liberty, Equality, Fraternity" all more or less spontaneously emerged from the actions of the people. In some cases, the revolutionary elite might try out a symbol in order to see how the public might respond. But the litmus test in each instance was the spontaneous adoption of the symbol by the people. This was also true of clothing, such as the type of trousers, shoes, or hat a person might wear. These constituted expressions of political sentiment through association with

---

[331] This was during the June 20, 1792, invasion of the Tuileries. Davidson, *French Revolution*, pp. 91–2. That incident was preceded by an incursion into the Legislative Assembly in which the demonstrators announced: "The people have arrived ... they wait for dignified recognition, finally, of their own sovereignty." Armed with "halberds, pikes, scythes, swords, spits, hatchets, rifles, cutters, knives, and pitchforks," as well as sabers, they proclaimed that "this isn't 2,000 men, but 20 million presenting themselves before you, an entire nation arming itself to fight tyrants, their enemies and yours." They marched through the hall for an hour and forty-five minutes. On the following day, the Legislative Assembly prohibited all such marches in the future. That worked for a time but other, even larger invasions of the hall occurred on March 9 and April 24, 1793. Alpaugh, *Non-Violence*, pp. 109–17, 136, 138. Also see Lefebvre, *French Revolution*, vol. 1, p. 124; Schama, *Citizens*, p. 604; Doyle, *French Revolution*, p. 112; Rude, *The Crowd*, pp. 98–102.

[332] Chapman, *French Revolution*, pp. 115–16.   [333] Lefebvre, *French Revolution*, vol. 1, p. 136.

[334] Lefebvre, *French Revolution*, vol. 1, p. 140.   [335] Hunt, *Politics, Culture, and Class*, p. 57.

[336] Schama, *Citizens*, p. 470. On the rhetorical importance of oaths in revolutionary rituals, see Hunt, *Politics, Culture, and Class*, p. 21.

factions and classes in popular culture.[337] Because they were not designed or premeditated, they were interpreted as possessing an authenticity reflecting the purity of the popular will and thus compelled their adoption by the revolution-ary elite.[338] On October 29, 1793, the National Convention even felt compelled to declare that freedom to dress as one wished was an individual right because the enforcement of social conformity had become so intense.[339] The General Will was also revealed by the aroused emotions of the people in reaction to speeches. Newspapers, pamphlets, and posters often had a similar effect when they encouraged a spontaneous alignment of popular sentiment with what appeared on the printed page.[340]

[337] In the ceremonial opening of the Estates-General, the nobles and clergy of the first and second estates wore traditional costumes reflecting their separate and distinct status in French society while the deputies of the third estate were dressed in plain black cloth. Their different modes of dress were dictated by royal protocol and custom. It was only in October 1789 that the deputies decided to formally abandon the uniforms of their respective orders. McPhee, *Liberty or Death*, p. 68; Schama, *Citizens*, p. 477. The costumes of the revolution, on the other hand, emerged as spontaneously generated popular fashion. Despite this respect for popular fashion, the Legislative Assembly in 1792 banned the wearing of religious uniforms outside of churches. By the end of 1793, only one clerical deputy was bold enough to wear clerical clothing in the National Convention. Israel, *Revolutionary Ideas*, pp. 481, 488.

[338] These symbols and associations took on a life of their own as they developed into practices that created a new and popular political culture that Hunt describes as the "chief accomplishment of the French Revolution." Hunt, *Politics, Culture, and Class*, pp. 15, 53–4, 72, 86. In her interpretation, the French Revolution created, instituted, and fostered the emergence of this new political culture in a process that sometimes had clearly identified agents and sometimes appears to have been the product of spontaneously evolving popular sentiment. On the cultural origins of Marianne and the red liberty cap (the Phrygian cap), see McPhee, *Liberty or Death*, pp. 167–8, 218. Although the Marseillaise and the cockade originated in spontaneous popular practice, the National Convention later turned them into state-sponsored and regulated sym-bols. On May 21, 1795, the display of all signs of political affiliation other than the tricolor cockade were prohibited and the Marseillaise was officially made the national anthem on July 14, 1795 (p. 281). The song was so emotionally inspiring that young girl students were "teaching" soldiers to sing the Marseillaise in Petrograd during a mutinous uprising in 1917. Sean McMeekin, *The Russian Revolution: A New History* (New York: Basic Books, 2017), p. 100. Close behind in popularity was the "Ça ira," in one version of which the second line was "Let's hang the aristocrats from the lanterns." Doyle, *French Revolution*, p. 128.

[339] McPhee, *Liberty or Death*, p. 242; Hunt, *Politics, Culture, and Class*, pp. 59, 81. Hunt also notes that in 1798 the Council of 500 considered making the wearing of the national cockade mandatory while prohibiting foreigners from wearing it. But this was long after the ideological intensity and ferment of the revolution had faded. Five years earlier, the Paris Commune ordered the arrest of any individual who was not wearing the cockade. This was on April 4, 1793, during the height of the Terror. Soboul, *The Sans-Culottes*, p. 189. On September 21, 1793, the National Convention ordered that all women wear the cockade. Andress, *French Revolution and the People*, p. 229.

[340] For instances in which oratory can be said to have contributed to the creation of "the People," see Schama, *Citizens*, p. 168. On literacy rates in revolutionary France and the role of printed matter generally, see Schama, *Citizens*, p. 180; McPhee, *Liberty or Death*, p. 49; Doyle, *French Revolution*, pp. 47–8; Israel, *Revolutionary Ideas*, p. 375; Burrows, "Books, Philosophy, Enlightenment," p. 79.

While they were usually spontaneously adopted, popular symbols alone could not make the masses into idealized "citizens." In order to educate and properly socialize the people, the revolutionary elite "manufactured" other symbols and rituals.[341] In the summer of 1790, for example, some of the foundation stones of the Bastille were carved into likenesses of the fortress and were sent as gifts to each of the departments.[342] The revolution also destroyed symbols of the *ancien régime*. In the days following the deposition of the king, for example, "mountains of statues, busts, portraits, coats of arms, emblems, and inscriptions glorifying monarchs, grandees, courtiers, aristocrats, and cardinals disappeared from sight across France."[343]

The most important of the manufactured symbols was the revolutionary festival.[344] As was the case with many elements of the French Revolution, the festival can be traced back to Rousseau, who had expressed a desire that the "patriotic celebrations" of the Swiss might "be revived" among the French because they accorded "with morality and virtue, which we enjoy with rapture and recall with delight."[345] During the revolution, festivals were organized in order "to make the republic manifest to the people, or the people manifest to itself," in harmony with Rousseau's principles.[346] For Robespierre, the organized festival was a kind of halfway house between the spontaneous expression of the General Will by the people in the streets (which could be corrupted by unvirtuous leaders) and the stifling formality of the national legislature (in which an authentic relationship with the spontaneity of the people was lacking). Properly designed and executed, the revolutionary festival could both educate the people through their participation in symbolic ritual and inspire them by aligning that symbolic ritual with their original "nature."[347]

The first and perhaps the greatest of these celebrations was the Festival of the Federation on July 14, 1790, the first anniversary of the storming of the Bastille.

---

[341] Hunt, *Politics, Culture, and Class*, pp. 12–14, 73–4.

[342] McPhee, *Liberty or Death*, p. 99. One of the stones was also carved into a bust bearing the likeness of Rousseau with an inscription on the base: "*Liberté, Égalité, Fraternité.*" In the annual celebrations of the fall of the Bastille, this bust was carried around the ruins. McDonald, *Rousseau and the French Revolution*, p. 156.

[343] Israel, *Revolutionary Ideas*, p. 262.

[344] Many things could serve as symbolic props for the revolution. On March 4, 1794, for example, Hébert cloaked the "Declaration of Rights" in black at the Cordeliers Club, ritually indicating that "the people" were now in a state of insurrection against the National Convention. When this insurgency was aborted, the "Declaration of Rights" was uncovered. Doyle, *French Revolution*, p. 269; Israel, *Revolutionary Ideas*, pp. 547–8. Schama reports that it was the bust of Liberty (not the "Declaration of Rights") that was veiled. Schama, *Citizens*, p. 815.

[345] Ozouf, *Festivals*, pp. 6, 31.

[346] Taylor, *Modern Social Imaginaries*, p. 123. Also see Hunt, *Politics, Culture, and Class*, pp. 23–4.

[347] Ozouf notes that the "festival was an indispensable complement to the legislative system, for although the legislator makes the laws for the people, festivals make the people for the laws." Ozouf, *Festivals*, pp. 8–9, 12, 198–203.

While sponsored and organized by the National Assembly, this festival was the most spontaneous and exuberant of all those held during the revolution. There were thousands of Festivals of the Federation staged throughout France, but the largest and most complex celebration was in Paris, where some 12,000 paid laborers radically transformed the Champ de Mars for the event. When, despite their efforts, preparation of the site fell behind schedule, thousands of citizens spontaneously joined them. The centerpiece of the festival was the renewal of patriotic oaths by the National Guard and, with the permission of the king, the royal regiments.[348] The latter were included because the minister of war decided that it would be impolitic to abstain and thus declared on June 4 that the king "has recognized in [the upcoming celebrations] not a system of private associations, but a gathering of wills of all the French for common liberty and prosperity." Once committed to the celebration, the royal family became prominent figures in the festivities as Marie Antoinette presented the Dauphin, outfitted in a National Guard uniform, to hundreds of thousands of people, all of them standing in pouring rain.[349]

Although they entailed funeral processions as opposed to festivals, the entombment of revolutionary heroes and the "great men" who had prepared the way for the revolution were also major and spectacular events. Mirabeau's death on April 2, 1791, so moved the National Assembly that it turned a then incompletely constructed church, already one of the largest buildings in Paris, into a mausoleum to be called the "Pantheon." The assembly reserved the right to select who would be entombed there and dictated that that honor could be conferred only after a person's death. On April 4, hundreds of thousands of people, including almost the entire membership of the National Assembly, escorted Mirabeau's body to the Pantheon. Voltaire soon followed him on July 10, 1791. Rousseau was an obvious candidate for entombment but he had despised Paris and thus ordered that he not be buried in that city. This wish was a major reason why his entombment was delayed by the National Assembly. Marat joined Mirabeau and Voltaire in the Pantheon after his assassination. Rousseau, despite his wishes, followed Marat less than a month later after disinterment of his body from its rural, bucolic setting.[350]

---

[348] Hunt contends that the ubiquitous practice of swearing oaths as part of the ritual of a revolutionary festival "commemorated and recreated the moment of the social contract; the ritual words made the mythic present come alive, again and again." Hunt, *Politics, Culture, and Class*, p. 27.

[349] On the Festival of the Federation, see Ozouf, *Festivals*, pp. 13, 16, 26, 33–60.

[350] Rousseau's widow supported the removal of his body to the Pantheon. On October 2, 1793, the National Convention decreed that Descartes' body should also be installed in the Pantheon but that was never done. Not all of Marat made it to the Pantheon because his heart "swung in grisly glory from a streamer" in the Cordeliers Club. On the entombment of Mirabeau, Voltaire, Marat, and Rousseau in the Pantheon, see Israel, *Revolutionary Ideas*, pp. 150–2, 170–1, 173–4, 558, 597–8; Scott, *Robespierre*, p. 217. On December 5, 1792, after Mirabeau's secret correspondence with Louis XVI had been discovered in a locked box, Robespierre

On November 10, 1793, the Paris Commune staged the Festival of Reason. The site was the great cathedral of Notre Dame, renamed the "Temple of Reason," and a shrine dedicated to philosophy was constructed where the high altar had previously stood. A solemn parade of "patriotic maidens in virginal white" was followed by the emergence of a woman in a red "Cap of Liberty" from the shrine. Symbolizing the "Goddess of Reason" and described by one observer as a "masterpiece of nature," she led city officials to the National Convention, where the president fraternally embraced her.[351] Although many deputies and Parisians welcomed this performance as a profound recognition of the supremacy of secular reason over the fantasies of religious belief, there were those, Robespierre among them, who balked at the idea that the revolution could or should be founded on atheism.[352]

One of those who balked was Antoine-Hubert Wandelaincourt, a clerical deputy. As the National Assembly drafted a new constitution, he had contended that the design of the new state should accord with "divine intentions." While Wandelaincourt conceded that "every legislator should by means of the laws summon the citizen to virtue," the state itself should recognize "a sacred and inviolable" commitment to the divine will because, as Rousseau had written in the *Social Contract*, only such a commitment could ensure political and social tranquility.[353] However, hostility to the Catholic Church made religion, particularly in its institutional forms, increasingly incompatible with the revolution.[354] Most importantly, many in the revolutionary elite viewed the Catholic Church as an "alien" institution directed by a foreigner (the pope). At

---

demanded that Mirabeau's body be removed from the Pantheon. The National Convention, however, did not order removal until late August or early September 1794. Schama, *Citizens*, p. 652; Doyle, *French Revolution*, p. 283. On February 8, 1795, as the winds of the revolution shifted, Marat was similarly removed from the Pantheon. As a pretext for its action, the National Convention now decreed that no one should be entombed until ten years after their death. Israel, *Revolutionary Ideas*, pp. 601–2; Doyle, *French Revolution*, p. 287.

[351] On the Festival of Reason, see Ozouf, *Festivals*, pp. 97–102.

[352] McPhee says that probably fewer than half of Parisians regularly took communion by the start of the revolution. McPhee, *Liberty or Death*, p. 8.

[353] Israel, *Revolutionary Ideas*, p. 363.

[354] In his first speech before the third estate, Robespierre warned the Church:

The clergy should be reminded of the principles of the early Church. The old canons provide for the selling of altar vessels to relieve the poor. But there is no need for such desperate remedies. All that is necessary is that the bishops and dignitaries of the Church should renounce that luxury which is an offense to Christian humility; that they should give up their coaches and give up their horses if need be; that they should sell a quarter of the property of the Church, and give it to the poor. (Scott, *Robespierre*, p. 48)

Perhaps the most serious problem that the Church presented to the revolution involved the infallibility of papal doctrinal authority and the consequent hierarchical organization of the clergy. As a competing source of political and social power, the pope, through the Catholic Church, clearly compromised what might otherwise have been the unhampered operation of the General Will. See, for example, Lefebvre, *French Revolution*, vol. 1, p. 40.

the same time, the Church was the proprietor of a reservoir of wealth upon which the National Assembly could draw while liberating the economy from feudal bonds.[355] While most of those who subscribed to Enlightenment principles were indifferent to privately held religious belief, public observance was often interpreted as an implicit endorsement of the *ancien régime*. The street leaders of the Parisian people went even further and attempted to root out even privately held religious belief by suppressing all public performance, requisitioning churches and putting them to use for secular purposes, informally chastising priests through popular action, and publicly committing the revolution to atheism.

Robespierre himself believed in a divinity that he (and many others) called "the Supreme Being." He also held that religious belief was an indispensable pillar in the maintenance of a healthy and stable society. Both of these views were reinforced by Rousseau's theoretical endorsement, as well as by a conviction that a "belief in the divinity and immortality of the soul" was necessary for the "moral fervor" Robespierre strongly preferred as an alternative to reason.[356] As a result, Robespierre's denunciation of those who supported the de-Christianization of French society was probably overdetermined and he described the Festivals of Reason as "ridiculous farces" organized by "men without honor or religion."[357] On November 21, 1793, Robespierre announced to the Jacobin Club that the popular beliefs of the people in a Supreme Being made religion vastly superior to the atheist pretensions of would-be and actual aristocrats.[358] Although the National Convention reiterated the revolution's commitment to religious freedom on

[355] Church property holdings were so vast "that space itself was Catholic: in Paris ... a quarter of the city's area was occupied by monasteries and convents." Furet and Richet, *French Revolution*, p. 19.

[356] Israel, *Revolutionary Ideas*, p. 498; also see p. 364. Stark summarizes Rousseau's interpretation of religion as encompassing these principles: "[T]here is a deity, all-powerful and all-good; there is a life after death with reward for the just and punishment for the wicked; the laws are sacred. Anyone who does not accept these propositions, being anti-social, should be banished." He goes on to quote Rousseau directly: "If anybody, after having publicly accepted these same dogmas, conducts himself as if he did not believe them, he shall be punished by death; he has committed the greatest of all crimes." Immediately following this passage, Stark comments: "At this point one can, almost bodily, see the stern figure of Robespierre looming up behind that of his master, throwing his shadow before him, and, behind Robespierre, the guillotine." Stark, "Literature and Thought," p. 66. On Robespierre's religious beliefs, see Jordan, *Revolutionary Career of Maximilien Robespierre*, pp. 195–9. As Robespierre put it: "If God did not exist ... it would be necessary to invent him" (p. 198). His religious beliefs, however, were entirely distinct from his attitude toward Catholicism, in which priests were to "morality what charlatans are to medicine" (p. 197).

[357] Schama, *Citizens*, p. 778. It is difficult to overstate the hostility of the de-Christianizers to religious belief and practice. Pierre Gaspard Chaumette, for example, contended that women went to church in order to breathe "the cadaverous odor of the temples of Jesus." Jordan, *Revolutionary Career of Maximilien Robespierre*, p. 194.

[358] Israel, *Revolutionary Ideas*, pp. 499–500; Doyle, *French Revolution*, p. 262.

December 6, 1793, popular repression of religious performances and those who presided over them continued.[359]

In what turned out to be one of his last official acts, Robespierre persuaded the National Convention to stage what became the Festival of the Supreme Being. In a speech delivered on May 7, 1794, he outlined "the relations between moral and religious ideas with republican principles." The central theme was that the "true priest of the Supreme Being is Nature itself, its temple is the universe; its religion virtue; its festivals the joy of a great people assembled under its eyes to tie the sweet knot of universal fraternity and to present before [Nature] the homage of pure and feeling ... hearts." When he finished, the convention obediently decreed that "the French people recognize the existence of the Supreme Being and the immortality of the soul" and subsequently ordered that a Festival of the Supreme Being be held on June 8, 1794. Robespierre was elected president of the convention just four days before the ceremony so that he might play a central role in the proceedings.

The festival itself was organized in such detail that it lacked all spontaneity and improvisation, qualities that the other festivals possessed at least to some extent. A gigantic symbolic mountain was constructed on the Champ de Mars with the ubiquitous tree of liberty at its summit. A mass procession led by Robespierre and the other deputies in the National Convention (many of whom were less than willing participants) moved through the streets of Paris to the festival site. A vast crowd had gathered there by the time Robespierre began his first, short address on the glories and challenges of God's work on earth. Carrying a torch that symbolized the light shining from deism, Robespierre then climbed up to the "hideous visage of atheism," which he set on fire. As it burned, a statue depicting "true philosophical wisdom" was revealed. Robespierre then delivered a second address in which he described atheism as a "monster" that the kings "had vomited on France." These proceedings were accompanied by musical arrangements composed for the occasion and a final hymn composed so simply that everyone present could join in the singing.[360]

By 1795, the National Convention had designated five annual festivals to be held on: January 21 (the execution of Louis XVI); July 14 (the storming of the Bastille); July 27 (the fall of Robespierre); August 10 (the deposition of the king); and September 22 (the proclamation of the republic). In October, five "moral festivals" were added, commemorating "Youth, Old Age, Spouses,

---

[359] Israel, *Revolutionary Ideas*, pp. 483–7, 490, 501.

[360] On the Festival of the Supreme Being, see Ozouf, *Festivals*, pp. 107–18; Doyle, *French Revolution*, pp. 276–7; Schama, *Citizens*, pp. 831–6; Jordan, *Revolutionary Career of Maximilien Robespierre*, pp. 199–201. After Robespierre's fall, most deputies thought that his "Cult of the Supreme Being" had to be discarded, even though they themselves were deists. Israel, *Revolutionary Ideas*, pp. 561–9, 604.

Thanksgiving, and Agriculture."[361] However, these events lacked the popular fervor and enthusiasm that had characterized earlier celebrations in which the people's embrace of the General Will had seemed to be so spectacularly manifest.

By this point, many deputies had concluded, some of them reluctantly, that society could not function in the absence of distinctions of class, occupation, and political identity. The utopian elimination of such distinctions (through, for example, universal display of the cockade, uniform personal attire, terms of address, and obligatory participation in public rituals) had revealed a disciplined regimen in which political and social purity triumphed over the effective direction of social and political action. They consequently came to believe that political and social purity had to be sacrificed if France were to survive. After Robespierre's fall, the revolutionary government ceased to make "radical appeals to the people," and symbols of their strength, such as the image of Hercules, were replaced by "abstract, arcanely allegorical, and ... enigmatic" emblems.[362] Some six or seven months later, elite extravagance in the display and consumption of fashionable clothing and fine food openly defied the principles of Jacobin austerity throughout Paris.[363] In the streets, "middle-class dandies who copied the clothes of the earlier court nobility, [strutted] about like peacocks." Known as the "Muscadins," they attacked those who wore clothing favored by the Jacobin sans-culottes, cut down Liberty Trees, howled during theatrical performances they did not like, and took over several of the sections in Paris. On November 9, 1794, they invaded the Jacobin meeting hall, breaking windows and beating those who happened to be there. Two days later, the National Convention closed the meeting hall for good.[364] At about the same time, the National Convention felt compelled to order the replanting of Liberty Trees in all those communes in which they had vanished, either because of neglect or vandalism, along with the punishment of those who had intentionally destroyed the trees.[365]

---

[361] Ozouf, *Festivals*, pp. 119–20, 175–8; McPhee, *Liberty or Death*, p. 300. On the rather secondary importance of the festivals of Châteauvieux and Simoneau that had been held earlier in the revolution, see Ozouf, *Festivals*, pp. 66–79.

[362] Hunt, *Politics, Culture, and Class*, p. 117.

[363] Israel, *Revolutionary Ideas*, p. 602. Under the Directory created in October 26, 1795, the revolutionary leadership moved to a palace, put on new and flamboyant official costumes, and instituted protocols that resembled those of the now defunct French court. Aston, *French Revolution*, p. 51.

[364] Anderson, *Daily Life*, p. 78; Israel, *Revolutionary Ideas*, pp. 599–600; Doyle, *French Revolution*, pp. 282, 284, 287; Furet and Richet, *French Revolution*, pp. 234–5, 238–9.

[365] Ozouf, *Festivals*, p. 339 n. 85. The notion of a "liberty tree" first arose in the American colony of Massachusetts in 1765. David Hackett Fischer, *Liberty and Freedom* (New York: Oxford University Press, 2005), pp. 19–33. The French may have thus borrowed the symbol from the American colonists. On the other hand, the colonists borrowed some of their own symbols from Cromwell's New Model Army (p. 35).

"THE PEOPLE"

In Rousseau's vision, "the people" would be citizens of a small city who would both recognize each other as equals and directly participate in politics within a common site. During the French Revolution, of course, it was never possible for politics to be conducted in that way. However, the vision was still powerful for three reasons. First, the revolutionary elite, including Jacobins, Girondins, and everyone else but the royalists, subscribed to the notion of "the people" and their "General Will" as the fount of political legitimacy. When Girondins identified "the people" as "the Nation" and viewed the national legislature as the vehicle for the General Will, they recognized the impossibility of direct, popular democracy. In rather sharp contrast, the Jacobins, including Robespierre, regarded the people of Paris as a register upon which could be read the authentic and naturally good instincts of an uncorrupted people. The people of Paris could not directly rule France but they could nonetheless coerce those who otherwise held that responsibility.

The second reason why Rousseau's vision was a powerful influence was that there were ambitious and talented political leaders who recognized that the people of Paris could constitute an independent and significant source of power outside formal political institutions. In pursuit of their political ambitions, these leaders exploited and thus reinforced the rhetorical shibboleths which the deputies of the National Assembly honored as ideological principles but often abhorred as canons of practical politics.[366] These principles prevented the National Assembly from using military force to protect its own sanctity when the populace invaded its precincts.[367] The last and perhaps most important reason was that the people of Paris themselves bought into Rousseau's vision, so much so that in several crucial instances they may have saved the revolution.[368] In bringing the king and the royal family to Paris from Versailles,

---

[366] On the popular societies that mobilized the people of Paris in direct action against the National Assembly, see Schama, *Citizens*, pp. 530–1.

[367] Once the National Assembly moved from Versailles to Paris, the revolutionary government was "at the mercy of Paris." Doyle, *French Revolution*, pp. 122–3, 220. An attempt to bring National Guard detachments from the provinces to the capital was rejected because Parisian deputies considered the proposal to be, in Israel's words, a "declaration of war" upon the people. Israel, *Revolutionary Ideas*, p. 281.

[368] The sans-culottes were indirectly influenced by "ideas which, as if by osmosis, circulated from the more cultivated to the humblest members of society; this explains how Rousseau's theories on popular sovereignty were vaguely shared by men who had never read the *Social Contract*." On Rousseau's influence among the sans-culottes, see Soboul, *The Sans-Culottes*, pp. 57, 59, 63, 87–8, 105–7, 243, 245. The sans-culottes particularly embraced Rousseau's injunction that "every law which the people themselves have not ratified is null and void" (p. 99). Also see Lefebvre, *French Revolution*, vol. 1, p. 127; Furet and Richet, *French Revolution*, p. 106. Other scholars are more skeptical. Israel, for instance, says that "there was simply no such thing as a coherent sans-culotte … ideology." He then adds that "the volatility and incoherence of populist sentiment … was indisputable." Israel, *Revolutionary Ideas*, pp. 628–9. On "the absence of class consciousness" among the sans-culottes, see Soboul, *The Sans-Culottes*,

for example, they transformed what had been a rather uncertain political stalemate into the revolutionary dominance of the National Assembly.

The sans-culottes were those who did not wear the knee breeches of the middle and upper classes, who worked with their hands in order to earn a living, and who, although most were literate, lacked a formal education.[369] According to the *Révolutions de Paris*, a leading Jacobin newspaper, the ideal member of the sans-culottes was "a patriot strong in mind and body ... he is the opposite [of] selfish and dislikes those who are such ... [A] republican ... who has only one passion, the lover of order and of equality, of independence and fraternity."[370] But this was an ideal that was seldom met in the social and political reality of revolutionary Paris.[371] Although their leaders were almost indistinguishable from deputies in the National Assembly in terms of their social origins and occupations, most sans-culottes were artisans, shopkeepers, and wage earners.[372] When mobilized in the streets of Paris, the sans-culottes most often demanded that the revolutionary state regulate the supply of grain

---

pp. 1, 23, 42–3, 62, 93. As Harkins notes, Rousseau's theoretical "stress upon a unitary society forced him away from any concept of class warfare." Harkins, "Intellectual Origins of Babouvism," p. 86. As a result, the Montagnards refused to openly appeal to the class interests of the peasants or the sans-culottes; see Lefebvre, *French Revolution*, vol. 2, pp. 113–14.

[369] There were approximately 10,000 clergy in Paris, along with 5,000 nobility and 40,000 "financial, commercial, manufacturing, and professional *bourgeoisie*." The remainder, classed as sans-culottes, composed some nine out of every ten Parisians. Although many of the sans-culottes occupied very diverse class positions, their common interest in the supply and price of bread proved to be "one of the most solid of the links that bound [them] together." Rude, *The Crowd*, pp. 12, 22.

[370] McPhee, *Liberty or Death*, p. 222. On the understanding of "fraternity" among the sans-culottes, see Soboul, *The Sans-Culottes*, pp. 153–8.

[371] An equally misleading characterization was promoted by Jacques-René Hébert, one of the popular leaders of the sans-culottes. In his paper, *Le Père Duchesne*, Hébert described a sans-culotte as a "foul-mouthed independent artisan craftsman, father of a family, shouldering responsibilities for politics at home while his sons fight on the frontiers, proclaiming his straightforward radical views on political issues." Paraphrased in Andress, *French Society*, p. 132. Also see Popkin, "Revolution and Changing Identities," pp. 243–5. In different ways, both images conformed with Rousseauian principles: the first as a representation of a faithful adherent of the thinker's precepts and the second because conventional civility and polite manners were the corrupt practices of "charlatans." Schama, *Citizens*, p. 734. For a description of "the official costume for a 'true patriot,'" including how conformity with its image altered Parisian fashion, see Anderson, *Daily Life*, p. 74. For a description of Hébert and the image he crafted of the typical sans-culotte, see Davidson, *French Revolution*, p. 181–2.

[372] The sans-culotte leaders were drawn from the professions and the ranks of comparatively well-to-do artisans. For a general description of artisans as a social class, see Andress, *French Revolution and the People*, chapter 2. On the class characteristics of the sans-culottes, see Soboul, *The Sans-Culottes*, pp. 2–45, 256–8. Soboul concludes that the "sans-culottes can be clearly defined only when compared to the aristocracy; when compared to the bourgeoisie, the distinction becomes less clear" (p. 20). For his part, Rude contended that the bourgeoisie were "more or less synonymous with urban middle classes – bankers, stockbrokers, merchants, large manufacturers, and professional men of every kind," while the sans-culottes in a "purely social sense" included "the small shopkeepers, petty trades, craftsmen, journeymen, labourers,

at fixed prices, require that the face value of the currency be honored in commercial transactions, and severely punish those who hoarded food supplies or otherwise speculated on the suffering of the people.[373] Hunger was thus a major factor driving their involvement in revolutionary politics, although their leaders often attached a broader political agenda to their demands.[374] In response, the revolutionary government provided bread to the people of Paris.[375]

Although the sans-culottes dominated about half of the forty-eight sections in Paris, the hardcore activists among them numbered, at most, some 3,000 men and women. In a crisis, however, their leaders could mobilize tens of thousands of armed people (the pike was the most common weapon carried in these demonstrations).[376] Although Robespierre envisioned the sans-culottes as "the people" from whom the General Will emanated, he was forced to compete for influence with popular leaders such as Hébert. This competition ultimately led him to subordinate rights in private property to a right to existence. In a speech delivered on December 2, 1793, for example, he declared: "The primary right is that of existence; the primary social law is therefore that which guarantees to all members of society the means for existing; all others are subordinate to these laws."[377] However, Robespierre never possessed the popular charismatic appeal that could mobilize and direct the people of Paris and they remained an unreliable political resource.[378] They were crucially important in the elimination of the Girondins but failed to rise up against the National Convention when the latter turned against him.

vagrants, and city poor." Rude, *The Crowd*, pp. 253, 256. More generally, see Andress, "Politics and Insurrection," pp. 401–17.

[373] Schama, *Citizens*, pp. 602–3.

[374] Hunt, *Politics, Culture, and Class*, p. 40; Sydenham, *The Girondins*, p. 167; Soboul, *The Sans-Culottes*, pp. 30, 45, 47–51, 59–60. As one revolutionary writer asked in 1789: What good was "peace and liberty to men dying of hunger? What use would a wise constitution be to a people of skeletons?" Schama, *Citizens*, pp. 331–2; also see pp. 308, 371. During the early days of the Russian Revolution, Alexander Kerensky toured Russian troops in an effort to raise morale for the fight against the Germans. After one of his speeches, "a simple soldier" asked him a similar question: "What good are land and freedom to me if I'm dead?" McMeekin, *Russian Revolution*, pp. 152–3.

[375] Soboul, *The Sans-Culottes*, p. 256. Doyle notes that bread composed three-quarters of the average person's diet and the poorest laborer spent, on average, between a third and half of his earnings on procuring it. Doyle, *French Revolution*, p. 22. On legislation regulating the supply, price, and content of bread during the revolution, see Israel, *Revolutionary Ideas*, p. 507.

[376] Schama, *Citizens*, pp. 720–1. Because of its symbolic and practical importance, Robespierre described the pike as "in a sense sacred." Davidson, *French Revolution*, p. 91. Also see Soboul, *The Sans-Culottes*, p. 102, 226–8. On the organization and political activities of the sections, see pp. 163–221.

[377] Soboul, *The Sans-Culottes*, p. 59.

[378] Jordan, *Revolutionary Career of Maximilien Robespierre*, p. 60.

From the very beginning of the revolution in the summer of 1789, street demonstrators targeted individuals whom they often arbitrarily identified as "enemies of the people," stringing them up from lamp posts or – sometimes and – parading their decapitated heads on pikes through the city.[379] The most dramatic and spontaneous of these demonstrations almost always involved violence. However, fewer than 100 of the 750 protests mounted by the sans-culottes in Paris during the revolution resulted in injury or death.[380] Most demonstrations were noisy, rowdy, and intended to intimidate the targets of their animus but, for all that, peaceful.

POPULAR DEMONSTRATIONS AND INSURGENCIES IN PARIS

The threat of popular violence in the capital was more or less omnipresent throughout the first five years of the revolution (see Table 4.4 for short descriptions of the major demonstrations in which the national legislature was either invaded and/or demonstrators summarily executed one or more people).[381] Some of these events, such as the fall of the Bastille, have already been described. This section briefly notes some of the other major incidents. For example, on August 10, 1792, the people of Paris, accompanied by detachments of the National Guard controlled by the sections of the city, assaulted the Swiss guards who protected the royal family. In a separate action, the monarchist Feuillants Club was also attacked. Several leading monarchists were killed and one of them, the editor of a royalist journal, had his head paraded on

---

[379] Schama, *Citizens*, p. 445. Sutherland suggests that "the *post-mortem* humiliation" of the crowd's victims, in the form of "decapitation, dragging the corpse, triumphal parades of severed heads, dismembering, and souvenir taking," had its origins in similar, although considerably more subdued, practices by the pre-revolutionary royal government. Sutherland, "Urban Violence," p. 279.

[380] In a very careful enumeration of popular protests in Paris, Alpaugh found that "only 7 percent" of "marches ever descended into bloodshed" (18 of 251) and only 12 percent of "street protests" became violent (88 of 754). "Threats of violence" were somewhat more frequent. Alpaugh, *Non-Violence*, pp. 3–5, 14. See pp. 211–52 for a list of all protests and marches during the revolution. McPhee notes that popular protest was endemic even before the revolution began. Citing Guy Lemarchand's work, he notes that "there were no fewer than 4,400 'troubles' in the countryside" between 1720 and 1788. Peter McPhee, "A Social Revolution? Rethinking Popular Insurrection in 1789" in Andress, *Oxford Handbook of the French Revolution*, p. 165. Whether or not these popular protests, along with changes in national institutions, constituted a "social revolution" is raised in a very different context by Gordon Wood: "In fact, it is now doubtful whether any such class upheaval occurred even in the French Revolution. If the French Revolution should turn out not to be a real revolution, after all, then there is obviously something wrong with our generic or sociological sense of what constitutes a revolution." Gordon Wood, *The Radicalism of the American Revolution* (New York: Vintage, 1991), p. 371n.

[381] For example, protestors marched through the Legislative Assembly on six occasions between April and June 1792. Alpaugh, *Non-Violence*, pp. 107–9.

TABLE 4.4. *Popular protest and violence in Paris and Versailles during the revolution*

Date of incident	Description	Ostensible motivation
June 30, 1789	Four thousand people storm a prison and release ten French Guards who had mutinied against the crown	Early manifestation of popular sovereignty and opposition to the king
July 14, 1789	Storming of the Bastille; several soldiers are killed; the commander of the garrison and the mayor of Paris are decapitated and their heads paraded through the city on pikes	Confiscation of gunpowder for muskets
July 22, 1789	The Intendant of Paris is decapitated and his heart ripped out of his chest; his head, along with that of his father-in-law, a former government official, is paraded through the city on a pike	The victims were accused of complicity in a plot to starve the city
October 5, 1789	People from Paris invade the National Assembly at Versailles	Demand for bread and punishment of troops who had trampled upon the revolutionary cockade
October 6, 1789	Two bodyguards are killed and decapitated at the royal palace in Versailles	Revenge for the killing of a man while the bodyguards were defending the royal family
July 17, 1791	Two men are killed on the Champ de Mars during a mass signing of a petition; fifty more people die when the National Guard attempts to disperse the crowd	The two men were suspected of attempting to sabotage the platform upon which the petition was to be signed
April 29, 1792	Fifteen hundred men armed with rifles march through the Legislative Assembly; there are five more invasions of the hall between April and June	Although these demonstrations were permitted by the assembly, the protestors were clearly demonstrating their ability to intimidate the deputies
June 20, 1792	Demonstrators parade through the hall of the Legislative Assembly and then, numbering more than 10,000 people, invade the Tuileries and accost the king in his apartment; they peacefully disperse after the king again swears loyalty to the constitution, puts on a liberty cap, and drinks the nation's health	Protest against the king's misuse of authority

Date	Event	Demand/Note
August 10, 1792	About 600 troops are killed while defending the royal family at the Tuileries; about a hundred of these soldiers are summarily executed	The troops had fired on people as they attempted to take possession of the royal family
September 2–6, 1792	Over 1,000 prisoners are taken from confinement and summarily executed	The prisoners were suspected of disloyalty to the revolution
May 1, 1793	Around 8,000 people declare that they are in a state of insurrection and march on the National Convention	Demands for price controls on bread and higher taxes on the wealthy
May 27, 1793	Sans-culottes invade the National Convention	Demands for abolition of a commission that had ordered the arrest of popular leaders
May 31, 1793	Sans-culottes again invade the National Convention	A variety of demands, the most important of which was for the arrest of Girondin leaders
June 2, 1793	About 80,000 people, including detachments of the National Guard, surround and lay siege to the National Convention	Demand that the National Convention order the arrest of the leading Girondin deputies
September 5, 1793	Thousands of sans-culottes invade the National Convention	Demands for emergency legislation and that the convention "make terror the order of the day"
April 1, 1795	Sans-culottes occupy the National Convention	Demand for "Bread and the Constitution of 1793"
May 20, 1795	Sans-culottes break into the National Convention and occupy the benches of the deputies; one of the deputies who attempts to bar their way is beheaded	Demand for "Bread and the Constitution of 1793"
October 4, 1795	Some 25,000 royalists, Catholics, and sans-culottes rise up against the National Convention and are dispersed only after hundreds are killed battling armed Jacobins and the regular army	Demand for new elections and prosecution of those who were responsible for the Terror

Note: This list contains only those incidents in which Parisians either invaded the hall of the national legislature or summarily took the lives of one or more people, between June 30, 1789, and October 4, 1795. The list is almost certainly incomplete.
Sources: For sources, see the text.

a pike.[382] The deposition and imprisonment of the king were followed, on September 2–6, 1792, by a coordinated assault on the city prisons led by section officials in which thousands of inmates, including many who had taken no part in politics, were killed.[383] The Princesse de Lamballe, a close friend of the queen, was decapitated and her head was taken on a pike to the Temple, where the royal family was incarcerated, so that Marie Antoinette would see it.[384] The demonstrators also impaled a nobleman and, while he was still alive, took him to the Legislative Assembly.[385]

On May 1, 1793, some 8,000 people from the Faubourg Saint-Antoine declared that they were in a state of insurrection and marched against the National Convention. There they presented a petition demanding that controls be imposed on the price of bread and that taxes be levied on the wealthy. The demands were accompanied by an ultimatum: "If you do not accept these measures, we shall declare ourselves, we who wish to save the nation, to be in a state of insurrection: 10,000 men have gathered outside the doors of the hall." Montagnards openly supported this insurgency in order to ensure sans-culotte aid in their competition with the Girondins. As a police spy concluded when filing his report, the "Jacobins know only too well that the people cannot be resisted when one needs them." On the following day, the convention passed

---

[382] Israel, *Revolutionary Ideas*, p. 257; Lefebvre, *French Revolution*, vol. 1, pp. 236–8; Doyle, *French Revolution*, pp. 189–90; Rude, *The Crowd*, pp. 104–7. While Robespierre did not publicly participate in the August 10 insurrection, Davidson concludes that he was one of its principal organizers. Davidson, *French Revolution*, pp. 98–9, 105. Thompson more or less agrees. Thompson, *Robespierre*, vol. 1, pp. 250–6. For a particularly careful explication of Robespierre's role, see Jordan, *Revolutionary Career of Maximilien Robespierre*, pp. 106–12. For Robespierre's own explanation of his relative lack of involvement in both the August 10 and September 2–5 events, see Robespierre, *Virtue and Terror*, pp. 41, 44.

[383] Schama describes the September massacres as "the oracular utterance of the General Will expressed in an oblation of blood and bone." Schama, *Citizens*, p. 639. For descriptions of the September massacres, see Doyle, *French Revolution*, pp. 191–2; Tackett, *Coming of the Terror*, pp. 211–14. A few days later, on September 9, a mob at Versailles violently took possession of fifty prisoners who were being moved to Paris from Orléans. The heads of forty-four of them were stuck on the gates outside the royal palace. McPhee, *Liberty or Death*, p. 162. While Israel concedes that "little documentary evidence" points to "the premeditated complicity of leading Montagnard politicians," he still concludes that they were largely responsible for the organization of the massacres. Israel, *Revolutionary Ideas*, pp. 271, 273. Thompson merely notes that, "[s]o far as is known, [Robespierre] never said a word or raised a finger against the massacres" and, in fact, attempted "to use them as a cloak for political assassination." Thompson, *Robespierre*, vol. 1, pp. 273–5. And, in fact, the Jacobin Club later accepted "responsibility for the September massacres," embracing them "as the result of revolutionary zeal" and transforming that interpretation into "a cardinal point of the Jacobin faith." Sydenham, *The Girondins*, p. 131; Thompson, *Robespierre*, vol. 1, p. 291.

[384] Andress, *French Revolution and the People*, p. 184. Her head was later taken to Marie Grosholtz (Madame Tussaud), who was compelled to take it into her lap in order to prepare a death mask. Chapman, *French Revolution*, p. 141.

[385] Alpaugh, *Non-Violence*, p. 133.

legislation imposing a maximum price on bread and granted local officials authority to search for and requisition hidden supplies.[386]

Less than a month later, on May 25, the Paris Commune sent a deputation to the National Convention and demanded abolition of a commission that had ordered the arrest of Hébert and other sans-culotte leaders. In response, Maximilien Isnard, a leading Girondin, met them head on: "I tell you in the name of the whole of France that if these perpetually recurring insurrections ever lead to harm to the parliament chosen by the nation, Paris will be annihilated, and men will search the banks of the Seine for traces of the city."[387] The next day, Robespierre urged the people of Paris to put an end to the commission by rising up against "the corrupt deputies" who had created it. However, the turnout on that day was small. On the following day, the Montagnards managed to attract more people who then invaded the convention and, by intimidating the deputies, compelled abolition of the commission. The sans-culotte leaders were then released. When the crowd dispersed, however, the Girondins demanded reconsideration of the commission's dissolution, alleging that some of the protestors had been able to vote illegally because they were intermingled with deputies in the convention hall. The commission was then reinstated.[388]

Responding to the National Convention's defiance, armed sans-culottes first confronted the General Council of the Paris Commune on May 31, 1793, and announced that its authority had been revoked by the "sovereign people" but could be reinstated if the council accepted a revolutionary program. This included: (1) new taxes on the wealthy; (2) the arrest of Girondin leaders; (3) the creation of an army of sans-culottes for the enforcement of revolutionary edicts; and (4) a wage of forty sous per day for sans-culottes bearing arms. After the council had endorsed this program, the sans-culottes marched to the National Convention. Girondins fought with them but the sans-culottes soon took control of the streets and entered the hall. Even though National Guard detachments, along with the sans-culottes, cut all communication between the convention and the rest of France, and even though armed sans-culottes were "standing about the aisles, waving pikes and rifles, cheering or scowling ominously," the deputies refused to comply with their demands. The sans-culottes then informed the convention that the "people" insisted that Marat and Robespierre be given authority over the future course of the revolution. Robespierre himself declared his support for their revolutionary program. After the deputies had deliberated for sixteen

---

[386] Doyle, *French Revolution*, pp. 229, 265; Israel, *Revolutionary Ideas*, p. 436; Soboul, *The Sans-Culottes*, p. 130. Hunger was a fact of life in Saint-Antoine because it was one of the poorest faubourgs in Paris. Davidson, *French Revolution*, p. 148.

[387] Sydenham, *The Girondins*, pp. 174–5.

[388] Schama, *Citizens*, pp. 721–2; Israel, *Revolutionary Ideas*, pp. 441–2. Israel states that this was "the first time" that Robespierre "directly instigated armed insurrection."

hours (from six in the morning until ten at night), the masses outside the hall dissipated. The deputies then referred their demands to the Committee of Public Safety and took no further action.[389]

Two days later, on June 2, the leaders of the Parisian sections mobilized some 80,000 people who surrounded the National Convention and demanded the immediate arrest of the leading Girondin deputies. Detachments from the National Guard (under the control of the sections) deployed cannons and forced deputies back into the hall when they tried to leave. Sans-culottes once again invaded the convention, accosting deputies in the aisles and occupying their benches. The siege lasted for hours until, finally, the National Convention ordered the arrest of the Girondin deputies, most of whom were still in the hall. After that vote, Pierre Vergniaud, one of those whose arrest had been ordered, offered "the Convention a glass of blood to gratify its thirst."[390]

On September 5, 1793, popular leaders utilized the authority of the Paris Commune to shut workplaces in the city in order to free the people for yet another assault on the National Convention.[391] With the formal backing of the Jacobins, thousands of people marched on the convention and invaded the hall. One of their leaders, Pierre Gaspard Chaumette, announced their purpose: "Legislators, the immense gathering of citizens come together yesterday and this morning ... has formed but one wish ... it is this: Our subsistence, and to get it, apply the law!" They specifically demanded the passage of emergency military and economic legislation that would enable newly created "Revolutionary Armies" to scour the countryside in a search of those who had hoarded food or otherwise harbored unpatriotic sentiments. Arriving later on the same day, a delegation from the Jacobin Club, led by Robespierre and accompanied by representatives from every one of the forty-eight sections in Paris, demanded that the imprisoned Girondins be put on trial. The deputies acceded to most of their demands, including a Jacobin insistence that the convention "make terror the order of the day." However, the convention refused to provide a guillotine on wheels for each of the newly created "Revolutionary Armies."[392]

---

[389] Schama, *Citizens*, pp. 722–3; Israel, *Revolutionary Ideas*, pp. 443–5; Doyle, *French Revolution*, p. 234.

[390] Israel, *Revolutionary Ideas*, pp. 425–6, 446–8; Doyle, *French Revolution*, p. 235; Schama, *Citizens*, pp. 723–4.

[391] Jordan noted that there was "an eclipse of the sun that threw a great darkness over the militants" as they prepared "to march on the Convention." Jordan, *Revolutionary Career of Maximilien Robespierre*, p. 176.

[392] McPhee, *Liberty or Death*, p. 212; Doyle, *French Revolution*, pp. 250–1; Davidson, *French Revolution*, p. 186. Israel's account downplays both the significance of this demonstration and Montagnard support for its leaders. Israel, *Revolutionary Ideas*, p. 505. For a discussion of whether or not the convention explicitly made "terror the order of the day," see Edelstein, "What Was the Terror?," p. 456.

A year later, in the second half of March 1795, the people of Paris marched on the National Convention on at least five occasions. On April 1, thousands of sans-culottes again invaded the hall, demanding "Bread and the Constitution of 1793," along with the release of those Montagnards who had been arrested after Robespierre's fall from power. After the National Guard arrived on the scene, the protestors were dispersed easily.[393] This was a prologue to one of the last mass insurgencies in Paris, in which the sans-culottes again broke into the National Convention on May 20, 1795. This time they carried, on a pike, the head of one of the deputies who had tried to prevent them from entering the hall. One of the demonstrators then ordered the deputies to "[g]et out of here; we are going to act as the Convention ourselves." For eleven hours, those sans-culottes who were able to squeeze into the hall harangued deputies with their now familiar demands for bread and the 1793 constitution. However, they more or less peacefully dispersed after regular troops and National Guard detachments massed in the nearby streets.

Thousands of sans-culottes again marched on the National Convention the next day and invaded the hall once more. Although they attempted, as before, to intimidate the deputies into granting their demands, they again left without accomplishing anything significant. This time, however, the National Convention retaliated by surrounding the center of the insurgency, the Faubourg Saint-Antoine, with troops and arresting thousands of those associated with the protests. Several dozen, including those who had murdered the deputy on May 20, were sent to the guillotine. Sixty-one Montagnard deputies were expelled from the convention, six of whom were tried for treason, convicted, and given death sentences (four committed suicide before they went to the guillotine).[394]

On October 4, 1795, a remarkably broad coalition of monarchists, Catholics, and sans-culottes rose up against the National Convention. Demanding new elections and punishment of those who had participated in the Terror, 25,000 people, including National Guard units controlled by the sections, marched through the streets of Paris. Although royalist sympathies probably motivated most of the protestors, they also mobilized under themes of direct democracy that were reminiscent of earlier demonstrations before Robespierre fell from power. They were met by armed Jacobins, detachments of the regular army, and artillery batteries commanded by Napoleon Bonaparte. After negotiations between the demonstrators and the convention's defenders broke down, Napoleon's cannons opened fire on the insurgents and

---

[393] Andress, *French Revolution and the People*, p. 235; Israel, *Revolutionary Ideas*, p. 605; McPhee, *Liberty or Death*, pp. 285–6.

[394] Soboul, *The Sans-Culottes*, p. 106; Andress, *French Revolution and the People*, p. 236; Israel, *Revolutionary Ideas*, pp. 608–10; Furet and Richet, *French Revolution*, pp. 248–52; Davidson, *French Revolution*, pp. 238–9; Rude, *The Crowd*, pp. 142–59. Israel calls the protests of May 20 and 21 "the biggest popular outbreak in Paris of the entire Revolution since 1792."

the ensuing battle between these more or less evenly matched forces continued for seven hours. Hundreds of people died in the fighting.[395]

In general, the French Revolution was not extraordinarily violent.[396] However, both mass executions in the provinces and the wending of carts through the streets of Paris as they carried the condemned to the guillotine were spectacular events in which the performance itself became a fundamental feature of the revolution. Schama, for example, concluded that "violence was not just an unfortunate side effect from which enlightened Patriots could selectively avert their eyes, it was the Revolution's source of collective energy. It was what made the Revolution revolutionary." He then goes on to say that this violence was, in part, the product of an "anticapitalist, antimodernist fury" that he describes as "Rousseau with a hoarse voice and sharpened with bloody-minded impatience."[397] But Schama's psychological interpretation of the appeal of violence to the masses probably inverts the relationship between summary executions and the ideology of the revolution. The revolution did not merely, if at all, release the inhibitions of the masses and revolutionary leaders as they struck down those who they viewed as their enemies. The revolution, instead, authorized political murder because it eliminated those who did not spontaneously, authentically, and unreservedly commit themselves to the realization of the General Will. In pursuit of the Rousseauian millennium, executions constituted a cleansing of the body politic in which second chances to prove your worthiness as a citizen were rare.[398] And, even where second chances appeared, many of the condemned refused to take them.

Schama also identified the "core problem of revolutionary government" as turning on "efforts to manage popular violence on behalf of, rather than against, the state." This was certainly the case for Robespierre and his Jacobin allies, but underpinning this problem was the even more intractable disjunction between, on the one hand, the revolution's legitimating doctrine of direct, unmediated expression of the General Will and, on the other hand, the

---

[395] Israel, *Revolutionary Ideas*, pp. 627–8; Rude, *The Crowd*, pp. 160–77.

[396] Edelstein, for example, points out that the body counts per capita in the American and French revolutions were similar. Edelstein, "What Was the Terror?," p. 465.

[397] Schama, *Citizens*, pp. 447, 531, 615, 618, 631–9, 859. The interpretation of violence varies quite a bit among historians. Some of them, like Schama, view street violence, mass executions, and the excesses of civil war in the Vendée as often gratuitous and, given what they view as the rather meager accomplishments of the revolution, inexcusable. Others see the same events as inevitable corollaries of significant and necessary social and political change. For brief reviews of the literature, see Schama, *Citizens*, pp. 791–2, 859–61; Edelstein, "What Was the Terror?," pp. 459–64. Also see Hanson, *Contesting the French Revolution*, pp. 162–70; Jack Censer and Lyn Hunt, "Imaging the French Revolution: Depictions of the French Revolutionary Crowd," *American Historical Review* 110: 1 (2005), p. 38. Soboul is somewhere in between. Soboul, *The Sans-Culottes*, pp. 130–1.

[398] On April 15, 1794, for example, Saint-Just justified this cleansing of the revolution of "traitors" and "moral corruption" as the primary task confronting the true revolutionary. Israel, *Revolutionary Ideas*, p. 557.

administrative necessities associated with ruling a nation of some twenty-eight million people. During the French Revolution, popular violence *was* democracy within the Rousseauian frame, both in theory because "the people" alone could authentically express the General Will, and in practice because blood shed by the people saved the revolution in several critical moments, such as the storming of the Bastille. Popular violence had to be managed because it could not be eliminated.[399]

CONCLUSION

Assuming that a declaration of principles and/or a formal constitution is a necessary element in the founding of a modern state, the French state was founded at least twelve times between 1789, when the Declaration of the Rights of Man and of the Citizen was decreed, and 1870, with the creation of the Third Republic. Although the drafting of new documents has become less frequent over the last century and a half, there have still been three new constitutions.[400] None of them, including the present constitution, have solved the unavoidable contradiction between the (mythical) sovereignty of the General Will and the reality that representative political institutions are necessary in a modern democracy. As a result, conflict between them became the endemic inheritance of the modern French state, with its many subsequent constitutions, coups, and political crises.[401]

The General Will is the only ground upon which sovereignty can be erected, but the conditions for its continuous revelation are incompatible with an organized state. The problem arises out of Rousseau's foundational dilemma:

---

[399] Schama, *Citizens*, p. 623. For a description of potential reforms that might have enabled the revolutionary government to "recapture ... the state's monopoly of authorized violence," see p. 707.

[400] Davidson, *French Revolution*, p. 248; Fitzsimmons, "Sovereignty and Constitutional Power," p. 213.

[401] In Arendt's view, the multiplicity of constitutions in the French Revolution and throughout the subsequent history of the nation evidenced "what should have been obvious from the beginning, namely that the so-called will of a multitude (if this is to be more than a legal fiction) is ever-changing by definition, and that a structure built on it as its foundation is built on quicksand." In that connection, she also describes the many constitutions that were created during and after the revolution as an "avalanche" in which "the very notion of constitution disintegrated beyond recognition." Arendt, *On Revolution*, pp. 117, 154–6. Taylor notes that the contradiction between the notion of the General Will and representative democracy could be resolved only "through some generally accepted forms of representative government" *if* those forms "at the same time become part of the popular social imaginary." He thus maintains that reason alone cannot resolve the contradiction between a large nation-state and direct democracy and must be supplemented, if not entirely displaced, by the emotional appeal of mythologized ideology. Taylor believes that "republican France" ultimately discovered a viable combination of these two things after the adoption of manhood suffrage. One could question this conclusion. Taylor, *Modern Social Imaginaries*, pp. 138–41.

The General Will can only be manifested by the people themselves in direct, mutually consultative communication *but* a city-state in which that kind of politics might be possible is clearly not a feasible model for a large nation-state.[402] Writing in 1965, Furet and Richet referred to "the prejudice against parliamentary institutions" as "a particularly strong tradition of French public life."[403] That tradition is still alive today because it is constantly fed by a profound contradiction in the French conceptualization of sovereignty.[404]

It is in precisely that way that the Declaration of the Rights of Man and of the Citizen in 1789 should be considered the founding of the French state even though it was in effect for only four years (two if we consider approval of the constitution of 1791 as its formal ratification).[405] The declaration melded the

---

[402] Bateman contends that

> a new generation of self-identified radical republicans gradually converged on a narrative of French political community that reinterpreted and reaffirmed republicans' commitment to popular sovereignty and universal suffrage [in the latter third of the nineteenth century]. They argued that (1) the revolution had regenerated France by redistributing property, creating a pantheon of heroes and a new political iconography, and establishing the sovereignty of the people as the defining feature of the nation. But (2) in a break with earlier republican traditions, this new generation insisted that the direct action of the people was no longer appropriate to modern conditions. Instead, the people must look to universal suffrage as the only appropriate manifestation of their sovereignty.

> David Bateman, *Disenfranchising Democracy: Constructing the Electorate in the United States, the United Kingdom, and France* (New York: Cambridge University Press, 2018), p. 276; also see pp. 290–3). This was but one of many attempts to reconcile the Enlightenment and Rousseau in French politics but, as Bateman notes, the Third Republic in which this vision was proffered did last much longer than other post-revolutionary regimes. As Bateman also notes, one of the enduring alternatives to republican regimes in the nineteenth century was a combination of monarchy and Bonapartism, but this was due to the fact that republican regimes, given the nature of the French founding, were so unstable. Also see Davidson, *French Revolution*, p. 246.

[403] Furet and Richet, *French Revolution*, p. 265.

[404] Napoleon overcame the problem of melding representative government and direct democracy by imagining that he himself was the embodiment of the General Will and could thus act both in the name of the people and as the people themselves. In Hunt's words, Napoleon "announced himself to be the voice of the people. In his view, there was no problem about the location of the Nation, charisma or society's center." Hunt, *Politics, Culture, and Class*, p. 48. But, as Arendt observes, "the burden or the glory of dictatorship" could only temporarily pose as "the nation-state's fictive ideal of unanimity." As she goes on to say, "it was not will but interest, the solid structure of a class society, that bestowed upon the nation-state ... its measure of stability." Arendt, *On Revolution*, pp. 154–5. In the French case, however, such a class-based solution has not been available because it so flagrantly violates the mythical ideal of the General Will as the foundation of state legitimacy. France has thus been condemned to alternate between the streets and the strongman.

[405] Bosher contends that "the National Constituent Assembly of 1789 established principles and a tradition, even though its own constitution was short-lived." Those principles have since evolved into "liberal doctrines" that continue to be grounded in their "eighteenth-century ideas of liberty and the General Will." Bosher, *French Revolution*, p. 272.

metaphysical conception of a "will of the people," the ritual granting of sovereignty to a new state, and the imbrication of a transcendent social purpose in that state. The problem was, as almost immediately became apparent, that a politically stable state could never actually be organized on the basis of the principles of that declaration. Because there was no role for history or tradition in the Declaration of the Rights of Man and of the Citizen, there was no way to cloak or obscure the contradiction between Rousseau's General Will and the governing of a large nation. And because "reason" (the root cause of hostility to history and tradition) has played such a privileged role in the conceptualization of the General Will, these contradictions are even more starkly on display than they would be if class, religion, or ethnicity had been invoked in the declaration.

As is the case with all founding assemblies, there was a moment at the very beginning of the revolution, after the third estate declared itself to be the "National Assembly," when the opening dilemma should have been evident. At that moment, there was no accepted leader, there were no procedural rules, and the members had not yet accepted their own credentials as representative agents of the people. But the dilemma that should have attended the creation of the National Assembly never surfaced. One reason is that, in effect, they tacitly accepted the crown's designations as their credentials, thus sloughing off the problem of how they could be considered representatives of the people to the king's agents (and, in that way, they also accepted the crown's conceptualization of "the people"). The problem of how to select a leader (a parliamentary officer) was resolved by rotating presidencies so that each presiding officer had little authority over the rest of the members. And, remarkably, the assembly was very slow to adopt parliamentary rules so that every member had equal rights in what was a very chaotic and often emotionally tumultuous setting. These decisions and practices served the deputies fairly well as long as the king provided a foil for their actions, but once the monarchy became moribund the dilemma reemerged in full view, starting with the question of who constituted "the people" and who were their agents.

Davidson lists seventeen "coups d'état" through which "the Revolutionaries steadily dismantled, piece by piece, the structure of institutional law which they had themselves created." He employs a somewhat broad notion of a "coup d'état" in constructing this list because he includes some actions undertaken by the people of Paris under the rubric of major "illegal" acts. Legality aside, he identifies acts and events that dramatically shifted the locus of political power during the revolution; the result of his analysis generally agrees with most narrative histories. Between the opening of the Estates-General and the deposition of the king on August 10, 1792 (the first of the seventeen coups), 1,193 days elapsed. Although this first period had violent moments and witnessed the steady weakening of the monarchy relative to the National Assembly, this was also the longest stretch of comparative political stability, comprising, as it

turned out, almost two-thirds of the entire period up to Robespierre's fall.[406]
From our perspective, the changing frequency of coups d'état on this list
correlates very well with the reemergence of the opening dilemma after the
deposition of the king.

Of all the foundings studied in this book, the French Revolution is the only
one in which most of the founders died violently before the new state was
established.[407] There are at least two ways in which we might interpret these
deaths as a response to this contradiction between the Rousseauian and
Enlightenment frames for the founding. On the one hand, we might see the
Terror, during which most founders were killed, as an avoidable response that
depended on the rise to dominance of Robespierre and those who favored a
Rousseauian architecture for the new revolutionary state. From this perspective, Robespierre, Saint-Just, and the other leaders of the Parisian masses used
the Terror to craft "an authoritarian populism prefiguring modern fascism"
that simply suppressed those favoring representative government.[408] In this
interpretation, the contradiction was, at least temporarily, resolved by eliminating one of the horns of the dilemma facing the revolution. It could have been
resolved in the same manner had their own horn been eliminated by the
Girondins. Under the latter interpretation, that would have happened but for
the tactical mistakes and accidents of fortune that afflicted the Girondins. We
might also add that the Girondin path would have probably resolved the

[406] Between May 5, 1789, when the Estates-General first convened and July 27, 1794, when
Robespierre was overthrown, 1,910 days elapsed. The average number of days elapsing
between the other sixteen coups is just under forty-five, with the eight shortest periods averaging
nine days. Davidson, *French Revolution*, pp. 259–60.

[407] Robespierre, for example, stated that the "founders of the Republic can only find peace in the
tomb." Although the passage can be interpreted several ways, one reading is that (1) there were,
in fact, "founders" but (2) the "founding" would not be completed during their lifetimes.
Jordan, *Revolutionary Career of Maximilien Robespierre*, p. 41. That interpretation is consistent with Robespierre's address to the convention on December 25, 1793, in which he described
the principles of revolutionary government, among them that "[t]he goal of constitutional
government is to preserve the Republic; that of revolutionary government is to found it." In
the same address, he also stated: "The foundation of the French Republic is not a game for
children." That indirect reference to the Terror was echoed in his description of the principles of
political morality on February 5, 1794 – "[I]ntimidate by terror the enemies of liberty; and you
will be right, as founders of the Republic" – and, in a slightly more upbeat tone: "[L]et us take
heart; this is the sanctuary of truth; here reside the founders of the Republic, the avengers of
humanity and destroyers of tyrants." Robespierre, *Virtue and Terror*, pp. 99, 115, 124. When
these passages are seen through the lens of martyrdom and self-sacrifice that preoccupied
Robespierre's vision of the future, the distinction between the "founders of the republic" and
the actual founding seems clear: Like the great Legislator imagined by Rousseau, the founders
would exit the stage at the very moment when their task was complete. As it turned out, all of
those whom Robespierre would have considered "founders of the republic," including himself,
exited the stage before the republic, as he conceived of it, was founded.

[408] Israel, *Revolutionary Ideas*, p. 695. "Montagnard populism resembled less a libertarian,
emancipating movement than an early form of modern fascism" (p. 221).

contradiction in favor of the Enlightenment without much of the violence that attended the Terror.

On the other hand, we might see the Terror as an inevitable consequence of the political logics, symbols, ideological totems, and practices that attended Rousseauian notions of the citizen, the Nation, and the General Will. Under the *ancien régime*, each of these had had a corresponding element (the subject, the kingdom, and the monarch) that rested upon the twin principles of divine right and absolutist authority. With the fall of the monarchy, those principles could no longer convey legitimacy upon the government and, in Hunt's words, "republicans set out to find new ways of putting their world together."[409] Those who favored the Enlightenment offered "reason" as a new foundation for the state but this had little popular appeal precisely because of its hostility to any conception of the sacred or eternal. Those who favored Rousseau, however, could easily and naturally ground state legitimacy in the metaphysical sovereignty of the people as expressed in the General Will. There was no contingency in this explanation because there was no real contest between these two alternatives. The problem was simply what to do with those who got in the way because of their devotion to Enlightenment principles. And the solution was the creation of a "rebuilt Committee of Public Safety" that "rapidly turned itself into the most concentrated state machine France had ever experienced." In the end, the revolution tried to invent "a new kind of politics, an institutional transference of Rousseau's sovereignty of the General Will that abolished space and time."[410]

---

[409] Hunt, *Politics, Culture, and Class*, p. 119. Earlier in her book Hunt describes four "inherent contradictions" that constantly subverted the revolution's "own basis of authority":

(1) While being political, it refused to sanction factional politicking. (2) While showing the power of rhetoric, it denied the legitimacy of rhetorical speech. (3) While representing the new community, it pushed toward the effacing of representation (in the name of transparency between citizens). (4) While referring to a mythic present, revolutionary rhetoric also had to explain the failures of the present, which it could only lay at the door of conspiracy-politics. (Hunt, *Politics, Culture, and Class*, pp. 48–9)

All of these can be attributed to Rousseau's influence. The only difficulty with this analysis of the internal inconsistencies *within* the Rousseauian tendency is that the very term "contradiction" implies (1) a commitment to logical order and (2) an intentional direction (an anticipated trajectory of social change), both of which are either very weak or entirely absent in the romanticism of Rousseauian ideology.

[410] Schama, *Citizens*, pp. 184–5, 755–6. While Israel sees fascist elements and contingency in the direction in which Robespierre took the revolution, Schama discerns a much more determinist and radical leftist trajectory. For example, Schama describes Saint-Just as "the very clay from which Leninism was to be shaped." But even Schama sees a few parallels with fascism. Referring to Jacques-Louis David, the great revolutionary artist, he says: "Albert Speer was not, then, the first to plan an architectural ideology around this kind of colossal collectivism" (pp. 535, 767, 830). (I might note that, in general, Schama prefers theoretical interpretations that involve surprise, contingency, and counterintuitive effects. See, for example, pp. 267, 275. From that perspective, the determinacy with which he views the authoritarian trajectory of the

Perhaps in recognition of the implacable contradictions arising from the abolition of space and time, Napoleon declared what in effect was a universal amnesty: "We must avoid all reaction in speaking of the Revolution. No man could oppose it. Blame lies neither with those who perished nor with those who have survived. There was no individual force capable of changing its elements or of preventing events which arose from the nature of things and from circumstances."[411] However, if Rousseau had been alive, Napoleon might have made an exception. As First Consul, Napoleon made a pilgrimage to Ermenonville, where the thinker's remains had been interred before they were removed to the Pantheon. Standing before the now empty tomb, Napoleon is reputed to have said: "It would have been better for the peace of France if this man had never lived."[412]

---

revolution might seem all the more pronounced.) Other historians see Babeuf as the culmination of the Rousseauian logic initiated by Robespierre. Babeuf, in fact, quoted several long passages from Rousseau in the defense he presented at his trial. Scott, *Defense of Gracchus Babeuf*, pp. 60, 62–4. Jeff Horn states that Karl Marx later accepted Babeuf's position "that only a powerful state with direct control of the economy could overcome the inherent exploitation of capitalism," while Lenin "claimed that he was following Babeuf's strategy when he orchestrated the October Revolution in 1917." Jeff Horn, "Lasting Economic Structures: Successes, Failures, and Revolutionary Political Economy" in Andress, *Oxford Handbook of the French Revolution*, p. 616. Marx and Engels openly acknowledged the work of Babeuf and his colleagues as directly contributing to the subsequent emergence of Marxism and the Communist movement in the nineteenth century. Israel, *Revolutionary Ideas*, p. 677. On Babeuf's political activities and ideology, see Andress, *French Society*, pp. 154–5; Harkins, "Intellectual Origins of Babouvism," p. 80; Doyle, *French Revolution*, p. 287; Israel, *Revolutionary Ideas*, pp. 600, 672. Others are less specific when tracing lineages. As Prince Petr Kropotkin said: "What we learn from the study of the Great [French] Revolution is that it was the source of all the present communist, anarchist, and socialist conceptions." Quoted in Scott, *Robespierre*, p. 258. Also see Arendt, *On Revolution*, pp. 40–1; Hunt, *Politics, Culture, and Class*, p. 3; Hanson, *Contesting the French Revolution*, p. 15. Taylor attributed the advent of "vanguard politics," as later practiced by the Bolsheviks, to Robespierre and his Jacobin followers. Taylor, *Modern Social Imaginaries*, pp. 124–5. From that perspective, we might note that while the French have created almost no public memorials to Robespierre, the Bolsheviks erected a monument to him in a garden next to the Kremlin soon after the October Revolution. In signing the decree authorizing the monument, Lenin lauded Robespierre's leadership of the Jacobins as "one of the highest summits attained by the working class in struggling for its emancipation." Jordan, *Revolutionary Career of Maximilien Robespierre*, p. 2. Quoting Bertram Wolfe, Jordan also stated that Robespierre, like Lenin "did not think of himself as a person looking for personal advantage or personal power, but as the selfless embodiment of a political line which was the only conceivably correct one" (p. 62). And Thompson, bringing the two leaders even closer together, stated that "on the political side, at least, Robespierre declares himself a Marxian revolutionist. Lenin himself might have penned his programme." Thompson, *Robespierre*, vol. 2, p. 34.

[411] Quoted in Doyle, *French Revolution*, p. viii.

[412] When queried why he thought that, Napoleon hedged just a bit: "[T]he future will tell us whether it would have been better if neither I nor Rousseau had ever lived." Miller, *Rousseau*, p. 202.

Almost by definition, all foundings of democratic states explicitly maintain that they have enshrined the will of the people at the very core of their constitution. At the most general level, the normative justification for this enshrinement appears to recognize no limits. For example, we could ask why the English, the Americans, and the French drew clear boundaries around their respective communities, boundaries that excluded other peoples while, at the same time, conferring upon their own peoples a specific and particular identity.[413] We could imagine that these boundaries merely carve up the world into separate enclaves but that, within each of them, the will of the people, along with its attendant institutions and practices, would be revealed and expressed in the same way. That similarity would arise from the fact that they all rest upon more or less the same body of democratic theory and principles. And, in fact, democratic states spend much of their political energy comparing their respective constitutions and practices with respect to such a metric. They monitor each other in a way that non-democratic regimes do not.[414]

A good case could be made that this mutual oversight has encouraged some convergence between democratic states in terms of suffrage expansion and individual rights, although the extent of that convergence could easily be exaggerated. One thing, however, is undeniable: With very rare exceptions, democratic states have not broken down those boundaries by combining with one another.[415] Non-democratic foundings, as will be discussed in the next three chapters, often have extraterritorial conceptions of the people (e.g., proletarians, Germans/Aryans, Shi'ites) that are uninhibited when it comes to crossing national boundaries. Democratic foundings, on the other hand, have produced remarkably resilient boundaries, in many cases due to the principle that the one thing a people cannot will is secession.[416] On the one hand, democratic foundings have denied the existence of a will of the people that transcends (what become) national boundaries. On the other hand, they have

---

[413] As has already been discussed, the drawing of boundaries involves confrontation with some aspects of the dilemma that attends all foundings: How do the founders decide, through a democratic process, who constitutes the people?

[414] There is one glaring exception to that statement: Communist regimes, after the proliferation of Eastern Bloc states following the Second World War, were often obsessed with their relative standing as "orthodox" exemplars of Marxist theory. However, both fascist and theocratic states, along with authoritarian regimes arising out of anticolonial independence movements, have been notoriously indifferent to variation in the ways in which other, apparently similar, states justified their sovereignty.

[415] Newfoundland did join the Canadian Confederation in 1949 and East and West Germany reunited in 1990. These very weak exceptions can be contrasted with the continuing strength of separatist movements in, for example, Spain, Great Britain, Canada, and Italy. The latter underscore the salience of boundaries in defining and permitting an authentic expression of the will of the people.

[416] Secession, of course, would be the founding event for a new conception of the people as a body capable of exercising a will.

also denied that there can be a will of the people separate and distinct from the national will.

The distinct and indivisible identity of the people presents no theoretical problems for the ancient English constitution because the will of the people, the state, and the transcendent social purpose to which the state is dedicated emerged within a mutually constitutive process. As a result, they are inextricably intertwined. Because there is no definitive moment in which the English state was founded, there is no event in which this melding occurred that might distinguish between an historical before and after. There is also no written text in which the provisions of the English Constitution were definitively set down in words. There are gestures, of course, to proclamations such as the Magna Carta (1215) and Declaration of Rights (1689), but these are flagrantly incomplete and hopelessly anachronistic. They also appeared long after the English state, people, and purpose had been melded in the mists of time. At best, they are minor corrections and embellishments of the customs and traditions that compose the ancient English constitution and, as such, only evidence steps in the evolutionary development of people and nation. And this explains why the English can only view the will of the people in distinctively national terms: The rights of Englishmen emerged – or, better stated, were revealed – in a long historical process that other peoples must undergo for themselves. The rights of Englishmen cannot be exported in a tidy package of political wisdom and they cannot, except in the broadest terms, be adapted in another cultural context. Although other peoples might learn some things from the English experience, particularly the virtues of incremental change in political principles, there is nothing the English can learn from other national experiences with democracy. The democratic suit must be tailored to the individual nation and the ancient English constitution fits its people as if it were (and it is) their very own skin.

The American founding would not have occurred had the English enfolded the colonists in the ancient constitution. But the English did not and, for that reason, the subsequent political crisis began as a fervent colonial affirmation of the rights of Englishmen not only as a just basis for political rule but, more to the point, as the *only* just basis for political rule. When this claim to English identity was categorically rejected by the mother country, the American founders had to find a way to retain this affirmation of the rights of Englishmen while recasting an identity for the colonists that would distinguish them from, as it were, Englishmen. The resulting contradictions were embedded in the hybrid Declaration of Independence and the institutional design set out in the United States Constitution, the former announcing the discovery of natural rights as the foundation of the ancient English constitution (rights violated by king and parliament) and the latter pragmatically innovating institutional filters that would make the will of the people a viable principle in the new American state (filters that mimicked English institutions that, less brutally justified in their sheer instrumentality, operated in much the same way).

For the better part of two centuries, the founding of the national state and its attending contradictions were viewed as the peculiar creation of the American people, with little application to the rest of the world beyond its oft-repeated dedication to the will of the people. But, beginning with the erection of new constitutions for Germany and Japan after the Second World War and, much more emphatically, the breakup of the Communist bloc in Eastern Europe in the last decade or so of the twentieth century, the lessons of the American founding became more than ready for export. By that time, the persisting influence of English institutions and practices had been thoroughly domesti- cated and their origins mostly forgotten, while the more brutally instrumental provisions and logics had been softened or eliminated by constitutional amend- ments and reinterpretation. However, while the forms of the American founding were now viewed as ready for export, the United States has never proposed a unification with another democracy and has even stiffened restric- tions on the incorporation of immigrants.

The French founding openly declared the universal rights of all men everywhere and abandoned all reverence for the peculiar customs and trad- itions of the nation in the name of reason (itself a fundamental principle with relevance and application everywhere in the world). Not surprisingly, the revolutionary elite in its earlier years believed that they had only to announce both rights and reason to the world and other societies would rise up and embrace them, either on their own or perhaps in some kind of federation with France. While these political principles proved to be a durable source of inspiration to those who would make a revolution else- where, the political institutions created by the French turned out to be a difficult product to export. This was largely because four elements uneasily cohabited with one another during the French founding: (1) a rhetorical invocation of "the people" that is as fulsome and unbounded as any in the history of the world; (2) the coincidence of democratic elections with, in practice, a full-blown dictatorship by committee; (3) abysmally low partici- pation in elections when they were held; and (4) the execution and exile of most of the nobility, clergy, and their allies because they would not agree that the creation of "liberty, equality, and fraternity" should be the tran- scendent social purpose of the new state.

Each of these presented problems when the French attempted to export their revolution. The rhetorical invocation of "the people" was undoubtedly sincere but irremediably broke its back on the question of whether or not the will of the people could be "represented" by elected delegates. The contest was never resolved between (1) the collective mobilization of the people of Paris who could present their demands without mediation (and therefore were a more authentic expression of the will of the people) and (2) the National Assembly, which was grounded in a much more conventional notion of parliamentary democracy. In fact, that contest became the opening through which a tyrannical dictatorship with all of its attendant and bloody repression of political dissent could emerge. Attempts to winnow the expression of the will of the people in the provinces, in turn, created an electoral process that both discriminated against the lower classes and, in addition, was too complicated and demanded too much time and energy for most people. The result was very low participation in elections even under a regime that fulsomely embraced the people as its very reason for existence. The most pragmatically successful element in the French founding was, somewhat ironically, the execution and exile of those members of the political elite who could not or would not embrace the new state. Although many of the exiles ultimately returned to France, their exclusion created an opening through which those who had no problem with giving at least lip service to the new regime could take their place or otherwise shunt them aside. Rather like Alexander Hamilton's bondholders after the American founding, the interests and claims of this new elite became bound up with the legitimacy of the new French state and its commitment to "liberty, equality, and fraternity."

Despite its grand rhetoric, the founding of the French state was profoundly contextualized by its historical and intellectual inheritance: the role of Rousseau in its conception of the "General Will" with all the contradictions that entailed when the revolutionary elite attempted to put it into practice; the recourse to a belief that the revolutionary elite could somehow "know" that General Will, even though the people were not yet ready (at least not entirely ready) to reveal it; the construction of filters on the electoral expression of the General Will that originated in this view that many people were not ready for democracy; and the recognition that the inheritance of class privilege from the *ancien régime*, along with its theoretical and practical claims, determined much of the variation in the way in which the revolution was received by the people. All of these elements made the French Revolution an historically distinctive and thoroughly contextualized event that, in turn, dramatically reduced its viability as a political export.

Once a democratic state has been founded, the transcendent social purpose that is melded into the creation of sovereignty justifies a winnowing of the content of the will of the people. In the French case, the constitutions that were serially created both during the revolution and in the centuries that followed represented attempts to craft institutions that would make otherwise free expression of the popular will compatible with the transcendent social purpose originally declared in the Declaration of the Rights of

Man and of the Citizen. These constitutions were, in one sense, attempts to keep up the fiction of a free expression of the popular will while making it impossible for the people to abandon the republic. In the United States, official discrimination against individual Communists and their party organization during and after the McCarthy era followed the same principle; in theory, the only thing that the people could not will was the abandonment of democracy and, for that reason, eliminating that option at the ballot box was perfectly compatible with the transcendent social purpose of the American state and society.

On the one hand, democratic states enshrine a particular conception of the people at the founding. As a result, there is a substantive component to the will of the people in that there is a particular people whose will is recognized. On the other hand, the transcendent social purpose that instantiates the will of this particular people also compels the creation of institutions (e.g., elections) through which the will can be revealed periodically in the future. These periodic revelations have several possible functions. For one thing, they confirm that the people still subscribe to the transcendent social purpose enshrined at the founding. (This is one reason why democratic states encourage their citizenry to vote; turnout is a "contentless" expression of continuing recognition of state legitimacy.) But these periodic revelations also allow the people to modify (but not reject) that original transcendent social purpose. As will be seen in discussion of the German case in Chapter 6, the Weimar Republic progressively abandoned democratic forms in repeated attempts to reconcile the (deeply divided) will of the people and it ultimately became a charade of democracy. Western democracies, if faced with a similar complexity of challenges, would almost certainly do the same thing.

This book, however, is not about the travails of Western democracy. It comes closest to that topic when I contend that a necessary condition for a stable democracy is that the "people" must be conceived as less comprehensive than the inhabitants of that space we call a nation. That necessity arises from the fact that the transcendent social purpose of the state not only authorizes the exercise of sovereignty but fixes an identity upon the people at the founding. The political elite who rhetorically construct the people at the founding are thus performing an essential political purpose when they, of necessity, link their conception of the will of the people to the identity of the people as a collective body. They perform this service regardless of whether they do so with the otherwise full panoply of democratic principles in mind or merely stumble through politics by serially trying out different formulations before settling on the one that seems most promising. Western democracies will never settle on the same conception of the will of the people because the identity of the people will always differ between nations; these different identities are a core attribute of the authentic transcendent social purpose that is embedded in the state. There is not and can never be a purely abstract and universal will of the people within the carapace of the nation-state. The valiant, unsuccessful attempt to create such a will during the French Revolution is conclusive proof of this impossibility.[417]

[417] It was in the spirit attending these attempts that Arendt saw deep and abiding links between the French and Russian Revolutions:

> Lenin was the last heir of the French Revolution; he had no theoretical concept of freedom, but when he was confronted with it in factual reality he understood what was at stake, and when he sacrificed the new institutions of freedom, the *soviets*, to the party which he thought would liberate the poor, his motivation and reasoning were still in accord with the tragic failures of the French revolutionary tradition. (Arendt, *On Revolution*, p. 56)

> McDonald, in contrast to Arendt, sees an "important distinction" between their underlying philosophies. In the Russian Revolution, the "works of Marx became the bible of a minority of a minority group, organized specifically and exclusively for political and revolutionary purposes," while, in the French Revolution, "Rousseau's works inspired no political parties, but exercised a profound influence upon men and women whose political opinions were widely different." McDonald, *Rousseau and the French Revolution*, p. 116. We should, however, interrogate McDonald's distinction in several respects. First, her reference to Marxist theory as the Bolshevik "bible" concedes the sincerity of their revolutionary commitment, including their belief that they were *not* "a minority of a minority group" in Russia. In addition, to note that there was general consensus on the importance of Rousseau's philosophy during the French Revolution is *not* the same thing as general agreement on how to implement that philosophy in the founding of the new state. It was in that implementation that profound problems arose.

PART II

THE FOUNDING OF NON-DEMOCRATIC STATES

We now turn to an examination of three non-democratic foundings: the instantiation of the dictatorship of the proletariat in the Russian Revolution; the emergence of the Third Reich as the enabler of the historical destiny of the German people; and the creation of an Islamic theocracy in the Iranian Revolution. In these, as in all modern foundings, the new state was dedicated to a clearly articulated transcendent social purpose. In most modern foundings, the announcement of this purpose prominently appears in the text of a new constitution. In democratic foundings, that purpose is understood to be something that the people can fully comprehend in the sense that they understand both what it is and how it can be collectively realized. As a result, the will of the people is thought to decisively determine the translation of the transcendent social purpose into the design of state institutions and principles. The founding elite, such as they are, does no more than record and translate the popular will that is revealed in a free and open democratic process.

In non-democratic foundings, however, the transcendent social purpose is viewed as vulnerable to misrecognition if it is legislated in what is conventionally regarded as a free and open democratic politics. Misrecognition of the transcendent social purpose is possible because the will of the people cannot be authentically revealed: Either the identity of the people is not yet correctly specified or social relations within the preexisting political community somehow distort the people's apprehension of what they must do. In either case, the will of the people must be refined and shaped after the state is created. For that reason, the revolutionary elite orchestrates a complex process in which (1) the people are viewed as generally aware of what it is that they should (and do) will with respect to the transcendent social purpose to which the state must be dedicated *but* (2) they are not competent to carry out the founding without the intervention of the revolutionary elite. While the revolutionary elite still utilizes the form of a legislative assembly to craft a constitution, the elite itself claims to manifest the popular will and thus, as political agent, oversees the melding of sovereignty, social purpose, and the will of the people when the new state is founded.

The popular will is always imperfect in that something invariably impairs its natural expression in majority rule. This imperfection means that there is always some disjunction between the conception of the popular will (1) as imbricated in the social purpose to which a state's sovereignty is dedicated and (2) as revealed in unconstrained majority voting. As a result, both democratic and non-democratic states "refine" the popular will by regulating its expression. This refinement assumes that the people could not accurately identify or effectively realize that transcendent social purpose – even after its recognition at the founding – in the absence of state intervention.

The possibility of misrecognition in democratic states is the primary justification for regulation of the conduct of elections. In the USA, for example, the federal and state governments regulate campaign contributions, require registration of voters at the polls, guarantee minority representation through the construction of district boundaries, certify candidates who may stand for election, set age and residency requirements for suffrage, and so forth. These regulations operate on the popular will by either regulating its formation (e.g., campaign contributions), policing its expression (e.g., imposing suffrage requirements), restricting the alternatives from which the people may choose (e.g., discriminating against minority party organizations, disqualifying individuals as candidates, or determining which issues might be the subject of a referendum), or compensating for deep-seated but improper opinions (e.g., racial and ethnic bias).

While there is no question that these things have a substantive impact on what is evidenced as the will of the people (e.g., in the outcome of elections), the declared purpose is to purify the popular will from contaminating influence without otherwise influencing what that will might express. For democratic states, the concept of misrecognition thus presumes the existence of a pristine popular will that can be revealed only if the political community eliminates or compensates for factors that would otherwise distort its manifestation. In theory, the will of the people is left undisturbed by these eliminations and adjustments; the authentic content (what the people would will) is merely revealed to the community. The transcendent social purpose in such states is thus dedicated to the identification and realization of the purified will of the people, along with those values and guarantees (e.g., freedom of the press) that facilitate the democratic process and make possible its reproduction through time.[1]

---

[1] The primary transcendent social purpose of democratic foundings is the dedication of the state to the *continued* and (theoretically) unfiltered control of the will of the people. Thus, the regulations described in the text apply to both the founding (when the popular will creates the state) and politics after the founding (when the popular will directs state policy). Misrecognition of the will

In non-democratic states, misrecognition of the transcendent social purpose occurs when the people have a general but imperfect understanding of what it is they should (and thus do) will. Here, the problem directly concerns content and only indirectly involves process. The content of what should be (and thus is) the will of the people can be (and is) revealed to those (in practice, the revolutionary elite) who are either trained, skilled, or gifted in its comprehension. This revolutionary elite utilizes the people's largely instinctual understanding of what they should (and thus do) will to mobilize them against the *ancien régime*, a regime that views any notion of the will of the people as, at best, irrelevant. The grounding for the revolutionary elite's privileged understanding of the will of the people is primarily historical, arising from comprehension of an unfolding, teleological trajectory in which the people play a central role as both object and participant. It is this role that the people can misrecognize even as they are summoned to instinctually realize their destiny. The primary task of the revolutionary elite is thus, in the first instance, to mobilize the people's instinctual understanding of their historical destiny in order to found the new state and then to ensure that this destiny is effectively realized. Part of that realization is the education and refinement of the people's understanding of their historical destiny in a process that is not consultative (in the manner of democratic states) but, instead, involves doctrinal instruction.

For example, in the Russian Revolution, Bolsheviks held that politically conscious workers could broadly recognize the historical role that their class must play but were nonetheless imperfectly aware of the proper political strategies and tactics that would realize their destiny. The actual content of the "dictatorship of the proletariat" was thus the responsibility of the vanguard party, which acted not as representatives of or in the name of the workers but as their correctly informed political consciousness. The Bolsheviks thus knew what it was that the workers should (and thus did) will even if the workers themselves might misrecognize the transcendent social purpose of the revolution (i.e., the historical destiny imbricated in the state in its founding).[2] At the founding of the Soviet state, this transcendent social purpose (the realization of the communist revolution as the next and final historical stage) was thus a technical matter whose theoretical preconditions and practical realization were perfectly known only to the vanguard party. As a result, the founding of the

---

of the people originates, for the most part, in the same potentially distorting influences both before and after the founding. The major difference is that, after the founding, the state itself can become a self-interested actor and thus a potentially distorting influence.

[2] Lenin and his Bolshevik colleagues viewed their party in the same way that Marx and Engels had before them: "an association of enlightened individuals operating beyond the bounds of conventional political activity [who] were charged with discerning the course of history and inspiring others to follow their lead." A. James McAdams, *Vanguard of the Revolution: The Global Idea of the Communist Party* (Princeton, NJ: Princeton University Press, 2017), p. 97.

Soviet state primarily involved the installation of the political consciousness of the working class as the elemental guide in realizing the communist revolution. And that political consciousness necessarily resided, in its perfected and thus practical form, in the vanguard party. Thus, in the first instance, the founding involved the inhabitation of the Russian state by the Bolshevik Party. Following the founding, one of the most pressing tasks was the instruction of the people in a proper understanding of and alignment with party doctrine (and thus what was *really* their own political consciousness).

The founding of the Third Reich enacted the people's recognition of the Leader who physically and theoretically embodied the will of the people. Like much of *Volkisch* thought, Nazi doctrine postulated an historical destiny for the German people, race, and nation. The German people should (and thus did) will this destiny, but alien and foreign influence had distracted them from their purpose. The task of the Nazi Party and Hitler, as Leader, was, in the first instance, to cultivate a proper awareness among the people of this destiny and to eliminate those social and political elements that were frustrating its realization. This awareness was inseparably intertwined with popular acclamation of Hitler as Leader because the purification of the German people, race, and nation would, inevitably, bring about the unification of people and Leader (in much the same way that the proletariat and the vanguard party became unified in the founding of the Soviet Union and, only slightly less so, in the way in which the Iranian religious community and Khomeini became one under the Islamic Republic). Politics, for the Nazis, was a process through which the Leader was revealed to the people, who, in turn, evidenced that revelation through increasingly enthusiastic public demonstrations and rising electoral support for the National Socialist Party. The founding of the Third Reich marked the point at which politics came to an end because the unification of the Leader and the will of the people under the auspices of and within the German state made realization of the German historical destiny a technical matter. The economy of purpose and the clarity of vision that the Leader could mobilize in pursuit of that destiny, along with the certainty that the Leader would himself will anything that the people should (and did) will, made further formal consultation with the people superfluous.

In the Iranian Revolution, the Shi'ite clergy held that even the most devout among the Iranian people could never be as enlightened with respect to God's will and purpose as religious scholars (the ulama). However, the devout could nonetheless recognize the spiritual merit and accomplishments of the ulama in connection with the major historical Shi'ite project: proper preparation of the religious community for the return of the Hidden Imam.[3] Although the people

---

[3] On the role of the Hidden Imam in Shi'i Islam, see Najam Haider, *Shi'i Islam: An Introduction* (New York: Cambridge University Press, 2014), pp. 145–66.

should (and thus did) will this proper preparation, their lack of training and imperfect spiritual enlightenment made misrecognition of what they actually willed unavoidable. Here, the problem took two forms. On the one hand, the people were inadequately trained as Islamic scholars and were thus likely to make mistakes in religious interpretation. This could be partially but not entirely corrected through religious training. On the other hand, this religious training could never transform the people into the anointed representative of the Hidden Imam on earth. Only the ulama could aspire to such a role, and, even for them, their role was only to recognize the one among them who might be so anointed.

The founding of the Islamic Republic thus created a theocratic state, ruled by the ulama, that would prepare the religious community for the return of the Hidden Imam. Just as there was no doubt that the Iranian people devoutly wished that their community would be so prepared, there was also no doubt that this was not a task that they could undertake themselves in all its fullness. The ulama constituted the spiritual consciousness of the people, inseparable from them within the religious community but also uniquely gifted in discerning the spiritual direction their community should take. After the founding, the people were to be further instructed in religious doctrine in order to refine and purify their understanding. But the people were also, within very strict limits, to be consulted with respect to the relative sanctity of individual members of the ulama. Unlike the Bolsheviks, the Shi'ite clergy insisted on a periodic demonstration of the people's instinctual awareness of their leaders' piety. The people, again within very strict limits, could detect sanctity but they were not competent to direct religious policy.

In all three foundings, the transcendent social purpose to which the state was dedicated was identical to the will of the people (as understood, realized, and later refined by the revolutionary elite). In each case, the authentic will of the people resided in a particular segment of the population defined by class, race, or faith: the proletariat in the case of the Soviet Union; those of German "blood" in the Third Reich; and devout Shi'a in Iran. These conceptions of the people excluded sizable portions of the population then living within national boundaries (e.g., the bourgeoisie, those whose ethnic identities were not German, and those belonging to other religious faiths). In that sense, the will of the people was not a "national" will as we commonly understand it. And for the same reason, there were also transnational extensions in each of these conceptions of the people: the international proletariat; German communities located in nations other than Germany; and devout Shi'a residing outside the political boundaries of Iran. These transnational extensions affected the way in which the state was founded by (1) making the will of the people practically inaccessible (e.g., because people in other nations could not participate in referenda or elections) and (2) conferring upon the state a transcendent social purpose that extended beyond the nation's boundaries. Thus, the Soviet state was dedicated to the promotion of a worldwide proletarian revolution in a founding in which workers in other nations could not participate directly.[4] The Third Reich was dedicated, in the first instance, to the incorporation of German communities then located outside Germany and, subsequently, to an expansion of German settlement in Eastern Europe. The Islamic Republic was similarly dedicated at its founding to the preparation of the Shi'ite religious community (and Muslim communities generally) for the return of the Hidden Imam.

These internal exclusions and external inclusions in the conception of the people made the nation-state itself an imperfect vehicle for registering and realizing the popular will because the political community and physical boundaries of the state were misaligned.[5] However, since the revolutionary elite could (and did) recognize and enact the popular will without formal consultation with the people, the main effect of this misalignment was to reinforce the subordination of the state to the revolutionary elite, both in the design of the new state and in its subsequent operation.

In the three foundings analyzed in the following chapters, connections are drawn between: (1) political beliefs as resident in the national culture before the revolution; (2) competition between ostensible representatives of those beliefs (usually competing parties) and between alternative beliefs (e.g., parliamentary democracy and religion); (3) the particular conception of those beliefs as articulated by the successful revolutionary party; and (4) the manner in which those beliefs were embedded in the founding by way of the revolutionary party. Each founding melded together: (1) the revolutionary party as the correct and full expression of the will of the people; (2) the transcendent social purpose to which the state is dedicated; and (3) sovereignty (the right to rule in the name of that transcendent social purpose). The most important elements in this process include: (1) the way in which the revolutionary elite competes with other parties (e.g., how those parties are conceived as opponents, in particular their respective relation to the historical destiny of the people); (2) the ideological explanations that the revolutionary elite construct as they make (what would otherwise be considered) tactical concessions in the competition for power; and (3) the manner in which the revolutionary party is positioned as both the embodiment of the will of the people and an infallible agent of their historical destiny.

---

[4] "Lenin was first and foremost an internationalist, a world revolutionary, for whom state boundaries were relics of another era and nationalism a distraction from the class struggle ... Russia was to him an accidental center of the first revolutionary upheaval, a springboard for the real revolution, whose vortex had to be Western Europe." Richard Pipes, *The Russian Revolution* (New York: Vintage Books, 1990), p. 352; also see pp. 396–7, 567–8, 668–9. Also see McAdams, *Vanguard of the Revolution*, p. 100.

[5] One of the central distinctions between non-democratic and democratic states is that the latter allow the people to decide, within limits, who should be included within the political community (i.e., as rights-bearing and participating members). Non-democratic states, particularly the three examined here, are founded upon a particular conception of the people that is unalterable precisely because it grounds their claim on sovereignty.

5

The Dictatorship of the Proletariat

The Russian Revolution

After Nicholas II, the Tsar of All the Russias, abdicated following mass demonstrations in Petrograd in March 1917, a committee of political leaders appointed by the Duma formed a Provisional Government.[1] At the same time, workers and soldiers created a Petrograd Soviet of Workers' Deputies (Petrograd Soviet) that both shared power with the Provisional Government and rapidly evolved into the leading component of the All-Russian Congress of Soviets.[2] After the destruction of the Tsarist autocracy, the Provisional Government and Petrograd Soviet thus became the only sources of legitimacy for the Russian state. Since none of the competing social forces mobilized within the Provisional Government and the Petrograd Soviet was strong enough to provide an effective social base, each was stalemated in what turned out to be a paralyzing competition for political dominance. This competition played itself out while the Bolshevik Party infiltrated the factory, the army, and

---

[1] The Duma was a representative assembly originally created as the monarchy's response to popular insurrections in the 1905 Russian Revolution. By 1917, changes in suffrage qualifications and the allocation of delegates had drastically reduced its democratic quality: The landed aristocracy alone chose half the deputies. Because it lacked popular legitimacy, the Duma became a nullity after the formation of the Provisional Government. However, "groups of its members continued to meet in 'private conferences,' where fulminations against anarchy and lawlessness were the regular order of the day." William Henry Chamberlin, *The Russian Revolution, 1917–1921*, 2 vols. (New York: Grosset & Dunlap, 1965), vol. 1, pp. 60–1, 189. Chamberlin later added that a "noteworthy weakness of the Provisional Government throughout the whole course of its career was the absence of any generally recognized national assembly on which it could lean" (p. 200).

[2] "Order No. 1" was published on March 1 by the Petrograd Soviet and directed soldiers to elect deputies to that body and to take possession of weapons and ammunition. The order also abolished the "salute" for enlisted men in their relations with officers. Sean McMeekin, *The Russian Revolution: A New History* (New York: Basic Books, 2017), p. 113. This order was reaffirmed on May 8 by "Order No. 8" (p. 148).

the navy. Once the party was confident of the support of the workers and troops in Petrograd, the Bolsheviks revolted against the Provisional Government, founded the new communist state under the auspices of the Soviet, and thus realized the ideological promise of a "dictatorship of the proletariat." In founding the communist state, the Bolsheviks yoked their claim on sovereignty to the party's dedication to carrying out a Marxist working-class revolution. They thus inhabited and gave a social purpose to a state apparatus that had been eroding while other social forces contended for control of the government.

The two most important events during the Russian Revolution were the abdication of the Tsar on March 15 and the Bolshevik revolt on November 7.[3] The first of these was brought on by spontaneous demonstrations demanding food that erupted in Petrograd on March 8.[4] Although these protests were not organized or led by any political party, they were not suppressed because the troops mutinied when ordered to fire upon the demonstrators. The leaders of the Duma soon concluded that only the Tsar's abdication would placate the demonstrators and thus allow the restoration of public order. After some delay, partially attributable to the fact that the Tsar was away from Petrograd at the time, Nicholas II abdicated in favor of his brother Michael Alexandrovich, the Grand Duke.[5] However, the Grand Duke, although more liberal and progressive than Nicholas, did not believe that he would enjoy enough support to rule effectively and refused to take the throne. That left the Duma leaders in control of the Russian state.[6] Representing the major parties in that chamber, they immediately formed a Provisional Government and dedicated that government to laying the foundation for the formation of a democratic state.[7] The founding

---

[3] When the revolution began, Russia still followed the old Julian calendar, which lagged by thirteen days behind the Gregorian calendar used in most of the world. For consistency, all dates cited in the text are based on the Gregorian calendar.

[4] Chamberlin described the popular movement that destroyed the Russian autocracy as "one of the most leaderless, spontaneous, anonymous revolutions of all time." He went on to say that, once the Tsar gave up the throne, "the Revolution may almost be said to have been made by telegraph, practically without resistance" as it spread throughout Russia. Chamberlin, *Russian Revolution*, vol. 1, pp. 73, 79, 85. Also see Edward Hallett Carr, *The Bolshevik Revolution, 1917–1923*, 3 vols. (New York: Macmillan, 1951), vol. 1, p. 70. For the role of hunger in the emergence of demonstrations in Petrograd, see Richard Pipes, *The Russian Revolution* (New York: Vintage Books, 1990), pp. 275–8, 330–1. In that respect, the parallel with Parisian popular protest during the French Revolution is striking.

[5] For the text of the Tsar's abdication, see Martin McCauley (ed.), *The Russian Revolution and the Soviet State, 1917–1921: Documents* (New York: Barnes & Noble, 1975), p. 13.

[6] On the Grand Duke's refusal to take the throne, see McMeekin, *Russian Revolution*, pp. 118–20.

[7] The proclamation through which the assumption of authority was announced to the Russian people was remarkably understated:

[T]he Provisional Government realizes its obligations to the State [and] takes upon its shoulders the task of implementing all the financial obligations of the State incurred by the old *regime*, such as payment of interest, payment of the state debts, obligations under treaties, payments to civil

of that democratic state was to be carried out through the election of delegates to the Constituent Assembly, which would write a new constitution. The Provisional Government and the promised election of a Constituent Assembly constituted the "democratic path" within the Russian Revolution.[8]

The alternative "non-democratic path" was more complicated. At about the same time that the Provisional Government constituted itself as the residual state authority, the workers and soldiers in Petrograd and throughout the rest of Russia were organizing Soviets.[9] Although the Soviets were class organizations (in the case of the soldiers' Soviets, the vast majority of the members were peasants who had been conscripted into the army), most of the party organizations and leaders favored a democratic state in which even the bourgeoisie would participate.[10] The "democratic" and "non-democratic" paths were thus intermingled at the beginning of the revolution because the Provisional Government and the All-Russian Congress of Soviets were both dominated by democratic parties, the former always more so than the latter. However, the relationship between the Soviets and the Provisional Government was often tense because the former pressed a class-based policy agenda (primarily land redistribution and an end to the war) that the more conservative Provisional Government either opposed or was reluctant to enact.[11]

servants, pensions and all other kinds of payment due by law, or treaty, or on some lawful foundation. On the other hand, all payments which are due to the public treasury, the taxes, customs, duties, and all kinds of payments must be paid as before into the public treasury until new laws are passed. The Provisional Government believes in the absolute necessity of the existing state departments being very careful in the expenditure of the money of the people. In order to emphasize this we must use the necessary measures for exercising active control. The magnitude of military expenditure at the present time, the increase of the state debt on account of the war, the increase of taxes, are all quite unavoidable.

James Mavor, *The Russian Revolution* (London: George Allen & Unwin, 1928), pp. 59–60.

[8] When the Provisional Government was proclaimed on March 7, it announced that its primary task was to "convoke the Constituent Assembly within the shortest time possible." McMeekin, *Russian Revolution*, p. 137. For an overview of the subsequent history of the Provisional Government, see pp. 137–9.

[9] For a succinct history of the origins of the Soviets in the 1905 Revolution and the role played by Soviets twelve years later, see Harold Shukman (ed.), *The Blackwell Encyclopedia of the Russian Revolution* (New York: Blackwell, 1988), pp. 135–7; Mavor, *Russian Revolution*, p. 130; Carr, *Bolshevik Revolution*, vol. 1, pp. 46–7. In 1917, the Soviets more or less systematically over-represented soldiers relative to workers in the apportionment of delegates, with, for example, one delegate awarded for every 250 soldiers and for every 1,000 workers in Petrograd. By April 11, when an All-Russian Congress of Soviets met in Petrograd, delegates "from 138 local Soviets, seven armies, thirteen rear units and twenty-six front units" were in attendance. Chamberlin, *Russian Revolution*, vol. 1, p. 112.

[10] In fact, Duma leaders may have consulted with the Executive Committee of the Petrograd Soviet when constructing the new Provisional Government. Mavor, *Russian Revolution*, p. 64.

[11] Prosecution of the war against Germany was viewed by the Constitutional Democrats (shortened to Kadets) and many Mensheviks and Socialist Revolutionaries as the nationalist precondition for state sovereignty. Their position thus paralyzed cooperation with other social forces because the geopolitical purposes of the war (honoring alliances with western powers and the goal of

The unelected Provisional Government nonetheless needed the Soviets because it lacked popular legitimacy; the elected Soviets, despite (or perhaps because of) their class basis, enjoyed much greater mass support.[12] On the other hand, the Soviets needed the Provisional Government because the officer corps of the Russian army and navy strongly preferred the latter as their commander-in-chief, because the Western powers were willing to recognize the Provisional Government as legitimate (and might well have balked at recognizing the Soviets), and because even the routine operations of the state bureaucracy demanded an expertise that many of the Soviet leaders lacked.[13] Both the Provisional Government and the Soviets anticipated that the election of a Constituent Assembly would resolve their uneasy bifurcation of responsibilities and social bases.

As a result, the Soviets were at first largely devoted to the founding of a democratic state, although the shape that state might have assumed would have been significantly, perhaps dramatically, different from the one preferred by the Provisional Government.[14] The major threat to a democratic founding came from the radicalism of the urban masses and the rural peasantry. Workers increasingly demanded influence over the management of factories while landless peasants illegally occupied land owned by the Russian nobility. Profiting from and abetting this radical trend was the Bolshevik Party, which (1) demanded that the Provisional Government hold elections for a Constituent Assembly that would create a new state; (2) organized mass demonstrations under the slogan "All Power to the Soviets"; (3) advocated a tripartite program of land redistribution, immediate peace with Germany and its allies, and "bread" for the people; and (4) insisted on the exclusion of bourgeois parties from all revolutionary political coalitions.[15] At the beginning of the revolutionary period, just after the abdication of the Tsar, the Bolshevik Party was insignificant in both size and influence.[16] However, as the war ground on and economic conditions steadily deteriorated, the Bolsheviks exploited increasing working-class distress and, later, rising disaffection within the army. Under

---

opening the Dardanelles and Bosporus to Russian traffic) were irrelevant to the immediate needs of the people for, among other things, food.

[12] Orlando Figes argues that "[a]t almost any moment between February and October [1917] the Soviet could have taken power and, although a civil war might well have been the outcome, its support was enough to ensure a victory." Orlando Figes, *A People's Tragedy: A History of the Russian Revolution* (New York: Viking, 1997), p. 359.

[13] Mavor, *Russian Revolution*, p. 131. On the tension between the Provisional Government and the Soviet, see, for example, George Vernadsky, *The Russian Revolution, 1917–1931* (New York: Henry Holt, 1932), p. 43; Carr, *Bolshevik Revolution*, vol. 1, p. 70; Chamberlin, *Russian Revolution*, vol. 1, p. 84.

[14] Vernadsky, *Russian Revolution*, p. 43.

[15] For descriptions of mass protests demanding bread for the people, see McMeekin, *Russian Revolution*, pp. 96–9.

[16] The Bolshevik Party, for example, played almost no role in the abdication of the Tsar. McMeekin, *Russian Revolution*, p. xv.

Lenin's leadership, the party consistently used tactical positions, such as support for the calling of a Constituent Assembly and participation in Duma elections, to further its ultimate goal of installing a "dictatorship of the proletariat" as the sole repository of state authority.[17]

The Bolshevik Party thus constituted the "non-democratic" path within the Russian Revolution, gradually adapting the Soviets to its purposes as the party captured the local Soviets that elected its delegates.[18] Even though the Bolshevik Party came to power by violently overthrowing the Provisional Government, the right of the "dictatorship of the proletariat" to rule Russia was legitimated by legislative assemblies that were similar in form and content to those that found democratic states. In order to see how and why this was so, we must briefly survey the several transformations in the construction of state institutions between the March demonstrations in Petrograd and the dissolution of the Constituent Assembly in January 1918.

The unfolding of the Russian Revolution can be analyzed in several different ways: as a dynamic competition between the Provisional Government and the All-Russian Congress of Soviets; as political contention between the major political parties; and as the popular mobilization of workers and soldiers behind the political program of the Bolshevik Party. As ways of understanding how the Soviet state was founded, all three of these perspectives are useful, but the most productive is political contention between the major political parties. Each of the party organizations was both strongly committed to a particular ideology and yet riven by internal divisions over the proper interpretation of what that ideology dictated in terms of political action and state formation.

On the right of the political spectrum stood the Kadets, who represented the rural gentry (large landholders) and urban bourgeoisie (e.g., shopkeepers, factory owners and management, and professionals) (see Table 5.1). The Tsarist autocracy had regarded the Kadets as "a liberal if not a radical party" but the Constitutional Democrats became, almost by default, "a bulwark of conservatism" after all the parties to its right disappeared following the Tsar's abdication.[19] In many respects, the Kadets modeled themselves on liberal

---

[17] On Lenin's conception of the Bolshevik Party's role in the revolution, and particularly what should be its political strategy and tactics, see A. James McAdams, *Vanguard of the Revolution: The Global Idea of the Communist Party* (Princeton, NJ: Princeton University Press, 2017), pp. 59–61, 71–101.

[18] The Petrograd and Moscow Soviets, for example, first evidenced Bolshevik majorities on September 13 and 18, respectively. Trotsky was elected president of the Petrograd Soviet on October 8. Chamberlin, *Russian Revolution*, vol. 1, p. 221. Also see McMeekin, *Russian Revolution*, pp. 200, 202–3.

[19] Chamberlin, *Russian Revolution*, vol. 1, p. 102. The absorption of the other conservative parties meant that the Kadet membership included some monarchists who wanted to reestablish the Tsarist autocracy and some authoritarians who preferred a military dictatorship to a socialist democracy.

TABLE 5.1. *Leading party organizations during the Russian Revolution: their social base and attitude toward the founding of a new state*

Party organization	Social base	Locus of power	Attitude toward the founding
Constitutional Democrats (Kadets)	Gentry and bourgeoisie	Provisional Government	Parliamentary democracy
Mensheviks	Urban intelligentsia	Provisional Government, state bureaucracy, Soviets, workers	Parliamentary democracy
Socialist Revolutionaries	Rural peasants and soldiers	Soviets, Provisional Government	Parliamentary democracy
Left Socialist Revolutionaries	Rural peasants and soldiers	Soviets	Proletarian dictatorship
Bolsheviks	Workers	Soviets	Proletarian dictatorship

Sources: Rosenberg, *Liberals in the Russian Revolution*, pp. 5–6, 123; Carr, *Bolshevik Revolution*, vol. 1, pp. 70, 109; Chamberlin, *Russian Revolution*, vol. 1, pp. 40, 102, 250, 327, 353–4; Mavor, *Russian Revolution*, p. 195.

parliamentary parties in Western Europe.[20] True to their name, the Kadets were devoted to procedural rigor and an almost meditative attitude toward legislative deliberation, so much so that they seemed at times to endanger their very survival by swaddling themselves in democratic etiquette.[21] As the only major

---

[20] "Venerating legal principles and a rule of law, holding individual civil liberties as precious values in themselves, seeking *political* democracy in the main, rather than *social* democracy or class leveling, Kadets represented in Russia what can generally be regarded as basic European liberal traditions." William G. Rosenberg, *Liberals in the Russian Revolution: The Constitutional Democratic Party, 1917–1921* (Princeton, NJ: Princeton University Press, 1974), pp. 5–6, emphasis in the original.

[21] Rosenberg describes the Kadets as persisting in the observance of correct parliamentary procedure and legislative courtesies even while the Bolsheviks were creating a new and powerful "antidemocratic reality" on the ground around them. On October 31, for example,

when a group of Mensheviks proposed that the Council deal with the urgent question of anarchy and counterrevolution, Kadets insisted the matter be sent first to a "special commission" for "analysis." At the moment they were doing so, moreover, party "whips" were moving around the floor, reminding Kadets "in even voices" that fees for their club were due, and telling them what commission meetings were scheduled.

This was a week before the Bolsheviks seized power. Rosenberg, *Liberals in the Russian Revolution*, p. 255. As Pipes put it, the Kadets and the Russian intelligentsia generally "regarded democracy, not as the product of a slow evolution of institutions and habits, but as man's natural condition." Pipes, *Russian Revolution*, p. 56. Their observance of correct parliamentary procedure and legislative courtesies was not an affectation but instead an enthusiastic embrace of the "natural" ways of politics.

political party that did not advocate socialism, the Kadets drew almost no support from workers, soldiers, and the peasantry. For this reason, and because their ideological commitments made them pariahs to much of the left, the Kadets were entirely locked out of the Soviets. However, the party enjoyed substantial influence in the Provisional Government and still held several ministries in the last Kerensky cabinet before the Bolsheviks revolted.[22]

The Mensheviks and the Bolsheviks were the two major Marxist parties and shared a working-class base in the major cities.[23] The Mensheviks also drew significant support from the urban intelligentsia and white-collar workers in the state bureaucracy. In terms of ideology, the Mensheviks contended that Russia had to pass through a "capitalist/democratic" stage in which the social and economic conditions for socialism would ripen before the proletariat could take power.[24] Although the Mensheviks were certainly to the left of the Kadets, the two parties were more or less natural allies in the steadily intensifying competition with the Bolsheviks. However, that alignment, along with their support for parliamentary democracy in general, made the Mensheviks vulnerable to Bolshevik charges that the party was a thinly veiled bourgeois organization committed to thwarting the creation of a revolutionary communist state.[25] When violent street demonstrations in July threatened to pull the Bolshevik Party into premature rebellion against the Provisional Government, Lenin argued that the attempt would fail because the masses still had faith in "the petty bourgeois capitalist-controlled policy of the Mensheviks and SRs

---

[22] Alexander Kerensky was prime minister in the Provisional Government during the three months immediately preceding the revolt.

[23] Both the Mensheviks and the Bolsheviks emerged as factions within the Russian Social Democratic Party, which had been founded in the last years of the nineteenth century. After an initial rupture in the Brussels–London Congress in 1903, the final split took place in 1912 when the Bolshevik Conference in Prague organized its faction into a separate party organization. Leszek Kolakowski, *Main Currents of Marxism* (New York: W. W. Norton, 2005), pp. 636, 731.

[24] The Menshevik program anticipated that the proletariat would ally with the bourgeoisie in order to overthrow the autocracy and, once the bourgeoisie was in power, the working class would constitute the main opposition to the capitalist government. Kolakowski, *Main Currents of Marxism*, p. 680. Left-wing parties vigorously debated whether or not Russia must pass through a "capitalist/bourgeois stage" before moving on to communism. If such a stage were necessary, there was debate about how long it would last and what form it would take. These questions, of course, were much more relevant to political programs in Russia than in more advanced western economies because Russian industry (and thus the size of the proletariat) was much less developed than in nations such as Germany, Britain, and France. Pipes, *Russian Revolution*, pp. 144–5, 346–7, 396–7.

[25] This interpretation was shared by one of the leading Kadets, who said that "the real preponderance in the Cabinet definitely belonged to the convinced supporters of bourgeois democracy." This was in early August when the Socialist Revolutionaries dominated the Provisional Government. Chamberlin, *Russian Revolution*, vol. 1, p. 187.

[Socialist Revolutionaries]."[26] From an ideological perspective, Lenin was simply conveying his own interpretation of the political situation within a Marxist schema. However, his interpretation was also easily adapted to the kind of sloganeering that constituted "reason in the streets" because it characterized the Mensheviks, the Provisional Government, and, in fact, any and all opposition to the Bolsheviks as "bourgeois" and therefore "counter-revolutionary."

The Mensheviks had significant internal disagreements, primarily over continued participation in the war against the Germans. The Internationalist wing opposed continuation of the war and, on this and other issues, often sided with the Bolsheviks. The Defencist wing supported the war and was that much closer to the Kadets in opposition to the Bolsheviks. However, when the Bolsheviks seized power, both Menshevik factions condemned the takeover for ideological reasons (as premature in terms of the historical development of Russia) and as an affront to socialist solidarity.[27]

Menshevik participation in revolutionary politics was largely determined by the party's doctrinal commitments and the declining popularity those commitments engendered. Menshevik insistence, for example, that Russia pass through a capitalist/democratic stage before reaching socialism committed the party to a reform program that became increasingly unpopular with the Russian masses. As the Bolsheviks relentlessly exploited their differences with this program by offering an immediate, sweeping social revolution as an alternative, the party increasingly drew industrial workers into their own ranks; as a result, the mass base of the Menshevik Party steadily shrank. By November, the party had become a head without a body and the prestige and standing of the Menshevik leadership among the nation's political elite were almost all that remained of the party's influence on events.

In response to their rapidly fading popularity in the streets, the Menshevik leadership became increasingly committed to parliamentary

---

[26] Carr, *Bolshevik Revolution*, vol. 1, p. 91. Also see Kolakowski, *Main Currents of Marxism*, p. 736; McMeekin, *Russian Revolution*, pp. 166–74. Pipes lists "three attempts at a putsch" in which "Lenin called out the mobs into the streets." The first two in May and July were more or less spontaneous demonstrations that the Bolsheviks stood ready to exploit opportunistically if the Provisional Government were likely to fall, the second more so than the first. However, both of these failed. The third, of course, was well orchestrated in every way by the Bolshevik Party and became the November Revolution. Pipes, *Russian Revolution*, p. 397. On the May demonstrations, see pp. 399–407. In contrast to the quote in the text, Pipes lays responsibility for Bolshevik involvement in the July demonstrations squarely on Lenin's shoulders, calling the party's participation his "worst blunder, a misjudgment that nearly caused the destruction of the Bolshevik Party" (p. 419 and, more generally, pp. 419–36). For descriptions of Bolshevik participation in the May and July demonstrations, also see Figes, *People's Tragedy*, pp. 394, 422–34.

[27] Leo Lande, "The Mensheviks in 1917" in Leopold H. Haimson (ed.), *The Mensheviks: From the Revolution of 1917 to the Second World War* (Chicago: University of Chicago Press, 1974), p. 94; Carr, *Bolshevik Revolution*, vol. 1, p. 112.

democracy as an end unto itself. At first, parliamentary forms appear to have been a means through which the capitalist/democratic stage could be effected by way of enabling bourgeois elements (i.e., the Kadets) to construct the appropriate political economy for the Russian state. However, as the Bolshevik threat became ever more manifest, Menshevik leaders increasingly utilized parliamentary forms as a way of constructing a broad coalition of socialist and non-socialist parties in opposition to the Bolsheviks and containing the threat they presented within formal legislative institutions. Whatever ambivalence the Mensheviks might have felt toward parliamentary democracy in March 1917 had vanished by the time the Constituent Assembly met in January 1918.[28]

The Socialist Revolutionaries enjoyed the support of the vast majority of the Russian peasantry and, because peasants comprised the bulk of the Russian army, of most of the troops mobilized for the war. This mass base made them by far the largest political party until they were suppressed by the Bolsheviks; however, their political program was very narrow, largely focused on the distribution of land to the peasantry.[29] Although the Socialist Revolutionaries were not a Marxist party, they did subscribe to a radical political ideology and, up until the overthrow of the autocracy, terrorist tactics.[30] Despite their size and the fervent devotion of their peasant supporters, the Socialist

[28] In the opening (and only) session of the Constituent Assembly, Irakli Tsereteli delivered a major speech in which he summarized Menshevik opposition to "anarchic attempts to introduce a socialist economy in a backward country" and argued that "the class struggle of the workers for their final liberation" could only be successfully realized within a political regime characterized by "popular sovereignty based on universal and equal suffrage." Carr, *Bolshevik Revolution*, vol. 1, p. 119.

[29] One estimate of class sizes in revolutionary Russia has placed the number of peasants (the social base of the Socialist Revolutionaries) at over a hundred million while the bourgeoisie (the social base of the Kadets) registered a comparatively paltry six million or so. The urban and industrial proletariat (the social base of the Mensheviks and Bolsheviks) comprised about twenty million people. Rosenberg, *Liberals in the Russian Revolution*, p. 123. If the outcome of the revolution had been dictated by numbers alone, the Socialist Revolutionaries would have built the new Russian state. On the Russian peasantry generally, see Pipes, *Russian Revolution*, pp. 91–120, 237. Pipes describes "Russian industrial workers" in 1900 as, "with minor exceptions, a branch of the peasantry rather than a distinct social group." This rather thick social integration of workers and peasants gave rise to thorny problems for Bolsheviks, in both the theory and the practice of proletarian politics.

[30] According to Chamberlin:

While the Socialist Revolutionaries were not blind to the changes in Russian life which had been brought about by the rapid development of capitalism in Russia during the last quarter, and especially during the last decade of the nineteenth century, they regarded the peasantry, rather than the industrial working class, as the main moving force for the revolutionary movement and placed the nationalization of the land and the confiscation of the landlords' estates for the benefit of the peasantry in the forefront of their demands. They also differed with the Marxian parties in advocating and practising individual terrorism. (Chamberlin, *Russian Revolution*, vol. 1, p. 40)

Revolutionaries were seriously handicapped in several ways. First, their support was largely concentrated in the rural expanses of Russia, far from the major cities where most revolutionary action took place. When the Bolsheviks mobilized Petrograd workers for an assault on the Winter Palace in November 1917, for example, there was no way that the Socialist Revolutionaries could oppose them by bringing their own mass base into play.

Second, most peasants had little or no education, had little understanding of social conditions and attitudes outside their villages, and were thus quite unsophisticated in terms of political doctrine or strategy. Although much of the leadership of the Social Revolutionary Party was as educated and urbane as their counterparts in the other parties, the gulf between the Social Revolutionary rank and file and their leaders was very wide.[31] When the Bolsheviks offered an immediate redistribution of land on terms that almost mimicked the Social Revolutionary program and combined that offer with withering criticism of Social Revolutionary support for the Provisional Government and parliamentary democracy, the peasantry flocked to the Bolshevik banner.[32] There was really only one demand that most peasants made in revolutionary politics, and that demand was that they be allowed to occupy the lands held by the Russian gentry. Much of that occupation ultimately occurred through spontaneous action when the gentry fled to the comparative safety of the cities.

The third and perhaps most debilitating handicap was the lack of unity within the Social Revolutionary Party. The commitment to land redistribution was the only programmatic element that held the party together. And even there unity was elusive because many party members were at least as committed to parliamentary democracy as they were to land reform and thus wanted to wait until the Constituent Assembly had formed a new state before formally redistributing landed estates to the peasantry. Others saw no reason to delay acting upon a demand that was both just on its face and inevitable in its realization. In addition, those Socialist Revolutionaries who were committed to continuing the war with the Germans anticipated that immediate reform would probably mean dissolution of the Russian army as peasant soldiers abandoned their units and rushed home to claim their share of land. In sum, immediate land reform, parliamentary democracy, and continuation of the war were mutually incompatible policies that divided the party into factions, but, unlike the Bolsheviks, there "was no Lenin to place an iron yoke of discipline on [what became an] inchoate organization."[33]

As a formal party organization, the Left Socialist Revolutionaries emerged only after the Bolsheviks overthrew the Provisional Government. In fact, when

---

[31] Chamberlin, *Russian Revolution*, vol. 1, p. 250; Vernadsky, *Russian Revolution*, p. 54.
[32] Chamberlin, *Russian Revolution*, vol. 1, p. 326.
[33] Chamberlin, *Russian Revolution*, vol. 1, p. 40.

elections were held for the Constituent Assembly in late November, the Socialist Revolutionaries fielded lists that still included their more radical colleagues. By that time, however, the Left Socialist Revolutionaries were already acting autonomously by refusing to leave the Second All-Russian Congress of Soviets when it endorsed the Bolshevik overthrow. Although they did not formally join the new government, they cooperated with the Bolsheviks in rejecting parliamentary democracy and demanding the immediate redistribution of land. They shared the same social base as their more moderate colleagues, but they were made of much ruder social material than the "sober, well-to-do peasants" and intellectuals who comprised the mainstream leadership of the party.[34] In Table 5.1, the Left Socialist Revolutionaries are categorized as preferring a proletarian dictatorship to parliamentary democracy, but that attitude toward the formation of the new state was a product more of their emphatic hostility toward parliamentary democracy than of their embrace of a Bolshevik-dominated dictatorship of the proletariat. That hostility kept them out of the Provisional Government. The only locus of power the party/faction enjoyed was in the Soviets.

Most of the leadership of the Bolshevik Party was either in exile or in Siberian prison camps at the beginning of the Russian Revolution. Until the leaders returned to Russia – and, in particular, to Petrograd – the party was not a significant factor in revolutionary politics and its program could only with difficulty be distinguished from that of the Mensheviks. All that changed when Lenin arrived in Petrograd on April 16. Four days later, on April 20, *Pravda* published his "April Theses," a set of doctrinal interpretations that subsequently guided the Bolshevik Party from that point until the November uprising.[35] The second of these theses clearly broke with the orthodox Marxist position assumed by both the Mensheviks and many Bolsheviks.

---

[34] Chamberlin, *Russian Revolution*, vol. 1, p. 353.

[35] Germany not only facilitated Lenin's transportation from Switzerland to Petrograd at the beginning of the revolution but also provided massive financial support to the Bolshevik Party after he arrived. McMeekin suggests that Germany's covert financial aid was a decisive factor in Bolshevik success. See McMeekin, *Russian Revolution*, pp. 125–36. Also see Erich Eyck, trans. Harlan P. Hanson and Robert G. L. Waite, *A History of the Weimar Republic: From the Collapse of the Empire to Hindenburg's Election*, vol. 1 (New York: Atheneum, 1970), p. 25. Lenin's "April Theses" are partially reprinted and analyzed in Carr, *Bolshevik Revolution*, vol. 1, pp. 79, 84, 86–7. In the theses, Lenin "flatly rejected" the position that Russia must "enter a period of extended bourgeois domination" after the fall of the Tsar, even though he had maintained that such a period was necessary on many previous occasions. This change in position occurred "after only one month of supposedly bourgeois rule!" McAdams, *Vanguard of the Revolution*, p. 87. The exclamation point is in the McAdams text. The "April Theses" initially encountered much opposition within the Bolshevik Party and only Lenin's prestige prevented outright rejection. Figes, *People's Tragedy*, pp. 387–8, 391, 393; for a description of factions within the Bolshevik Party, see pp. 392–3.

The peculiarity of the current moment in Russia consists in the *transition* from the first stage of the revolution, which gave power to the bourgeoisie as a result of the insufficient consciousness and organization of the proletariat, *to its second* stage, which should give the power into the hands of the proletariat and poorest strata of the peasantry.

Rejecting all cooperation with the Provisional Government, Lenin urged his party to actively educate and thus persuade the masses that "the Soviet of Workers' Deputies is the *one possible* form of revolutionary government" once it was no longer "subject to the influence of the bourgeoisie." The fundamental goal of the party was

[n]ot a parliamentary republic – a return to that from the Soviet of Workers' Deputies would be a step backwards – but a republic of Soviets of Workers', Poor Peasants' and Peasants' Deputies throughout the country, growing from below upwards.

The clear implication, as Carr put it, was "that the moment when the Bolsheviks, by means of mass education, secured a majority in the Soviet would be the moment of the passing of the revolution into its second, or socialist, phase."[36]

By late October the Bolsheviks were ready to seize power. By that point they had full control of the most important Soviets (including Petrograd) and of most of the military units in and around Petrograd, as well as broad support among workers in the major cities. On October 22, the Petrograd Soviet passed a resolution of "no confidence" in the Provisional Government and formed a War-Revolutionary Committee that the Mensheviks accurately described as "a staff for seizing power." Although the political implications were clear, the Bolsheviks made no attempt to conceal these measures, nor did they deny their portent. This was so much the case that the official Kadet newspaper on November 1 started a daily column with the heading "Bolshevik Preparations" for taking power. And one member of the Bolshevik Central Committee publicly remarked that "we are openly preparing an outbreak."

Chaired by Leon Trotsky, the War-Revolutionary Committee coordinated the deployment of Russian military and naval units. In an almost bloodless coup, the Bolsheviks occupied the major transportation, communication, and government centers on the evening of November 6, and, at 10 o'clock the following morning, they announced that the "Provisional Government is overthrown" and that the "authority of the State has been transferred to the hands of the organ of the Petersburg Soviet of the Workmen's and Soldiers' Deputies – the War-Revolutionary Committee, which is at the head of the Petersburg proletariat and garrison."[37]

---

[36] Carr, *Bolshevik Revolution*, vol. 1, p. 79. Also see McMeekin, *Russian Revolution*, pp. 131–2. The formal title of the "April Theses" was "On the Tasks of the Proletariat in the Present Revolution."

[37] Mavor, *Russian Revolution*, p. 156.

In the early morning of November 8, Trotsky announced the fall of the Provisional Government to the Petrograd Soviet. Lenin also spoke to the Petrograd Soviet, explaining that "the overthrow" meant

that we are going to have a Soviet government. We will have our own organ of authority without any participation of the *bourgeoisie*. The depressed masses will build up an authority for themselves. The old state apparatus is going to be broken up, and a new apparatus of administration, in the form of the Soviet organization, is going to be built up. From to-day a new phase in the history of Russia begins, and this *third* Russian Revolution, as a final result, is to bring the victory of socialism.[38]

The Petrograd Soviet then passed a resolution approving the actions of the War-Revolutionary Committee and acknowledged its authority pending the establishment of a Soviet government. All that remained to be done at that point was the capture of the Winter Palace, where a few government ministers were sheltering.

It was no coincidence that the Second All-Russian Congress of Soviets was also meeting in Petrograd on the night of November 7–8.[39] When the Congress passed a resolution assuming authority over the Russian state, the Bolshevik coup thereby became a Soviet government. In its second session on the evening of November 8, the Congress issued a decree:

To establish for the administration of the country, until the Constituent Assembly provides otherwise, a Provisional Workers' and Peasants' Government, which is to be named "The Soviet of the People's Commissars." The management of the different branches of the life of the State is entrusted to commissions, the personnel of which secures the accomplishment of the programme announced by the congress, in close contact with the mass organizations of the working men, working women, sailors, soldiers, peasants, and employees. The governmental authority rests with the *collegia* of the chairmen of these commissions, viz. with the Soviet of the People's Commissars.[40]

The Congress then appointed the Soviet of the People's Commissars (each commissar was responsible for a policy area in much the same way that ministers would be in a parliamentary regime) and named Lenin as chairman.[41]

When the First All-Russian Congress of Soviets had convened in June, the Bolsheviks had comprised only a little under 13 percent of the delegates (see Table 5.2). As the third largest party, the Bolsheviks were less than half the size of either the Mensheviks or the Socialist Revolutionaries. By November,

[38] Mavor, *Russian Revolution*, p. 160, emphasis in the original.
[39] The Bolshevik coup had, in fact, been scheduled to take place just before the convening of the Second All-Russian Congress on November 7. Carr, *Bolshevik Revolution*, vol. 1, p. 98. Also see McMeekin, *Russian Revolution*, pp. 207–9. On Bolshevik involvement in the calling of the Congress and the election of delegates, see Pipes, *Russian Revolution*, pp. 474–7.
[40] Mavor, *Russian Revolution*, p. 162.
[41] Mavor, *Russian Revolution*, pp. 144–7, 156, 160–2; Rosenberg, *Liberals in the Russian Revolution*, pp. 130, 260; Chamberlin, *Russian Revolution*, vol. 1, pp. 297, 308–12, 320–3, 326–7.

TABLE 5.2. *Party strength in the All-Russian Congress of Soviets and Constituent Assembly*

June 1917 Congress of Soviets	November 1917 Congress of Soviets	January 1918 Constituent Assembly
Socialist Revolutionaries (285)	Socialist Revolutionaries (55)	Socialist Revolutionaries (410)
Mensheviks (248)	Mensheviks (56)	Mensheviks (16)
Bolsheviks (105)	Bolsheviks (323)	Bolsheviks (175)
Other parties (139)	Left Socialist Revolutionaries (70)	"National groups" (86)
Unaffiliated parties (45)	Unaffiliated and minor parties (58)	Kadets (17)

Note: Ukrainian nationalists comprised most of the "national groups" elected to the Constituent Assembly.
Sources: Carr, Bolshevik Revolution, vol. 1, pp. 89, 110; Mavor, *Russian Revolution*, p. 169, n. 17.

however, the Bolsheviks could claim almost 60 percent of the Second All-Russian Congress of Soviets, a majority further buttressed by the support of the Left Socialist Revolutionaries (who by then had become a formally organized party).[42] Because the Bolsheviks thoroughly dominated the Congress of Soviets, this became the legislative assembly that founded the Soviet state and, for that reason, was the legislative assembly that capped the "non-democratic" revolutionary path.

The abdication of the Tsar had ended the old regime and thus constituted a revolution. But the transfer of sovereignty to the new Provisional Government was more or less a default result of the Tsar's abdication and thus did not found a new state. With the important exception of the Bolsheviks, all parties in the revolutionary coalition expected and favored the election of a Constituent Assembly. That assembly would then found the new state by writing a constitution that would both legitimate its rule and instantiate a post-revolutionary settlement. However, elections to the Constituent Assembly were repeatedly postponed by the Provisional Government. They were finally held on November 25, soon after the Bolshevik uprising, and they did not go well for the Bolsheviks.[43] They elected just under a quarter of the 704 delegates while their chief rivals, the Socialist Revolutionaries, won almost 60 percent of the

---

[42] The Bolshevik majority became even greater when many of the Menshevik and Socialist Revolutionary Party members protested the coup by leaving the Congress. McMeekin, *Russian Revolution*, pp. 213–15.

[43] Most elections did not go well for the Bolsheviks. In early September 1917, for example, the party polled only 33.3 percent of the votes in the municipal election in Petrograd, its home base. The party did somewhat better in Moscow but was still short of a majority there as well. Pipes, *Russian Revolution*, pp. 465–6.

seats.[44] If the Constituent Assembly had been permitted to draw up a constitution, it would have become the legislative assembly that capped the "democratic" revolutionary path.

However, the Bolsheviks had no intention of permitting the Constituent Assembly to draft a new constitution. The purely instrumental reason for their rejection of the assembly was clear: the party controlled the Soviets, much of the army and navy, the city of Petrograd (in which the assembly was to meet), and the major posts in the government ministries. Given that they had already declared their own revolution and now wielded most of the authority of the Russian state, the Constituent Assembly was nothing but a threat to their rule. But the doctrinal justification for Bolshevik rejection of the Constituent Assembly nonetheless sheds light on the party's understanding of the new Russian state's social purpose.

Most of the doctrinal principles that informed the party's strategy originated, of course, with Lenin. While Russia was not yet ready for a communist revolution in March, Lenin believed that conditions were more than ripe by late October.[45] In that short span of time, the economic base of Russia had certainly not changed significantly, so this ripening had little or nothing to do with the fundamental material preconditions for a communist revolution. But the attitude of the Russian masses had changed in ways that strengthened the Bolshevik Party not only in the streets but also in the Soviets, the factories, and the Russian military. There was thus a link between popular public opinion (democracy) and the strategy of the party: the former both legitimated and enabled the latter. When Lenin presented the party's new land policy to the Second All-Russian Congress of Soviets one day after the Bolsheviks seized power, he attributed its doctrinal heterodoxy to the following fact: "As a democratic government, we cannot evade the decision of the popular masses, even if we were not in agreement with it." Even once the Bolsheviks were in power, the "vital first steps of the regime were . . . taken under the banner not of socialism, but of democracy."[46]

Lenin wanted to postpone the elections to the Constituent Assembly but was overruled by the party.[47] When the returns revealed a massive defeat, the Bolsheviks considered suppressing the Constituent Assembly by not allowing it to convene. Nikolai Bukharin argued against suppression because, as he put it, "constitutional illusions are still alive in the broad masses." However, he did advocate expulsion of the Kadets and of a sufficient number of the other

---

[44] The Kadets were the only bourgeois party participating in these elections and were severely handicapped by Bolshevik suppression of their newspapers, disruptions of party meetings, and arrests of their leaders. Aside from this interference, the elections were remarkably free and fairly conducted. Chamberlin, *Russian Revolution*, vol. 1, p. 365.

[45] On the October Revolution, see Pipes, *Russian Revolution*, pp. 439–505.

[46] Carr, *Bolshevik Revolution*, vol. 1, p. 106.   [47] Carr, *Bolshevik Revolution*, vol. 1, p. 109n.

delegates so that the assembly would simply ratify the new Bolshevik regime.[48] On December 26, 1917, Lenin anonymously published his "Theses on the Constituent Assembly" in *Pravda* in which he analyzed the Bolshevik seizure of power the previous month and concluded that the Constituent Assembly was now an anachronism. Because "the constituent assembly is the highest form of the democratic principle" in a "bourgeois republic," the party's support for the assembly under the Tsarist autocracy had been "fully legitimate."

However, once the Tsar was overthrown and a bourgeois government assumed power, the Bolsheviks had properly insisted that "a republic of Soviets is a higher form of democratic principle than the customary bourgeois republic with its constituent assembly" and was, in fact, "the only form capable of assuring the least painful transition to socialism." On the one hand, once the transition from Tsarist autocracy to parliamentary democracy had occurred, the historic mission of "revolutionary social-democracy" became the instantiation of the dictatorship of the proletariat (in the form of the Bolshevik Party). This instantiation could most effectively be achieved through the agency of the Soviets once the masses became conscious of the actual alignment of class forces and revolutionary possibility. On the other hand, these developments had also encouraged a proper understanding of their own class position among the bourgeoisie and their agents, the Kadets. Their completely reasonable and anticipated hostility to the Bolshevik Revolution had eliminated any "possibility of resolving the most acute questions in a formally democratic way."

There was thus an inevitable collision looming between the political orientation of the Constituent Assembly and "the will and interest of the toiling and exploited classes who [have begun] the socialist revolution against the bourgeoisie." For these reasons, Lenin concluded, "any attempt, direct or indirect, to look at the question of the Constituent Assembly from the formal juridical standpoint, within the framework of bourgeois democracy," was a betrayal of the socialist revolution because it failed to properly "appraise the October rising and the tasks of the dictatorship of the proletariat." If the Constituent Assembly, once it met, did not unconditionally accept "Soviet power" and support the "Soviet revolution," the ensuing "crisis ... can be solved only by revolutionary means."[49]

On January 2, 1918, the Bolshevik government announced that the Constituent Assembly would convene on January 18; and, on January 4, it set January 21 as the date for the Third All-Russian Congress of Soviets. On January 16, two days before the Constituent Assembly was to meet, the Central Executive Committee of the All-Russian Congress of Soviets approved a

---

[48] In Carr's words, Bukharin's recommendation would have turned "the Left rump into a 'revolutionary convention'" that then would have symbolically effected "the transition from bourgeois to socialist revolution through the agency of the Constituent Assembly." Carr, *Bolshevik Revolution*, vol. 1, p. 113n. Also see Figes, *People's Tragedy*, p. 513.

[49] Carr, *Bolshevik Revolution*, vol. 1, pp. 113–14.

"Declaration of Rights of the Toiling and Exploited People" and peremptorily demanded that they be adopted by the assembly. The Central Executive Committee also requested that the assembly formally recognize that its members had been elected before the "masses" had risen "against the exploiters." Because the masses had not "yet experienced the full force of the resistance of the exploiters in defence of their class privileges [and] had not yet undertaken in practical form the building of a socialist society," they had mistakenly elected delegates whom they now realized did not reflect their true class interests. For that reason, "the Constituent Assembly would think it fundamentally incorrect, even from the formal standpoint, to set itself up against the Soviet power."

In other words, the Constituent Assembly should naturally conclude that it had become an anachronism and had no other option than to support the Bolshevik regime. The Committee therefore asked the Constituent Assembly to announce: "Supporting the Soviet power and the decrees of the Council of People's Commissars, the Constituent Assembly recognizes that its tasks are confined to the general working out of the fundamental principles of the socialist reconstruction of society."[50]

When the Constituent Assembly finally convened on January 18, Yakov Sverdlov, acting in the name of the Central Executive Committee, shoved aside the oldest delegate, who, in accordance with tradition, was about to open the proceedings. Sverdlov then presented the Central Executive Committee's resolutions, asking that they be immediately considered and adopted. The Assembly rejected the resolutions and elected Victor Chernov, a Socialist Revolutionary, as presiding officer (he defeated Marie Spiridonova, a Left Socialist Revolutionary backed by the Bolsheviks). What then followed can be viewed as either one of the most interesting, if aborted, foundings in world history or, alternatively, as a tragic farce. Although a large majority of the delegates were opposed to the new Bolshevik regime, the galleries were crowded with Bolshevik workers and sailors who were armed and had been drinking heavily. They pointed their weapons at the delegates and made threatening catcalls while the Socialist Revolutionaries and delegates belonging to the other minor

---

[50] Carr, *Bolshevik Revolution*, vol. 1, p. 117. On January 17, *Izvestiya* reprinted another committee resolution that underlined the imperative nature of these requests:

On the basis of all the achievements of the [November] revolution and in accordance with the Declaration of Rights of the Toiling and Exploited People adopted at the session of the Central Executive Committee on January 3, 1918, all power in the Russian republic belongs to the Soviets and Soviet institutions. Therefore any attempt on the part of any person or institution whatever to usurp this or that function of state power will be regarded as a counter-revolutionary act. Any such attempt will be crushed by all means at the disposal of the Soviet power, including the use of armed force. (Carr, *Bolshevik Revolution*, vol. 1, pp. 117–18)

By this point, the Bolsheviks had outlawed the Kadets and had arrested some of the more prominent moderate leaders of the Socialist Revolutionaries. As a result, some of the resistance to the November Revolution had already been suppressed.

parties made parliamentary motions, debated resolutions, and otherwise attempted to go about the business of founding a democratic state. After the Bolshevik delegates left the chamber, their seats on the chamber floor were taken by now quite rowdy workers and sailors who continued to insult and provoke the credentialed delegates.[51] Finally, the sailor who commanded the military guard in the hall approached Chernov on the dais and told him that the Constituent Assembly must adjourn.[52]

CITIZEN SAILOR: I have been instructed to inform you that all those present should leave the Assembly Hall because the guard is tired.

CHAIRMAN [CHERNOV]: What instruction? From whom?

CITIZEN SAILOR: I am the commander of the Taurida Guard. I have an instruction from the commissar.

CHAIRMAN: The members of the Constituent Assembly are also tired, but no fatigue can disrupt our proclaiming a law awaited by all of Russia. [Loud noise. Voices: "Enough, enough!"]

CHAIRMAN: The Constituent Assembly can disperse only under the threat of force. [Noise.]

CHAIRMAN: You declare it. [Voices: "Down with Chernov!"]

CITIZEN SAILOR: I request that the Assembly Hall be immediately vacated.

The delegates then hurriedly cleared up the parliamentary business that was before them as "more Bolshevik Troops crowded" into the hall. After twenty minutes or so, they adjourned and left the chamber. Lenin later described this "dispersal of the Constituent Assembly by Soviet authority [as] the complete and open liquidation of formal democracy in the name of the revolutionary dictatorship."[53]

When the delegates returned to the Tauride Palace the following day, they found armed guards blocking the doors. The Constituent Assembly never met again. As a theoretical commentary on foundings, we should note that the delegates in the Constituent Assembly persistently asserted that they were in touch with and were exercising the will of the Russian people even as their assembly was first surrounded by and eventually physically infested with Bolshevik roughnecks. The symbolic role of the Constituent Assembly in the founding of a Russian state demanded a neutrality toward – almost an insensibility to – the acts of personal intimidation directed at them. Their persistence in adhering to parliamentary protocol in the face of a malicious display of potential violence was not a charade; it was a ritual form necessary to their very identity and purpose. As a ritual that could enact a democratic founding, it was

---

[51] Mavor, *Russian Revolution*, pp. 195–8.

[52] Carr believed that the order to close the session came directly from Lenin. Carr, *Bolshevik Revolution*, vol. 1, pp. 119–20; Chamberlin, *Russian Revolution*, vol. 1, p. 370.

[53] Pipes, *Russian Revolution*, pp. 553–4, 556; on the Constituent Assembly generally, see pp. 537–57. For a description of the events leading up to its convocation and the proceedings when it met, see Figes, *People's Tragedy*, pp. 507–9, 513–18.

necessary that those delegates believed in what they did and that the consequences of that belief materialized in actual political practice – necessary but not, in this case, sufficient.

On January 19, 1918, the same day that the delegates found the doors to the Tauride Palace blocked by armed guards, the Central Executive Committee announced the dissolution of the Constituent Assembly. The Committee attributed its decision to the changing alignment of historical class forces within Russia and the consequent need to cleanse state institutions of bourgeois influence, unequivocally committing those institutions to the control of the dictatorship of the proletariat:

At its very inception, the Russian revolution produced the Soviets of Workers', Soldiers' and Peasants' Deputies as the only mass organization of all the working and exploited classes capable of giving leadership to the struggle of these classes for their complete political and economic emancipation.

Throughout the initial period of the Russian revolution the Soviets grew in number, size and strength, their own experience disabusing them of the illusions regarding compromise with the bourgeoisie, opening their eyes to the fraudulence of the forms of bourgeois-democratic parliamentarism, and leading them to the conclusion that the emancipation of the oppressed classes was unthinkable unless they broke with these forms and with every kind of compromise. Such a break came with the October Revolution, with the transfer of power to the Soviets ...

The October Revolution, which gave power to the Soviets and through them to the working and exploited classes, aroused frantic resistance on the part of the exploiters, and in putting down this resistance it fully revealed itself as the beginning of the socialist revolution.

The working classes learned through experience that old bourgeois parliamentarism had outlived its day, that it was utterly incompatible with the tasks of Socialism, and that only class institutions (such as the Soviets) and not national ones were capable of overcoming the resistance of the propertied classes and laying the foundations of socialist society.

Any renunciation of the sovereign power of the Soviets, of the Soviet Republic won by the people, in favour of bourgeois parliamentarism and the Constituent Assembly would be a step backwards and would cause a collapse of the entire October Workers' and Peasants' Revolution ...

Outside the Constituent Assembly, the parties which have the majority there, the right-wing Socialist-Revolutionaries and the Mensheviks, are waging an open struggle against Soviet power, calling in their press for its overthrow and thereby objectively supporting the exploiters' resistance to the transition of land and factories into the hands of the working people.

Obviously, under such circumstances the remaining part of the Constituent Assembly can only serve as a cover for the struggle of the bourgeois counter-revolution to overthrow the power of the Soviets.

In view of this, the Central Executive Committee resolves: The Constituent Assembly is hereby dissolved.[54]

---

[54] McCauley, *Russian Revolution*, pp. 184–6.

The Bolsheviks did not contest the fact that the delegates to the Constituent Assembly had been democratically elected. Nor did they challenge the notion that a state must be founded in accordance with the "will of the people." However, they lodged objections against bourgeois interpretations of what a "democratic election" might be and how the "will of the people" should be constituted.

Both challenges originated in the Bolshevik conception of the connection between history and political consciousness. At every historical stage, there was a "correct" correspondence between political consciousness and the material conditions of a class. In March 1917, the proletariat participated in a bourgeois revolution that destroyed the Tsarist autocracy and brought into existence a parliamentary democracy. However, Russian workers were not yet fully conscious of the fact that this parliamentary democracy was but a temporary way station on the road to socialism. Bending to that political reality, the Bolsheviks supported the calling of a Constituent Assembly as a way of unmasking the bourgeois class orientation of the Provisional Government (because the latter was, in fact, reluctant to put at risk state policies, such as prosecution of the war with Germany, by holding elections). Bolshevik support for the Constituent Assembly was thus a means of educating the masses and did not involve a commitment to conventional democratic elections. When this education had created a correct political understanding of the historical moment within the proletariat, the Bolsheviks overthrew the Provisional Government.

On the one hand, the Bolsheviks knew that the proletariat had come to correctly understand what should be done because party cadres were in close contact with workers and soldiers who, in many cases, wanted more immediate, radical action than the party thought was prudent. The development of revolutionary consciousness was thus monitored in the streets, the factories, and the barracks. On the other hand, the Bolsheviks wanted, if possible, to demonstrate this consciousness by way of formal, organized political action, action that took the form of the election of delegates by the local Soviets throughout the nation. So, when elections to the Second All-Russian Congress of Soviets resulted in a clear majority for the Bolsheviks, this allowed the party to claim that the Congress represented the "will of the people" and could thus legitimate the seizure of power that occurred just before it convened.

The Congress was, of course, a legislative assembly. And, aside from the exclusion of the bourgeoisie from the franchise (a small fraction of the population) and the class basis of constituencies, the Congress was democratically elected. In these respects, the founding of the Soviet state resembled more conventional democratic foundings. But the Bolsheviks grounded their conceptualization of the "will of the people" in a correct, doctrinal understanding of historical class destiny. The proletariat had to approximate that understanding or there could be no socialist revolution. But perfection of that understanding, in terms of how the state should be constructed and how society should be transformed, was the task of the Bolshevik Party as the vanguard of the revolution.[55] Leon Trotsky described what he thought the new socialist individual would become once the party completed its mission:

Man will, at last, begin to harmonize himself in earnest ... He will want to master first the semi-conscious and then also the unconscious processes of his own organism: breathing, the circulation of blood, digestion, reproduction, and, within the necessary limits, will subordinate them to the control of reason and will. Even purely physiological life will become collectively experimental. The human species, the sluggish *Homo sapiens*, will once again enter the state of radical reconstruction and will become in its own hands the object of the most complex methods of artificial selection and psychophysical training ... Man will make it his goal to master his own emotions, to elevate his instincts to the heights of consciousness, to make them transparent ... to create a higher sociobiological type, a superman, if you will ... Man will become incomparably stronger, wiser, subtler. His body will become more harmonious, his movements more rhythmic, his voice more melodious. The forms of life will acquire a dynamic theatricality. The average human type will rise to the heights of an Aristotle, Goethe, Marx. And beyond this ridge, other peaks will emerge.[56]

Among many other things, the proletariat would become doctrinally sound and self-sufficient, able to flourish within the new communist society while fully comprehending its fundamental logic and theoretical grounding.

The party thus became the vehicle for realizing the "dictatorship of the proletariat" as it pursued the construction of the new state and the transformation of society. And, because only the party could act upon a correct understanding of these things, individual preferences, as an expression of individual "wills," were irrelevant (or even counter-revolutionary).[57] After the party decided upon a policy, often by voting as individuals, political discipline demanded individual conformity with the decision.[58] The party as a collective

---

[55] This complicated relationship between revolutionary action and the maturation of the "will of the people" predated the creation and rise of the Bolshevik Party. In 1879, for example, a small band of Socialist Revolutionaries formed a terrorist group called the People's Will whose mission was to enlighten, persuade, and raise the consciousness of workers and peasants by assassinating leading political figures. This terrorist band was not "authorized" by the people in the sense of asking their consent before acting; instead, it was dedicated to revealing to the people what they, in fact, willed by violently exposing the oppressive relations that pervaded Russian society. Pipes, *Russian Revolution*, pp. 142–3, 358–9.

[56] Pipes, *Russian Revolution*, p. 137.

[57] For instances in which Lenin was either in the minority with respect to a party decision or faced strong disagreement before getting his way, see Rosenberg, *Liberals in the Russian Revolution*, p. 271; Carr, *Bolshevik Revolution*, vol. 1, p. 109n; Pipes, *Russian Revolution*, pp. 388, 393–4, 402, 404, 415, 439, 470–3, 482–5, 508, 511, 518–19, 524, 575, 583–4, 586–7, 592–3. As McAdams put it: "No one seriously questioned Lenin's status as a first among equals. Nevertheless, his associates still firmly believed that revolutionary decision making was a collective enterprise. They were comfortable disagreeing with Lenin on nearly every issue and expected that their views would be taken seriously." McAdams, *Vanguard of the Revolution*, p. 98.

[58] For the most striking instance of party discipline, see Carr, *Bolshevik Revolution*, vol. 1, p. 109.

TABLE 5.3. *Legislative assemblies attending the founding of the Soviet state*

Legislative assembly	Claim on legitimacy	Role in the founding of the state
Second All-Russian Congress of Soviets (November 8, 1917)	Election by workers and soldiers	Proclamation of a Provisional Workers' and Peasants' Government, naming the People's Commissars (Lenin as chairman, etc.).
Central Executive Committee (January 16, 1918)	Election by Soviets of Workers', Soldiers' and Peasants' Deputies	"Russia is declared a republic of Soviets of workers', soldiers' and peasants' deputies. "All power in the center and locally belongs to these Soviets." (Part of the Declaration of Rights of the Toiling and Exploited People)
Third All-Russian Congress of Soviets (January 23, 1918)	Election by workers, peasants, and soldiers	Approved dissolution of the Constituent Assembly and Declaration of Rights of the Toiling and Exploited People. Also adopted a resolution – "On the Federal Institutions of the Russian Republic" – that stated: "The Russian Socialist Soviet Republic is created on the basis of a voluntary union of the peoples of Russia in the form of a federation of the Soviet republics of these peoples."
Fifth All-Russian Congress of Soviets (July 10, 1918)	Election by workers, peasants, and soldiers	Adoption of the Soviet Constitution, including the Declaration of Rights of the Toiling and Exploited People as a preamble.

Sources: Vernadsky, *Russian Revolution*, p. 162; Carr, *Bolshevik Revolution*, vol. 1, pp. 108, 110, 117, 121, 123, 150.

was the only unit that could identify and act upon a correct understanding of the historical moment.[59]

[59] This insistence on the absolute authority of the party over doctrinal interpretation made the Soviet founding rather unique in its inclination to disown its founders. For example, the official history of the Communist Party (written long after the revolution) notes that only Grigory Zinoviev and Lev Kamenev opposed the party's decision in late October to prepare for the overthrow of the Provisional Government: "They asserted that the working class was incapable of carrying out a Socialist revolution; they sank to the position of the Mensheviks, who were championing the bourgeois republic. This was a betrayal of Socialism. The capitulatory position of Zinoviev and Kamenev was no accident. Their treachery was the direct outcome of all their

While most foundings are dramatic events that are easily recognized as breaks with the past, the durability of their claims on state sovereignty are often neither immediately obvious nor uncontested. In the Russian Revolution, the legitimation of the Bolshevik uprising by the Second All-Russian Congress in November was, in retrospect, clearly a founding, but many of those who witnessed the event and its immediate aftermath believed that the attempted takeover would fail. As the Bolsheviks consolidated power, there were at least three other legislative assemblies that could conceivably be interpreted as playing a role in the founding of the Soviet state (see Table 5.3). The most dramatic of these was the Bolshevik refusal to allow the newly elected Constituent Assembly to meet in January 1918. Soon after that, the Third All-Russian Congress of Soviets both formally denied the legitimacy of the Constituent Assembly and affirmed the Bolshevik takeover in November. By comparison, the adoption of a formal constitution by the Fifth All-Russian Congress of Soviets on July 10, 1918, was almost an afterthought.[60] In fact,

opportunist vacillations." And Trotsky, who did not vote against the resolution but, instead, "insisted on its being postponed until the Second Congress of Soviets was convened," was accused of assuming a position "tantamount to wrecking the insurrection, for the Socialist-Revolutionaries and Mensheviks might postpone the Congress, and that would have enabled the Provisional Government to concentrate its forces by the time the Congress opened, so as to smash the insurrection." B. N. Ponomaryov et al., trans. Andrew Rothstein, *History of the Communist Party of the Soviet Union* (Moscow: Foreign Languages Publishing House, 1960), p. 252. Despite their condemnation decades later, all three of these dissenters were elected to the seven-member Political Bureau and subsequently played leading roles in the Bolshevik Revolution. Chamberlin, *Russian Revolution*, vol. 1, p. 292. Also see McMeekin, *Russian Revolution*, p. 203. On Lenin's tolerance of dissent within the party, see Pipes, *Russian Revolution*, pp. 349–50, 511.

[60] The constitution did, however, formally define, primarily by exclusion, the proletariat:

[T]he following categories [were prohibited] from voting or running as candidates in soviet elections: [1] Persons using hired labor with the aim of extracting profit (this covered kulaks, as well as urban entrepreneurs and artisans), persons living off unearned income (dividends from capital, profits from enterprises, rent from property, and so forth)[; 2] Private traders and middlemen[; 3] Monks and priests of all denominations[; 4] Former employees and agents of the Tsarist police, secret police, and special corps of gendarmes[; 5] Members of the former Imperial family, the House of Romanov.

Sheila Fitzpatrick, *Everyday Stalinism: Ordinary Life in Extraordinary Times: Soviet Russia in the 1930s* (New York: Oxford University Press, 1999), p. 117. The will of the people (the proletariat) was thus the will of those who were not excluded from voting or standing as candidates in elections. However, this was only theoretically interesting because the same constitution also provided that the Bolshevik Party (as the embodiment of the proletarian will) would be the only organization fielding candidates in those elections. The elections themselves were thus redundant exercises. The constitution also promised the "abolition of all exploitation of man by man" and, through socialism, a distribution of "the prosperity of the exploiters" to the "working people." Rogers Smith views these promises as instrumental appeals to the loyalty of the people, which, of course, they were. But they were also commitments which were deeply embedded in Bolshevik ideology. Rogers Smith, *Stories of Peoplehood: The Politics and Morals of Political Membership* (New York: Cambridge University Press, 2003), p. 60.

Bolshevik doctrine strongly implied that there was no need for a social contract when the party itself both embodied the will of the people and constituted the state. The idea that the party should or could contract with itself was a contradiction in terms.[61]

---

[61] Carr reported that Lenin's writings in the months preceding adoption "will be searched in vain for any reference to constitution-making." This indifference was rooted in doctrine. Carr, *Bolshevik Revolution*, vol. 1, p. 125. After the founding, however, the Soviet Union continued to conduct elections that, while reaffirming the supremacy of the Communist Party as the only legitimate embodiment of the "will of the people," otherwise took a number of different forms. Mark B. Smith, "Popular Sovereignty and Constitutional Rights in the USSR's Supreme Soviet Elections of February 1946"; Gleb Tsipursky, "Integration, Celebration, and Challenge: Soviet Youth and Elections, 1953–1968"; Stephan Merl, "Elections in the Soviet Union, 1937–1989: A View into a Paternalistic World from Below"; Thomas M. Bohn, "'The People's Voice': The Elections to the Supreme Soviet of the USSR in 1958 in the Belorussian Capital Minsk" all in Ralph Jessen and Hedwig Richter (eds.), *Voting for Hitler and Stalin: Elections under 20th Century Dictatorships* (Frankfurt: Campus Verlag, 2011), pp. 59–78, 81–99, 276–306, 309–30.

6

Blood and Soil

The Founding of the Third Reich

Adolf Hitler was sworn in as chancellor of the Weimar Republic just before noon on January 30, 1933. Before taking office, the Nazi leader had consented to an alliance with a conservative party in which the latter would hold most of the cabinet seats in the new government. While their coalition would not enjoy a majority in the Reichstag, there had been minority governments and cabinets before this one. And the chancellorship Hitler was assuming was not the most powerful office under the Weimar Constitution; that position was held by Field Marshal Paul von Hindenburg, who had soundly defeated Hitler in the presidential election the previous year. The Field Marshal, in fact, retained authority to dismiss the chancellor and his new government at any time. In all respects, the ritual surrounding Hitler's oath complied with the formalities of the Weimar Constitution as they had been performed by previous chancellors as they took office. In these respects, the event that ushered Hitler and the Nazi Party into power appeared to be nothing more than another round in the play of parliamentary politics. However, that evening, tens of thousands of uniformed storm troopers, men of the SS (*Schutzstaffel*, Hitler's Praetorian guard), and other members of right-wing paramilitary organizations marched through the streets of Berlin in celebration.[1] As they saluted the new chancellor, there was no doubt that they embraced his assumption of power as a new founding for the German state.

Hitler and the Nazi Party came to power under rules and procedures laid down by the Weimar Constitution. Those rules and procedures had originally been created with the hope that, in time, the German people would come to invest parliamentary democracy with a legitimacy that would make respect for

---

[1] Richard J. Evans, *The Coming of the Third Reich* (New York: Penguin Books, 2005), pp. 307, 310; Peter Fritzsche, *Germans into Nazis* (Cambridge, MA: Harvard University Press, 1998), pp. 139–42.

the rules of the political game more important than the identity and policies of those who won and lost elections. Although that game had recently been played in a way that sometimes stretched those rules, there was still a wide societal consensus on the kind of actions that would transgress the bounds set by the constitution. At the time Hitler became chancellor, many people viewed the Nazi Party as a legitimate player in the political game.

Even so, by 1933, most of the delegates elected to the Reichstag, including those belonging to the Nazi Party, had little or no respect for the parliamentary democracy that had been created by the Weimar Constitution. Those delegates played the political game in order to replace it with something else, although there was little agreement on what that something else might be. From that perspective, Hitler and the Nazi Party came to power while abiding by the rules of a political game that they fully intended to destroy. And there, too, they were not alone.

A paradox thus attends the founding of the Third Reich. On the one hand, Hitler and the Nazi Party sought to cloak their assumption of power in legitimacy by abiding by the rules of a political game for which they had obvious and unmitigated contempt. On the other hand, once in power, they almost immediately destroyed that political game, replacing it with a radically different system of governance. Why did they abide by the rules of a political game they despised when obedience to those rules implied the possibility that they might never attain power? That question naturally leads to a second: Why, once they attained power under the rules of that political game, did they destroy it? If those rules brought them power, why not continue to practice politics within that political game? The answers to these questions reside in how they and German society conceived of the will of the people.

German society contained at least four different, competing conceptions of the will of the people in the years between the creation of the Weimar Constitution and Hitler's assumption of power. One of these, the Leninist conception of the dictatorship of the proletariat, is already familiar to the reader as the driving force behind what became the Russian Revolution. Embodied in the German Communist Party, this construction conceived the popular will as something that would only fully manifest its intent after the impending proletarian revolution had brought the party to power. Until then, the German Communist Party, like the Nazis, played the game of parliamentary democracy but, unlike the Nazis, their participation was not motivated by a belief that the game would bring them power; they instead believed that participation was the best way of spreading their doctrinal commitments among the masses while sabotaging parliamentary democracy from within.

A very different conception of the popular will formed the beliefs and practices of those who subscribed to parliamentary democracy, both in abstract theory and as constructed under the Weimar Constitution. Although they had substantive commitments that varied enormously, ranging from political allegiance to the Catholic Church to pursuit of an ostensibly Marxist social democracy, they formed the core elements of most Weimar governments before

Hitler became chancellor. For them, the popular will was manufactured and manifested in democratic elections and uninhibited parliamentary debate.

Yet another conception of the popular will was the property of what was left of an *ancien régime* that yearned for the reestablishment of the German monarchy and, more practically and realistically, an authoritarian state grounded in the prestige and discipline of the national army. This conception interpreted the popular will as favoring the interests and needs of the German nation as recognized by the landed aristocracy, high-ranking officers in the military, and those who controlled the largest firms in the industrial economy. In their view, parliamentary democracy at best muddled the expression of the popular will in endless and pointless political debate. At worst, electoral competition between the major parties divided the people into petty interests and fragmented the nation into hostile factions. Although they blamed democracy for these effects, their solution (authoritarian rule by the nation's elite) assumed that the masses should never actively participate in politics regardless of the form the political system might take. In their conception, the popular will was manifested as an immanent desire for social order, national unity, and a prominent role for the German nation in the world at large. The German people willed these things even though they could not reach them through their own volition. On the one hand, democracy and democratic practices were not necessary for discovering the content of the popular will because that was already known. On the other hand, the popular will was both muddled and frustrated by the petty squabbles that attended parliamentary democracy.[2]

The fourth and final conception of the popular will resided in the ideology and practice of the Nazi Party. Like those who proposed the establishment of an elite-dominated authoritarian state, the Nazis believed that parliamentary democracy fragmented the nation and thus prevented the German people from fully realizing their innate racial and cultural superiority. But the Nazis pushed this logic further by asserting that the realization of this superiority on the national and world stage was the rightful historical destiny of the German race, people, and nation.[3] Upon coming to power, the Nazi Party proposed to

---

[2] See, for example, George L. Mosse, *The Crisis of German Ideology: Intellectual Origins of the Third Reich* (New York: Grosset and Dunlap, 1964), p. 283.

[3] Nazi ideology distinguished between the German race (those who possessed the requisite genetic material to be considered Aryan), people (those who identified with the Aryan community), and nation (the state that enabled the Aryan community to pursue its rightful historical destiny). While recognizing that race, people, and nation were different things before the party assumed power, the goal was to make them synonymous by expelling from Germany those who did not belong to the Aryan race, by persuading those who were Aryan that their highest allegiance was to the Aryan community, and by encompassing all German-speaking Aryans, including those then residing in other countries, within a unified German nation. There was an unsolved question with respect to the other Nordic peoples who undoubtedly belonged to the Aryan race but had little or no affinity with German culture. Stanley G. Payne, *A History of Fascism, 1914–1945* (Madison: University of Wisconsin Press, 1995), p. 157.

remold the German state in such a way that the power of the German people could materialize this destiny. In this respect, Nazi ideology was similar to traditional German conservative thought. However, unlike the authoritarian elite, the organization of the Nazi Party was itself merely a vehicle for the true embodiment of the popular will: the Leader.[4] The Leader, in his person and his conscious spirit, both embodied the popular will (in the sense that he was the material personification of the German people and thus could will only what they willed) and led the people (in the sense that he correctly identified and then acted upon those measures that would realize the historical destiny of the German race, people, and nation – in effect, telling the people what it was that they willed).

As a theoretical device, the notion of the Leader relieved or eliminated several tensions that would have otherwise plagued the Nazi Party. First among them was the tension between Hitler's absolute, personal domination of the party organization and the party's pretensions as a popular movement of the people. The Nazi Party presented Hitler's popularity as incontrovertible evidence that he, as the Leader, personally embodied the will of the German people. As an extension of the Leader's own persona, the Nazi Party thus became merely a vehicle for realizing that will. From that perspective, Hitler's complete domination of the party organization perfected that party organization as a means for implementing the popular will. In sum, Hitler's popularity empirically demonstrated that the Nazi Party was the vehicle for enacting the popular will and, at the same time, made Hitler's personal control of the party organization not only reasonable but logically imperative.

This formalization of Hitler's charismatic appeal as one of the central pillars of party ideology also entailed the subordination of the various interests and sectors of the German nation to the Leader's (and thus the popular) will.[5] The Nazi Party sometimes proposed policy platforms that contained planks that appealed only to particular, narrowly circumscribed interests. However, if the party had relied only upon such planks in their campaigns, the Nazis would have fared no better than any of the mainstream democratic parties. The notion of the Leader reconciled the practice of democratic politics (e.g., Nazi Party appeals to narrow interests in the electorate) with the party's ultimate goal of abolishing democracy as a necessary step in materializing the historical destiny of the German people.[6] In theory, the Leader ostensibly tolerated appeals to

---

[4] See, for example, the formal definition of "Leader" in Research Institute for Military History, *Germany and the Second World War. Volume I: The Build-up of German Aggression*, trans. P. S. Falla, Dean S. McMurry, and Ewald Osers (Oxford: Clarendon Press, 1990), p. xxvi.

[5] Listening to one of Hitler's speeches was "a mystical experience: one of affirmation, or indeed transcendence; he was both the monarch and the high priest of a faith in which the nation was the core article of belief." Nicholas O'Shaughnessy, *Selling Hitler: Propaganda and the Nazi Brand* (London: Hurst, 2016), p. 4.

[6] "It was the leader who in his person united state and the *Volk*: he was the living embodiment of the ideology and, through the state, the executor of actions necessary to safeguard the innermost

narrow interests as illustrations of how every element in the German nation would prosper when the party came to power. But the emphasis was not on how interests would prosper but on how they would be reconceived once the German people were unified under the authority of the Leader.

As was the case with those who supported parliamentary democracy, the Nazi Party interpreted elections as a manifestation of the will of the people.[7] In that sense, the returns registered how well the Nazis had performed as they attempted to convince voters of their party's right to rule. The party also anticipated that victory in those elections was the way in which it would come to power. But election campaigns were also, and sometimes primarily, opportunities in which the masses could express their growing adulation for the Leader; this adulation, duly confirmed in ever greater numbers of votes for the party, was evidence that the people were coming to recognize that they and the Leader were one and the same.[8] Nazi campaigns became grand spectacles in which the Leader presided over ecstatic demonstrations of fealty, subordination, and a mass abandonment of personal identity. Although the Nazi Party still had to win elections, the elections themselves served as stages upon which the Leader performed a role utterly hostile to the individualism central to conventional conceptions of a democratic will.

As long as the party improved its performance in these elections, the campaigns also demonstrated the inevitability of the Leader's assumption of power. This inevitability was, of course, central to party ideology in that the German people must inevitably recognize that their historical destiny could be realized only through their unification with the Leader. Although the German people may not at first recognize Hitler as the Leader who would unify, declare, and carry out the will of the people, party ideology anticipated this recognition as an historical necessity. Corroborating election returns, in the form of increasing proportions of the electorate casting votes for the Nazi Party, were thus confirmation of this expectation.[9]

---

purpose of the race. He was, therefore, both lawmaker and judge." George L. Mosse, *Nazi Culture: Intellectual, Cultural and Social Life in the Third Reich*, trans. Salvator Attanasio (New York: Schocken Books, 1981), p. 319.

[7] Richard J. Evans, *The Third Reich in Power* (New York: Penguin Books, 2005), pp. 44–5.

[8] During the runoff election for president in 1932, for example, Nazi papers raised "Hitler's own person ... to even greater heights of pseudoreligious intensity." One provincial paper approvingly quoted Hitler as saying that "I believe that I am God's instrument to liberate Germany." A headline in the *Volkischer Beobachter*, the official organ of the Nazi Party, claimed that "[t]he National Socialist movement is the resurrection of the German nation," while filling "its pages once again with pictures of Hitler and the adoring masses." Dietrich Orlow, *The History of the Nazi Party, 1919–1933* (Pittsburgh, PA: University of Pittsburgh Press, 1969), p. 252.

[9] As a consequence of these beliefs, Hitler "was deeply concerned, one might say even paranoid, about popular opinion." Robert Gellately, *Backing Hitler: Consent and Coercion in Nazi Germany* (Oxford: Oxford University Press, 2001), p. 257.

At the founding of the Third Reich, it was neither Hitler nor the Nazi Party that inhabited the German state but the German race, people, and nation. Hitler merely embodied the will of the people and the party organization was the vehicle through which they would realize their historical destiny. Once the German state was founded on those principles and beliefs, there was no longer any need for democracy. This, in outline, is how the popular will came to be instantiated in the German state at the founding of the Third Reich. In the rest of this section, we explore these themes in more detail, beginning with the establishment of the Weimar Republic and the kind of political system that it created. We then move on to a description of the Weimar party system, juxtaposing the varying interpretations that the party system placed on the will of the people, including how that will was expressed. This section also describes the principles of German conservative thought and how Nazi ideology both grew out of that tradition and came to supplant it. Finally, we turn to the founding of the Third Reich both as a moment in which the will of the people was melded into the German state and as an event manufactured by opportunistic exploitation of political possibility.

THE FOUNDING OF THE WEIMAR REPUBLIC

The Weimar Republic was founded in much the same way that most modern republics have been founded. Calling itself the Council of People's Delegates, a revolutionary committee emerged after Germany conceded defeat during the First World War. Dominated by the Social Democratic Party, this revolutionary committee organized elections to the Constituent Assembly (also known as the National Assembly) which was then elected on January 19, 1919.[10] Friedrich Ebert, the head of the provisional government, welcomed the delegates to Weimar in a manner that easily conformed to the most orthodox requirements of democratic foundings.

The National government through me extends its greeting to the Constituent Assembly of the German nation ... The Provisional Government owes its mandate to the Revolution. It will place this mandate back into the hands of the National Assembly. In the Revolution the German people rose against an antiquated and collapsing rule of force ... As soon as its right of self-determination has been assured, the German people will return to the way of legality. Only by parliamentary discussion and decision can the unavoidable changes in the economic and social spheres be produced, without which the Reich and its economic life must perish. It is for this reason that the National Government extends its greeting to this National Assembly as the highest and sole Sovereign in Germany. We are done forever with the old kings and princes by the grace of God ... With the certainty of a republican majority in this Assembly, the old ideas of a

---

[10] All citizens, including women, who were at least twenty years of age could vote in this election. Erich Eyck, *A History of the Weimar Republic*, trans. Harlan P. Hanson and Robert G. L. Waite (Cambridge, MA: Harvard University Press, 1962), vol. 1, p. 61.

God-given dependence are eliminated ... The German people are free, they shall remain free and govern themselves for all time to come.

Ebert then declared: "The National Assembly is the expression of the will of the German Nation; it alone has from now on the right to decide, it alone has the responsibility for Germany's future."

Just a few days after it convened, the Constituent Assembly returned the favor by adopting a provisional constitution that, among other things, legitimated Ebert as the president of the government of the Republican Reich. Later, when the permanent constitution was approved, the preamble declared that "[t]he German People, united as a Nation ... has given itself this Constitution."[11] All of these elements conformed to the common practice of democratic foundings: the unlimited and exclusive sovereignty of the constituent assembly as the embodiment of the national will, the reciprocal legitimation of the government authority that calls the constituent assembly into being, and the affirmation of the product of their deliberations as nothing other than the materialization of the national will (after which the constituent assembly dissolves).

The Constituent Assembly began deliberations in Weimar, Germany, on February 6 and about six months later, on July 31, approved what became known as the Weimar Constitution in a vote that was, in hindsight, deceptively lopsided. The democratic parties of what became the parliamentary center of German politics cast 262 votes for the constitution. One or more of these parties would participate in every governing coalition until the last year before Hitler assumed power. Opposing adoption were seventy-five delegates drawn

---

[11] Johannes Mattern, *Principles of the Constitutional Jurisprudence of the German National Republic* (Baltimore, MD: Johns Hopkins Press, 1928), pp. 82–5. At another point in his analysis, Mattern gave an interpretation of the preamble that dramatically limited the individual consent that otherwise might be read into this founding. In his view,

[the term] German people [did] not signify the mere total of individual Germans in a numerical sense, but the German people, conscious of their membership in the German Nation, and united in the determination to enforce its will upon the individual members of the body politic. The Republican Constitution, created by them as the expression of this will, is not identical with the creation of their union, but rather the manifestation of the political will of the Nation expressed in the form of law. (Mattern, *Principles of the Constitutional Jurisprudence*, pp. 149–50)

Put another way, Mattern insisted that German people had materialized their unity as a nation in the founding in a way that limited both the scope of individual consent and the protections (e.g., political rights) that might otherwise be offered individuals against the claims of the state. Schmitt held a somewhat similar view, arguing that the "unity of the German Reich does not rest on these 181 articles [in the Weimar Constitution] and their validity, but rather on the political existence of the German people. The will of the German people, therefore something existential, establishes the unity in political and public law terms beyond all systematic contradictions, disconnectedness, and lack of clarity of the individual constitutional laws." Carl Schmitt, *Constitutional Theory* (Durham, NC: Duke University Press, 2008), p. 65.

from the conservative right and the Independent Socialists. These two ideological extremes, along with the Nazi Party that emerged afterward, would
combine to bring down the democratic order created by the constitution. In
1919, the conservatives were still recovering from the fall of the Kaiser and the
defeat of the German army. The Independent Socialists formally composed the
left wing of the Social Democratic Party, but, in practice, they were all but
autonomous. They would later become the German Communist Party.[12]

The Weimar Constitution resembled its predecessor in many respects. The
major difference was the transfer of "constituent power ... from the dynastic
legitimacy of the German princes to the German people." In place of the Kaiser,
the constitution created a president who would be directly elected under universal suffrage. A majority coalition in the Reichstag would nominate a candidate for chancellor who would be appointed by the president.[13] Of the two
offices, the president clearly carried more authority. Not only was the president
directly elected by the people (and could thus pose as their spokesperson
without intervening accountability to a particular political party or coalition
of parties) but he could also appoint or dismiss the chancellor and dissolve the
Reichstag by calling for new elections. But the most important and fateful
power held by the president resided in what became the notorious Article 48,
which read, in part:

If public safety and order in the German Reich is materially disturbed or endangered, the
National President may take the necessary measures to restore public safety and order,
and, if necessary, to intervene by force of arms. To this end he may temporarily suspend,
in whole or in part, the fundamental rights established in Articles 114, 115, 117, 118,
123, 124, and 153.

The National President must immediately inform the Reichstag of all measures adopted
by authority of Sections 1 or 2 of this article. These measures shall be revoked at the
demand of the Reichstag.

The emergency powers thus made available to the president permitted the
suspension of individual political and civil rights, the use of the military and

---

[12] Eyck, *History of the Weimar Republic*, vol. 1, p. 68. On the split within the Social Democratic
Party, including discussion of support for parliamentary democracy by the majority wing, see
Stefan Berger, *Social Democracy and the Working Class in Nineteenth and Twentieth Century
Germany* (Harlow: Longman, 2000), pp. 96–101. Also see Eric D. Weitz, *Weimar Germany:
Promise and Tragedy* (Princeton, NJ: Princeton University Press, 2013), pp. 15–20, 27–33.

[13] Christoph Mollers, "'We Are (Afraid of) the People': Constituent Power in German
Constitutionalism" in Martin Loughlin and Neil Walker (eds.), *The Paradox of
Constitutionalism: Constituent Power and Constitutional Form* (New York: Oxford University
Press, 2007), p. 91. On the framing and provisions of the Weimar Constitution, see Eyck,
History of the Weimar Republic, vol. 1, pp. 64–77. On the constitutional history of Germany
before the First World War, including the relationship between the popularly elected Reichstag
and the Kaiser, see p. 88. Also see, Evans, *Coming of the Third Reich*, p. 80. On the transition
between the pre-war and Weimar Constitutions, see Mattern, *Principles of the Constitutional
Jurisprudence*, pp. 71–82.

police in restoring and maintaining public order, and the ability to issue ordinances by decree that superseded and went beyond the statutory law enacted by the Reichstag. The ability of the Reichstag to revoke these measures was fatefully hamstrung by the president's authority to dissolve the chamber and call for new elections. If the Reichstag was not in session, the president could rule the nation with all the authority of an extraordinarily powerful dictator. In one of the painful ironies attending Hitler's rise to power, it was Friedrich Ebert, the Social Democrat most responsible for creating a parliamentary democracy under the Weimar Constitution, who first made extensive use of these emergency powers.[14]

While Article 48 should be attributed to a lack of faith in the capacity of a democratically elected parliament to rule effectively, the other major flaw in the Weimar Constitution can be traced back to a principle that the people should rule in all the fullness of the particularity of their beliefs. The system of proportional representation set down in the Weimar Constitution and then implemented in the Franchise Law of April 27, 1920, virtually guaranteed parliamentary representation to any political party that drew as little as 1 percent of the total vote. Under this system, minor parties of all kinds flourished, some of them dedicated to the interests of narrow economic sectors and occupations, others to regional identities.[15] The major parties offered differing conceptions of the proper relationship between the German state and people, some of them condemning Weimar democracy while presenting full slates of candidates to the electorate. Under the low threshold for parliamentary

---

[14] Mattern, *Principles of the Constitutional Jurisprudence*, pp. 485–8, 499; Evans, *Coming of the Third Reich*, p. 80. By invoking Article 48, Ebert intended to enable the survival of democracy in the face of serious political and economic challenges. He nonetheless set precedents that were later used to bring down the democratic system that he tried so hard to create and protect. Karl Dietrich Bracher, *The German Dictatorship: The Origins, Structure, and Effects of National Socialism*, trans. Jean Steinberg (New York: Praeger, 1970), p. 170. Also see Thomas Childers, *The Nazi Voter: The Social Foundations of Fascism in Germany, 1919–1933* (Chapel Hill: University of North Carolina Press, 1983), pp. 52–3. On the ability of the president to suspend freedom of speech and freedom of the press under Article 48, see Modris Eksteins, *The Limits of Reason: The German Democratic Press and the Collapse of Weimar Democracy* (London: Oxford University Press, 1975), p. 70.

[15] Because proportional elections rewarded electoral strategies that cultivated strong loyalties by economic sectors, social classes, and religion, such parties and loyalties thrived in Weimar politics. Nazi electoral strategy (1) tactically responded to these groups by claiming that their parties were not serving them well (and the Nazis could do better) and (2) strategically reformulated group identities so as to stress their common membership in and contributions to the *Volk*. By stressing a common German identity and the Nazi Party as the vehicle for realizing a common German destiny, the party both weakened the sectarian exclusivity of group identities and cloaked the inconsistencies in the Nazi political program (which, in many instances, offered material benefits to some groups while imposing material costs on other groups to whom the party was also appealing). One of the most serious of these inconsistencies involved the clash of interests between white-collar unions (employed, for example, by department stores) and small businesses (who also had conflicting interests over wages and work rules).

representation, none of these parties had much reason to compromise their principles as they competed for votes. In fact, intense competition in the electoral arena almost compelled them to differentiate their platforms from one another while promising staunch commitment to those principles.

Proportional representation thus splintered the party system in a way that discouraged the emergence of effective political leaders who might have otherwise been prominent figures in the public arena and could have bridged, through the art of compromise, policy differences in what was always a cobbled-together parliamentary coalition. The resulting instability of parliamentary coalitions often made effective governance almost impossible.[16] And the absence of major party leaders made contestation for the presidency a matter of personalities in which ostensibly non-political figures had a strong advantage over those enmeshed in what appeared to be petty squabbles between parliamentary factions.[17] The immediate beneficiary was Field Marshal Paul von Hindenburg, a military hero of the First World War, who was elected president after Friedrich Ebert's death. His election has been called "a disaster for the democratic prospects of the Weimar Republic."[18]

Compared with other foundings, the creation of the Weimar Republic was extraordinarily weak.[19] Although there was significant support in Germany for parliamentary democracy (particularly within the Social Democratic and centrist bourgeois parties), conservative and far-left ideologies mobilized passions far more effectively. Because the Allies insisted that the monarchy be abolished, conservatives viewed the new constitution as an alien imposition. In addition, because the democratic parties that wrote the constitution were also the parties that made the peace, their loyalty to the interests of the German nation could be challenged. These things were made far worse by the fact that the Versailles Treaty that made that peace imposed extremely harsh

---

[16] "Between 13 February 1919 and 30 January 1933 there were no fewer than twenty different cabinets, each lasting on average 239 days." Evans, *Coming of the Third Reich*, p. 83.

[17] Eyck, *History of the Weimar Republic*, vol. 1, pp. 69–71; Childers, *Nazi Voter*, pp. 42–3; Rudolf Heberle, *From Democracy to Nazism: A Regional Case Study on Political Parties in Germany* (Baton Rouge: Louisiana State University Press, 1945), p. 4. For a slightly less critical evaluation of proportional representation in Weimar Germany, see Evans, *Coming of the Third Reich*, pp. 83–4.

[18] Hindenburg's candidacy was the product of his national prominence and deep divisions between the conservative parties that prevented agreement on anyone else. While Hindenburg might be viewed as non-political in the sense that he was not directly affiliated with any of the organized political parties, he was hostile to democracy and increasingly sought ways of evading the inconvenience of parliamentary government. Ultimately, of course, Hindenburg appointed Adolf Hitler to the chancellorship. Evans, *Coming of the Third Reich*, pp. 81–3.

[19] Eyck, for example, states that Ebert himself "knew that the German Republic could not be born in less auspicious circumstances or at a less auspicious time." Eyck, *History of the Weimar Republic*, vol. 1, p. 45.

and ultimately unworkable terms on Germany.[20] Governing the nation meant complying with the terms of this treaty, which, in turn, became a precondition for the survival of democracy. In combination, these responsibilities crucified the democratic center as the far right and the far left sought to effect their own, radically undemocratic foundings. Divisions within the democratic center only made matters worse as the Weimar Constitution came to stand for procedural formality in politics with little commitment to substantive values such as freedom, equality, or national identity. Thus emptied of content, the Weimar Constitution never melded the popular will with the sovereignty of the national state.[21]

THE WEIMAR PARTY SYSTEM

Of all the political parties that competed for votes during the life of the Weimar Republic, the German Democratic Party (DDP) was the strongest proponent of democracy as an end unto itself.[22] Strongly committed to civil liberties, women's rights, and parliamentary debate, the party drew support from the German intelligentsia, pacifists, moderate industrialists, and the Jewish community (see Table 6.1).[23] The party also enjoyed the support of export-oriented industrialists because of its consistent opposition to tariff protection.[24] While the party leadership was composed of notables (many of them from circles outside of politics), most of its electoral support was drawn from the middle class, particularly white-collar workers, civil servants, and the proprietors of small businesses.[25] Aside from its promotion of democracy, the party stressed the need to resolve class differences and thus positioned itself as a likely coalition partner with the much larger Social Democratic Party, with which it

[20] For a more skeptical interpretation of the importance of the Versailles Treaty on German politics, see Fritzsche, *Germans into Nazis*, pp. 151–4.

[21] Evans, *Coming of the Third Reich*, pp. 59, 88. On the impact of the Versailles Treaty on German politics, see pp. 60–8, 75. Also see Eyck, *History of the Weimar Republic*, vol. 1, pp. 80–128.

[22] The initials stand for Deutsche Demokratische Partei. For an account of the party's creation and social composition, see Eyck, *History of the Weimar Republic*, vol. 1, pp. 59–60.

[23] William Brustein, *The Logic of Evil: The Social Origins of the Nazi Party, 1925–1933* (New Haven, CT: Yale University Press, 1996), p. 111. However, Jewish support fell off sharply after 1930 when the party moved to the right (p. 39). Hamilton estimated that more than half of German Jews voted for the DDP before then. Richard Hamilton, *Who Voted for Hitler?* (Princeton, NJ: Princeton University Press, 1982), p. 248.

[24] Brustein, *Logic of Evil*, pp. 37–8.

[25] Wolfram Wette, "Ideology, Propaganda, and Internal Politics as Preconditions of the War Policy of the Third Reich" in Research Institute for Military History, *Germany and the Second World War*, vol. I, p. 58. Although he was not active in party affairs, Max Weber supported the DDP until his death in 1920. Hamilton, *Who Voted for Hitler?*, p. 247. He even indicated a willingness to stand for election to the Constituent Assembly in 1919 but was passed over by party leaders because they were more comfortable with other men. Eyck, *History of the Weimar Republic*, vol. 1, pp. 61–2.

TABLE 6.1. *Characteristics of the major political parties in the Weimar Republic*

Party	Core social base	Orientation toward democracy and the Weimar Republic	Preferred basis for the sovereignty of the German state
Communist (KPD)	Working class; after the onset of the Great Depression, the unemployed	Hostile	Soviet organization of the state and economy using the Soviet Union as a model
Social Democrat (SPD)	Working class	Favorable	Supported the Weimar Republic; procedurally correct and legalistic
Democrat (DDP)	Middle-class; intelligentsia; export-oriented sectors of the economy	Favorable	Supported the Weimar Republic; emphasis on democratic principles and political rights
Catholic (Zentrum)	Catholics; hierarchy of the Catholic Church; particularly strong in Bavaria	Favorable	Supported the Weimar Republic, although weakly after 1930; often emphasized separation of church and state; federalism
German People's (DVP)	Bourgeoisie; industrial elite	Indifferent	Supported the Weimar Republic until 1929; an authoritarian regime thereafter
Nationalist (DNVP)	Large landowners; Lutherans; Lutheran Church; veterans; particularly strong in eastern Germany and Prussia	Hostile	Restoration of the German Empire, constitutional monarchy, and elitist respect for the traditional social order
Nazi (NSDAP)	Small farmers; shop keepers; independent artisans; students; particularly strong in rural areas of northern Germany	Hostile	Organization of politics and state authority under an all-powerful "Leader" who would embody and enable the rightful historical destiny of the German race, people, and nation; "blood and soil" nationalism

often cooperated in parliamentary deliberations and governing coalitions.[26] However, the rise of the Nazi Party after 1928 eroded German Democratic Party support within the middle class and the party gradually moved to the right in a vain effort to stem its losses.[27] In 1930, the party merged with the right-leaning Young German Order and adopted a new name: Deutsche Staatspartei (DSP). Even after these attempts to refashion its image, however, the party campaigned in the 1932 Reichstag election under a banner demanding "the preservation of the republic and democracy" and urged its supporters to "fight hard for the republic."[28] The primary narrative behind the DDP is one of an almost unremitting decline that almost exactly paralleled that of the Weimar Republic. As one writer put it, the German Democratic Party, "the favorite of liberal intellectuals then and now, had the most auspicious beginning of the republic's new parties and the most abject end."

If the DDP was the first pillar of Weimar democracy, the Catholic Center Party (the Zentrum) was the second. Although Catholicism might have generated its own party organization in any case, the Zentrum owed much of its cohesion and vitality to Bismarck's *Kulturkampf* in the 1870s, during which the German state blocked clerical appointments, banned the Jesuits, and arrested or deported hundreds of priests. In 1877, the Catholic Church was even declared an "enemy of the Reich." Although Bismarck later reversed many of these policies, Catholics overwhelmingly supported the Zentrum as their main line of defense against discrimination and repression by the German state. For its part, the hierarchy of the Catholic Church more or less sponsored the party as its vehicle in German politics.[29] Because religion was the primary foundation for the party and because Catholics were distributed along the full breadth of the German class spectrum, the Zentrum encompassed farmers, industrial workers, middle-class shopkeepers, white-collar employees, those who could claim noble lineage, and the leaders of large corporations. It even had a regional wing, the Bavarian People's Party, that was independent of the main organization. With respect to the main cleavage in German politics, the Zentrum presented itself as an alternative somewhere between capitalism and socialism in much the same way as did the Nazis. In fact, the Zentrum has been described as the "Catholic Volkspartei" because of its emphasis on the superseding salience of German Catholicism over all other forms of identity and interest.[30]

Unlike the DDP, however, democracy was more a means than an end for the Zentrum and its commitment to parliamentary governance was contingent on whether or not it promised to protect the Church. In a stable democracy, an alliance with the democratic parties of the center would have guaranteed

[26] Childers, *Nazi Voter*, pp. 38, 62–4.   [27] Childers, *Nazi Voter*, p. 190.
[28] Childers, *Nazi Voter*, pp. 135–6, 204.   [29] Childers, *Nazi Voter*, pp. 24–5.
[30] Hamilton, *Who Voted for Hitler?*, pp. 146, 252; Brustein, *Logic of Evil*, p. 40; Childers, *Nazi Voter*, pp. 41–2, 114.

religious tolerance and a tolerable détente with German nationalism. In fact, its flexible policy commitments (outside of issues involving the Church) made the Zentrum a natural coalition partner in the Weimar period and the party participated in every government up until 1930 (see Table 6.2).[31] However, the Zentrum found the Nazis abhorrent. In 1924, for example, the Zentrum accused the Nazi Party of harboring "a fanatical hatred of Christians and Jews" arising from its preference for the "old Wotan cult" of German antiquity over "Christian faith and Christian virtue."[32]

The Zentrum's secure confessional base meant, on the one hand, that it would never become the dominant force in German politics (there were far too many Protestants for that to happen) and, on the other hand, that its electoral support was fairly immune from the increasing popularity of the Nazi Party.[33] But this insularity did not mean that the Zentrum would remain fully committed to parliamentary democracy. As Richard Evans notes, the Catholic Church "saw a turn to a more authoritarian form of politics as the safest way to preserve the Church's interests from the looming threat of the godless left" – and where the Church would go, the Zentrum would have to follow.[34]

The third and largest pillar of Weimar democracy was the Social Democratic Party (Sozialdemokratische Partei Deutschlands or SPD). As they had been since the 1870s, the Social Democrats were still formally committed to Marxist ideology but in practice the party leadership was no longer either socialist or revolutionary. Their electoral base resided in the organized working class, particularly the large industrial unions, and their policy commitments generally favored industrial workers.[35] However, those policy commitments were often relegated to second place behind the party's support for parliamentary democracy. That support made them a natural coalition partner for the Zentrum and the German Democratic Party but also meant that the Social Democrats had to fend off the German Communist Party, which openly competed for the loyalty of radical workers.[36] The Social Democrats clearly recognized the threat that the Nazi Party posed to both their constituency and democratic government. In 1930, for example, party members serving in the Reichstag issued a remarkably prescient description of Nazi intentions:

---

[31] Childers, *Nazi Voter*, p. 190; Heberle, *From Democracy to Nazism*, p. 2.

[32] Childers, *Nazi Voter*, pp. 114, 258. On Nazi attempts "to reassure Catholics, and indeed all Christians, that the *volkisch* movement was a friend of religion," see p. 114.

[33] Childers, *Nazi Voter*, p. 266.

[34] Evans, *Coming of the Third Reich*, pp. 90–1, 94, 250, 255, 258, 262. On the Zentrum's turn to the right in the years just before the Nazi takeover, see Childers, *Nazi Voter*, pp. 260–1.

[35] By allying with the Zentrum during the life of the Weimar Republic, "the SPD managed to build one of the most advanced welfare states of the world." Berger, *Social Democracy*, p. 140.

[36] Hamilton, *Who Voted for Hitler?*, pp. 285–6; Childers, *Nazi Voter*, p. 191.

TABLE 6.2. *Composition of governments and cabinets under the Weimar Republic (1923–33)*

Chancellor (party)	Dates in office	NSDAP	DNVP	DVP	Zentrum	DDP	SPD	KPD
Wilhelm Marx (Zentrum)	November 30, 1923–January 15, 1925			X	X	X		
Hans Luther (non-partisan)	January 15, 1925–January 20, 1926		X	X	X	X		
Hans Luther (non-partisan)	January 20, 1926–May 17, 1926			X	X	X		
Wilhelm Marx (Zentrum)	May 17, 1926–January 29, 1927			X	X	X		
Wilhelm Marx (Zentrum)	January 29, 1927–June 29, 1928		X	X	X			
Hermann Müller (SPD)	June 29, 1928–March 30, 1930			X	X	X	X	
Heinrich Brüning (Zentrum)	March 30, 1930–May 30, 1932				X	X		
Franz von Papen (no party)	May 30, 1932–December 3, 1932							
Kurt von Schleicher (army general)	December 3, 1932–January 30, 1933							
Adolf Hitler (NSDAP)	January 30, 1933							

Note: Popular names for the political parties: NSDAP (Nazi); DNVP (Nationalists); DVP (German People's); Zentrum (Catholic); DDP (Democrats); SPD (Social Democrats); KPD (Communists). The last four chancellors (Brüning, Papen, Schleicher, and Hitler) were appointed by President Hindenburg even though they enjoyed only minority support in the Reichstag. Papen resigned from the Zentrum when he became chancellor.

Source: Most of the information in the table was taken from Eyck, *A History of the Weimar Republic,* vol. 1, p. 342; vol. 2, p. 489.

A Hitler government would aim to follow the Italian example by destroying all workers' organizations and creating a long-term state of siege. It would abolish freedom of the press and of assembly and other political rights, bringing about a permanent danger of civil war at home and a foreign war of revenge. This would mean the economic collapse of Germany and the end of an independent German nation, with all the frightful consequences that would ensue for the working people.[37]

However, their commitment to the legalistic forms and procedural formalities of democracy prevented them from resorting to force. As the Weimar Republic governments became increasingly authoritarian, the SPD supported those governments in an attempt to block even more frightening alternatives, particularly the assumption of power by the Nazis.[38] By that point, the party had all but abandoned the social policy interests of the working class as it tried to use the last shreds of the Weimar Republic as a shield against the radical right.[39]

The Social Democratic Party has sometimes been held responsible – if any party can be held responsible – for the assumption of power by the Nazi Party. A brief recounting of the party's possible failings and mistakes can, in fact, double as a description of the nature of Weimar politics in general. For one thing, the party has been accused of "not taking seriously enough the threat posed by anti-Semitism" and even, on rare occasions, permitting "anti-Semitic stereotypes to creep into ... their entertainment magazines." Anti-Semitism had been endemic in German society since at least the late nineteenth century, but it only became politically pathological when combined with German nationalism, particularly the rightist fixation on the German race, people, and nation after the First World War. So this charge should be widened to encompass *volkisch* nationalism generally. The problem for the Social Democrats is that their involvement in the making of the peace at Versailles fatally compromised their nationalist standing. They could make plausible and, with hindsight, utterly convincing arguments why nationalist policies, ambitions, and ideologies were problematic but they could not offer an alternative conception of identity to a nation prostrated and humiliated by foreign military power. Thus, the pragmatism with which they approached the Allies undercut their nationalist credentials from the very beginning of the Weimar Republic. Against this backdrop, the SDP's failure to directly confront anti-Semitism was clearly secondary to the party's inability to reconcile democracy and nationalism during the Weimar

[37] Wette, "Ideology, Propaganda, and Internal Politics," p. 67.
[38] Berger, *Social Democracy*, pp. 131–2. "If any one party deserved to be called the bulwark of democracy in the Weimar Republic, it was the Social Democrats." Evans, *Coming of the Third Reich*, p. 89.
[39] In attempting to explain its support for the Brüning cabinet to party members, the SPD said: "We fight for this state ... because we know that the moment the black-red-gold flag [of the republic] sinks, the red flag of socialism will fall along with it. It must be clear ... that the republic and the working class are bound together for life and death." Childers, *Nazi Voter*, p. 251. Backing Brüning meant that the SPD had to tolerate rule by presidential decree under Article 48 of the Weimar Constitution (p. 192). Also see Berger, *Social Democracy*, p. 130.

Republic – and the Allies, not the SDP, were directly and primarily responsible for that inability.

The party's formal commitment to Marxist principles might also be considered a mistake.[40] The SPD's strong support for parliamentary democracy raised many questions involving ideological consistency and made formal participation in a bourgeois government running a capitalist economy at least awkward. However, the Social Democrats probably had no alternative. If they abandoned Marxism and became a left-liberal party, their electoral base in the industrial working class would have been easy prey for the German Communist Party. If they instead pursued a more radical strategy and condemned capitalist democracy, the party would not have been able to support democratic alternatives to the radical right and may even have invited military repression. From that perspective, the SPD's formal commitment to Marxism and practical support for democracy squared a circle that made the Weimar Republic viable. This, too, was not a failing that brought the Republic to ruin.

As a governing party, the SPD was directly responsible for creating several precedents that, while well intentioned, were later cited by the Nazi Party once Hitler took power. One of them, use of Article 48 of the constitution, has already been mentioned. The other was the creation in 1922 of a special court, appointed by the president, for the prosecution and punishment of right-wing violence. This legislation had a number of nasty features that reappeared after 1933, including a provision that gave retroactive legitimacy to summary executions. Furthermore, the special court turned out to be ineffective in achieving its central purpose (which was to remove trials of right-wing defendants from a German judicial system that was unwilling to aggressively prosecute them). While use of Article 48 and the creation of this court might be considered mistakes, the Social Democrats did recognize two facts of German politics that made life difficult for the democratic left and, thus, for the Weimar Republic. One was the problem of reconciling the demands of the Allies under the Versailles Treaty with German public opinion in a deeply divided multiparty system. The other was the consistently hostile attitude of the German military and judiciary to the Republic itself. That attitude favored severe repression of leftist violence while more or less tolerating rightist brutality.[41] In fact, much of the violence committed by the right simply went unpunished. Finally, there should be at least some doubt that the Nazis crucially relied on these precedents when they transformed the Weimar Republic into the Third Reich.

---

[40] Berger, *Social Democracy*, pp. 102, 118; Brustein, *Logic of Evil*, pp. 112–13.

[41] Evans, *Coming of the Third Reich*, pp. 134–5; Bracher, *German Dictatorship*, pp. 110–11. The increasing aristocratic composition of the officer corps during the Weimar Republic made the army ever more hostile to parliamentary democracy over time. Warren B. Morris, Jr., *The Weimar Republic and Nazi Germany* (Chicago: Nelson-Hall, 1982), p. 79. More generally, see Mark Jones, *Founding Weimar: Violence and the German Revolution of 1918–1919* (Cambridge: Cambridge University Press, 2016), pp. 328–38.

The Social Democrats have also been accused of losing "touch with political reality" when the party strongly supported Hindenburg over Adolf Hitler in the 1932 presidential election. While it is certainly the case that the SDP thus backed a candidate who was both generally hostile to the Republic and particularly antithetical to their party and the working class generally, by that point there was simply no alternative candidate who could have blocked a Nazi assumption of power.[42] If the Social Democrats had abstained, Hitler would have probably won easily.[43] Such criticism naturally raises the question of whether and when the Social Democrats should have resorted to extra-parliamentary measures such as a general strike or armed resistance. If there was a point at which these tactics might have forestalled or prevented a Nazi takeover, that point was long gone by the 1930s. The Iron Front, the paramilitary units led by the SDP, were simply no match for Nazi brownshirts or the right-wing Steel Helmets.[44] And the German army, even under Versailles restrictions on size, would also have come in on the side of the right. Civil war was thus a losing proposition for the Social Democrats, who, in any case, had little stomach for bloodletting.[45]

---

[42] In endorsing Hindenburg, *Vorwarts*, the official SPD newspaper, urged the party faithful to vote for the lesser of two evils: "And if you don't do it out of love, do it out of hate [for the] Fascists." Anna von der Goltz, *Hindenburg: Power, Myth, and the Rise of the Nazis* (New York: Oxford University Press, 2009), p. 162. As a result of the SPD's support and the rise of Hitler's popularity with conservatives, "the best statistical predictor of a vote for Hitler in 1932 was," paradoxically, the "vote for Hindenburg in 1925." Benjamin Carter Hett, *The Death of Democracy: Hitler's rise to Power and the Downfall of the Weimar Republic* (New York: Henry Holt, 2018), p. 139. Also see Goltz, *Hindenburg*, pp. 144–6.

[43] As Eyck put it: "[E]ven the most dubious of men had to admit that Hindenburg's candidacy had been the only thing that kept Hitler from being elected President of Germany in 1932." Eyck, *History of the Weimar Republic*, vol. 2, p. 360. In general, Eyck was quite critical of the Social Democrats even while conceding that they were among "those very Germans who were most clearly committed to democracy" (pp. 163–5, 461).

[44] Created in 1924 by the Zentrum, DDP, and Social Democrats, the Reichsbanner became the largest paramilitary organization in Weimar Germany. However, even after its transformation into the Iron Front, it was no match for its right-wing counterparts. Wette, "Ideology, Propaganda, and Internal Politics," pp. 62–3. One of the largest of the right-wing paramilitary organizations was the Stahlhelm (Steel Helmet) which had enrolled over a million men by 1927. The Reichsbanner had more members but the Stahlhelm, the largest of Germany's veterans' organizations, was both better trained as a fighting organization and enjoyed much stronger ties to the German military. Morris, *Weimar Republic*, pp. 79–80.

[45] At the final SPD conference on June 19, 1933, one of the party leaders who had argued against civil war painfully admitted that he now regretted his decision:

It is gruesome, when I think of it today, what blood I thought had to be avoided in July 1932 ... I could not justify what, in my opinion, would have been needlessly spent blood of our followers. Now I have to tell you, nothing was avoided thereby. Now it will be an ocean of blood and tears. From this enemy no mercy is to be expected. I cannot do much more. But you have to do what your conscience dictates. It is worth the effort.

If a party can be held responsible for the Nazi assumption of power, it was not the Social Democratic Party. The Zentrum and the German Democratic Party cannot be held responsible either. The German Communist Party, however, is certainly a contender for this dubious honor. Founded in December 1918 by Rosa Luxemburg and Karl Liebknecht, the Communist Party (Kommunistische Partei Deutschlands or KPD) advocated a "dictatorship of the proletariat" modeled upon Bolshevik Soviets that would abolish capitalism. For the Communists, parliamentary democracy was neither a means nor an end; it was a bourgeois deception. Election campaigns were merely opportunities for proselytization in which success was measured in ideological conversions instead of votes.[46]

The primary focus of party activity was on preparations for the working-class revolution that Communist doctrine considered imminent. The first revolutionary attempt to found a Soviet-style state began in Berlin on January 6, 1919, just days before the Constituent Assembly was scheduled to convene. That uprising was put down by workers aligned with the SPD and the Freikorps, a right-wing paramilitary organization. The second attempt was initially led by "bohemian intellectuals" who proclaimed a Bavarian Soviet Republic in Munich in April. The Communists rather belatedly joined this revolt but it, too, was put down by the Freikorps. The third attempt occurred when the Communists organized a "Red Army" in the Ruhr as a response to a right-wing putsch. The German army suppressed the Communists in this uprising. The Communists rose up a fourth time in March 1921, only to be put down again by the army with help from the police. The last attempt to create a Soviet-style state occurred in Hamburg in 1923 and became "the fifth revolutionary disaster since the founding of the party."[47] After 1923, the

This was three days before Hitler banned the Social Democratic Party. On the heavy odds that the SPD would have faced if it had chosen to revolt, see, for example, Hamilton, *Who Voted for Hitler?*, pp. 280–1. Evans refers to each of the Social Democratic failings or mistakes discussed in the text but often qualifies them in one way or another. Evans, *Coming of the Third Reich*, pp. 29–30, 88–9, 137, 255, 276, 279, 286–7, 319, 320–1, 361. Evans also observes that the SDP only reluctantly adopted emotionally rousing electoral tactics that the Nazis had perfected long before them. "If the Social Democrats were to have stood any chance of beating the Nazis at their own game [involving the use of symbols, formulaic greetings, party salutes, and impassioned political slogans], they should have started earlier" (pp. 289–91). Also see Jost Dulffer, *Nazi Germany, 1933–1945: Faith and Annihilation* (London: Arnold, 1996), p. 21; Berger, *Social Democracy*, pp. 132–3.

[46] Berger, *Social Democracy*, p. 97; Evans, *Coming of the Third Reich*, p. 57. For an overview of the class composition of KPD membership, see Conan Fischer, *The German Communists and the Rise of Nazism* (New York: St. Martin's Press, 1991), pp. 129–32.

[47] Hamilton, *Who Voted for Hitler?*, pp. 288–97; Weitz, *Weimar Germany*, p. 91; Sheri Berman, *Democracy and Dictatorship in Europe: From the Ancien Regime to the Present Day* (New York: Oxford University Press, 2019), pp. 238–9, 241–2. On the Freikorps, see Fritzsche, *Germans into Nazis*, pp. 122–6; Payne, *History of Fascism*, p. 161.

Communists continued to organize but they did not again directly challenge the German state.

Given this revolutionary activity and the uncompromising radicalism of party doctrine, no one underestimated Communist hostility to the Weimar Republic and the KPD became an ominous specter that haunted both the democratic center and the far right.[48] Although each uprising clearly demonstrated the impotence of the Communist movement, both in terms of the small number of followers fully committed to a revolutionary experiment and an inability to exploit political opportunity, middle-class imagination increasingly viewed the Marxist left as the major threat to political stability and thus focused on those parties that promised the most effective response to that threat.

One of the most important effects of Communist doctrine was thus to encourage a kind of revolutionary adventurism. This adventurism was, of course, further encouraged by the revolutionary success of the Soviet Union, which provided a model to be emulated by the German Communist Party. Public apprehension stimulated by KPD adventurism inevitably strengthened the far right in electoral politics and the primary beneficiary was the Nazi Party. However, the Soviet Union became more than a model as the KPD increasingly fell under the spell and, thus, the control of the Communist International (Comintern). Once that occurred, the KPD became a creature of Moscow and was no longer an autonomous political party. Under the Comintern's direction, the KPD systematically downplayed the gravity of the Nazi threat even though it was one of the primary reasons for that party's rising popularity. Viewing the Nazi Party as "simply a manifestation of the final crisis of monopoly capitalism," the KPD focused its attention on its primary competitor for worker allegiance, the Social Democratic Party.[49]

In 1929, the KPD coined a new term, "social fascism," which referred to the mechanization and organizational consolidation of industry as a strategy for the maximization of monopoly profits. The collateral effects of this strategy included widespread unemployment and a major crisis for the capitalist system. But the KPD alleged that the most politically important consequence was the creation of a privileged labor aristocracy that aligned itself with the capitalist order against the proletariat. This aristocracy was represented in the workplace by labor unions affiliated with the Social Democratic Party, which also defended their interests (and therefore the interests of the capitalist class) in politics. The SPD thus became "the vanguard of fascism" and the most

---

[48] Hamilton, *Who Voted for Hitler?*, p. 299.

[49] However, Stalin had read a Russian translation of *Mein Kampf* and was well aware of the gravity of the Nazi threat to the Soviet Union. Wette, "Ideology, Propaganda, and Internal Politics," p. 22. Once the Nazi Party took power, Stalin sought to buy time by cooperating with the new regime and even tolerated without protest the destruction of the German Communist Party. Bracher, *German Dictatorship*, p. 198. Also see Wette, "Ideology, Propaganda, and Internal Politics," pp. 72, 75–7; Evans, *Coming of the Third Reich*, pp. 242–3, 314, 326–7.

important enemy of the proletariat. In the 1930 election, the KPD warned workers that they had to choose between a "Fascist Dictatorship or proletarian dictatorship ... Fascism or bolshevism." Contending that "the Nazis ... cannot govern without the help of the SPD," the Communists claimed that these two "fascist" parties were tacitly cooperating in an effort to "hold back the masses" through promulgation of "an anti-capitalist demagogy." The SPD was thus conflated with the Nazi Party in a way that made cooperation between the two working-class parties utterly impossible.[50]

The German Communist Party was probably not in a position to choose whether or not to cooperate with the Social Democrats. Both Marxist doctrine and the captivating success of the Bolshevik revolution tied the party to the Soviet Union in a way that made autonomous action in German domestic politics almost inconceivable.[51] But the Soviet Union and, in particular, Stalin could have chosen to target the Nazi Party, instead of the SPD, as the primary threat. Whether that would have prevented Hitler's assumption of power is questionable, but at least a united working-class front would have increased the probability. As things stood, it is difficult to conceive of a plausible Communist strategy that would have strengthened Nazi prospects more than the one the KPD actually adopted.

Sharing responsibility for the Nazi takeover were the conservative parties on the right wing of the political spectrum. One of these, the German People's Party (Deutsche Volkspartei or DVP), was too small to have much of an impact. Just after the end of the First World War, the DVP and the German Democratic Party had considered a merger. As the two most bourgeois, liberal parties, they shared a middle-class constituency and a combination seemed natural. However, they went their separate ways with the more conservative DVP publicly favoring a constitutional monarchy and otherwise more closely aligning itself with the interests of big business. Drawing around 10 percent of the vote in the early years of the Weimar Republic, the DVP was led by Gustav Stresemann, who almost single-handedly kept the party within the democratic center. When he died in 1929, the German People's Party moved to the right, became openly hostile to the Weimar Republic, and declined into irrelevance as the Nazi Party absorbed most of its constituency.[52] By that time, whatever strategy the party might have chosen would not have made any difference.

---

[50] Childers, *Nazi Voter*, pp. 181–3; Fischer, *German Communists*, 102–11, 164; Berger, *Social Democracy*, pp. 105, 111. One of the reasons why tarring the Social Democrats with "social fascism" was an attractive strategy was that, as Berger notes, some four out of every five KPD members was unemployed (p. 109).

[51] Evans, *Coming of the Third Reich*, pp. 93–4. Comintern domination of the KPD also weakened the party's appeal among German workers. Brustein, *Logic of Evil*, pp. 136–7.

[52] Childers, *Nazi Voter*, pp. 38, 137; Hamilton, *Who Voted for Hitler?*, pp. 31, 240–2; Wette, "Ideology, Propaganda, and Internal Politics," p. 54; Brustein, *Logic of Evil*, pp. 34–5; Evans, *Coming of the Third Reich*, pp. 95–6.

While the German People's Party might be exonerated because its mistakes were made when it had become irrelevant, the same is not true of the much larger German Nationalist People's Party (Deutschnationale Volkspartei or DNVP). Created in November 1918 through an amalgamation of conservative parties, the DNVP inherited the core principles and interests of the traditional Prussian aristocracy. These combined the landed elite's contempt for democracy, bourgeois modernism, social equality, and pacifism with a deep, reflexive respect for noble birth, military bearing, national identity, and the reserved manners of old wealth. The DNVP drew support from the same groups that had previously backed the Kaiser: the Prussian landed elite (along with agrarian proprietors generally), the military, high-level civil servants, and those who controlled heavy industrial corporations. In elections, these elements were complemented by large sections of the Lutheran Church and its congregants. Regionally, the Nationalists were particularly strong in East Prussia, where their elite base was concentrated.

The Nationalists did consent, on occasion, to participate in parliamentary coalitions with the bourgeois parties. But the Marxist commitments of the SPD and their working-class constituency made even the most tentative political cooperation extremely difficult. Although President Hindenburg was not formally identified with any party, there was never any doubt that his Prussian estate, noble birth, and high military rank made the Nationalists his natural home. While the Nationalists occasionally toyed with the idea of abandoning the Weimar Republic by turning Germany into a constitutional monarchy, their most feasible goal was an authoritarian regime backed by the German military. Toward the end of the Weimar Republic, this option was constantly on the table as Hindenburg tried to find a solution to increasing political instability.[53]

The Nationalists paved the way for the Nazi rise to power on two levels. One was on the plane of party ideology, which is discussed briefly here. The other occurred during the actual moment of Hitler's ascension to the chancellorship and will be discussed later. In terms of party ideology, there were five primary points at which Nazi and Nationalist understandings of politics met: the construction of nationalism and national interest; the unifying role of *volkisch* cultural identity; anti-Semitism as an organizing principle of state and society; the identification of "Bolshevism" as the primary enemy of the German people and nation; and the necessity of strong, authoritarian leadership. On these things there was enough general agreement between the two parties that many voters had trouble distinguishing between them. Although the Nationalists nonetheless attempted to draw advantageous distinctions between their positions and those of the Nazi Party, that effort failed for several reasons. For one thing, the Nazis possessed a much more effective propaganda machine and, in

---

[53] Childers, *Nazi Voter*, pp. 40–1, 74; Hamilton, *Who Voted for Hitler?*, pp. 20–1, 31, 233; Evans, *Coming of the Third Reich*, pp. 20, 94–5.

Hitler, an unmatched spellbinding orator. Both the machine and the orator presented a moving target that was extremely difficult to pin down when the Nationalists attempted to start a serious debate over policy issues. Far more ominously, the Nationalists vastly underestimated the gravity of the Nazi threat. The elite leadership of the DNVP thought that they could control the plebian (although largely middle-class) masses arrayed behind the Nazi Party by overawing or outmaneuvering Hitler, who, they believed, was merely a popular politician of little sophistication and pliable principles.[54]

With respect to the construction of nationalism and national interest, the Nationalists and the Nazi Party agreed on three essential principles: repudiation of the conditions imposed on Germany by the Versailles peace settlement; recovery of German lands lost in that settlement and a general unification of all German communities within the German nation (e.g., the absorption of Austria); and the military conquest of "living space" in Eastern Europe for the expansion of the German people. While neither party specifically identified which nations would be compelled to make room for German settlers, Poland was an obvious target.[55] The only real difference between the two parties was the aggressiveness with which they intended to pursue these goals, and even there the difference was, to all appearances and representations, slight.

Underlying the strong nationalist orientation of both parties was an organic conception of the German people as a race and a nation.[56] This conception emerged out of *volkisch* culture and its premise that authentic German values and identities must be cultivated by resisting the cosmopolitan influence of the nation's largest cities, where foreign ideas and peoples had diverted the *volk* from their cultural traditions.[57] While *volkisch* themes had been around for

---

[54] However, Kater notes that many "academics and well-educated professionals" joined the NSDAP when it was first formed because Nazi pageantry, symbolism, and rhetoric had

a certain esthetic appeal for the intellectual, an appeal that was as much grounded in his hatred of what were considered the vulgarities of Bolshevism as in his contempt for late nineteenth-century bourgeois liberalism, which he looked upon as degenerate. Many ... delighted in the unsophisticated behavior of Adolf Hitler and his cronies and thought it fashionable to identify themselves with such earthy ways.

After 1924, however, most intellectuals "found it difficult to associate with a party that so openly despised them and insulted their sensibilities." Michael Kater, *The Nazi Party: A Social Profile of Members and Leaders, 1919–1945* (Cambridge, MA: Harvard University Press, 1983), pp. 29, 47–8.

[55] The Stahlhelm, for example, so blatantly displayed its intentions toward Poland that the French and the Poles lodged diplomatic protests with the German government. Wette, "Ideology, Propaganda, and Internal Politics," p. 27.

[56] Following Stanley Payne, "organic" refers "to concepts of society in which its various sectors are held to bear a structured relationship to each other that serves to define and delimit their roles and rights, taking precedence over the identities and rights of individuals." Payne, *History of Fascism*, p. 13n.

[57] The German term *Volk* neatly conflated the different elements that composed the object of nationalist feeling: "People, race, nation, ethnic stock." From that perspective, *volkisch* was an

some time, they took on political significance during and after the unification of Germany in the last third of the nineteenth century and had deeply penetrated popular culture by the 1920s. They were immeasurably strengthened by trench warfare during the First World War, which generated the "myth of the war experience," a mystification of combat and self-sacrifice that claimed that a "sacred union" had been forged between those who had fought for the German nation. Violence, military discipline, obedience to command, and nationalism were thus bound up with German nationalism in a way that made authoritarian leadership a natural implication.[58] In politics, these beliefs and orientations neatly aligned with the rural, agrarian base and strong military traditions of the Nationalist Party. In all these things, there was little difference between the Nationalists and the Nazis.

The Nationalists, however, stressed the importance of Christian values, particularly those associated with the Protestant churches.[59] The Nazis, on the other hand, were much more concerned with aligning religious worship with an authentic German spirit and sometimes even suggested a resurrection of the ancient German gods. For these Nazis, Judeo-Christian beliefs and moral philosophy were an alien intrusion into the natural spirituality of the German people. The Nationalists condemned this "call for a return to the pagan cults of the old Germans" as a rejection of the Bible.[60]

Reinforcing *volkisch* understandings of the destiny of the German people was a broad and, at times, intense anti-Semitism that identified the German Jewish community as everything that the German people were not.[61] In its political manifestations, anti-Semitism rested on three primary and apparently contradictory beliefs: that Jews composed the international network that

---

adjective "[p]ertaining to the *Volk* (with racialist, mystical, and sentimental-traditionalist over-tones); patriotic, nationalist." Research Institute for Military History, *Germany and the Second World War*, vol. I, p. xxvii. Also see Orlow, *History of the Nazi Party*, p. 19n. Most German workers were not attracted to *volkisch* beliefs, both because Marxist doctrine regarded those beliefs as rank superstition and because *volkisch* tenets tended to reinforce the class hierarchy. Mosse, *Crisis of German Ideology*, pp. 262–3. On the reaction of the bourgeois middle class to radical cultural movements in art, literature, music, and sexual permissiveness, see Evans, *Coming of the Third Reich*, pp. 120–9. For the increasing political implications and applications of *volkisch* identity during and after the First World War, see Fritzsche, *Germans into Nazis*, pp. 110–12, 198–202.

[58] Payne, *History of Fascism*, pp. 161–3. Also see Wette, "Ideology, Propaganda, and Internal Politics," pp. 15, 25–6. On the importance of wartime experience in the trenches to Nazi Party members, see Orlow, *History of the Nazi Party*, pp. 47–9, 88.

[59] Wette, "Ideology, Propaganda, and Internal Politics," pp. 41–2.

[60] Childers, *Nazi Voter*, p. 115. On the ancient and mystical elements in *volkisch* and Nazi conceptions of the German racial community, see Mosse, *Crisis of German Ideology*, p. 90, 116–20.

[61] For an analysis of the increasing conflation of anti-Semitism, social Darwinism, belief in the moral and biological superiority of the German race, and state-centered nationalism from the middle of the nineteenth to the early twentieth centuries, see Bracher, *German Dictatorship*, pp. 13–45.

directed the increasingly exploitative operations of advanced capitalism in the form of colossal industrial corporations and international financial institutions; that Jews were the theoreticians who had developed and refined Marxist doctrine both as a theoretical edifice and as an predatory political movement; and that both of these projects (not too strong a word) threatened the identity and very survival of the German nation and, in more biological versions, the integrity of the Aryan race.[62] The implications of this rejection of Jews and Judaism were made more urgent by charges that organized Jewry secretly or not so secretly dominated national and international politics.

In 1920, for example, the Nationalists urged a return to "Christian values and German family life" while insisting that the "ominous Jewish predominance in the government and public life ... has increased steadily" since the creation of the Weimar Republic. Four years later, the Nationalists attempted to bridge the class chasm in rural Germany by condemning the policy and cultural orientation of the democratic center: "Whether estate owner or small peasant, both are threatened by the antiagrarian policies of the black-red-yellow parties ... If you don't give your vote to the Nationalists, then you can't be surprised if the Jewish, consumer viewpoint wins the upper hand and leads to the ruin of agriculture." In 1931, the DNVP similarly promised that the party would "resist the subversive, un-German spirit in all forms, whether it stems from Jewish or other circles. We are emphatically opposed to the prevalence of Jewdom in the government and in public life, a prevalence that has emerged ever more continuously since the revolution."[63] Even so, there was daylight between the racial beliefs held by the Nationalists and their ostensibly apolitical Stahlhelm allies, on the one hand, and the Nazis, on the other.[64]

---

[62] Bracher, *German Dictatorship*, p. 39. Despite the apparent contradiction, Childers described "the linkage of Jews with both Marxism and capitalism [as] the ideological foundations of Nazi electoral strategy in 1924." Childers, *Nazi Voter*, p. 106.

[63] Childers, *Nazi Voter*, pp. 41, 76. White-collar workers formally enrolled in unions aligned with the Nationalist Party were particularly receptive to Nazi appeals (pp. 89–90). Also see Evans, *Coming of the Third Reich*, p. 95.

[64] In 1924, the Stahlhelm leadership declared: "The Stahlhelm fights for the German *Volk* and therefore for the renewal of the Germanic race; it fights to strengthen German self-consciousness so that foreign racial influences will be eliminated from the nation." The Stahlhelm also distinguished between Aryans and Jews, regarding the latter as ineligible for German citizenship. In these things, the organization's ideology was virtually indistinguishable from Nazi doctrine. However, the Stahlhelm also believed that some Jews who had lived in Germany for several generations were acceptable as permanent residents and that a distinction should be drawn between "racism of blood and racism of spirit," rejecting the former and endorsing the latter. These more "moderate" attitudes led the Stahlhelm to regard the Nazis as dangerous racial fanatics. The organization's predilection for aristocratic rule cemented these differences. Mosse, *Crisis of German Ideology*, pp. 255–6. Sixty members of the Reichstag belonged to the Stahlhelm in 1928; fifty-one of the sixty also belonged to the DNVP. Wette, "Ideology, Propaganda, and Internal Politics," p. 24. Also see Payne, *History of Fascism*, p. 161. The German Youth Movement spurned the Nazis on very similar grounds, rejecting Hitler for "his

Both parties linked Jews to the Communist menace, although the Nazis tended to depict this connection in more sinister terms and contended that Jewish direction of the Communist conspiracy was unequivocally hostile to the racial destiny of the German people. The two parties also diverged with respect to those workers who were attracted to the Communist Party. The Nationalists viewed German politics in class terms and more or less wrote off industrial workers as a lost cause. While the party tried to win working-class votes by appealing to nationalist, religious, and traditional social values, especially deference to titled elites, Nationalists did not directly compete with the Communists on the latter's terms.[65] While hostility between the KPD and the NSDAP was very real and doctrinally rooted among their respective party elites, the Nazis viewed German workers as fully fledged members of the German race, people, and nation and thus sought to change the way in which they viewed class relations.[66] Although the party vacillated in how these class

vulgar tastes, his fanaticism, and his 'proletarianization' of the party" (p. 275). Also see Kater, *Nazi Party*, p. 142.

[65] In many respects, Nazi ideology cannot easily be described in conventional class terms.

[T]he ideology of the Nazi revolution was based upon what were presumed to be Germanic traditions; while the revolution looked to the future, it tried to recapture a mythical past and with it the old traditions which to many people provided the only hope of overcoming the chaos of the present ... In reality the morality which National Socialism offered as typically Germanic was the bourgeois morality of the nineteenth century: the sanctity of the family, of marriage, and of the unostentatious, dedicated life. Dedicated to the *Volk*, not to the making of money. (Mosse, *Nazi Culture*, p. xxvi and, more generally, pp. xxix–xxxii)

Mosse describes "National Socialism [as] a religion; the depth of the ideology, the liturgy, the element of hope, all helped to give the movement the character of a new faith ... Nazism was a total world view which by its very nature excluded all others" (p. xxi). On the difficulty traditional parties had when placing the Nazis on the conventional left–right political spectrum, see Childers, *Nazi Voter*, p. 111.

[66] Although the Nazis never abandoned hope that they might be able to attract the support of the working class, their program held little appeal for most workers. For one thing, National Socialist hostility to the concept of an inevitable conflict of interest between capitalists and workers seemed out of step with the reality that industrial workers confronted in their daily lives. Nazi opposition to the formation of labor unions, a corollary to their hostility to class conflict, was similarly off-putting. Nazis were also indifferent to labor strikes, the major tactical weapon in the working-class arsenal. What the Nazis offered the worker in place of these things was an anti-Semitism that pitted the Aryan German worker against the "internationalist Jew." However,

[the] worker simply did not understand the Nazis' association of Semitism with high-volume capitalism and undue profit gains. He did not find himself in danger of seduction by international Jewry, whose representatives he did not even recognize, except, perhaps, for those at the helm of the unions, and the union leaders were generally trusted. The worker rarely read Jewish-controlled newspapers, and if he did, it was beyond his capabilities to determine in what sense they were "Jewish" and why, by virtue of that fact, they were "bad." He could not visualize "Judas, the World's Enemy" ... who had supposedly been preying on the workers of Europe since the outbreak of the Great War. (Kater, *Nazi Party*, pp. 20–2)

relations were depicted, the Nazis were much more willing than the Nationalists to view corporate capitalism, especially the financial sector, as hostile to the general interests of the German people. In this respect, Nazi rhetoric often resembled Communist slogans when describing the expression of elite interests in German politics.[67] Because both parties attempted to appeal to the working class and shared a common interest in the destruction of the Weimar Republic, tactical cooperation between them might not seem surprising. And at the mass level there was both a great deal of fluidity in membership, some real collaboration in political action and strike activity, and even fraternization. When the Nazis finally came to power, many ostensibly Communist workers even moved en masse into the National Socialist Party.[68] All of these things were simply inconceivable as possibilities for the Nationalists.

When Alfred Hugenberg became party leader in 1928, the Nationalists became a much more authoritarian organization with both an ideational and practical affinity for the "leadership principle."[69] The model for both Nationalists and President Hindenburg was Otto von Bismarck, who, along with the Kaiser, ruled Germany for almost three decades in the late nineteenth century. During that period, Bismarck unified the German states and then consolidated the new nation. That achievement effectively attached nationalist sentiment to the concepts of strong personal leadership and martial spirit that became second nature to the Nationalist Party.[70] While this favorable attitude toward strongman rule was shared by the Nazis, the ideological basis was very different. Where the Nationalists placed a strong leader within a consensus constructed and grounded within traditional elite beliefs and relations, the

---

[67] Fischer, *German Communists*, p. 194.

[68] In May 1927, "Goebbels, in a phrase that the Communist leader, Ernst Thalmann, could not have bettered, described the Berlin police as 'the pimp ... of capitalism.'" Orlow, *History of the Nazi Party*, p. 87. On the similarity of Nazi and Communist rhetoric, see Fischer, *German Communists*, p. 106. Childers reported that "Communist rhetoric" was so "stridently nationalist in tone and content ... [that] *Vorwarts* [the leading SPD newspaper] branded the KPD 'more National Socialist than Hitler.'" Childers, *Nazi Voter*, pp. 181–3. On competition for working-class support between the two parties, see Fischer, *German Communists*, pp. 129–30, 132, 146–7. On the frequency with which individual workers switched membership between the two parties, see Fischer, *German Communists*, pp. 131, 137; Kater, *Nazi Party*, pp. 53–4. Kater also noted that turnover in the Nazi Party membership was very high generally (p. 34). On turnover among Nazi storm troopers, see Richard Bessel, *Political Violence and the Rise of Nazism: The Storm Troopers in Eastern Germany, 1925–1934* (New Haven, CT: Yale University Press, 1984), p. 47. On strike cooperation between the National Socialists and Communists, see Eyck, *History of the Weimar Republic*, vol. 2, pp. 186, 433; Morris, *Weimar Republic*, p. 175. On tactical political collaboration, see Fischer, *German Communists*, pp. 148, 189. On the movement of Communist workers into Nazi ranks after Hitler assumed power, see Fischer, *German Communists*, p. 191. On violence between Communist and Nazi paramilitary organizations, see Fischer, *German Communists*, pp. 148–53; Payne, *History of Fascism*, p. 170; Brustein, *Logic of Evil*, p. 170; Bessel, *Political Violence and the Rise of Nazism*, pp. 76–7.

[69] Payne, *History of Fascism*, p. 163; Evans, *Coming of the Third Reich*, p. 95.

[70] Evans, *Coming of the Third Reich*, p. 13.

"Leader" contemplated in Nazi ideology was beholden to no one except the German race, people, and nation, and, since he was the embodiment of those things, the "Leader" was effectively free of those things as well.[71]

There were three primary differences between traditional conservatism and Nazi principles in that the former (1) emphasized Christianity as the foundation of the German state, (2) held that the state should respect the rule of law, and (3) viewed military or civil service to the state as "a noble duty inherent in citizenship." Where conservatives "tended to endow the state with the character of a super-individual personality, the nature of which could not be explained in terms of a mere covenant of the citizens," the Nazis elevated the "community of the people" so that it became an "ultimate ethical value" that contradicted and largely supplanted Christian belief. In addition, the identification of the Leader with the German people made the rule of law unnecessary and largely irrelevant since the Leader's commands flawlessly enacted the popular will.[72] Finally, the primacy of the Nazi Party as an extension of the Leader's personality reduced state service to a secondary role.[73] These were important differences

[71] In Hermann Göring's words:

In this first year of Nazi rule the German people is assembled in unanimous, unswerving loyalty to the state, the race (*Volk*), and the German nation to which we all belong. Every difference is wiped away. The barriers of class hatred and the arrogance of social status that for over fifty years divided the nation from itself have been torn down ... Finally, the idea of the national community rises above the ruins of the bankrupt liberal-capitalist state. (quoted in Berman, *Democracy and Dictatorship*, p. 234)

In this passage, "state" should be understood as synonymous with the "Leader."

[72] The most important theorist of this relationship between the Leader and the will of the German race, people, and nation was Carl Schmitt, who, as paraphrased by Mosse, proposed that "the leader, the corporations, and, indeed, the whole *Volk* participated in a mystical racial unity that engendered identical attitudes and values. The common denominator [of this unity was] the Aryan race." Schmitt, *Crisis of German Ideology*, p. 285. Schmitt contended that "the Nazi system was not to be a mere dictatorship from above, but was supposed to be based upon a truly democratic principle of government" because the "Fuhrer and *Volk* were equal in kind" in that

they shared the same race and blood; the human nature of each individual German and that of his leaders was thought to be identical. Therefore their aims must be identical as well, as both wanted to fulfill themselves by bringing about the true Germanic State ... Leader and led were a part of the same organic *Volk*. What distinguished the leader from the masses was his ability to make them conscious of their peoplehood and to lead them toward its fulfillment. (Mosse, *Nazi Culture*, pp. xxxvi–xxxvii)

There was, in Schmitt's words, "an unconditional similarity of racial stock between leader and followers. The continuous and truthful contact between leader and followers and their reciprocal loyalty rest upon this racial similarity. Only this similarity of racial stock can prevent the leader's power from becoming tyranny and despotism ... this concept of similarity of racial stock penetrates all systematic juridical considerations" (p. 326).

[73] Heberle, *From Democracy to Nazism*, pp. 15–20. For conservative nationalists, "the concept of the unity of will of the State, i.e., the concept of the legal personality of the State," was nothing more than an enabling juristic "fiction which we must accept for the better understanding of our

but they were mostly matters of degree, not open contradictions, before Hitler took power and transformed them into practice.

After 1928, the Nationalist Party adopted ever more extreme positions as it competed with a surging Nazi Party in the electoral arena.[74] Even as it moved to the right, however, the DNVP still regarded the Nazis as a young and vigorous upstart, certainly not yet ready to rule the nation but nonetheless a mobilizing force in German politics that could reach constituencies that were immune to the rather staid appeals of aloof Nationalist elites. While their campaign rhetoric converged, the Nationalists distinguished between what must be said in political combat from what must be done as state policy. And they assumed that Hitler and the Nazi Party were guided by the same principle. Little did they imagine that it was the stump rhetoric that the Nazis were carefully moderating because their intentions with respect to state policy were too extreme for public discussion. So Nationalist campaign positions were probably more extreme than what they would have done had they ruled the state and Nazi rhetoric was more moderate than their actual intentions. As a result, they ended up in about the same place from the perspective of the individual voter.[75] This perceived similarity was strongly reinforced by the DNVP tendency to propose authoritarian alternatives to parliamentary democracy.[76]

The electoral history of the Weimar Republic was dominated by two related trends (see Table 6.3). On the one hand, there was the remarkable rise of the Nazi Party that almost literally exploded in size after the onset of the Great Depression. On the other hand, there was the concomitant decline of the bourgeois parties of the right and center (the DNVP, DVP, DDP, and most of the splinter groups). Although close analysis of the election returns suggests that the Nazis drew votes from all class factions in German society, the major element driving party expansion was the consolidation of elite and bourgeois

---

legal order." In one of the more unfortunate projections of Germany's future development, they believed that this concept was not "likely to serve as a basis for the glorification of the State" because it was nothing more than "an auxiliary construction" intentionally designed by jurists and thus "our own creature." Mattern, *Principles of the Constitutional Jurisprudence*, p. 102.

[74] Childers, *Nazi Voter*, p. 190.   [75] Hamilton, *Who Voted for Hitler?*, pp. 26, 150–1.

[76] Wette, "Ideology, Propaganda, and Internal Politics," pp. 23, 28. The quasi-authoritarian governments that ruled Germany prior to Hitler's assumption of power did not view the Nazis as a benign competitor. In December 1931, for example, Chancellor Heinrich Brüning warned the nation:

Although the leader of the National Socialists has emphasized the legal methods and goals of his political intentions, nevertheless one cannot ignore the sharp contrast to these assurances provided by the violent assertions of no less responsible leaders of this same party who continue to incite Germans to senseless civil war and to diplomatic follies. When one declares that one intends to break down legal barriers once one has come to power in legal ways, then one is no longer observing legality, particularly if clandestine plans are simultaneously being made for revenge. (Eyck, *History of the Weimar Republic*, vol. 2, p. 341)

TABLE 6.3. *Percentage of the vote cast for the major political parties in Reichstag elections (1924–33)*

Election	Nazi NSDAP	Nationalist DNVP	German People's DVP	Catholic Zentrum	Democrats DDP	Social Democrats SPD	Communists KPD	Other Splinter
May 4, 1924	6.5	19.5	9.5	16.6	5.7	21.6	12.6	8.3
Dec. 7, 1924	3.0	20.5	10.1	17.3	6.3	26.0	9.0	7.8
May 2, 1928	2.6	14.2	8.7	15.2	4.8	29.8	10.6	13.7
Sep. 14, 1930	18.3	7.0	4.9	14.8	3.5	24.5	13.1	14.4
July 31, 1932	37.3	5.9	1.2	15.7	1.0	21.6	14.3	3.2
Nov. 6, 1932	33.1	8.5	1.8	15.0	1.0	20.4	16.9	4.7

Note: Commonly used party names are in the first row; the initials are for the formal German names. For the purposes of this table, these designations ignore party schisms, defections, mergers, and other (usually minor) changes in party organization and titles.
Source: The percentages are taken from Childers, *Nazi Voter*, pp. 58, 61, 125, 141, 209, 211. Almost identical percentages can be found in Hamilton, *Who Voted for Hitler?*, p. 476. The major difference is that the latter breaks out the Bavarian People's Party from the Zentrum total and includes their votes in the "Other" category.

sectors under Nazi leadership.[77] The Zentrum, with its similar construction of politics as a communal expression of the Catholic faithful, was relatively untouched by the National Socialist expansion. So were the working-class parties of the left, although there the Social Democrats were slowly losing ground to the implacably radical Communist Party.[78] As a result of this growing polarization between the bourgeois middle class and radicalized workers, the Nazi and Communist parties drew more than half of all votes cast in the Reichstag election in July 1932, and together held a majority of the seats. Since both parties were firmly committed to the destruction of the Weimar Republic (and, for that matter, each other), it was not possible to cobble together a parliamentary majority that might have abided by democratic practice and norms. By that point, there was little or no hope of resurrecting a stable foundation for Weimar democracy even if President Hindenburg and his advisers had wanted to make that a project.[79]

TACTICS, STRATEGY, AND IDEOLOGY OF THE NAZI PARTY

Electoral competition in the Weimar Republic was primarily based on occupation and the particular economic interests associated with occupation. While there were other narrowly framed appeals to religious affiliation, women, and youth, a party's strength usually rested on the material concerns of the occupational and class characteristics of its membership.[80] Within this highly fragmented party system, there were, however, broad class categories that shaped much of the perception of both parties and voters. Most Germans, for example, belonged to what has been described as the "lower class," composed of workers, peasants, and others possessing little wealth and income (see Table 6.4). In addition to the 55 percent of the population in this class, another 43 percent resided in the various strata of the "middle class," including white-collar workers, small proprietors, landowning farmers, and those who lived modestly off their investments or property holdings. The very small remainder composed the nation's elite: titled nobility, the owners and directors of large corporations, the professoriate in major universities, and the highest rungs of

---

[77] Childers, *Nazi Voter*, p. 178. On the decline of the DNVP after 1928, see p. 133. On the cross-class appeal of the Nazi Party, see Evans, *Coming of the Third Reich*, p. 9; Dulffer, *Nazi Germany*, p. 10.

[78] On the relative indifference of Catholic and working-class voters to the Nazi Party, see Dulffer, *Nazi Germany*, p. 11; Evans, *Coming of the Third Reich*, pp. 262–3.

[79] "After 20 July 1932 the only realistic alternatives were (1) a Nazi dictatorship or (2) a conservative, authoritarian regime backed by the army." Evans, *Coming of the Third Reich*, p. 287. Also see Childers, *Nazi Voter*, p. 208. On the erosion of electoral support for the parties that had created the Weimar Republic, see Morris, *Weimar Republic*, p. 81. On the growth of anti-democratic parties, see Evans, *Coming of the Third Reich*, pp. 93–4, 96.

[80] Childers, *Nazi Voter*, p. 10.

TABLE 6.4. *Socioeconomic class and support for the Nazi Party*

Socioeconomic class	Percentage of all gainfully employed adults and students	Percentage of those who joined the Nazi Party in 1933	Reasons for supporting or opposing the Nazi Party
Lower-class: Skilled and unskilled workers, including those employed in traditional and artisanal crafts	54.6	30.7	Most workers accepted some variant of a Marxist class struggle as their understanding of politics and therefore found Nazi principles hostile to their material interests; in addition, the anti-Semitic elements in the Nazi program were not relevant to daily life.
Lower-middle-class: Self-employed artisans and craftsmen; professionals without academic degrees; lower-rung white-collar workers and civil servants; owners and operators of small businesses and shops; and self-employed farmers and fishermen.	42.6	57.1	Many in this class were attracted to nationalist stands; in addition, economic uncertainty, status anxiety, and perceived class competition led many to become virulently anti-Semitic as both an explanation for their plight and outlet for their frustration; farmers were also attracted to the material aspects of the Nazi program.
Elite: High-ranking managers in large firms; high-ranking civil servants holding academic degrees; senior students in prep schools or universities; entrepreneurs; titled aristocrats; the very wealthy; and those wielding political authority.	2.8	12.2	Many students were First World War veterans who blamed Jews for the German defeat; high-ranking civil servants and other elements in the economic elite supported the Nazis as a bulwark against Bolshevism although they were reluctant to formally join the party; opposition to the Weimar Republic and parliamentary democracy in general was common.

Source: The percentage of each class as a proportion of all gainfully employed adults and students was calculated from the 1933 national census. The percentage of each class as a proportion of all those who joined the Nazi Party in 1933 was calculated from a sample of membership lists. Both are taken from Kater, *Nazi Party*, pp. 241, 252. Other information in this table is abstracted from Kater, *Nazi Party*, pp. 2–3, 5–12, 20–3, 26–9. Also see Mosse, *Nazi Culture*, p. 346.

the state bureaucracy.[81] The National Socialist Party performed least well among industrial workers in Germany's largest cities. However, skilled workers were significantly more likely to vote for the National Socialists and become active party members than were unskilled laborers.[82]

Within the vast and diverse German middle class, Nazi support was particularly strong among the proprietors of small businesses, small farmers, shopkeepers who had difficulty competing with large department stores, craftsmen, the lower ranks of white-collar workers, pensioners, and those of modest means who primarily lived on income generated by their financial assets and real-estate holdings.[83] As Karl Bracher noted, this middle-class orientation extended to the composition of the 107 Nazis elected to the Reichstag in 1930, "sixteen [of whom] had a commercial, handicraft, or industrial background; twenty-five were employees; thirteen were teachers; twelve, civil servants; fifteen, party functionaries; eight, ex-officers; twelve, farmers; one, a clergyman, and one, a pharmacist." By 1932, 230 National Socialist delegates now included "fifty-five employees or workers, fifty farmers, forty-three from business, handicraft, and industry, twenty-nine party functionaries, twenty civil servants, twelve teachers, and nine ex-officers."[84]

However, Nazi strength within the German middle class varied in two obliquely related ways: The party was much stronger in rural communities than it was in large cities and the Nazis polled much better among Protestants than Catholics. Within Germany's largest cities, moreover, the Nazi vote was significantly correlated with class: elite neighborhoods gave the party its best showing, followed by middle-class areas, with working-class quarters bringing up the rear.[85] While many upper-class and elite sympathizers supported the Nazis without formally joining the party, open affiliation increased significantly in the period just before the Nazi takeover.[86]

---

[81] These figures are the result of a very careful explication of the class structure in Germany between the wars by Kater, *Nazi Party*, p. 12. On the construction and interpretation of class categories, see pp. 2–3, 6–12.

[82] Kater, *Nazi Party*, pp. 22–3, 35–6; Childers, *Nazi Voter*, p. 257. On elements of the Nazi program that appealed to workers, see p. 246.

[83] Kater, *Nazi Party*, pp. 26–7, 39, 42–4, 229; Childers, *Nazi Voter*, pp. 4, 159, 166, 264–6, 277; Bracher, *German Dictatorship*, p. 152; Evans, *Coming of the Third Reich*, p. 264. For critical reviews of the literature identifying those portions of German society that voted for the National Socialists, see Hamilton, *Who Voted for Hitler?*, pp. 9–36; Brustein, *Logic of Evil*, pp. 2–9.

[84] Bracher, *German Dictatorship*, pp. 152, 183.

[85] Hamilton, *Who Voted for Hitler?*, pp. 37–8, 40–1, 50, 90–1, 121, 421; Dulffer, *Nazi Germany*, p. 11.

[86] On upper-class and elite membership in the Nationalist Socialist Party, see Kater, *Nazi Party*, pp. 28, 62–3. On differences between the characteristics of Nazi Party membership and electoral support by voters, particularly the underrepresentation of civil servants as enrolled members compared with the votes they gave the party, see Childers, *Nazi Voter*, p. 12. On the growth of Nazi Party membership, see Dulffer, *Nazi Germany*, pp. 9–10.

Within the German elite, university professors and upper-class students were particularly drawn to the Nazi Party. In fact, so many students joined the National Socialists that German universities became one of the primary bastions of Nazi strength and influence. While one of the attractions for students was sponsorship of athletic and martial organizations, Nazi anti-Semitism also "blended smoothly with the tradition of Jew-baiting" in "university seminars and student fraternities."[87] Despite their often virulent anti-Semitism, civil servants occupying the higher rungs of the government bureaucracy were not particularly attracted to the Nazi Party. They were much more comfortable with the more traditional and aristocratic DNVP and only moved toward the Nazis fairly late in the life of the Weimar Republic. In fact, just before the Nazi takeover, only one in ten of "all German civil servants" had joined the party.[88]

The Nazi Party came to power by combining opportunistic electoral tactics, strategic combinations with established traditional elites, and the construction of an encompassing ideology that bound increasing numbers of Germans to the charismatic leadership of Adolf Hitler. As an electoral organization, the National Socialist Party was very decentralized and most campaign material reflected the local context of political competition and differences in the composition of the electorate. There was quite a bit of trial and error as the party adjusted its message "in the light of reports received from the field."[89] In the 1924 election, for example, the National Socialist Party offered the worker "surprisingly specific ... social and economic" reforms such as "the restoration of the eight-hour day ... giving labor a voice in the formulation and conduct of company policy as well as a profit-sharing scheme carrying the weight of law. The party also favored action to prohibit the hiring of women and juveniles in large plants."[90]

As an appeal to farmers in 1930, Hitler crafted an "official party proclamation" that placed specific policy proposals within the broader context of what had become the Nazi vision for rejuvenating the German nation.[91] Within that

---

[87] Kater, *Nazi Party*, pp. 27–30, 69. Kater suggested that "[h]alf of the entire German student body may have joined the Nazis by 1930" (p. 44). Also see Wette, "Ideology, Propaganda, and Internal Politics," pp. 37–8, 40.

[88] Kater, *Nazi Party*, pp. 29–30, 48–9, 59, 69–70; Childers, *Nazi Voter*, pp. 172, 229. Even as late as 1932, the Nazis did not make many explicit appeals to civil servants as a potential voting bloc (pp. 238–9).

[89] Hamilton, *Who Voted for Hitler?*, p. 421.

[90] Childers, *Nazi Voter*, pp. 110–11 and, more generally, p. 175. For a broad discussion of Nazi programmatic appeals that emphasizes their opportunistic qualities, see Bracher, *German Dictatorship*, pp. 144–6.

[91] Many scholars have cited the ambiguities, inconsistencies, and generalities of Nazi electoral appeals as evidence that the party did not have a clearly defined program or, in a stronger formulation, did not know what policies a Nazi state would adopt if it came to power. The question is not whether the Nazis had an overarching socioeconomic program or whether the particularities of that program appealed to some groups (because of their material interests) more than others but whether the overarching program was designed solely or even primarily for

vision, agriculture was described as playing a – if not the – central role because increasing agricultural production would enable the German people to feed "ourselves from our own land and soil." Agricultural self-sufficiency would create a more prosperous rural economy that, in turn, would provide a home market for German industry, reduce dependence on exports, and enhance the German peasantry's natural role as the "mainstay of the people's health," as well as "the nation's fount of youth and the backbone of its military strength" in the coming struggle for living space.[92] The party's policy positions thus mixed specific commitments that promised narrow benefits to particular sectors of the German electorate with broad ideological goals that subordinated those sectors to what the party (and many ordinary Germans) believed to be the historical destiny of the German race, people, and nation.[93] Hamilton, for example, maintained that the primary election themes driving the expansion of the National Socialist Party were "debt relief in the countryside and anti-Marxism in the cities." While "there was a persistent focus on the Jews with their supposedly deleterious effect on German culture and institutions," anti-Semitism was distinctly secondary to the central focus on economic survival of small farmers and class conflict in large cities.[94]

Before the Great Depression, the Nazis were an almost irrelevant after-thought among the many extremist parties arrayed to the right of the DNVP, just one of many splinter parties attempting to exploit popular hostility to the Weimar Republic. Because the party was weak and because Nazis often expressed an ambivalent attitude toward corporate capitalism (in the vernacu-lar, "big business"), industrial leaders did not embrace the National Socialist

---

the purpose of appealing to such interests. For example, the Nazi proposal to resettle the German peasantry on farms in the East (e.g., Poland) certainly appealed to the narrow material interests of landless or otherwise impoverished farmers but the proposal itself was a primary element in the larger project of realizing the proper destiny of the German race (*Lebensraum*) along with the slightly less broad goal of lessening German dependence on the importation of food (autarky) and thus freeing the German nation from economic constraints as it pursued that destiny.

[92] Hans-Erich Volkmann, "The National Socialist Economy in Preparation for War" in Research Institute for Military History, *Germany and the Second World War*, vol. I, p. 191. On the central place of the rural peasantry in Nazi ideation, see p. 190. Also see Evans, *Coming of the Third Reich*, p. 435. For examples of the practicality and material specificity of Nazi appeals to farmers and farm laborers, see Kater, *Nazi Party*, pp. 41, 70–1. Those appeals, however, were not always easily reconciled with Nazi ideology. Childers, *Nazi Voter*, p. 179.

[93] Payne, *History of Fascism*, p. 167. Also see Brustein, *Logic of Evil*, pp. 22–3, 51, 101, 147–55. Brustein's "central thesis is that the mass of Nazi followers were motivated chiefly by common-place and rational factors – namely, their material interests – rather than by Hitler's irrational appeal or charisma" (pp. xii). However, he adopts a very broad, expansive interpretation of "material interests." See, for example, pp. 141, 143, 145, 155–6. Gellately also downplays Hitler's charismatic appeal. Robert Gellately, *Hitler's True Believers: How Ordinary People Became Nazis* (New York: Oxford University Press, 2020), pp. 10–11.

[94] Hamilton, *Who Voted for Hitler?*, p. 422.

Party until a few months before Hitler assumed power.[95] The tension between the particular positions assumed by the Nazi Party and its ideological commitments presented a similar problem for industrialists, devout Christians, and landed nobility.

The Nazi program, adopted in 1920, was quite radical, proposing among other things:

the abolition of the treaties of Versailles and Saint-Germain ... return of the former German colonies; a racially regenerated Germany free from Jewish influence; a strengthened executive and a single parliament; a new German common law free from Roman taint; abolition of the professional army and formation of a national army; cultivation of national fitness by means of physical education and compulsory games and gymnastics; work for all in the interest of the common good which takes precedence over individual good; abolition of unearned income; nationalization of large concerns; communalization of large shops to the benefit of the small tradespeople; suppression of newspapers transgressing against the common weal; respect for the rights of the two great religious confessions in so far as they constitute no menace to the morale or ethical sense of the Germanic race or to the existence of the state.[96]

On one point, the Nazis were quite explicit: "Only a people's comrade [*Volksgenosse*] can be a citizen. Only a person of German blood, irrespective of religious denomination, can be a people's comrade. No Jew, therefore, can be a people's comrade."[97] Otherwise, the Nazis trimmed their sails by reassuring the great industrialists that the party would not abolish the capitalist system, comforting Christians that the party was neither heathen nor atheist, and denying any intention of breaking up landed estates.[98] These opportunistic (and insincere) concessions aside, one of the most remarkable traits of the National Socialist Party was just how consistently it held to the principles of the program adopted in the early years of its existence. Many of these early commitments were still guiding party (and German state) policy right up until the fall of the Third Reich.

One of those commitments was the party's promise to bring down the Weimar Republic. But there was significant tension in how the National Socialists viewed, on the one hand, their ideological commitment to dismantle

---

[95] Kater, *Nazi Party*, pp. 45, 63–4. On growing support among the German elite generally, see pp. 70–1. Also see Evans, *Coming of the Third Reich*, pp. 172–3; Volkmann, "The National Socialist Economy," pp. 188–9; Orlow, *History of the Nazi Party*, p. 110.

[96] Rohan d'Olier Butler, *The Roots of National Socialism, 1783–1933* (New York: Howard Gertig, 1968), pp. 222–3.

[97] Hett, *Death of Democracy*, p. 99.

[98] Morris, *Weimar Republic*, p. 157; Orlow, *History of the Nazi Party*, p. 137. This trimming even extended to some of the most central elements of Nazi ideology. Once the National Socialists became a major party, for example, Nazis became "increasingly careful not to frighten ordinary people by preaching dire tactics against Jews. Similarly, the goal of war to achieve [living space for the German people] while destroying the Soviet Union was normally not mentioned." Payne, *History of Fascism*, p. 167. Also see Brustein, *Logic of Evil*, p. 57–8.

the republic once they took control of the German state and, on the other, the role of the Weimar Republic as a means for attaining power. As a means for attaining power, the Nazis played by the parliamentary and electoral rules and by so doing hoped to demonstrate that Hitler and the National Socialist Party visibly represented the popular will of the German race, people, and nation. This demonstration was pragmatically necessary because the Nazis knew, after the failure of the Munich putsch in 1923, that they would never come to power by way of an armed revolution.[99] But it was also ideologically necessary in that the Leader must be publicly recognized by the German people as the embodiment of the popular will. Elections, as long as the Nazi Party continued to expand its share of the votes, thus materially demonstrated a growing recognition of Hitler as the Leader while providing a legal platform upon which the party could spread its ideology. In that way, Nazi political campaigns were a logically incompatible but nonetheless effective mixture of narrow appeals to the interests of specific social and economic groups, public speeches and demonstrations intended to mobilize potentially sympathetic voters, and strident condemnations of the very democratic practices and norms that made the first two politically relevant.[100]

All of this was on public display for anyone who cared to look. Just before the 1928 Reichstag election, for example, Joseph Goebbels published an article in which he contemptuously ridiculed the alacrity with which the Weimar Republic had provided the means for its own destruction.

We go into the Reichstag in order to acquire the weapons of democracy from its arsenal. We become Reichstag deputies in order to paralyze the Weimar democracy with its own assistance. If democracy is stupid enough to give us free travel privileges and per diem allowances for this service, that is its affair ... We'll take any legal means to revolutionize the existing situation. If we succeed in putting sixty to seventy agitators of our party into the various parliaments in these elections, then in [the] future the state itself will supply and finance our fighting machinery ... Mussolini also went into parliament, yet soon thereafter he marched into Rome with his Black Shirts ... One should not believe that parliamentarism is our Damascus ... We come as enemies! Like the wolf tearing into the flock of sheep, that is how we come.

After his election to the Reichstag, Goebbels assured the party faithful that he had not been brought within the ambit of democratic practice.

I am not a member of the Reichstag. I am a holder of immunity, a holder of travel privileges ... We were elected against the Reichstag, and we will carry out our mandate

---

[99] For a succinct description of the conspiracy to overthrow the Weimar Republic that led up to the Munich putsch in November 1923, see Orlow, *History of the Nazi Party*, pp. 42–5. Also see Evans, *Coming of the Third Reich*, pp. 189–94; Eyck, *History of the Weimar Republic*, vol. 1, pp. 273–7, 295–7.

[100] Hitler, for example, used an airplane to campaign throughout the length and breadth of Germany in what was, for that time, an extraordinary personal engagement with the mass public. Evans, *Coming of the Third Reich*, p. 288.

in the sense of those who furnished that mandate ... A holder of immunity has free admission into the Reichstag without having to pay amusement tax. He can, when Mr. Stresemann tells about Geneva [negotiations with foreign powers], pose irrelevant questions, as for example whether it is a fact that Stresemann is a Freemason and married to a Jewess. He reviles the "system" and in return received the gratitude of the Republic in the form of seven hundred and fifty marks monthly salary – for faithful service.[101]

After the 1930 Reichstag elections in which the Nazis became, for the first time, one of the major political parties, "107 deputies clad in identical brown shirts marched into the chamber [and] answered with [a] resounding 'Here! Heil Hitler!' to the roll call of members."[102] They faced off against seventy-seven "disciplined and well-organized Communists" who responded to their own names with a "Red Front Heil!" Together they made the Reichstag "virtually unmanageable" as they raised "incessant points of order, chanting, shouting, interrupting and demonstrating their total contempt for the legislature at every juncture."[103]

NATIONAL SOCIALIST IDEOLOGY

Nazi ideology has been dismissed as a "conglomerate of ideas and precepts, of concepts, hopes, and emotions" that both lacked internal consistency and misappropriated the ideas of other thinkers, most prominent among them Friedrich Nietzsche.[104] With the important exception of Hitler's autobiographical *Mein Kampf*, the Nazi movement did not have an authoritative text from which to deduce proper political principles, the specification of long-term goals, and the rank ordering of possibly competing values.[105] But it did not need one.

---

[101] Bracher, *German Dictatorship*, pp. 141–2. Also see Wette, "Ideology, Propaganda, and Internal Politics," p. 83; Evans, *Coming of the Third Reich*, p. 451. Before the 1930 election, the Nazis had only twelve seats in the Reichstag.

[102] In 1931, a Reichstag committee report "showed that four hundred different legal charges were pending against the 107 National Socialist delegates." Eyck, *History of the Weimar Republic*, vol. 2, p. 298.

[103] Orlow, *History of the Nazi Party*, p. 190; Evans, *Coming of the Third Reich*, p. 275.

[104] Bracher, *German Dictatorship*, pp. 22, 28–9. Also see Evans, *Coming of the Third Reich*, pp. 258–9. On the misappropriation of Nietzsche, see pp. 39–40; Mosse, *Nazi Culture*, pp. xxvii, 93–4. An exception to the absence of ideology is Gellately, *Hitler's True Believers*, pp. 39–40.

[105] The only other text that merits mention was Alfred Rosenberg's *The Myth of the Twentieth Century*, which appeared in 1930. This book made him "one of the chief theorists of national socialism." Morris, *Weimar Republic*, p. 117; Bracher, *German Dictatorship*, p. 90. For summary interpretations of the contents of *Mein Kampf* and Hitler's thought generally, see Payne, *History of Fascism*, pp. 157–8; Wette, "Ideology, Propaganda, and Internal Politics," pp. 18–23; Dulffer, *Nazi Germany*, pp. 15–17; Mosse, *Nazi Culture*, pp. 1–4. Mosse notes that "*Mein Kampf* was required reading in the schools of the Third Reich" once the Nazis came to power.

The central premise of the Nazi movement was the concept of the Leader as an infallible "agent of history" who would realize the destiny of the German race, people, and nation. The reciprocal relation that underpinned this concept required the full, absolute, and unwavering dedication of the Leader in realizing that destiny in return for which the German people gave their full, absolute, and unwavering obedience to the Leader. This way of depicting the relation, however, overstates the distinction between the Leader and the people because this was not a social contract in which reciprocal obligations were formally exchanged by conscious, self-aware individuals. Instead, the Leader and the people were merely different aspects of the same organic whole. Within this organic whole, it was just as impossible to conceive of a Leader who might betray the historical destiny of the people as it was that the people might somehow fail to recognize and obey the instructions of the Leader. Put another way, the Leader was not commanding the people and the people were not obeying commands. The Leader was simply a superhuman figure, verging on what would normally be considered the divine, who possessed a miraculous and unerring ability (beyond rational explanation or dispute) to instinctively identify those measures and policies that would realize the historical destiny of the German people.[106] This combination of oracular omnipotence on the part of the Leader and complete organic alignment of the people with what the Leader revealed meant that Nazi ideology could be and was quite spare: Whatever the Leader desired was correct and true, including what might appear to the uninitiated to be contradictions or logical impossibilities.[107]

Several consequences followed from this notion, some of them rather mechanically facilitating and others more theoretically abstract. Among the former was the Leader's absolute authority over the organization of the party. The Leader stood at the center of an inspired circle that extended outward, in the first instance, to his most trusted lieutenants, then to the more numerous ranks of local party leaders, ordinary members of the party, those who sympathized with, supported, and voted for the party, and, finally, the German people at large in all their fullness (including those residing under foreign governments). But the practical consequence of the concept of the Leader, both before and

---

[106] On October 1925, a somewhat excitable Joseph Goebbels wrote in his diary: "I read Hitler's book [*Mein Kampf*] from cover to cover, with rapacious excitement! Who is this man? Half plebeian, half god! Really the Christ, or only John the Baptist?" Dulffer, *Nazi Germany*, pp. 14–15.

[107] Orlow, *History of the Nazi Party*, pp. 4–5, 300–1; Dulffer, *Nazi Germany*, p. 29; Bracher, *German Dictatorship*, pp. 47, 100, 147–9. Bracher concludes that "leader worship" as articulated in Nazi doctrine and belief

proved to be the most effective part of a propaganda which promised not only victory and greatness but also salvation and security. Long before 1933, a wealth of grotesque practices and religious fervor testified to the quasi-religious impact of the Leader propaganda, as, for example, obituaries in which the name of Hitler was invoked in place of the name of the Lord. (Bracher, *German Dictatorship*, p. 148)

after the Nazis took power, was the complete subjugation of the party apparatus to Hitler's control. There was dissent from time to time but dissent always presented a simple choice for the would-be rebel: either a full recantation of faulty belief and a return to the party fold or exile.[108]

A second consequence was the Leader's ability, within this understanding, to delegate authority without accepting responsibility. One of the most remarkable characteristics of the National Socialist Party was its simultaneous pursuit of many diverse and often potentially contradictory projects. The Nazis, for example, organized the people by economic sector, by gender, by age, and by class. They held meetings and distributed propaganda directed at each and all segments of German society and monitored the responses they received. This apparent decentralization within a very authoritarian party organization permitted experimentation with themes and ideas without calling into question the infallibility of the Leader. Those themes and ideas that failed to produce results were simply the mistakes of well-meaning subordinates who, once they had received further guidance from the Leader, corrected their beliefs.

In many ways, this was the perfect design for an authoritarian party bent on revolution that was nonetheless compelled to compete in democratic elections. On the one hand, the party organization was a supple, opportunistic electoral machine whose major purpose was the generation of votes. In this respect, the party molded itself to the forms and interests of German society as they then existed. On the other hand, the party organization was nothing more than the vehicle through which the Leader would manifest his embodiment of the popular will and the historical destiny of the German people.[109] In an address to the Dusseldorf Industrial Club almost exactly a year before he assumed the chancellorship, Hitler painted a picture of Weimar democracy that in some ways applied to his own party: "Either we shall succeed in hewing a nation hard as iron out of this hotchpotch of parties, federations, associations, world views, caste feelings and class madness, or the lack of this internal unity will ultimately destroy Germany."[110] First the party, then the nation.

A third consequence was the relatively egalitarian ethos in the Nazi Party – at least compared with other parties on the right. The concept of the German race, people, and nation did not discriminate against lower-class origins, the poorly educated, youthful inexperience, or the less intelligent. The only necessary qualifications for a successful party career were "unerring devotion to the party and unquestionable loyalty to the leader."[111] The abandonment of

---

[108] Orlow, *History of the Nazi Party*, p. 10.
[109] Orlow, *History of the Nazi Party*, pp. 200–1, 301; Bessel, *Political Violence and the Rise of Nazism*, p. 61.
[110] Dulffer, *Nazi Germany*, p. 13.
[111] Heberle, *From Democracy to Nazism*, p. 9. For a description of citizenship qualifications in the Third Reich, see Mosse, *Nazi Culture*, pp. 335–6. Upon taking power in 1933, "the Nazis proposed to build a unified racial community guided by modern science." Underpinning that

individual identity that accompanied absolute submission to the Leader stripped members of those social characteristics, such as elite status or intellectual achievements, that might otherwise have prevented full submersion in the collective German people. Here, too, the concept of the Leader both facilitated party operations (by perfecting internal party unity and discipline) and visibly confirmed doctrinal theory (as it made the party organization into a microcosm of what Germany was to become in the future).

The concept of Leader, of course, was intimately entwined with idea of the German people or *Volk*. Neatly summed up in the phrase "blood and soil," *volkisch* thought had long posited an organic unity arising out of the cultivation of the traditional lands of the German people, a shared language and culture that had been collectively constructed and preserved, and an ethnic past characterized by rightful self-assertion, valor, and honor. In the competition for supremacy between nations, these things demonstrated not only that the German people *will* prevail in that competition but that they *should* prevail as a matter of rightful destiny.

Urging the incorporation of all German-speaking peoples in Europe within one nation, a pan-German movement both developed the ideological justification for this project and articulated the political measures necessary for achieving that goal.[112] One of the latter was an aggressive foreign policy in order to recover "lost" German territory and then further expand the boundaries of the German nation so that it would encompass the entirety of the German people.[113] Another was the emergence of a national leader who, like Otto von Bismarck, would have the strength and vision to lead the German people in pursuit of this expansionary project. While this involved a much softer notion of centralized authority than the Nazi conceptualization of the Leader, the parallel was nonetheless clear. In both these ways *volkisch* thought underpinned Nazi political ideology.

Volkisch thought was also quite antagonistic to anything that tended to divide the *Volk* into hostile groups. In German politics, those divisions came in three primary forms: class, occupation, and religion. With respect to class, the Nazis constantly attacked Marxist ideology as a lethal threat to German unity.[114] By stressing the natural solidarity of the *Volk* within their shared historical destiny, the Nazis rendered individual self-interest illegitimate and could propose an ideological frame that sought to span the otherwise massive

---

vision were the categories set down the 1935 Nuremberg racial laws. Peter Fritzsche, *Life and Death in the Third Reich* (Cambridge, MA: Harvard University Press, 2008), pp. 76–7, 83. Those Germans with "four Aryan grandparents" qualified for an "Aryan passport."

[112] Mosse, *Crisis of German Ideology*, p. 301; Evans, *Coming of the Third Reich*, pp. 3, 177, 450; Heberle, *From Democracy to Nazism*, pp. 7–8n.

[113] Mosse, *Nazi Culture*, p. xxvii.

[114] Nazis, however, seldom attacked the economic elite. In one of those rare attacks, they charged that the Nationalists had "robbed the poorest people in the *Volk* of their property and savings, but they protected the princes." Childers, *Nazi Voter*, pp. 227.

class chasm that divided German politics into a left and a right.[115] The National Socialists succeeded so completely that they could rightfully claim "the coveted mantle of *Volkspartei*" by 1932.[116] Although most workers and Catholics chose to remain outside the party fold, the Nazis had at least made major inroads into every class, religious group, and occupation in the German electorate.

Religion posed special difficulties for the Nazis in that Christianity neither was authentically German in origin nor promoted compatible ethical principles. While Martin Luther could be embraced as a kind of "Germanic hero" and the "prophet of a Nordic religion," St. Paul was viewed as having fatally intro- duced Judaic elements into Christian theology that were not only foreign to German culture but also threatened racial purity. The Old Testament could not be salvaged, for example, and the New Testament was tolerable only if Christ were "redefined as an Aryan." The party experimented with the construction of a new "Christian" church that would be more compatible with its interpret- ation of *volkisch* beliefs but, in the end, did not seriously attempt to reconceive the religious commitments of the German people. In return, many pastors and priests either accommodated themselves to the rise of the Nazi Party or even found virtues in National Socialism that could be endorsed from the pulpit. There were more Protestants than Catholics in that latter category.[117]

The Nazis were more uncompromising in their anti-Semitism, which had more racial than religious overtones. Jews made up about 1 percent of the population and had, with the exception of religion, assimilated into German society. Even the religious divide was quite porous, with frequent instances of intermarriage between Jews and Christians and conversions of Jews to Christianity. Preferring to participate in mainstream parties, particularly those on the left and center of the political spectrum, Jews had never formed their own sectarian party. Despite these things, anti-Semitism was also a staple of

---

[115] As Goebbels put it, "the class parties of the right and left must be overcome and a new way opened for the creation of a genuine people's party" that would replace "the false patriotism of the bourgeoisie" with a "steely nationalistic toughness" and "the false socialism of the Marxists with a true and unsentimental socialist justice." Marxism was particularly condemned by the Nazis on two counts. First, its democratic character "destroys all creative powers in the *Volk*" through "the immoral terror of the majority." In addition, its international pretensions "obliter- ates *Volk* and nation and [thus] severs the roots of our organic existence." Childers, *Nazi Voter*, pp. 103, 179–80. For Social Democratic and Communist responses to Nazi appeals for working-class support, see p. 107.

[116] Childers, *Nazi Voter*, p. 266.

[117] Morris, *Weimar Republic*, p. 117; Kater, *Nazi Party*, p. 66; Mosse, *Crisis of German Ideology*, pp. 307–8; Mosse, *Nazi Culture*, pp. xxxi–xxxii, 235–40. The German people had to choose, Carr quotes Hitler as saying, between "the Jewish Christ creed with its effeminate pity-ethics or a strong heroic belief in God in nature, in God in our own people, in God in our destiny, in our blood." Hitler clearly chose the pagan beliefs that preceded Charlemagne's conversion of Germany to Christianity. William Carr, *A History of Germany, 1815–1945* (New York: St. Martin's Press, 1969), p. 376.

German culture and had been for at least half a century.[118] The major contribution of Nazi ideology to anti-Semitism was an insistence on a biological basis to a distinction between Jewish and German identities that implacably and forever condemned Jews to racial inferiority while interpreting their presence in Germany as a visible and continuing threat to the racial purity of the German people.[119] Because religion – and, indeed, any known system of conventional ethics – balked at the clear, if unspoken, implications of this biologically grounded anti-Semitism, the Nazis cited the rather large literature on social Darwinism as support for a national eugenics program in order to strengthen and purify the German race.[120] In this way, anti-Semitism was given a "scientific" basis that further objectified and thus dehumanized Jews while denying them any possibility of continued existence, let alone membership, in the German community. By designating a very small minority as a potentially fatal threat to national survival, the National Socialist Party insisted on the relegation of other internal divisions (such as class or religion) to a lower order of politics while raising, in the name of the *Volk*, the necessity of German racial unity to the highest conception of statecraft.[121]

As a corollary to anti-Semitism, this emphasis on eugenics and German racial purity posited very different roles for men and women. Men were warriors and women raised children. The service women could perform as part of the *Volk* was neatly summed up in the Nazi slogan *Kinder, Kuche, und Kirche* (children, kitchen, and church). When the Nazis created a national women's organization in the summer of 1931, it was dedicated to the cultivation of "a German women's spirit which is rooted in God, nature, family, nation, and homeland." The unavoidable and intended implication was that the involvement of women in society and the economy should be restricted to

---

[118] Evans, *Coming of the Third Reich*, pp. 3, 21–44, 151–2, 164–71, 188, 257.

[119] On the Nazi "dichotomy of Jew and German," see Orlow, *History of the Nazi Party*, p. 6.

[120] Childers noted that the Nazis, in fact, turned the relationship between anti-Semitism and religious ethics on its head by asserting in a *volkisch* leaflet that "the real test of a [political] party's Christianity is its stance on the Jewish question." Childers, *Nazi Voter*, p. 116. On the implementation of anti-Semitic policies once the Nazis took power, see Gellately, *Backing Hitler*, pp. 4, 24, 25–31, 121–50.

[121] Mosse, *Crisis of German Ideology*, pp. 292, 294, 302; Evans, *Coming of the Third Reich*, pp. 38, 173–4; Childers, *Nazi Voter*, pp. 79, 105–6, 267. For the origin of "scientific" racism and other aspects of Nazi ideology, see Payne, *History of Fascism*, pp. 202–3; Andrew D. Evans, *Anthropology at War: World War I and the Science of Race in Germany* (Chicago: University of Chicago Press, 2010). Bracher has emphasized an elitist dimension of the Nazi interpretation of *volkisch* ideology in that the "coming revolution was not meant for this popular mass but for a new elite of racially superior leaders. Their rule and victory over Jews and other 'inferiors' – the true *volkisch*-racist revolution – remained the only genuine kernel of Hitler's ideology, regardless of the proclamations of National Socialist doctrine and propaganda; almost everything else was utilitarian, Machiavellian power politics." Bracher, *German Dictatorship*, p. 181. This, of course, was not how the National Socialists publicly presented their program.

activities that would support husbands and nurture children. Alienated by the radicalism of Nazi ideology, most women were slow to warm to the National Socialists. However, by 1930, the party was drawing as many (and perhaps more) votes from women as it was from men.[122]

While the Nazis spanned the gender divide by widening it, party ideology generally emphasized the common destiny of the *Volk* in order to downplay and even dismiss as dangerously fantastical the major divisions in German society arising from class, occupation, and religion. And there is, in fact, evidence that the Nazis were even able to penetrate the working-class base of the Communist Party by using the collective identity of the *Volk* as a solvent on class identity.[123] *Volkisch* ideology also buttressed Nazi attempts to construct a middle path between capitalism and socialism by condemning both as products of Jewish conspiratorial design and influence.[124] The purification of the German race would thus also enable the emergence of a *volkisch* economy in which true Germans would finally be free to realize their own aspirations within their encompassing collective destiny. What this would mean exactly for those who led giant corporations, held vast landed estates, or relied on labor unions to shore up their interests on the industrial shop floor was unclear. But the demonization of the Jews as responsible for class conflict and economic difficulties generally enabled strikingly different sectors of German society to coexist within the National Socialist Party (see Table 6.4).[125]

This, then, was the conception of transcendent social purpose to which the Third Reich was dedicated at its founding: the realization of the historical destiny of the German race, people, and nation as revealed in the self-evident superiority of the *Volk*, to be carried into fulfillment under the guidance of the Leader. Several practical elements need to be mentioned in conjunction with this theoretical construction. The first is the storm troopers who publicly demonstrated the discipline, vigor, and martial valor of the Nazi movement.[126] Neatly attired in brown-shirted uniforms, storm troopers were almost always

---

[122] Childers, *Nazi Voter*, pp. 117–18, 239, 259–60, 267; Brustein, *Logic of Evil*, pp. 55–6; Kater, *Nazi Party*, pp. 148–9, 151; Dulffer, *Nazi Germany*, p. 10; Evans, *Coming of the Third Reich*, pp. 129, 213, 262.

[123] Fischer, *German Communists*, p. 130.

[124] On the Nazi attempt to create "'a third path' between Marxist centralized state planning and laissez-faire capitalism," based, in part, on "Keynesian economics," see Brustein, *Logic of Evil*, pp. 52–4, 61, 91, 120. For a detailed description of Nazi economic ideas and policy proposals before Hitler came to power, see Volkmann, "The National Socialist Economy," pp. 173–82. Contending that "the central ideological postulate for an extension of German living-space [*Lebensraum*] provides the key to their economic-policy thinking," Volkmann generally stresses the logical coherence, expansive vision, and detailed specificity of the Nazi economic program.

[125] Kater, *Nazi Party*, p. 29; Childers, *Nazi Voter*, pp. 66–8, 119–20, 152–3, 218–19, 245, 247, 262; Payne, *History of Fascism*, p. 155.

[126] On the storm troopers and other paramilitary organizations, see Hamilton, *Who Voted for Hitler?*, pp. 319, 328, 444–5; Bessel, *Political Violence and the Rise of Nazism*, pp. 44–5, 75–6; Evans, *Coming of the Third Reich*, pp. 73, 275, 285; Fischer, *German Communists*, pp. 153–7.

present in lecture halls and meeting rooms when a Nazi official addressed a crowd. During elections, they would distribute campaign literature and march in serried discipline through the public streets. But their most influential role during the Weimar Republic was probably their willingness to do battle with their left-wing counterparts, particularly the Communist Red Front. While much of this violence did not rise above ordinary thuggery, there was still a ritualized form that harmonized with the general ethos of party philosophy. For example, the class commitments of the Communist Party dictated – above and beyond the Red Front's relative weakness as a paramilitary force – a defensive strategy in which their paramilitary units primarily protected working-class neighborhoods against the "fascist" threat. The Communists would have considered the notion of an active defense of the neighborhoods of their bourgeois and elite class enemies quite absurd.[127] The Nazis, on the other hand, considered the entire "nation" to be their appropriate and legitimate stalking ground and viewed storm trooper intrusions into working-class neighborhoods as simple expressions of their claim to represent the entire *Volk*. As a result, much of the violence between Nazi and Communist paramilitary units took place in the working-class areas of industrial cities.[128]

The paramilitary units deployed in Weimar politics were generally most violent and effective in direct correlation with the integrity and radical quality of the new founding they wanted to give to the German state. Thus, the Communists and National Socialists were able to field what were in effect small armies dedicated respectively to the workers' revolution and the realization of the racial destiny of the German people. The Nationalists fielded a somewhat less effective force in the form of the Stahlhelm because their commitment to monarchy or authoritarian rule was less complete. While well-armed and disciplined, the Stahlhelm did not have a well-defined political project to promote. The Social Democrats organized the Reichsbanner but their commitment to parliamentary democracy severely compromised their ostensible support for a Marxist revolution. The Reichsbanner thus ended up defending the Weimar Republic, a project that was clearly inconsistent with street violence and would not have whetted the bloodlust of Social Democrats even if it had

---

[127] Street violence was ritualized in another way as well. "On the whole, considering the political philosophies and the size of the organisations involved, the number of dead and seriously injured during the political battles of the early 1930s seems evidence less of an uncontrolled civil war fought on Germany's streets than of a series of incidents in which the rules of the game generally were understood and respected." Bessel, *Political Violence and the Rise of Nazism*, p. 96. For a detailed account of storm trooper violence in the eastern Prussian provinces in the years before the Nazis came to power, see pp. 75–92, 95.

[128] Fischer, *German Communists*, pp. 148–9, 153–4. On casualties resulting from street violence between paramilitary units sponsored by the various political parties, see Evans, *Coming of the Third Reich*, pp. 269–70; Hett, *Death of Democracy*, p. 127.

been.[129] And the bourgeois parties of the center fielded only token organizations or none at all.

All of the major political parties had symbols and rituals that set them apart from the others. But none were as richly endowed in such things as the Nazis. The most important and ubiquitous symbol was the hooked cross or swastika, which could be utilized alone or displayed within a white circle signifying nationalism upon a red background that stood for socialism. Although the historical origins are unknown, by the time the National Socialist Party adopted the swastika it had come to symbolize the superiority of the German race, with strong nationalist and anti-Semitic overtones. The swastika was often attached to standards and carried en masse as uniformed party members marched through the streets. There was also the rigidly extended, upward-sloping Nazi salute, often accompanied by "Heil, Hitler!," through which Nazis publicly demonstrated their fealty to party and Leader.[130] Nazi symbols and ritual forms were often adopted from those previously used by *volkisch* groups, Christian churches, and the Italian fascist movement under Mussolini.[131] But their combination and the intensity of feeling that they evoked were unique. As Wolfram Wette notes, their impact "helped to dethrone the intellect and liberate emotions," particularly within the highly ritualized setting in which the party would present its speakers.

At the beginning of a mass meeting the [storm troopers] would perform a martial entry with banners, military music, and the roll of drums, and form up with their swastika flags and standards into a "speaker's guard of honour." Then battle-songs were sung to get the audience into the right mood before the speaker appeared. When he did so, often after several hours of waiting, the tension was released in tumultuous cries of "Sieg Heil."[132]

If the effect had been less dramatic, all of this might be dismissed as mere propaganda, a kind of political spectacle on a par with nineteenth-century torchlight parades in the USA. But the impact was far more powerful and disembedded party converts from prosaic reality, so much so that "they no longer lived in [conventional German] society, but saw themselves only as simultaneous destroyers of the old and builder of the new."[133]

---

[129] Bessel, *Political Violence and the Rise of Nazism*, p. 79.

[130] After Hitler assumed power, this salute became more or less ubiquitous throughout Germany but tended to decline in frequency over time. Fritzsche, *Life and Death*, pp. 19–24.

[131] On the swastika and other Nazi symbols, see Morris, *Weimar Republic*, 114–15; Evans, *Coming of the Third Reich*, pp. 40, 43, 159, 171, 174, 184–5, 212–13, 290; Bracher, *German Dictatorship*, pp. 87–8; Wette, "Ideology, Propaganda, and Internal Politics," pp. 85–6. Much of the structural design of the party was similarly adapted from the cellular form of Communist organizations. Childers, *Nazi Voter*, pp. 120–1.

[132] Wette, "Ideology, Propaganda, and Internal Politics," p. 86.

[133] Orlow, *History of the Nazi Party*, p. 277; also see pp. 2–4. Orlow goes on to say that this process "progressively disengaged a politically articulate German from the pluralist values of

As a vehicle for the dissemination of Nazi belief, nothing was superior to a mass meeting in which the *Volk* were symbolically and virtually represented by the sheer number of people. Once they were gathered in the presence of party symbols and personnel, the speaker's address appealed to the lowest common denominator shared by the audience. These appeals further evoked the common feeling and destiny that bound together the *Volk* and, for many Germans, a Nazi speech thus entailed the discovery of a new and transcending identity that trivialized their own self-interested lives. As a propaganda technique, most Nazi speeches were necessarily simple in that the same anti-Semitic, nationalist, anti-Bolshevik tropes were repeated over and over again. This repetition not only drove home the party's primary themes but also avoided raising issues that might divide the audience along conventional political lines.[134] Hitler himself framed his speeches as an appeal to individuals who felt socially isolated and lonely, offering them, in his own words,

the picture of a great community, which has a strengthening and encouraging effect on most people ... If, on leaving the shop or mammoth factory, in which he feels very small indeed, he enters a vast assembly for the first time and sees around him thousands and thousands of men who hold the same opinions; if, while still seeking his way, he is gripped by the force of mass suggestion which comes from the excitement and enthusiasm of three or four thousand other men in whose midst he finds himself; if the manifest success and the consensus of thousands confirm the truth and justice of the new teaching and for the first time raise doubts in his mind as to the truth of the opinions held by himself up to now – then he submits himself to the mystic fascination of what we call mass suggestion.[135]

the Weimar Republic and reengaged him in the values of the [Nazi] myth" (p. 300). As Orlow notes, those who joined the party after 1930 when the Nazis became a major force in German politics often did not go through this transformative process; their allegiance to the party was much more contingent and self-interested compared with early converts (p. 187). The allegiance of these new supporters was further weakened by the fact that many of them had not participated in elections before they voted for the Nazis. Evans, *Coming of the Third Reich*, p. 261. For examples of Hitler's charismatic "spell" over party members, see Evans, *Coming of the Third Reich*, pp. 224, 227; Payne, *History of Fascism*, pp. 159–60.

[134] This same apprehension lay behind Nazi reluctance to create labor unions that might otherwise have improved their appeal to workers. Any emphasis on "bread-and-butter" issues would segment the party membership and thus weaken its symbolic alignment with the *Volk*. For similar reasons, Hitler steadfastly refused to enter into any parliamentary coalition in which the National Socialists would not be the dominant partner. Orlow, *History of the Nazi Party*, pp. 103, 308. The rapid growth of the Nazi Party after 1931 encouraged the proliferation of special interest factions, so much so that the National Socialists "consistently" prohibited the formation of those representing "mere" economic interests. Orlow, *History of the Nazi Party*, p. 199.

[135] Wette, "Ideology, Propaganda, and Internal Politics," pp. 83–6. The quote is from *Mein Kampf*. Also see Bracher, *German Dictatorship*, pp. 97–8; Evans, *Coming of the Third Reich*, p. 168.

While these propaganda techniques might appear to provide little sustenance for a revolutionary founding, the mass ideology upon which states are founded is never very complex. As a result, the Nazi invocation of the historical destiny of the *Volk* and the derivative conception of the Leader were more than sufficient for the founding of the Third Reich.[136]

THE FOUNDING OF THE THIRD REICH

The last three years of the Weimar Republic combined democratic elections to the Reichstag with the appointment of chancellors and cabinets that did not enjoy parliamentary majorities (and thus largely ruled, with the cooperation of Hindenburg, through presidential decree). The last cabinet supported by a parliamentary majority resigned on March 27, 1930.[137] Since there was no way to construct a majority government with the materials at hand, President Hindenburg appointed Heinrich Brüning, one of leaders of the Zentrum Party, as chancellor.[138] On July 16, 1930, Brüning's government was condemned by a large majority of the Reichstag (256 to 193). Brüning then declared an emergency, invoking Article 48 of the Weimar Constitution and ruling by presidential decree. Frustration with a fractious Reichstag also led Brüning to call for new parliamentary elections. The National Socialists subsequently stunned Germany by drawing over 18 percent of the vote, thus becoming the second largest party (after the Social Democrats).[139] From this point on, Reichstag elections were seen as a "rolling of the dice" in which the Nazis might, in fact, come to power without entering into a parliamentary coalition. The Social Democrats, in particular but not alone, were especially wary of this possibility and pragmatically acquiesced to quasi-authoritarian rule by the nationalist right in order to prevent the Nazis from coming to power.

[136] For the origin and meaning of the term "Third Reich," which came to designate the impending founding of the new German state, see Morris, *Weimar Republic*, pp. 151–2.

[137] Evans describes the fall of Herman Muller's government, "the beginning of the end of Weimar democracy." Evans, *Coming of the Third Reich*, p. 247. Also see Hamilton, *Who Voted for Hitler?*, p. 254.

[138] On Brüning's service as chancellor, see Eyck, *History of the Weimar Republic*, vol. 2, pp. 253–77; Morris, *Weimar Republic*, pp. 160, 164–5; Evans, *Coming of the Third Reich*, pp. 250–1, 255.

[139] For a description of the organization and strategy of the Nazi campaign in the September 1930 Reichstag election, see Childers, *Nazi Voter*, pp. 137–40. On the political impact of the election, see Evans, *Coming of the Third Reich*, pp. 259–60.

Major events preceding Hitler's appointment as chancellor of the Weimar Republic

1930: March 27. The "Grand Coalition" cabinet resigns. President Hindenburg appoints Heinrich Brüning chancellor. This is the first of three governments that does not enjoy a majority in the Reichstag.

1930: September 14. Nazis win 107 seats in the Reichstag election and thus become the second largest political party.

1931: February–October. The Reichstag is adjourned because the proceedings had become so chaotic no legislative business could be conducted.

1931: March. Brüning announces restrictions on freedom of the press.

1932: March 13–April 10. First and second (runoff) presidential elections, both of them primarily contests between Hindenburg and Hitler. Hitler polls 30 percent in the first and 37 percent in the runoff. Social Democrats support Hindenburg as the lesser of two evils.

1932: April 13. Hindenburg issues a presidential decree outlawing Nazi storm troopers. Franz von Papen later lifts the ban.

1932: May 30. Brüning resigns as chancellor. Hindenburg appoints Franz von Papen in his place.

1932: July 29. Papen bans public political meetings.

1932: July 31. Reichstag election. Nazis win 230 seats, thus becoming the nation's largest political party.

1932: August 9. Papen decrees that the killing of a political opponent "out of rage or hatred" is punishable by death.

1932: September 12. The Reichstag votes "no confidence" in the Papen government, 512 to 42 with five abstentions.

1932: November 6. Reichstag election. Nazi support declines but it still remains the largest party.

1932: December 3. Papen resigns. Hindenburg appoints General Kurt von Schleicher as chancellor.

1933: January 30. Hitler sworn in as Reich chancellor.

Source: Most entries were taken from Evans, *Coming of the Third Reich*, pp. 247, 250–1, 269–70, 275, 283, 285–7, 299–302, 318, 336, 341, 343–4, 351, 358–9, 364–5, 367–8, 372.

During the presidential elections in 1932, the Social Democratic Party supported Hindenburg in both the first contest and the subsequent runoff. Hitler lost but drew 37 percent of the vote against Hindenburg in the second election.[140] The Nazis again drew 37 percent of the vote in the Reichstag elections

---

[140] On the politics surrounding the 1932 presidential election, see Evans, *Coming of the Third Reich*, pp. 277, 281. On the artifice through which Hitler became a German citizen (and thus qualified to run for president), see Morris, *Weimar Republic*, pp. 166–7.

in July. Because the Nazis were now the largest party in the Reichstag, Hermann Göring became the presiding officer.[141] In the meantime, Brüning had resigned and Franz von Papen, a Catholic and a titled aristocrat with a landed estate, had been appointed chancellor.[142] A member of the Zentrum with pronounced authoritarian leanings, Papen was forced to resign from his party when he took office. By now, the Reichstag was almost entirely irrelevant to the government, a fact amply demonstrated when, on September 12, over 90 percent of the members voted in favor of a "no confidence" motion. Papen, with Hindenburg's consent, then dissolved the Reichstag and scheduled new elections. When these were held in November 1932, National Socialist support fell but the Nazis remained the largest party.

Because it was now clear that Papen had not found a solution to the governance problem, Hindenburg replaced him with General Kurt von Schleicher, who had previously been responsible for the army's relations with the civilian government. The next two months were consumed in the development and presentation of competing plans for resolving the now persistent, unending political crisis.[143] As chancellor, Schleicher attempted to put together a rather innovative, quasi-socialist program that might appeal to both the left and the traditional right.[144] However, this program only alienated the wealthy elite while being spurned by the left, and Schleicher was left with no political base other than the army. As Hindenburg's personal friend, Papen still enjoyed access to the aging president and proposed that he appoint Hitler as chancellor but surround him with traditional conservatives in the cabinet.[145] Papen himself became vice-chancellor. However, the National Socialists were awarded the Ministry of the Interior, and the new Minister of Defense, sponsored by the army, subsequently proved to be

---

[141] On the political impact of the July 1932 Reichstag election, see Evans, *Coming of the Third Reich*, pp. 293–4; Morris, *Weimar Republic*, p. 175; Orlow, *History of the Nazi Party*, p. 279.

[142] Evans calls Papen's appointment as chancellor "the end of parliamentary democracy in Germany." For an account of Papen's service as chancellor, see Evans, *Coming of the Third Reich*, pp. 283–6, 296–8.

[143] On the complex negotiations and political maneuvers as Schleicher and Papen vied for Hindenburg's favor in the months before Hitler came to power, see Morris, *Weimar Republic*, p. 179; Dulffer, *Nazi Germany*, pp. 25–6; Evans, *Coming of the Third Reich*, p. 306.

[144] On Schleicher's service as chancellor, see Evans, *Coming of the Third Reich*, pp. 301–2; Morris, *Weimar Republic*, pp. 176–7.

[145] In retrospect, it is very difficult to imagine how the conservatives could have been so confident that they could dominate this Nazi government but confident they were – at least some of them. Papen, for example, is reported to have said: "Within two months we will have pushed Hitler so far into a corner that he'll squeak." Evans, *Coming of the Third Reich*, p. 308; Dulffer, *Nazi Germany*, p. 26. On the contingencies that may very well have prevented the Nazis from coming to power, see Evans, *Coming of the Third Reich*, pp. 161, 325–7, 442–3. Evans concludes that "a military regime of some description was the only viable alternative to a Nazi dictatorship" by July 1932. Also see Dulffer, *Nazi Germany*, p. 26; Payne, *History of Fascism*, pp. 178–9; Bracher, *German Dictatorship*, p. 202.

very sympathetic to the Nazis. With these two ministries, the National Socialists gained control of the major security forces of the now dying Weimar Republic. In the first instance, this control meant that Nazi paramilitary units could move against their partisan enemies with impunity; soon, the uniformed agencies of the German state joined them. These ministries, in addition to the chancellorship, enabled the founding of the Third Reich.

But that founding did not take place on the morning of January 30, 1933, when Hitler was sworn in as chancellor. In fact, the proceedings unfolded much as they had when previous governments had taken office.[146] The Nationalists, now a much diminished force, formally joined the Nazi parliamentary coalition and took over many of the ministry posts, with their leader, Alfred Hugenberg, occupying those pertaining to economic policy and agriculture.[147] Their participation gave the Nazi-led coalition a thin democratic veneer, although the two parties together controlled only a minority of the seats in the Reichstag. So, although the original transfer of power to the Nazis was certainly the decisive event in bringing about the founding of the Third Reich, in itself it did not constitute a founding. In fact, from the Nazi perspective, the immediate response to Hitler's assumption of the chancellorship might well have been a sigh of relief.[148]

The new National Socialist regime immediately began to consolidate its hold on power. On February 4, President Hindenburg was persuaded to issue a "Decree for the Protection of the German Nation," empowering Hitler and his new ministers to prohibit public assemblies and censor publications. Then, on February 27, the Nazis received an unexpected boon when an apparently deranged anarchist carrying Communist leaflets set fire to the Reichstag,

---

[146] This event did not constitute the founding despite the fact that it was subsequently called the "*Machtergreifung*," defined as the "seizure of power." From the "Glossary of German Terms" in Research Institute for Military History, *Germany and the Second World War*, vol. I, p. xxvi.

[147] Evans, *Coming of the Third Reich*, pp. 307–8, 316. Hugenberg, however, appears to have had immediate regrets. The day after entering Hitler's new governing coalition, he reportedly said: "[Y]esterday I committed the biggest blunder of my life. I allied myself with the biggest demagogue in the history of the world." Hamilton, *Who Voted for Hitler?*, p. 240.

[148] Dulffer, *Nazi Germany*, p. 27. For an interpretation that views Hitler's appointment as chancellor "as one of history's most tragic ironies" in that "the party's electoral support had begun to falter," see Childers, *Nazi Voter*, p. 269. Orlow similarly concluded that, by "the end of 1932, [the Nazi Party] was well on its way to the rubbish pile of history. Its demise was delayed, but that was principally the work of Papen and the German conservatives." Orlow, *History of the Nazi Party*, p. 308. Also see Bessel, *Political Violence and the Rise of Nazism*, p. 26. On the fragility of National Socialist electoral support and Nazi fears that the party might have peaked in the July 1932 Reichstag elections, see Evans, *Coming of the Third Reich*, pp. 295, 299–301. However, Gellately maintains that "the Nazis were not doing as poorly in the elections as some historians have suggested" and that, once Hitler took power, "a social consensus emerged in favour of Hitler and Nazism within months." Gellately, *Backing Hitler*, pp. 3, 12. For maps and graphic descriptions of the changing electoral strength of the NSDAP between 1924 and 1933, see Michael Freeman, *Atlas of Nazi Germany: A Political, Economic, and Social Anatomy of the Third Reich* (London: Longman, 1995), pp. 27–37, 43.

burning it to the ground. The Nazi regime instantly sprang into action and began to arrest Communists throughout Germany. Hindenburg supported suppression of the KPD and, ultimately, other political parties by signing the "Reichstag Fire Decree," which suspended most civil liberties otherwise protected by the Weimar Constitution and permitted the central government to take over local governments.[149] On March 5, a new election of delegates to the Reichstag was held. In order to allow Communist candidates to stand for election and thus split the left vote with the Social Democrats, the Nazis delayed an official ban on the Communist Party until the votes had been cast. Then, on March 6, the Communist Party was declared illegal.[150] Two weeks later, what turned out to be the first of many concentration camps was opened at Dachau to house political prisoners, most but not all of them Communists.

Major events in the consolidation of power after the Nazi takeover

1933: February 4. Hindenburg issues a "Decree for the Protection of the German Nation" that gives the new Nazi government the authority to prohibit public assemblies and to censor publications.

1933: February 27. Marinus van der Lubbe, a Dutch anarchist, burns down the Reichstag.

1933: February 28. Hindenburg signs a decree drafted by Hitler suspending provisions in the Weimar Constitution that protected freedom of speech, freedom of the press, the right of assembly, personal liberty and privacy, and property rights, as well as permitting the central government to take over local governments.

1933: February 28. The state government in Bavaria bans Communist meetings and shuts down the Communist press.

1933: March 1: Publication of Social Democratic newspapers is temporarily banned for two weeks. This ban is renewed every two weeks until it becomes permanent.

1933: March 5. Reichstag election.

1933: March 6. The Communist Party is officially banned.

1933: March. Interior Minister Frick orders that Nazis be appointed in place of elected government ministers in federated states.

1933: March 20. What turns out to be the first concentration camp in Germany opens at Dachau.

---

[149] Evans, *Coming of the Third Reich*, pp. 328–33. On Hindenburg's presidential decrees of February 4 and 28, see Wette, "Ideology, Propaganda, and Internal Politics," pp. 89–90. Following Ernst Fraenkel, Hett calls the decree "the constitutional charter" of the Nazi regime. Hett, *Death of Democracy*, p. 6.

[150] Evans, *Coming of the Third Reich*, pp. 11–12.

(*cont.*)

1933: March 23. The Reichstag passes the Enabling Act that confers unilateral law-making authority upon Hitler (as Reich chancellor). The act renders the Reichstag and President Hindenburg more or less powerless.

1933: May 10. The German government seizes the Social Democratic Party's assets and property.

1933: June 22. The Social Democratic Party is officially banned.

1933: June 26. Reichstag deputies and other political officials belonging to the Bavarian People's Party (allied with the Catholic Zentrum) are arrested.

1933: June 28. After the government prevents its Reichstag deputies from serving, the leaders of the State Party formally dissolve the party.

1933: June 29. The German Nationalist Front (formerly the Nationalist Party) formally dissolves itself.

1933: July 1. The Nazis sign an agreement (the Concordat) with the Vatican under which priests are prohibited from engaging in political activity and the Zentrum is to be disbanded.

1933: July 5. The Zentrum formally dissolves and encourages its political officials to join the Nazi Party.

1933: July 4. The leader of the People's Party announces the dissolution of the party.

1933: July 14. Hitler decrees that the National Socialist German Workers' Party is the only legal party in Germany and that the founding or maintaining of other party political organizations is illegal.

1933: December 1: The Ministry of the Interior declares that the Nazi Party is now unified with the German state.

1934: August 1. A law is passed combining the offices of Reich president and Reich chancellor under Adolf Hitler.

1934: August 2. President Paul von Hindenburg dies.

1934: August 19. A plebiscite approves Hitler's self-appointment as head of state following Hindenburg's death. Almost 90 percent (89.9) of the votes support Hitler.

Source: Most entries were taken from Evans, *Coming of the Third Reich*, pp. 42–3, 328–33, 335–6, 339–42, 344–5, 351, 358–9, 364–5, 367–8, 372.

The March 5 Reichstag election was held as part of the agreement that brought the Nazis into power because Hitler wanted to confirm the party's right to rule through a public demonstration of the popular will. While previous Reichstag elections had involved violence, they had still met the minimal procedural and contextual conditions required for a democratic choice. But the election held on March 5, 1933, did not.[151] The Communist and Social Democratic Parties, for example, were almost completely prevented from conducting public campaigns, including ordinary activities such as the distribution of leaflets. Many Communist Party members and candidates, in fact, had already been detained by the government. Nazi storm troopers, on the other hand, were enrolled as auxiliary police officers and authorized to carry firearms as they marched through the streets and harassed political opponents. Despite Nazi intimidation and violence, the Communists still polled a little over 12 percent of the vote and the Social Democrats almost held their own with eighteen. The Nazis came in with just under 44 percent and increased their representation in the Reichstag from 196 to 288 seats. As their allies, the Nationalists polled about 8 percent, winning one more delegate to go with the fifty-one they already had. But that was just enough to give the Nazi-led coalition a majority of both the popular vote and seats in the Reichstag. Given the advantages enjoyed by the National Socialist Party, this was not a superb performance but it still, albeit superficially, qualified as a victory and, more importantly, a popular endorsement of the new regime.[152]

[151] For a map of regional Nazi strength in the March 5, 1933, election, see Frank Omland, "'Germany Totally National Socialist' – National Socialist Reichstag Elections and Plebiscites, 1933–1938: The Example of Schleswig-Holstein" in Ralph Jessen and Hedwig Richter (eds.), *Voting for Hitler and Stalin: Elections under 20th Century Dictatorships* (Frankfurt: Campus Verlag, 2011), p. 256. For a good summary of the 1930, 1932, and 1933 elections, including the political context in which they were conducted, see Ivan Ermakoff, *Ruling Oneself Out: A Theory of Collective Abdications* (Durham, NC: Duke University Press, 2008), pp. 5–18.

[152] The consensus among scholars seems to be that the election results were clearly but not entirely tainted by Nazi violence and political intimidation. Hamilton, for example, questioned their "validity and significance" and did not view the voting patterns as worthy of further analysis. Hamilton, *Who Voted for Hitler?*, p. 4. Also see Evans, *Coming of the Third Reich*, pp. 339–40; Eksteins, *Limits of Reason*, p. 266. Morris called the election "semifree." Morris, *Weimar Republic*, p. 183. Payne echoed that judgment. Payne, *History of Fascism*, p. 174. The stakes behind the question of how much violence and intimidation added to the Nazi vote total are fairly significant. In a highly proportional electoral system, 44 percent would be a remarkably good showing and, since the Nazis ran in partnership with the Nationalists, the governing coalition did manage to draw a majority of the votes and, thus, earned the right to rule. On the other hand, that majority was almost certainly "manufactured" at the margin by undemocratic practices carried on by both the Nazi Party and, what was rapidly becoming the same thing, the German state. Without those practices, the Nazis and the Nationalists would not have gained a majority of the vote. But this does not mean that there was a "democratic majority" that was somehow suppressed in this election because the Communists, who drew one out of every eight votes, were just as committed to destroying the Weimar Republic as were the Nazis. From that perspective, there was no democratic majority to be had, no matter how the election had been conducted. In March 1933, we might therefore conclude that there was no popular, majority basis for either continuing the existence of the Weimar Republic or for founding an alternative state. If the popular will in such a situation should be interpreted as a plurality expression of the citizenry, then the Nazis clearly had the best claim on power, with or without violence.

The March 5 election set the stage for the founding of the Third Reich because the returns created a parliamentary majority that was committed both to destroying the Weimar Republic and to concentrating central state authority in Hitler's office. The vehicle for both purposes was to be an amendment to the Weimar Constitution that would grant all legislative authority to the chancellor, thus eviscerating the Reichstag of political influence. Loosely modeled on similar measures that had temporarily and for limited purposes granted legislative authority to previous chancellors, this amendment was entitled the "Law to Relieve the Distress of the People and Reich," or, more commonly, the Enabling Act.[153] While the amendment granted Hitler the power to rule Germany by decree for the next four years, passage required the presence of two-thirds of the members of the Reichstag to meet the quorum requirement and, in addition, the support of two-thirds of the members who voted. The Nazi-led parliamentary coalition held only a bare majority of the seats.

The first step in manufacturing the required two-thirds majority was taken when Hermann Göring, the presiding officer, ruled that those Communists who had been elected to the Reichstag on March 5 were no longer legitimate members. Because their party was now illegal, these delegates had not shown up to claim their seats. However, the Communists still constituted part of the Reichstag's official membership and thus composed part of the quorum requirement even if they were absent. Göring's extraordinary and almost certainly illegal ruling reduced the quorum requirement by fifty-four members and also enhanced the proportion of seats occupied by the Nazi-led parliamentary coalition. But their majority was still not large enough. One problem was the Social Democratic Party, which still fielded ninety-four delegates, every one of whom was unalterably opposed to passage of the Enabling Act.[154] In order to reach the necessary two-thirds majority, Hitler opened negotiations with the Zentrum, which was led by a priest, Ludwig Kaas. These discussions revolved around assurances for the autonomy of the Catholic Church, particularly in Bavaria where the Church had long been a major political force. In return, the Zentrum would provide the additional Reichstag support for passing the Enabling Act.[155]

With the Zentrum now on board, the Communists outlawed, and members of the smaller parties intimidated into submission, the Nazis could confront the Social Democrats. In a scene reminiscent of the convocation of the Constituent

---

[153] Payne, *History of Fascism*, p. 175. For description of the adoption of the Enabling Act, see Ermakoff, *Ruling Oneself Out*, pp. 17–20. For descriptions of previous enabling acts and their political context, see Mattern, *Principles of the Constitutional Jurisprudence*, pp. 486, 492–5, 501.

[154] The SDP had elected 120 delegates but "some were in prison, some were ill, and some stayed away because they feared for their lives." Evans, *Coming of the Third Reich*, p. 351.

[155] Evans, *Coming of the Third Reich*, pp. 351–2. For a detailed description and analysis of the Zentrum's decision to support the Enabling Act, including contingencies that led to that decision, see Ermakoff, *Ruling Oneself Out*, pp. 64–75, 94–117, 133–46, 211–26, 245–76.

Assembly in St. Petersburg fifteen years earlier, the Nazis lined the sides and
rear of the Kroll Opera House with uniformed, armed storm troopers and SS
men. The auditorium itself was festooned with swastikas and other Nazi
emblems. As one Social Democrat later reported: "Wild chants greeted us:
'We want the Enabling Law!' Young lads with the swastika on their chests
looked us cheekily up and down, virtually barring the way for us. They quite
made us run the gauntlet, and shouted insults at us like 'Centrist pig,' 'Marxist
sow.'"

As he presented the Enabling Act to the Reichstag, Hitler first promised to
respect the autonomy of the established churches and claimed credit for suppressing the Communist scourge. The absence of every KPD delegate must have
weighed heavily on the minds of the other delegates as Hitler now warned those
who might oppose passage of the Enabling Act. In a scene already drenched in
menace, adrenaline, and auguries of the terror yet to come, Hitler announced
that the "government of the nationalist uprising" was "determined and ready
to deal with the announcement that the Act has been rejected and with it that
resistance has been declared. May you, gentlemen, now take the decision
yourselves as to whether it is to be peace or war."

The most memorable speech, however, belonged to Otto Wels, the leader of
the Social Democratic delegation. Surrounded by his party colleagues, who
were, in turn, surrounded by storm troopers, Wels began with the observation
that "[f]reedom and life can be taken from us, but not honour." He then
continued with what in many ways appeared to be a valedictory address in
which the closing passage was both wistful and, perhaps unreasonably, considering the circumstances, hopeful.

In this historic hour, we German Social Democrats solemnly profess our allegiance to the
basic principles of humanity and justice, freedom and socialism. No Enabling Law gives
you the right to annihilate ideas that are eternal and indestructible. The Anti-Socialist
Law [of the late nineteenth century] did not annihilate the Social Democrats. Social
Democracy can also draw new strength from fresh persecutions. We greet the persecuted
and the hard-pressed. Their steadfastness and loyalty deserve admiration. The courage
of their convictions, their unbroken confidence, vouch for a brighter future.[156]

As Wels ended, the auditorium broke out in pandemonium as the disciplined
and mannered applause of the vastly outnumbered Social Democrats was
swallowed up in a Nazi din of contemptuous taunts, bullying ridicule, and
shrill laughter.

Hitler had seen an advance copy of this address and had prepared his
response. "You think," he noted, "that your star could rise again!
Gentlemen, Germany's star will rise and yours will sink ... Germany shall be
free, but not through you!" After a few more short speeches, 444 votes were
cast in favor of the Enabling Act and only ninety-four delegates, all of them

[156] Evans, *Coming of the Third Reich*, pp. 352–4.

Social Democrats, dared to oppose passage.[157] With all legislative and executive power now consolidated in the hands of their Leader, the Nazis had succeeded in founding the Third Reich and the Weimar Constitution was now a dead letter, so much so that the Nazis never found it necessary to write a new document to replace it.[158]

The most remarkable characteristic of the founding of the Third Reich was Nazi insistence on observing the proper forms of a democratic process for which they had the utmost and unmitigated contempt. The party ran candidates in Reichstag elections and campaigned for votes with techniques and appeals that matched the democratic parties of the center in style and orientation. Hitler was appointed chancellor in a formally orthodox procedure that recognized him as the leader of the largest party in the Reichstag. In turn, he called for a new election so that his minority coalition might immediately be put to the test. The returns gave the coalition a majority in the Reichstag and thus legitimated Nazi rule as the will of the people. At that point, Nazi ideology did not see the need for more elections because the Leader had now come to power, the people and Leader were now one, and the task at hand was to realize the historic destiny of the German people, race, and nation. Democracy, with all its splintering and divisive appeals to narrow interests and individual identities, was not only unnecessarily distracting but positively harmful.

However, the Nazis did hold plebiscites in which the people were given an opportunity to approve major state decisions and policies.[159] For example, on November 12, 1933, a national plebiscite approved Germany's withdrawal from the League of Nations. On August 19, 1934, another plebiscite

---

[157] Evans, *Coming of the Third Reich*, pp. 352–4. As Evans notes, the majority was so large that even the participation of the missing Communist and Social Democratic delegates could not have prevented passage.

[158] "The Enabling Law ... has rightly been described as the constitution of National Socialist Germany." Berger, *Social Democracy*, p. 136n. Just after passage, Carl Schmitt, one of the leading constitutional theorists in Germany and "an influential supporter" of the new Nazi regime, declared that the Enabling Act had brought into being a "completely different kind of government" that marked the end of party competition. The content and design of the new political order would, according to Schmitt, be determined by the Leader. Evans, *Coming of the Third Reich*, p. 371. In July 1933, a few months after passage of the Enabling Act, Schmitt publicly praised the Nazis for having "gotten rid of parliamentary democracy and political parties." Hett, *Death of Democracy*, p. 213. On the importance of the Enabling Act as the decisive event in the Nazi takeover, see Evans, *Coming of the Third Reich*, p. 349; Dulffer, *Nazi Germany*, pp. 33–4; Robert Thomson Clark, *Fall of the German Republic: A Political Study* (New York: Russell and Russell, 1964), pp. 486–8. Bracher went on to say that the importance of the Enabling Act also lay in the fact that its formal legality made "willing collaborators [of] the civil service and the courts," both of which were essential elements in routinizing terror and intimidation through which the Nazis purged German society of opposition elements. Bracher, *German Dictatorship*, pp. 194, 197, 210.

[159] Evans, *Coming of the Third Reich*, p. 121.

approved Hitler's self-appointment as president following Hindenburg's death. This was a particularly important step because it formally combined the presidency and the chancellorship and thus eliminated all need to distinguish between them. Almost nine in every ten votes were cast in favor. On March 29, 1936, a plebiscite approved German reoccupation of the Rhineland. This one would have passed even if the Nazis had not been in power. In April 1938, a similar plebiscite approved union with Austria and the Nazi regime generally. None of these were, of course, binding. And all of them were conducted in a way that made opposition extraordinarily dangerous. As exercises in the demonstration of power, the plebiscites evidenced the almost complete dominance of the National Socialist Party in German political life. However, from the perspective of Nazi ideology, these plebiscites evidenced the organic unity of the people and the Leader in a display that did not logically exclude the use of intimidation when applied to those who, for whatever reason, were not of the *Volk*. Although democratic in form, these were not occasions in which the will of the people was consulted but, instead, demonstrations attesting to the unstoppable force created by the organic union of the people with the Leader. They were thus spectacles in which undemocratic practices such as violence and intimidation were as proper and expected as the casting of a ballot.[160]

Since there could be only one organic unity of Leader and people, the other political parties with their charlatan pretenders were not only useless but treasonous. They were not, however, eliminated all at once. Instead, they were eradicated serially in a pattern similar to the consolidation of power in both the Soviet Union and, as we shall see, the Iranian Islamic Republic. The process in those cases had begun with the party most hostile to the designs and intentions of the new state. For the Nazis, this was the KPD; the Communists, of course, had already been banned when the Enabling Act was passed. Then came the Social Democratic Party, whose assets and property were seized on May 10. The party itself was proscribed on June 22. The Bavarian People's Party, allied with the Catholic Zentrum and sharing its doctrinal commitments, was rendered politically impotent by arrests on June 26. Three days later the Nationalists, the ostensible partner in the Nazi Reichstag coalition, voluntarily dissolved. Finally, after the Nazis and the Vatican signed the Concordat, the Zentrum also disbanded on July 5 and, as a token of goodwill, encouraged its political officials to join the Nazi Party. On July 14, Hitler decreed that the National Socialist Party was the only legal political party in Germany and that

---

[160] On the role of referenda after the founding of the Nazi state, see Markus Urban, "The Self-Staging of a Plebiscitary Dictatorship: The NS-Regime between 'Uniformed *Reichstag*,' Referendum and *Reichsparteitag*" in Jessen and Richter (eds.), *Voting for Hitler and Stalin*; Omland, "Germany Totally National Socialist," pp. 42–7, 254–71.

all political activity by other party organizations was prohibited. Finally, on December 1, the Ministry of the Interior declared that the Nazi Party was now unified with the German state, symbolically substantiating the consolidation of Leader, people, race, and nation.[161]

From a procedural perspective, all of these things were at least tainted by illegal actions, some of them collateral to the consolidation of power in Nazi hands (e.g., street violence and assassinations) and others that were flagrant violations of existing law. But prior governments had set at least weak precedents for most of the process through which the Nazis seized power. There were, for example, pre-Hitlerian precedents for suppression of a free press, the dissolution of freely elected governments in the states, the exercise of authoritarian powers under Article 48, the prohibition of members of selected political parties from employment in the civil service, and the banning of paramilitary units associated with the major political parties.[162] The Nazis were, however, extraordinarily aggressive in their use of these precedents and their combination under one regime constituted an entirely new and different political order.[163]

The Nazis opportunistically used the forms and processes of Weimar democracy in order to build their movement and advance their claims on power. And while we might view their exploitation of these forms and processes as a cynical (and thus insincere) strategy, the fact is that they found a way to integrate formal democracy into their ideological expectations as a form of revelatory discovery and subsequent presentation of the Leader to his people. And that was the crux of the connection: The emergence and public acclamation of the Leader was more or less consistent with formal democratic practice in that the display of popular recognition in the form of rallies, marches, demonstrations, and symbolic acts (e.g., the Nazi salute) was compatible with, even affirmed by, the casting of ballots (as long as the party more or less steadily increased its proportion of the votes).

However, as the party came ever closer to assuming power, the ideological need for conforming to democratic practice radically declined. On the one

---

[161] On the destruction of the Weimar party system, see Evans, *Coming of the Third Reich*, pp. 344, 358–9, 364–6; Dulffer, *Nazi Germany*, pp. 34–6; Morris, *Weimar Republic*, p. 192; Hamilton, *Who Voted for Hitler?*, p. 260. For a description of the negotiations between the Catholic Church and the new Nazi regime that led to the Concordat, see Evans, *Coming of the Third Reich*, pp. 363–6.

[162] Eksteins, *Limits of Reason*, p. 248; Dulffer, *Nazi Germany*, p. 21; Kater, *Nazi Party*, pp. 42–3; Also see Hamilton, *Who Voted for Hitler?*, pp. 279–80; Morris, *Weimar Republic*, pp. 188–9; Evans, *Coming of the Third Reich*, p. 344.

[163] For detailed recitations of the illegal acts through which the Nazis first assumed power and then consolidated their hold on the German state, see Bracher, *German Dictatorship*, p. 211; Evans, *Coming of the Third Reich*, pp. 452–4.

hand, the party had already irrevocably "recognized" the Leader and, as the proximity to power increased, the problem was not how to persuade the last necessary increment of the German public to support the National Socialist Party but, instead, how to manipulate the political situation so that others would grant the party an opportunity to rule. In this respect, the proportional system of representation was absolutely essential in that it made parliamentary coalition-building the expected and almost unavoidable method of creating and sustaining governments. The Nazis, for that reason, did not have to have a majority of the votes in a democratic election in order to (conventionally) legitimate their assumption of power. What they needed was enough votes to make them the largest political party and, then, a willing coalition partner to put them over the top. In some ways, these requirements were no different than those confronting the democratic political parties of the center. The difference was that, once power was gained, the Nazis always intended to abolish democratic practice and forms. And any informed observer could not have failed to see that that was their intention.[164]

Passage of the Enabling Act melded the *Volk* and the German state within an organic unity symbolized, materialized, and actualized by the Leader.[165] The notion of "consent," so vital to social contract theory, vanished at the founding since the will of the *Volk* and the Leader could never diverge; they were one and the same. The will of the people was registered at the founding as a now self-evident fact, but it, too, vanished at the founding as a separate element in state theory. The will of the people folded neatly and completely into the absolute authority of the Leader, who was now at one with the German people, race,

---

[164] Scholars have discussed at length the question of whether or not the events leading up to the Nazi assumption of power constituted a "revolution." There is no consensus. For a sampling of views, see Evans, *Coming of the Third Reich*, pp. 456–60; Evans, *Third Reich in Power*, pp. 16, 120–1; Dulffer, *Nazi Germany*, pp. 36–7; Payne, *History of Fascism*, p. 204; Bracher, *German Dictatorship*, p. 7.

[165] Consistent with this notion of organic unity between the people and the Leader, much of the process through which the Nazis consolidated power took the form of "coordination" (*Gleichschaltung*), "a metaphor drawn from the world of electricity, meaning that all the switches were being put onto the same circuit, as it were, so that they could all be activated by throwing a single master switch at the centre. Almost every aspect of political, social and associational life was affected, at every level from the nation to the village." Evans, *Coming of the Third Reich*, p. 381. The Nazis attributed residual political resistance within the German people to foreign and alien (often Jewish) influence. One of the most pressing tasks confronting the new government was thus, as Goebbels put it, to mold the people so that they would begin "to think as one, to react as one, and to place itself in the service of the government with all its heart" (p. 397). Along with other elements of Nazi ideology, this project led almost naturally into, first, the isolation of Jews and other alien elements from the rest of the German people, then the denial of their civil and political rights, their incarceration in camps, and, finally, their routinized extermination. The Holocaust was thus intimately connected with the purification and organic unification of the *Volk*. Also see Dulffer, *Nazi Germany*, pp. 39–40.

and nation.[166] The founding thus obliterated the major principles of democratic theory in the same moment they framed and evidenced the new foundation of the German state.

---

[166] After the Nazis had consolidated power, the role of the Leader was formally developed in a way that, on the one hand, fully explained where the Leader stood within party cosmology while, on the other, placed no limits on how the Leader might or should exercise power. In 1939, for example, Ernst Rudolf Huber wrote in his *Constitutional Law of the Greater German Reich* that the Leader represented "the united will of the people" and, for that reason

[the] authority of the Leader is total and all-embracing: within it all resources available to the body politic merge; it covers every facet of the life of the people; it embraces all members of the German community pledged to loyalty and obedience to the Leader. The Leader's authority is subject to no checks or controls; it is circumscribed by no private preserves of jealously guarded individual rights; it is free and independent, overriding and unfettered. (Evans, *Third Reich in Power*, p. 44)

7

Islamic Theocracy

The Iranian Revolution

On January 7, 1978, Daryush Homayun, the Shah's Information Minister, published an article in a semiofficial newspaper in which he described Ayatollah Ruhollah Khomeini as "an adventurer, without faith, and tied to the centers of colonialism ... a man with a dubious past, tied to the more superficial and reactionary colonialists." Writing under a pseudonym that in no way disguised the regime's authorship, Homayun accused Khomeini of accepting money from the British in return for his public attacks on the Shah's reform program. Rioting broke out the following day in the holy city of Qom after the regime's security forces attempted to suppress protests by theological students. Some seventy people were killed in the next two days. Thus began the Iranian Revolution.[1]

The targets of the riots and protests that soon followed eloquently traced the connection between Western-style modernization and the Shah's reform program while unambiguously manifesting popular hostility to both of them. On February 18, at least twenty-seven people died and 262 were injured in a riot in Tabriz, where "cinemas, liquor stores, restaurants, banks, hairdressing salons," and the headquarters of the regime's political party were attacked. On August 19,

---

[1] Nikki R. Keddie, *Modern Iran: Roots and Results of Revolution* (New Haven, CT: Yale University Press, 2003), p. 225. In 1983, Sussan Siavoshi interviewed an anonymous protest leader who described the Qom incident as

A turning point in many respects. First of all, the secular leaders had no role in initiating the demonstration. Second, slogans used by the demonstrators were clearly voiced in religious language. And third, the regime's severe reaction convinced many people that the most feared enemy from the regime's point of view was the religious community and that therefore the religious opposition must be the most powerful of all opposition.

Sussan Siavoshi, *Liberal Nationalism in Iran: The Failure of a Movement* (Boulder, CO: Westview, 1990), p. 138.

480 people perished when an arsonist set fire to the Cinema Rex in Abadan.[2] On September 8, martial law was declared in Tehran as troops killed hundreds of protestors in what was later called Black Friday. On November 4, about a dozen students died in protests at Tehran University. The next day, protestors burned "[b]anks, hotels, cinemas, showrooms," and the Ministry of Information while guerrillas attacked police stations throughout the city. The army watched but did nothing. During this period, strikes and slowdowns by public employees in government offices and state-owned enterprises increasingly paralyzed both bureaucratic routine and economic activity.

On December 10 and 11, these protests and strikes culminated in massive parades in Tehran that ostensibly commemorated the martyrdom of Imam Hussein. Over two million marchers called for the immediate abdication of the Shah and the impending end of the Pahlavi dynasty was now obvious. On December 30, the Shah asked Shapour Bakhtiar, a prominent liberal leader, to become prime minister. Bakhtiar agreed to take the post only if the Shah agreed to leave Iran and the Shah subsequently left for Egypt on January 16, 1979. However, because Bakhtiar had negotiated with the regime, his former allies in the liberal, secular wing of the protest movement deserted him. After several fruitless attempts to bargain with Khomeini (who was in Paris), Bakhtiar finally allowed the ayatollah to return to Iran. After sixteen years in exile, Khomeini arrived in Tehran on February 1. Three million people turned out to celebrate his return. Three days later, Khomeini appointed a provisional government led by Mehdi Bazargan, a "Muslim liberal." At the same time, Khomeini stated that the primary task of the provisional government would be to arrange for a popular referendum authorizing an Islamic Republic.[3] That referendum would be followed by the election of a constituent assembly that would draft a new constitution and, after that, the election of a new parliament. Although all of this appeared to conform to the precepts of a democratic founding, Khomeini left no doubt that this one would be different.

---

[2] Regime opponents renamed the movie theater "Kebab House of the Sun of the Aryans" after a royal title the Shah had created in an attempt to imitate Louis XIV. Said Amir Arjomand, *The Turban for the Crown: The Islamic Revolution in Iran* (New York: Oxford University Press, 1988), pp. 117–18. Several years later, a Muslim fundamentalist was convicted of setting this fire. One of the witnesses who had been aware of his guilt stated that he, the witness, had withheld information from the police "[f]or the sake of Revolution." Suroosh Irfani, *Iran's Islamic Revolution: Popular Liberation or Religious Dictatorship?* (London: Zed Books, 1983), p. 180n.

[3] Khomeini's theoretical comprehension of the form that this Islamic Republic might take evolved over the years he spent in exile in Iraq. For surveys of his thinking, see Mojtaba Mahdavi, "The Rise of Khomeinism"; Amr G. E. Sabet, "*Wilayat al-Faqih* and the Meaning of Islamic Government"; and Behrooz Ghamari-Tabrizi, "The Divine, the People, and the *Faqih*" in Arshin Adib-Moghaddam (ed.), *A Critical Introduction to Khomeini* (New York: Cambridge University Press, 2014), pp. 56–8, 70–85, 221–6.

As a man who, through the guardianship [*velayat*] that I have from the holy lawgiver [the Prophet], I hereby pronounce Bazargan as the Ruler, and since I have appointed him, he must be obeyed. The nation must obey him. This is not an ordinary government. It is a government based on the *shari'a*. Opposing this government means opposing the *shari'a* of Islam and revolting against the *shari'a*, and revolt against the government of the *shari'a* has its punishment in our law … it is a heavy punishment in Islamic jurisprudence. Revolt against God's government is a revolt against God. Revolt against God is blasphemy.[4]

When the military declared its political neutrality, the Bakhtiar government fell on February 11. After that, the revolutionary movement, led by Ayatollah Khomeini, controlled the Iranian state.[5]

All modern states, even those that would not usually be categorized as democracies, are founded in rituals through which sovereignty, the will of the people, and a transcendent social purpose are melded together as the foundation of state authority. The Islamic Republic of Iran was founded in two such rituals, one the precursor to the other. On March 30–31, 1979, the Iranian people voted in a national referendum asking them whether they wanted the new state to be an "Islamic republic" or a monarchy. Over 98 percent of those who voted favored the founding of an Islamic republic. A little more than eight months later, on December 2–3, a second national referendum asked the Iranian people whether the newly drafted constitution should be the basis of that Islamic republic. Over 99 percent of those who voted approved adoption of the new constitution. Although there were other significant events and moments attending the founding of the Islamic Republic, these two were the most important. On their face (and from a particular perspective), they were unequivocal expressions of the popular will as it founded a new state. However, that new state, ostensibly founded by mass democratic rituals, was not to be a democracy.

As in the Russian case, there were two paths the Iranian Revolution might have taken. One of them would have led to a more recognizably "Western-style" democracy in which political competition and public debate were not tightly regulated or controlled by the state. The other led, as it turned out, to a theocracy in which religious doctrine and members of the clergy dominated society and the state. The leading forces favoring the democratic path were the National Front and the Liberation Movement, which drew their strength from urban professionals and civil servants. The National Front was a "bourgeois democratic or reformist social democratic organization" whose leader, Karim Sanjabi,

[4] Baqer Moin, *Khomeini: Life of the Ayatollah* (New York: St. Martin's Press, 1999), pp. 203–4.
[5] Houchang E. Chehabi, "Religion and Politics in Iran: How Theocratic Is the Islamic Republic?," *Daedalus* 120: 3 (1991), p. 74; Arjomand, *Turban for the Crown*, pp. 121–2, 134; Keddie, *Modern Iran*, pp. 234, 238; Jahangir Amuzegar, *The Dynamics of the Iranian Revolution: The Pahlavis' Triumph and Tragedy* (Albany: State University of New York Press, 1991), p. 291; Dilip Hiro, *Iran under the Ayatollahs* (London: Routledge and Kegan Paul, 1985), p. 90.

met with Khomeini in Paris and afterward produced a declaration stating that both Islam and democracy would be basic principles underlying the post-revolutionary state.[6] This declaration went a long way toward reassuring the National Front that the new regime would resemble the social democracy that secular liberals desired. That reassurance, in turn, made them very reluctant to negotiate a compromise solution with the Shah in which the latter would have retained as least some role in the government. Aside from some of the Marxist organizations and parties, the National Front was probably the most secular political element in the revolutionary coalition.

Mehdi Bazargan, who later led the first revolutionary government, was a founding member of the Liberation Movement when it emerged in Iranian politics in 1961. While most of its original leadership was drawn from the National Front, the organization insisted that state authority be compatible with Islamic principles and that political participation by devout Muslims and the clergy was morally imperative. For most of the period leading up to the revolution, the Liberation Movement both supported the monarchy and advocated liberalization of the regime. However, political suppression gradually pushed the Liberation Movement toward more radical positions and its disaffection helped alienate the urban middle class from the regime.[7]

Ironically, perhaps, much of the new urban middle class in Iran was the byproduct of the Shah's modernization program. That meant that much of the impetus for a more Western-style democratic polity had been created by a regime that suppressed its claims for greater political participation in the government.[8] That suppression then pushed liberal, secular organizations into coalition with the fundamentalist clergy, an embrace that not only smothered liberal democratic elements in Iran but also reversed or stalled what had been the modernizing thrust of the Shah's reform program.

In 1977, the "new middle-class sectors" represented only 18 percent of the population. As in the Russian Revolution, these sectors threw up many articulate, pragmatic, and experienced political leaders, but the revolutionary settlement was largely shaped by street demonstrations in which the middle class was far outnumbered by other sectors historically tied to the clergy: the "traditional" bourgeoisie (e.g., the bazaar merchants), who made up about

---

[6] On Khomeini's rather deceptive moderate pronouncements while in Paris, see Mohammad Ayatollahi Tabaar, *Religious Statecraft: The Politics of Islam in Iran* (New York: Columbia University Press, 2018), pp. 69–70; Moin, *Khomeini*, pp. 195–8, 219. While repeatedly emphasizing the depth and sincerity of Khomeini's religious belief, Moin also notes the many instances in which Khomeini opportunistically trimmed his sails. On Khomeini's carefully considered strategy, see, for example, pp. 68–9.

[7] Hossein Bahiriyeh, *The State and Revolution in Iran, 1962–1982* (New York: St. Martin's Press, 1984), p. 174; Mohsen M. Milani, *The Making of Iran's Islamic Revolution: From Monarchy to Islamic Republic* (Boulder, CO: Westview Press, 1988), pp. 143–4; Keddie, *Modern Iran*, pp. 233–4; Siavoshi, *Liberal Nationalism*, p. 158.

[8] Arjomand, *Turban for the Crown*, p. 108.

10 percent of the population; the working class (33 percent); and the peasantry (36 percent).[9] The position assumed by these sectors was also a byproduct of the Shah's policies. For example, modernization had negative implications for the traditional organization of the economy overseen by merchants who sold their wares and services in urban bazaars. The Shah responded to their protests with policies that increasingly marked them as retrograde opponents who should be eliminated.[10] As was the case with the new middle class, both repression and policy pushed the traditional bourgeoisie into the arms of the clergy; however, the link between the Islamic clergy and bazaar merchants was already strong and longstanding.[11]

The backbone of the massive street demonstrations in 1978 was composed of illiterate or semiliterate, unskilled peasants who had migrated to the cities and worked in the informal, part-time economy at the margins of the modern industrial and service sectors.[12] These migrants lived in slums on the outskirts of the cities where they raised very large families and adopted lifestyles characterized by some of the aspects of modern life (e.g., television and popular fashions) while otherwise retaining a very traditional relationship with Islam and the Islamic clergy. Khomeini and the fundamentalist clergy called them the "dispossessed" and frequently described them as "oppressed" and "innocent." Although Khomeini never stated exactly what should be done to relieve the miseries of the migrants, he nonetheless persuasively blamed the regime's modernization policies for their suffering. These migrants far outnumbered skilled, industrial workers in the Iranian economy and, along with bazaar merchants, composed the "core social basis" of the Iranian Revolution.[13]

In all these ways, the political economy that structured the Iranian Revolution was the product of reforms and policies that dated back half a century to the founding of the dynasty in 1925 by Reza Shah Pahlavi, the

---

[9] Arjomand, *Turban for the Crown*, p. 281.

[10] Misagh Parsa, *Social Origins of the Iranian Revolution* (New Brunswick, NJ: Rutgers University Press, 1989), p. 94; Theda Skocpol, "Rentier State and Shi'a Islam in the Iranian Revolution," *Theory and Society* 11: 3 (1982), p. 272. Hiro has described the Iranian bazaar as a network of "wholesalers, commission agents, brokers, middlemen, merchants, money-changers, workshop owners, artisans, craftsmen, apprentices, shopkeepers, shop assistants, hawkers, peddlers and porters" into which much of both the working class and the clergy were thickly embedded. Hiro, *Iran under the Ayatollahs*, p. 375n.

[11] This was and is a reciprocal relationship in which "the bazaris are dependent on the clergy to legitimate them and their economic activities, and the clergy depend on the economic power of the bazaris for support, in part to establish and maintain their schools and religious buildings as well as religious activities in general." Masoud Kamali, *Revolutionary Iran: Civil Society and State in the Modernization Process* (Aldershot: Ashgate, 1998), p. 187. Also see Arjomand, *Turban for the Crown*, p. 15; Skocpol, "Rentier State," pp. 270, 272, 274; Keddie, *Modern Iran*, p. 226.

[12] Keddie, *Modern Iran*, p. 232.

[13] Kamali, *Revolutionary Iran*, pp. 175–8, 181–3; see pp. 199–203 for a description of the role of marginalized urban migrants in particular revolutionary events.

Shah's father. Those economic and social policies shaped and in some cases brought into being sectors that remodeled the political landscape and produced the political demands that now characterized the modernizing nation. However, those changes tended, from the Shah's perspective, to increase resistance to his reform agenda faster than they created sympathetic constituencies. There was thus a gap between what was expected to be a long-term strengthening of popular support for economic and social change (arising out of the modernization program as new sectors supporting change were created and traditional sectors opposing change atrophied) and short-term political opposition to reform.[14]

The Shah attempted to bridge that gap by creating a secret police, the SAVAK, that employed some 60,000 people who routinely beat, whipped, burned, and executed those who opposed the regime.[15] By 1975, Amnesty International described Iran as having "the highest rate of death penalties in the world and a history of torture which is beyond belief."[16] Intense repression on this scale dissolved what might otherwise have been a natural inclination to support or at least tolerate the Shah's rule when challenged by the fundamentalist clergy. Many of the Shah's problems were thus of his own making in that he either gratuitously attacked or insulted many of these social groups while neglecting other classes that might have been willing to support the regime if given a larger role in the making of its policies.[17]

Whatever chance that the Iranian Revolution might have resulted in the founding of a democratic state was probably eliminated by the Shah's reliance on repression.[18] Even without repression, secular liberals and their Islamic allies constituted a fairly small minority of Iranian society and their own hopes

---

[14] The Shah's program intended to modernize society by modernizing the state and the economy. Because the modernization of society was a precondition for releasing the will of the people in national politics, the regime anticipated that will by centralizing authority in the monarchy. The dilemma facing the Shah was that modernization of society prematurely created a popular demand within the urban middle class for democratic participation that could not be accommodated without fatally undercutting the regime program. Political mistakes and miscalculations by the Shah (understandable mistakes and miscalculations as evidenced by American diplomatic traffic) then pushed secular and leftist groups into a tacit (because undernegotiated) alliance with Khomeini and the fundamentalist clergy. For a similar interpretation of the relationship between modernization and the Iranian Revolution, see Ali Gheissari and Vali Nasr, *Democracy in Iran: History and the Quest for Liberty* (New York: Oxford University Press, 2006), pp. 55, 65.

[15] The SAVAK was originally created in 1953 with the assistance of the CIA in order to eliminate the underground organization of the Tudeh, the Communist party in Iran. Arjomand, *Turban for the Crown*, p. 73.

[16] Hiro, *Iran under the Ayatollahs*, p. 96; Irfani, *Iran's Islamic Revolution*, p. 151.

[17] On the inseparability of modernization and the Shah's political mistakes as causes of the revolution, see James A. Bill, "Power and Religion in Revolutionary Iran," *Middle East Journal* 36: 1 (1982), p. 26.

[18] Arjomand, *Turban for the Crown*, p. 6.

thus depended on the continued political demobilization of migrant workers and the peasantry. And that demobilization depended to a large extent on the attitude assumed by an Islamic clergy that was far from monolithic in either its doctrinal principles or its political philosophy.

SHI'A ISLAM

All Muslims believe that Muhammad was "God's Messenger" whose preaching, when set down in writing, became the Qur'an, the holy book of Islam. The two great sects within Islam, the Sunnis and Shi'as, share three additional beliefs: monotheism, resurrection, and the existence of prophets. However, Shi'as also have two beliefs that distinguish them from Sunnis: the Imamat and a particular conception of justice.[19] The vast majority of Iranians are Shi'as and almost all of them are followers of Twelver Shi'ism, in which the fundamental tenet is that there have been twelve imams chosen by God to lead the Islamic community. Each of the twelve descended from the Prophet through his daughter, Fatima. The last of these, the Imam Mahdi, vanished in 870 CE when he was five years old.[20] For seventy years afterward, he maintained contact with believers through regents. When the last of these regents died in 940 CE, communication with the Twelfth Imam ended and what is known as the Greater Occultation began. However, Shi'as believe that the Hidden Imam will return "at the end of time to impose godly justice."[21]

Shi'as believe that legitimate authority can be exercised only by the imam. In the absence of the Twelfth Imam (who now resides in an inaccessible, non-earthly plane), any claim to the right to rule over the faithful is illegitimate unless the person making that claim can conclusively demonstrate that he acts on behalf of the Hidden Imam. Those who can most persuasively demonstrate that connection are the Grand Ayatollahs, the highest-ranking members of the Shi'ite clergy. Each Grand Ayatollah has the right to form an independent judgment on religious questions and a responsibility to thus guide the faithful in the absence of the Hidden Imam. Each member of the faith chooses one of the Grand Ayatollahs as their guide, unquestioningly accepting their interpretations of Islamic law and doctrine as "emanating indirectly from God and the Hidden Imam" and donating money for the support of mosques and other religious institutions associated with the ayatollah they have chosen.[22] For most of Iranian history since Twelver Shi'ites were invited into Persia in the early sixteenth century, the clergy and the monarchy enjoyed a (sometimes uneasy)

---

[19] Hiro, *Iran under the Ayatollahs*, pp. 9, 12.

[20] Adib-Moghaddam, *Critical Introduction*, pp. xviii–xix. Khomeini descended from the Seventh Imam of the Ahl a-Bayt, Imam Musa al-Kadhim, and thus from the Prophet (p. xxi).

[21] Milani, *Making of Iran's Islamic Revolution*, p. 46; Kamali, *Revolutionary Iran*, pp. 22–3.

[22] In 1982, for example, there were ten Grand Ayatollahs. Irfani, *Iran's Islamic Revolution*, pp. 11–12, 18n; Sabet, "*Wilayat al-Faqih*," p. 77.

symbiotic relationship. The monarchy needed the clergy in order to legitimize its rule because it otherwise could not claim to act on behalf of the Hidden Imam. The clergy needed the monarchy in order to maintain and routinize its own, more material relationship to the people (e.g., in the form of religious taxes that supported mosques and centers of theological learning).

The Shah's modernization program inevitably brought social and cultural change to Iran and much of that change made the Islamic clergy uncomfortable. Many of them, in fact, were horrified by the presence of American military advisers, the distribution of Western movies and other cultural media, the adoption of Western fashions that did not respect traditional Islamic mores, and the Shah's increasingly indifferent, if not openly hostile, attitude toward the clergy.[23] However, most of the clergy did not become involved in politics even after Khomeini was exiled in 1964. As a result, most of the regime's suppression fell upon either secular or lay Islamic organizations that advocated liberalization of the political system. Mosques thus remained solely places of worship, quiet sanctuaries in which people could safely gather and communicate with one another. When the revolution came, the thick distribution of mosques throughout Iranian society, the close ties between the clergy and the bazaar, and the devout beliefs of much of the peasantry and working class transformed mosques into a national network that underpinned and shaped popular mobilization against the regime. In fact, the Shah's repression of what would have been more secular and lay Islamic alternatives meant that the mosque network was the only social structure through which the masses could be brought into politics.[24]

THE REVOLUTIONARY MOVEMENT

Under the Shah, Iran had turned into a "rentier state" that funded modernization, military expansion, and most social welfare policies out of oil revenues that flowed almost exclusively into government coffers. This reliance on outside, foreign revenues meant that the regime never developed close ties with Iranian society and, as long as repression was effective, could safely ignore popular sentiment. In many ways, the Shah was personally responsible for his regime's isolation. For example, the Shah's agrarian reform program had enabled much of the independent peasantry to buy land, thus making them yet another class that had been created by the regime's modernizing policies. He could have easily nurtured the landowning peasantry as an extension of the regime's social base; instead, he rather gratuitously branded them an obsolescent impediment to progress by publicly stating, in 1975, that "Iran's small and

---

[23] For a summary of regime policies during the 1960s and 1970s that either ignored or targeted clergy interests and relations with Iranian society, see Keddie, *Modern Iran*, p. 222; Skocpol, "Rentier State," pp. 82–3.

[24] Parsa, *Social Origins*, pp. 190, 301, 306.

relatively unproductive farmers are an extravagance that the country can no longer afford."[25] The Shah's absolutist temperament only increased the regime's isolation by transforming the monarchy into the sole target of mass opposition.[26]

The revolutionary movement that deposed the Shah has been described as a

"rainbow" coalition of avowed Marxist-atheists, liberal agnostics, non-practicing Moslems, progressive Islamic elements among intellectuals and students, social demo-crat followers of former Prime Minister Mossadeq, Islamic-Marxist reformers, the established Shi'ite hierarchy (with different objectives and involvement), and, finally, Islamic fundamentalists and hard-line disciples of Ayatollah Khomeini. Participants in street marches and demonstrations included *déclassé* aristocrats, old-time politicians, disgruntled job-seekers, small businessmen, new industrialists, urban workers, and idle hangers-on.[27]

Once the Shah was gone and the military had returned to the barracks, this coalition almost immediately began to break up.[28] As the coalition disinte-grated, the various elements articulated differing visions of what they wanted the new Iranian state to be. We are less interested in those visions than we are in how they connected those visions to what they conceived to have been the "will of the people." In every case, that vision and the conception of the "popular will" were intimately related.

The National Front, for example, conceived of the popular will from a liberal perspective. While conceding that the influence of the Shi'ite clergy and the strength of Islamic sentiment in society would mean that there could be no strict separation of church and state in Iran, most leaders of the National Front still advocated a more or less secular social democratic political system in which religious institutions and the clergy would stand aloof from politics. As is the case with most Western liberals, the political system would be primarily process-oriented in that a free press, open political competition, and universal suffrage would enable a largely uninhibited expression of the popular will.

The Liberation Movement also preferred the construction of a more or less liberal democratic regime, but it would have imposed more constraints on the exercise of the popular will in the form of mild regulation of electoral competi-tion and a privileged position for the clergy with respect to oversight of legislation that implicated areas already covered by Islamic law (e.g., Shari'a). Their orientation would have centered expression of the popular will more

---

[25] Arjomand, *Turban for the Crown*, p. 107.   [26] Skocpol, "Rentier State," pp. 269–70.

[27] Amuzegar, *Dynamics of the Iranian Revolution*, p. 14. Amuzegar described the "collective, and somewhat incongruous, objective of the [revolutionary] coalition [as] a government of national unity – at once Islamic, nationalist, democratic, egalitarian, bourgeois, nonaligned, socialist, and economically self-sufficient. It was in the truest sense of the word, a government of all things to all men" (p. 18).

[28] On the fracturing of the revolutionary coalition, see Jerrold D. Green, *Revolution in Iran: The Politics of Countermobilization* (New York: Praeger, 1982), pp. 142–4.

squarely within the Shi'ite mainstream of Iranian society by excluding more secular policies and possibilities. At the margin, the Liberation Movement overlapped with the Mujahedin-e-Khalq, an armed, leftist guerrilla organization that favored the creation of "an egalitarian Islamic society through fusion of Islam and Marxism." The Mujahedin envisioned a radical restructuring of property relations prescribed, as they saw it, in both the Qur'an and in Marxist theories of historical materialism. The Islamic movement, from its perspective, was the vanguard of a social revolution that would naturally adopt, over time, a more orthodox Marxist program. It thus already anticipated what the popular will in Iran desired as an historical outcome and would have tailored regulation of the political expression of that will in such a way that it would have produced that outcome. Whether or not popular opinion at the present moment properly reflected that will had no relevance (aside from tactical considerations of how to conduct revolutionary politics and operations).[29]

More orthodox Marxist-Leninist organizations such as the Fedai Khalq (an armed guerrilla organization similar to the Mujahedin) and the Tudeh (a formally organized political party aligned with and strongly influenced by Moscow) were more secular in their orientation but even more restrictive with respect to the range of ways in which the "will of the people" might be expressed.[30] The vast majority of the membership of the Tudeh and the two guerrilla organizations came from students who were or had been enrolled in universities and other educational institutions. Like the urban middle class from which they came, they were the product of the Shah's modernization policies that had, in this instance, more than doubled student enrollment during the 1970s. For those belonging to these organizations, "the revolution itself was the supreme redemptive act and would automatically produce the ideal society through their agency in the vanguard."[31] Although the left was a major influence upon the modernizing middle class in Iran, it failed to penetrate the bazaar

---

[29] For a detailed and sympathetic history of the Mujahedin-e-Khalq that severely criticizes the secular Marxist wing, see Irfani, *Iran's Islamic Revolution*, pp. 89–115. For links between the Mujahedin and the modernist clergy, see Milani, *Making of Iran's Islamic Revolution*, pp. 146, 148–9. For the Mujahedin's changing relationship with Khomeini's revolutionary program, see Moin, *Khomeini*, pp. 176–8.

[30] Gheissari and Nasr write:

[The] strongest voices in the modern middle class and among intellectuals and students were associated with the Left ... The Left was not a pro-democracy force in the 1970s; its world-view was collectivist and was not primarily concerned with the rule of law, civil liberties, or individual rights. Rather, it saw the rhetoric of democracy as a means to an end. It was strongly antistate, favored class war and revolution, and promised a utopian state. (Gheissari and Nasr, *Democracy in Iran*, pp. 67, 68)

Also see Asghar Schirazi, trans. John O'Kane, *The Constitution of Iran: Politics and the State in the Islamic Republic* (London: I. B. Tauris, 1997), p. 294; Moin, *Khomeini*, pp. 58, 160, 167, 172, 218, 240.

[31] Arjomand, *Turban for the Crown*, p. 106.

or the working class, both of which remained devoted to fundamentalist Islamic beliefs. This failure ultimately drove the Mujahedin and the Fedai Khalq back into armed opposition once fundamentalist consolidation of the Islamic Republic began in earnest. All of the above groups – whether they be secular liberals, Islamic radicals, or Marxist guerrillas – assumed that the "people" encompassed all who lived within the national boundaries of Iran. Not so the separatist groups representing the nationalist aspirations of Kurds, Turkomans, Arabs, and Baluchis, who advocated either complete independence (thus constructing an entirely separate people that might express a will) or regional political autonomy (a radical constriction of the will of the people at the national level).[32]

Given the variety of ways in which the post-revolutionary state was envisioned and the resulting incompatibility between their interpretations of how the will of the people should be purified by way of electoral regulation, policy injunctions, and constitutional prohibitions, the founding of the Iranian state would have been complicated even without the participation and influence of the Islamic clergy. However, as it turned out, the clergy became the almost hegemonic force behind the founding as it first tentatively compromised with other elements of the revolutionary coalition, then almost unilaterally imposed a largely theocratic design upon the constitutional assembly, and finally eliminated, often by force and violence, competing political formations that refused to yield to clerical rule. We will turn to an account of how that transpired in a moment. First, though, we need to describe political attitudes and positions within the clergy itself, because the Shi'ite ulama was far from united on questions involving the relation between church and state.

THE ULAMA

The highest clerical rank in Twelver Shi'ism is occupied by a *marja'e taqlid* (source of imitation), who draws upon the Qur'an and Islamic religious traditions as he legislates the proper relationship between Islam and temporal affairs. Each *marja'e taqlid* draws to himself followers who accept and obey him as the authoritative interpreter of Islamic thought. His interpretation takes the form of judgments and rulings, which are usually codified and published.[33] A mullah only becomes a *marja'e taqlid* after many years of scholarly training and study during which he must demonstrate his piety through exemplary conduct and ascetic discipline. He must also attract a following, a community of believers, who declare him to be their guiding authority with respect to

---

[32] For a brief review of the political ideologies associated with different elements of the revolutionary coalition, see Hiro, *Iran under the Ayatollahs*, p. 103.

[33] Milani, *Making of Iran's Islamic Revolution*, pp. 138, 330; Moin, *Khomeini*, pp. 32–4. *Maraja'e taqlid* are more commonly referred to as "Grand Ayatollahs." Hiro, *Iran under the Ayatollahs*, p. 376n.

Islamic principles and law.[34] Accompanying this declaration is a commitment by the faithful to pay religious taxes to the *marja'e taqlid*. These taxes are then used to fund religious schools, to aid the poor and sick, and to maintain mosques and other religious centers. Under Shi'i tradition, no *marja'e taqlid* can impose his interpretations and rulings upon any other *marja'e taqlid*. Each is formally equal to and autonomous of the others. In addition, their number is limited only by their individual ability to attract enough followers to form a self-sustaining community. In combination, these two principles guarantee that Twelver Shi'ism contains a diversity of doctrinal perspectives (encouraged by the implicit competition between *maraja'e taqlid* for followers) and a rather polycephalic clerical hierarchy (with each of the lower ranking clergy aligned with one of the *maraja'e taqlid*).[35]

In the period before the revolution, Shi'i interpretations of Islam's relation to state authority could be divided into three distinct but, in practice, often overlapping perspectives: fundamentalist, modernist, and orthodox. The fundamentalists held the state responsible for increasing immorality in Iranian society and declining religious devotion of the people. As leaders of this faction (not an inappropriate word), Ayatollahs Khomeini and Montazeri condemned the Shah's modernization program as the reason decadent Western mores had taken hold among the faithful. When their opposition became openly political, the Shah attempted to suppress them. At that point they became irrevocably hostile to the regime and viewed formal clerical political power, in some form, as the only remedy for Iran's slide into decadence and wickedness.

Modernists, such as Ayatollah Mahmoud Taleqani, viewed modernization as beneficial or, regardless of its benefits, inevitable. The problem was the Shah's regime and that problem could be solved by creating a healthier and more organic relationship between the people and the state. As a political movement, clerical modernists attracted many followers who believed that Shi'ism and Marxism could be reconciled in that Shi'ism "could fulfill Marxist ideology's historic function and become a material force." From that perspective, Shi'ism was grounded in a "creed of justice" in which concern for

---

[34] Arjomand, *Turban for the Crown*, p. 16.

[35] Bill, "Power and Religion," p. 23; Chehabi, "Religion and Politics in Iran," p. 80; Milani, *Making of Iran's Islamic Revolution*, p. 154; Siavoshi, *Liberal Nationalism*, p. 192; Kamali, *Revolutionary Iran*, pp. 28, 30; Martin Riesebrodt, trans. Don Reneau, *Pious Passion: The Emergence of Modern Fundamentalism in the United States and Iran* (Berkeley: University of California Press, 1998), p. 149. As a result, the number of followers that an ayatollah attracted was a major factor in the prestige he possessed within the clerical hierarchy. The involvement of the people in thus creating this hierarchy might also provide an opening for (heavily constrained) influence in the selection of the Supreme Leader for the Islamic state. See, for example, Sussan Siavoshi, *Montazeri: The Life and Thought of Iran's Revolutionary Ayatollah* (Cambridge: Cambridge University Press, 2017), pp. 203–4.

the poor became a leading guide for action.[36] There would be a role for the clergy in the politics of the state but that role would have been one of facilitation as opposed to domination.[37]

In rather sharp contrast to both the fundamentalists and modernists, the orthodox clergy, led by Ayatollahs Khorasani and Golpayegani, preferred to stand aloof from politics. While they, too, deplored the changes taking place in Iran, they continued to subscribe to the traditional role of the clergy in Iranian politics: tacit support for the ruling regime in return for clerical autonomy in religious matters and the administration of Islamic institutions.[38] After the death of Ayatollah Borujerdi in 1961, an orthodox leader who had openly cooperated with the regime, the Shah became increasingly less interested in upholding the state's end of this reciprocal relationship. By the mid-1970s, it was not at all clear that the orthodox had a viable strategy for maintaining the clergy's place in Iranian society.[39]

Because the fundamentalists became the most important force driving the Iranian Revolution, we must closely examine their perspective on the proper relationship between state sovereignty and the will of the people. Because his thought so strongly influenced the revolution and so completely dominated what became his political faction, that examination must focus on Ayatollah Khomeini. Ruhollah Musavi Khomeini was born in 1902. In 1919, he became a disciple of Ayatollah Ha'eri and went with him to Qom two years later. After years of study under Ha'eri, Khomeini became a respected member of the clergy in his own right. In 1930, he married the daughter of a wealthy ayatollah and that union subsequently produced five children, two sons and three daughters.[40] His political activity began in 1944, when he published an open

[36] Gheissari and Nasr, *Democracy in Iran*, pp. 70–1; Milani, *Making of Iran's Islamic Revolution*, pp. 139–40, 144.
[37] Describing the thought of Ayatollah Taleqani, Keddie writes:

Human laws (*'urf*) are fragmentary, limited by history, and subject to change. They are easily diverted by a tyrannic power; are influenced by passions; and must be applied by coercion. Only Islam is the perfect legislator – it encourages reason to follow the path of God instead of misleading it; frees man from the slavery of human customs; teaches all to distinguish good from evil; and makes of a man controlled by passions a controller of himself. Because of these qualities, Islamic law (*fiqh*) is not accessible to all; only mujtahids can decide its application. (Keddie, *Modern Iran*, p. 197)

[38] Milani, *Making of Iran's Islamic Revolution*, p. 138. For a slightly different categorization of the clergy in this period, see Kamali, *Revolutionary Iran*, p. 180.
[39] Riesebrodt, *Pius Passion*, p. 149; Milani, *Making of Iran's Islamic Revolution*, p. 138. For the historical origins of the traditional relationship between church and state in Twelver Shi'ism, see Arjomand, *Turban for the Crown*, pp. 15, 75, 79; Gheissari and Nasr, *Democracy in Iran*, p. 69.
[40] One of the sons, Mustapha, was apparently poisoned by SAVAK agents in October 1978. He was killed in retaliation for an unsuccessful assassination attempt on the Shah's sister. Hiro, *Iran under the Ayatollahs*, p. 69.

letter to the clergy encouraging them to condemn public immorality. In that same year, Khomeini published a book, *Secrets Exposed*, as a response to the writings of a disciple of Ahmad Kasravi, an anticlerical intellectual. In this book, Khomeini contended that "attacks on religious leaders help to destroy the country and its independence." But most of his criticism was directed at Reza Shah (Mohammad Reza Shah's father and the founder of the Pahlavi dynasty), whom he characterized as an enemy of Islam. Although some parts of the book appeared to tolerate rule by a monarch hedged about with constitutional limitations, Khomeini concluded that, "apart from the royalty of God, all royalty is against the interests of the people and oppressive; apart from the law of God, all laws are null and absurd. A government of Islamic law, controlled by religious jurists (*faqihs*) will be superior to all the iniquitous governments of the world."[41]

During the 1950s, Khomeini became a disciple of Ayatollah Borujerdi, the most influential cleric in Iran. Since Borujerdi was very conservative and supported the Shah's regime, Khomeini was politically inactive. After 1960, however, he again began to criticize the regime, this time as a teacher of ethics in Qom. After Borujerdi passed away in 1961, Khomeini became a *marja'e taqlid* in his own right and soon after began to publicly attack the regime.[42] In January 1963, the Shah proposed that a national referendum be held on reform principles; this subsequently became known as the "White Revolution." Two months later, Ayatollah Khomeini publicly charged that the Shah was attacking Islam. Khomeini's criticism both initiated active clerical resistance to the Shah and gave him leadership of that movement.

On June 3, 1963, Khomeini gave a speech in Qom ridiculing the Shah as a spineless puppet of forces that he did not comprehend:

Let me give you some advice, Mr. Shah! Dear Mr. Shah ... Maybe those people [advisers and the government in power] want to present you as a Jew so that I will denounce you as an unbeliever and they can expel you from Iran and put an end to you! Don't you know that if one day some uproar occurs and the tables are turned, none of these people around you will be your friends. They are friends of the dollars; they have no religion, no loyalty.

Khomeini also called upon the "commanders of the great Iranian army, its respectable officers, and its noble members" to join in the "salvation of Islam and Iran." The next day he was arrested. The day after that, demonstrations and riots broke out throughout Iran.[43] After intervention by other Grand Ayatollahs, Khomeini was released and placed under house arrest. When Khomeini again attacked the regime the following year, he was exiled to

[41] Keddie, *Modern Iran*, p. 192.   [42] Hiro, *Iran under the Ayatollahs*, pp. 49, 51.
[43] Milani, *Making of Iran's Islamic Revolution*, pp. 91–2.

Turkey. From there, he later moved to Najaf in Iraq, one of the holiest cities in Shi'ite Islam. There he remained until 1978, when he left for Paris.[44]

While in Iraq, Khomeini continued his political opposition to the Shah by making public declarations in which he linked the regime, Western imperialism, and Zionism. His pronouncements were widely circulated inside Iran in the form of tape cassettes. During this period, a book, *Islamic Government*, was compiled from lecture notes taken down by his students. In this book, Khomeini asserted that both monarchy and "dynastic succession" were alien to Islam and thus concluded that the Shah's regime was illegitimate. Instead of monarchy, Khomeini stated that Islamic law, as laid down in the Qur'an and tradition arising out of the Prophet's practice, contained "all the laws and principles needed by man for his happiness and perfection." Until the return of the Hidden Imam, the only people who can interpret Islamic law are Muslim jurists and, thus, it is they who should govern the people. Khomeini called upon the ulama to purify Islam by exposing the corrupting influence of Western thought and ways. Those among the clergy who supported the regime were to be ostracized and condemned.[45]

At the heart of Khomeini's political thought was his theory of *Velayat-e Faqih* (Guardianship of the Jurist). Lodging supreme political authority with the clergy, this doctrine radically revised the traditional Shi'a conceptualization of the proper relationship between mosque and state. Under the traditional conceptualization, only the return of the Hidden Imam could inaugurate "just rule." Because all worldly governance would be imperfect in the absence of the Hidden Imam, the ulama should stand apart from politics until his return and the proper role of the ulama was thus restricted to the protection and propagation of Islam. While that might include advice to those who ruled and, in extremis, political intervention by the ulama, the clergy should normally remain aloof from the impurity unavoidably associated the exercise of government authority.[46]

Khomeini found theological justification for the direct assumption of political power by the ulama in the practical realities of creating and maintaining a devout Islamic community. First, he noted that Islamic law could not reform and purify society unless it was enforced publicly. The achievement of human happiness through the establishment of a devout Islamic community thus necessitated the exercise of state authority. Second, Khomeini observed that God had given the community Islamic law by revealing the Shari'a and the

---

[44] Irfani, *Iran's Islamic Revolution*, p. 84; Arjomand, *Turban for the Crown*, pp. 72, 85–6; Shaul Bakhash, *The Reign of the Ayatollahs: Iran and the Islamic Revolution* (New York: Basic Books, 1984), p. 30.

[45] Keddie, *Modern Iran*, pp. 191–4.

[46] Gheissari and Nasr, *Democracy in Iran*, p. 69; S. M. A. Sayeed, *Iran before and after Khomeini* (Karachi: Royal Book Company, 1999), p. 44; Milani, *Making of Iran's Islamic Revolution*, pp. 149–54.

teaching and practice of the Prophet. Once those revelations had been received, they required political rule by the ulama because only the clergy could properly interpret and thus execute Islamic law. Third, in the absence of the Hidden Imam, responsibility for representation of God's will unavoidably devolved upon the ulama. To shirk this responsibility for the sake of a fictitious religious purity was itself a transgression of Qur'anic commands. Since the Shari'a and the teaching and practice of the Prophet were both fully revealed and covered the entirety of those areas that must underpin the creation and maintenance of a purified Islamic community, Islamic law would be more or less self-executing.

What was needed, then, was a strong leader who could carry out what had already been decided and ordained by God. While there was some room for consultation among the ulama (even, perhaps, taking the form of an assembly of clerics), the proper form of an Islamic government should concentrate authority in a single leader, the most learned and devout among the ulama.

If a deserving jurist is endowed with these two qualities [justice and knowledge of Islamic law], then his regency will be the same as enjoyed by the Prophet in the governing of the Islamic community, and it is incumbent on all Moslems to obey him.[47]

That leader thus accepts a political authority identical to that exercised by the Prophet and the imams. Although the latter are far superior to the ulama in terms of spiritual virtue, the political authority associated with the enforcement of Islamic law is otherwise the same.[48]

All of this was in turn grounded in Khomeini's conception of "reason," which had originally appeared in his anonymously published book *Kashf al-Asrar (The Discovery of Secrets)* in 1942. Referring to a hypothetical secular person who had contempt for Islamic thought, Khomeini wrote:

This irrational person has taken it for granted that religious people have trampled upon the rule of "reason" and have no regard for it, thus revealing his own ignorance. Is it not religious people who have written all our books on philosophy and the principles of jurisprudence? Have they not looked upon thousands of philosophical and theological issues in the light of reason and intellect? Is it not these leaders of theology who consider reason as one of the binding issues?

However, Khomeini carefully noted that this conception of reason was not an invitation to a debate on the interpretation of religious doctrine; instead, he urged

---

[47] Bakhash, *Reign of the Ayatollahs*, p. 38.
[48] Sayeed, *Iran before and after Khomeini*, pp. 46–50. Sayeed concludes that Khomeini's political thought should be read "as an ideology ... a synthesis of seminal ideas and symbols, more action oriented than metaphysical ... a conceptual framework to render political strategy intelligible" (p. 64). On the nature of Islamic law in Khomeini's thought, also see Farzin Vahdat, *God and Juggernaut: Iran's Intellectual Encounter with Modernity* (Syracuse, NY: Syracuse University Press, 2002), pp. 163–4; Arjomand, *Turban for the Crown*, pp. 98–9.

the protectors of Shi'a orthodoxy to "smash in the teeth this brainless mob with their iron fist" and "trample upon their heads with courageous strides."[49]

Khomeini's political thought thus exploited Twelver Shi'ism's millennial preoccupation with the ultimate return of the Hidden Imam and, in the meantime, the primacy of spiritual leadership in the construction of a proper Islamic society.[50] The ulama were the regents who must rule in his absence. The assumption of power by the religious leader was humbled by the knowledge that he would govern only in place of the Hidden Imam. Because Islamic law was already known in its fullness, the leader was merely the agent of a self-executing divine will; in effect, the leader would have neither a personal will nor individual ambition. One of the popular slogans of the insurgency emphasized this temporary regency: "The Revolution shall continue until the return of the

---

[49] Moin, *Khomeini*, p. 63.

[50] On the connection between belief in the return of the Hidden Imam and Khomeini's theory of the state, see Moin, *Khomeini*, pp. 153–6. For a more general, critical review of Khomeini's theory, see Hamid Mavani, *Religious Authority and Political Thought in Twelver Shi'ism from Ali to Post-Khomeini* (London: Routledge, 2013), pp. 142, 178–210. Mavani cites, with approval, Mohsen Kadivar's conclusion that Khomeini's principle of "*Velayat-e Faqih*, be it of religious or civil order, appointive or elective, absolute or conditional, lacks credible religious foundation" in Islamic thought (p. 141). Najam goes even further, concluding that Khomeini had placed himself "far outside the mainstream of the Twelver Shi'i scholarly tradition." Najam Haider, *Shi'i Islam: An Introduction* (New York: Cambridge University Press, 2014), p. 213. Although the validity of the *Velayat-e Faqih* principle was denied by many Islamic theorists, Khomeini nonetheless utilized the concept to make unqualified obedience to the Islamic state a religious obligation of the faithful: "[T]he government, which is part of the absolute deputyship of the Prophet, is one of the primary injunctions of Islam and has priority over all other secondary injunctions, even prayers, fasting and hajj." For that reason, the "preservation of the Islamic Republic is a divine duty which is above all other duties. It is even more important than preserving the Imam of the Age (*Imam-e-asr*), because even the Imam of the Age [i.e., the Hidden Imam] will sacrifice himself for Islam" (p. 182). Also see Tabaar, *Religious Statecraft*, pp. 52–4; Haider, *Shi'i Islam*, pp. 208–13. For Khomeini's lectures on the proper nature of the Islamic state, delivered to students before the Iranian Revolution, see National Technical Information Service, *Islamic Government* (Springfield, VA: US Department of Commerce, 1979). In many respects, the writings of Grand Ayatollah Hossein Ali Montazeri, who was Khomeini's student and follower, are a better guide to the latter's theory of the Islamic state, including the grounding of the *Velayat-e Faqih* in the "four authoritative pillars" of Islamic thought: "the Quran, *hadith*, consensus, and reason." In contrast to other forms of government, including democracy,

Islamic government is an entity that has the authority to implement divine laws and fulfill the interest of the people in accordance with Islamic standard. The Islamic government is not a dictatorship, and that is why the Islamic ruler is called *emam* [leader], *vali* [governor], and *ra'i* [shepherd]. He is an *emam*, because he is a role model for the society, he is a *vali*, because he administers the affairs of the people, and he is a *ra'i* because he is an ever present protector of people from harm. In our view the ruling position is not one from which the ruler can extract glory or put burden on people, instead we see it as an entity that fulfills the interest of the community, an entity that frees people from the shackles of imitation, customs, and all other [oppressive norms] that have been imposed on them. (Siavoshi, *Montazeri*, pp. 201–2 and, more generally, 197–233)

Mehdi, the Lord of the Age." For the fundamentalist clergy and their followers, "the revolution was heading towards a divine destination and to that end they ... sought to eliminate evil and promote revolutionary/religious virtue." The revolution itself heralded the imminent return of the Hidden Imam. In preparation for that return, the Islamic community must be purified and made ready; all vestiges of the immorality and corruption of the Shah's regime must be eradicated. Many of Khomeini's followers began to call him the "Imam," thus placing him somewhere in the Shi'ite pantheon. And there were rumors that Khomeini himself had been in direct communication with the Hidden Imam and that his leadership of the revolution thus validated the movement as the expression and realization of God's will. Those who opposed the revolution were not mere political rivals but were "apostates" who "had to be dealt with according to the religious code of sin."[51]

Although most of the other Grand Ayatollahs came to oppose the Shah's regime and supported the revolutionary movement, they never accepted Khomeini's theological innovations as correct or even plausible interpretations of Shi'ite belief. While their reservations were rarely made public, they dismissed his theory of clerical leadership, his apparent rejection of collegial consultation among his peers in the Shi'ite hierarchy, and, perhaps most of all, his insistence that the clergy become directly involved in the exercise of political authority.[52] The strongest criticism came from Ayatollah Shariatmadari, whose numerous Azeri-speaking followers dominated much of the northwest corner of Iran. Of clerical involvement in politics, Shariatmadari said: "In Islam there is no provision that the ulama must absolutely intervene in matters of state." Such intervention was only justified when parliament was likely to pass a law that violated the Shari'a or no secular leader could maintain social order. Otherwise, the ulama should not "involve themselves in politics ... We [the clergy] must simply advise the government when what they do is contrary to Islam ... It is the duty of government to govern. There should be no direct interference from spiritual leaders."[53] Shariatmadari was providing only a careful summary of traditional Shi'ite teaching, teaching that, in practice, limited the forms in which the other leading Shi'ite ayatollahs could openly

[51] Bahiriyeh, *State and Revolution in Iran*, pp. 174–6; Gheissari and Nasr, *Democracy in Iran*, pp. 87–8; Chehabi, "Religion and Politics in Iran," pp. 72, 75; Milani, *Making of Iran's Islamic Revolution*, p. 326; Arjomand, *Turban for the Crown*, pp. 6, 99, 101, 103, 177–88. Although Khomeini apparently never explicitly embraced "the charismatic title of Imam with its subtle millenarian connotations," Arjomand observes that he used its appeal in order to strengthen the fundamentalist movement. On Khomeini's ostensible pretensions to "the status of an Imam" and popular references to that status, see Moin, *Khomeini*, pp. 157, 200–1, 206, 227, 229, 284, 292. Moin himself repeatedly refers to Khomeini as "Imam" (pp. 203, 205, 241, 307).

[52] Sayeed, *Iran before and after Khomeini*, pp. 178–9, 181; Riesebrodt, *Pius Passion*, p. 150; Chehabi, "Religion and Politics in Iran," p. 73.

[53] Hiro, *Iran under the Ayatollahs*, pp. 117–18. Also see Schirazi, *Constitution of Iran*, pp. 47–8; Milani, *Making of Iran's Islamic Revolution*, p. 267.

express and otherwise act upon their dissent. Khomeini's entry into politics thus engendered little *political* opposition from the conservative clergy even though they rejected his doctrinal innovations and clearly comprehended his political intent.

What is more difficult to understand is the warm embrace that Khomeini received from secular democrats and the radical left. As Amuzegar notes, "Khomeini's politics and philosophy were an open book to all who cared to know them . . . But, like Hitler's *Mein Kampf* . . . the ayatollah's master plan for Iran was either misread or disbelieved." In the end, Khomeini simply "did exactly what he always wanted to do."[54] During the summer months of 1978, those middle-class Iranians who had come to accept Western notions of democracy and political debate euphorically celebrated after mass demonstrations apparently compelled the regime to embark upon what they believed would be a self-sustaining liberalization of national politics. They seriously misjudged the situation in at least four ways: (1) They believed that the masses who participated in these demonstrations shared their political values; (2) they assumed that Ayatollah Khomeini would observe the traditional Shi'ite orientation toward politics and return to a quiet life of religious study once the crisis was over; (3) they anticipated that the Shah would adopt reform measures that would enable him to retain the monarchy with sharply circumscribed powers; and (4) if the Shah failed to liberalize the regime, they expected the subsequent revolution to assign social democrats a major role in shaping the new state. On each of these things, they were emphatically and categorically mistaken.[55]

THE IRANIAN REVOLUTION

Revolutions and foundings are often, if not always, very different things. A revolution must assemble a broad coalition that either tolerates or supports the overthrow of an existing regime. In the Iranian case, that coalition was held together by personal hostility to the Shah and his security agencies. Because the regime rested on a very narrow social base primarily composed of the royal family, high-ranking state officials and their retainers, and the military, there was very little popular support for the Shah when the revolutionary movement began to demonstrate its strength in the streets. But the streets were deceptive because they displayed only passionate and broad hatred of the regime.

One of the most effective insurgent tactics was to schedule mass demonstrations so that they coincided with the observance of mourning for fallen

---

[54] Amuzegar, *Dynamics of the Iranian Revolution*, p. 260. Also see Milani, *Making of Iran's Islamic Revolution*, p. 206.

[55] Keddie, *Modern Iran*, p. 230. Arjomand views the acquiescence by the liberal intelligentsia in fundamentalist leadership of the revolution as a more or less Faustian bargain arising out of recognition of the clergy's influence over the masses and admiration for the ulama's often courageous opposition to the Shah. Arjomand, *Turban for the Crown*, p. 97.

comrades. Under Shi'i tradition, mourning anniversaries were observed at forty-day intervals after death. Since everyone knew when someone had been killed in a previous demonstration, the interval and thus the next occasion for a demonstration was public knowledge and required little in the way of formal arrangements. In addition, both devout and secular elements in the revolutionary coalition could demonstrate under color of a religious observance that effectively blended their respective commitments. Finally, the regime could not repress funereal rituals without risking a massive reaction among those who could be mobilized only by an unmistakable transgression of Islamic practice. The net result was a splendid tactic that both united the movement and outmaneuvered the regime but was otherwise rather devoid of real meaning and substance.[56]

As expressions of the will of the people, demonstrations rely on simple slogans as mobilizing themes and visible displays of sentiment. As a result, they did not provide much evidence of the kind of state that the masses wanted to erect once the revolution had succeeded. That was an advantage in that every element in the revolutionary coalition could rally around slogans proclaiming "liberty and social justice" as principles that the Shah had transgressed. And almost every group in the coalition accepted religious imagery as a way of communicating with the masses they led. As a result, the bland ideological themes displayed in the streets could be interpreted by almost everyone in the revolutionary coalition in a way that seemed to favor their own particular goals.[57] However, despite their shared opposition to the Shah, there was little agreement within the coalition with respect to the founding of the new revolutionary state. For many in the coalition, that discovery would come later as a very unhappy surprise.

During the revolutionary crisis of 1978 and the early part of 1979, Khomeini cloaked his goals in public rhetoric that comforted the more secular and leftist elements in the coalition.[58] When asked in September 1978 what would be entailed in the establishment of an Islamic government, Khomeini categorically denied that "religious leaders should themselves run the affairs of government" because they should only "lead people in defining their Islamic demands." As for the possibility that he himself would be involved in the new government, Khomeini stated that "neither my age, nor my desire, nor my [religious]

---

[56] Keddie, *Modern Iran*, p. 226; Siavoshi, *Liberal Nationalism*, p. 138; Mhamed Heikal, *The Return of the Ayatollah: The Iranian Revolution from Mossadeq to Khomeini* (London: Andre Deutsch, 1981), pp. 88–9.

[57] Amuzegar, *Dynamics of the Iranian Revolution*, p. 35; Milani, *Making of Iran's Islamic Revolution*, p. 134; Arjomand, *Turban for the Crown*, p. 103; Gheissari and Nasr, *Democracy in Iran*, p. 66.

[58] Milani, *Making of Iran's Islamic Revolution*, p. 206; Gheissari and Nasr, *Democracy in Iran*, p. 69; Keddie, *Modern Iran*, p. 240.

position permits such a thing." His role and that of the ulama would be restricted to "guidance and counseling" in order to ensure that "there were no deviations and people were not subjected to oppression." Khomeini even went so far as to say that women would be free to choose "their profession, activities, and destiny" under the Islamic government.[59] Around the same time, Khomeini told a French newspaper reporter: "We are for a regime of total liberty. The future regime of Iran has to be one of liberty. Its only limits will be, as in any other state, the general interest of society, but also considerations of dignity."[60]

In an attempt to relieve apprehension that the clergy intended to take over the government, Khomeini distinguished between the routine, technical policies of a government and those that affected Islam as a spiritual community.

There are certain matters which are executive affairs such as urban planning and traffic regulations. These are not related to [Sacred] Law, and it is beneath the dignity of Islam to concern itself with them; they are not related to basic laws. In Islam there is no room for the institution of basic laws and if an assembly is installed it will not be a legislative assembly in that sense, but an assembly to supervise government. It will deliberate [and determine] the executive matters of the kind I mentioned and not basic laws [which are already laid down by Islam].

Here, Khomeini was speaking in the midst of a revolutionary crisis in which he was endeavoring to hold together a diverse coalition that would compel the government to permit his return to Iran.[61]

Amuzegar has described Khomeini's revolutionary strategy as "four-pronged": (1) demonizing the Shah as hostile to Islam and morally aligned with American and Israeli interests; (2) evoking religious and communitarian sentiment within the military so that the troops ultimately became undependable props for the Shah's regime; (3) mobilizing the faithful behind strikes and boycotts of state agencies in order to paralyze government operations; and (4) veiling his plans for an Islamic government behind a platitudinous rhetoric stressing the humility and democratic ethos of the ulama. This strategy succeeded because, from the very beginning of the revolutionary crisis, Khomeini and other fundamentalist leaders were widely recognized as the most unequivocal and radical opponents of the Shah's regime.

By 1978, Khomeini had constructed a subterranean empire resting upon the network of mosques that spanned Iran, the clergy he had trained and taught who now preached in many of these mosques, his followers who could now be mobilized by these clerics, and the religious taxes that these followers paid into his religious institutions and operations. Using this personal empire, Khomeini

---

[59] Irfani, *Iran's Islamic Revolution*, p. 84.   [60] Chehabi, "Religion and Politics in Iran," p. 76.
[61] From an interview in Paris on January 2, 1979, shortly before Khomeini returned to Iran. Arjomand, *Turban for the Crown*, pp. 148–9.

could communicate with much of the Iranian citizenry without being monitored by either the Shah's regime or those in the revolutionary coalition who subsequently became his political competitors.[62]

When the revolutionary crisis broke out in January 1978, the most articulate and visible leaders were liberal democrats whose demands most resonated with the educated middle class in the major urban centers, most particularly Tehran. Even before the street demonstrations began, the intelligentsia was politically active in organizing open-letter campaigns and holding public poetry readings in which reform themes played a prominent role. While these activities were not viewed as threatening by the regime, they did establish liberal democrats as the most well-known leaders of the reform movement inside Iran. Khomeini, it should be remembered, was still in exile.[63] In some ways the prominence of the liberal intelligentsia played into Khomeini's hands, because he well "understood the game of numbers. Though the Iranian middle class was prominent in the economy and dominated intellectual and political debates, it was far smaller than the lower middle classes." And it was the relative silence of the lower middle classes that lulled the liberal democrats into thinking that it was they who would lead the reform movement to victory.[64]

Nothing underscored this delusion more dramatically than the climactic street demonstrations in Tehran on December 10-11, 1978. On December 10, the modernist Ayatollah Taleqani and Karim Sanjabi, the liberal democratic leader of the National Front, marched at the head of a column of almost one million demonstrators that took six hours to pass through the center of Tehran. The next day, they again led a demonstration, but this time the number of marchers had doubled, now totaling almost two million. On both occasions, Taleqani and Sanjabi figuratively led protests largely composed of Khomeini's supporters. These same demonstrators who followed Taleqani and Sanjabi through the streets of Tehran later enabled Khomeini to reject both Taleqani's and Sanjabi's visions for a post-Shah polity. Although they were riding a tiger that they believed was of their own making, it was Khomeini's creation and his to command.[65]

The massive demonstrations in Tehran in December spelled the end of the Shah's regime. At the end of the month, he had appointed Shapour Bakhtiar

---

[62] Amuzegar, *Dynamics of the Iranian Revolution*, pp. 36, 259. Also see, Hiro, *Iran under the Ayatollahs*, p. 100.

[63] Arjomand, *Turban for the Crown*, p. 108; Siavoshi, *Liberal Nationalism*, p. 137.

[64] Gheissari and Nasr, *Democracy in Iran*, p. 69. After August 1978, demonstrators drawn from Khomeini's natural constituency of the urban poor, unskilled workers, and the lower middle class increasingly outnumbered those groups hitherto drawn to the moderate opposition. However, the leadership of these demonstrations was still composed of liberal democrats and the Islamic left. Siavoshi, *Liberal Nationalism*, p. 141; Kamali, *Revolutionary Iran*, pp. 193, 197.

[65] This was the first occasion in which Khomeini activated his theological network to bring into the city large numbers of demonstrators from the surrounding villages. Hiro, *Iran under the Ayatollahs*, p. 84.

prime minister of a transitional government and two weeks after that the royal family left Iran for Egypt. On February 1, Khomeini returned to Iran. Ten days later Bakhtiar's government was replaced by one appointed by Khomeini. The revolution had been completed but the founding was yet to come.

From Khomeini's perspective, there were three events that cumulatively constituted the founding of the Islamic Republic of Iran. Taken alone, Khomeini might have considered each of them as sufficient for the purpose of formally melding sovereignty, the will of the people, and a transcendent purpose within the new state. However, facts on the ground ultimately compelled Khomeini to found his republic in a fairly conventional manner. The first event that might have founded the new state was the mass demonstrations that brought down the Shah. Here, Khomeini could cite the huge rally in Tehran on December 11, 1978, where some two million people approved by acclamation a "seventeen-point charter" that demanded abolition of the monarchy, accepted Khomeini as leader, and approved the formation of an Islamic government.[66] Michel Foucault, who was in Tehran at the time, regarded that display as a very rare but nonetheless unmistakable "real-world" manifestation of the popular will.

Among the things that characterize this revolutionary event, there is the fact that it has brought out – and few peoples in history have had this – an absolutely collective will. The collective will is a political myth with which jurists and political philosophers try to analyse or to justify institutions, etc. It's a theoretical tool: nobody has ever seen "the collective will" and, personally, I thought that the collective will was like God, like the soul, something one would never encounter. I don't know whether you agree with me, but we met in Tehran and throughout Iran, the collective will of a people. Well, you have to salute it, it doesn't happen every day.

However, Foucault also pointed out that "this collective will has been given one object, one target and one only, namely the departure of the shah."[67] From that perspective, mass demonstrations that occurred before the Shah was overthrown were too closely linked to the revolution to constitute a founding.

---

[66] According to Bakhash:

> Later opposition claims notwithstanding, Khomeini in Paris had not pledged to permit the people a free choice on the form of government that would replace the monarchy. He took the position, rather, that the people had already voted in a "referendum" for an Islamic republic by taking part in the great anti-shah demonstrations, or that a referendum would be held, but only to confirm a choice already made. (Bakhash, *Reign of the Ayatollahs*, p. 72)

> Also see, Hiro, *Iran under the Ayatollahs*, pp. 84–5; Arjomand, *Turban for the Crown*, p. 134.

[67] Ali M. Ansari, *Iran, Islam, and Democracy: The Politics of Managing Change*, second edition (London: Chatham House, 2006), pp. 41–2. Ansari suggests that "what Foucault was witnessing was the social manifestation of the myth of political emancipation, which had finally come of age." On Foucault's experiences in revolutionary Tehran and his interpretation of the Islamic insurgency, see Behrooz Ghamari-Tabrizi, *Foucault in Iran: Islamic Revolution after the Enlightenment* (Minneapolis: University of Minnesota Press, 2016), pp. 55–74.

Within the revolutionary coalition there were radically different interpretations of the kind of state the demonstrators actually wanted to replace the Shah and each of those interpretations could be said to have contributed to the success of the revolution.

To put those competing interpretations to rest, Khomeini called for a national referendum on the establishment of a new Iranian state. Aside from whether or not a successful founding could be made through a simple, one-sentence referendum, there were two important questions that had to be settled. The first question involved the title of the new state; the second whether citizens would be offered alternative choices. Khomeini settled the first question when he spoke to a great crowd in Qom on March 1, 1978. "What the nation wants," he said, "is an Islamic republic: not just a republic, not a democratic republic, not a democratic Islamic republic. Do not use this term, 'democratic.' That is the Western style."[68] Implying that democracy might have no place in a properly constructed Islamic republic, Khomeini also said: "Democracy is another word for usurpation of God's authority to rule."[69] Later, in urging people to support the referendum, Khomeini again defended the title he had chosen, "Not the 'republic of Iran,' nor the 'democratic republic of Iran,' nor the 'democratic Islamic republic of Iran,' just the 'Islamic Republic of Iran.'"[70] By that time, "democratic" had become a somewhat dangerous code word for the liberal elements in the revolutionary coalition. On the one hand, the adjective seemed to open up a range of political debate and possibility as the new state was constructed. On the other, as Khomeini noted, "democratic" was associated with the Western impulses and doctrines that were anathema to the fundamentalist clergy.[71]

The question of whether or not the people should be offered alternatives in this referendum was settled in much the same way. The conservative Ayatollah Shariatmadari and many others insisted that the Iranian people should have more than one political system as choices.[72] Other groups with more secular or Marxist leanings, such as the Democratic National Front, the Fedai Khalq, and the Mujahedin-e-Khalq, thought that voters should be asked to vote on a constitution once one had been drafted so that they might better know what kind of government they were approving. These demands were rejected and the ballot simply asked voters: "Do you favor an Islamic Republic or a monarchy?" Fearing that the impending endorsement of an Islamic republic would further marginalize them, the Democratic National Front, the National Front, the Fedai Khalq, and the Kurdish separatist parties

---

[68] Bakhash, *Reign of the Ayatollahs*, p. 73. Khomeini added: "We respect Western civilization, but will not follow it." Hiro, *Iran under the Ayatollahs*, p. 108.

[69] Hiro, *Iran under the Ayatollahs*, p. 106.   [70] Arjomand, *Turban for the Crown*, p. 137.

[71] Keddie, *Modern Iran*, p. 234.

[72] Ayatollah Shariatmadari, for example, preferred that the referendum ask voters "What kind of political system would you prefer?" Hiro, *Iran under the Ayatollahs*, p. 118.

boycotted the referendum. Since a vote for the monarchy would have been a vote for the Shah's (now defunct) regime, over 98 percent of all those who voted chose an Islamic Republic.[73]

Khomeini probably regarded this referendum as an expedient tactic that was somewhat at variance with his own political belief. The latter was perhaps better articulated in his 1963 opposition to the Shah's proposed referendum on the "White Revolution" in which he stated that a "referendum or national approval has no validity in Islam ... and the voters should have sufficient knowledge to understand what they are voting for. Consequently, a large majority [of Iranians] do not have the right to vote [for the referendum]."[74] The faithful would never know enough to decide whether or not a political decision might transgress upon Islamic law. That was the task of the clergy. The referendum on whether Iran should become an "Islamic Republic" skirted this problem only because the ballot constructed the choice in such a way that voters would overwhelmingly endorse clerical rule.

As foundings go, this referendum might have been conclusive had the fundamentalist clergy been able to impose their own vision of what an "Islamic Republic" should be. But this was not the case for several reasons. For one thing, the fundamentalist design for government encompassed a dominant role for a clerical "leader" of the faithful and that principle was strongly opposed by almost every Grand Ayatollah other than Khomeini. In addition, clerical institutions under Shi'ite tradition provided rather poor models for the governance of a complex, industrializing society. The lack of a good model was perhaps most problematic when it came to distinguishing between routine, technical policies that could be administered by specialized bureaucracies and those matters that the clergy would have to decide because they implicated and thus possibly transgressed upon Islamic law. Because the boundary between these two was not always obvious, defining and policing the distinction between them demanded institutions more intricate and predictable than the charismatic organization of a theological seminary.

Finally, and perhaps most importantly, Khomeini himself did not seem to have a clear idea of the kind of state he wanted to create.[75] As long as he remained far and away the most dominant political influence in Iran, he seemed to be inclined to "muddle through" as he developed a conception of what an Islamic Republic should be. In many ways, this muddling was reactive in that he simply created temporary political arrangements in order to reject institutions and policies proposed by his political opponents.[76] However, at some point this

---

[73] Milani, *Making of Iran's Islamic Revolution*, p. 261; Bakhash, *Reign of the Ayatollahs*, p. 73. The left-leaning Democratic National Front had spun off from the National Front.

[74] Milani, *Making of Iran's Islamic Revolution*, p. 91.

[75] Arjomand, *Turban for the Crown*, p. 150.

[76] See, for example, Keddie, *Modern Iran*, p. 245.

incremental and somewhat haphazard process would have to be rationalized if it were to institute the basis for a stable political order.

In early June, Khomeini celebrated the sixteenth anniversary of the 1963 uprising against the Shah in a speech that warned the intelligentsia not to oppose clerical rule:

Those who did not participate in this movement have no right to advance any claims ... Who are they that wish to divert our Islamic movement from Islam? ... It was the mosques that created this Revolution, the mosques that brought this movement into being ... So preserve your mosques, O people. Intellectuals, do not be Western-style intellectuals, imported intellectuals; do your share to preserve the mosques.[77]

By mid-July, the provisional revolutionary government had drafted a new constitution that was rather unoriginal in its major provisions. Although the monarchy was eliminated, the framework was remarkably similar to the former 1906 constitution that both Shahs had more or less turned into a dead letter during their reigns. The draft provided for a strong presidency, a parliament, and a Council of Guardians that would be responsible for ensuring that all legislation was compatible with Islamic law. Only five of the twelve members of this council would be clergy. The other seven, a majority, were to be laymen. Everything considered, this would have been a strikingly mild version of what should have been considered possible under the rubric of an "Islamic republic." Nonetheless, many of the same groups that had been critical of the referendum now opposed the draft. Others, such as Ayatollah Shariatmadari, the National Front, and the Freedom Movement, gave it their support. For his part, Khomeini only demanded that the draft be changed so that women would be ineligible for judgeships and the presidency. Otherwise, he approved the draft and recommended that it be submitted to a vote of the people without revision.[78]

Sayeed describes the draft as "neither enough Islamic nor secular" and thus falling "short of the expectations both of the secular and religious factions." With the proposed constitution taking fire from both sides, Khomeini worked out a compromise through which an Assembly of Experts would be elected to revise the framework.[79] This met the demands of the secular parties because they anticipated that they would be able to liberalize the document's restrictions

---

[77] Arjomand, *Turban for the Crown*, p. 137. As Arjomand notes, Khomeini's hostility to the intelligentsia was not surprising since he had repeatedly announced that "the *complete eradication* of Occidentalism, or Western cultural influence" was one of his two most important political goals (the other was "the establishment of an Islamic theocracy") (p. 138, emphasis in the original).

[78] Milani, *Making of Iran's Islamic Revolution*, pp. 261–2.

[79] Khomeini's support for the Assembly of Experts might have been anticipated because he had previously declared, on the day after returning to Iran, that "it is our duty to continue this movement until all elements of the Shah's regime have been eliminated and we have established a Constituent Assembly based on the votes of the people and the first permanent government of the Islamic Republic." Vahdat, *God and Juggernaut*, p. 164.

on human rights, social welfare guarantees, and democratic participation. Islamic radicals, on the other hand, wanted to move the framework in a much more theocratic direction.[80] With the election of the Assembly of Experts scheduled for August 3 and the secular parties already in the field, Khomeini mobilized the clergy by insisting that revision of the draft constitution was both their prerogative and their obligation.

This right belongs to you. It is those knowledgeable in Islam who may express an opinion on the law of Islam. The constitution of the Islamic Republic means the constitution of Islam. Don't sit back while foreignized intellectuals, who have no faith in Islam, give their views and write the things they write. Pick up your pens and in the mosques, from the altars, in the streets and bazaars, speak of the things that in your view should be included in the constitution.[81]

The vastly outnumbered and fragmented ranks of the secular parties proved no match for Khomeini's ulama.

THE CONSTITUTION OF THE ISLAMIC REPUBLIC OF IRAN

The Assembly of Experts was in many ways equivalent to what in more secular contexts would be called a "constituent assembly." It was composed of seventy-three members elected from constituencies throughout the nation and was entrusted with the "high politics" of crafting a fundamental law. As it turned out, fifty-five of those seventy-three members belonged to the clergy.[82] Although the assembly adopted rules that required a two-thirds majority for approval of each provision in the new constitution, the clerics had little

---

[80] Sayeed, *Iran before and after Khomeini*, pp. 167–8. In a clear demonstration of who was the better judge of political reality, Hashemi-Rafsanjani, one of Khomeini's most loyal supporters, asked Mehdi Bazargan and Abo Hassan Bani-Sadr: "Who do you think will be elected to a constituent assembly? A fistful of ignorant and fanatic fundamentalists who will do such damage that you will regret ever having convened them." Arjomand, *Turban for the Crown*, p. 150.

[81] Arjomand, *Turban for the Crown*, p. 151.

[82] Although most of these clerics would have been elected in any case, their numbers were enhanced by the decision of the National Front, the National Democratic Front, and Shariatmadari's Azeri-based Muslim People's Republican Party to boycott the election in protest against clergy control of the media, violent attacks on their headquarters and candidates by the Hezbollah (a militant organization loyal to Khomeini), and anticipated voting fraud by the provisional revolutionary government. However, the election itself was remarkably free of disruption. Milani, *Making of Iran's Islamic Revolution*, p. 262; Hiro, *Iran under the Ayatollahs*, p. 119. For an itemized list of voting irregularities, see Schirazi, *Constitution of Iran*, pp. 31–2, 43n. However, several of the problems that Schirazi cites seem to be either minor or attributable to the fact that much of the electorate was both uneducated and devoutly religious: Because they were uneducated they needed assistance in completing the voting ritual (e.g., filling in the ballot) and because they were devout they depended on clerics for that assistance. Although the voting was largely peaceful, fundamentalists later replaced twelve elected members of the opposition with members belonging to Khomeini's Islamic Republican Party. Bahiriyeh, *State and Revolution in Iran*, pp. 150–1.

difficulty in dominating the legislative process. The only problems arose in coordinating the actions of fundamentalists, who were rather untrained in the art of deliberative politics. However, as it turned out, some of Khomeini's former students turned out to be surprisingly adept at what were normally secular parliamentary arts.[83]

The Assembly of Experts convened on August 19 and finished its deliberations on November 15, 1979. During those three months, the convention racked up around 560 hours in formal sessions. The mandate given to the Assembly of Experts had been to "review" the original draft of the constitution within thirty days, making such corrections and changes that it thought would improve the document. Once it convened, however, the assembly basically started from scratch and ignored the time limit that had been set on its deliberations.[84] When the members had finished, they had produced an almost entirely new document. That document opened with a long, discursive introduction that basically recited the history of the revolution and then laid out the constitutional framework of the new Islamic Republic in 175 separate articles.[85]

Although the introduction mentions the referendum in which "Iranian people declared their final and firm decision" to create "the Islamic Republic," most of the text recounts other ways in which the popular will was manifested during the revolution:

Thus it was that the awakened conscience of the nation, under the leadership of that precious *marja'-i taqlid*, Ayatullah al-Uzma Imam Khomeini, came to perceive the necessity of pursuing an authentically Islamic and ideological line in its struggles ...

The Islamic Revolution of Iran was nurtured by the blood of hundreds of young believers, women and men, who met the firing squads at dawn with cries of *"Allahu akbar,"* or who were gunned down by the enemy in streets and marketplaces ...

Commemorations of the martyrs of the Revolution, on the seventh and fortieth days after their death, like a series of steady heartbeats brought greater life, ardor, and enthusiasm to this movement, which now was unfolding across the country ...

The common sight of mothers with infants in their arms running toward the scene of battle and the barrels of machineguns demonstrated the essential and decisive role played by this major segment of society in the struggle.

After slightly more than a year of continuous and steadfast struggle, this sapling of a revolution, watered by the blood of 60,000 martyrs and 100,000 wounded and disabled, not to mention billions of tumans' worth of property damage, came to bear fruit amidst loud cries of "Independence! Freedom! Islamic government!"

---

[83] Sayeed, *Iran before and after Khomeini*, pp. 168–9.

[84] As Mohsen Milani notes, the American Constitutional Convention in 1787 had similarly exceeded the narrow mandate under which it had been created and thus provided ample precedent for the Assembly of Experts' aggressive reinterpretation of its prerogatives. Milani, *Making of Iran's Islamic Revolution*, p. 263.

[85] For an analysis of the constitution's provisions, see Schirazi, *Constitution of Iran*, pp. 8–19.

In the course of its revolutionary development, our nation has cleansed itself of the dust and impurities that accumulated during the tyrannical regime and purged itself of foreign ideological influences returning to the intellectual positions and authentic world-view of Islam. It now intends to establish an ideal and model society on the basis of Islamic criteria ...

[T]he Constitution provides the necessary basis for ensuring the continuation of the Revolution at home and abroad. In particular, in the development of external relations, the Revolution will strive, in concert with other Islamic and popular movements, to prepare the way for the formation of a single world community, in accordance with the Qur'anic verse *"This your nation is a single nation, and I am your Lord, so worship Me"* (21:92), and to assure the continuation of the struggle for the liberation of all deprived and oppressed peoples in the world.[86]

The first article then announces: "The form of government of Iran is that of an Islamic Republic, which received an affirmative vote from the Iranian people on the basis of their longstanding belief in the Qur'anic government of truth and Justice, after their victorious Islamic Revolution led by the eminent *marja'-e taqlid*, Ayatollah al-Uzma Imam Khomeini." Article 2 lays out the ideological basis of the Islamic Republic, characterizing it as

a system of government based on belief in:

   a. the One God (as stated in the Islamic creed "There is no god but God"), His exclusive possession of sovereignty and the right to legislate, and the necessity of submission to His commands;
   b. divine revelation and its fundamental role in the expounding of laws;
   c. the return to God in the hereafter, and the constructive role of this belief in man's ascending progress toward God;
   d. the justice of God in creation and legislation;
   e. continuous leadership and guidance, and its fundamental role in assuring the continuity of the revolution of Islam;
   f. the exalted dignity and value of man, and his freedom, joined to responsibilities, before God;

which secures equity, justice, and political, economic, social, and cultural independence, and national solidarity, by recourse to:

   a. continuous *itihad* of the *fuqaha* possessing the necessary qualifications, exercised on the basis of the Book of God and the Sunna of the Ma'sumin, upon all of whom be peace...[87]

---

[86] *Constitution of the Islamic Republic of Iran*, trans. Hamid Algar (Berkeley, CA: Mizan Press, 1980), pp. 14–18.

[87] *Constitution of the Islamic Republic of Iran*, pp. 26–7. Ijtihad is "the deduction of particular applications of Islamic law from its sources and general principle by a religious scholar who possesses the appropriate qualifications." The *fuqaha* are scholars "of the Islamic religious sciences, especially jurisprudence." The Sunna is "the normative practice of the Prophet Muhammad." The *ma'sumin* are "those divinely endowed with the attribute *'ismat*, i.e., freedom from error and the commission of major sin; in Shi'i Muslim belief, the Prophet, his daughter Fatima, and the Twelve Imams."

The Introduction and the first two articles thus clearly but indirectly associate the March referendum with the founding of the Islamic Republic.

Because an Islamic Republic was dedicated to realizing God's commandments and because those commandments were divinely revealed only to those clerics who manifested qualities of scholarship and piety, only those clerics could rule over an Islamic society. As rulers, those same clerics would be responsible for and guided by interpretations of Islamic law and the tradition of the Prophet. Those interpretations would determine the substance of state policy not as a political prerogative associated with ruling but as logical deductions from scripture and tradition. In sum, the Iranian people had dedicated state sovereignty to the clergy, who, in turn, had dedicated themselves to interpreting and realizing the commands of God. These decisions were irreversible in the first instance because the Iranian people did not possess the scholarly knowledge and doctrinal training necessary to determine and execute God's commandments. But, even more to the point, reversing these decisions was simply inconceivable because no people, once embarked on the path to righteousness (e.g., the creation and purification of a just Islamic society), would ever knowingly choose to deviate from that path. However, they might unwittingly commit an error. And it was the role of the clergy to make sure that such errors were either suppressed (as heretical possibilities) or corrected (as misunderstandings of God's command). With respect to the clergy, it was similarly inconceivable that clerics possessing a thorough understanding of Islamic law and sublime piety would ever mislead the people. In fact, once the new republic was up and running, even to suggest that clerics might dishonor themselves by violating their divine responsibilities was itself heresy.

The remaining 173 articles worked out the details of how God's commandments, as revealed through Islamic law and scholarship, were to be institutionally realized in state policy. Here, there are three primary areas of interest with respect to the founding of a non-democratic state: the authority of the Supreme Leader, the relationship of the Supreme Leader to the rank and file of the Islamic clergy, and the relationship of both of them to the Iranian people. As we shall see, there are apparent contradictions in some of these arrangements but they do not seem to be as inconsistent as some have suggested.[88]

The Supreme Leader is the Hidden Imam's representative on earth: During the Occultation of the Lord of the Age (may God hasten his renewed manifestation!), the governance and leadership of the nation devolve upon the just and pious *faqih* who is acquainted with the circumstances of his age; courageous, resourceful, and possessed of administrative ability; and recognized and accepted as leader by the majority of the people.[89]

---

[88] For a sampling of those who have noted contradictions in the Iranian constitution, see Ansari, *Iran, Islam, and Democracy*, pp. 45–6; Schirazi, *Constitution of Iran*, pp. 1, 37, 52–3; Sayeed, *Iran before and after Khomeini*, pp. 44, 67; Vahdat, *God and Juggernaut*, p. 180.

[89] Article 5, *Constitution of the Islamic Republic of Iran*, p. 29.

Although we will return to how a majority of the people recognize and accept the leader in a moment, the Assembly of Experts left no doubt that this question was already settled at the time they drafted the constitution:

Whenever one of the *fuqaha* possessing the qualifications specified in Article 5 of the Constitution is recognized and accepted as *marja'* and leader by a decisive majority of the people – as has been the case with the exalted *marja'-i taqlid* and leader of the revolution, Ayatullah al-Uzma Imam Khomeini – he is to exercise governance and all the responsibilities arising therefrom.[90]

By universal acclamation, the Iranian people had already recognized Khomeini as the Supreme Leader. In fact, both his recognition and the role he was given predated the constitution because they were organically determined by the relation between the Islamic community and their God. In effect, the constitution was merely enshrining the Supreme Leader within the apparatus of the Islamic Republic (as opposed to creating an office and allocating prerogatives to the person who occupied that office).[91]

The Supreme Leader's authority is so extensive that whoever occupies the office is constrained only by the ideational constraints of Shi'ite tradition.[92] For example, he appoints almost all of the high posts in the judiciary; exercises almost complete command of the armed forces (including the power to declare war); approves the candidates who stand for election to the presidency and, once a candidate has been elected, approves his election; dismisses the president if the latter fails to perform well; and selects the members of the Council of Guardians (half of the twelve members directly and the others indirectly through a process in which the Supreme Leader plays a major role).[93] The Council of Guardians, in turn, regulates the conduct of elections to the Majles (the Iranian parliament), approves candidates who may stand for election to the

---

[90] Article 107, *Constitution of the Islamic Republic of Iran*, p. 66.

[91] The authority assigned to the Supreme Leader under the Iranian constitution has sometimes been compared to that of a philosopher king in Plato's Republic. See, for example, Gheissari and Nasr, *Democracy in Iran*, p. 86; Sayeed, *Iran before and after Khomeini*, p. 45; Milani, *Making of Iran's Islamic Revolution*, p. 152; Ansari, *Iran, Islam, and Democracy*, p. 47. On the origins of the Supreme Leader in Khomeini's pre-revolutionary writings, see Schirazi, *Constitution of Iran*, p. 55.

[92] For an interpretive summary of the Supreme Leader's authority, see Milani, *Making of Iran's Islamic Revolution*, pp. 264–5. On the consolidation of power in the Supreme Leader after adoption of the constitution, see Schirazi, *Constitution of Iran*, pp. 61–85. For a detailed chart depicting "State Structures of the Islamic Republic of Iran" that illustrates the centrality, autonomy, and authority of the Supreme Leader (*Faqih*), see Cheryl Benard and Zalmay Khalilzad, *"The Government of God": Iran's Islamic Republic* (New York: Columbia University Press, 1984), p. 119.

[93] Article 91. The six members who are not directly appointed by the Supreme Leader are "to be elected by the National Consultative Assembly from among the Muslim jurists presented to it by the Supreme Judicial Council." Two of the five members of this Supreme Judicial Council are appointed by the Supreme Leader; the other three are "chosen by all the judges of the country." *Constitution of the Islamic Republic of Iran*, p. 60.

Majles, and approves (or rejects) legislation passed by the Majles. Several of these powers are shared with other appointed bodies but the Supreme Leader himself appoints their members. In effect, most of the government apparatus is susceptible to the Supreme Leader's control if he chooses to influence its decisions. Given his role as the Hidden Imam's representative on earth, there is little ideational justification for limiting the Supreme Leader's powers.[94] That includes his term in office: The Supreme Leader serves until the end of his natural life.[95]

The Supreme Leader's relations with other clerics can be divided into three areas: relations with other Grand Ayatollahs and ayatollahs outside the government; relations with those clerics who occupy official posts in the government; and relations with those clerics who select a new Supreme Leader. The Supreme Leader's relations with high-ranking clergy outside the government is left more or less untouched by the constitution. In Shi'ite tradition and custom, the Supreme Leader may be the first among equals outside of government but he also may not be. The clerical hierarchy is polycephalic and each Grand Ayatollah is largely independent and autonomous from the others. Although the constitution does engender a political practice that has implications for the organization and operation of the Shi'ite clerical community outside of government, the constitution does not formally intrude the government into the selection of clerical leaders, the operation of theological schools, the staffing of mosques, or the scholarship and rulings produced by clerics. Although it would be too simplistic to say that the clergy have inhabited the government but not vice versa, that roughly summarizes

---

[94] As Hiro put it, the Supreme Leader "does not rule according to his own will" and thus his rule cannot be "dictatorial." Hiro, *Iran under the Ayatollahs*, p. 117.

[95] After the Assembly of Experts had created the post of Supreme Leader and specified his powers, the Italian journalist Oriana Fallaci asked Khomeini what the implications of this arrangement might be for popular democracy in Iran.

Fallaci's question: In drafting the new constitution, the assembly of experts passed one article . . . by which the head of the country will have to be the supreme religious authority. That is you. And the supreme decisions will be made only by those who know the Koran well – that is, the clergy. Doesn't this mean that, according to the constitution, politics will continue to be determined by the priests [clergy] and no one else?

Khomeini's answer: This law, which the people will ratify, is in no way in contradiction with democracy. Since the people love the clergy, have faith in the clergy, want to be guided by the clergy, it is right that the supreme religious authority should oversee the work of the prime minister or of the president of the republic, to make sure that they don't make mistakes or go against the Koran.

Khomeini then added: "[T]he word Islam does not need adjectives such as democratic. Precisely because Islam is everything, it means everything. It is sad for us to add another word near the word Islam, which is perfect." (Skocpol, "Rentier State," pp. 277–8)

For more of the interview, see *International Herald Tribune*, October 15, 1979, p. 5.

the relationship. The Supreme Leader exercises no more authority over the clerical community outside of government than the prestige he has earned through scholarship and piety.[96]

The situation is quite different with respect to the Supreme Leader's relations with clergy who are given posts within the government. Many of those posts are reserved for clerics and every post may be filled by a cleric. Either directly or indirectly (through bodies that he appoints), the Supreme Leader makes almost all of these appointments. Because the Council of Guardians determines who is eligible for election to the Majles, the Supreme Leader can prevent a cleric from serving there as well. In all these ways, there is a very strict clerical hierarchy within the Islamic Republic that is quite at odds with the structure of the traditional clerical community outside of government. The Supreme Leader can impose an orthodoxy within government that would be beyond his reach in the rest of society.

Because the Supreme Leader is mortal, the constitution provides for the selection of a replacement. There would be no difficulty if, as was the case with Khomeini, the Iranian people designated a successor by acclamation. However, if this is not the case

experts elected by the people will review and consult among themselves concerning all persons qualified to act as *marja'* and leader. If they discern outstanding capacity for leadership in a certain *marja'*, they will present him to the people as their leader; if not, they will appoint either three or five *marja*'s possessing the necessary qualifications for leadership and present them as members of the Leadership Council.[97]

These "experts" must be members of the clergy. Only those whose candidacies are approved by the Council of Guardians and the Supreme Leader may be chosen "by the people" in elections. In that and other ways, the popular will is very constrained. After it is constituted, the Assembly of Experts (it takes on the same name as the constitutional convention) may change the way in which "experts" are selected.[98] Thus, if the Supreme Leader is still alive, he will play a very large and perhaps determining role in the selection of his successor. But the successor himself is not in a position to influence his selection. The role played by the people, in keeping with the ideational justification for clerical rule, is largely to signal their willingness to delegate the selection of a new Supreme Leader to "experts" who better understand Islamic law and are in a better

---

[96] The decentralized organization of the clerical network outside the Iranian state has, however, subsequently come under criticism by those who would like to see the Islamic Republic centralize the operation of religious institutions, including the training of students and the collection of revenue. See, for example, Schirazi, *Constitution of Iran*, p. 260.

[97] Article 107, *Constitution of the Islamic Republic of Iran*, p. 66.

[98] Article 108, *Constitution of the Islamic Republic of Iran*, p. 67. The text in this article is unclear. It could be read as granting full autonomy to the Assembly of Experts in regulating the manner of their election and the vetting of their candidacies, but that interpretation seems unlikely.

position to evaluate the piety of those who might be eligible.[99] However, if no one person seems qualified to serve alone, the "experts" may select several clerics to serve collectively as a "Leadership Council."

The election of "experts" for the selection of a new Supreme Leader is one of several instances in which the constitution provides for popular election. These are all briefly described in Article 6:

In the Islamic Republic of Iran, the affairs of the country must be administered on the basis of public opinion expressed by means of elections, including the election of the President of the Republic, the representatives of the National Consultative Assembly [the Majles], and the members of councils, or by means of referenda in matters specified in other articles of this Constitution.

However, the eligibility of candidates is so tightly controlled by either the Supreme Leader or bodies dominated by his appointees that "public opinion" can be expressed only within a fairly narrow range of alternatives. Within this range there can be and has been intense political competition, but the constitution purifies the will of the people by restricting the range of alternatives before that competition begins. Once purified in this way, the will of the people can be appropriately and productively expressed.

Given the high priority placed by the constitution on creating situations in which the Iranian people can consent (by way of elections or referenda) to rule by the clergy, we might reasonably ask why the constitution provides for any elections at all.[100] As the introduction notes, the Iranian people in a "final and firm decision" had endorsed the founding of an Islamic Republic and, in that act, requested that they be governed by God's commandments as divinely revealed to the clergy. Interpreted in that way, the Islamic Republic seems to have no place for elections in any form.[101] Part of the answer probably lies in an attempt by the Assembly of Experts to appease more liberal elements in the revolutionary coalition, although by that point they were already so marginalized as to be almost irrelevant. Part of the answer may also lie in the representation of the Islamic Republic in the world at large, where popular consent would have been interpreted differently (e.g., as more or less regularly expressed in

---

[99] For an example of how this interpretation surfaced during deliberation in the Assembly of Experts, see Schirazi, *Constitution of Iran*, p. 37.

[100] On the incompatibility of popular democracy with the teachings of Twelver Shi'ism, see Amuzegar, *Dynamics of the Iranian Revolution*, p. 120.

[101] Ayatollah Beheshti presided over debate in the Assembly of Experts and was the primary author of Article 5, which created the Supreme Leader. Referring to popular democracy during discussion of this article, he took the following position: "In the present system the leadership and legislation cannot be left to the majority at any given moment. This would contradict the ideological character of the Islamic Republic." Beheshti "thus rejected democracy as un-Islamic on the grounds that the people could fall into error. In his view a state that had to take account of the voice of the people would have to submit to laws that were influenced by such errors." Schirazi, *Constitution of Iran*, p. 35.

elections as opposed to a "one time only" grant of authority to the clergy). But the major reason lies in the nature of Shi'ite Islam, in which popular opinion has traditionally played a major role in determining the clerical hierarchy. We return to this later.

First, though, we should at least mention a few issues that seem inconsistent with the ostensible purpose of an Islamic Republic. Shi'ite Islam, like most religions, recognizes the political borders of nations as artificial, if unavoidable, boundaries dividing the faithful.[102] Article 10 of the constitution emphatically endorses this view in relation to the fundamentalist project of exporting religious revolution.

In accordance with the verse "This your nation is a single nation, and I am your Lord, so worship Me," all Muslims form a single nation, and the government of the Islamic Republic of Iran has the duty of formulating its general policies with a view to the merging and union of all Muslim peoples, and it must constantly strive to bring about the political, economic, and cultural unity of the Islamic world.[103]

Article 12 states that the "official religion of Iran is Islam" but then immediately restricts that designation to "the Twelver Ja'fari school of thought," further specifying that "this principle shall remain eternally immutable." While this is not surprising given the basis of the government's founding, it does seem to be a little at odds with the goal of "merging and union of all Muslim peoples." That goal also seems compromised in the same article when the constitution states that other "Islamic schools of thought ... are to be accorded full respect, and their followers are free to act in accordance with their own jurisprudence" and to run their own schools. However, they only enjoy full autonomy, as religious communities, where they "constitute a majority" of the local population. Even more incongruously, the "Zoroastrian, Jewish, and Christian Iranians" are designated as "recognized minorities" and, in addition, are guaranteed representation in the Majles.

Zoroastrians are presumably tolerated because theirs is an ancient faith practiced by the Persian (now Iranian) people. Judaism and Christianity are both faiths distantly related to Islam and followed by significant numbers of Iranians. In addition, religious toleration has long been one of the fundamental tenets of Islam. So both political reality and religious doctrine can explain these exceptions. The incongruity arises between the emphasis in Article 10 on the revolutionary export of Twelver Shi'ism and the recognition and incorporation of religious diversity in Iran.[104] Why should Iran bother to export Twelver Shi'ism if religious conversion to the one true faith is not at least strongly encouraged at home? What exactly is being exported by the Iranian state that religious missionaries could not do as well or even more effectively? The

---

[102] Vahdat, *God and Juggernaut*, p. 163.
[103] *Constitution of the Islamic Republic of Iran*, p. 31.
[104] See Articles 12, 13, and 64, *Constitution of the Islamic Republic of Iran*, pp. 32, 52.

problem seems to lie in the nature of the purification of Islamic society that the revolution was meant to undertake. Most of that purification involved the rejection of Western values and cultural influence and, thus, a cleansing of alien elements that had infiltrated traditional Iranian society. From that perspective, religions that had long been followed by a minority of Iranians could be tolerated because they were not Western in origin. However, this cleansing of alien elements grated against the self-image of the revolution, which prided itself as both "modern" and "devout." And that was the primary reason (along with more jihadic traditions) for the emphasis on the dedication of the state to bringing about the "political, economic, and cultural unity of the Islamic world."

This dedication also seems at odds with the one passage in which nationalism clearly rears its head. Article 115 lays out the criteria determining the eligibility of those "religious and political personalities" who can serve as "President of the Republic": "Iranian origin; Iranian nationality; administrative and managerial capacities; a good past record; trustworthiness; piety; convinced belief in the fundamental principles of the Islamic Republic of Iran and the official school of thought of the country."[105] Since the constitution has already, in Article 110, stated that the Council of Guardians will evaluate "the suitability of candidates for the presidency" before they are permitted to stand for election, and since the Supreme Leader in practice controls the Council of Guardians, most of these criteria might seem superfluous because they would not significantly constrain either the Council of Guardians or the Supreme Leader. Neither can be overruled within the Iranian state. But the first two criteria, "Iranian origin" and "Iranian nationality," are not superfluous because they are facts almost always set down in official documents long before men might become presidential candidates. By making both those born outside the political boundaries of Iran and those who are not Iranian citizens ineligible for the presidency, the constitution clearly constrains the Council of Guardians and the Supreme Leader because they are not permitted to approve a candidate who does not possess an Iranian birth certificate or Iranian citizenship.

Viewed against the rest of the constitution, particularly the more theocratic elements, these restrictions appear a little anomalous in at least two respects.[106] First, they recognize limitations on the spiritual enlightenment of the Council of Guardians and the Supreme Leader in that they are not permitted to approve a candidate who is in other respects a pious believer in Twelver Shi'ism (among the other qualities set forth in the article). But, more importantly, the nationalist criteria emphatically and voluntarily impose a political boundary within the Islamic community. Other parts of the constitution that have nationalist implications, such as the creation of a national army, might be explained away as

---

[105] *Constitution of the Islamic Republic of Iran*, pp. 70–1.
[106] See, for example, Ansari, *Iran, Islam, and Democracy*, p. 46.

impositions forced upon Iran by the political reality of the international system of nation-states. But that same political reality cannot justify the nationalist restrictions placed on eligibility for the presidency.[107]

ADOPTION OF THE CONSTITUTION AND CONSOLIDATION OF THE ISLAMIC REPUBLIC

The Iranian people were asked to approve the constitution in a referendum held on December 2–3, 1979. Over 99 percent of the 15,785,956 voters who cast ballots favored adoption.[108] Although a large majority would have approved the constitution in any case, the margin was swelled by the occupation of the US embassy in Tehran by "Students Following the Line of the Imam" on November 4. The ensuing hostage crisis brought down the provisional revolutionary government of Mehdi Bazargan, who had become, by default, a relatively liberal figure because of the continuing marginalization of secular and leftist elements in the original revolutionary coalition. His fall thus enabled the fundamentalists to further tighten their grip on state institutions. In addition, the occupation of the embassy unleashed nationalist sentiment that rallied around Khomeini and the fundamentalists as the only leaders who could stand up to the United States and thus defend the revolution from foreign intervention.[109]

The fundamentalists had begun to consolidate their control of the revolution even before the constitution was ratified.[110] During the summer of 1979, they either shut down opposition newspapers or took them over. The

---

[107] Khomeini seems to have played only a marginal role in the work of the Assembly of Experts. Arjomand, for example, describes the legislative deliberations as "largely independent of the personal inclination of the participating ayatollahs" in which the primary task was "working out the full logical and institutional implications of Khomeini's theocratic idea in the framework of the modern nation-state. This impersonal process, a novel rationalization of the political order, unfolded in the form of the constitution making of the clerically dominated Assembly of Experts." Arjomand, *Turban for the Crown*, p. 151. The best account of the assembly's deliberations appears in Schirazi, *Constitution of Iran*, pp. 35–55. Although some of the debates were vigorously contested, the decisions were remarkably consensual. Schirazi reports, for example, that an average of sixty-six votes were cast on roll calls taken in the assembly, of which an average of only two dissented from the majority while four, again on average, abstained (p. 55n). For a general survey of the origins of the constitution, see Ali Rahnema, "Ayatollah Khomeini's Rule of the Guardian Jurist" in Adib-Moghaddam, *Critical Introduction*, pp. 97–114.

[108] Hiro, *Iran under the Ayatollahs*, p. 120. The Muslim People's Republican Party, Ayatollah Shariatmadari, and the National Front supported a boycott of the referendum. Milani, *Making of Iran's Islamic Revolution*, p. 279. Referring to the provision for a Supreme Leader in the constitution, Ayatollah Shariatmadari lamented: "We seem to be moving from one monarchy to another." Hiro, *Iran under the Ayatollahs*, p. 139.

[109] Keddie, *Modern Iran*, p. 248; Arjomand, *Turban for the Crown*, p. 139.

[110] Gheissari and Nasr, *Democracy in Iran*, p. 80.

fundamentalists already controlled the radio and television networks because they had been regulated by the state before the revolution and had thus fallen into fundamentalist hands as part of the "spoils of war."[111] As part of this first stage in the consolidation of the revolutionary regime, they also joined with the Marxist left in purging liberal democrats from their political coalition. Many of the supporters of the National Front and the National Democratic Front were educated middle-class professionals and they now emigrated from Iran by the hundreds of thousands. Their exodus helped the fundamentalists suppress demands for democratic participation.[112] Once liberal democrats had been purged, the fundamentalists turned their attention to the Marxist left and drove them from the coalition. On August 16, for example, Khomeini warned the nation: "Let no one expect that the corrupt and American or non-American left will be able to reappear in this country ... We gave them time and treated them mildly in the hope that they would stop their devilish acts ... We can, when we want, in a few hours throw them in the dustbin of death."

On July 20, 1980, the Mujahedin-e-Khalq issued a statement that blamed Khomeini's religious pretensions for the split. "Mr. Khomeini is so convinced of his divinity that he sees any opposition to himself as opposition to God, Islam and the Holy Quran ... Although he thinks he is deputizing for the Twelfth Imam, we have never accepted him in that role." By this time, the leftist guerrillas had returned to the underground and had begun to assassinate fundamentalist leaders.[113] However, Khomeini found the Tudeh, the Moscow-oriented communist party, useful because it continued to interpret the revolution as "an anti-imperialist petty bourgeois ... precursor to socialist revolution" and thus supported the fundamentalist project.[114] The last stage of consolidation involved the silencing of the conservative clergy who opposed Khomeini. By that point, Ayatollah Shariatmadari was the only real threat. Shariatmadari's Muslim People's Republican Party was suppressed, his residence was attacked, and Khomeini's followers stripped him of his status as a Grand Ayatollah as punishment for secretly collaborating with the Shah during the revolution.[115]

---

[111] Hiro, *Iran under the Ayatollahs*, p. 128; Arjomand, *Turban for the Crown*, p. 138; Milani, *Making of Iran's Islamic Revolution*, p. 263.

[112] Keddie, *Modern Iran*, p. 243.

[113] Hiro, *Iran under the Ayatollahs*, pp. 128, 188–9; Bakhash, *Reign of the Ayatollahs*, p. 219.

[114] Hiro, *Iran under the Ayatollahs*, p. 229; Keddie, *Modern Iran*, p. 254. For the official line of the Tudeh, see Hiro, *Iran under the Ayatollahs*, p. 203. The fundamentalists tolerated the Tudeh until 1983 when it, too, was brutally suppressed.

[115] Chehabi, "Religion and Politics in Iran," p. 82; Arjomand, *Turban for the Crown*, p. 140; Hiro, *Iran under the Ayatollahs*, pp. 140–1, 218; Sayeed, *Iran before and after Khomeini*, pp. 178–9; Bakhash, *Reign of the Ayatollahs*, p. 67; Milani, *Making of Iran's Islamic Revolution*, pp. 279–80. For the opposition of some of the other Grand Ayatollahs to Shariatmadari's defrocking, see Irfani, *Iran's Islamic Revolution*, p. 230.

One of the last refuges of political dissent was the universities, but these, too, fell in the opening months of 1980 when they were forcibly occupied by Khomeini's followers during the Iranian "Cultural Revolution." The professors and students were expelled (some of them killed) and the universities were closed.[116] Noting that secular scholarship had no place in the Islamic Republic, Khomeini concluded: "If we extensively survey all the universities in the world, we will see that all the troubles that have afflicted mankind have their roots in the university."[117]

Soon after Khomeini's return to Iran, the fundamentalists began to systematically execute their opponents. The first executions were, in fact, carried out on the rooftop of a building in which Khomeini was holding court.[118] Convictions were speedily obtained because Khomeini decided that public trials, defense counsel, and judicial due process should not stand in the way of the will of the people. An insistence on such procedures before prisoners were executed reflected "the Western sickness among us" because "criminals should not be tried; they should be killed."[119] By the summer of 1981, executions were routine.[120]

Much of the political suppression that helped to consolidate the revolutionary regime was carried out by the Party of Allah (the Hezbollah), a loosely structured organization directly controlled by the fundamentalists. A pamphlet put out by one of the government ministries described a typical Hezbollahi as

a wild torrent surpassing the imagination ... He is a maktabi [one who follows Islam comprehensively], disgusted with any leaning to the East or West. He has a pocketful of documents exposing the treason of those who pose as intellectuals. He is simple, sincere and angry. Stay away from his anger, which destroys all in its path. Khomeini is his heart and soul ... The Hezbollahi does not use eau de cologne, wear a tie or smoke American

---

[116] Arjomand describes Khomeini as having conducted a "massive *Kulturkampf* against the Westernized intelligentsia," of which the assault on the universities was a part. Arjomand, *Turban for the Crown*, p. 87. Also see Hiro, *Iran under the Ayatollahs*, pp. 159–60; Keddie, *Modern Iran*, p. 250.

[117] Irfani, *Iran's Islamic Revolution*, p. 205.   [118] Moin, *Khomeini*, p. 207.

[119] Bakhash, *Reign of the Ayatollahs*, p. 62.

[120] On September 9, 1981, Khomeini gave these executions a scriptural basis: "When Prophet Muhammad failed to improve the people with advice, he hit them on the head with a sword until he made them human beings." Hiro, *Iran under the Ayatollahs*, p. 196; also see pp. 106–7. "Men and women were killed for everything from drug and sexual offenses to 'corruption on earth,' from plotting counter-revolution and spying for Israel to membership in opposition groups." Bakhash, *Reign of the Ayatollahs*, p. 111; also see pp. 59, 111–12, 220–30. For a close analysis of 863 executions of members of secular communist political organizations between 1981 and 1983, see Ali Mirsepassi, *Intellectual Discourse and the Politics of Modernization: Negotiating Modernity in Iran* (New York: Cambridge University Press, 2000), pp. 171–5. This analysis does not include 9,368 executions of those belonging to the Mujahedin-e-Khalq because that organization was Islamic. The Tudeh was still legally operating during this period and thus none of its members were killed.

cigarettes ... You might wonder where he gets his information. He is everywhere, serving your food, selling ice-cream.[121]

No one knows how many people died during the Iranian Revolution. For the period between January 1978 and February 1979, the estimates range from several thousand to as many as 40,000.[122] And thousands more died in street fighting and executions after the Shah was overthrown.

Many of the people who fought for the revolution died for principles and ideas that did not find their way into the founding of the Islamic Republic. In fact, many of them died at the hands of the Islamic Republic itself. Their deaths underscore the necessary distinction between revolutions and foundings. Revolutions are usually backward-looking; in this case, the unifying element for the revolutionary coalition was an almost stupefying hatred of the Shah and the regime he had built.[123] Once the Shah was gone, that hatred was not of much use as a basis for founding a new state.

As the almost universally recognized leader of the revolution, Ayatollah Khomeini was in the best position to shape the founding and, as most analysts and scholars agree, he made the most of his opportunity. Although there are moments of hesitancy in which he appears to have underestimated fundamentalist strength, he made no serious mistakes as he first confronted the Shah, then balanced and maneuvered against the several elements of the revolutionary coalition, and finally went up against his opponents among the conservative clergy. His opponents, on the other hand, made many errors, most of them arising out of a serious misapprehension of Khomeini's ultimate goals and the strength of the political resources at his command. Theda Skocpol has called the Iranian Revolution a "social revolution" in which there is a "rapid, basic" transformation "of a country's state and class" structure and "its dominant ideology ... carried through, in part, by class-based upheavals from below." However, she also adds that "idea systems and cultural understandings in the shaping of political action" played an inordinately large role in the Iranian social revolution.[124] Because social revolutions erupt from below, the masses often have only a vague conception of the kind of state they want to found in place of the *ancien régime*. This vague conception creates an opening for the revolutionary leadership as it seizes (and sometimes creates) the moment of victory in which the *ancien régime* falls and then defines, often through force and violence, what the political goal of the revolution actually will be.

The primary opponents of the revolutionary leadership are usually liberals and democratic socialists who would create a political process in which the

---

[121] Hiro, *Iran under the Ayatollahs*, pp. 242–3. Compare this description with Jacques Rene Hebert's depiction of a typical sans-culottes during the French Revolution on page 307.

[122] For a sampling of estimates, see Arjomand, *Turban for the Crown*, p. 120; Bill, "Power and Religion," p. 28; Hiro, *Iran under the Ayatollahs*, p. 94.

[123] Amuzegar, *Dynamics of the Iranian Revolution*, p. 10.

[124] Skocpol, "Rentier State," pp. 265–6, 268.

popular will is elicited from society, as opposed to imposed upon it. However, the creation of a political process that elicits the popular will invariably slow down or even reverse much of the radical impetus that throws up a social revolution in the first place. Realizing that fact, those revolutionary leaderships that are willing to make much stronger and imperative assumptions of what constitutes the popular will and to advocate the erection of strong, centralized state institutions as instruments for the imposition of that will end up founding the new revolutionary state.[125] Much of this interpretation appears to fit the Iranian Revolution rather well.[126]

What does not fit quite as well is the "ideational content" of the Iranian founding, specifically its thick underpinnings in Islamic theology and its formal incorporation of the Shi'ite clergy in state administration. Although there is usually some overlap, church and state are almost always separate institutions in modern societies. When they are combined, the political system is called a theocracy in which, in its ideal form, "God is recognized as the immediate ruler and His laws are taken as the legal code of the community and are expounded and administered by holy men as His agents."[127] This certainly fits Khomeini's conception of the Islamic Republic, but, in practice, this conception has been undermined, first, by the absence of a strict clerical hierarchy in Shi'ite Islam and, second, by disagreement within the clergy on its proper relation to the state.

From that perspective, the "linchpin of the theocratic component of the constitution" was the hegemonic authority of the Supreme Leader, who possesses an ostensibly direct relation to God through the agency of the Hidden Imam. The creation of such an office, along with the mobilization of the clergy as the Supreme Leader's subordinates, represented "a clear attempt at church building" in that it erected, in practice, an ecclesiastical institution within the

---

[125] Skocpol, "Rentier State," p. 276. Khomeini himself offered an interpretation of the Iranian Revolution that placed it alongside other popular revolts: "The great reformist movements in history did not possess power at their inception ... The cadres of the [reformist] movement would draw the attention of the people to oppression and awaken them to the dangers of submitting to the rule of the tyrants, then the people became the active force which sweeps all the obstacles in its way." Hiro, *Iran under the Ayatollahs*, p. 117. In the Iranian case, the goal of the reform movement was the establishment of an Islamic Republic and the cadre was the fundamentalist clergy.

[126] However, Skocpol does say that the broad consensus on the Shah's ouster strongly distinguished the Iranian Revolution from its French, Russian, and Chinese antecedents in that "a mass-based social movement" intended "to overthrow the old order" from the very inception of the revolution. Skocpol, "Rentier State," p. 267.

[127] The quotation is taken from Vernon Bognador (ed.), *The Blackwell Encyclopaedia of Political Institutions* (Oxford: Basil Blackwell, 1987), p. 610. Reprinted in Chehabi, "Religion and Politics in Iran," p. 69. Chehabi, however, hastens to add that neither Shi'ite Islam in general nor the fundamentalist clergy in particular "strictly ... constitute a church in the sociological sense." For a definition of a church, he cites Max Weber, *Economy and Society*, eds. Guenther Roth and Claus Wittich (Berkeley: University of California Press, 1978), p. 1164.

state itself.[128] Regardless of whether or not we call the result a theocracy, the social purpose of the Islamic Republic is the realization of God's will on earth through the creation of a just and pure Islamic community.[129] And that social purpose is very different from the more worldly goals of most social revolutions in which revolutionary upheaval intends the reshaping of a materialist social order. In the Iranian case, the social purpose of the purification of society (by eliminating alien, evil elements) is to prepare the way for a supernaturally dictated millennium.

As already noted, the constitution of the Islamic Republic assumes that the Iranian people have already made a "final and firm" decision to grant the clergy and, in particular, the Supreme Leader the right to rule. This grant rests on the public demonstrations that overthrew the Shah, referenda that designated the Islamic Republic as the preferred form of government, the election of members to the Assembly of Experts that wrote the constitution, and the referendum through which the people approved that constitution. The political theory underlying the concept of the Islamic Republic is grounded in two broad principles: (1) that the people wish to constitute and perfect an ideal Islamic community on earth in preparation for the return of the Hidden Imam; and (2) that the people realize that only the clergy can interpret and execute Islamic law and the practice of the Prophet through which this ideal community can be realized. Since Khomeini and the fundamentalists who followed him viewed Islamic law and the practice of the Prophet as an infallible and exhaustive guide to all those matters relating to the construction of an ideal Islamic community, there was no need for further manifestation of the popular will.[130] Those matters that government undertook that were irrelevant to the construction and governance of an ideal Islamic community could be safely entrusted to specialists who would efficiently and capably run the material infrastructure of the nation (e.g., construct and maintain highways, hospitals, and water systems). Those matters that involved the spiritual and moral health of the community must be the prerogative of the clergy.[131]

---

[128] Chehabi, "Religion and Politics in Iran," p. 77.

[129] For hesitation in classifying Iran as a theocracy, see Chehabi, "Religion and Politics in Iran," pp. 81, 83, 87; Gheissari and Nasr, *Democracy in Iran*, pp. 3, 100. Other scholars do not hesitate. Parsa, *Social Origins*, p. 2; Bahiriyeh, *State and Revolution in Iran*, p. 177.

[130] As Schirazi puts it, once the Islamic Republic is up and running, the "people are not active subjects of the state but the state's objects." Schirazi, *Constitution of Iran*, p. 55.

[131] The construction of this ideal Islamic society necessitates the inculcation of "a spiritual unity that characterizes the entire community" and that inculcation, in turn, requires an "ideological conversion" that will produce "morally virtuous human beings ... The shaping of the economic and political relations of society through the medium of social control leads to the creation" of the conditions under which this ideological conversion will occur. Sayeed, *Iran before and after Khomeini*, p. 64.

Khomeini himself justified the founding of the Islamic Republic as a reflection of "the will of the people and the precepts of Islam."[132] With respect to the latter, he said:

The law of Islam, divine command, has absolute authority over all individuals and the Islamic government ... In Islam, then, government has the sense of adherence to law; it is law alone that rules over society. Even the limited powers given to the Most Noble Messenger (upon whom be peace) and those exercising rule after him have been conferred upon them by God.

An Islamic Republic under which sovereignty (the right to rule) can belong only to God is the most popular (in the sense of consensual agreement) form of government because the "body of Islamic laws that exist in the Quran and the *Sunnah* [tradition of the Prophet] has been accepted by the Muslims and recognized by them as worthy of obedience. This consent and acceptance facilitates the task of government and makes it truly belong to the people." There is thus no ambiguity concerning what the people want in the form of the laws that will govern society because they are already laid down in an Islamic law and tradition that the people have ratified en bloc when the Islamic Republic was founded.[133]

There was thus no role for a popularly elected legislative assembly in Khomeini's political theory because such a body could only introduce error into what would otherwise be clerical imposition of God's design. As Khomeini wrote: "Since Islamic government is a government of law, knowledge of the law is necessary for the ruler, as has been laid down in tradition."[134] A popularly elected legislative assembly would inevitably introduce error either by electing lay members who did not possess a proper understanding of Islamic law (and thus made mistakes) or by elevating clerics of lesser scholarly distinction over their brethren who were better able, through superior training and piety, to preside over the Islamic community. With respect to the latter, only the clergy could properly evaluate the scholarship and piety of their peers.

However, Shi'ite Islam does provide a significant role for public opinion in the elevation of clerics within the Shi'ite hierarchy. As we have noted, as one

---

[132] Vanessa Martin, *Creating an Islamic State: Khomeini and the Making of a New Iran* (London: I. B. Tauris, 2000), p. 165.

[133] Najibullah Lafraie, *Revolutionary Ideology and Islamic Militancy: The Iranian Revolution and Interpretations of the Quran* (London: Tauris Academic Studies, 2009), pp. 68–9. As Sayeed puts it, the "sovereignty of God and unconditional obedience to the body of law embedded in the *Quran* and the *Sunna*, gives this apparently authoritarian government a semblance of democracy." Sayeed, *Iran before and after Khomeini*, p. 50.

[134] Kamali, *Revolutionary Iran*, p. 159. "Khomeini rejected the idea of human legislation, and therefore also of legislatures, on the grounds that, because true consciousness and justice were not within the province of humans, they had no right to 'forge' legislation." Clerics, on the other hand, would be only a conduit for God's commands. Vahdat, *God and Juggernaut*, p. 163. Also see Schirazi, *Constitution of Iran*, p. 55.

precondition for becoming a Grand Ayatollah, a cleric must attract a following of believers who are willing to accept their spiritual guidance in the interpretation of Islamic law and other religious matters. These believers then contribute to the support of their Grand Ayatollah through the payment of religious taxes. These funds enable their spiritual leader to create and maintain religious academies and other institutions that contribute to the wellbeing of the Islamic community. But the key point here is that believers choose which cleric that they follow, a choice that is unrestricted as long as the cleric has undergone extensive training under one or more ayatollahs and has demonstrated a superior understanding of Islamic law in his own writings.[135]

There is thus at least an analogical basis for recognizing the will of the people as an influence on state policy after the founding of the Islamic Republic. If we imagine, for a moment, that members of the Majles bear a similar relation to the people that an ayatollah does to his followers (e.g., both are voluntarily chosen by their followers as their leader and representative), then a democratic election merely becomes the means through which these followers make known their choice.[136] Similarly, the range of alternatives from which followers must choose is strongly constrained. In the case of ayatollahs, those whom believers may choose to follow must have completed years (often decades) of religious training and study in which their scholarship, piety, and personal character are monitored by a collective, clerical elite that, through informal means, determines whether or not they qualify as a possible "source of imitation" for believers. The vetting process in the case of those who stand for election to the Majles is much shorter but is nonetheless equally rigorous. That process also involves many of the same characteristics that qualify a cleric for religious leadership.

The Iranian constitution provides only that the "qualifications of electors and candidates, as well as the method of election [to the Majles], will be specified by law."[137] That law was laid down, in the first instance, by the Supreme Leader (Khomeini) when he assigned to the interior ministry and revolutionary council responsibility for determining who could vote and who

---

[135] "[T]he institution of *mujtahid* [Islamic scholar] has been one of the most democratic and populistic in the comparative history of religion. Every practicing Shi'i has in effect to choose one particular cleric to pray behind and is free to choose whomever he wishes. The process is one of consensus and of democracy at the very grassroots of society." Bill, "Power and Religion," pp. 23–4.

[136] Let me hasten to add that an ayatollah who has attracted a following among the devout enjoys a prestige far, far greater than an ordinary member of the Majles. In addition, while religious issues play a prominent role in Iranian politics, more secular dimensions of public policies are much more prominent in political competition than they are in the selection and elevation of Islamic clerics. The analogical similarity that is suggested in the text is thus very limited in scope. On the other hand, it still provides some rationale for consulting, albeit in a very constrained fashion, public opinion even after the founding of a theocratic state.

[137] Article 62, *Constitution of the Islamic Republic of Iran*, p. 51.

could run for election.[138] The Majles later amended this law in 1984 by assigning most responsibility to the Council of Guardians, which was up and running by that time. (Because the Council of Guardians can reject legislation passed by the Majles, it necessarily played a large role in creating this new election law.) Under the revised regulations, candidates must demonstrate to the Council of Guardians that they possess good character, are loyally devoted to the Islamic Republic, and support the principle of clerical rule (particularly the role and authority of the Supreme Leader). The Council of Guardians disqualifies those candidates who do not meet these criteria. Once the election is held, a majority of the Majles must accredit the member's election. Once a member is accredited and begins to serve, he can be expelled from the Majles for violating the rules of good conduct. In addition to these rather institutionalized methods of screening candidates and members, there have also been attacks and threats of attacks by armed groups affiliated with the regime, particularly the Hezbollah, which have discouraged some of those who have been elected from attempting to serve in the Majles.[139]

All states refine the will of the people by limiting the right to vote and creating qualifications that restrict who may stand for election. In addition, most legislative bodies can expel members or otherwise regulate their membership. These are all refinements of the collective will of the people in that they define who is recognized as belonging to that collective (i.e., who is qualified to vote), which candidates the will of the people can select (i.e., who can stand for election), and so forth. As refinements of the will of the people, they channel politics in particular directions.[140] Both democratic and non-democratic states recognize the will of the people as a fundamental legitimating justification for sovereignty. The major difference between these two kinds of states lies in the degree to which they insist on refining that will after the state has been founded. In Iran, the fundamentalists have made demonstrated loyalty to their theocracy a major condition of the eligibility of candidates who may stand for election. In doing so, the state ensures that the people cannot err when they choose one candidate over another because all candidates have been vetted before the

---

[138] For the regulations under which the first Majles was elected, see Bahman Baktiari, *Parliamentary Politics in Revolutionary Iran: The Institutionalization of Factional Politics* (Gainesville: University Press of Florida, 1996), pp. 63–9.

[139] Schirazi, *Constitution of Iran*, pp. 86–91. "[O]n the opening day of the 5th Majles, Hezbollah, in a letter to MPs, threatened to search out any 'liberals' among them, drag them into the streets and there bring them before a revolutionary court" (p. 91). Also see Baktiari, *Parliamentary Politics*, pp. 109–11.

[140] There are many other aspects of constitutions that also restrict the range and shape the quality of the will of the people, such as protections for individual rights, federal arrangements that divide sovereignty, and appointment (as opposed to election) of important officials who staff state institutions.

people vote.[141] In the same way, all ayatollahs have been vetted before the faithful may choose to follow them.[142] A liberal democracy creates a "society of citizens." The Islamic Republic recognizes a "society of believers." In such a society, "the prerogatives of the faith supersede those of the citizen" and "the aim of politics and law" is "to protect the faith and the society of believers, not to empower citizens."[143]

CONCLUSION

The Soviet state, the Third Reich, and the Islamic Republic of Iran all arose from non-democratic foundings. But each of them nonetheless involved representations of the will of the people as legitimations for their creation. Here we compare and contrast aspects of these three foundings, demonstrating how each one can be traced back to particular conceptions of the will of the people – what it is that they should, must, and thus did will.

We begin with the leader of the revolutionary elite because an examination of that role implicates much of the relationship between the elite and the transcendent social purpose instantiated at the founding (see Table 7.1). The most relevant dimensions upon which the three leaders can be compared are their relative doctrinal fallibility and their relation to the revolutionary elite as a whole. Lenin, for example, was certainly regarded as the preeminent leader of the Bolshevik Party but he was not considered an infallible guide in either the making of tactical decisions or doctrinal interpretation. In part, but not entirely, his relation to the party was his own doing in that he insisted that the vanguard (Bolshevik) party was the collective repository of "correct understanding" of Marxist doctrine. Individuals (including Lenin himself) could err but the party, as a collective, could not. Once the party had made a decision, individuals must conform or leave the party. Leon Trotsky contended that it "was no accident ... that the Bolshevik Party had a leader of genius" during the revolution because a "revolutionist of Lenin's makeup and breadth could be the

---

[141] Within the Iranian constitution, the problem of reconciling the expression of the will of the people with the elimination of error is most acute in the selection of the Supreme Leader. Given the quasi-divine status of the leader as the representative on earth of the Hidden Imam, the assignment of any role to the people in his selection is quite problematic. However, the restrictions placed on who may stand for election to the Assembly of Experts that selects the Supreme Leader effectively means that the selection is controlled by the clerical elite. The will of the people is so refined or purified by these arrangements that its expression is well within the bounds of Islamic orthodoxy as understood and interpreted by the fundamentalist clergy. Schirazi, *Constitution of Iran*, p. 35.

[142] The people are also protected from exposure to error through restrictions on the expression of political and religious opinion. Article 24: "Publications and the press are free to present all matters except those that are detrimental to the fundamental principles of Islam or the rights of the public," *Constitution of the Islamic Republic of Iran*, p. 37.

[143] Gheissari and Nasr, *Democracy in Iran*, p. 31. Although the authors were referring to politics in the early twentieth century, their characterization still aptly describes contemporary Iran.

TABLE 7.1. *Characteristics of the founding of the Soviet Union, the Islamic Republic of Iran, and the Third Reich*

Founding	Leading figure	Role in the revolution	Transcendent social purpose of the new state	Manner in which the popular will is evidenced	Enemies of the founding
Soviet Union	Vladimir Lenin	Leader of the vanguard party of the proletarian revolution	Carry out the transition from capitalism to communism	Support in the streets and the barracks for the vanguard party	Bourgeoisie and the capitalist class generally, Russian nobility and Tsar
Third Reich	Adolf Hitler	Leader of the *Volk*	Unify and mobilize the German people, race, and nation in pursuit of their historical destiny	Support in rallies and elections for the National Socialist Party and Hitler in particular	Jews, Communists (and Marxists generally), those who wish to create a liberal democracy
Islamic Republic of Iran	Ayatollah Khomeini	Shi'ite cleric closest to the Hidden Imam	Prepare the religious community for the return of the Hidden Imam	Support in the streets for Khomeini and an Islamic Republic	Atheists, heretics, those who advocate modernization of Iranian society (e.g., intelligentsia)

Note: This table depicts the characteristics of each founding from the perspective of the founders (e.g., from the perspective of the National Socialist Party in the founding of the Third Reich).
Source: Earlier versions of Tables 7.1 and 7.2 appeared in Richard Bensel, "The Founding of Nondemocratic States" in John L. Brooke, Julia C. Strauss, and Greg Anderson (eds.), *State Formations: Global Histories and Cultures of Statehood* (New York: Cambridge University Press, 2018).

leader only of the most fearless party, capable of carrying its thoughts and actions to their logical conclusion." However, without "the Party Lenin would have been as helpless as Newton and Darwin without collective scientific work." The making of the revolution was thus the working out of a science in which, Trotsky goes on to say, the "Bolshevik leadership would have found the right line of action without Lenin, but slowly, at the price of friction and internal struggles."[144] At the founding, it was thus the Bolshevik (soon the Communist) Party that was melded into the Soviet state. Lenin, as first among equals, was simply a member of that party.[145]

Ayatollah Khomeini, on the other hand, was infallible because he had been chosen by the Hidden Imam as the latter's emissary on earth. However, Khomeini's infallibility was theoretically limited to those policies that directly affected the spiritual health and purity of the religious community. Other matters, such as the placement of sewer lines or management of the financial system, were considered technical questions that could, however competently decided, involve error and, in any case, were beneath the dignity of the ayatollah. On spiritual questions, however, Khomeini was infallible. The ayatollah's relations to the revolutionary elite were complex. On the one hand, the clerics who supported the Iranian Revolution were themselves "experts" on spiritual matters (as evidenced by their titles in the constitutional assembly). When they wrote the constitution for the Islamic Republic, they, in fact, cited that expertise when they assigned themselves primary responsibility for selecting the next Supreme Leader (a selection conditioned by the possibility that God and the Hidden Imam had identified one among them for that role).

On the other hand, once a Supreme Leader had been identified, there could be no justification for opposing him on spiritual matters because he willed only that which God willed. Khomeini's relations with the revolutionary elite were, however, complicated by the fact that many clerics joined the revolution without fully subscribing to the entirety of his doctrinal interpretation of the Supreme Leader's role in the new Islamic Republic. Some of these dissidents were purged from the clergy and others were silenced. But the absence of either a consensus among the clergy on doctrinal questions or a commitment to conform with Khomeini's interpretation (once it became known) meant that there was much more ideological variation among clerics than among Bolsheviks. From that perspective, the founding of the Islamic Republic

---

[144] Leon Trotsky, *Stalin: An Appraisal of the Man and His Influence*, ed. and trans. Charles Malamuth (New York: Grosset and Dunlap, 1941), p. 205.

[145] The reality, of course, was quite different. As Pipes put it, the Soviet Union "has been from the beginning to an unusual extent a reflection of the mind and psyche of one man: his biography and its history are uniquely fused." This fusion, in turn, was of Lenin's own making in that he was "unwilling to distinguish himself from his cause or even to concede that he had an existence separate from it[, and] his life, as he conceived it, was at one with the party's." Pipes later added: "[T]he Bolsheviks were bound together, not by what they believed, but in whom they believed." Richard Pipes, *The Russian Revolution* (New York: Vintage Books, 1990), pp. 341, 389.

instantiated Ayatollah Khomeini personally, as opposed to a loosely defined revolutionary elite, as the interpreter of the will of the people (or, what amounted to the same thing, the will of God). Those clerics who were loyal to Khomeini were incorporated largely in the form of an abnormally large personal retinue.[146]

In rather sharp contrast to both Lenin and Khomeini, Adolf Hitler was regarded as an infallible authority on all aspects of German social, economic, and political life. Because he embodied the historical destiny of the German people, race, and nation (and thus the popular will of the German people), Hitler could only will what the German people should, must, and did will. However, as Leader, Hitler could see more clearly how the historical destiny of the German people could be realized than the people themselves. This inerrancy underpinned both the organic unification of Leader and his people and the Leader's relationship to the revolutionary elite. That elite, embedded in the National Socialist Party, simply became the extension of the Leader, facilitating, in the first instance, his rise to power and, subsequently, his management of state operations (which were also an extension of the Leader). This organic unification of Leader, party, people, and state was so complete that, unlike the Islamic Republic, the Third Reich never contemplated how Hitler's charismatic authority might either be transferred to another person upon his death or be transformed into rational, systematic bureaucratic processes. At the founding, the Leader, party, and people were, as an organic whole, simultaneously imbricated into the state (which, itself, became part of that organic unification under the direction of the Leader).

In all three instances, there was a core revolutionary cadre that was drawn to the movement by its founding principles: class (Russian), race (Germany), and religion (Iran). The mass public was integrated into the founding first and foremost by this cadre and its leaders. However, for many, if not most, of the mass public, other interests and other beliefs were just as important as those proffered by the cadre and its leaders. Their adherence to the revolutionary party was thus far more conditional than that of the cadre and, in the end, while the mass public brought the regime into power and thus enabled the founding of a new state, this outcome was not exactly what the "democratic will" (as far as the mass public was concerned) had in mind. At the founding, it was the beliefs most concretely and fervently held by the cadre and leaders of the revolutionary party that became the transcendent social purpose to which the new state was dedicated. For the cadre and leaders, the revolutionary tasks were, on the one hand, to attract a mass following by any means possible (including misrepresentation of the intended political program and the

---

[146] In this respect, the constitution of the Islamic Republic anticipated the routinization of what necessarily began as Khomeini's charismatic rule, almost as if the clerics had read Max Weber's discussion of the transformation of charismatic leadership into rational bureaucratic forms. Weber, *Economy and Society*, vol. 2, pp. 1121–5.

construction of proposals that appealed only to narrow segments of the public) and, on the other hand, to interpret that mass following as an expression of a popular will that endorsed – indeed compelled – adoption and instantiation of its principles in the founding of a new state. The inevitable tension between these two tasks meant that each founding was thus always slightly off-center and had to be "purified" once the revolutionary party had taken power.

In each instance, the transcendent social purpose to which the new state was to be and, in fact, was dedicated involved the realization of a specific historical destiny. In what became the Soviet Union, this destiny was the historically inevitable communist revolution, ultimately global in scope, in which proletarians would capture the state, abolish bourgeois/capitalist social relations, and then dissolve as a class in what would, in the end, become an ungoverned (in the sense of formal political processes) society. The agent for realizing this destiny was the Bolshevik Party, which both embodied, as a vanguard, the historical impulse to revolution and strengthened that impulse by promoting a proper understanding of Marxist doctrine.[147] Since this understanding was necessarily incomplete when the revolutionary opportunity arose, the party acted in advance, as it were, of the will of the people. In terms of evidence of the existence of that will, all that was needed were popular demonstrations of the revolutionary impulse in a form that recognized the leadership of the vanguard party. Because they were a bourgeois device that could only fragment and distort that impulse, democratic elections were a sham. In practice, the sufficiency of the popular will (in terms of the strength and integrity of the revolutionary impulse) was the primary and exclusive concern of the vanguard party: the proof of the pudding was in the eating (i.e., whether the revolution succeeded). Once the new state was founded, the people would be taught what it was that they should, must, and did will when they revolted against the old order.

In the Iranian Revolution, the historical destiny of the Shi'ite religious community was a devout embrace of the impending return of the Hidden Imam. The transcendent social purpose of the new state was the purification of the religious community in preparation for that return. While this purification was the duty and responsibility of all devout Shi'ites (and was thus what the religious community should, must, and did will as a people), only the clergy and, above all others, Ayatollah Khomeini knew precisely how this purification was to be effected. Here, too, the people knew instinctually (e.g., in their feelings of revulsion when confronted with "modern" social mores) what had to be done. However, unlike the Bolsheviks, the clergy could not wait for the revolutionary impulse to mature because God's will was already manifest.

---

[147] "Impulse" here refers to the almost instinctual rejection of the capitalist order and the erection of a socialist society in its stead. As such, it involves little more than a complete repudiation of the existing social and economic order along with enthusiastic acceptance of the leadership of the vanguard party.

While the focus was on the religious community's recognition of Ayatollah Khomeini as the emissary of the Hidden Imam, this recognition was not something that could be evidenced through democratic elections (in part because such elections allowed the irreligious and infidel to participate and in part because, as a political process, they diverted and fragmented the attention of the religious community with "modernist" issues and forms). In place of elections, massive street demonstrations established Ayatollah Khomeini's pre-eminent spiritual authority by acclamation and thus underpinned the founding of the Islamic Republic. By the time the Assembly of Experts was elected, popular acceptance and recognition of this spiritual authority was already radically shaping the terms of what might have been democratic political competition. Once the Islamic Republic was founded, purification of the religious community commenced, including religious instruction, the suppression of impure elements, and the reformulation of relations between the devout and the clergy.[148]

The founding of the Third Reich was more complicated in that the revelation of the will of the people required a more sustained and intense engagement with democratic elections. From the Nazi perspective, political campaigns occasioned huge displays of emotional feeling that materially manifested the voluntary subordination of individual identity to the collective destiny of the German people, race, and nation, while the election returns demonstrated growing acceptance of Adolf Hitler as Leader (as evidenced in ever larger proportions of the votes received by the National Socialist Party). While these elections also placed growing numbers of uniformed Nazis in legislative halls throughout Germany, including the Reichstag, Nazis did not play the parliamentary game of compromise and coalition-building that normally weaves the fabric of democratic governance. Their presence in legislative chambers was instead used to demonstrate the contempt of the German people for democracy as a process that weakened, diverted, and otherwise frustrated the collective unity of the German people. While elections were thus occasions for evidencing the will of the people, they also paved the way to the assumption of power by the Leader. However, they were emphatically not an instrumental means of achieving substantive goals before the Leader assumed power. After the founding, the Leader presided over a purification of the German people that, while emphasizing race in the place of religion, is otherwise remarkably similar to the Iranian Revolution in its rejection of "modernist" social mores and beliefs.

All three foundings thus rested on a profound conception of the will of the people as an instinctual force driven by historical destiny and yet imperfect in

---

[148] To some extent, these things preceded the founding of the Islamic Republic, because clerics viewed purification as a religious duty regardless of whether or not it was carried out under state auspices.

both its expression and its understanding of what it is that should, must, and will be done. In each founding, the revolutionary elite had a perfect understanding of that historical destiny and proceeded to meld that understanding into the forms and content of the new state. In each instance, the people (i.e., proletarians, Germans, or Shi'ites) had to be purified of impure elements (e.g., the bourgeoisie, Jews, or non-believers) as a necessary step toward enhancing the expression of the popular will.[149] Doctrinal education was also a step in that direction in that, once properly trained, the people were expected to recognize and willingly subscribe to the historical destiny as prescribed in Marxist thought, *volkisch* theory (as refined in Hitler's *Mein Kampf*), or Khomeini's scholarly writings. However, the understanding of the people of their own historical destiny could never be brought up to the level of the revolutionary elite until that historical destiny had been realized (i.e., worldwide proletarian revolution, the return of the Hidden Imam, or the global triumph of the German race). It is this subordination of the people to the revolutionary elite that makes each of these a non-democratic founding.

In all three foundings, the new states and the states they replaced were more or less necessary incidentals of history because the "people" spanned national boundaries and because there were those who resided within those national boundaries who were not of the people. The historical destiny attending each founding recognized this incidental nature by prescribing a transcendent social purpose in which the state-as-nation-state was clearly an imperfect instrument: the world revolution of the proletariat, the absorption of all Shi'ites (and Muslims) in one religious community, and pan-German unification and

---

[149] In each case, the unity of the revolutionary coalition (to which the founding revolutionary elite belonged) originally rested on unmitigated rejection of the existing regime (i.e., the Tsar, the Weimar Republic, or the Shah). After the founding (in a process that was already underway), the revolutionary elite progressively eliminated the other parties in the coalition (starting with those on the right in Russia and on the left in Iran and Germany). In all three instances, the revolutionary party eliminated competing parties one by one, beginning with those parties furthest from the revolutionary elite and then encompassing those that had earlier been allies. In one sense, this was a clearly instrumental strategy of "divide and conquer" that necessarily began with those party organizations whose goals most diverged from those of the revolutionary elite (because those organizations would otherwise have most readily seen the writing on the wall with respect to their own fate if the process of elimination had started elsewhere). In another sense, however, this strategy was also profoundly ideological in that purification of the people should necessarily begin with a purging of the most impure elements and influences among them. As Martin Niemoller, a pastor who was himself imprisoned by the Nazis, painfully reminisced: "First they took the Communists, but I was not a Communist, so I said nothing. Then they took the Social Democrats, but I was not a Social Democrat, so I did nothing. Then it was the trade unionists' turn, but I was not a trade unionist. And then they took the Jews, but I was not a Jew, so I did little. Then when they came and took me, there was no one left who could have stood up for me." Richard J. Evans, *The Third Reich in Power* (New York: Penguin Books, 2005), pp. 232–3.

TABLE 7.2. *The constituting event in the founding of the Soviet Union, the Islamic Republic, and the Third Reich*

Constituting event	Significance of the event	Content of the founding
Soviet Union: The endorsement by the Second All-Russian Congress of Soviets of the Bolshevik overthrow of the Provisional Government	Confirmed the validity of the revolution led by the vanguard party	Melded the popular will (as embodied in the Congress of Soviets), the vanguard party of the proletariat (the Bolsheviks), and the transcendent social purpose (realizing the historical destiny of the proletariat by carrying out the communist revolution) in the new Soviet state
Third Reich: Passage in the Reichstag of the Enabling Act	Conferred all legislative authority on the Leader	Melded the popular will (as embodied in the Reichstag election), the Leader (Adolf Hitler), and the transcendent social purpose (realizing the historical destiny of the German people, race, and nation) in the new Third Reich
Islamic Republic: Ratification of the new constitution by national referendum	Created the Islamic state	Melded the popular will (as embodied in Iranian electorate), Shi'ite clerics (followers of Ayatollah Khomeini), and the transcendent social purpose (purification of the religious community in preparation for the return of the Hidden Imam) in the new Islamic Republic

Notes: In each case, there were several other events that could be considered as "constituting" the founding. The ones chosen for inclusion in this chart marked the turning points after which the respective revolutionary elites no longer believed that eliciting further demonstrations of the will of the people was necessary in order to consolidate the new state. Since they considered the new state to have been properly founded, the will of the people was henceforth organically represented in the new state, making further consultation of the popular will (as something distinct from the state) superfluous.

expansion. In each case, national boundaries were at least arbitrary, plastic conventions, if not irrelevancies imposed by a hostile world order.[150]

In democratic foundings, the state becomes the content of the social contract between the people (as individuals) and the political community they create. In non-democratic foundings, there has been no social contract because the people (as individuals) are completely folded into the political community as an historically destined collective (see Table 7.2). The founding of the state is merely the formal recognition of that collective and the revolutionary elite that bears, perfects, and will realize the historical destiny of the people. Non-democratic foundings thus do not mark the transition from a state of nature (a pre-political society of individuals) into a political community organized and governed by a state. The political community has always existed as an historically authorized and destined collective. The erection of a state at the founding is merely an incidental step in realizing that historical destiny.

As an incidental step, all the elements that would otherwise pose an opening dilemma at a democratic founding are already well-settled facts: (1) the identity of the people and who is authorized to represent their will; (2) the identity of the leader who is authorized to recognize proposals and place them before the founding assembly; and (3) the rules through which the leader is selected and the members of the assembly are recognized as representatives of the people. In fact, the legislative assembly that enacts the founding is almost a ritual formality because all these elements have already been prescribed in the historical destiny of the people (as interpreted and presented by the revolutionary elite). There is thus no "sleight of hand" through which the opening dilemma is resolved because the opening dilemma never existed in the first place.

---

[150] There were, of course, differences in the way in which each founding regarded these boundaries as potentially encompassing a people. For the Bolsheviks, every nation would ultimately (if it did not now) contain a proletariat that would revolt and overthrow the capitalist order. National boundaries would thus disappear when the communist historical destiny had been realized. For Shi'ites, the religious community was spatially concentrated in just a few nations. The community could expand through religious conversion and *jihad*, but, although expansion by these means was a religious duty of the faithful, political boundaries demarcating the limits of the religious community were not necessarily destined to disappear until the return of the Hidden Imam (when they would become utterly irrelevant). For Nazis, the German people, race, and nation were biologically grounded in the blood. Conversion (say from a Pole to a German) was thus ruled out as impossible. While this ineradicable racial identity, along with the spatial concentration of Germans in Central Europe, would appear to make national boundaries both relevant and useful, Nazi ideology posited a German racial superiority so supremely dominant that recognition of national boundaries would have been the idle parlor game of weaker races and their nations. The German people, for their part, would have taken whatever lands and resources that they needed regardless of where they were located. Put another way, national boundaries require a mutual recognition of those residing on both sides of the perimeter. The Nazis would never have participated in that mutual recognition because they were emphatically opposed to a world order in which national boundaries set limits on the destiny of the German people.

8

Conclusion

All modern foundings embody myths, fictions, and abstractions that enlist mass support for the state's sovereign right to rule.[1] While symbolically indispensable, these fictions are grounded in metaphysical assumptions that cannot be constructed or referenced as empirical realities.[2] These assumptions shape and determine how the popular will is conceived. All modern states thus claim that their sovereignty rests upon a foundational popular consent, a consent wrapped in myth and fiction.

Each founding is unique in the sense that to believe in the myths attending a particular founding (say, the United States) is to deny belief in the others. In some instances, we can tolerate and even respect the abstractions that underpin the sovereignty of another nation. The extent of that toleration might arise, for example, from their particular social and political results (e.g., a stable political

---

[1] In a tract published posthumously in 1642, Sir Dudley Digges contended that there was no such thing as a popular will because

> for the people, to speak truly and properly, is a thing or body in continual alteration and change, it never continues one minute the same, being composed of a multitude of parts, whereof divers continually decay and perish, and others renew and succeed in their places ... they which are the people this minute, are not the people the next minute.

Quoted in Edmund Morgan, *Inventing the People: The Rise of Popular Sovereignty in England and America* (New York: W. W. Norton, 1988), p. 61. Under Charles I, Digges served as ambassador to Russia and member of parliament. Also see A. James McAdams, *Vanguard of the Revolution: The Global Idea of the Communist Party* (Princeton, NJ: Princeton University Press, 2017), p. 93.

[2] This interpretation has several (ultimately distracting) parallels with Schmitt's approach to foundings. Carl Schmitt, *Constitutional Theory* (Durham, NC: Duke University Press, 2008), including Ellen Kennedy's "Foreword" and "An Introduction to Carl Schmitt's *Constitutional Theory*: Issues and Context," pp. 9, 13, 45, 59, 67, 70, 74–6, 78, 83, 125–6, 279.

order and/or practical guarantees for individual freedom), but we nevertheless cannot embrace their myths as our own.[3]

The founding of the English state, for example, is irretrievably shrouded in the mists of history (see Table 8.1). The original people are identified as Anglo-Saxons and we are told that their political beliefs and practices were precursors to the "rights of Englishmen." But precisely when Anglo-Saxons became the "English" people is unclear. Some would say that they were already "English" when they crossed the North Sea and invaded the British Isles. Others would contend that it was their experience after the migration, especially interaction with the native Britons, that made them English. Either way, it was within the emergent English identity that the rights of Englishmen emerged. The myths and abstractions that underpin this shrouded history thus give the ancient English Constitution two of its three legs: a people and a transcendent social purpose. The last leg, the birth of the English state, was created by the emergence of the first king of England who ruled over the great majority, if not all, of the English people. But the English people were slow to unambiguously identify themselves as such and the contenders for the title of the first king of England were equally slow to name the realm that they ruled "England." This raises few problems for a founding that, unlike the others we have studied, interprets the melding of people, state, and transcendent social purpose as a process of mutually constitutive creation.

In true Whiggish tradition, the rights of Englishmen are simultaneously refined and revealed in the changing historical relations between the people and the state. The strength of the English state is that its myths are shrouded in the mists of history and this shroud allows them to be creatively imagined (even as historians debate the details). The weakness is that these same beliefs do not encompass the Irish (who left after the First World War) or the Scots (who are contemplating leaving as this book is written).

The American Revolution, on the other hand, anticipated (and rather heroically hoped) that the design of the new national state would generate a proper political identity. The colonists originally embraced an English identity that, they believed, awarded them all the rights of Englishmen in return for loyalty to the crown. At the beginning of the political crisis that would ultimately lead to the American Revolution, the colonial elite, in fact, constructed more elaborate English abstractions than their counterparts in the mother country. When they were told, in so many words, that they were not encompassed within the ancient English Constitution, the American revolutionary elite was compelled to construct another identity for the colonists, one that would call upon the familiar rights of Englishmen that they had seen as their birthright before their

---

[3] We should also note that to call into question the myths, fictions, and abstractions that attended the founding of one's own state is a fundamentally revolutionary act. And that is true even if that questioning does not propose a new set of myths, fictions, and abstractions to replace the old ones.

TABLE 8.1. *Comparison of the six foundings*

The founding	The people	Transcendent social purpose	Founding event	Founding elite	Resolution of the dilemma connecting the will of the people to the founding
England	English	Rights of Englishmen	Historical emergence of the first king of England	Anglo-Saxons	Mythical reconstruction of history in which custom and tradition exhibit no precise beginning
United States	American colonists	Will of the people	Declaration of independence/ ratification of the Constitution	Socially and economically prominent gentlemen	Assertion by fiat that the founding elite represent the will of the people combined with retrospective ritual ratification
French Republic	French	General Will and the rights of man	Declaration of the rights of man/beheading of Louis XVI	Members of the French Assembly	Belief held by members of the French Assembly that they collectively embodied the General Will of the people
Soviet Union	Proletariat	Communist revolution	Second All-Russian Congress	Bolshevik Party	Marxist theory, amended by Lenin, that posited the Bolsheviks as the vanguard party of the proletariat
Nazi Germany	Germans/ Aryans	Destiny of Germans/Aryans	Passage of the Enabling Act	Nazi Party	The designation, through mass displays of recognition, of the Leader who will fulfill the historical destiny of the German/Aryan people
Islamic Republic	Shi'ites	Preparation for the return of the Twelfth Imam	National referendum on the new constitution	Shi'ite clergy who followed Ayatollah Khomeini	Religious doctrine through which the Shi'ite clergy and Khomeini in particular were assigned responsibility for reforming society and the state

rejection by the mother country while, at the same time, articulating a transcendent social purpose that would vitalize the new state they hoped to form. The result was a hybrid founding that, on the one hand, rhetorically announced "that all men are created equal" and, on the other, instantiated English traditions and customs in the pragmatic design of its institutions. The American founding is in some ways fundamentally incoherent. Its durability may be primarily due to a fortuitous geographical context – just enough pressure from competing nations in the international arena to induce the unification of the thirteen states but not so much that its jerry-built structure would collapse when challenged.[4]

There is always something contingent about the shape that a national identity assumes after a founding, partly depending upon the kind of political institutions that are erected, partly depending on how the transcendent social purpose is imagined, and partly depending on the political practices that these two things engender once the state and its relations to the people are up and running. The French Revolution presumed that the rights of man were natural (as did the English), but also universal (unlike the English). The French revolutionary elite also presumed that the natural virtue of the people would be released through the proper design of political institutions – much like the Americans, although the Americans were much more pragmatically experimental than the French.

The Bolsheviks picked up on the French notion of the duty of the revolutionary elite to act as a proxy for the popular will, and they also interpreted the natural identity of the people to be a product of the trajectory of history. However, the Bolshevik conception of the proletarian revolution was much more focused on the proper economic framework of state–society relations, as opposed to the correct design of political institutions as an expression of the (for the French) General Will. While the Nazis borrowed much less from the French than did the Bolsheviks, they, too, viewed the identity and destiny of the German people as fixed (outside of history) and thought that both identity and destiny would be realized through the proper construction of political institutions (the melding of the Führer with the will of the people). Shi'ite revolutionaries also saw identity as fixed, but, for them, the will of the people was doctrinally determined (as the voluntary acquiescence of the devout to the will of God). But in all three of these non-democratic foundings there is still a notion, expressed in different ways, that the design of political institutions aids (and may be essential to) the proper orientation of the people toward their transcendent social purpose, and thus toward state authority.

It is clear that these foundings were not entirely independent of one another. However, that interdependency rapidly decreases as we sequentially move

---

[4] A possibility suggested by Zachary Elkins, Tom Ginsburg, and James Melton, *The Endurance of National Constitutions* (New York: Cambridge University Press, 2009), p. 162.

through the historical order. The American founding is simply unimaginable without reference to the colonial experience with the customs and traditions of the ancient English Constitution. The French Revolution owed less to the American founding than the latter did to the English.[5] However, the American founding still shaped the French Revolution through the direct participation of thousands of Frenchmen in the war for independence and through the American creation of symbols and declarations that the French revolutionary elite could borrow and imitate, especially the demonstration that a written constitution could meld together the will of the people, a transcendent social purpose, and the sovereignty of a new state.[6] The French contribution to the founding of the Soviet Union was much less significant but the Bolsheviks still learned how to manipulate depictions of "the will of the people" so that they yielded the political outcome that they believed desirable. Lenin himself probably borrowed some of Robespierre's techniques with respect to both presenting himself as the incarnation of the revolutionary ethos and posing as the first among equals within a cohesive vanguard party.[7] The Nazi and Shi'ite

[5] On the general influence of the American Revolution on other nations, see Jonathan Israel, *The Expanding Blaze: How the American Revolution Ignited the World, 1775–1848* (Princeton, NJ: Princeton University Press, 2017).

[6] Georges Lefebvre, *The French Revolution from Its Origins to 1793* (New York: Columbia University Press, 1969), vol. 1, pp. 145–7; William Doyle, *The Oxford History of the French Revolution*, second edition (New York: Oxford University Press, 2002), pp. 63–4. However, not everyone in the National Assembly believed that the American experience was relevant for the French. In the debate over the Declaration of the Rights of Man and of the Citizen, a monarchist deputy contended that

American society, newly-formed as it is, consists wholly of property-owners already accustomed to the idea of equality who have encountered none of the problems of feudalism on the soil which they are now cultivating. Such men were obviously prepared for the responsibilities of total freedom, since their social background made them perfectly suited for democracy. But we, gentlemen, have as our fellow-citizens a vast multitude of men with no property who depend for their living on security in their work, the maintenance of civil order and constant protection by the state ... It is my belief, gentlemen, that is it essential in a great empire such as ours for men placed by fate in a position of dependence to understand the just limits of natural liberty rather than to hope for an extension of those limits.

François Furet and Denis Richet, trans. Stephen Hardman, *French Revolution* (New York: Macmillan, 1970), p. 88. This is an early formulation of the "no feudalism in America" thesis, but it did not persuade the assembly. For other comparisons between the American and French Revolutions, see Simon Schama, *Citizens: A Chronicle of the French Revolution* (New York: Alfred A. Knopf, 1989), p. 354; Hannah Arendt, *On Revolution* (New York: Penguin Books, 2006), p. 82; Lynn Hunt (ed.), *The French Revolution and Human Rights: A Brief Documentary History* (Boston: Bedford Books, 1996), p. 51.

[7] On links between the French and Russian Revolutions, see, for example, Furet and Richet, *French Revolution*, pp. 97–8. Pipes contends that the French Revolution provided much of the logic, tactics, and ideological presumptions that the Bolsheviks, and particularly Lenin, utilized in their own revolution. Richard Pipes, *The Russian Revolution* (New York: Vintage Books, 1990), pp. 129, 733, 737n, 789–93, 798, 808. In 1903, more than a decade before the Russian

foundings, however, were almost entirely independent of all the others. The only aspect they share with the other four is the necessity to somehow empirically demonstrate that their revolutionary program was, in fact, willed by the people. While that demonstration was strongly predetermined by the political processes dictated by Hitler and Khomeini, we should note that the process through which popular consent is elicited is always manipulated in order to produce a favorable outcome. It is just that some of these manipulations grate more harshly on our Western sensibilities than others.

The form and role of the constitution also differed in these six foundings. In the American case, the constitution pragmatically adjusted the competing interests of an otherwise cohesive political elite. In its attempt to elicit popular consent, that political elite certainly recognized the opening dilemma, particularly the problem of how to imagine that the Constitutional Convention had been authorized by the people. During the convention itself, they wrestled with the problem of identifying the transcendent social purpose of the new state as something that the people willed, because, for one thing, the people could not "will" all subsequent public policies. Some of these policies, usually in the form of "rights," could be embedded in the constitution, but most had to be left unspecified, subject only to the operation of the state apparatus as it enacted transient expressions of the popular will. The founders also had to design a ratification procedure for the document they had crafted, one that would empirically and theoretically substantiate their claim that deliberations in the convention had reflected the will of the people. All of these aspects were pragmatically resolved in ways that recognized the dilemma that always attends a founding.

The opening dilemma posed by the Constitutional Convention, for example, would not have been resolved had the convention been formally authorized by the Continental Congress to draft an entirely new constitution. That authorization would only have pushed the question back to the original convocation of the Congress itself. And, if the founders had postulated that the colonial assemblies had somehow legitimately authorized the convocation of the Continental Congress, that would only have pushed the question back to the creation of the colonial assemblies. Ultimately, the logic of legitimation would have inexorably invoked the origins of the British crown in the deep recesses of history – not very promising theoretical ground upon which to justify rebellion against the king.

Similar problems attended the claim that the opening dilemma was somehow resolved retroactively. Under that alternative, the constitution is transformed into an unauthored proposal whose genesis is of no importance because it was simply a suggestion put before the people. What mattered was how the people

---

Revolution, Leon Trotsky "sarcastically" compared Lenin to Robespierre during a debate at the Second Congress of the Russian Social Democratic Labor Party. Trotsky thought that Lenin was undermining party unity. McAdams, *Vanguard of the Revolution*, p. 77.

disposed of that suggestion once it was handed over to them for their consideration. That approach contended that the constitution can be and was appropriately "ratified" as the will of the people.[8] Aside from the problem that the constitution was presented to the people as a more or less "take it or leave it" proposition (which implied that the founders had assigned themselves a role much like Rousseau's "lawgiver" who was above and beyond the people with respect to knowledge and virtue), this interpretation of the ratification process only moves the opening dilemma to the state conventions.[9] While the state assemblies pragmatically resolved the dilemma by announcing a time and place for each convention, as well as a process for selecting delegates, the theoretical justification for these acts rested on their own authorization to articulate the will of the people. This problem was veiled because the assemblies, despite their theoretical inadequacy as authorizing institutions, enjoyed the affection and respect of their respective peoples. That respect and affection made the ratification process viable in practice, but it was nonetheless a logically incoherent method of substantiating the will of the people with respect to adoption of the constitution.

[8] As Frank puts it: "Madison's navigation of the attending dilemmas of popular authorization resisted the turn to metaphysical abstraction and the appeal to a transcendent or immanent absolute. In his approach to the problem of constituent power, Madison insisted on the productive irreducibility of institutional mediation and the performative elicitation of a retrospective authorization by the people." Jason Frank, "'Unauthorized Propositions': *The Federalist Papers* and Constituent Power," *Diacritics* 37: 2–3 (2007), p. 103. Put another way, Madison (and many other founders) denied that it was possible for the people to collectively participate in the drafting of a constitution and, for that reason, "institutional mediation" was necessary. That claim, in turn, deflected attention from whether or not the Constitutional Convention had been authorized to do the drafting (the question arising from the opening dilemma) to "retrospective authorization by the people," which, of course, was resolved in much the same way. Where Frank says "productive," I would say "pragmatic and effective." Also see pp. 105–6. Frank presumes that "the people" actually exist as an intentional, self-actuating, and self-realizing collective. See, for example, this passage on p. 118: "[T]hese [popular] enactments attend democratic claims made in seemingly everyday or ordinary political settings." It is presumed that "the people" existed, as a self-conscious actor, before they were manifested in these "enactments." Put another way, there is an essentialist conception of "the people" that places their identity outside of politics. In general, democratic theorists almost always make a presumption of this kind.

[9] Rousseau states that "the lawgiver ... has no authority to do what he sets out to achieve." Frank, "'Unauthorized Propositions,'" p. 114. That was not quite the case with the American founders, who were designated "delegates" by their respective states (although the purpose for which they were designated by the states was peremptorily abandoned as soon as the Constitutional Convention met in Philadelphia). In Rousseau's vision, the people are immediately present in the venue where the "laws" are declared and thus collectively "receive" them without the mediation of representation by agents. And because the lawgiver is altruistically motivated and has no personal interest in the outcome (because he will leave once the laws are declared), the alignment of the laws with the transcendent social purpose of the people (i.e., the instantiation of the "General Will" as the arbiter of their collective destiny and the purpose of their community) is more or less guaranteed. On all these points, the American founders differed from Rousseau's "lawgiver." See, for example, pp. 116–17.

Many political theorists have recognized the problematic role of the will of the people in the American founding, particularly the hubris, if we can call it that, motivating the opening line: "We, the People of the United States, in Order to form a more perfect Union." Few of these theorists would declare the constitution to be illegitimate because it did not democratically resolve the opening dilemma (although some would regard the legitimacy of the constitution to be impaired for more substantive reasons, particularly the implicit sanction of slavery). They thus recognize that no founding can be thoroughly democratic because the opening moves must be made by arbitrary fiat. That leaves up in the air the question of how we might evaluate the American (or any other) founding.

We might, for example, evaluate the American founding by examining the political virtue of the founders. This was one of the most common arguments made by advocates of ratification: The participation in the convention of the most prestigious among the American elite implied both that the founders were able to recognize and act upon the will of the people *and* that the document they drafted was very likely to be the best that could be produced. Because evaluation of the political virtue of the founders has waxed and waned over the centuries, this does not seem to offer a very stable result. Evaluation of the substantive provisions of the constitution fares even worse because arrangements such as the Electoral College and the awarding of two senators to every state regardless of population have become inconsistent with what have become more direct and expansive notions of the way in which a democratic will should be expressed. We might also evaluate the American founding purely by its results in terms of the stability of the political order that it created, the substantive policies that have grown up around the American state, and the collective values that these things have engendered in the people. We actually do all of these things. However, all of them leave the legitimacy of the constitution (and thus of the founding) up in the air because none of them identify the transcendent social purpose that the people, in 1789, (ostensibly) embedded in the new American state.

The secret deliberations in the American Constitutional Convention pragmatically adjusted the competing interests of the delegates, the states they represented, the classes to which they belonged, and, lastly, the people at large. The American founding thus took on the aspect of a comprehensive "bargain" in which most people in what became the nation could find something that appealed to their interests. The ancient English Constitution was similar but, in contrast to a single event, it has pragmatically adjusted competing interests over centuries of political decision-making as the state laid down political precedents, customs, and traditions. The French Revolution was very different because there was neither a revolutionary party that could convincingly embed a transcendent social purpose in the new state nor a unified political elite that could pragmatically adjust its internal conflicts of interest. The French had plenty of constitutions but none of them became definitive in terms of melding the people, the transcendent social purpose, and the sovereignty of the state. The Russian, German, and Iranian revolutions all drafted and adopted detailed constitutions but, in each case, they merely instantiated the revolutionary party as the ruling authority and it was the latter, not the constitution, that claimed to embody the transcendent social purpose. In some respects, then, this sequence from the English to the Iranian founding records a more or less steady decline in the salience of the rule of law as a legitimating principle for state sovereignty and a corresponding rise in the charismatic role of revolutionary parties and their leaders.

In all six cases, the emotional embrace of the ritual performance in which the purpose, the will of the people, and sovereignty were melded was both imagined and demonstrated.[10] For the English, this embrace was taken for granted because it had occurred in "time immemorial." To ask for empirical evidence for the original founding process was to challenge the state's legitimacy. The Americans, even with limited suffrage eligibility, mediation by the thirteen states, and the presumptuous process through which the constitution was constructed, were closer to the ideal through which a people might consent to the founding of a new state. The weakness of the revolutionary elite vis-à-vis the thirteen states was a major factor behind the openness with which they sought public consent. The French possessed the most elaborate ideological justification for the primacy of the unmediated will of the people (the General Will) but could not settle on a definitive process through which that will might construct and enable the institutions of the new state. As a result, French revolutionaries repeatedly consulted the people in elections and other ways only to ignore and, even more frequently, repudiate what those consultations revealed.

The Bolsheviks were much less concerned with the emotional resonance of the people than with the way in which it could be translated into political power. While the French came to believe that they knew what the people willed, even if the people were not ready to express that will, the Bolsheviks held that the doctrinal understandings of the political party, as the vanguard of the proletariat, *was* what the people willed. As a result, events in which the will of the people was ostensibly expressed were choreographed in such a way as to produce preordained results. There was, however, still an element of popular consultation in that the working class had to display at least some indication that Russia was historically "ready" for the communist revolution. For the

---

[10] Foucault contends that emotional embrace of the founding complicates the subsequent performance of the tasks of politics: "It is a law of history that the simpler the people's will, the more complex the job of politicians. This is undoubtedly because politics is not what it pretends to be, the expression of a collective will. Politics breathes well only where this will is multiple, hesitant, confused, and obscure even to itself." Quoted in Behrooz Ghamari_Tabrizi, *Foucault in Iran: Islamic Revolution after the Enlightenment* (Minneapolis: University of Minnesota Press, 2016), p. 61. On this, Foucault and Schmitt are in perfect agreement.

Bolsheviks, it was not Marxist *theory* that was at risk but its application to 1917 Russia. We can thus imagine that Bolsheviks might have conceded that the Russian proletariat had failed the test and that a "doctrinally correct" revolution could not occur at that time.

For the Nazis, that test involved popular recognition of Adolf Hitler as the Führer, the Leader who embodied the historical destiny of the German people. Popular demonstrations, mass rallies, and election returns were interpreted as evidence of the relentless increase in popular support for Hitler and the Nazi Party. Once in power, the identification of the will of the Führer with the will of the people made political conformity mandatory. It is not clear whether the Nazis would have accepted evidence that the people were indifferent toward or rejected Hitler as their Leader since there was no other candidate waiting in the wings to replace him. The problem was a little different for the founding of the Islamic Republic in Iran. There, devout Shi'ites, somewhat like the proletariat in Russia, had to demonstrate that they regarded the Shi'ite clergy who followed Khomeini (and, even more importantly, Khomeini, himself) as the anointed intermediaries between the people and the Twelfth Imam. In this respect, the Iranian founding paralleled that of the Soviet Union. However, Khomeini himself also took on some of the leadership qualities that had been ascribed to Adolf Hitler in the founding of the Third Reich.

Because of these differences, it is clear that none of the six foundings could accept any of the others as entirely compatible with their own, either as precedents or as theoretical logics. But they all share a common core in the sense that the people were imagined, albeit in very different ways, to have consented to the founding of the respective states.[11] In addition, in each instance this consent was imagined to have arisen, at least in part, from an intuitive understanding by the people of the transcendent social purpose to which the state should be dedicated. This intuitive understanding could be demonstrated in rational political behavior (most closely illustrated in the American founding), but, in all these cases, it was also revealed in the emotional resonance between the people and that transcendent social purpose. That emotional resonance arose out of the "natural character" of the people, inextricably intertwined with what was presented as their historical destiny. In each case, the founders cited the emotional resonance of the people as confirmation that the melding of the will of the people, the transcendent social purpose, and

[11] The melding of a transcendent social purpose, the will of the people, and the granting of sovereignty create what we might term a "Platonic form" in that this becomes the normative ideal that underpins the possibility of a mutually constitutive relationship between a people and a state. The details of the things that enter into the melding always (and apparently must) vary, but the abstract form is constant. In many ways, this interpretation is similar to Max Weber's concept of an "ideal type," although the normative element would be (at least largely) absent in the latter. In fact, because meldings are necessary only within a particular historical stage (i.e., post-feudal, mercantile, and industrial capitalism), they are in that respect closer to an ideal type than to a Platonic form.

the creation of the state's sovereign right to rule conformed to other aspects of the people's understanding of the world (e.g., Geertz's seamless web of meaning).

This conformity did not grow out of a calculated decision in the sense that a rational choice theorist would read into a symbol its implications for an individual's personal interests. In each instance, there was, to be sure, a rich and complex theoretical grounding for the symbolic displays and mythological formations that accompanied the founding. The English, for example, had a numberless phalanx of theorists who explained the intricacies of the common law and the ancient constitution. While Edmund Burke was perhaps the greatest of all those who took it upon themselves to theoretically relate custom and tradition to the state's right to rule, all of them proposed that the details of the English founding had been lost in the mists of history. However, this was a strength, not a weakness, because, whatever these fictions and myths might have been in the beginning, they were considered to have been validated by experience. There were some quasi-mythological personalities who graced historical events, such as King Arthur and his Round Table, but they were as much the occasion for as the protagonist in constitutional formation.

While many of the symbols and principles of the English founding were coopted by the United States, the American revolutionaries could not pretend that their founding was shrouded in time immemorial because the process was on full public display. While the United States had James Madison, Thomas Jefferson, and Alexander Hamilton among its most prominent theoreticians, none of them were decisive or even essential articulators of the founding ethos. Of the foundings studied here, the American was the most instrumentally pragmatic, combining the emotional appeal of the English inheritance with a rational appraisal of human possibility originating in an understanding of social reality.[12] There was certainly creative innovation in both symbolic theory ("all men are created equal") and institutional design (e.g., sharing sovereignty between the national and individual states).[13] But necessity was the parent of

---

[12] Hannah Arendt convincingly argues that the claim made by the revolutionary elite as they seek to overthrow the existing government owes much of its content and design to the regime it replaces. The transcendent social purpose of the new state is thus strongly shaped by the historical context in which the struggle with existing political authority occurs. What she does not say, however, is that revolutionary elites invariably deny that influence as they seek to ground the new state in the will of the people. She also does not say that this influence is much weaker in non-democratic foundings in which a complex and well-articulated ideology motivates the revolutionary elite. Arendt, *On Revolution*, pp. 146–7.

[13] Arendt, for example, has contrasted the American and French Revolutions from this perspective: "What appeared to be most manifest in this spectacle [the French Revolution] was that none of its actors could control the course of events ... [In] the course of the American Revolution ... the exact opposite took place [and] the sentiment that man is master of his destiny, at least with respect to political government, permeated all its actors." In the French Revolution, on the other hand, we can see "the impotence of man with regard to the course of his own action." Arendt, *On Revolution*, p. 41.

political imagination in this instance. There is also something about the prominent role of "the rule of law" in both the English and the American foundings that suppressed charismatic possibility (e.g., George Washington, who certainly had gravitas, had much more importance as a symbol to be deployed than as an oracular theoretician to be consulted). In many ways, the English and the American foundings made the rule of law the transcendent social purpose willed by the people.[14]

The non-democratic foundings, on the other hand, all had protagonists who combined popular charismatic appeal and an extraordinary ability to attribute a common purpose to their respective people: The Soviet Union had its Lenin, the Nazis had their Hitler, and Iran had its Khomeini. There were complications in these foundings, complications that arose, in part, out of the theoretical problem of linking the charismatic appeal of the leader to the natural will of the people and, thus, to the revolutionary program. That problem was more serious for the Bolsheviks than for the Nazis or Shi'ites because Marxist theory did not provide as much theoretical space for charismatic leaders.[15] But it seems nonetheless clear that each of these leaders became, in their own time, a mythological icon of the revolution that they led.

The French Revolution is a bit of an outlier compared with the other five. There was certainly an extensive theoretical foundation for the revolution in which Rousseau was extremely important. But Rousseau's thought also introduced a theoretical problem that appeared to be irresolvable: How could a nation as large as France conduct politics with the immediacy and thick consultation among citizens of a city-state? Into that conundrum stepped Maximilien Robespierre, who proposed that he, through his willingness to sacrifice himself as the embodiment of the General Will, should guide the revolution to its destiny. However, Robespierre never possessed the charismatic appeal that might have enabled completion of this (theoretically incoherent) project, and his execution brought the revolution to an end.[16]

---

[14] However, the role of the rule of law as a primary founding principle may be responsible for the ability of Great Britain and the United States to revise provisions in their respective constitutions without resorting to formally designated conventions. Formal procedures, such as judicial review, combined with the constant recitation of broad foundational principles have allowed adaptation in these states without sacrificing the intense attachment of the citizenry to their constitutions. See, for example, Elkins, Ginsburg, and Melton, *Endurance of National Constitutions*, p. 164.

[15] On Lenin's charismatic appeal, see Pipes, *Russian Revolution*, p. 348. However, the potential contradiction between Lenin's personal charisma and Marxist theory was almost entirely suppressed by his own, personal subordination to the revolutionary project (which, of course, he was primarily responsible for designing) (p. 350). Once Lenin had died, the Soviet regime "inaugurated a deliberate policy of deifying Lenin which ... would turn into a veritable state-sponsored Oriental cult" (p. 812).

[16] The French Revolution marked a global transition in the political history of states for many reasons. As Pipes put it:

If modern states could have been founded upon reason and logic alone, symbolic displays such as the Liberty Tree and George Washington's selfless virtue would have been superfluous. These symbolic displays do not constitute logical arguments because an explicit articulation of their meaning would be always incomplete and contestable. Symbolic displays elicited an emotional response from the people precisely because (1) they allowed, even compelled, the people to imagine that, despite loose ends, the state would be properly dedicated to their transcendent social purpose and (2) the people intuitively understood and embraced that purpose, an understanding and an embrace that were evidenced in their emotional response to these symbols. Founders, for that reason, cannot simply choose those symbols that appear likely to further their designs; instead, they must draw upon the cultural heritage of the people.

Even when the new state is up and running and thus able to "manufacture" symbols such as flags, monuments, and patriotic songs, these are not merely pragmatic signs for coordinating collective life. For example, the plaque placed on the podium when the president makes an announcement is not simply a convenient signal that the president will appear at that place and in that role; instead, it is a culturally laden emblem of the embodiment of the will of the people in American democracy.[17] Put another way, symbols and performances

---

Post-1789 revolutions have raised the most fundamental ethical questions: (1) whether it is proper to destroy institutions built over centuries by trial and error, for the sake of ideal systems; (2) whether one has the right to sacrifice the well-being and even the lives of one's own generation for the sake of generations yet unborn; (3) whether man can be refashioned into a perfectly virtuous being.

He then concludes that "revolutionary struggles" after 1789 have not been "over politics but over theology." Pipes, *Russian Revolution*, p. xxiii. Pipes would have been more correct if he had said "over a theology of history." And from that perspective it is somewhat ironic that the French Revolution, which was hostile to history as a source of political principle, has engendered such powerful successors in which historical destiny is the primary driving force.

[17] As one of the leading analysts of American politics has put it: "Elections stand at the core of American political life. They provide ritual expression of the myth that makes political authority legitimate: We are governed, albeit indirectly, by our own consent ... The mythical and practical components of elections meet at the point where electoral constraints are supposed to make leaders responsive and responsible to the public." Gary C. Jacobson, *The Politics of Congressional Elections*, eighth edition (Boston: Pearson, 2013), p. 1. Schmitt, from a very different perspective, contended that a fully participatory democracy empties politics of all meaning.

In the United States of America and in other Anglo-Saxon countries, complicated machines with registers and buttons were invented in order not only to ensure electoral and voting secrecy institutionally, but also to provide it additional mechanical guarantees. It is fully conceivable that one day through ingenious discoveries, every single person, without leaving his apartment, could continuously express his opinions on political questions through an apparatus and that all these opinions would automatically be registered by a central office, where one would only need to read them off. That would not be an especially intensive democracy, but it would provide a proof of the fact that the state and the public were fully privatized. It would not be public opinion, for even the shared opinion of millions of private people produces no public opinion. The result is only a sum of private opinions. In this way,

associated with the creation and exercise of political sovereignty must be grounded in popular beliefs that enable a connection between the exercise of raw political power and the cosmological order that created both the people and the state. As a result, the space in which the transcendent social purpose of the state resides is a supranatural realm where logic, if pressed very far in any direction, must immediately succumb to contradiction.

There are symbols and performances that, at any point in time, reaffirm the alignment of the state with the transcendent social purpose that it ostensibly enacts. The receptivity of the citizenry to these symbols and performances, in turn, measures the viability of that alignment. When they are effective, they carry both much more and much less meaning than mere appearances might suggest: much more because they involve a wide-ranging sublimation of the self to the society encompassing the state; much less because that same sublimation of the self strips the symbols and performances of most consciously imputed meaning. This last point is very important in that the individual has suspended self-interested calculations of loyalty, obedience, and identity in proportion to their enthrallment by the symbols and performances that connect the state to the popular understanding of the cosmological order. All of this means that we can easily overinterpret the specific content of a symbol (e.g., Marianne) when, in fact, the most important point is that it is consensually and thus unconsciously accepted. That acceptance, in turn, explains how a society turns the exercise of raw political power into a cosmological mandate. Marianne, as a visual symbol and representation, is both the entirety and only a small part of how that is done.

The relatively loose fit between the emotional resonance of the people, their cultural understanding of the world, and the symbolic displays that accompany the founding explains in large part why the founders in these six cases, particularly their revolutionary allies, rarely got what they wanted from their revolution. The English case is an exception because the founders did not even realize that they were founders (rather like Romulus and Remus in Rome, the founders were mythological fictions). To say that King Arthur was either happy with or disappointed in the founding of the English state and nation would involve much more imagination than is usually the case.[18] The American founding was different. For example, George Washington ultimately

lost all hope for democracy. Party spirit, he said in 1799, had destroyed the influence of character in politics. Members of one party or the other now could "set up a broomstick" as candidate, call it "a true son of Liberty" or a "Democrat" or any other epithet that will suit their purpose, and the broomstick would still "command their votes in toto!"

no common will arises, no *volonté générale*; only the sum of all individual wills, a *volonté de tous*. (Schmitt, *Constitutional Theory*, p. 274)

[18] The entry in B. B. Woodward, Late Librarian to the Queen, and William L. R. Cates, *Encyclopaedia of Chronology, Historical and Biographical* (Boston: Lee and Shepard, 1872) reads: "Arthur, *British Prince, (mythic)* – said to have defeated the Saxons at Mount Badon, 516?" (p. 125).

Three years later, Alexander Hamilton concluded that "this American world was not made for me," which was just another way of saying that "this American world" had not turned out in the way he had wanted. Jefferson, for his part, lived long enough to be "frightened by the popularity of Andrew Jackson, regarding him as a man of violent passions and unfit for the presidency." All of them, along with many other founders, realized that their efforts had produced a very different republic than the one they had originally thought they had designed.[19]

In the French case, Bonaparte was not quite what Rousseau had in mind, destruction of the monarchy was not complete, and, of course, many of the founders had been executed by their colleagues even before Bonaparte took power. In the Soviet case, all except hardcore Bolsheviks were disappointed (or, as in the French case, killed). In the Nazi case, all who were not hardcore Nazis thoroughly devoted to Hitler were shunted aside. In the Iranian case, all those who were not devoted to Khomeini's interpretation of Shi'ite doctrine were disillusioned (many of them killed, particularly his Marxist allies). However, the Iranian case may have come closest to what the founders had in mind with the American case a close second.

Part of the disappointment of the founders in their product can be traced back to the opening dilemma that all founding assemblies must confront. The most important difficulty attending the melding is that the will of the people cannot, either in theory or in practice, be manifested before the people themselves have been declared to be a political community. This political community, however, cannot be constituted in the absence of a manifestation of the popular will. Resolution of this dilemma is impossible in logic and theory. In practice, a political agent must prescribe the way in which the popular will can be manifested and, by way of that prescription, identify who will act in the name of the people. Although the people can neither identify nor "make" themselves, the founding elite must construct fictions and abstractions that assert that, in fact, the people have done so. But these fictions subsequently take on a life of their own and become the political playthings of those who exercise or want to exercise power in the new state.

When delegates convene in a constitutional assembly, they are agents authorized to represent the will of the people. The process through which they have been selected has already presumed what the people demand as their transcendent social purpose because that purpose played a fundamental role in defining who the people are. For example, in the founding of the Soviet Union, only workers and peasants were identified as "the people" before delegates were selected (in a process that was strongly manipulated). As agents of the people, the founding elite construct a new state in accord with the transcendent social

---

[19] Gordon S. Wood, *The Radicalism of the American Revolution* (New York: Vintage, 1991), pp. 366–7.

purpose that has already dictated the identity of "the people" and with what must be embedded in the constitution in order to legitimate the granting of sovereignty. At this point, non-democratic foundings sometimes submit the new constitution to a national referendum in which the people demonstrate their consent to the formation of the state. However, that referendum is invariably structured in such a way that the outcome is preordained.

In non-democratic foundings, manipulation of the conditions under which the referendum is conducted is appropriate because (1) the founding assembly has already embedded the transcendent social purpose into the new constitution and (2) many people do not yet have a proper understanding of what that purpose should be. Thus, on the one hand, a referendum is unnecessary because the people have already consented even though they may have to be further educated before they realize that they must consent. On the other hand, a freely debated and implemented referendum would put the new constitution at risk because at least some of the people are not yet politically enlightened. A constrained referendum in which the outcome is predetermined thus becomes a ritual essential to the political education of the people (as opposed to a mutual consultation with an otherwise free political community). In any event, the state of nature in which the people is imagined to be free to consent has long since vanished. Ironically, perhaps, democratic foundings have been less apt to submit their new constitution to a public referendum than non-democratic foundings.

All democratic foundings are celebrated as the fount in which the will of the people, sovereignty, and the political order are melded. However, the convening of a new and sovereign constitutional convention is also often regarded with extreme apprehension for several reasons. One is that many in the elite, and also the citizenry at large, no longer believe that "the people" can be trusted to devise a new constitution because they are no longer sufficiently virtuous. It is better, for that reason, to limp along with an old founding that may have lost resonance with the citizenry than to take chances by calling for a new constitutional convention. In addition, a durable political order over time creates its own legitimacy in the sense that the citizenry come to prefer political stability to the risks that might attend changes in the state's commitment to the transcendent social purpose. This profoundly conservative perspective explains why the ancient English Constitution and the United States Constitution have weathered many a political crisis: Both of them have found ways of incrementally changing the terms of the original founding without revising, at one sitting, the entire panoply of institutions, rights, and principles associated with their respective states.[20]

[20] In the American case, this raises an interesting question: Does the emphasis on originalism and textualism by many conservative jurists and constitutional theorists increase, in the long run, the necessity of a new founding? If the only way to change (update) the founding of a democratic state were to convene a new constitutional convention, would that encourage these jurists and theorists to at least entertain the possibility of such a convention?

A related but more fundamental reason for reluctance to hold a new convention is that the citizenry (and certainly the political elite) realize that a successful founding requires the negotiation of many difficult issues, including resolution of the opening dilemma, that make the outcome of a new constitutional convention quite risky and unpredictable. For example, a new founding must reconsider the conception of the people, rearticulate the transcendent social purpose, and revise the notion of popular consent. All of these then become contingent outcomes that may very well depart from those now operative under the old regime. As these negotiations proceed, all of the myths, fictions, and abstractions that have shrouded the previous founding in democratic glory will be called into question. As part of their grade school experience, American children color in Betsy Ross' flag or tape Thanksgiving turkeys to the classroom window as they are incorporated into American political culture. What would that indoctrination look like in the midst of a full-scale constitutional convention?

In any event, a new constitutional convention, if one were to be held in the United States today, would be much more freewheeling and open than the 1787 proceedings in Philadelphia. Such a convention would be both entrancing as political theater and certain to provoke great anxiety throughout the polity.[21] In addition, it would most probably fail to engender the kind of myths and abstractions that bind together a people. All these reasons are ultimately reducible to an apprehension, sometimes explicit but often implicit, that the will of the people can be a dangerous and unreliable fiction when actually put in play. And that explains why foundings are almost always preceded by revolutions: The motivation behind a founding needs to be very high.

Non-democratic states would run similar risks if they attempted a refounding, but a new constitutional convention is almost inconceivable because the transcendent social purpose of the state has already been identified and permanently embedded in the constitution and state institutions. For non-democratic states, it is the education and political orientation of the people that must be properly managed, as opposed to a perfecting revision of the constitution. For democratic states, the priorities are usually reversed but the cultivation of supportive beliefs among the citizenry is nonetheless important. In fact, it is because democratic elites fear that they have failed to cultivate proper attitudes in their citizenries that they view a new constitutional convention with such anxiety.

---

[21] Ordeshook has argued that the construction and history of "Western constitutions" can provide lessons in constitution-making for newly democratizing nations. He also contends that many of those lessons can be derived from the American experience. However, those lessons seem not to have been learned by the citizenry of the United States. Their fear of themselves as the collective makers of a new constitution in fact suggests that those lessons have not been learned very well anywhere in the West. Peter Ordeshook, "Are 'Western' Constitutions Relevant to Anything Other than the Countries They Serve?," *Constitutional Political Economy* 13 (2002), pp. 3–24.

As already noted, non-democratic foundings invariably assume that the people must be educated even after they have consented to the formation of the new state. Because the people have not fully or correctly understood the transcendent social purpose that they have nonetheless embedded in the new state, one of the most pressing tasks after the founding is to improve the understanding of the people. The people, of course, are thought to fervently desire that improvement as well. This education is recognized as one of the most important functions of the new state.

Democratic foundings, on the other hand, tend to presume that the will of the people is naturally and fully formed at the moment of founding. The problem is not with the character or content of the will but with its authenticity when revealed through the operation of state institutions. Democratic foundings thus anticipate that their founding constitutions may be imperfect and might need some revision in the future. Put very broadly, non-democratic foundings presume that it is the *people* who need to be perfected while democratic foundings presume that it is *state institutions* that must be refined.

We should, however, qualify this distinction in several ways. First, it applies most strongly to the moment of the founding; in practice, the distinction between democratic and non-democratic states begins to blur a bit once the state is up and running because the state itself becomes a participant in political life. As a participant, even democratic states repress popular sentiment that might undermine their own viability.[22] Second, the distinction tends to understate the extent to which democratic states manufacture the "perfection" of the popular will at the founding by excluding some portions of the population from participation and, after the founding, by educating the citizenry into a proper understanding of, for example, American "ideals." Finally, there is a kind of middle ground between the extremes of the democratic and non-democratic dichotomy, a ground occupied, for example, by the French Revolution during its agonized search for political stability.

Although this takes us some distance away from the primary themes of this book, it might also be suggested that failure to directly confront the apprehension that a new constitutional convention might go awry has undermined the cultural legitimacy of the original founding and, thus, the stability of the political and social order. One symptom of this decay can be seen in the discrepancy between the apprehension with which Americans regard a refounding of their own state and the enthusiasm and alacrity with which democratic foundings are used as a justification for military adventures abroad. These military adventures found states in which the opening dilemma disappears into a welter of theoretical assumptions about how the founding assembly should be constructed and what it should be permitted to decide. The best part of the

---

[22] The most common example of such repression is the almost universal hostility to secession by otherwise democratic states. This hostility strongly reifies the identity of "the people" as an indivisible collective with equally strong commitments to a particular set of national boundaries.

Rousseauian model of continuous conversation with a freely expressed democratic will – what was once the hallmark claim of American democracy – is
nowhere to be found in these American-imposed experiments.

Whenever a constitutional assembly is convened for the purpose of founding
a new state (e.g., in Iraq or Afghanistan), readers of this book should pay close
attention to how that assembly is created and the procedures through which it
organizes itself. What are the myths, fictions, and abstractions that cloak the
opening dilemma? How closely aligned are these abstractions with the formal
process of constitution-making? Are there discrepancies between the conception of the popular will and the transcendent social purpose embedded in the
new state? To what extent are the people thought to be competent to recognize
what it is they will and how does the organization of the new state compensate
for any lack of competence?

But all these questions pale against a larger one: Has the increasing rationalization of modern society in the West made new democratic foundings much
more difficult because the citizenry simply cannot suspend disbelief when myths
and abstractions are deployed? Are modern states thus much more likely to be
founded in non-democratic contexts where the symbolic deployment of these
things is much more effective than in the West? These questions lead to the most
important question of all: If myths and abstract beliefs are necessary for a stable
political community, how do we instrumentally create such things in a democratic society when the entire apparatus of intellectual and scientific culture
seems to be dedicated to exposing them as fantasies?[23] It could be that we have
exhausted this paradigm by relentlessly pursuing its implications for political
practice and institutional design, and, as a result, have finally revealed its
metaphysical vulnerability in the modern world.

---

[23] Although he has his own interpretation of what should be the transcendent social purpose of a
democratic state, I take this question to be the central focus of Rogers Smith's *Stories of
Peoplehood: The Politics and Morals of Political Membership* (New York: Cambridge
University Press, 2003).

Index

CPSIA information can be obtained
at www.ICGtesting.com
Printed in the USA
LVHW050016170123
737223LV00001B/29